ENDURANCE AND ENDEAVOUR

RUSSIAN HISTORY

1812–1992

J. N. WESTWOOD

FOURTH EDITION

OXFORD UNIVERSITY PRESS

Oxford University Press, Walton Street, Oxford OX2 6DP
Oxford New York
Athens Auckland Bangkok Bogota Bombay
Buenos Aires Calcutta Cape Town Dar es Salaam
Delhi Florence Hong Kong Istanbul Karachi
Kuala Lumpur Madras Madrid Melbourne
Mexico City Nairobi Paris Singapore
Taipei Tokyo Toronto
and associated companies in
Berlin Ibadan

Oxford is a trade mark of Oxford University Press

Published in the United States by
Oxford University Press Inc., New York

© Oxford University Press 1973, 1981, 1987, 1993

First published 1973
Second Edition 1981
Third Edition 1987
Fourth Edition 1993

British Library Cataloguing in Publication Data
Data available

Library of Congress Cataloging in Publication Data
Data available
ISBN 0-19-873103-5

5 7 9 10 8 6

Printed in Great Britain
on acid-free paper by
Biddles Ltd
Guildford and King's Lynn

AUTHOR'S PREFACE

Although this Fourth Edition is much enlarged, the purpose of the book remains the same; that is, to provide as much information as possible, readably and reliably. As before, the author hopes that many readers will regard its narrative chapters simply as an introduction to the long Bibliography that follows them, in which the number of titles now approaches one thousand, evidence both of the interest in the subject and of the research that is still being pursued. The practice of slipping items of fact and opinion into the Bibliography has been continued, partly because it encourages the reader to look at those pages and partly because it provides a place for material that would fit awkwardly into the main text.

This edition has an extra chapter to cover the Gorbachev years. The revelations of those years provided new detail but it has not been necessary to revise the judgements of the book, because western historians already had an accurate knowledge of what had been going on. However, in this edition, thanks to that new openness, it has been possible to dispense with scores of protective devices of the 'probably', 'perhaps', and 'it would seem' type.

CONTENTS

1. *Eighteen Twelve and After*

1812

WHEN Russians talk of the war of 1812 they do not mean the war in which Washington was burned by the British, but the war in which, apparently, Moscow was burned by the Russians. This war between the French republican empire and the Russian tsarist empire was as remarkable a high-spot in the history of the latter as it was a low-spot in the history of Napoleon. For Russia, it was one of those rare moments in history when almost all people, serfs and lords, merchants and bureaucrats, put aside their enmities and realized that they were all Russians. Russia, sometimes called 'a state without a people', seemed to become, for a few precious months, one people, and never quite forgot the experience.

Five years previously, in 1807, Tsar Alexander I had made peace with Napoleon after losing more battles than he could afford and after becoming dissatisfied with his British allies. This peace was made at the celebrated meeting on a river raft at Tilsit, and entailed Russia's desertion of her ally Prussia, as well as her adherence to Napoleon's Continental System. Neither of these elements were approved by Alexander's subjects, and both he and the treaty became unpopular in Russian society. Betrayal of Prussia was regarded as dishonourable, while the Continental System, which meant the virtual cessation of Anglo-Russian trade, damaged many influential merchants and landowners, for Russia was already becoming a grain exporter, and north Russia traditionally supplied the British navy with its masts, rope, and sails.

True, the Treaty of Tilsit gave Alexander a free hand in Finland. He conquered that territory from the Swedes, and from 1809 until 1917 Finland was part of the Russian Empire, having a semi-independent status as a grand duchy. But this success did not mollify Alexander's critics at home. The Tsar, moreover, was himself becoming more and more wary of his new friend Napoleon, and in any case it is probably true that he had signed the treaty only because he had little choice and wanted time to gain strength for a final struggle against the French. For his part, Napoleon had several real and imagined grievances, and it soon became evident that the fine sentiments expressed at Tilsit had lost their meaning. Alexander prepared for the conflict by securing his flanks; he signed a treaty with Sweden and brought to a temporary close Russia's Danubian quarrel with Turkey. Napoleon prepared an invasion army and in June 1812 led it into eastern Poland, where he met Alexander's final peace envoy and sent him back with a negative answer.

Alexander had chosen to appoint himself commander-in-chief of the Russian armies in the field. But his advisers, remembering Alexander's disastrous intervention in 1805 which had given Napoleon his great victory at Austerlitz, persuaded him that he could do most good by going to Moscow and rallying the country. This left the minister of war, Barclay de Tolly, in command. Barclay was with the 1st Western Army, and the 2nd Western Army was under Bagration. The latter, senior to Barclay in military rank, was now subordinate to him by virtue of Barclay's ministerial rank. This situation was no doubt the basic cause of Bagration's hostility to his commander, expressed in occasional backbiting and intrigue.

Bagration was not a Russian, but a Georgian. He had learned the military trade fighting in what were already Russia's traditional battlegrounds. He had fought in the Caucasus against tribes resisting Russian encroachment, against the Turks on the south-western frontier, and against Sweden; Russia at the turn of the century was still expanding and meeting resistance as she did so. But Bagration's greatest glory, and one which probably made him feel superior to Barclay, was his outstanding record as a commander under the greatest of all Russian generals, Suvorov, in the Italian and Swiss campaigns of 1799. Unlike Barclay, he had the reputation of a fiery and irrepressible warrior, but Barclay's contribution to the Russian army was far greater. Although no stranger to the battlefield, Barclay was more an organizer and thinker. In 1809, after service against the Turks, French and Swedes, and having attained the rank of General of Infantry, he became governor of the Finland he had just helped to conquer. Then in 1810 he became war minister and immediately began to strengthen the army; he wrote a manual of generalship, tightened army organization, built strongpoints, and doubled the size of the army. Like Bagration, Barclay was not a true Russian. His Scottish ancestors had been among the hundreds of skilled foreigners recruited by Russian rulers in the seventeenth century to serve as officers, technicians, or administrators. His family had settled at Riga in the Baltic provinces where the gentry, which was the ruling class and which provided the Russian Empire with many of its most notable administrators, was of German origin.

Barclay could speak Russian only badly, although this was less of a handicap than it might seem, for Russia's upper gentry, the class which provided high officers and administrators, regarded Russian as the language of the common people. Top people spoke French, or if not French, German.

As Barclay's army slowly retreated eastwards from Vilna, it was joined by the 2nd Army retreating north-eastwards. Under Bagration's skilful leadership the 2nd Army had beaten off attacks by its French pursuers; thus Napoleon had failed in his attempt to prevent the union of the two main Russian armies. However, the Emperor of the French still hoped to achieve his original intention, to win an early decisive victory and thereby persuade Alexander to become his ally again. The French army was now approaching Smolensk, the westernmost city of Russia proper (as distinct from White Russia). Napoleon expected that the Russians would make a real stand here, but they did not. Barclay merely fought a very stiff rearguard action and after fighting withdrew from the city, having burned much of it.

In the circumstances the policy of retreating and avoiding a decisive battle was the only possible course. Although intensive recruiting was being carried out it would obviously be some time before Russia could convert her manpower superiority into military superiority. In the meantime, withdrawal forced Napoleon either to abandon his enterprise or to push on and thus extend his supply lines. The Russian military leaders were familiar with Wellington's strategy in the Peninsular campaign and realized it was well suited for Russia. Both Barclay and Alexander favoured a policy of retreat well before the 1812 campaign started. But neither Alexander nor Barclay had anticipated the strength of public opposition to their strategy. In St. Petersburg, Alexander was now at the lowest point of his popularity. He was blamed for making peace with Napoleon in 1807, a peace which had dishonoured Russia and had not finally saved the country from French attack, and he was blamed for retreating before Napoleon. Especially was he criticized for entrusting his armies to Barclay, a foreigner who did not understand how precious was every inch of Russian soil. After Smolensk had been relinquished without any attempt at what the St. Petersburg gentry considered a proper fight, Barclay's position became untenable. Alexander replaced him with General Kutuzov. However, Barclay continued to serve under Kutuzov and his policy was not abandoned. Kutuzov, a hero of the Turkish wars and a self-styled pupil of Suvorov, was by this time too old for his job. He was sixty-seven, so fat that he could hardly walk, gluttonous, in ill-health and within eight months of death. But he had the virtue of being really

Russian and of enjoying the complete confidence of public opinion. St. Petersburg society and the army officers would accept a retreat ordered by Kutuzov more readily than a retreat ordered by Barclay.

Meanwhile, Napoleon's Grande Armée was shambling across the Russian plains. It was a long, hot summer and thousands of soldiers succumbed to heat exhaustion before it was decided to march only at night. Discipline had degenerated. Supplies were short. Evidently, Napoleon's quartermasters had counted on scavenging to meet a large part of their daily requirements, but the retreating Russians left behind them little that was edible. Most successes that were achieved in foraging were made by the more experienced French soldiers and this, added to the stingy paternalism of the French quartermasters when distributing supplies to the contingents of their allies, intensified the hostility of the non-French towards the French. The horses suffered even more from the supply shortage; many of them died from bad feeding, while others were themselves eaten by the soldiers. By the end of August many of the non-French troops were barefoot and their dust-caked uniforms little better than rags. Stragglers were numbered in the thousands; some of these were merely ill, for typhus and dysentery were spreading, but the majority were lagging behind voluntarily as a tactical preliminary to desertion and return home. Above all, water was short. The few good sources were usually tainted; occasionally a corpse or an amputated limb would be found in a spring or pond, deposited by the retreating Russians and perhaps recalling to the French soldiers Napoleon's utterance at Smolensk: 'how sweet smells the corpse of an enemy!'

Thus, despite the legend of the subsequent retreat from Moscow, it was the advance which caused most damage to the invaders. There was never any need for the Russian army to fight a set-piece battle, for Napoleon's forces were disintegrating day by day. However, Kutuzov was persuaded by public opinion, pressure from St. Petersburg, and the enthusiasm of his junior officers, to make one stand before Moscow. Thus occurred the battle of Borodino, a bloody contest which was strategically quite unnecessary but which was undertaken because to surrender Moscow without a fight was unthinkable. Although Peter the Great had made St. Petersburg the official capital, in the minds of Russians Moscow was still the traditional capital.

So in early September the Russian army stopped retreating and formed up in a defensive position on high ground near the village of Borodino, commanding the Smolensk–Moscow highway about seventy miles west of Moscow. The Russian forces numbered about 120,000, of whom 10,000 were hastily raised and half-trained militia sent out from Moscow.

Barclay commanded the right wing and Bagration the left, with the Russian HQ in the centre. Wisely, Kutuzov passed the battle well out of cannon range, consuming cold chicken and champagne.

By this time the French army had shrunk from the half-million, with which it had begun the campaign, to a mere 130,000, and was already slightly inferior to the Russians in artillery. Napoleon decided to make a frontal attack on the opposing positions, probably fearing that otherwise the Russians would be tempted to retreat once more and deny him his long-desired victory. At the end of a hard-fought day, in which positions changed hands time after time, the Russians began a slow and orderly withdrawal. Although the French had won the battlefield they had not won the war, for they had not destroyed the opposing army. At Borodino, which Napoleon later adjudged his most expensive and terrible battle, the French suffered 30,000 casualties and the Russians 40,000 (some Russian historians give the French casualties as 68,000; some French historians give the Russian casualties as 60,000). Bagration was mortally wounded and died some weeks later at his country estate. Barclay, as though conscious of his recent unpopularity, deliberately exposed himself in the battle, emerging a hero and uninjured.

Why Napoleon failed to win his expected victory has remained a controversial issue, which some historians have avoided by claiming that Borodino was in fact a French victory. The fundamental fact is that the two armies were closely matched in strength and that Napoleon on this occasion was not able to win a smashing victory by taking advantage of poor generalship on the part of his opponent. There was one critical point in the battle when Napoleon could have turned the tide by committing his reserve, the Imperial Guard. However, despite the urgings of his generals, he did not do this and lost his chance. It has to be remembered, too, that Napoleon was unwell at the time. Moreover, the greater part of his army had been afflicted with chronic diarrhoea since entering Russia. This ailment was almost catastrophic for the cavalry, for reasons which do not need to be explained. One French cavalry lieutenant, writing to his wife about the battle, made this comment:

> I had again become afflicted by the diarrhoea which had so tortured me at Smolensk, and this day I experienced one of the worst imaginable agonies. For I wanted neither to leave my post nor dismount. I dare not say what I did to get rid of that which was tormenting me, but in the process I lost two handkerchiefs.[1]

A week after Borodino, Napoleon stood on a hill overlooking Moscow and, according to an eye-witness, was exceedingly contented. With

---

[1]   *Vie de Planat de la Faye, Souvenirs, lettres et dictées* (1895), 82.

Moscow in his grasp, he thought that Alexander would sue for peace, leaving him free to master the rest of the world. This showed a crucial misjudgement of Alexander and of Russia; shortly after this the Tsar told one of Napoleon's peace envoys that he would rather grow potatoes in Siberia than submit to the French Emperor.

By arrangement between the two sides, the Russian army left Moscow through one gate while the French entered it through another. Instead of crowds on the streets and a welcoming deputation, Napoleon met empty streets and silence. Almost all the population of Moscow had left, taking the most transportable valuables and food along with them. This was an unusual and unnerving experience for Napoleon, and so was the fire of Moscow which broke out shortly after the French arrived. Moscow was built of wood, except for a few mansions and public buildings. After four days of burning, during which a lack of fire pumps and the indiscipline of the occupying troops made fire-fighting ineffectual, about four-fifths of the city was uninhabitable. The difficulty in properly housing his troops, added to the anxiety about his supply lines, forced Napoleon to quit Moscow. He waited a few weeks, hoping that Alexander would negotiate, then gave the order to leave.

The Russians believed (and still do) that it was the French who set fire to Moscow to vent their frustration at finding so little to loot and to eat in the city. Among Russia's allies, the belief grew that the fire was an act of noble self-sacrifice on the part of the Russians, prepared to destroy what they valued most for the sake of defeating Napoleon. After the war the then governor of Moscow, Rostopchin, found himself lionized in European society, which believed that it was he who had issued the order for the burning. Responding to this flattery, Rostopchin openly claimed that he had been responsible. However, on returning to Russia, where the fire of Moscow was regarded as a dastardly act, he found that his claim had made him very unpopular. Accordingly, he denied his complicity. The truth of the matter has never been reliably established, but the balance of probability suggests that it was indeed Rostopchin who was responsible. After all it was he who, before leaving Moscow, ignited his own house and ordered the removal of the city's fire pumps.

The French left Moscow in mid-October, with the intention of returning west by a route more southerly than their approach road. The Russian army when it abandoned Moscow had not moved north, so as to cover St. Petersburg, but had chosen a far better strategy, moving south and then west so as to threaten Napoleon's communications and to have access to the food supplies of the fertile south. The French Emperor hoped that *en route* he would meet the Russian army and win a victory which might not be decisive but would at least camouflage his humiliation. On leaving Moscow he ordered the blowing-up of the Kremlin, but this order was not fulfilled, because the fuses were wet. Another unfulfilled order forbade officers and men to burden themselves with loot; when the *Grande Armée* left Moscow it resembled more a caravan of carpet traders than an army. Some officers had found Russian carts and carriages which they loaded with all kinds of furniture, pictures, and wines.

A week after leaving Moscow there was a heavy engagement with Kutuzov, resulting in both sides retiring to lick their wounds. Napoleon was forced to retreat along the road by which he had advanced, via Borodino with its still-unburied corpses. Although Kutuzov, to the disgust of the British general who was attached to his headquarters, avoided close engagements with his retreating opponent, Cossacks and partisans were quick to bring a bestial death to stragglers or lagging detachments. The first snow fell in the first week of November. Neither the cavalry nor the artillery had been supplied with winter horseshoes and it was not long before most of the army's horses disappeared. Without horse transport the supply situation became catastrophic and more men dropped out by the roadside. At the end of November the Russians were outmanoeuvred for a few precious hours, enabling most of the army to cross the river Berezina, but thousands of stragglers and camp followers were killed at this point, drowned, trampled underfoot by their comrades, or massacred by Russian guns. It was not until early December that the really cold weather set in. Contrary to the impression given by Napoleon's apologists, there was no early winter that year and the French were not defeated by the cold. The cold, when it came, only finished the job. In the final count, probably four-fifths of the half million men who followed Napoleon into Russia were lost, and only a few of these died from cold.

After the crossing of the Berezina and the onset of below-zero temperatures, Napoleon left the remains of his army and went on ahead back to France. 1812 had not been a good year for him. For Alexander and for Russia, on the other hand, 1812 had been a great year. It was not simply a military triumph; it seemed to be a demonstration of moral strength. Earlier, the government had feared that invasion would spark off widespread peasant revolts, but this had not happened and the people and government had, for once, stood shoulder to shoulder.[2] Thus the Russians were right to call this campaign the Patriotic War, and there is some justification for choosing 1812 as the starting point for a history of modern Russia.

[2] There were, however, one or two minor revolts, typically by peasants in areas not threatened by the invasion, who resisted call-up.

The Tsar in Europe

As soon as Napoleon's rearguard left Russian territory Alexander had to decide whether to rest on his laurels, or to pursue the French until they were irrevocably defeated. Despite opposition at home, Alexander decided to continue the war, and personally took over his troops at Vilna. This decision was bad for the Russian economy, but Alexander was unable to resist the opportunity of leading his victorious army to liberate Europe, from a godless tyrant. It appealed to his vanity, his thirst for military glory, his liberalism, and his newly acquired piety.

The French defeat in Russia, and the incursion of Alexander's troops into central and western Europe, prompted a shifting of alliances, and in 1813 the victorious armies (Russian, Prussian, and Austrian), after winning the battle of Leipzig,[3] triumphantly entered Paris. The subsequent treaty, thanks to Alexander's influence, was not ungenerous towards the former enemy; Napoleon was allowed to exercise his talents as sovereign of Elba, and France was allowed to keep her 1792 frontiers. Before approving the restoration of the Bourbons, Alexander insisted that the latter should grant their French subjects some kind of constitution. After the treaty was signed Alexander visited England, where he received a genuine welcome from the people but not from the ruling class. At the ensuing Congress of Vienna, Alexander was opposed on a number of points not only by the British but especially by the Austrians. At one stage the erstwhile allies, far from organizing a peaceful Europe, were themselves on the edge of war. But unity was restored, and strengthened when Napoleon returned to France in 1815.

In the ensuing campaign, Russian troops did not participate at the battle of Waterloo, but they made a second entry into Paris, where they were welcomed almost as liberators. The Russians had been preceded by the Prussian army, which was bullying the Parisians and preparing to blow up the Pont d'Ièna (a bridge named after Napoleon's victory over the Prussians in 1806; the Prussians, insulted, had decided to punish the bridge rather than rename it). The calming effect of Alexander's arrival, his unconcealed sympathy for the French people in the previous year's negotiations, his fine presence and his ability to please, made the Russian Tsar a folk-hero not only in France but in most of Europe. When he went home he took with him a great reputation; and left behind 30,000 Russian troops who stayed until 1818 as part of the allied garrison in Paris and eastern France. It was some of these troops, influenced by their stay abroad, who a few years later would be plotting to murder Alexander.

[3] Of the estimated 50,000 Allied casualties, about 22,000 were Russian.

Russian society in 1812

The total population of the Empire when Napoleon invaded was forty-one million (see table, p. 600). Thus even at this time Russia had seemingly enormous manpower reserves; the population of Great Britain was eighteen million and that of the USA eight million. But the structure of Russian society and of the Russian economy ensured that the human potential of the Empire was not efficiently utilized.

Muscovite Russians ('Great Russians') made up only about half the total. Of the others, the largest group were the Ukrainians (sometimes, to their distaste, called 'Little Russians'). These dwelt in the south-western part of the Empire, with Kiev and Kharkov their best-known cities. At one time they had been under Polish rule, but in 1654 their leaders had opted for allegiance to Moscow. Their language was very similar to Russian, and it seems likely that the difference between them and the Great Russians was less in 1812 than it became later. On the northern border of the Ukraine was Byelorussia or Belarus ('White Russia'), similarly one of the eastern Slavic nations, but less populous than the Ukraine.

One other group which was predominantly Slavic were the Cossacks. The name Cossack means 'free warrior', and certainly freedom and warfare were the distinguishing preoccupations of these people. Their territory was mainly in the south of European Russia, around the lower and middle courses of the rivers Don and Dnieper. They were descended principally from Russian ancestors who had fled either from Muscovy or from Poland, from the former to evade serfdom or other hardships, from the latter to avoid oppression from the Catholic Church and non-Russian overlords. The communities they established were on the borders of the Polish and Muscovite lands, and served as a first line of defence against alien peoples, notably the Turks. Apart from fighting off invaders, the Cossacks also found themselves resisting the expansion of Muscovy, but were often compelled either to become subjects of the tsar as the latter incorporated their lands into his own territory, or to move further on. In this situation the Cossacks developed into a tough, savage, and volatile people, jealous of their freedoms, great fighters on horseback, and running their affairs by a riotous form of democracy with elected headmen. In the rebellions of the previous two centuries Cossacks had played a leading part, but in the eighteenth century they had begun to lose their autonomy. The Russian government allowed them their land and did not impose serfdom, but it did demand military service. One by one the Cossack communes in the Empire were converted to military units; each Cossack male was required to serve in the army, providing his own horse. Contrary to the general belief, the Cossacks did not provide outstanding cavalry units, but they excelled in pursuing a beaten enemy and in looting. From the political point of view they changed during the nineteenth century from an independent and vaguely hostile people into one of the most loyal and ruthless supports of the regime.

Of the non-Slavic peoples, the Germanic, Jewish, and Finnic were the most important; Jews (see p. 127) were rare except in the western borderlands. Essentially there were two Finnic groups; the Finns of Finland (and their kinsmen in Estonia), and the remnants of the Finnic tribes which had originally inhabited Muscovy. The latter had been mainly absorbed by the incoming Slavs to whom they passed on some of their physical features, but there remained isolated pockets of them. The Germans, who like the Cossacks played a role in the Empire out of all proportion to their numbers, could also be divided into two groups. Of little political importance were the German settlers who had moved with governmental approval and privileges to the lower Volga and south Russia, where by hard work and intelligent methods they became prosperous farmers, arousing the envy of their neighbours. The Baltic Germans were an entirely different group. They had settled during the twelfth and thirteenth centuries in what is now Estonia and Latvia, and had become the ruling class of landowners while the original inhabitants became an inferior labouring class. With their knightly origins, or at least a tradition of social superiority, and their German method and diligence, they supplied the Empire with many of its leading figures: soldiers, sailors, governors, and administrators. They tended to be unpopular among true Russians, partly because of envy but partly because in the eighteenth century several ruling empresses had employed them on a large scale as favourites, advisers, and taxgatherers, and many of them had abused their responsibilities.

There were numerous Mongols residing within the Empire. They were mainly the remnants of the Tartars who, in the thirteenth century, had invaded the early Russian settlements and held the Russian people as tribute-paying subjects for two centuries. The Tartars had not settled within the Russian borders, but they had established communities outside, notably Kazan and Astrakhan, which had fallen into Russian hands as Muscovy expanded in the fifteenth and sixteenth centuries. Other non-Europeans lived in Siberia which, although not highly valued by St. Petersburg and largely unexplored, was part of the Empire and contained a variety of pagan tribes, including Red Indians,[4] of whom little was known at this time.

[4] *Arctic*, Vol. 22, 71.

Of the total population, only about 4 per cent lived in towns; and the definition of town included hundreds of settlements which were little more than villages. There were only two cities with a population of more than 100,000. These were St. Petersburg (308,000) and Moscow (270,000). There was a great gap between these two, which were genuine cities, and the next most important towns, all of which had less than 60,000 inhabitants. St. Petersburg had been the capital of the Empire for a hundred years, and by 1812 most of its public buildings were complete. Architecturally, it was European, in accordance with the westernizing tastes of its founder, Peter the Great. Moscow, on the other hand, was traditionally Russian, with its Kremlin and old churches. This difference was reflected in the inhabitants of the two cities. The people of St. Petersburg considered the Muscovites to be a trifle primitive, while the citizens of Moscow regarded St. Petersburg society as slightly alien and vaguely suspect. Many regarded Moscow as the 'real' capital, certainly the spiritual capital, and the habit was developing of referring to 'the two capitals'. Tsars were crowned in Moscow.

Of the total population, less than 2 per cent belonged to the nobility, a term which embraces a wider range of status than in the west, and which may be regarded in Russian history as synonymous with gentry. Another 2 per cent covered the priests and emergent middle class, leaving the peasantry as 96 per cent of the total population. The nobility included a small aristocracy, but consisted mainly of average and small landowners. At the beginning of the nineteenth century the nobility was at the peak of its privilege. The aristocracy was mainly families which could trace their ancestry back to Rurik, the reputed founder of the Russian state ten centuries previously, or to one or two other ancient rulers of lands since absorbed by Russia. These used the title of prince, but because titles were inherited by every child of a family, princely rank was losing its exclusiveness. Close relatives of the tsar were called grand princes, often translated as grand dukes.

Up to the time of Peter the Great the majority of the gentry inherited their land and title, and performed state tasks. But the tsars did distribute state land, and the peasants on that land, to non-nobles who entered their service as soldiers or administrators. Possession of this land made the new owner one of the gentry. Because in Russia land was plentiful but labour scarce, it became the practice to tie peasants to the land they worked. On privately owned land they would work both for their own subsistence and also for their owner, who would thus be sustained while he attended to his state duties. Thus depriving the peasants of their freedom to move (that is, making them serfs) had some justification originally.

Peter the Great, with his insatiable need for more soldiers and administrators, effected a change in the nature of nobility. For a time it seemed that whereas previously the state had obtained most of its servants from the ranks of the nobility, henceforth it would fill the ranks of the nobility with its servants. Peter insisted that merit and not nobility should determine a person's role in government service, and that when commoners reached responsible positions (that is, a rank) they should automatically receive gentry status. To this end, and to make his civil service as prestigious and attractive as his military service, he introduced his celebrated Table of Ranks. With amendments, this remained in force until 1917 and gave a man precedence not because of his blood, but because of his job. Henceforth, every rank in the administration would be equivalent to an existing rank in the army so that, for example, a provincial secretary would have equal status with an army second lieutenant, and top civil servants could style themselves 'general', and wear an appropriate uniform. There were fourteen ranks; the upper eight automatically conferred hereditary, and the lower six non-hereditary, nobility. (Under Nicholas I the non-noble but privileged title of 'honoured citizen' would be introduced as reward for achievement, especially in commerce, learning, and the arts.)

Thus by the time Alexander became tsar there were six types of gentry: the aristocrats; nobles of inherited title; nobles holding foreign titles; nobles created by royal patent; nobles who had obtained their title by attaining a rank in the bureaucracy; and those who had been ennobled on gaining an officer's commission. The aristocrats tended to regard the last three groups as upstarts, and also looked down on the barons included in the nobles of inherited title; the title of baron, like that of count, was Germanic, and introduced by Peter mainly to reward merchants or industrialists. It was the aristocracy which, towards the end of the eighteenth century, set the fashion of speaking French rather than Russian, of sending its children to French-oriented schools, or hiring French tutors, cooks, and dressmakers. This frenchification, and the wearing of European-style instead of traditional Russian clothing, soon spread to the middle ranks of the gentry.

By Alexander's time the gentry had been relieved of the obligation to serve the state, but the serfs had not been relieved of the complementary obligation of serving their lords. Hence much of the rural discontent of this time. But most of the gentry did in fact serve, although usually for shorter periods, partly out of habit and partly because those who had never entered state service lost important privileges. Most gentry had only small estates; about one-third possessed fewer than ten male serfs, and another third between ten and thirty. Although small in numbers, the gentry were the dominant force in political life. In the eighteenth century it was palace revolutions carried out by Guards officers, themselves from the upper ranks of the gentry, which deposed and imposed the succession of unlovable characters who occupied the throne. It was the Guards officers who had murdered Paul and installed Alexander. Obviously, as even the tough Catherine discovered, any tsar wishing to retain his title could not afford to antagonize the gentry. This is why both Catherine and Alexander failed to fulfil their wish and promise to do something for the serfs. Yet despite the political power of the gentry, which was due partly to the absence of a substantial middle class whom the tsar might play off against the nobility, the individual Russian gentleman had very much less personal freedom than his western counterpart.

There were two main types of peasant: privately owned peasants (serfs), who comprised rather more than half the total; and state peasants, who were rather less than half the peasant population,[5] and who lived on land which had not yet been distributed to private owners, being still the property of the state. All lived hard and unrewarding lives, but the serfs were clearly the worst off. A serf was simply the property of his owner, virtually a slave. He could be bought or sold, made to work in a factory, had no meaningful legal rights, and in the worst cases was completely at the mercy of his owners, who could have him flogged to death, sent to Siberia, or conscripted for twenty-five-years' service in the army. Most of the gentry were not brutal, a few for moral or economic reasons actually gave their serfs freedom, yet most treated their serfs rather as they might treat their domestic animals. Sometimes serfs were compelled to work six days a week on their lord's land, leaving only Sunday for work on their own allotment; and at some periods and places they could be flogged for working on Sundays. Somewhat more fortunate were those who, instead of providing labour, paid a regular rent in cash or kind. Others were compelled to work in factories; they might be attached to workshops established by their lord on the estate, or they might be hired or sold to factory-owners elsewhere. Some were taken as domestic servants by their owner. Others, luckier, were allowed to seek their fortunes as hired workers in the towns, remitting part of their wages to their landowner.

As will be shown later, there were economic as well as moral reasons why serfdom was undesirable. Alexander took few positive measures, and those he did take (like his ban on newspaper advertisements of serfs for sale) were easily circumvented. But he did forbid the extension of serfdom to his recently acquired territory in Poland and Finland. This was a

[5] By mid-century state peasants outnumbered serfs.

considerable step forward, because serfdom had been extended to the Ukraine only a few decades previously. Later, Nicholas I similarly forbade the spread of serfdom to Siberia; any serf who could escape and settle in Siberia unapprehended became a state peasant. Yet Alexander continued the practice, which he acknowledged to be wrong, of giving state land to favourites and supporters, thus converting state peasants to privately owned serfs. But his gifts were never quite as generous as those of his grandmother Catherine, who gave away peasants by the thousand to her various lovers.

The gentry and the clergy were exempt from personal taxation, but the peasants were not. In 1825, the government's revenue of 393 million roubles included 115 million derived from the peasants' poll-tax, while the 118 million from indirect taxes on alcoholic beverages also came mainly out of the peasants' pockets. On the other hand the peasants benefited little from the corresponding 393 million roubles of government expenditure. Fifty-four million of this went on state debts, and eighteen million on court expenses. The army took 152 million and the navy twenty-one million. The ministry of finance took no less than eighty-eight million, of which much was no doubt expended on tax-gathering administration. After deducting fifteen million for the ministry of the interior, five million each for justice and foreign affairs, which had little business with the peasantry, and twelve million for contingencies, there was left about seventeen million for services which might directly or indirectly benefit the peasant: transport, education (four million), and posts.

An additional four million roubles went to the Orthodox Church and could be regarded as money spent on behalf of the masses. For the Russian people was a religious people. The tsar (the 'Preserver of the Dogmas') and most Russians belonged to the Russian Orthodox Church, although the Baltic gentry usually remained Lutheran. Foreign brides of sons of tsars adopted the Orthodox faith. At times in Russian history the Orthodox Church became a great patriotic force, symbolizing the common tradition and experience of the Russian people. Together with serfdom, autocracy, and the army, the Church was one of the great forces which made Russia what it was, shaping Russian attitudes and behaviour for nearly ten centuries.

The Church

The Greek Orthodox faith was adopted by the Kievan Russians in AD 989, by order of their Grand Prince Vladimir. This was the most important event in the history of the Russian people. Among other things, it cut Russia off from Catholic Europe; Russia never had a real Renaissance, although certain of her rulers tried to impose one. Nor did she experience an intellectual exercise like the Reformation; she did have a religious schism but this was intellectually primitive.

At first, Greek priests and teachers supervised the affairs of the Russian Church, but after the fall of Constantinople the native Russian clergy, aided and abetted by the tsars, asserted itself. Moscow was proclaimed the 'Third Rome' ('and a fourth there shall not be'), and a century later the Metropolitan of Moscow was elevated to the dignity of Patriarch. Some historians see in the concept of Moscow as the city of God, and in the Russians' belief that only they held the true faith, a spirit of Messianism which persisted into the Soviet period. Certainly the Russian Orthodox believer felt that somehow God liked him better than he liked other Christians, and in the nineteenth century the defenders of the principle of autocracy exploited this feeling by emphasizing that the tsar was God's favourite lieutenant on earth. The expression Holy Russia conveyed all this. The philosopher Soloviev would later observe that whereas a Frenchman, wishing to express all that was best in France, would speak of *la belle France*, and an Englishman would talk of *olde England*, Russians would speak of Holy Russia. This was not a political or aesthetic ideal, but moral and religious. Dostoevsky, speaking through Shatov in *The Possessed*, went further:

A nation only remains a nation when it has its own God and uncompromisingly rejects all the other gods in the world, and when it believes that with its God it will conquer and drive out all other gods from the world . . . But there is only one truth, so only one nation can have the true God, even though other nations may have their own great gods. The Russian people is the only 'God-bearing' nation . . .

In the early sixteenth century there had been a struggle between those priests who deplored the Church's rich landholdings and its role in temporal affairs, and the official leadership of the Church. The latter, relying heavily on the concept of heresy for moral strength and on the tsar's forces for physical strength, suppressed the dissidents, only to fall victim to a permanent schism in the seventeenth century. This schism, which created the problem of the Old Believers, was provoked by Patriarch Nikon, who enforced the correction of rituals which, according to Greek scholars, had become corrupted either through time or during their transfer from the Greek to the Russian Church. Among the issues which became burning issues was whether two or three fingers should be used in the blessing, and how Jesus should be spelled in the Cyrillic alphabet. The Old Believers were those who, despite persecution, insisted on keeping the old practices unchanged, and violently opposed foreign interference in Russian tradition. Over the succeeding centuries, the persecuted Old

Believers established their own communities which, according to foreign travellers, were cleaner, better kept, and more prosperous than the villages of the Orthodox. For the Orthodox Church, the schism meant not only the existence of a rival faith, but a loss of power; before Nikon the Church was frequently dominant in affairs of state, but his reliance on the state for help in chastising his priestly opponents led to a weakening of the Church's influence. This weakening was followed a few decades later by Peter the Great's abolition of the office of Patriarch and the creation of the Holy Synod. The latter, headed by an Over Procurator (a layman appointed by the tsar) enabled the government to keep a close eye on the Church. Catherine the Great further increased state influence by taking much of the Church land and, in partial substitution, giving state salaries to the bishops; that is, bringing the higher clergy into the pay of the state.

The subservience of the Church to the state, and the corresponding willingness of the state to serve the Church, seemed to intensify in the nineteenth century. The Sermon on the Mount well expresses the philosophy which the Church taught its members. Some of this teaching was not open to misinterpretation. 'Blessed are the merciful for they shall obtain mercy' is a concept which underlies the charity of the typical Russian; not simply the easy charity of alms-giving but the readiness to regard, say, a criminal as unfortunate rather than evil. The influential writings of Makarenko, the Soviet educationist, on the possibilities of social redemption for hardened criminals would be well within this tradition. On the other hand, 'Blessed are the meek, for they shall inherit the earth' was a text easily misused to persuade the flock that sufferings imposed by an arbitrary state were in accordance with God's scheme. The place of the Church in Nicholas I's ideology of 'Orthodoxy, Autocracy, Nationalism' will be described in Chapter 2. For emphasis, here is an extract from the catechism used in the schools and churches of Nicholas's Russia:

Response: . . . God commands us to love and obey from the inmost recesses of the heart every authority, and particularly the Emperor.
Question: What examples confirm this doctrine?
Response: The example of Jesus Christ himself, who lived and died in allegiance to the Emperor of Rome, and respectfully submitted to the judgement which condemned him to death . . .

After the death of Alexander II in 1881, the Orthodox Church, with Pobedonostsev as Over Procurator, would eagerly support the autocracy and obtain state aid to persecute Jews, Old Believers, and the various sects. Although some nineteenth-century revolutionaries were priests, sons of priests, or seminary students, most of the clergy preached submission.

The Russian Orthodox clergy was divided into two classes, the white and the black. The black clergy were monks, occupied with various monastic works (including the preservation of what learning the Church possessed), and provided the bishops and other high dignitaries. The white clergy were the parish priests. Unlike the celibate black clergy they were required to marry (but could not re-marry) and, in imitation of Christ, wore long hair and beards. Ideally, they were expected to possess a good strong voice: the more leonine the priest, the more his parishioners respected him. The priest was attached to one church for all his working life and received a negligible salary. In the villages he lived almost like a peasant, keeping his own livestock and regarding the local landowner as a very superior being. His income depended on how much he could squeeze from his flock for baptisms, marriages, burials, blessings, and devil-exorcisings. Although he was a graduate of a seminary or theological school, he did not have much learning, but he knew by heart the holy texts and it was these which he retailed, without interpretation, to his congregation. Most parishioners, even the most ignorant, regarded the priest as a church functionary, someone who performed necessary services, rather than as a spiritual guide. This meant that the Orthodox tended to decide for themselves what was good and what was bad: few Russians, for example, took seriously all the admonitions of their priests, but they did celebrate with great fervency such meaningful ceremonies as Christmas and, especially, Easter.

The holy man (*Starets*) who was such a feature of Russian spiritual life was not necessarily a monk, although he would settle in or alongside a monastery. A top-class holy man would typically be a rough, ascetic, semi-literate, eccentric, pious, speak-his-own-mind-to-anybody character. Because of his evident spirituality and understanding, all kinds of people would come to him with all kinds of problems. However, the Russian religious mind, which tended to confuse ignorance with holiness and naïvety with purity, did not always distinguish the genuine holy man from inferior imitations.

A really famous holy man would bring both fame and riches to the monastery which harboured him. Many were canonized. The creation of saints was simpler in the Orthodox Church than elsewhere. Later, under Nicholas II, canonization became so common that it lost part of its glory: it was sufficient for leading figures in a locality to clamour loud and long enough for a defunct bishop or holy man of that locality to be promoted to sainthood. The lucky corpse would then be disinterred and placed on public view in some kind of glass case. Traditionally the strongest claimant for sainthood was a revered holy man in the vicinity of whose corpse miracles were observed.

Theologically, the Orthodox Church was characterized by its denials of the issuance of the Holy Ghost from the Son of God, of papal infallibility and primacy, of the concept of purgatory, and of indulgences. It was cautious in its use of the word transubstantiation. In the 1839 catechism this word would be regarded as only one of several alternatives, and the catechism, while maintaining that the bread and wine were truly of the body and blood of Christ, refrained from explaining *how* they were thus transformed; this was a secret which only God could understand. Outwardly, the Church approved the worship of relics, and accepted pilgrimage as a significant act of worship. These characteristics continued into the Soviet period. Half a century after the Bolshevik Revolution, pilgrims in their thousands would still be ambulating each year all over Russia, smearing their kisses over the glass cases containing the remains of saints.

Apart from the Old Believers, there were numerous sects. Among them were the *Doukhobors* ('spirit-wrestlers'), hard-working and quite prosperous, whose refusal to acknowledge the temporal government and its works (including military service and state education) led to government persecution. Towards the end of the century, with the help of Tolstoy and others, many Doukhobors emigrated to western Canada, where their relationship with officialdom was as thorny as it had been with St. Petersburg. Other sectarians were the *Khlysty* ('whips') who liked to flog each other; the 'gapers' who prayed with open mouths so that the Holy Spirit might enter into them; the 'wanderers', who were always on the move in search of God's truth; and the 'jumpers', who prayed while jumping so that their prayers would be closer to God. Alexander I was more tolerant of religious eccentricity than his successors. After all, he liked to regard himself as enlightened.

Alexander I

Napoleon called Alexander 'the Northen Sphinx' and 'a real Byzantine', and it is true that Alexander was easy to misunderstand. But his apparent inconsistency was perhaps due to a conflict of two consistencies, his fear of disorder and his wish for improvement (a conflict which plagued his successors too). In retrospect, it seems that his ideas and his thoughts led their own lives independently of what Alexander happened to say at any particular time. Superficially, he seemed at different times to be an ardent liberal or a reactionary militarist. In conversation he was usually charming and agreeable. To some he seemed a complete diplomat, and to others a complete hypocrite. Physically he was most handsome: tall, of fine bearing, and with attractive blue eyes. These characteristics were presumably inherited from his mother, a German princess. All the later Romanovs were graced, more or less, with the same physical appeal.

Alexander's liberalism was a result of his education and of his earlier friends. His grandmother, Catherine the Great, had provided him with a Swiss tutor who was sympathetic, among other things, to the ideals of the French revolutionaries. The young Alexander was quick to adopt the feelings of his tutor, although he probably did not think about them very deeply. As a young man he acquired friends of progressive outlook, including one who had actually worked among the Jacobins in Paris. In the early years of his reign he discussed with these friends the best means of translating intentions into practice: how to end the brutalizing institution of serfdom without losing the support of the landowning and serf-owning gentry, how to give freedom to the Poles while keeping them attached to Russia, how to give some political rights to the people while maintaining the principle of autocracy.

Alexander at one time had toyed with the idea of renouncing his rights to the succession and going with his wife to live an idyllic life on the banks of the Rhine. However, as soon as he was tsar he showed no interest in relinquishing his authority and this, basically, was why his liberal intentions were so disappointing in realization. Towards the end of his reign, influenced by pious advisers, he dropped some of his liberal pretensions, but not all of his liberal friends. In general, although historians may have treated Alexander too kindly, he was one of the better tsars. Certainly his improvements rarely touched the heart of a problem, but only one of his four successors surpassed him as a reformer.

It is not hard to suggest where Alexander's militarism originated. Both Tsar Peter III, his officially presumed grandfather, and Paul I, his father, had been admirers of all things Prussian, and especially of the Prussian army. Peter III was never happier than when drilling and manoeuvring and inspecting his miniature army of wax soldiers; he even organized a proper field court-martial and ceremonial hanging for a palace rat which had been discovered nibbling one of these toys. Paul, to the dismay of his generals, had prussianized the Russian army, composing his own drill manual on Prussian principles, and designing Prussian-type uniforms and hairstyles for his troops. As a young man Alexander had assisted his father on the parade ground and derived as much satisfaction as Paul in barking out orders, staging meticulous inspections, listening to bands playing, and watching regiments marching.

Alexander acceded in 1801, at the age of twenty-four. There seems little doubt that he had throughout his twenty-four-year reign two burdens on his conscience. Like his grandmother Catherine, he came to the throne as a result of violence, for his father had been murdered by Guards officers wishing to enthrone Alexander. The latter had acquiesced in the conspiracy, persuading himself that his father would be merely deposed, not killed. Secondly, it is quite likely that Alexander had no more right to the throne than had his grandmother; the inheritance of Paul, Alexander and the subsequent so-called Romanovs depended on whether Paul had really been the son of the feeble Peter III, husband of Catherine. Paul was probably Catherine's son, but Catherine by blood had been merely a German princess. She had numerous lovers, and one of these was probably Paul's father. Thus the claims of Paul and subsequent tsars to a divine right to rule were associated with a very questionable past.

The Tsar's advisers: Golitsyn and Arakcheyev

After 1812 the two most influential advisers of the Tsar were A. N. Golitsyn and Arakcheyev, both of whom had been long acquainted with Alexander and held responsible posts. In the difficult days of personal unpopularity and French invasion it was Golitsyn who had led Alexander to the tranquillity of Bible-reading. Alexander, who regarded Golitsyn as an old friend, had appointed him Over Procurator of the Holy Synod in 1803. This government post was one of the most influential in the Empire, and Golitsyn enhanced the office by making himself Alexander's unofficial spiritual adviser. On Golitsyn's urging, in 1812, the Tsar approved the foundation of the St. Petersburg Bible Society by Scottish members of the similar British society. This soon became the Russian Bible Society; its first president was Golitsyn and its most important achievement was the translation of the Old Church Slavonic Bible into Russian. Since Bible-reading could never become popular among illiterates, many of those who had formerly opposed education of the common people changed their minds, and the Bible Society was able to establish several schools for the poor. Because Alexander was known to favour it, all official doors were opened for the Society, and by the time it ceased operations in 1824 it had 289 branches in the Empire.

In 1817 Golitsyn became head of a new ministry of spiritual affairs and education, while remaining Procurator. In this post, while managing public education in a spirit of religious fanaticism, he showed great tolerance towards the many minor religions and sects of Russia (except the Jesuits, who had converted his nephew into an ardent Catholic, and whom, for ostensibly educational reasons, he then expelled from Russia). For the dignitaries of the Russian Orthodox Church such tolerance was unpardonable, as was Golitsyn's reputed sympathy for freemasonry. Arakcheyev, ever jealous of the Tsar's ear, was also seeking ways to unseat his rival. In 1823 an unsavoury and secret alliance was formed between Arakcheyev and the Metropolitan of St. Petersburg. Arakcheyev unearthed as their instrument a monk, Photius, whom Golitsyn had once dismissed from the chaplaincy of a cadet unit, and who was now groomed for the role of holy man. Photius was brought to the capital, was said to have performed one or two satisfactory miracles and, like Rasputin ninety years later, made a great impression in St. Petersburg society. His friends fixed for him an audience with the Tsar, at which the holy man's eloquence evidently shook Alexander, for there followed a ban on secret societies and free-masonry, which Photius had described as enemies of the true faith. Later, Photius had a three-hour interview with Alexander, who called him 'God's envoy'. On this occasion the monk assured the Tsar that there were all sorts of plots afoot, and that the Russian Bible Society was at the centre of them all. The result was the replacement of Golitsyn and the end of the Bible Society. Henceforth Arakcheyev would have no rivals.

Arakcheyev had been a loyal servant of Paul, helping him to prussianize the Russian army. His devotion to Paul's memory no doubt helped him in his dealings with Alexander, who had a bad conscience over his father's murder. In the early part of Alexander's reign Arakcheyev was inspector of artillery, and his improvements did much to prepare the army for its encounter with the French. From 1808 to 1810 he was minister of war. He claimed to be absolutely devoted to Alexander, but it was a very jealous devotion. He was reputed to be of great integrity, an unusual quality among Russian officials. His first care was his military colonies. At the time of his rivalry with Golitsyn he was only content when the Tsar seemed to be paying more attention to the military colonies than to Golitsyn's Bible Society.

Justification for the military colonies was primarily economic. Russia had emerged from the Napoleonic Wars militarily and politically triumph-ant but economically shattered. Although intelligent measures had been taken to subsidize the ravaged areas and to end inflation, the government was heavily indebted at home and abroad. Yet Russia was intent on play-ing the role of a great power, with a correspondingly great army. The milit-ary colonies (which had been tried before 1812, against Arakcheyev's advice, but were expanded only after 1815) were villages whose active male inhab-itants were householding peasants (who worked the fields) and soldiers (who were billeted on the householders). The householders, like everybody else, were under military discipline and, in addition to their economic functions, were drilled and given elementary military training. The soldiers were similarly expected to help in the fields or village workshops. In this way a large standing army could be made economically self-sufficient.[6]

[6] For more on the military colonies, see *The Journal of Modern History*, Vol. 22 (1950), 205–19.

The troops in these colonies were, at first, veteran soldiers, and were billeted on householders who were chosen from men of good character aged from eighteen to forty-five years. Other inhabitants became a reserve. Young children were enrolled, uniformed, and separated from their parents as 'cantonists' to undergo education in military schools. Men over forty-five were required to serve as auxiliaries. Villages thus militarized were on lands belonging to the state, and despite the colonies' unpopularity with the peasants (who in effect found themselves conscripted, together with their families), by 1825 they provided over one-quarter of the army's soldiers. Neither Alexander nor Arakcheyev would tolerate resistance, even though several revolts indicated that the draftees were unhappy.

The villages were often provided with new huts and good furniture, as well as hospitals and churches, all at government expense. Nevertheless the peasants hated them, for they combined the hard labour of agricultural life with the harsh discipline and lack of leisure of army life. In many villages agricultural work was neglected by uncomprehending commanders, but in others, modern and efficient farming was pursued. This efficiency, and perhaps the open and hidden subsidies, enabled the colonies to become, on average, quite prosperous. In a sense they were a primitive form of planned economy. Girls were directed to marry prescribed bachelor soldiers, for example, and Arakcheyev fixed a production target of one baby per year per family. (Wives who failed to fulfil this plan were fined, as were those who miscarried, gave birth to dead babies, or produced daughters instead of sons.) The colonies made an important contribution, both in men and supplies, to the wars of the late twenties, but because of disaffection they lost favour subsequently. They were finally abolished in 1857, having in their final decades provided labour gangs not only for local factories but also for railway-building. Nicholas I established several new colonies, mainly in vulnerable border areas, before he became disillusioned with them.

One reason for the unpopularity of the colonies was the character of their chief. Arakcheyev was virtuous, religious, and honest, but he was also uneducated and sadistic. He tended to appoint men of similar character to command the individual colonies, and the result was a regime of savage and brutal repression. Arakcheyev described himself proudly as 'a truly Russian uneducated gentleman', which was true but did not reveal that he was also decidedly eccentric. He was known to weep on hearing a sad story, yet take delight in ordering the whipping of an errant little girl. He would melt into sentimentality on hearing nightingales sing, and then order all cats to be hung for fear that they might silence this music. In Paul's time he had torn off with his own hands the whiskers of a defaulting

soldier. A doctor in one of the military colonies later testified that Arakcheyev had a twisted psychology and suffered from a 'deep disturbance of
the whole nervous system'. When, in 1819, he suppressed a serious revolt
in one of his colonies, he wrote to Alexander that he had been torn
between two courses. On the one hand he had to act 'decisively' and on
the other hand he had to decide what he should do as a good Christian.
Having 'called on the help of Almighty God' he decided to run the offenders twelve times each through a gauntlet of 1,000 men. As a result,
twenty-five of the delinquents died, which is not surprising since each was
entitled to 12,000 blows. Alexander replied, 'I know exactly how your
sensitive soul must have suffered in these circumstances.' At the end of the
reign the normally dutiful Arakcheyev was neglecting his responsibilities
as he wallowed in a period of depression following the death of his
mistress. This lady was a sadist in her own right, and some ill-treated serfs
finally cut her throat. Arakcheyev wrote despondently to Alexander for
sympathy, and wore around his neck a scarf soaked in her blood.

Russia and the world

Under Alexander, Russia attained a position in Europe which was not to
be regained until 1945. She was victorious in war, had extended her
frontiers almost into central Europe, enjoyed the reputation of liberator,
and had the most powerful army in the world. Yet before Alexander died
Russia's reputation as champion of the oppressed had evaporated, for the
Tsar by his actions proved to be the champion of the oppressors.

Having settled the Polish question as well as his allies at the Vienna
Congress would allow, and having earlier in his reign consolidated the
territorial gains which his grandmother had made in the Black Sea area at
the expense of Turkey, Alexander felt free to play the role of arbiter of
Europe. The foundation for his policy had been laid in 1815 by the
Quadruple Alliance and the Holy Alliance. The Quadruple Alliance,
signed by Britain, Austria, Prussia, and Russia on the morrow of their
triumph over France, contained an article foreshadowing the concept of
the 'summit conference': periodic meetings of rulers and foreign ministers
were proposed to discuss problems which might threaten the peace of
Europe. Five such meetings (congresses) were held, the last being in 1825,
by which year the British had dropped out and the French had been
admitted. As for the Holy Alliance, this was a product of Alexander's new
piety. He had reached the conclusion that peace, justice, and charity in
Europe could be preserved only if rulers would allow themselves to be
guided by the principles of peace, justice, and charity. A document en-
shrining this Christian platitude was prepared and circulated. Most of the

European sovereigns signed it, although without treating it quite as reverently as did Alexander.

The Holy Alliance has been blamed for the suppression of the rebellions against oppressive rulers in Spain, Portugal, Naples, Piedmont, and Greece. In reality, it was the system of congresses introduced by the Quadruple Alliance which enabled Alexander and his fellow-rulers to co-ordinate their actions against what were genuine liberation movements. As he grew older and holier, Alexander came to believe more and more strongly in a worldwide revolutionary conspiracy, working to overthrow the monarchs whom God had appointed to watch over the interests of the peoples. The wave of revolutions of 1820 and 1821 were discussed at the congresses, and Alexander not only urged his fellow-rulers to intervene but, undeterred by an 1820 mutiny in his own élite Semeonov Guards, offered Russian troops to help them. Making grateful use of Alexander's approval, but tactfully declining his troops, Austria and France marched, respectively, into Italy and Spain, suppressing the revolutionary governments and restoring the former rulers. However, because of opposition from Britain, Alexander's wish to dispatch troops to restore Spain's disintegrating South American empire was not fulfilled.

The Greek rebellion was not so easily dealt with. What happened was that a former Greek officer of the Russian army, Ypsilanti, entered the Turkish Danubian provinces with a band of followers. Much of his support came from the recently founded Russian city of Odessa, where there was a substantial Greek population. Because he had entered from Russia, the Greek inhabitants of the Turkish provinces believed he had Russian support and met him with open arms. However, after some successes, Ypsilanti's difficulties with the local Roumanian inhabitants caused his rebellion to fail; but not before another rebellion had been ignited in Greece proper. Alexander was torn between his sympathy for the Greeks and his anti-revolutionary fervour and promises. He chose the latter, condemning the Greek rebels and thereby making himself very unpopular at home, for Russia was a traditional friend of the Greeks and traditional enemy of the Turks. When the latter murdered the Patriarch of the Greek Orthodox Church as he was celebrating Easter, popular indignation in Russia was intensified. But Alexander stood firm, although he made several unsuccessful diplomatic moves to settle the issue. Eventually Greece won her freedom in 1830, with some help from Alexander's successor. Ironically, Alexander's foreign minister at the time of the Greek revolt, Capodistrias, was himself a Greek and later became the first elected president of Greece.

Although the western frontier was stable, a Russian army of 50,000 men was kept busy in the Caucasus. The 'pacification' of this region, stubbornly resisted by mountain tribesmen, would continue for many decades. In Central Asia the great period of Russian expansion towards India was yet to come, while in North America there was a regression. Russian settlers had been in what is now Alaska, Oregon, and California long before the United States became interested in these territories. Tsar Paul I had chartered the Russian America Company (and bought his family some shares in it), and by 1812 an armed trading settlement, Fort Ross, had been established about fifty miles north of San Francisco. However, the Russian fur trade in this area was threatened by Yankee traders, who not only collected furs, but brought shiploads of rum and guns for the local Indians. In 1821, under pressure from the Russian America Company (and perhaps to protect his own investment), Alexander issued an order granting a monopoly to the Russian traders. Even when Russia sent a warship to enforce this order, there was little immediate reaction in the USA; the Pacific still seemed remote to Americans of that time. However, it was not long before lobbying by those New England traders who had most to lose from the Russian monopoly whipped up a semblance of popular indignation. Because relations between the two nations were friendly, an agreement was negotiated which protected the rights of existing Russian trading posts but acknowledged that the territory surrounding them was 'unclaimed'. It was while studying this problem that the Secretary of State, Adams, evolved the principle of reserving future American colonization for the Americans. This principle, somewhat elaborated, was inserted in President Monroe's address to Congress, and became known as the Monroe Doctrine.

Alexander had always been sympathetically interested in American affairs. The US Constitution had inspired some of his own constitutional dreams, and the American failure to eliminate slavery discouraged him in his scheme to free the Russian serfs. He corresponded with Jefferson, and met Adams when the latter was American minister in St. Petersburg. But original American respect and admiration for Alexander diminished when the latter seemed to discard his liberal sentiments. By 1821 Jefferson was describing Alexander as 'the very leader of a combination to chain mankind down eternally to oppressions of the most barbarous age.'[7]

Alexander the constitutionalist

There was a big difference between the constitutionalism which Alexander preached abroad, and the autocracy which he practised at home. But in

[7] From a private letter, quoted in M. M. Laserson, *The American Impact on Russia 1784–1917* (Collier, 1962), 134.

the case of Poland Alexander did demonstrate a willingness to transform
promises into realities.

The history of Poland has always been closely tied to that of Russia.
Though both are Slavic nations, their relationship has usually been more
baleful than brotherly. Their differences are rooted in Poland's link with
the west (and hence with the Renaissance and Reformation) through the
Roman Catholic Church; this drew her apart from Russia, whose traditional cultural links were with Byzantium through the torpid Orthodox
Church. Lacking indisputable natural frontiers, the shape and the size of
Poland have been continuously variable. At its peak the Polish Commonwealth contained an enormous territory stretching from the Baltic to the
Black Sea and including Lithuania, White Russia, and the Ukraine. It was
the two latter lands, where an Orthodox and Russian population was
ruled by a Catholic and non-Russian gentry, that caused most of the
Russo-Polish wars, until in 1795, by the last of the Polish Partitions,
Poland was divided between Austria, Prussia, and Russia. But although
the state of Poland had been thus eliminated, the nation of Poland lived
on, and until 1918 patriots were struggling for a reunited and independent
Poland. Moreover, among what until 1945 could be termed the Polish
ruling class, there were many who dreamed not simply of an independent
Poland, but of a re-conquest of the old Polish empire, preferably by means
of a glorious cavalry charge at sunset.

Alexander felt that the dismemberment of Poland, over which his
grandmother Catherine presided, had been a shameful act. One of his
closest friends, Czartoryski, was himself Polish, and no doubt sustained
Alexander's sympathy for the Poles. At the Congress of Vienna, Alexander
had been thwarted in his wish to 'reunite' the Poles, although Russia had
been granted the Duchy of Warsaw, which Napoleon had earlier created
from Prussian Poland (see map, p. 595). Towards the end of 1815, while at
the peak of his popularity, Alexander presented his Poles with a constitution. This made the former Duchy of Warsaw a kingdom (the tsar of
Russia being the king of Poland) with a bicameral parliament. Thus, those
Poles who were now in the Russian Empire were politically better off than
their compatriots in Austria and Prussia, although they had neither true
independence nor a truly popular assembly. It was a promising start,
especially after the creation of a Polish army, commanded by the Tsar's
brother, Constantine.

Alexander regarded his Polish constitution as a pilot-project for an
eventual constitution for Russia proper. He had previously made some
changes in the mechanism of government; he had introduced ministries,
and instructed his gifted adviser Speransky to prepare a draft constitution.

However, only one significant innovation of this constitution had been adopted, the Council of State. Alexander felt that the prerequisite for a constitution was the abolition of serfdom but, not feeling strong enough to antagonize the gentry, he had been able to do little for the serfs. The gentry had persuaded Alexander to dismiss Speransky in 1812, but a few years later the Tsar ordered another of his advisers to draft another constitution. This, which borrowed some federal features from the US constitution, was similarly unused. Alexander probably realized that there were too many problems to be solved before a worthwhile constitution would be workable: serfdom, illiteracy, the shortage of educated and honest administrators. In any case, Alexander did not seek a true constitutional monarchy; the popular assemblies he envisaged would not initiate or veto legislation, they would merely discuss it. Over the next century Russia would remain an old-fashioned benevolent despotism, enduring a chronic shortage of first-rate benevolent despots. Effective power remained in the hands of the tsar, who took advice from his friends and family as well as from his recognized advisers. He could issue laws single-handed, but usually worked through the Committee of Ministers. The ministers were appointed by and were personally responsible to the tsar. As for the newly introduced Council of State, whose members were nominated on the basis of age and experience, this studied draft laws and passed on its conclusions to the tsar, who was in no way compelled to abide by its counsel.

But, although Alexander could not abolish serfdom, he had already improved the prospects for better government by creating a new educational system, whose best graduates were expected to join the administration.

Education

The course of Russian education had been eccentric, and would remain so. Some of the early tsars of Muscovy, realizing how geography and history had retarded the intellectual development of their people, had imported foreign teachers and sent Russian students abroad. Some, like Peter the Great and Catherine, had allocated substantial funds for opening schools in Russia. But other rulers, like Paul, considering education subversive, took an exactly opposite line, expelling foreign teachers, banning the import of foreign books, proscribing the teaching of certain subjects, and allowing no students to go abroad.

Alexander's statute on education of 1804, which laid the organizational foundation of a comprehensive state system, was probably influenced by his friend Paul Stroganov, who was familiar with French educational ideas. While it may be true that, in terms of new schools founded, Catherine's educational policy was more fruitful than Alexander's, it was the scheme of 1804 which permitted, in fact generated, the growth in numbers and quality which would be a feature of Russian education throughout the nineteenth century. Essentially, the statute prescribed the division of Russia into six educational districts.[8] Each educational district would be administered by a curator, in close touch with the ministry of education which Alexander had established. In each district there was to be a university, which would supervise the educational activities in that district. Each university would train teachers for, and derive students from, higher four-year secondary schools (gymnasiums) which would serve the main towns. In their turn the gymnasiums would be linked with the next level, the district two-year schools. Finally, at the base of the educational pyramid, were the parish schools, providing a one-year elementary course.

The six universities were to be Moscow (founded 1755); St. Petersburg (founded 1819); Dorpat, an old institution promoted to university status and devoted to instruction in German for the benefit of the Baltic provinces; Vilna, which was in formerly Polish Lithuania and was doing for the local Poles what Dorpat was doing for the Baltic Germans; Kazan and Kharkov, both of which were established almost immediately. Each university was to have attached to it a teachers' training institute, the students of which were required to sign a pledge that they would teach in the state system for six years after graduation. University regulations were quite liberal, and there was provision for sending the very best students abroad for postgraduate study. Some of the precepts included in the statutes were also progressive. Teachers were told to rely on their own diligence and method rather than on 'the excessive labour' of their pupils, to concentrate not on fact-cramming but on imparting understanding and curiosity, to make their lessons entertaining and never to give way to anger. In the curricula practical and technical subjects were emphasized. A higher status for education was achieved not only by improving teachers' salaries, but by finding, in 1819, a place in the Table of Ranks for qualified persons; a degree student was in the 14th Rank (one rank below an army ensign) and could rise successively to the 8th Rank granted to holders of doctoral degrees (equivalent to an army major, and conferring hereditary nobility).

While on the university level the plans were achieved, not all the proposed schools were opened. By 1825 the main towns had their gymnasiums, about fifty of them, but the district and especially the parish schools were well below their targets. In fact parish schools, which depended mainly on the charity of landowners and the Church for their funds,

---

[8] By 1914 there were fifteen educational districts.

probably numbered only about 600. In terms of pupils, there were about 5,000 students in the gymnasiums, 30,000 in the district schools, and perhaps 30,000 in the parish schools. As for the six universities, these had nearly 1,700 students. All these figures were an improvement on those of 1804, but compared to the total population were still tiny.[9] However, as will be noted later, if schools outside the supervision of the ministry of education were included, the total number of pupils would be at least trebled.

In the universities teachers and researchers were of a high quality, and in Alexander's time were largely recruited from foreign, especially German, institutions. Although some of the best-known professors took the trouble to learn Russian, most did not. It was the practice to conduct lectures in Latin. This caused resentment among the students, who needed to study Latin to enter university, but rarely knew it well enough to gain maximum benefit from the lectures. Moreover, such concentration on a dead language seemed opposed to the progressive image of the university system; there was a certain weirdness, for example, in using Latin to instruct gentlemen-farmers in scientific agriculture.

That the schools directly under the ministry of education only accounted for about one-third of the total pupils is evident from the following figures: in 1825 there were about 265,000 pupils in Russia; of these, almost 70,000 were in the ministry's institutions, over 100,000 in military schools, another 50,000 or so in church schools, and more than 40,000 in specialized schools. The military schools' total was composed predominantly of the seven-to-eighteen-year-olds born to parents in the military colonies and taken for education and training at the age of seven. Among the special schools were those providing secondary education for orphans and girls, which were supervised by the Tsar's mother. In addition, there were already a few factory schools, financed by progressive industrialists (private funds played their part also in the state system; Kharkov University was financed by a local landowner).

In higher education the universities were supplemented by purely technological or professional institutions. These were the responsibility of the appropriate ministries, but, as time passed, the ministry of education began to interest itself in them. Some of the best known were founded before Alexander's time. Peter the Great on his visit to England, for example, had recruited two teenage students of Christ's Hospital to found a Russian school of navigation. The Mining Institute, which like several other specialized colleges of that period still exists under a different name, was

---

[9] For a note on educational statistics, see p. 549.

founded in the reign of Catherine. In Paul's time were founded the first medical school (the Military Medical Academy), and the Institute of Transport Engineers. Among institutions founded in Alexander's reign were a second forestry institute, several provincial military cadet schools for the nobility, the Main School of Engineering, the Mikhail Artillery School (whose first director was a rocket expert), and also the Corps of Pages to educate sons of the élite. With the exception of the cadet schools, these were all at St. Petersburg, helping to make that city the undisputed academic centre of the Empire. Alexander's reign was marked also by a flourishing of scientific societies and journals. The Academy of Sciences was reformed, making it a purely research and disseminating body with no teaching responsibilities. To existing learned associations, like Catherine's Free Economic Society, were added several similar organizations, including the Physics–Mathematics Society, the Moscow Naturalist Society, and the Moscow Agricultural Society. These held meetings and published journals to discuss and spread the latest advances in their fields.

After 1815 Alexander had an understandable but regrettable desire to transform education in the same way that he imagined his Holy Alliance had transformed international relations. He found no lack of helpers, for the war had caused many besides the Tsar to turn towards religion and away from secularism and liberalism. Apart from those of genuine religiosity, there were those who had always been against education, and others who were only too anxious to jump on the most promising bandwagon. It was henceforth from the pious and the careerists that ministers of education and educational district curators were appointed. In 1817, so as to make the educational system dependent more on the Church than on the state, the ministry of education under Golitsyn was enlarged to become the ministry of spiritual affairs and education. Golitsyn's policy was to intensify at all levels the study of the Bible and of dead languages, usually at the expense of technical and commercial courses. With his approval, purges were carried out in the universities; professors who had trained abroad were excluded, students and teachers were forbidden to study abroad, the Jesuit establishments were closed and the Jesuits expelled from Russia. More important still, obsessed pious conservatives were appointed to the educational district curatorships. Because the educational system was well co-ordinated and centralized, these few men were able to dominate education in their districts from the university down to the parish school.

The most celebrated of these devoted reactionaries was Magnitsky, who earlier had been sent to 'inspect' Kazan University. After a week's sojourn there he had produced a report for the ministry, alleging that the University was infected 'with the repugnant spirit of deism', and that all the

professors deserved exemplary punishment. Magnitsky had no doubt that
the University should be destroyed, but his report did give two choices:
'This destruction can be done in two ways: (a) by stopping the operation
of the University or (b) by publicly demolishing it. I would prefer the
latter.' The ministry decided not to kill Kazan University. It prescribed
instead a fate worse than death, appointing Magnitsky curator of the
Kazan educational district. He at once settled down to his task which was,
as he described it, 'the purging and humbling of the University, in my
capacity as a Russian and Christian'. His first step was the removal of
most professors, and the hiring of new ones on the basis of their moral
credentials. The first part of this programme he easily achieved but, because news travels fast in academic circles, he was unable to find replacements who were willing, virtuous, and qualified. He finally abandoned
academic qualifications and appointed a collection of pharmacists, country doctors, schoolteachers, and governesses. To rule Kazan University
Magnitsky devised a system which is suggestive of the commander-and-
commissar dual leadership of the Red Army a century later. The Rector
was retained, with responsibility for the academic programme, but alongside him was appointed a Director, responsible for political and moral
affairs. This Director became a sort of watchdog, and forced the Rector
into a more-or-less insignificant role. In the University's regulations, composed by Magnitsky, the Director was enjoined to examine students' exercise books, listen to their conversations, observe their prescribed daily
prayers, introduce them to religious literature in their spare time, remind
them that virtue is rewarded not only in heaven but also by the government, and above all root out any freethinking. Students who would not
conform wore a label on which was written 'sinner'; they were put in cells
('solitude rooms') whose walls were decorated with paintings of the Day
of Judgement. During incarceration, fellow-students would pray for the
delinquents each morning before lectures. Care was taken to shield the
students from harmful lectures. Magnitsky divided the sciences into two
categories: 'positive science' (religion, law, natural and mathematical
sciences), and 'visionary science' (philosophy, political science, ethics).
The first group had an unchanging content, whereas the visionary sciences,
according to Magnitsky, changed their content every twenty years, although not simultaneously in each country. Efforts were made to protect
the first category from contamination by the second, and teachers of the
latter were ordered to emphasize the frivolity and insignificance of their
subjects; a notice overhung the chair of the professor of philosophy,
bearing Paul's words 'Beware lest any man spoil you through philosophy
and vain deceit'. Lecture notes were inspected and had to conform with

Magnitsky's requirements. In geometry, the triangle was represented as a symbol of the Trinity and the hypotenuse described as 'the expression of the union of heaven and earth'. Subversive books, including those advancing the theories of Newton and Copernicus, were removed from the University's library.

Around Magnitsky there grew what would in modern times be called a personality cult. He was awarded an honorary degree whose parchment proclaimed him 'the celebrated guardian angel of the Russian church'. At university ceremonies the Rector would praise the genius and piety of 'the beloved Mikhail Leontevich Magnitsky'. The other educational districts did not have curators of quite this calibre, but the pattern was similar. Enrolments fell. The universities lost respect among the public. After his fall Golitsyn was replaced as minister by Admiral Shishkov, who regarded literacy as a first step towards subversion. Nor did he have a high regard for education in general. He compared it to salt: too much spoils the taste. The educational system survived these trials, but the spirit of repression which typified Alexander's last years led directly to the attempted revolution of 1825.

The Decembrist Revolt

Apart from occasional revolts in the military colonies, and the normal frequency of small-scale peasant disturbances, Alexander reigned untroubled by serious rebellions. Thus he was luckier than his grandmother, who had faced the peasant revolt of Pugachov, which at one stage had seemed to threaten the regime. And, like Catherine, he died a natural death. But only just; by dying in late 1825 he forestalled a serious conspiracy which had scheduled his assassination for May 1826. The conspirators were later referred to as Decembrists, because their revolt occurred prematurely in December 1825 during the confusion caused by Alexander's death.

The Decembrist conspirators were of liberal inclination, and their background was Russian freemasonry and the Russian army. Catherine at first had encouraged progressive ideas, but had lost her enthusiasm when the French Revolution showed that liberal thought could be dangerous. In intellectual circles, however, liberal ideas were kept alive, and a few Russians of the gentry class were familiar with the works of west European philosophers and political economists. Freemasonry, though banned from time to time, flourished in Russia, and the masonic orders had a wide range of members. The concept of service and charity which they usually emphasized could not fail to prompt criticism of the state of affairs in Russia. The masonic lodges, where men were treated as equals irrespective of their official rank, in effect were semi-secret societies where those of similar views could meet and make plans. Although Alexander in 1822 banned all freemasonry, it was too late to prevent some of the masons forming new and completely secret societies with revolutionary aims.

Prominent among those who realized that drastic changes were needed were Russian army men, especially those who had been in the army of occupation in France. Guards officers were perhaps the most active of these, but there were men from ordinary regiments, including non-commissioned officers and even some privates.

They had observed conditions in France, where there were no serfs, where there was relative freedom of speech and of the press, where there were regular judicial processes, where there was a constitution of sorts, and where new ideas circulated and were openly discussed. When these military men returned home they viewed the bestiality and arbitrariness of Russian life no longer as a background, but as foreground, and their bitterness was sharpened by the patriotic posturings of reactionaries like Rostopchin, who were playing the role of war heroes while praising traditional Russian society and describing the French as barbarians. One returning veteran later wrote:

Seeing the insipid life in St. Petersburg and listening to the babblings of old men praising the past and deprecating every progressive step was unbearable. We were a hundred years from them.[10]

The first of the revolutionary societies was founded in 1816, in response to Alexander's failure to perpetuate the spirit of 1812. By 1825, through a series of foundings, dissolutions, and amalgamations, there were two significant societies, the Southern and the Northern. The aspirations of these two were not quite the same; the southerners were more radical than the northerners of St. Petersburg. For geographical reasons contact between the two societies was only intermittent. Their aims included the replacement of the autocracy by a representative type of government, the abolition of serfdom, and judicial reform. The Southern Society, the nucleus of which was made up of army officers serving in the Ukraine, produced a programme composed by its leading member and intellectual, Colonel Pestel. This envisaged a republic, the abolition of class differences, and the division of land into 'social' and 'private' segments. A leader of the Northern Society, N. Muravyov, advocated a constitution somewhat similar to the American; the emperor would have similar powers to those of the US president, there would be civil liberties, police officials would be elected, classes and titles would be abolished, but property would be a pre-requisite for office-holders.

[10] I. Yakushkin, *Zapiski* (1925), 11.

Inside the membership of each society there was a variety of attitudes and aptitudes. On one extreme were those who felt that the Tsar could be retained and persuaded to carry out the necessary reforms. On the other extreme was a handful of men with a thirst for violence. There were romantic hotheads seeking martyrdom, and cautious intellectuals hating the idea of bloodshed and counselling a step-by-step programme. Most members, as the complement of their love of Russia, had at least a trace of chauvinism, which is probably why they were especially hurt by Alexander's grant of constitutions to the Finns and Poles.

There were rumours, never completely disproved, that Alexander's official death in 1825 was stage-managed, that in fact the Tsar did not die but went away to lead a quiet secluded life as a Siberian holy man. But these rumours came later, and had no connexion with the chaos in St. Petersburg when the news of his death arrived. He died while on a Black Sea vacation with his wife, and the news took one week to reach the capital. Since Alexander had no legitimate children, the succession passed to his brothers. In St. Petersburg Nicholas swore allegiance to his elder brother Constantine, who was in Poland, although he knew that Constantine had earlier renounced his rights following a morganatic marriage. This renunciation had remained a family secret and Nicholas presumably swore allegiance, aware that it was he who was intended to be the next tsar, because he feared confusion and disorder if there was a period of uncertainty; but for two weeks Constantine, while refusing the throne, would not make a clear public renunciation. The members of the Northern Society, well-informed of palace secrets, decided that they would never again have an equally good opportunity, and hastily planned a revolt.

The plan adopted was to persuade the capital's garrison that an oath of allegiance to Nicholas would be an act of treason, that Constantine was the true heir and the report of his renunciation false. This argument was a betrayal of the aims and purity of the Northern Society, for not only was it a lie, but it also portrayed the conspirators as defenders rather than enemies of the autocracy. The plan also meant that the whole action had to be carried out in the interval between the anticipated announcement of Nicholas's accession and the ceremony of swearing-in the soldiers. Nicholas, who had some inkling of the plot (partly from an English soldier serving in the Russian army), acted intelligently and courageously throughout. After stationing some of the more reliable troops at strategic points, he arranged to have the announcement of his accession (the reading of a formal manifesto to the assembled Senate) made early in the morning. The sleepy senators were collected before sunrise and the ceremony finished well before eight o'clock. The troops were to swear their new allegiance before noon, so the conspirators had only a few hours in which to act.

The plotters persuaded some units to march to the Senate Square and clamour for Constantine. This was according to the plan, but had been made pointless since the Senate's part in the accession had already been played. Despite this, the conspirators kept their men outside the Senate, where they were joined by a trickle of additional soldiers and sailors. There were occasional mild clashes between the insurgents and loyal troops. Crowds, which soon gathered, showed some hostility to Nicholas, but the conspirators, who after all were of the gentry, did not encourage them for they had no intention of letting their revolution fall into the hands of a common mob. The previously appointed leader of the revolt never turned up, being occupied in wringing his hands in private. Many of the loyal troops would have joined the revolt if the rebels had shown more activity, but on-the-spot leadership was provided by a high-voice officer with a lisp, who failed to change the rebels' plan and seize the initiative. By late afternoon there had been few casualties, although the governor of the city had been killed by one of the more bloodthirsty of the conspirators. Nicholas, wishing to clear up this dangerous situation before nightfall, gave the insurgents one more chance to surrender and then called on his artillery. After three salvos the revolt of the Northern Society was over. Pestel had been arrested on the eve of the revolt, thanks to informers' reports. After the revolt those members who had fled, and members of the Southern Society, began to be arrested. Some of the southern officers aroused their troops and for a week tramped ineffectively about the Ukraine at the head of a semi-revolutionary semi-army. Then, after a bloody confrontation with loyal forces, they surrendered.

The Decembrists failed because they were divided among themselves, had made no real preparations for their revolt, refused to make use of discontent among the masses, and were mentally prepared in advance for a glorious failure. Yet the respect in which they were held by later revolutionaries was justified. Despite the pathetic course of their rebellion, it was the first of a series which in less than a hundred years was to topple the regime. It was unprecedented for the gentry and the army to make a rebellion not for themselves but for a better society and to ally themselves with intellectuals. It was also the end of a tradition, for never again did the Guards officers stage a revolution. In the past they had engineered many palace revolutions, overturning one tsar to replace him by another. In this, their last coup and one of their few failures, they had aimed at something higher.

2. The Russia of Nicholas I

Nicholas I and his reign

WHEREAS historians have dealt perhaps over-generously with Alexander I, they have tended to over-condemn his brother Nicholas I. Nicholas was in a permanent state of struggle against his personal limitations, sincerely trying to do what was right and failing not through lack of will but through lack of perception. The thirty years of Nicholas's rule are regarded as a particularly dark period of Russian history but, while repression and militarism were certainly dominant, it was nevertheless a period noteworthy for intellectual and creative achievement, and for economic and technical advance.

The decisive event of Nicholas's long reign was the Decembrist Revolt. This shook him, and was the main cause of his irrational nervousness in subsequent years. The later twenties were the honeymoon years: there were some steps to improve government, to codify the laws, to help the state peasants; there was a successful war against Persia, support of Greek independence, and another successful war against Turkey; there were relatively good relations between the regime and the intellectuals, relaxed censorship, and a political police concerned with public welfare as much as with security. Then came 1830 and the overthrow of the King of France. Then 1831, when cholera struck Russia for the second successive year and Poland rebelled against the Tsar. From 1830 the honeymoon was over. Fear of revolution determined policy. There was growing internal repression. Friends became enemies and Turkey became a friend. Poland was russified. Jews and other minorities were hard-pressed. After 1848, when revolutions in Europe were again accompanied by a murderous cholera in Russia, the pressure grew heavier. Nicholas not only stood firm, unlike his fellow-rulers in Austria and Prussia, but sent his army into Europe to help suppress revolution: to Wallachia in 1848 and Hungary in 1849, thus enabling the hard-pressed Ottoman and Habsburg dynasties to retrieve their fortunes. Then came the unwanted war in the Crimea, and

Nicholas's Russia was shown to be, if not a giant with feet of clay, at least a very ineffective giant.

Nicholas was born nineteen years after his brother Alexander. As with many another noble Russian child (including his contemporary, Pushkin), the main influence on Nicholas's formative years was his nurse. Like Pushkin, Nicholas learned from his nurse how to be a Russian; how to write Russian, how to pray in Russian, how to feel like a Russian, how to dislike the Poles like a Russian. (But whereas Pushkin's nurse was Russian, Nicholas's was Scottish.) When Nicholas was seven he was transferred to the care of male tutors, supervised by a general who, apart from being a Baltic German, had the additional disadvantage of believing that education was a process of forcing young men to do things against their will, using the whip if necessary. With this inauspicious start, Nicholas's unusual personality is hardly surprising. He insisted on order, neatness, and regularity, and was uneasy when these were disturbed. With these traits it is small wonder that Nicholas later felt most at ease among army officers, all the more so as the only subjects for which he showed any academic interest were the military sciences. It is possible that if he had been treated more wisely he would have learned more; later in life he showed a certain intellectual curiosity in theology and history. But his tutors' methods simply made him stubborn, less open to new ideas, hostile to learning. His formal education ended when he was fifteen. His brother, the Tsar, refused to allow him to take part in the 1812 campaign, but in 1814, Nicholas, as a young officer, was with the Russian army in Paris, where he derived great enjoyment from the endless ceremonies and parades. After this, Nicholas travelled in Europe; in England he was unimpressed by Parliament but deeply impressed by the Duke of Wellington. Then, at the age of twenty, tall and handsome, he returned home and was appointed commander of a Guards brigade, where he played an agreeable role in restoring discipline to its pre-war level.

In later life Nicholas surrounded himself with army officers. These were the type of men that he felt he could understand and trust—believers like him in an orderly chain of command, with each link accepting and demanding complete subservience of inferior to superior; participators like him in a life which was organized, regular, and capable of perfection; possessors like him of the military mind, with its lightning grasp of the superficial. Nicholas emphasized that his profession was the army by wearing uniform more or less permanently. When necessarily out of uniform at night he consoled himself by sleeping on an army bed. On one visit to Windsor he surprised his royal hosts by requesting, immediately on arrival, straw from the stables to fill his army mattress.

By marrying a Prussian princess, Nicholas added one more German element to the regime. This marriage, though planned as an act of state to buttress the alliance of Russia and Prussia which had defeated Napoleon, was, or became, very successful, even though towards the end of his life the Tsar allowed himself the luxury of one or two mistresses. The marriage led to frequent contact with Prussia, which he came to admire and imitate. He even showed some sympathetic interest in the Lutheran church, despite his Orthodox piety. Nicholas spent much of his reign travelling through his Empire, inspecting not only his troops but all kinds of institutions. But these progressions were so rapid, and the foreknowledge of his arrival so sure, that local officials were usually able to conceal the evils and abuses which such visits were intended to reveal. He did not enjoy his life. He considered that the office to which God had called him was a crushing burden. He was sustained only by a strong sense of duty, which enabled him to plod on until the end, which was a bitter end. He died, aged fifty-eight, with great dignity, perhaps sustained by anticipation of the ceremonies and parades in the better world to come.

Nicholas's subordinates and their duties

Nicholas soon dispensed with the services of men like Magnitsky and Arakcheyev, but other advisers of Alexander were retained. These included some of the bright young liberals of a quarter-century earlier, now grown older and less liberal. In a secret committee formed at the start of the new reign and containing many of Alexander's counsellors, possible governmental reforms were discussed, but few of them were carried out. One overdue reform, the codification of the laws, was executed by Speransky with his usual technical efficiency. In the past, Russian laws had been often obscure. There had been a codification in the mid-seventeenth century, but since then many laws, both old and new, had been forgotten. By rediscovering some of these laws, and recording them, Speransky made the legal apparatus less uncertain, and revealed certain duties, like those of nobles towards their serfs, which had been conveniently forgotten.

One of Alexander's advisers retained by Nicholas was Kiselev, who reorganized and improved the life of the state peasants. Kiselev was a veteran of 1812, and therefore very acceptable to Nicholas. Another ex-soldier was Kankrin, a German in Russian service who had been an excellent quartermaster-general in 1812 and later served as minister of finance under Alexander and Nicholas for twenty-one years. He was a capable man, though sometimes ultra-conservative, and his work will be mentioned in Chapter 3. As time passed, Nicholas's inner circle included an increasing number of military men; one such was Kleinmikhel, a trusted colleague of the Tsar, whose energy and ability to see the heart of a problem was accompanied by a certain ruthlessness. He had been a protégé of Arakcheyev, and succeeded the latter as supervisor of the military colonies. Kleinmikhel was a man who got things done, and a man who killed his workers through hard driving and negligence (as happened when he was organizing the construction of the St. Petersburg–Moscow railway). He earlier had attracted the Tsar's admiration by the speed with which he carried out the rebuilding of the Winter Palace after a disastrous fire; for this he received a gold medal inscribed 'Zeal Overcomes All'. Later, Kleinmikhel was a useful go-between for Nicholas and his mistresses, and he found good homes for the illegitimate children resulting from these liaisons. In 1842 he became director of transport and public buildings, and he retained his influence until the death of Nicholas in 1855.

Another ex-officer, a cavalry officer of the worst type, was Protasov, who became Over Procurator of the Holy Synod. He concentrated on outward appearances, expecting his department and the Church to function in the smooth way that military organizations were believed to function. He neglected both high matters, such as questions of theology, and low matters, like the upkeep of parish schools. He did, however, broaden the curriculum of seminaries and prescribe Russian instead of Latin as the language of instruction. Uneasy in the presence of learned dignitaries, he preferred the company of the simple-minded. He refused to approve the publication of a commentary in Russian on the Bible, recommending that future priests should not be taught the dangerous habit of appraising holy texts, but should simply learn them by heart, and in Church Slavonic, as had always been the practice. The Church under Protasov played a great part in the russification of the Empire's non-Russian nationalities. In Poland and the western Ukraine the Uniate Church[1] was gradually dissolved by Orthodox proselytizing and administrative pressures. The Catholic Church continued to be tolerated, as were the Armenian, Protestant, Moslem, and Buddhist religions, but all these came under the authority not of the Holy Synod, but of the ministry of the interior. Those Russian intellectuals who were attracted to Catholicism had little opportunity for propaganda inside the Empire, but several went abroad; one Moscow professor went to Ireland to combat Protestantism. Protasov, with the approval of the Church, exerted his main pressure on the Old Believers and on the various sects which had grown out of the Orthodox faith. In some respects these were treated by the Orthodox authorities rather as the

[1] The Uniate Church had been founded in 1596 to attract, towards Poland and Roman Catholicism, the Slavic and Orthodox inhabitants of the Ukraine and Byelorussia. It recognized the authority of the Pope but conducted services in Slavic languages.

Soviet government would later treat the Orthodox. While they were granted freedom of conscience, they were not allowed to proselytize. Their communities, chapels and cemeteries were attacked, sometimes fiscally and sometimes physically. They reacted by becoming more stubborn and, probably, more numerous. By the 1850s there may well have been ten million such dissidents, although the figure published by the government was less than one million.

General Paskevich, who came nearest to the traditional concept of court favourite, had been Nicholas's commander when the future Tsar was starting his army service. The respect which the young Nicholas had felt for him remained and, despite his faults, Nicholas supported him in the intrigues which were continuously simmering in the army and war ministry. As a result, Paskevich rose to be commander-in-chief, even though better generals were available. He did have some organizing talent, but in his campaigns he emerged victorious only because his opponents were more incompetent than he. In war it seemed that he was only at ease when in retreat; he retreated when enemy troops advanced, believing that they would not dare to do so unless they were certain of their superiority; he retreated when the enemy was out of sight, anticipating an attack from an unexpected direction; he was even known to retreat when the enemy retreated, fearing a ruse.

Perhaps the characters who did most to shape Nicholas's reign were the two loyal Germans, Nesselrode and Benckendorff. The latter, as originator and head of the Third Section, will be described later. As Nicholas's adviser on foreign affairs, Nesselrode's main contribution was persuading the Tsar to have second thoughts whenever he was on the verge of declaring war or mobilizing his army to meet some threat he saw in Europe. Revolutions abroad were feared by Nicholas almost as much as revolutions at home, being regarded as a threat to legitimacy and very infectious. Some observers have attributed the outbreak of the Crimean War to the absence of Nesselrode's influence. Being a Protestant, his advice was not sought in the dispute with Turkey over the protection of Orthodox Christians in the Ottoman Empire.

It was Uvarov, the intellectually gifted minister of education, who first used the slogan 'Orthodoxy, Autocracy, Nationality' in a report he wrote. Evidently the Tsar liked it, as did Uvarov himself, and thus was born the ideology known as 'official nationality'.

Orthodoxy

'Official nationality', as expressed simply in the three-word slogan 'Orthodoxy, Autocracy, Nationality', provided the ideological justification for the ambitions and actions of the government, and was supposed to be a guideline for the ambitions and actions of the people. It was popularized by a host of journalists, professors, courtiers, and priests. Most of these popularizers were not hacks or opportunists, but did believe in the concept they were expounding, although not all interpreted the concepts the same way. Their arguments, though one-sided and in retrospect mistaken, were not an insult to the intelligence of their audiences. Their opposition to democracy, to revolution, and to nationalism was not irrational, but the dangers they saw in change could not be evaded simply by avoiding change. The error of the ideologists was that at a time when the world was in a state of rapid transformation they chose, not to guide the forces of change, but to block them.

As 'Orthodoxy, Autocracy, Nationality' was a prescription and justification for changelessness, it was appropriate that Orthodoxy was listed first. When ideologists during Nicholas's reign talked of Orthodoxy being the foundation of the Russian state, they had in mind several factors, apart from the comforting conservatism of the Church. At its simplest, Orthodoxy implied firm faith in God and the concept of a divine will; it was this faith and this concept which bolstered Nicholas throughout his unsought and unhappy reign. On another level the Orthodox Church was shown as something peculiarly Russian, as the special gift which Holy Russia possessed and wished to share with Christians and non-Christians. For Russians, including Nicholas, Russia's God was special. The messianic trait of the Russian character, the praiseworthy desire to do good to the rest of the world, has been often noticed. The idea of Orthodoxy was perhaps the most powerful message the Russians had in tsarist times, but it was never well-received, although it was transmitted energetically in Poland and the western borderlands, where Nicholas's government and the Church strove to drive out the Catholic and Uniate churches as part of the russification policy.

Thirdly, there was Orthodoxy as a standard of behaviour. As already pointed out, Nicholas took this seriously, his habitual severity frequently being mitigated by his appreciation of Christian charity. There were other responsible personages who followed the Tsar's example, but most of them were far more interested in another of Orthodoxy's attractions, its function as a solid prop of the regime. For them, just as the tsar was the defender of the faith, so the Church should be defender of the tsar. It was the Orthodox priests who, once a year and in every church until the reign of Alexander II, publicly and emphatically pronounced a curse on 'those who do not believe that the Orthodox monarchs have been elevated to the throne thanks to God's special grace, and that from the moment they are

anointed with the holy oil, are infused with the gifts of the Holy Ghost'.[2]
And it was an Orthodox metropolitan who proclaimed to Catherine the
Great that God 'hath seen Thy pure heart . . . and Thy sinless ways,'[3] a
testimonial which would seem to cast doubt on God's all-knowingness.

Autocracy

The second string in the bow of the ideologists was Autocracy. This had
several implications, but its essence was that the tsar expected the willing
and total submission of his subjects, just as God expected the tsar's willing
and total submission. From this, historians and journalists developed
other justifications of autocracy. The Christian autocrat was the Christian
conscience of his people; with absolute power, the ruler was able to soften
the impact of the law in individual cases, thus humanizing something
which would otherwise be impersonal and standardized; all his subjects in
his presence were equal; he could reward the deserving and break the
undeserving. The autocrat was also entrusted by God with the task of
keeping the people down; the Russians were great as a people but were
dangerous if not kept under tight control. The people had sometimes to be
forced to do what was good for them; they needed a father who would
love them even while punishing them. The tsar was also the great co-
ordinator; only a strong one-man rule could cope with a phenomenon like
Russia with its immensity, diversity, and potential wealth. Other nations,
especially Protestant nations, might prosper with representative governments, but this was not true of Slavic or Latin countries, whose peoples'
volatility required strong and concentrated direction. Thus the tsar and
his executive were very necessary and they had to be severe. One journalist
compared the tsar's ideal harshness with the pepper which every good
salad needs. In foreign affairs, the concept of autocracy was associated
with that of legitimacy; any attempts to overthrow the 'legitimate' (that is,
dynastic) rulers of foreign states were felt to be threats to the principle of
autocracy, hence directly or indirectly opposed to Russia's true interests.

All these arguments in favour of Russian autocracy contained their
grain of truth, but ignored the possibility that other and better means might
be available to supply the virtues attributed to the concept. It is true, for
example, that Russia was a land difficult to govern, but there were other
solutions apart from autocracy. Also, the arguments contained a good
deal of wishful thinking; one instance is the claim that all subjects were
equal in the presence of the tsar, which was obviously not the case in practice. Furthermore, like the other elements of the three-element ideology,

[2] J. S. Curtiss, *Church and State in Russia* (Columbia University Press, 1940), 28.
[3] Ibid., 27.

the whole philosophy was pessimistic. It provided an intellectual justification for repression, by pointing out human weaknesses and Russian failings which needed to be controlled. But control could have been exercised by means other than police and prisons, which after all only treated the symptoms of unrest.

When Nicholas and his publicists talked of autocracy, Peter the Great was never far from their minds; Peter, the super-autocrat, who drove his people hard to create a new empire and a new Russia. Peter's shortcomings were ignored, as was the possibility that his real achievements were a long way short of his intentions, and that in the long run he might have achieved more by encouragement than by harshness. Many of Nicholas's publicists were historians, and it was easy for them to justify autocracy by drawing on historical examples. They showed how great peoples like the Romans had declined after rejecting hereditary autocrats, and how strong rulers like the Ivans and Peter had brought Russia far from its beginnings as an obscure village on the banks of the River Moscow. Nicholas admired the more despotic tsars, especially Peter, and identified himself with them, just as did his successor exactly a century later. In view of what came later, it is also interesting that from adulation of the office of tsar there grew, on the part of the more tasteless and opportunistic publicists, a 'personality cult' around Nicholas himself, although this was against the latter's wishes. One historian even proposed that Russia should be renamed 'Nicholaevia'.

Nationality

Whereas Orthodoxy and Autocracy were terms easy to define and defend, Nationality could be, and was, interpreted in several ways. At its simplest, Nationality signified the union of Orthodoxy and Autocracy: Orthodoxy plus Autocracy equals the Russian nation. But perhaps a better translation would replace the word Nationality with the word Russianism, for this is what the ideologists usually meant. They claimed, rightly, that Russia was not just one of the European states, but that it was something special, something different from other European countries because of its history. Many arguments were advanced to bolster this idea. Some of these were interesting (e.g., Russia's rulers were always closer to the people than in the west because a shortage of stone meant that princes could not build castles); some were twisted (e.g., western states were created by conquest, whereas Russia grew by absorption, hence western nations are based on hate whereas Russia is founded on love); others were exaggerated (e.g., the Russian language has subtleties which give its users a great advantage over other peoples in the formation and exchange of ideas). Yet despite distortions and exaggerations, the essential truth was there, that Russians, because of their unique history and geography, have a different character and temperament, different beliefs, ambitions and fears, and a different outlook. Shevyrev, who taught Russian literature at Moscow University, warned against western cultural influence; the west was like a man with a lethal infectious disease, enveloped in poisonous vapours, whom Russians embraced at their peril. Others, like the conservative poet Tyutchev, claimed to see a polarization, and like Shevyrev used concepts and language which would be echoed in the 1940s:

In Europe for a long time already there have existed just two real forces, revolution and Russia. These two forces are now opposed to each other and tomorrow they may enter into combat. No negotiations or treaties between them are possible: the existence of one means the death of the other! . . . Russia, country of faith, will not lose her faith at the decisive hour. She will not shrink from the greatness of her calling, she will not shirk her mission. And when could this mission be more clear and obvious? One could say that God has written it in fiery characters across the storm-darkened sky; the west is disappearing, all crumbling and perishing in this general conflagration . . . And when over this enormous ruin we see rising up like a Holy Ark this still vaster empire, then who will doubt its mission, and shall we, its children, lose faith and spirit?[4]

From the acceptance of Russia as a unique phenomenon other ideas followed, varying according to the character of their proponents. Those of messianic temperament felt that the Russian idea was so good it should be shared with the rest of the world. Those whose thinking was more in accord with that of Nicholas pointed out the virtues of Russian life, rooted in Autocracy and Orthodoxy, and warned against any changes; why change something which is already fundamentally perfect? Many went further and claimed that the concept of serfdom was something essentially Russian, the complement to autocracy, the keystone of Russian society which must not be tampered with.

The messianic upholders of Russianism were often in disagreement with the government. Although the Tsar pursued a policy of russianizing the non-Russian parts of his Empire he did so more for purposes of obtaining a good military-style standardization than for ideological reasons. When the russianizers began to demand, in print, the russification of the Baltic provinces, whose German nobility provided Nicholas with his most trusted servants, they were condemned by the Tsar. After all, as Nicholas remarked, whereas the Russian nobility merely served the Empire, the Baltic nobility served the Tsar. Many of the russifiers shared the spirit of

---

[4] F. Tyutchev, *Polnoye sobraniye sochinenii* (1913), 295, 306. These lines are taken from an article written during the European revolution of 1848.

nationalism, the more romantic kind of nationalism, which was abroad in western Europe. They in no way wished to impose Russianism on other countries, upholding the right of peoples to form their own states. Rather illogically, however, they denied this right to non-Russian peoples inside the Empire, these people should russify themselves, or be russified by others.

This was the beginning of that period in which intellectuals liked to classify each other as either Slavophils or Westernizers. Westernizers were those who believed that the traditional Russian ways of life could be a handicap, and the sooner Russia caught up with the West the better. The Slavophils, influenced by the German romantics, opposed westernization and idealized Russia's distinctiveness. Some Slavophils later embraced Panslavism, dreaming of a united Slavic world led by Russia and with its capital at 'Tsargrad' (Constantinople). Westernism, Slavophilism (and Panslavism) should be regarded as useful generalizations for attitudes, rather than for clear-cut groups. A person holding Slavophil views might also hold a few Westernizer views, or be a former or future Westernizer, and vice versa. Only later, at certain times, would there be animosity between the spokesmen of the two trends; they were agreed about much (for example, that the existing regime was unsatisfactory) and their most essential differences concerned religion and history. Westernizers admired Peter the Great and tended to be atheists, while Slavophils worshipped the Russian God and believed that Peter had taken the wrong road. Although the controversy between the two trends of thought was perhaps over-dramatized and over-personalized, it did reflect the eternal question which faced philosophizing Russians: was Russia of the East or of the West, or could she be simply Russia?

The Panslavists' brand of patriotism was not always welcomed by Nicholas. Their ambition to use Russian power to liberate the Slavic peoples living under Austrian, Turkish, or Prussian rule was considered not only dangerous, but incompatible with Nicholas's opposition to the overturning of traditional regimes. The Slavophils also had their demerits in the opinion of Nicholas and the proponents of Nationality, even though some of the Tsar's ministers had Slavophil sympathies. The Slavophils, openly or by implication, belittled Peter the Great when they advocated a return to the purity of old Russian society and its traditions. Their opponents, the Westernizers, were in this respect more palatable. Nor did the Westernizers hint, as did some Slavophils, that Nicholas was not a true Russian, but three-quarters German, and therefore not capable of properly appreciating the Slavs. However, the Westernizers were dis-tasteful in other ways, for they implied that Orthodoxy and Autocracy and Nationality were not quite the virtuous necessities portrayed by the regime's publicists.

Government

Although one of Nicholas's first acts as Tsar was to entrust a secret committee with the examination of governmental institutions, no fundamental changes were made. But the processes of central government did in fact change, even though the institutions seemed unaltered. At first, Nicholas seemed to enhance the importance of the Committee of Ministers by insisting that its members put duty first and attend sessions regularly and punctually. One secretary was dismissed for tampering with the messages passing between the Committee and Nicholas. However, the slowness of the official channels, and Nicholas's desire to have all strings in his own hand, caused him to by-pass the regular processes. He did this by expanding the functions of his own Imperial Chancery. This he organized into sections, each dealing with a particular field which otherwise would have been in the purview of a ministry. The head of each section was answerable to the Tsar, not to any minister. The best known of these sections was the Third Section, which administered the political police and gendarmerie. Nicholas's insistence on participating in all important decisions meant that he was overloaded with work, for, despite his protests, minor matters also came before him, presumably because few officials had the courage to decide what was important and what was not. Not surprisingly, his method of government meant that some departments or ministries were often unaware of what was going on in their own fields.

Because of its diversity and size Russia has always been difficult to govern, and this was especially so in Nicholas's time, when the Empire was almost at its greatest extent and railways and the telegraph were only just appearing. There was one notable change in provincial government under Nicholas, whereby control of the provinces was simplified. Henceforth a provincial governor was directly responsible to the minister of the interior, and had direct control over his provincial board. The former office of governor-general, directly answerable to the tsar, was retained in only a handful of distant or exceptional provinces. But continuing centralization of control meant that increasing amounts of provincial paperwork were submitted to St. Petersburg, so much so that senior men in the ministry were overloaded. Thus it could happen that an important question sent by a provincial governor would be decided by some junior official or clerk in St. Petersburg.

Dishonesty and corruption, always common in the tsarist bureaucracy, flourished under Nicholas, even though he punished severely in those cases which came to his notice. Laziness and large-scale dishonesty were found mainly in the upper and middle ranks; the minor officials and clerks, overloaded with paperwork and underpaid, had to be content with bribe-taking. This bribery was well-established and regarded almost as normal; citizens requiring a service had to give a tip of a standard amount (if they forgot, they were sternly bidden 'Don't forget to say thank you'!) But although the bureaucracy had more than its fair share of crooks and bullies, the majority of its officials were perhaps more to be pitied than resented, and this should be remembered when reading the many writers who complained about them. Herzen, who at one time worked in a provincial government office, had this to say:

> One of the saddest consequences of Peter's revolution was the development of the official class. An artificial, hungry, and uneducated class, capable of doing nothing but 'serving', knowing nothing apart from official forms, it is a kind of civilian priesthood, celebrating divine service in the law-courts and the police forces, and sucking the blood of the people with thousands of greedy, unclean mouths. . . . There, somewhere in sooty offices which we hurry through, shabby men write page after page on grey paper, and make copies on embossed paper—and persons, families, entire villages are outraged, terrified, ruined. A father is sent to exile, a mother to prison, a son to the army—and all this breaks over their heads like thunder, unexpected and usually undeserved.[5]

Herzen also described the local governor, one Tyufyayev:

> A governor's power tends to increase in direct ratio to the distance from Petersburg . . . Tyufyayev was a true servant of the Tsar. He was well regarded, but not well enough. Byzantine servility was unusually well combined in him with official discipline. The annihilation of self, the renunciation of will and thought before authority was combined with harsh oppression of subordinates.[6]

The bureaucratic attitude, the subordination of the individual to the requirements of officials' convenience, routine, and obsessions, has been a constant theme in Russian history and a constant trial to the ordinary people of Russia. In the Soviet period this 'bureaucratism' persisted, despite sincere efforts to eliminate it.

One other feature of the bureaucracy was its role in bringing the euphemism to a fine art. Among the thousands of reports and surveys laboriously composed by officials, penned by clerks, and annotated by superiors, there were few in which a spade was called a spade. Unpleasant facts were not described as such, although an experienced official was able

[5] A. I. Gertzen, *Byloye i dumy* (1946), 134. The provincial bureaucracy was markedly inferior to the central bureaucracy, with fewer nobles, fewer educated men, and poorer promotion prospects.

[6] Ibid., 126, 134. Herzen's *My Past and Thoughts* is available in English (Knopf, 1968). The first two of the four volumes describe his Russian experiences and are good bedtime reading, but a pinch of salt should be kept handy.

to read between the lines of fancy and obscure prose. Thus, as a source of information, the bureaucracy was imperfect. Its statistics were also questionable, especially those supplied by small provincial departments.

Conservative though it was, the bureaucracy in mid-nineteenth-century Russia was in reality a great force which got things done, even though inefficiently. Its social composition was changing; whereas at the beginning of the century its leading officials tended to be former army officers, by 1850 about three-fifths of the two capitals' top bureaucrats had been in the civil service all their working life. German officials had lost some of their preponderance, although they still held about 15 per cent of the upper posts in St. Petersburg. Taking the central and provincial offices together, about two-fifths of the bureaucrats were sons of nobles, and about one-third sons of junior officers or of junior bureaucrats. Sons of priests, especially evident in the provinces, accounted for about one-fifth. It was the sons of nobles who tended to rise to the most influential positions. This was not because of their wealth; money helped, but about half the sons of nobles in the service possessed no serfs (serf possession being a measure of wealth and corresponding roughly to land possession). The key to success was education, especially since a specific degree of education now entitled an entrant to join the service at a specific rank. But of course the sons of nobles had better access to education; about one-third of them had higher education and another tenth could claim some 'snob' education such as a lycée or the Corps of Pages.[7]

Internal enemies, and the Third Section

When the western press referred to Nicholas as the 'Royal Gendarme' it was not without cause. Nicholas's Russia, especially after 1848, did resemble a modern police state, with strict censorship, numerous informers, arbitrary arrests, preventive punishments, and frequent denunciations of allegedly subversive citizens. That Nicholas's motives are understandable is hardly a mitigation of his ultimate responsibility for this. Nevertheless, it should be noted that, because the regime's repression hit literary, and therefore vocal, circles in particular, its impact was probably exaggerated; certainly, observers wrote of the misery of the peasants of this time, but this misery was a habitual misery and unconnected with the Third Section.

The apparatus of a police state was mobilized to sniff out and crush conspirators who were believed to be active all over Russia, but who in fact simply did not exist. Yet Nicholas had no way of knowing that during his rule there would be no serious plot. His reign started with the

---

[7] For a discussion of the social composition of the bureaucracy, see *Slavic Review*, Sept. 1970, 429–43.

Decembrist Revolt, which was rooted in that part of society believed most loyal, the army. That the end of the Decembrists was also the end of serious conspiracy could not be known; Nicholas feared that the Decembrists were a beginning rather than an end. Immediately after the revolt there had been a wave of arrests in the capital, involving people who for one reason or another were under suspicion. In all, 121 accused came before the special court. Only 4 per cent were executed, yet because the hangings were the first held in public in St. Petersburg for many decades the sentences seemed unduly severe. Not only were there five hangings (actually seven, for stretched ropes caused two to be hanged twice), but long terms of penal servitude and exile were inflicted on those considered less guilty. Because of Nicholas's interference, some of the most guilty received light sentences, while at least one of the hanged was relatively innocent. In time, public opinion, which among older people at least had been against the rebels, moved to the side of the victims. This change occurred after it became clear that Nicholas would never grant amnesty to the exiles, and after the wives of the prisoners had dramatically given up their comfortable lives and followed tradition by going to Siberia to share their husbands' hardships.

Despite countless arrests of groups and individuals during Nicholas's reign, the Third Section suppressed only two major dissident groups, neither of which was a threat to the regime. In 1847 a Ukrainian society, which was partly an expression of Slavophilism and partly of Ukrainian nationalism, was suppressed, and the opportunity was taken to sentence the Ukrainian nationalist poet Shevchenko to ten years' exile as a private soldier. Articles on Ukrainian history or in the Ukrainian language disappeared, and even the adjective *Ukrainian* became suspect. This suppression of Ukrainian national feeling aroused no great protest from the St. Petersburg and Moscow intellectuals; their concern for the freedom of peoples did not extend to the Little Russians. The second alleged conspiracy unearthed by the authorities was revealed in 1849, and thus coincided with a renewal of Nicholas's alarm that the revolutionary spirit might spread from the west into Russia. This was the Petrashevsky circle, which discussed current affairs from a reformist and sometimes radical viewpoint. The Petrashevsky circle was in no sense planning rebellion, but fifteen members received the death sentence, including the novelist Dostoevsky. At the place of public execution the death sentences were, at the last possible moment, commuted to exile. Paradoxically, this act of mercy, because of its circumstances, was considered an act of cruelty. There is little doubt that the whole drama was planned, but was less an act of cruelty than a reflection of Nicholas's view of himself as father of the

Russian people: a 'let's teach them a lesson they'll never forget and then let them go' attitude.

The Third Section, administering the 'higher police', was established in 1827, and carried out the investigations and arrests of suspected subversive elements. Political police were not new to Russia. As early as the seventeenth century, Russian embassies abroad included a clerk who reported secretly to the tsar on the activities of the mission's leading officials. Under Peter the Great especially, it was the duty of every citizen to inform the authorities of any overheard abuse of state or tsar, and this led to an increasing flow of denunciations. The number of false accusations increased, particularly after rewards were offered. The investigators had too little time to deal with all these cases and, since they were afraid to release suspects without proper investigation, many innocents languished and died in gaol. The secrecy surrounding these government operations encouraged negligence; nobody was held publicly responsible for the death of long-held suspects, or for their expiry under torture. Alexander I ostentatiously abolished the political police, but in fact continued to use it under a different name. He later established a ministry of police, whose agents spent many of their working hours defending their role against the ministry of the interior, which continued to regard internal security as its own affair. Alexander, probably fearful of a plot against his life, had many of his associates watched, including Speransky and the pious Magnitsky. At one period Alexander even had the minister of police watched by a team of informers. Double agents, intriguers, and power-seekers flourished, which was one of the reasons why much information about the Decembrists' conspiracy never reached responsible officials until it was too late. With so much doubtful information arriving daily, the report of conspiracy in the army was not given the prompt attention it warranted.

Benckendorff, who became the first chief of the Third Section, submitted to Nicholas the plan on which this new political police organization was based. Familiar with the French secret police, which had a high reputation at that time, Benckendorff wished the new organ of state security to be loved and respected by the population. Thus a great effort was made to separate the gentlemanly side of the organization from its more squalid informing and shadowing departments. Incorporating the civil and military gendarmerie, the Third Section offered promising careers to gentlemen-officers. For these, public respect was to be one of the main inducements to join the service. For the informers, on the other hand, high rewards would be offered, and it was hoped that these inducements might bring forth a larger number of aspirants, so that the lowest types of character could be dispensed with. To emphasize the freshness and purity of the Third Section's better side, bright blue uniforms and white gloves were prescribed. Thus attired, the new gendarmes were sent out, not only on security work, but on behalf of the public welfare. Some, especially in the provinces, unmasked bullying and thieving local officials who had been exploiting the people. Such efforts did for a few years convince many Russians that the Third Section's gendarmerie was a genuine friend of the people.

While in practice there was hardly any activity barred to the Third Section, its main tasks were the shadowing, investigation, arrest, and punishment of people considered dangerous; observation and documentation of foreigners in Russia; investigation of 'heretical' religious communities; preliminary investigations of counterfeiting; supervision of prisons, camps, and other penitentiary institutions; and provision of general information, especially on the state of public opinion. After its early years, the welfare functions of the organization were overshadowed by its repressive and underground operations. Well before the alarming year of 1848 the Third Section was shadowing about two thousand persons annually. At times it insisted on participating in censorship and also acted as the regime's public relations organizer, placing unsigned articles favourable to Nicholas in compliant newspapers both at home and abroad. It received petitions addressed to Nicholas, investigated them, and sent both the petitions and the comments on to the Tsar (Nicholas insisted that he should see all petitions addressed to him). With these petitions, plus denunciations and reports on suspected persons, the Third Section in some years dealt with more than 15,000 cases. Even though it expanded, its officials were overloaded, and more and more suspects were arrested, detained, or exiled, not because they were known to be guilty, but because conceivably, in the future, they might become guilty. Third Section officials, who were always polite to their victims, on occasion assured the latter that, although they might be innocent, they should be grateful for their detention for it protected them from temptation. Several false rumours or denunciations were started by government officials, wishing to damage their rivals; sometimes the Third Section helped in the fabrication of such cases and sometimes it was the victim of them. Ordinary people had every incentive to invent accusations, for a denunciation upheld by the investigators could bring the denouncer freedom if he were a serf, promotion if he were a soldier or official, land and title if he were of the middle class. Even after Nicholas ordered that false denunciations should be punished, the flood of accusations continued. Because only a few of the more gifted or experienced investigators could tell intuitively whether a denunciation was in good faith, because punishment was simpler than investigation, and because no chances could be taken, a victim of a denunciation had all the odds against him unless he knew influential people who could intervene on his behalf. But once a victim had served his sentence, he could return and take up his life again with no discrimination against him.

The Third Section, but not the secret police as such, was finally abolished by Nicholas's successor, Alexander II. By that time the Third Section obviously had failed to keep the promise of its early years when, among other things, it had attracted officials of good character, had advocated the freeing of the serfs as a contribution to public order, and had recommended the amelioration of censorship. It never succeeded in eliminating from its ranks the odious characters whom the 'higher police' tend to attract in all countries, and this in turn led to dishonesty, false accusations, adulterated evidence, bribery, and an atmosphere of suspicion and fear among the population, the government, and the Third Section itself. Yet even at its worst it hardly approached the mechanical ruthlessness which characterized the secret police of several regimes in the twentieth century.

Education and scholarship

After the death of Alexander, men like Magnitsky lost their influence and were replaced by others who, though reactionary, had certain positive qualities. Uvarov, who was minister of education for most of the reign, was a genuine scholar, and his passion for the classics, and for oriental studies, was reflected in the curricula of the gymnasiums and universities. The European upheavals of 1830–31 and 1848 had as damaging repercussions on education as in other fields. In 1831 there was a drop in university enrolment of about one-third, followed in 1835 by new regulations which made the educational curators directly subordinate to the minister of education, thus by-passing the university councils. At the same time new professorial appointments became subject to prior ministerial approval. In 1849 it seemed at one point that all the universities would be closed down. A new university statute was introduced, student numbers were cut (there were 4,006 university students in 1848, but only 3,018 in 1850), tuition fees were raised (partly to make it harder for commoners to receive a higher education and thus raise themselves above their 'proper station'), inspectors of morals were attached to all universities, and students were added to the growing list of professionals required to wear a uniform. Students were also required to have a special style of haircut, apparently so that they could be easily recognized in any civil disturbance. It was at this time that Uvarov felt himself forced to resign, being replaced by a man rather more reactionary and considerably less cultured.

The departure of Uvarov was followed by a pruning of his beloved classics courses, giving more time for practical and technical subjects. (But Greek was not finally eliminated until the early twentieth century, and Latin only after 1917.) There were further encroachments on academic freedom. Professors not only had to hand in for approval their lecture notes, but there were informers who would denounce them if they departed from their text in the lecture itself. Philosophy could be taught only by a priest. There was a similar stiffening of control in the schools, to each of which, earlier, had been appointed a school inspector to watch over morals and political opinions. In gymnasiums, additionally, monitors were appointed to supervise the dormitories, and these reported any dangerous tendencies to the inspector.

The propagation of new ideas was what the authorities particularly wished to avoid; Uvarov himself had stated that his ambition was to build dams to stop the flow of new ideas into the Empire, and thus 'prolong Russia's youth'. Yet intellectual life was by no means dead. New ideas refused to be suppressed. Perhaps the most advanced in the exchange of ideas was Moscow University, which was, and would remain, the biggest (with 1,200 students in 1855, and 10,000 by 1909). Perhaps because it was in a culturally sophisticated city, 400 miles from the St. Petersburg bureaucracy, this university seemed less restricted than others. Even when philosophy was in 'safe' hands, the ideas of the German philosophers, so fascinating to that generation of students, could be imbibed from friends, from banned foreign books (which scholars were usually allowed to obtain) or from teachers in other fields. Herzen, who studied science at this university, later wrote that he learned from the professor of agronomy more about German philosophy than about agricultural science. Moscow University, though academically the responsibility of its rector, was also the concern of the city's governor. He, however, was an easy-going army officer and was probably genuinely disturbed when students were arrested by the Third Section. He also believed that a university was organized like an army, according to Herzen:

> It was long before he could get used to the impropriety of there being no lecture if a professor was ill; he thought the next on the list should step in, so that Father Ternovsky sometimes had to lecture in the clinic on female diseases and Richter, the gynaecologist, had to lecture about the Immaculate Conception.[8]

By the mid-nineteenth century the predominance of Germans and other foreigners in the higher teaching posts began to wane, except at Dorpat. A typical university teacher would have had German instructors when a

---

[8] Gertzen op. cit. 57.

student, would have studied in Europe for his doctorate, and then returned to teach in a Russian university. Despite interference and restrictions, the Russian university teacher had a better life and more opportunities than most other Russians. The lot of the junior teachers was improved by the introduction of a new rank, the *Dotsent*. This rank, which still exists, gave status to those who had the qualifications for a professorship, but had not yet obtained it.

In the humanities, philosophy was perhaps the subject which suffered most under Nicholas. In fact, the chair of philosophy at Moscow University was abolished in the late twenties. History, on the other hand, flourished. Nicholas himself was keenly interested in Russian history, and chairs in this field were first established under his influence. One of the most intelligent supporters of the regime and its ideology, Pogodin, even felt able to write that the historian represents the 'crowning achievement' of a nation, for it is through the historian that a nation learns to understand itself. This eulogy would have carried even more weight if Pogodin had not been himself a professor of history.

But despite the emphasis on history, and the scope and excellence of oriental studies (which remained a permanent characteristic of Russian universities), it was in the sciences that Russian teachers and researchers were mainly distinguishing themselves. Moscow had its chairs of technology and of farm management. St. Petersburg had courses on magnetism and electricity which were unmatched in the outside world. Kazan had the mathematician Lobachevsky who, apart from rescuing his university from the damage done by Magnitsky, is recognized as one of the great names in non-Euclidean geometry. It was in this period that the Pulkovo observatory, which would play its part in the Russian space programme a century later, was established by the Academy of Sciences. The St. Petersburg chemist Zinin was making discoveries useful for the production of aniline dyes, and experimenting with nitro-glycerine. One person who benefited from his work was Alfred Nobel, who subsequently developed dynamite (the Nobel family was working in St. Petersburg during the Crimean War, but returned home in relative poverty when the ending of that war resulted in the termination of their weapons contract). By the mid-nineteenth century, too, Russian mathematicians were very advanced in their studies of the theory of numbers and probability. Mechanical computers were being successfully constructed in St. Petersburg. In the new field of electricity, four St. Petersburg professors, of whom Lenz was the best known, were leading the world in the evolution of electric motors and the telegraph. Contrary to popular belief, Russian scientists deserve credit for laying the world's first practical electric telegraph; this was the

St. Petersburg to Kronstadt link of 1835, followed by the much longer St. Petersburg–Warsaw line of 1839. Both of these were for military purposes.

One of the best-known names in Russian education and science at this time was that of Pirogov, pioneer surgeon and educator. Known in the west, when known at all, as the doctor who dressed Garibaldi's wounds and the experimentalist who persisted long and unsuccessfully in inducing anaesthesia by injecting ether through the anus, Pirogov's real achievement is obscured. In 1836 he was professor of surgery at Dorpat, and already contributing, through experimentation and publication, to the solution of many problems faced at that time by surgeons and anatomists. He then became an army doctor, and in the Caucasus campaign of 1847 became, apparently, the first person to use ether for battlefield operations. In the Crimean War he became famous for bringing, against all the odds, some degree of organization into the chaotic and deadly military hospitals. In this he was assisted by the first female nurses to enter active service with the army (Russia, too, had her Florence Nightingales). From 1858 to 1861 he was curator of the Kiev educational district, and brought a fresh and broad mind to work on the problems of public education. Some of his ideas were incorporated in Alexander II's educational reforms. He also started the first Russian Sunday school, at Kiev. Unlike western models, this was concerned not with teaching the scriptures but with reading and writing, and aimed at those for whom Sunday was the only free day. These Sunday schools were very successful, with about 300 being founded before their popularity aroused suspicion during the reign of Alexander II; they were then put under governmental and church control. As for Pirogov, he fell into official disfavour and was transferred to a lesser position in the early sixties, probably because he was too imaginative and too popular.

Literature and the arts

During the eighteenth century, common spoken Russian developed into a literary language, but it was the poet Pushkin who transformed Russian into one of the world's great languages. Since it is the language rather than the content of Pushkin's work which is so exquisite, he is difficult to appreciate in translation. But he did for Russian what Shakespeare did for English and Dante for Italian. He gave poetic meaning to the simplest Russian words and phrases, showing that the language of the common people was as rich and as flexible as any other vernacular. Of noble, but not rich, family, Pushkin achieved some fame during Alexander's reign through his *Ode to Freedom* and his authorship of some of the most witty and cruel epigrams about Arakcheyev. These circulated among St.

Petersburg society and resulted in his expulsion from the capital. Nicholas allowed him as an act of grace to return to St. Petersburg, but his relationship with the Tsar and government was uneasy. He was killed in a duel at the age of thirty-seven. In his relatively short life he had written, among many others, *Evgenii Onegin*, a novel in verse; the Shakespeare-style play, *Boris Godunov*; a novel, *The Captain's Daughter*, about the Pugachov Rebellion; and the poem, *The Bronze Horseman*, celebrating the awesome greatness of Peter the Great. He also composed a multitude of epigrams and a few works which, because of their content, were not widely distributed; his *Gavriiliada*, for example, portrayed the seduction of the Virgin Mary by, almost simultaneously, the Holy Ghost, the Serpent, and the Archangel Gabriel.

Almost within hours of Pushkin's death, verses entitled *The Death of a Poet* were circulating in manuscript. In this indignant and very talented poem, scorn and revulsion was heaped on the moronic and idle young nobles who, unable to appreciate the damage they had done, were responsible for Pushkin's death. An old lady, fearful of revolution, sent a copy to Nicholas, and an investigation was ordered. The author was a twenty-three-year-old Guards officer of Scottish ancestry, Mikhail Lermontov. Nicholas, irritated not only by the poem but by the thought that a Guards officer should waste his time writing poetry, ordered Lermontov's reduction to the ranks and transfer to the Caucasus. When he returned to the capital after this first expulsion, Lermontov's experiences fighting the Caucasian tribesmen and seducing the Caucasian tribeswomen provided the material for a stream of superb poems, stories, and songs written in the Romantic spirit. Lionized by St. Petersburg society, writing erotic poems for fellow-officers, dancing, drinking, and seducing, Lermontov led a short and reckless life before being killed in a duel. In his best-known prose piece, *A Hero of our Time*, Lermontov portrayed what later would be called a 'Superfluous Man'. In this story the hero is a highly talented young officer who seems to have already experienced everything which life has to offer. He runs recklessly after all kinds of diversions, usually involving women or violence or both. He finishes by asking himself why he, talented and courageous as he is, could not have done something better with his life. The Superfluous Man, whose life is futile because society gives him no scope for his talent, was destined to be a favourite subject of Russian novelists.

Gogol, a Ukrainian writing in Russian, first attracted attention with his semi-humorous, semi-fantastic tales of Ukrainian peasant life, but his best-known works were the novel, *Dead Souls*, and the play, *The Government Inspector*. In the latter, which the censor wished to ban but which

Nicholas liked and allowed, bitter fun is poked at corrupt officials of provincial government. The characters, the liars, hypocrites, posers, swindlers, bullies, and other official types, were familiar to the audience but had never before been portrayed so exactly or so amusingly; the play's illumination of the evils of the bureaucracy is perhaps what Nicholas liked, for he was aware of the deficiencies of his administrators.

In this period romantic painting superseded the school known as Russian classicism. Bryullov's enormous canvas, *The Last Days of Pompeii*, was probably the first Russian painting to attract worldwide acclaim; it was sadly overrated by the fashionable public and soon forgotten, except in so far as it inspired Bulwer Lytton's famous novel. Of greater permanent interest, especially to historians, are those painters who depicted scenes from Russian life. Of these, Venetsianov and the former Guards officer, Fedotov, were the most important; they led Russian painting into the age of critical realism. Fedotov's painting, *The Decoration, or a Bureaucrat the Morning after Receiving an Honour*, appears to have been the first painting to be cut by the censor. It portrayed an official, brutalized, soulless, and arrogant, standing in his dressing gown and haircurlers, trying on his new medal. To the public which flocked to see it in 1848, this picture seemed to express the essence of heartless decoration-seeking officialdom. The censorship appeared to share this impression, for when prints were made it insisted that the medal be taken out of the picture.

Music did not escape the attention of the censor (at one period musical scores were suspect, as potential secret codes). Nevertheless, there was a blossoming of Russian talent in the person of Glinka, who based his work on traditional church and folk music, rejecting the imitative and foreign-inspired work of his less distinguished contemporaries. In general, music was highly appreciated in St. Petersburg and Moscow. Guest artists from the west were often heard, and in the capital there was a permanent Italian opera company. The richer nobility maintained their own orchestras and Russian choirs were already being praised by foreign critics. One musical event in 1833 was the introduction of the first Russian national anthem. Hitherto, on ceremonial occasions abroad, the Tsar had been greeted with the British anthem, which Nicholas found mildly humiliating. Apparently the new anthem proved popular, for at the coronation of Alexander II two decades later it was sung three times over during the fireworks display, the first time modestly with 1,000 voices, the second time somewhat louder with the addition of massed choirs and military bands, and the third time more emphatically, accompanied by cannon salvos 'fired by means of an electro-galvanic apparatus'. But the words seemed little more advanced than those of the British anthem formerly used:

God, save the Tsar!
Mighty and strong reign for our glory;
Reign for the dread of our enemies,
O Tsar of the Orthodox Faith!
God, save the Tsar!

The critics and commentators

Literary criticism began to flourish under Nicholas, its most noted practitioner being Belinsky. Probably Russia's most influential critic, Belinsky
had been excluded from Moscow University after his professors had decided he lacked sufficient intellect. He then became one of the very few
Russians who made their living by writing (almost all Russian writers were
landowners). It was he who recognized that a specifically Russian literature was emerging, worthy of comparison with the literary heritage of western nations. It was he, too, who, towards the end of his thirty-seven-year
life, popularized the description 'critical realism' as a feature and as a
standard of judgement of Russian literature. By realism he meant simply
the description of things as they are. By critical he meant socially responsible; the writer had a duty to illuminate the seamy side of life in the hope
of encouraging dissatisfaction and hence improvement. Critical realism
therefore implied that a writer was to be judged above all by the content,
the social implications, of his work. Belinsky wrote that Russia's 'salvation'
lay neither in mysticism nor piety nor asceticism but in enlightenment and
humanity, in sharing the successes of western civilization.

A key work was Chaadayev's *Philosophical Letter* (actually there were
eight of these, but only the first was published). Chaadayev, a former
Guards officer and participant in the 1812 campaign, published this article
in 1836, startling governmental and intellectual circles. Chaadayev was
declared to be mentally defective, the editor of the newspaper which published it was exiled, and the overworked censor who had passed it was
expelled from government service. Chaadayev took a distinctly pessimistic
view of Russia's past and present. He cast doubts on the assumption that
Russia, though behind the west, would eventually go through the same
processes as the west had undergone. He pointed out that since Russia
had a quite different history, with no Renaissance, no Reformation, and
no Roman Law, there was no guarantee that she would pass through the
same stages as the west. He later implied that Russia's future lay in
following the west, but modifying western experience so as to fit Russian
realities. Thus Chaadayev was in a certain sense the harbinger of those
Russian revolutionaries, like the Populists and Lenin, who saw the importance of modifying western concepts before applying them in Russia, as

opposed to others, like the Decembrists and the Mensheviks, who seemed content to imitate the west.

The question of Russia's destiny was the preoccupation of minds other than those of Chaadayev and those who thought like him. In a sense, Russia was the Superfluous Man of Europe; so much power, so much capability, but unable to find the opportunity of using these advantages for the general welfare. Proponents of Official Nationality, as already mentioned, thought that Russia should remain as she was in order to serve as a shining example for the rest of the world. When Chaadayev, in his *Philosophical Letter*, wrote that Russia's past was empty, her present intolerable, and her future non-existent, Benckendorff replied that 'Russia's past is admirable, her present more than magnificent: while so far as her future is concerned, it cannot be grasped by the most audacious imagination'.[9] This was a very eloquent eulogy of Russia, especially as it came from a Baltic German writing in French.

At this period discussion groups and literary circles were the only effective way of circulating and developing new ideas. Friends of intellectual bent would join together regularly for a partly social, partly instructive, meeting. The most fruitful of these circles, where not only ideas, but banned books and handwritten manuscripts, might circulate, were usually quite informal. German philosophy, including Hegel, was very fashionable, as well as French socialist thought. Intellectuals were very few in Russia at this time, and were concentrated in the two capitals. For most of them, their most important audience was themselves. As might be expected, the Third Section was not slow to insinuate its informers into these circles, and many participants were arrested. Among them was the young Herzen who, after release from exile, emigrated in 1847. Already known as a gifted and persuasive writer and journalist, he became the inspiration of the left-wing of the Westernizers. He claimed that Russia would only move forward after power had been transferred from the upper classes to the people, and after science, socialism, and freedom had replaced repression. After witnessing the 1848 revolutions, and personally discovering that western democracy meant the replacement of one big tsar by a multitude of little tsars, Herzen changed his views somewhat. He advocated the inclusion of truly Russian features, like the commune, in the society of the future, so that the dangers inherent in western democracy might be avoided by drawing on Russia's experience. From 1856, Herzen was in London, publishing his Russian newspaper *Kolokol* (*Bell*). This included items received from correspondents inside Russia describing, among other

[9] Quoted in S. Monas, *The Third Section* (Harvard University Press, 1961), 169.

things, bureaucratic frauds and injustices. It was smuggled into Russia
and attained an influential, though necessarily limited, circulation there.
But after 1863, when Herzen supported the Poles in their rebellion against
Russia, he lost influence among Russian radicals; when Russian intellectuals talked of freedom they usually meant freedom for themselves, not for
the Poles. Nevertheless, and despite the widening gap between Herzen and
the younger revolutionaries, he may be said to have been the forerunner of
later revolutionary movements. In particular, his advocacy of blending
modern western civilization with the old Russian elements inspired the
emergent Populists.

Bakunin, one of Herzen's contemporaries, was also discomfited by the
fate of the Polish revolt, and henceforth devoted himself to European
affairs. Regarded as the inspirer of modern European anarchism, Bakunin
was originally simply a revolutionary democrat. Sometimes classed as one
of Russia's 'repentant nobility', he had participated in the European
revolutions of 1848–9, and had been extradited to Russia and exiled to
Siberia, whence he escaped abroad in 1861. It was not until after this, his
final departure from his homeland, that he became a real anarchist.
Bakunin's ideas reached Russia through returning emigrés and through
his *Peoples' Cause*, an anarchist periodical smuggled into Russia and read
largely by students. Although his excitable personality hindered the development of an anarchist movement in Russia, most shades of revolutionary opinion absorbed anarchist ingredients. Bakunin never had a strong
organization, but he became the inspiration of young revolutionaries; he
was something of a hero, having participated in so many glorious failures,
while his advocacy of the destruction of the state was congenial to those
many Russians who resented the rigidity and repression of the government.

Censorship

The strict censorship under which writers worked during most of Nicholas's
reign was by no means an innovation. The last years of Alexander's reign
witnessed a stricter control than the early years of Nicholas. It is true that
a censorship law introduced in 1826 enabled the authorities to ban almost
anything if they so chose, but it was not applied as strictly as it could have
been, and in 1828 new and lenient regulations were introduced, reflecting
the short-lived honeymoon between the Tsar and literary circles. The
censors were instructed not to interfere with certain kinds of publication;
most of the censors were themselves either part-time writers or at least in
sympathy with writers, the latter being usually in favour of some kind of
censorship, and the new law, which made the censor, not the writer or

publisher, responsible once approval had been given, was regarded as a measure of protection against post-publication prosecution. But the Third Section gradually encroached on the censorship preserves of the ministry of education; after the upheavals in France and in Poland in 1830–1, and especially after 1848 and the Petrashevsky affair, censorship was strict, unfair, and often absurd.

The atmosphere in which writers and publishers worked can best be conveyed by some examples. Thus, under Alexander's censorship, a work mentioning that certain mushrooms were poisonous had to be changed when the censor pointed out that, since mushrooms were habitually eaten by the peasantry during Lent, they were therefore sacred and to claim that they might be poisonous was sacrilegious. Under Nicholas a poet who referred to his 'divine muse' was told that divinity was not an earthly quality. A cookery book was not allowed to refer to free air in the oven, because 'free air' sounded revolutionary. Medical textbooks could not show diagrams of the body. In fiction the bad end awaiting the villains had to be clearly shown. The newspaper editor who wrote and printed a rather critical review of the play *The Hand of the Almighty Saved the Fatherland* found himself detained and his newspaper (and hence his livelihood) suppressed; Nicholas had liked the play so much that he had seen it several times, and was therefore insulted by the review. Articles on serfdom were not allowed, and even the word itself was banned for a time. Descriptions of poverty in Russia were not permitted. Information on events in Poland and Finland could only be printed if it had first appeared in official government publications. Similarly, news of western Europe, after 1848, could only take the form of reprints from the Prussian newspapers. Magnitsky, fighting the good fight in his enforced retirement, wrote *Instructive Extracts from the history of contemporary West Europe, Revealing the True Cause of the Catastrophes tormenting it, as an example for Young People and for Minds not yet infected with the Foreign Cholera of the Spirit of the Time* but even with this title the book was banned by Benckendorff, who said its publication would mean the printing of a number of harmful opinions. Writers and potential writers and people suspected of being writers could be shadowed, detained for days or weeks in the nearest guardhouse, imprisoned, exiled, or, like Chaadayev, certified as insane.

Only three periodicals were banned in Nicholas's reign, but the publication of a far larger number of proposed newspapers and monthlies was not allowed to start. To such requests Nicholas typically replied that there were already enough on the market. The two best periodicals, *The Contemporary* and *Notes of the Fatherland*, were never banned, even though their articles were by no means as uncritical as the Third Section wished. The latter believed that the respect in which these journals were held by a reading public athirst for good commentary would cause a very undesirable public indignation in the event of their suppression. On the other hand, the owner and writers of the subservient newspaper *Northern Bee* were not immune from suspicion, shadowing, and incarceration in guardhouses, even though its publisher was a proponent of Official Nationality, offered to serve as an informer, would always give space to unsigned propaganda articles produced by the Third Section, and forwarded to the latter denunciations against competing editors, publishers, and writers.

Because serious discussion of social issues was so limited by censorship and so distorted by 'official' writing and information, it was in fiction that, in the nineteenth century as in the twentieth, Russian writers presented, frequently obliquely, new ideas which otherwise would never have reached a large audience. In modern Russian history there is often more truth to be found in fiction than in non-fiction, and the novel had a more important influence on public opinion than in other countries. This meant extra responsibility for novelists; entertainment and virtuosity were not enough, as Belinsky had emphasized. The 'thick' monthly periodical with long, thoughtful and solid articles in its chosen field was becoming popular, and it was in literary journals of this type that most serious fiction was first published; successful serializations would later be published in book form. In Nicholas's time, periodicals (and newspapers) were reaching a wider audience, but circulations were still small. Because costs were low and prices quite high, books and journals could be published in small editions. Many good periodicals had fewer than 500 subscribers.[10] In intellectual circles, censorship was mitigated by the hand-copying and circulation of original works, some of which remained unprinted for decades. Chaadayev's *Philosophical Letter* circulated in this way among hundreds, if not thousands, of readers for seven years before its appearance in print.

The army

The Russian army, with about one million men, was the largest in Europe. Although it called up only 1 to 2 per cent of eligible males each year, the conscripts served for twenty-five years. Thus to be selected as a conscript was a tragedy for the individual, and also for his family, which was unlikely to be ever reunited. A man could be chosen at any age between

---

[10] In 1846, under unenterprising editorship, *The Contemporary* had 233 subscribers. After becoming more radical, it increased this to 3,100 (plus street sales) in 1848. After the death of Nicholas, journals were allowed openly to discuss current affairs, and *The Contemporary's* subscribers reached a peak of 6,500 in 1861.

twenty and thirty-five. Landowners could send their serfs as recruits if they gave trouble, village communes could send men who were unpopular or did not pay their proper share of taxes, courts could sentence men to army service, while richer peasants could bribe the selectors, or hire substitutes. Men exempt from poll-tax (nobles and others) were likewise exempt from conscription.

Two incentives were used to create good soldiers: corporal punishment and Christianity. It was an article of faith that perfection in drill could only be obtained by beating almost to death any soldier who was less than perfect. Christianity was an asset in terms of morale rather than of training. Church services were frequent, regular, and compulsory for all except certain minorities. After the horrors of the parade ground they were a great relaxation, providing with their ritual and music a real inspiration and sense of togetherness, while also promoting patriotic feelings. In wartime, the priests who blessed the bayonets preached that to die fighting for the Holy Tsar was a joyous experience. But most soldiers died not in battle but from disease, aided by negligence, malnutrition, and hardship. In the quarter of a century preceding the Crimean War, Russia lost more than one million soldiers through causes other than battle.[11]

Until the Crimean War, the Russian army was trained to fight battles like Borodino. The potential battlefield was vaguely envisaged as an immense ballroom, over which bodies of troops in close order would perform a complex minuet as they prepared for the climax, a decisive bayonet charge. The main event in the peacetime Russian army was the annual manœuvres, which traditionally took place in the training grounds of the western borderlands. Manœuvres, however, is an inaccurate term, for under Nicholas the emphasis was on parades and inspections. Units marched and evolved under the eyes of the Tsar, who was quick to detect a line which was not quite straight, a turn which was not quite ninety degrees, or a soldier whose spine was not quite rigid. This spirit spread downwards so that officers of all ranks were judged, not by the fighting qualities of their men, but by their perfection on parade. But such parades were regarded as good training for war, for it was laid down that in battle the advances, assaults, and other manœuvres would be carried out in the same way, with the same close order, the same symmetry, the same rigidity, and, apparently, the same quasi-goose step.

The mass bayonet attack was regarded as the supreme battle-winning tactic, which is one reason why musketry training was neglected. It was believed that in battle a cavalry charge would put to flight an enemy

[11] J. S. Curtiss, *The Russian Army under Nicholas I* (1956), 248–51.

softened up first by artillery and then by bayonet attack. The cavalry officers, especially the senior officers, were almost entirely to blame for the poor showing of their men in the Crimean War. Like the infantry officers, they had concentrated on performing brilliantly at parades. Their horses, fed on oats and beer, were magnificently glossy and plump but when, at one annual manœuvres, Nicholas ordered the cavalry to do everything at the gallop, 700 horses died in one day from unaccustomed exertion.[12] The engineers and the gunners were excellent by any standard, and this excellence remained a feature of the Russian army both before and after the 1917 Revolution. Perhaps because of the inadequacies of Russian small arms, the artillery was expected to play a decisive role in the opening stages of a battle. The engineers, in fortification and in sapping, were superior to those of other armies and already made use of electric detonators in the 1850s. A Russian textbook of fortification was translated and used at this time by several European armies.

The engineers and gunners recruited the more intelligent men, both as officers and as other ranks. Infantry and cavalry officers were usually of poor quality. Certainly, there were some good, or potentially good, officers, but it was usually not these who reached the top. The innovator was regarded with hostility, and so was an officer who read too many books or who trained his men for war rather than parades. Anti-intellectualism was the ruling characteristic of the officer corps, reflecting Nicholas's success in steering the army away from politics. Many Russian officers were former officer-cadets (junkers). These were youths of noble birth and of doubtful education who would serve in the ranks and then receive commissions after two or more years' service. Although it is true that a fraction of these had some kind of higher education, the majority were dull, spoiled children for whom the army seemed to offer the only suitable respectable employment. A better officer was produced by the various four-year cadet corps establishments which had blossomed under Alexander, and continued to flourish under Nicholas.

In any army there can be found corruption and peculation. In the Russian army these were on a grand scale. It was not a case of the occasional cook, say, who would issue less than the rations and sell the surplus to traders. It was a case of the regimental commander who would spend less than his approved food budget and pocket the difference. It was a case of high officers who would use their men as workers in their own private projects. It was engineers who would inflate cost estimates for proposed structures. It was medical officers who would keep patients in bed as long

12 Ibid., 137.

as possible, prescribing fancy diets and wines for them which they would consume themselves. In all cases it was the officers, sometimes the sergeants, who profited, the ordinary soldier who suffered. The regimental cash box, containing soldiers' savings as well as supply funds, was a frequent victim. Leo Tolstoy, who as a young officer served in the Crimean War, included this passage in *Hadji Murat*, one of his short stories:

> After they finished smoking the soldiers began talking.
> 'They say the commander has been at the cash box again,' one of them remarked lazily. 'He lost at cards, you know.'
> 'He'll pay it back,' said Panov.
> 'Of course he will. He's a good officer,' Avdeev agreed.

The scale of the Russian army's inadequacies was attributable to the nature of Russian society, and to the army's misfortune that for fifty years it never lost a war. It was only the Crimean War, when Russia found herself fighting against foes stronger than the Poles, Persians, and Turks, that revealed the rot to a wide public. Nicholas was ultimately responsible for this failure, because he claimed to be an autocrat and a professional soldier. Yet he saw further than his high officers (whom, admittedly, he selected). It was Nicholas who ordered the better treatment of recruits, who urged the investigation of the medical and supply services, who released after only fifteen years' service conscripts with unblemished records, who pointed out that soldiers should be trained in fieldcraft, and who tried to instil some commonsense among the cavalry officers. That his urgings were largely ineffective was due, not so much to his own shortcomings, as to the traditional difficulty faced by Russian rulers of ensuring that their instructions were carried out in their absence.

Russia at war

A short victorious war is the temptation of many regimes, especially of those which feel unsure of themselves. Nicholas was blessed with two such wars at the start of his reign, against Persia and against Turkey. The Persian war was purely and simply a result of Russian expansionism in the Caucasus. Not content with the previous conquest of Georgia and Azerbaizhan from the Persians, Russia claimed still more territory from the Shah. The latter's 1826 counter-attack was defeated, and in 1828 a peace treaty brought Persian Armenia into the Russian Empire. The central, mountainous part of the Caucasus would be outside Russian control for several more decades. However, some progress in the 'pacification' of this region was made during the reign. By cutting down the forests which sheltered the villages of dissident tribesmen, the hostile territory was reduced, while new forts helped to contain sudden attacks sweeping down from the mountains. But one of Nicholas's favourite projects, the securing of the Black Sea coastline by a series of forts, was defeated by malaria.

Nicholas's second short war involved the settlement of the Greek problem, bequeathed by Alexander I. Russia in 1827 agreed with Britain and France to impose a treaty whereby the Turks would acknowledge Greek self-government. The Sultan was slow to agree, and a combined fleet of Russian, French, and British ships attacked and destroyed his fleet at Navarino. Despite this, the Sultan remained obstinate. Nicholas, with tacit French and British approval, sent his army into the Turkish Danubian possessions. The Tsar himself joined his troops, but was honest enough to leave the army after the first campaign, openly admitting that his presence did more harm than good. A further campaign was more successful, although losses from disease and negligence were high. There were also Russian advances in Transcaucasia. The end result was a treaty giving Russian ships free passage on the Danube and through the Straits. Greece was declared independent in 1830. After this war Russia became a friend of Turkey, for Nicholas did not wish to see the fall of the long-established dynasty in Constantinople. When the Sultan was threatened by his Egyptian subjects, Nicholas sent the Black Sea fleet to help him; the result was the retreat of the Egyptians and an even more favourable Russo-Turkish treaty. Despite ups and downs, partly caused by British intrigues, Russo-Turkish relations remained peaceful. In 1841, Turkey, Russia, and four other European powers signed the Straits Convention, which specified that Turkey would allow no foreign warship to pass the Straits, except when Turkey was at war. This gave Russia as much security as she could reasonably expect without herself occupying the Straits.

When, in 1830, the king of France was overthrown, Nicholas feared the spread of revolution. And not without reason, for just as the Tsar was contemplating the dispatch of Russian troops to put down the revolt of the Belgians, itself sparked by the events in Paris, he found himself faced with insurrection within his own Empire, in Poland. Nicholas had hitherto accepted the Polish constitution, although he did not like it. Nevertheless many Poles were dissatisfied and were intent on winning complete independence, as well as the restoration of Lithuania. In 1830 conspirators shot at a general whom they mistook for Grand Duke Constantine, the Viceroy. The ensuing revolt was slow to take fire, partly because Constantine, long resident in Poland, was a Polonophile and refrained from using force against the rebels. However, intransigence on the part both of Nicholas and the more extreme of the rebels made hostilities inevitable. Czartoryski, Alexander's old friend, was among those who joined the rebel government.

The Russian army moved in, but faulty tactics and inherent deficiencies robbed it of an early victory. Moreover, its commander and thousands of soldiers (and also Constantine) died of cholera. After Paskevich took over command, a slow advance was achieved, but Russian successes were due more to quarrels among the Poles than to Paskevich's generalship. After Warsaw was captured some rebels, including Czartoryski, emigrated to Paris, where they carried on propaganda against Russia and for Polish independence. As for Russian Poland, its constitution was abrogated, it was ruled more and more by St. Petersburg bureaucrats, its universities were closed, and the Russian language was imposed in official institutions.

In 1848 there was another revolution in France which led to upheavals so widespread that Nicholas was sufficiently alarmed to issue a strong, almost demented, warning to the revolutionaries of Europe; 'Give heed, O ye peoples, and submit, for God is with us!' When his friend and ally the King of Prussia had to compromise with the rebels, he was pained, and announced that if Prussia became a republic he would consider it his duty to send in Russian troops to restore the throne. He did send in the Russian army to enable the Emperor of Austria to suppress the revolt of the Hungarians under Kossuth, the Tsar's zeal on this occasion being heightened by the knowledge that among the ranks of the Hungarian rebels were many Poles. The Russian army lost 10,000 men in this campaign, of whom about 9,000 died from disease; Paskevich was partly to blame for these deaths, as he had failed to provide adequate medical services. Earlier, Russian troops had entered Roumania to help the Turks suppress a revolutionary government there.

It was Nicholas's wish to convert friendship with Turkey to influence over Turkey which led to the Crimean War. Certainly Russia did not desire this war, and was only partly to blame for it. Nicholas had anticipated, and dreaded, the break-up of the Turkish Empire, and had earlier tried to agree with other powers on how to deal with this when the time came; he thought he had made it clear that Russia did not want Constantinople, but could not tolerate any other power establishing itself there. After the quarrel about the respective rights of Orthodox and Catholic priests in the Holy Places under Turkish rule had been settled, Russia demanded the right to 'protect' Christians in the Turkish Empire. To emphasize this demand, Russian troops entered the Danubian provinces, and this led to a Russo-Turkish conflict. The Russian fleet annihilated the Turkish navy at Sinope (having attacked when the incompetent and unsuspecting Turks were at anchor, the Russian admiral, Nakhimov, was immediately accused in the British press of committing an atrocity). French and British ships moved in to prevent a possible Russian landing near Constantinople, and then, in 1854, France and Britain declared war.[13]

In the ensuing conflict the deficiencies of the Russian army proved to be more crippling than the deficiencies of the Allied armies. The Russian officers were usually more incompetent than their French and British opposite numbers. The Russian commander-in-chief, the timid and apprehensive Paskevich, persistently opposed the sending of reinforcements to the Crimea, in case the Austrians should decide to attack the western frontier. Even when specifically ordered to do so by Nicholas, he only went through the motions of doing so. In some other respects he opposed Nicholas's suggestions, although in retrospect it seems that Nicholas had a sounder appreciation of what was needed than either Paskevich or the other leading generals. The best Russian generalship was provided by the handful of admirals who assumed commands on land. Nakhimov virtually took command of the defence of Sevastopol, during which he was killed.

The Allied landing in the Crimea was followed by a Russian defeat at the Battle of the Alma (1854). The war then developed into a costly contest over the possession of Sevastopol, whose value was more symbolic than strategic. After a year's siege the Russian army withdrew from this fortified base, and peace followed in 1856. The Treaty of Paris was not excessively burdensome to Russia; her bargaining position had been improved by military successes against Turkey in the Caucasus, and by Anglo-French differences. The greatest sacrifice was the acceptance that the Black Sea should be neutralized; this meant that Russia could not have a fleet there whereas Turkey, similarly restricted, in wartime would have no difficulty in bringing in her own or her allies' warships from the Mediterranean. Russia also lost influence in the Danubian region, which was soon to see the creation of a new state, Roumania. The autocracy was in no danger, even though the war had demonstrated the incompetence of its generals, the inefficiency of its officials, and the dishonesty of its army supply merchants. All the same, Russia could no longer be regarded, as she had been since 1812, as the dominant power of Europe.

Nicholas had died before this, in 1855. Appropriately, he died from over-inspecting; already having a cold, he insisted on carrying out a military inspection in February and was rewarded with pneumonia. Being worn out and disappointed, he did not show much resistance and died calmly some days later, having apologized to his heir for his failure to leave the

---

[13] For a serious study of the causes of the Crimean War, a good start would be the article by B. D. Gooch in *American Historical Review*, Vol. LXII (1956), 33–58, which surveys a century's historiography on the subject.

affairs of state in proper order. Decades later, the celebrated geographer and anarchist leader, Prince Kropotkin, recalled Nicholas's death:

On February 18 the local police distributed bulletins among the houses informing us of the Tsar's illness, and inviting the population to go to church to pray for his recovery. Actually the Tsar was already dead and the authorities knew this . . . but because right until the end nothing had been said of the Tsar's illness they considered it necessary to gradually prepare 'the people'. We all went to church and prayed very fervently . . . [two days later] we did learn of the death of Nicholas I. When the news spread, our own and neighbouring households were gripped with fear. It was said that at the market 'the people' seemed very suspicious-looking, and not only expressed no regret but on the contrary expressed dangerous thoughts . . . the landowners expected a serf rising at any minute, a new Pugachov revolt.

At this time in the streets of St. Petersburg intellectuals hugged one another, telling each other the good news. All forecast that there would be an end to the war and to the terrible conditions which had been created by 'the iron tyrant'.[14]

But not everybody rejoiced at the Tsar's death. Among those who were saddened was Queen Victoria, who wrote that she had not forgotten friendlier times. The Queen's opinion of the Tsar, written in 1844, still seems perceptive:

He is stern and severe—with fixed principles of duty which nothing on earth will make him change; very clever I do not think him, and his mind is an uncivilised one; his education has been neglected; politics and military concerns are the only things he takes great interest in; the arts and all softer occupations he is insensible to, but he is sincere, I am certain, sincere even in his most despotic acts, from a sense that it is the only way to govern; he is not, I am sure, aware of the dreadful cases of individual misery which he so often causes, for I can see by various instances that he is kept in utter ignorance of many things, which his people carry out in most corrupt ways, while he thinks that he is extremely just.[15]

[14] P. Kropotkin, *Zapiski revolyutsionera* (1966), 60.
[15] A. C. Benson, and Viscount Asher. *The Letters of Queen Victoria 1837–1861* (John Murray, 1908), II, 14.

3. *Tsar and Serf*

Alexander II

BORN in 1818, bombed in 1881, Alexander II at his accession was thirty-six, and was destined to reign for twenty-six years. Nicholas I had ensured that his son and heir was better prepared than he had been for the high office which awaited him. From the age of six to sixteen, Alexander's education was supervised by a broad-minded army general. Beating was not considered the best way to instil knowledge; the tutors were expected to be tolerant and to gain Alexander's interest. The academic side of the heir's education was supervised by the poet Zhukovsky, whose concern for the well-being of the common people is presumed to have been the source of Alexander's own sensibilities. Thus his upbringing not only equipped him with such essentials as a knowledge of languages, of history and of the duties of a ruler, but also with a perceptive and humane attitude towards the world in general. At the age of nineteen he started on his travels. He was the first member of the royal family to visit Siberia, where his encounter with the lives of convicts and exiles led to a certain improvement in their lot after he became tsar. Then to Europe, where he became engaged to a German princess, the marriage taking place in 1842. Some years later he visited the Caucasus, and won a St. George Cross for bravery when mountain tribes launched an unexpected but unsuccessful attack on his party.

With the possible exceptions of Khrushchev and Gorbachev, no Russian ruler brought so much relief to so many of his people as did Alexander II, autocratic and conservative though he was. His father had groomed him for the succession by appointing him to a number of committees and councils, including the Council of State and committees dealing with serfdom, railways, and others. In these, his opinion was often contrary to those of the more liberal members. In Nicholas's many absences, Alexander was left in charge of routine state affairs. Thus when he came to the throne he was already familiar with procedures and problems, and he knew much of his Empire at first hand. Although not immune to the superficial attractions of military life, he was not quite so passionate a soldier as his father. He inherited from his father and his tutors an honesty of character and loyalty to subordinates, but he was milder, more sensitive, and more patient than his father. He was still, however, an autocrat rather than a leader.

The main events of his reign were, first and very foremost, the freeing of the serfs; then, and partly in connexion with this reform, real changes in local government, justice, education and the army. Ironically, and perhaps naturally, these reforms and the freer atmosphere were followed by new and strong manifestations of the revolutionary movement. The 'Tsar Liberator' also had to cope with two burdens which had afflicted his father: cholera and the Poles. These trials seemed to lead to a certain reaction on Alexander's part, and there was a partial return to tactics of repression. However, just before his assassination and having, as he thought, succeeded in calming the Empire, Alexander was preparing a new series of reforms. Among these was the grant of some political influence to the people. Throughout the reign there was steady economic progress, expansion in Central Asia, some attempt to overcome the financial consequences of the Crimean War, and a continuation of railway building. In foreign affairs there was a rather unnecessary war against Turkey, but Alexander was able to avoid other large-scale conflicts. As Tsar, his biggest failure was his heir.

Apart from his advisers and ministers, Alexander was influenced by his brother Constantine, whose importance may have been underestimated. As Nicholas's second son, Constantine had been groomed for a career in the navy, and it was he who from 1855 carried through the reform of the Russian fleet. Steam began to replace sail at a fast rate, the number of sailors kept on shore was reduced, paperwork was thinned out, and corporal punishment strictly controlled. Officials of above-average intelligence were appointed to the navy ministry. In 1862 Constantine was appointed Viceroy of Poland and endeavoured to take a moderate line with the Polish nationalists. However, the latter tried to assassinate him, and the words and deeds of extremist Poles and extremist Russians made it impossible for him to avoid the 1863 Polish revolt. He remained navy minister and Chairman of the Council of State until the death of Alexander. He continued to have great influence, although his liberal inclinations were not strong enough to prevent the reaction of Alexander's later years. Perhaps his biggest contribution was in the early years of the reign, when he did much to ease the passage of the statutes designed to free Russia from her shameful and harmful tradition of serfdom.

The Russian peasant at mid-century

Long before the Crimean War it had been recognized that Russia's main problem was the peasant problem, but the landowning nobility, on which the tsarist state depended for its administrators and officers, was opposed to any radical social reconstruction in the countryside. The nobles had a generally free hand in supervising their serfs; so long as they found their quota of conscripts, so long as they produced their serfs' taxes on time, and so long as they did not abuse their privileges too notoriously, they were free (unlike industrialists) from government interference. The serfs were the nobles' affair, and that other large group, the state peasants, were the affair of those appointed to administer them. Thus official Russia, westernized Russia, could ignore the real Russia; only when the peasantry flared into revolt was it noticed. It lived its own life. It had few cultural links with the urban classes. It was the 'dark people', sometimes described as being alienated from 'society' although it was the latter which was alienated from the peasantry, and thus from traditional Russia.

Discussion of the Russian peasantry can only be generalized because, although there was much that was typical, there was little which was invariable. One broad distinction will be made, but to give a complete and true description of peasant life would require a volume for each province. The broad distinction is geographical: European Russia can be divided into the wooded, clayey north and centre on the one hand, and the fertile and almost treeless south on the other. The latter includes the region of the Black Earth, which stretches from the south-western borderlands into Asiatic Russia, narrowing as it does so. While very fertile, it has unreliable rainfall and hence fluctuating harvests. The distinction between the grain-surplus south and the grain-deficit north and centre was always import-ant; industrial goods and timber moved south, while grain moved north.

The rationale of serfdom, that is, the tying of the peasant to the land he tilled, was that it ensured labour (and hence income) to the landowning noble, enabling the latter to devote himself to serving the state. The enserfment of the peasants had been gradual, but by the middle of the seventeenth century the peasant and his descendants were legally obliged to remain on the land of their master. When the state granted land to new or old nobles for services rendered, the peasants on that land were transformed from state peasants into serfs.

Thus the serf served the noble and the noble served the tsar, an equation having some apparent justice, since serving the tsar was no light matter. But no sooner had serfdom become a fact than the nobility began seeking ways to alter the equation. For most of the eighteenth century the tsars felt dependent on the nobility (there was hardly a middle class to whom they could appeal, and the peasants did not count), and in 1762 Tsar Peter III was persuaded to acknowledge that the nobility was no longer *obliged* to serve. The equation was broken, and the serfs expected release from their own corresponding obligations. But the anticipated *ukaz* was never issued and the peasants, believing that it had been promulgated but had been hidden from them by the landowners, became resentful. Hitherto, peasant revolts had been localized though frequent, but in the reign of Catherine the Great the intensified discontent expressed itself in Puga-chov's rebellion, which lasted two years and threw official Russia and the nobility into a panic. Of the several impulses which drove later tsars to seek better conditions for the peasantry, fear of a repetition of Pugachov's rebellion was probably the strongest.

In 1850 almost half the peasants were serfs.[1] State peasants outnum-bered them, and usually led a better life. After Catherine and Paul, the practice of making gifts of thousands of state peasants to favourites (that is, transforming them into privately owned serfs) more or less ceased, while the confiscation of church lands by Catherine had converted the church's serfs into state peasants. The state peasantry was administered by crown appointees, some of whom were as bad as the worst landowners, but for most state peasants life was bearable. Serfdom was most prevalent around Moscow and in the south. North and north-central Russia were still largely inhabited by state peasants, and there was no serfdom in Siberia (a century later this was still reflected in the more independent character of Siberian and northern peasants).

Serfs cultivated the land allotted to them, and in recompense for the use of this land they were required to work also on the land reserved for the use of the landowner. Three days a week was probably the average re-quirement but in the worst cases, and in busy weeks, this might be doubled (which meant that the serf could not properly look after his own land). There were no fixed rights or obligations for the peasantry. A landowner could increase his serf's dues and duties, he could seize their property, he could forbid their buying from, selling to, or working with persons outside the estate, he could make them into domestic servants, sell them either separately or with their families, force them to marry so as to breed more serfs, or forbid them to marry disapproved partners. Except in cases of murder or banditry, the landowner administered rural justice and could send troublesome serfs to Siberia or into the army. Whipping was com-monplace. Although there were many landowners who were kindly,

---

[1] See Table 1 on p. 600.

educating and sometimes liberating favoured serfs, there were others who were brutal; social isolation and almost absolute power led some land-owners to excesses which in other circumstances they would have found revolting. Probably the worst-off peasants were those with an absentee landlord. Some nobles had never even seen their estates, and many more only visited them rarely. Such estates were entrusted to bailiffs who all too often were dishonest and tyrannical.

Some nobles were very poor. Some possessed no serfs at all. There were villages divided between a dozen or so nobles. On the other hand there were the well-to-do:

At that period the wealth of a landowner was measured by the number of 'souls' he possessed. 'Souls' meant male serfs, women did not count. My father was a rich man, he had more than 1,200 souls in three different provinces . . . in our family there were eight persons, sometimes ten or twelve; fifty servants in Moscow and sixty or so in the country did not seem too many . . . the dearest wish of every land-owner was to have all his requirements supplied by his own serfs. All this was so that if a guest should ask, 'What a beautifully-tuned piano! Did you get it tuned by Schimmel's?' the landowner could reply, 'I have my own piano-tuner.'[2]

Englishmen travelling through Russia often compared Russian peasant life, not always unfavourably, with the condition of the Irish. But many foreigners were shocked by the condition of the poorer peasants. An American wrote that the village poor,

generally wanting the comforts which are supplied to the Negro on our best-ordered plantations, appeared to me to be not less degraded in intellect, character, and per-sonal bearing. Indeed, the marks of physical and personal degradation were so strong, that I was irresistibly compelled to abandon certain theories not uncommon among my countrymen at home, in regard to the intrinsic superiority of the white race over all others.[3]

Some landowners tried to help themselves and their serfs by introducing better methods. But the peasants would listen to their new instructions, nod their heads gravely, and then go away to perform their tasks in exactly the way they and their forbears had always performed them. This passive resistance to change was the despair of the improving landowner, who tended to relapse into apathy after a few years of vain effort. In the twentieth century both the tsarist and Soviet governments realized the value of gentle persuasion by example, but both surrendered too often to the dangerous temptation of enforced change.

Serfdom might have deprived industry of a labour force had not more and more landowners allowed their serfs to substitute regular money payments for the labour obligation. Even though such serfs still belonged

---

[2] P. Kropotkin, *Zapiski revolyutsionera* (1966), 60.
[3] J. Stephens, *Incidents of Travel in the Russian and Turkish Empires* (1839), II, 38.

to their master, who could recall them if he wished, this did enable them to seek factory work afield, or stay in the village and devote themselves to handicraft or local industry. Also, many landowners started their own estate factories, using serf labour and local raw materials. Others sold batches of serfs to city industrialists, while state peasants could be drafted to factory work.

Although landowners in the private lands and officials in the state lands had virtually full administrative power over their peasants, in most parts of Russia they delegated authority to the peasant commune (*mir*) and its assembly of heads of households. For urban Russians the *mir* was 'discovered' in the nineteenth century by the German traveller and writer von Haxthausen, who declared that it was not simply a village institution but also an object of veneration; the *mir* was the voice of the people gathered together, and Orthodox Christians believed that when they were in congregation they were in close relationship with God. How ancient was the *mir*, and whether it was unique to the Slavs, was hotly disputed in the nineteenth century. But certainly it was a democratic and egalitarian institution, even if, somehow, the richer members often seemed to have more influence than the poorer. The peasants' preference for egalitarian collectivism was shown in one of the most important functions of the *mir*, its allocation of the peasants' land. It was the *mir* which decided who should get what. The basic principle was equality. The amount of land allotted to a household depended on the size of that household. The quality of the allotments had to be equal, and this was usually achieved by dividing each of the various qualities of land into strips, and ensuring that households received strips of each quality. Pastureland and meadow were kept for common use, because animals could not be expected to stay on particular strips. For some peasants, especially in the south-west, their strip allocation had become permanent and hereditary, but for the majority of Russian peasants there were periodic redistributions to allow for changes in the size of households. From the point of view of equality, this system was excellent. From the economic point of view it was pathetic. Where there were periodic redistributions, peasants tended to exhaust their strips rather than improve them. Everywhere, the uncultivated boundaries between strips occupied a considerable area of the fields, sometimes as much as one-fifth. Strips were often so narrow that there was not room to turn a plough. Peasants might walk hundreds of extra miles each year because their strips were so scattered. Each arable operation had to be identical and carried out at the same time on each strip; for example, it was impracticable for cattle to be grazed on the stubble of a harvested strip if other strips were uncut or planted with

cabbages. Thus there was little scope for an enterprising peasant to experiment with improved methods.

The *mir* fixed the dates for the main arable operations and also allocated the burden of taxes and labour services among its constituent households. Sometimes, too, the *mir* would rent or purchase additional land
from the landowner or from the state. After Emancipation many functions formerly belonging to the landowner were transferred to the *mir* or
its elected elder. That it was possible for the *mir* to dissolve an unsatisfactory marriage, despite the Church's cherished monopoly of divorce, shows
how far the peasantry was allowed to lead a life of its own, largely outside
state law and social convention.

At meetings of the *mir* assembly decisions, typically, were unanimous; a
dissenting minority would eventually allow itself to be persuaded, thus
creating a consensus. Everyone would then work to implement the decision. Subsequent Russian attitudes to democratic procedures would be
affected by this tradition.

Except in the Black Earth south the peasantry relied heavily on non-
agricultural income. Apart from animal husbandry, agriculture, and fishing, there were local handicraft industries, while many males left home in
the quiet season to seek temporary jobs afield. Almost everywhere the
land was farmed on the three-field system (fallow; winter grain; spring
grain). In the Black Earth region wheat was the predominant winter crop,
with rye elsewhere. Oats was the usual spring crop. The peasant staples
were rye bread, and porridge (*kasha*) made from oats, buckwheat, or
wheat. The traditional cabbage soup of the north and centre was less common in the south, where *borshch*, (beetroot soup) was typical. Little meat
was served outside soup, but fish was common. The traditional drink was
kvas, a rye-based beer, although towards the end of the century tea was becoming popular, with a few of the better-off families possessing a samovar.
At festivals and celebrations vodka was drunk, and relative delicacies like
pies and pancakes were served.

Russian villages were usually situated near the bank of a lake, river, or
stream. Typically the village was a line of unpainted wooden huts along
each side of a main 'street' which was unpaved and undrained. Traditionally, the household consisted of the 'big' family, which included the two
parents, grandparents, and the sons, daughters-in-law, and grandchildren.
But at mid-century the big family was giving way to the small one, as sons
preferred to start their own households, even though this was less economical. The oldest non-senile male was head of the family, the registered
householder, and as such a voter in the *mir* assembly. Children began to
help with the work not long after they learned to walk. In the big family

the least enviable status was that of daughter-in-law, who was dominated by the mother and often treated like a slave; if her husband was conscripted for twenty-five years' service she had little reason to continue living, but usually stayed on to lead a dog's life with her in-laws. The tradition still persisted of the father-in-law assuming the conjugal rights of a conscripted son.[4] But despite the low status of women (reflected, among other ways, by entrusting the pigs to their exclusive care as well as by numerous proverbs and sayings, like 'The hair is long but the brain is short'), efforts were made to help widows. Villagers might work on a holiday to help someone unable to help herself. When food became short, as it often did after Christmas, those who had food might share it with those who had not. Life was brutish, but not lacking compassion. The Russian village was not dull, even though it seemed dull to outsiders. It was just different; compared to urban life it offered simpler and fewer diversions but not necessarily fewer satisfactions. There could be no greater contentment than knowing in September that for the next year there would be bread enough.

The 1861 reform and after

Alexander I did little for the serfs, although he knew that something should be done.[5] Nicholas I issued some decrees to help them, which were mainly ignored. But Nicholas did succeed in helping the state peasants, giving the poorer more land, taken from the richer. Nicholas also pointed out that if the peasants' lot was not ameliorated they would rebel and take what they wanted. After the Crimean War the nobles could not deny that the Russian social structure was archaic and inefficient. A few nobles were beginning to have doubts about the ethics of serfdom. A few others had realized that serf labour was less productive than freely hired labour. Many no doubt recalled that Pugachov's rebellion of discontented peasants had resulted in the cutting of many noble throats; when, in 1856, Alexander II told an assembly of nobles that it would be better for serfdom to be abolished from above, rather than from below, they knew exactly what he meant. Nevertheless, the average landowner did not welcome the Emancipation Statutes which were promulgated five years later; they had been opportunistically pushed through by Alexander at a time when the nobility was in disarray.

Not for the last time in Russian history, the government, having decided on the measure, instructed those to whom it was distasteful to

---

[4] E. Elnett, *Historical Origins and Social Development of Family life in Russia* (1926), 133.

[5] But he showed the world that his heart was in the right place by manfully condemning, at the Congress of Aix, Negro slavery.

discuss the best manner of its implementation. Throughout Russia, committees of nobles were formed to evolve their collective opinion on how emancipation should be achieved. It is doubtful whether their opinions were accorded much attention in St. Petersburg, but the committees made it easier for the nobility to accept the idea of emancipation, especially as the nobles were also expected to supervise the local execution of whatever measures were passed. For the average noble, watching from afar the debates of his representatives, the whole affair was alarming and mystifying. Arina Petrovna, a landowner in Saltykov-Shchedrin's novel, *The Golovlov Family*, was not at all untypical:

> The first blow to Arina Petrovna's power was not so much the abolition of serfdom, but rather the preparations which preceded it. At first just rumours, and then the landowners' assemblies with their petitions, then the provincial committees, then the editing committees. All this wore her out and confused her. Arina Petrovna's not infertile imagination played with innumerable petty details. For example, she was suddenly struck with the question, 'what do I call Agashka in future? Agafyushka perhaps? Or perhaps I'll have to be very respectful and call her Agafeya Fedorovna' . . .
>
> At the time the committees were dissolving, Vladimir Mikhailich died. . . . His last words were, 'I thank God for calling me now, so I won't have to stand before Him among a rabble of serfs!'

Like most compromises in Russia, the 1861 Emancipation Statutes were received with great displeasure by those affected. But the autocracy succeeded, where transatlantic democracy failed, in ending bondage without civil war. That the Tsar's intention had been announced in 1856, with the legislation appearing in 1861, was not proof of foot-dragging, but a reflection of the enormous complexity of the problem. The attempt to be fair to all, despite the innumerable variations and special cases and local circumstances throughout Russia, meant that the legislation was extremely detailed. Only the basic principles will be mentioned here.

The fundamental principle was that the serf was to be given not merely his freedom, but also land to go with it. There was no intention of creating a landless proletariat by a stroke of the pen. This fundamental principle led to the fundamental weakness of the reform, which was the unavailability of enough land to satisfy everybody, and the consequent failure to reconcile the peasants' beliefs regarding land ownership with the legal facts of land ownership. Whereas legally the land belonged to the landowners in areas of serfdom, the peasants, ignorant of the law, had always believed that the land rightfully belonged to those who worked it. Under the 1861 statutes serfs were freed and (typically) their communes received in trust the land they habitually worked for their own account. What usually happened was that the landowners received treasury bonds in compensation for the land they were required to cede to their former serfs, and the latter were in turn required to recompense the Treasury by a series of forty-nine annual redemption payments. The average area per peasant varied according to the locality and was worked out by local committees. To the peasant, who believed that the land was rightfully his, it seemed that he was being compelled to buy his own property. Many, if not most, believed that their true protector, the Tsar, had ordered that they be given their land without payment, but the nobles were concealing this instruction. Moreover, the valuation placed on the peasants' land allocation was often higher than the product of that land justified. To the nobles, especially of the centre, land over-valuation seemed logical because it was not so much the land as the labour of the serfs living on that land which had been of value to the landowner. But the peasantry felt it was monstrously wrong.

The Emancipation was not an instant settlement; it took years to put into practice. Many peasants were in no hurry because they anticipated that the land to be received would be more of a burden than an asset; it was too small to support them but entailed heavy tax and redemption payments. The Statutes did provide that, with the landowner's agreement, a serf could obtain exemption from the redemption payments by accepting one-quarter instead of a full land allocation, but not many took advantage of this. Village communes were generally held responsible for the redemption payments: through their right of issuing or withholding passports for travel over twenty miles they could hold back peasants who were in arrears. It was intended that the commune should hand over the allotted strips to a peasant when his redemption payment was complete.

State peasants were not forgotten; in 1866 they were given the option of purchasing their land in the same way as the former serfs or of remaining as they were, as tenants.

Most nobles, especially in the less fertile regions, felt that they were badly hit by the Emancipation. In the Black Earth region, however, their committees had succeeded in reducing the peasants' allocations to well below the national average, so that a peasant, to make both ends meet, had to work for much of the year as a hired labourer on the noble's remaining land. Many nobles, unable or unwilling to make the required adaptation to a system of hired labour, began to live permanently in town, renting out their land to the peasants and thereby demonstrating that they were nothing but parasites in the agricultural economy. Other nobles did adapt themselves; some worked large estates with modern methods and provided much of Russia's increasingly important grain exports. Some of the shrewder peasants followed their example, buying the lands of poorer

neighbours and farming it individually. But the *mir* still limited the freedom of most peasants to experiment, or to develop their holdings before
redemption payments were completed. The laws remained unclear for
most peasants; there had been no precise statement of basic peasant rights
and obligations, which often meant that the peasant still had to do what
he was told if he did not want a whipping.

Despite its imperfections the Emancipation was an enormous step forward. In succeeding decades additional changes were made to remedy some
of its inadequacies. But peasant dissatisfaction, expressed in periodic disturbances and, sometimes, refusal to accept the land allotments, was never
eliminated. The widespread failure of the peasants to make their redemption payments on time is hardly surprising in view of the general poverty.
On certain occasions, such as the birth of a royal heir, tax and redemption
arrears were cancelled. The redemption period was extended and finally,
in 1906, the payments still outstanding were written off. Meanwhile, to
help the more prosperous peasants to buy more land (often from the
nobles), the Peasant Bank was established; by the turn of the century the
richer peasants were acquiring land rapidly, while the poorer were selling
their holdings and becoming wage-earners. After the bad famine of 1891,
the ministry of agriculture was set up, and one of its functions was to
encourage better methods. On the other hand, because the peasantry was
alleged to be resentful, indolent, disrespectful, unruly, and intoxicated,
Alexander III approved the appointment of so-called land captains to
maintain discipline in rural areas. These, often retired army officers,
varied widely in character, but their function everywhere was to replace
the authority which before the Emancipation had been wielded by the
landowners. Answerable to St. Petersburg, they could override the decisions of the *mir* and, with the police, keep the countryside under strict
control.

The 1905 rebellion was preceded by several years in which peasant
disorders were more widespread than usual. Especially in the Black Earth
region there were risings, sometimes planned by the *mir*, in which peasants
burned the local noble's buildings and divided up among themselves his
stock and implements. Long after the urban rebellion of 1905 had been
suppressed, the countryside was still inflamed. The hangings and floggings
of Stolypin (see p. 165) only brought peace to the countryside in 1907. It
seems likely that in 1905 itself it was not the urban disorders but the
peasant risings which most alarmed the government. One minister, at
least, toyed with the idea of compulsorily buying out the landowners, so
as to provide more land for the peasants. For Russian governments there
was nothing sacred in private property. The land had been distributed by

the tsar, and what one tsar had given another could take away. Catherine's nationalization of church lands, Alexander II's forced purchase of land-owners' land in 1861, as well as the subsequent expropriations of the Soviet period, shared a common background.

Industry and railways

The 1861 Emancipation can be considered as the loosening of a chronic log-jam. Many improvements which serfdom had prevented were now, not only possible, but seen to be urgent. There were also effects which were not immediately perceptible. One such effect was the new possibility of Russia overcoming her industrial backwardness as peasants were slowly drawn into new patterns of life and work.

For most of the reign of Nicholas I, economic policy had been in the hands of Kankrin. The latter was a genuine self-made man, a German who had arrived penniless in Russia after dropping out from a second-rate university. Having no influential friends, knowing no Russian, he received noble's rank from Paul I, but no job. But by making himself an expert on successive current problems he attracted attention and climbed high. His economic policy was characterized by a quiet determination to do noth-ing; he felt the economy would develop slowly as it had in the past, and there was little the government could do about it. Nicholas had more faith in government intervention and sometimes overruled his elderly minister. This was especially evident in the question of railway-building, with Nicholas pushing through a construction programme over the opposition of Kankrin.

Apart from railways, the main economic questions in Nicholas's reign had been the stabilization of the currency and the problem of raising enough money from taxes to pay for government expenditure. Both these seemed to be on the verge of solution when the Crimean War broke out and made the situation worse. In retrospect, it is clear that what Russia needed was industrial development, for with growth and prosperity taxes would have yielded more, yet seemed less burdensome. But the spon-taneous industrial revolution which was transforming western Europe had not spread to Russia; if it had, it would not have been welcome to a government which foresaw the dangers of an emerging proletariat. Private enterprise was usually reluctant to engage in industrial undertakings; whereas foreign entrepreneurs were eventually persuaded to invest their capital and knowledge in large-scale industry, the natives preferred the field of commerce because trade and speculation in Russian conditions seemed to offer higher profits with less risk. It was more profitable to use capital to build up a stock of imported products for re-sale than to produce those products at home. It was this lack of industrial enterprise which had persuaded previous rulers, like Peter the Great, that the only way to ensure a supply of strategically necessary goods (such as iron for cannon and textiles for uniforms) was for the state to set up its own factories, or to subsidize private producers. Thus the concept of state intervention in Russian industry was well established.

Towards the end of his reign, Nicholas felt he had to respond in some way to the benefits which Russia was receiving from the move towards free trade in the west. The result was the tariff of 1850, which included some significant reductions. However, some industries remained highly protected; notably, there was a total prohibition of iron imports to protect the technically backward Urals industry. One feature of the new rates was that they favoured Russian cotton weavers but not cotton spinners. Unlike weaving, which was still a domestic industry, spinning was Russia's nearest approach to the industrial revolution at this time; around St. Petersburg and Moscow there were numerous spinning mills with all the characteristics of factory industry, including an emergent proletariat which was badly fed, badly housed, and therefore dangerous.

It would not be until 1882 that a small and overworked factory inspectorate would be established. Under Nicholas I and Alexander II, badly treated workers did occasionally send petitions to the tsar. In most cases the response was punishment of the signatories, arrest of the ringleaders, and quiet government persuasion of the management to improve conditions. Although this was in keeping with the concept of the benevolent autocrat, it probably tended to alienate workers from the system.

Under Alexander II, Russian industry underwent a notable expansion, both in old and new branches. The textile industry continued to develop, and very large factories were founded. Many of these were owned and run by the British; the interest of Lancashire in the Russian industry began in the forties, when Britain relaxed her controls over the export of textile machinery. When the American Civil War cut cotton supplies, the acreage under cotton in Turkestan was enormously extended, and henceforth Russia derived most of her raw cotton from within her own frontiers. Foreign entrepreneurs were also largely responsible for the transformation of Russian metallurgy. The old Urals ironworks, which had produced high quality but expensive iron by the charcoal process, were dwarfed in the sixties by the iron and steel industry of the Donets Basin. It was John Hughes, aided by technicians and workers from his South Wales homeland, who showed what could be done by modern methods. Apart from the local ore, he exploited the hitherto-untouched coal seams of the Donets region, helping to create what would become Russia's richest source of high quality coking coal.[6] Another fuel, oil, was also becoming practical. The Nobel brothers established a modern oil industry around Baku in the Caucasus. Hitherto the local oil had been dug by hand and transported in leather pouches on camelback but, after a few decades under the Nobels, the region was covered with mechanically bored oil wells, there was a local refinery, and river and rail tankers were carrying the products all over European Russia. In engineering, Russia noticeably lagged behind the west, and it was only through import restrictions and tariffs that the home products could compete with imports. However, there did exist some state and foreign-managed works producing a reliable range of products; railway equipment was often home produced.

Russian railway-building had started under Nicholas I. The first public railway had been the twenty-five-kilometre Tsarskoye Selo railway from the capital to Pavlovsk, where public entertainments were promoted in order to encourage passenger traffic. Builder of the Tsarskoye Selo railway was Gerstner, an Austrian whom Slavophils claimed was a Slav. His railway, finished in 1837, was an immediate success, even though the native birchwood used as fuel produced showers of sparks and complaints by smouldering passengers.

Nicholas I had a better appreciation of railways than his advisers, who preferred to develop further the canal system. He was especially impressed by the speed with which the Liverpool and Manchester railway had carried troops to suppress rebellion in Ireland, for he had his own Irish problem in Poland.[7] For the most important railway project, the St. Petersburg–Moscow railway, the American engineer Whistler was invited to Russia as a consultant. Although the Tsarskoye Selo railway was of six-foot gauge, Whistler recommended for future construction a five-foot gauge. The Russian railway gauge thereby became three and a half inches wider than the European standard. The St. Petersburg–Moscow railway was opened in 1851, having been built by army engineers and serf labour to very high technical standards. Rolling stock was built in a state engineering works leased to American entrepreneurs.

Under Alexander II the government drew up successive plans for railway construction; like most of Europe, but unlike Britain and the USA, the railway network was planned, and there was no duplication of lines between any two points. At first, when the government offered concessions

---

[6] For more on Hughes and the city he founded (Iuzovka, later Donetsk) see *Economic History Review*, XVII, 564–9 or, at book-length, T. Friedgut, *Iuzovka and Revolution*, Vol. 1 (1989).

[7] He began building the St. Petersburg–Warsaw Railway, in 1851, mainly for strategic reasons.

to build the lines it wanted, there were few takers. Foreign investors had doubts about Russian financial stability, while domestic capitalists knew they could make higher profits in trade. Thus the practice developed whereby the government guaranteed the annual dividend on the shares of new private railway companies. In this way investors, assured of dividends whether or not the lines were profitable, were encouraged to put their money into railways. But this and other devices left wide loopholes for the sharp practitioner, and fortunes were made by some of the railway 'kings', at government expense. In some cases a railway company was better off making a loss than making a profit.

Foreign investors, especially French, and foreign engineers played a large but not exclusive role in building Russian railways. Foreign equipment was also imported, for although the government granted various concessions to encourage the domestic production of rails, rolling stock and steel-work, Russian entrepreneurs were reluctant to engage in this business. Nevertheless, in the long run the railway programme did much to stimulate the fuel, metallurgical, and engineering industries. In the nineties, more than four-fifths of new locomotives were home-built.

Growth of Russian Common-carrier Railways

	Mileage	Freight traffic (million tons)
1866	3,000	3
1883	14,700	24
1903	36,400	76
1913	43,900	158
1956	74,600	1,371
1990	91,600	3,872

Source: J. N. Westwood, *A History of Russian Railways* (1964), and Radio Moscow.

The government fluctuated in its preference for private or state railways. In 1867 it sold its St. Petersburg–Moscow railway to private interests, and Alaska to the USA, to raise money for more railways; it was a heavy investor in private lines, for frequently the latter could not raise enough capital from private sources. By 1900 the preference was definitely for state-owned and state-managed railways, and by 1917 only a few lines were still in private hands.

4. *Thaw*

Towards popular government

THE optimistic and relaxed decade which followed Alexander's accession could well be described as a thaw following Nicholas's winter. Although discussions about serfdom dominated the early years, time was found for other matters; Russians were even permitted to smoke on the streets of St. Petersburg. After the question of serf emancipation had been settled, other major reforms followed which did not, however, fully satisfy the optimists. Especially over-optimistic were those of the gentry who, envying the political rights and responsibilities of the English squire, sought to popularize in Russia the ideas of British liberalism. These men, an active minority of the nobles, felt that Russia needed a more popular form of government (in which, of course, they would play an important role), and that the nobles' traditional privileges were outmoded. In 1862 an assembly of the nobility of Tver Province in an address to the Tsar announced their rejection of the idea that nobles should remain free from taxation or continue to automatically hold the key positions in the state service. Thirteen of these nobles, meeting separately, called for a classless elected popular assembly, and were duly rewarded with incarceration in the Peter–Paul Fortress at St. Petersburg. One of the earliest acts of Valuev as minister of the interior was to forbid assemblies of nobles commenting on anything but local matters.

Nevertheless, the government in 1864 introduced a measure of self-government in local affairs. It organized in most provinces local assemblies called *zemstva* (singular: *zemstvo*). There were two levels of these. At the lower level were the district *zemstva*, containing the separately elected representatives of the nobles, the townsmen, and the peasants. Because of the electoral arrangements the nobility held about 40 per cent of the seats and the peasants, vastly more numerous, slightly less than 40 per cent, with townsmen and clergy holding the rest. This disproportion was even more marked in the superior level of *zemstva*, those at provincial level. The membership of the provincial *zemstvo* was elected from the district *zemstva* of that province. Both types of *zemstvo* had as chairman the local marshal of nobility, and both elected an executive for day-to-day decisions. The government later placed restrictions on the *zemstva*'s powers of local taxation, and in addition they were required to carry out with their own funds some of the tasks formally reserved for the central government. But despite these and other restrictions, the institution flourished until the October Revolution. In public education, public health and welfare, local economic development, road-building (and in at least one case, railway-building) the *zemstva* did good work. Their knowledge of local conditions and of local people enabled them to do a good job where a St. Petersburg official would have failed. Much of their work lived on after 1917. In the 1990s, for example, local hospitals built by the *zemstva* could still be observed, fulfilling their original function. In 1870 a somewhat similar system was granted to the cities, which were provided with a town council elected by property-holders. These city governments were never allowed to control the city police, which remained under the control of the ministry of the interior, but many of them did good work in such spheres as urban roads and transport, street lighting, garbage disposal, drainage and water supply.

The success of the *zemstva* demonstrated that the people were indeed capable of looking after their own affairs. The failure to follow up this success with a parallel widening of public participation in central government had unfortunate consequences. That Russians could make a success of new, untraditional institutions, provided they could see the benefits, was demonstrated not only by the *zemstva* but also by the new judicial system of 1864.

Judicial reform

Probably the blackest aspect of Nicholas's reign had been the virtual impossibility for the ordinary Russian of obtaining justice in the courts. It is true that Speransky had codified Russian laws, but the way those laws were administered and applied made them meaningless. This was a situation which Nicholas had inherited from two centuries of neglectful rulers. The Decembrists had placed reform of the judicial system high on their list of priorities, and rightly so. Even amid the inherent injustices of a society based on serfdom, there was no excuse for the wrongs and the cruelties inflicted on innocent citizens by an institution which in theory was intended to protect them.

Under Nicholas there was an amazing number and variety of courts, and cases could be transferred from one to another almost endlessly. It was quite common for a case to drag on for two or three decades before being settled. In any judicial system it is difficult, if not impossible, to avoid favouring members of a particular class, usually those who can afford to wait and can afford to try every loophole the law offers. But in Nicholas's Russia the dilatory procedures alone made recourse to law ruinous for anyone who had no strings to pull. The supreme judicial body was the Senate, which could hear final appeals. Below this there were various courts of appeal, and on the lowest level a multiplicity of courts of first instance. Most judges were quite untouched by legal training, and more than half were illiterate. This illiteracy was in fact assumed in the regulations, which stated that if all the judges of a court were illiterate the court secretary was empowered to write down their decision. This placed power in the hands of the secretary, especially as all evidence was written. The police were also granted great power under the system. Apart from carrying out preliminary inquiries, they had the right in some cases to levy fines. Since both the court secretaries and the police relied on bribes to maintain the standard of living to which they considered they were entitled, it is evident that the majority of court decisions depended on the respective financial resources of plaintiff and defendant. A particularly glaring example of the temptations to abuse police power was the provision that, if a murderer was not found, the police could levy a collective fine on the inhabitants of the locality.

The most obvious feature of the system was its devotion to formality. There was a certain procedure for every circumstance, and every procedure was based on bureaucratic rather than human considerations. This was especially evident in the way judgement was made. An accused never saw his judges, nor they him. All evidence was written. It was presented to the judges as a pile of documents, and they assessed these according to the rules of evidence. The most weighty evidence was a confession. In the absence of a confession, mutual corroboration of two independent submissions was considered especially strong evidence. Then, in descending order of reliability, the rules detailed the other kinds of acceptable evidence. A litigant under these rules was well advised to present evidence of an educated male noble, or, if a noble was unobtainable or unbribable, of a priest of the Orthodox faith. The preference given to the word of a male over that of a female, of a nobleman over a priest, and of a priest over a layman was accepted as natural and traditional, but could only lead to abuses. In his memoirs, Aksakov mentions the case of a landowner whose main interest was raping his female serfs. He had only progressed through the first fifteen years of his programme when he was strangled by some of his victims. When the case came to court, neighbouring nobles testified that their late lamented friend was 'of decent behaviour, as was to be expected of a noble Russian gentleman', and this testimony, according to the rules, was the strongest presented.[1] So the women were convicted, and their sentence, 100 lashes and Siberian forced labour, was particularly harsh because in the scale of punishments it was more serious for a serf to kill a noble than vice versa, even if the vice was versa.

The whole procedure of justice, which was inquisitorial and secret, meant that even a wise and well-intentioned judge was no guarantee of a fair decision. The documents which reached the judges, and which would accompany the case as it went from court to court and from judge to judge, were unreliable, being the product of police methods of persuasion or of venal secretaries. Since the judges never met the accused, the evidence was unlikely to be challenged.

Military courts were sometimes used to try civilians. They were faster, and a more convincing deterrent. Under Nicholas I this practice became widespread; arson, crimes by civilians in the company of soldiers, and riotous behaviour by peasants in the presence of military guards, were among the cases handled by the army courts.

Alexander II had always seen the necessity for judicial reform, but it was not until after Emancipation that he began to treat the question with any enthusiasm. The Judicial Reform, enacted in 1864, ensured that the public welfare would henceforth be the main concern of the Russian courts and of Russian law. The Reform introduced several concepts quite new to Russia, and apparently out of keeping with Russian tradition and with the autocratic regime. Yet despite this, and despite the opposition of conservative circles, the changes were readily accepted and proved a great success right from the start. In brief, the Reform simplified the organization of the court system and introduced the principles of separation of powers, public and oral proceedings, and the jury system.

The reorganization of the courts entailed the replacement of the multifarious existing institutions by a system which, in general, meant that a case started in a lower court could be transferred on appeal to only one, or sometimes two, other courts. Each province was to have its court, and appeals from this were to be heard in one of the ten Palaces of Justice. The final court of appeal was the Senate, although not all cases could go that high. Some courts remained outside the new system, and this was to prove a weakness. These included church courts (which among other things had exclusive jurisdiction in divorce cases), military courts,[2] and the special

---

[1] I. S. Aksakov, *Sochineniya*, Vol. IV, 657.

[2] Military courts were confined to military cases. But from 1878, in the face of revolutionary activities, they were used to try civilians who used force against the authorities; by that time the military courts had themselves been reformed; their advantage was that they did not encourage inflammatory speeches by the accused.

local peasant courts which tried minor offences. After 1872 a special department of the Senate was entrusted with 'crimes against the state', which gave the government better opportunity to deal with political enemies in a way it considered fitting. Two provisions of the new code provided additional loopholes for arbitrary action, or inaction, against the whole principle of the Reform. One article gave the 'administrative power' (that is, the bureaucracy) the right to 'take measures . . . in order to prevent and limit . . . felonies and misdemeanours'. This gave the authorities the power of 'administrative' arrest or exile: under this provision a person could be exiled, without court intervention, in order to *prevent* him committing a crime. Another article, while allowing officials to be tried for abuses of their powers, insisted that their superiors' approval was a prerequisite for a case to be brought. This meant that a miscreant official could be protected from justice by the head of his department. However, even in the worst periods of reaction in the next two reigns, the government was unable to use these loopholes as much as it wished. The principles of the 1864 Reform became so firmly and so rapidly ingrained in the Russian consciousness that failure to observe them always aroused protest.

In the new courts, while documentary evidence was not excluded, the parties were expected to present oral evidence. Moreover, in criminal cases, not only the evidence but the testimony of witnesses and experts had to be given orally, so that all aspects of the case put together in the preliminary investigation could be challenged and tested in open court. Preliminary investigation, supervised by a magistrate, was to remain hidden from public view, but the new provision for full publicity of court proceedings gave substantial protection to the accused. Even though the latter was unrepresented while the police collected evidence and witnesses against him, he could challenge such testimony in court and could, at his own expense, summon witnesses in his defence against any unforeseen evidence. As further safeguard, voting on the verdict by juries was kept secret, so as to protect them from threats of violence.

The first public session of the civil courts appears to have taken place in the Senate in October 1865, in the presence of the minister of justice. On this occasion the available seats were by no means filled by the public. However, in the provincial courts there developed a great demand for seats; there were fewer competing entertainments. It was not long before the simple fact of public access began to result in speedier trials, more business-like judges, and less frequent attempts by the police or administrators to pervert the course of justice. Full publicity, oral testimony, and the controversial procedure made the fabrication of false evidence a risky enterprise.

The controversial principle, the arguing out of a case by prosecutor and defender, would have meant less if at the same time the jury had not been introduced for major criminal cases. In most respects the jury functioned as in the Anglo-Saxon countries, but not always. The new code stipulated that the jury would decide not on the unanimity principle, but according to a majority. In those cases when the vote was equal there would be a Not Guilty verdict. Decision by majority was by many considered un-Russian, for there had been a centuries-old tradition (in the village commune, in ancient Novgorod, and elsewhere) that only a consensus could justify an action or decision. However, the reason for rejecting the unanimity principle was itself very Russian; it was argued that one juryman should not be allowed to thwart the will of eleven others. Jury members recorded their vote by secret ballot, and their decision was conveyed to the court in writing in response to a written question from the judges. If all three judges believed that the accused was innocent they could, if the jury found him guilty, hold another hearing with a fresh jury; but only once.

An interesting and sometimes criticized feature of the juries in Russia was that they regarded themselves as representing, not only the public interest, but also the public conscience. Once an accused was found Guilty the judges enjoyed little flexibility in sentencing. The Russian jury sometimes overcame this problem by finding an accused Not Guilty, if it believed that the penalty in the given circumstances would be too great. It would do this even if the accused had admitted his guilt and there was no doubt at all that he had committed the crime; for the Russian jury there was a distinction between legal guilt and moral guilt and the latter sometimes had priority. In some rare cases the jury might even contrive to change the offence.[3] For example, if it was presented with incontrovertible evidence that an accused had been stealing horses yet felt that circumstances gave him some excuse, it might, in answer to the judges' question 'Do you find the accused Guilty to the charge of horse-stealing?' reply 'The accused is found Guilty of stealing rabbits'. In this way an accused could be found guilty but the severity of his punishment reduced.

As for the judges, the principle of separation of powers enhanced their status; they were appointed for life and were normally irremovable. When special circumstances made the disciplining of a judge essential, the process was in the hands, not of a government agency, but of the judges of a superior court. Also, so as to discourage the re-emergence of a bribable judiciary, salaries were high. Although judges were appointed by the tsar, the list of candidates from which he chose was compiled by the judiciary.

³ S. Kucherov, *Courts, Lawyers, and Trials under the last three Tsars* (1953), 70.

The introduction of the controversial procedure obviously entailed the provision of a pool of trained men to fill the positions of defending and prosecuting counsel. In other words, Russia had to have a Bar. Despite opposition to the creation of a recognized new professional class of lawyers, Alexander gave his consent to the establishment of the Russian Bar. In this way not only the supply of counsel was ensured, but also their supervision and standards of professional conduct. Those who opposed this innovation were correct, in so far as the Russian lawyers became the most effective and vocal body of liberally inclined men in the Empire. The profession not only worked intelligently and effectively for reform, but also provided several revolutionary leaders. Trained in the art of persuasion, professionally involved both with officialdom and the seamy side of Russian life, the lawyer was a natural leader in the movement towards reform. Shortly before the class was extinguished by the Revolution, it began to supply from its ranks some of the better parliamentarians of the Duma. In the courts, high-handed administrators were frequently humiliated by defending lawyers.

Another innovation of 1864 was the justice of the peace. This likewise was an immediate success. Elected by the local *zemstvo*, the justice of the peace dealt with small cases where the parties desired a quick, comprehensible, inexpensive and on-the-spot decision. For the humble worker or peasant who demanded justice but was afraid to get himself entangled in the courts, the justice of the peace provided exactly what was needed. It was not long before these men, or at least most of them, became a firmly rooted and respected institution in their respective localities. They were so successful, especially in their protection of the small man against local officials, that they were eliminated by Alexander III's government and not reinstated until 1912. The justice of the peace, like the jury, like irremovable judges, like the Bar, was resented by those who regarded justice as something dispensed by rulers rather than something administered by society for the benefit of society.

Not only the ultra-conservatives but, later, many of the revolutionaries deprecated the new judicial system. Some revolutionaries no doubt did so on the principle that reforms to make life more bearable were harmful because they made revolution less likely. Others, placing exaggerated emphasis on the few occasions when justice was seen to be dispensed in favour of a particular class, proclaimed that the system was simply a new system of exploitation devised by and for the bourgeoisie. The lawyer Lenin, however, was not entirely opposed to the innovations which had been introduced in 1864. Looking back with a century's perspective, it seems clear that the Judicial Reform of 1864 was not only a great innovation

accepted as a blessing by the vast majority of Russians, but also introduced one of the world's better judicial systems.

It was not long before the restraining force of the new system made itself
felt by administrators, and particularly by those officials who had hitherto
scorned individual rights in their quest for convenience, bribes, or power.
As this class of person found itself checked by the courts, resentment
developed, but remained largely ineffective. With a few exceptions, for the
remainder of the Romanov dynasty, lawyers had complete freedom of
speech in the courts and their words were reported in the newspapers. Since
so many of the accused were directly or indirectly the victim of government
action, defence counsel could hardly avoid pointing out the injustices inflicted by the regime. The effect of this was heightened by the eloquence of
many lawyers, and the tolerance of many judges; the latter would permit
discussion of government actions in court if these were at all relevant to
a case.

The Vera Zasulich case of 1878 demonstrated how, by introducing the
Judicial Reform, the government had cut a great deal of ground from
under its own feet. This was the *cause célèbre* not only of the reign but of
the century. It was the practice to try 'crimes against the state' in the
special courts prescribed. These courts were part of the regular system, and
were public, but defence and prosecution argued their case not before a
jury, but before five judges from the local judiciary and four elected 'class
representatives' (in a provincial court these would be two leaders of the
nobility, a town mayor, and a peasant elder). To avoid publicity the
government also made great use of its power of 'administrative arrest' to
exile those regarded as potentially dangerous. However, since both these
practices had been highly criticized, the Vera Zasulich case was referred to
a regular St. Petersburg court.

The accused in the case, the twenty-eight-year-old daughter of an army
officer, had shot and wounded the governor of St. Petersburg, General
Trepov. When the case came up, the minister of justice asked the presiding
judge to obtain a conviction. The latter, however, rejected this interference,
secure in the knowledge of his irremovability. At the trial, defence counsel
pointed out that Vera had shot Trepov because she had been greatly upset
and moved by a recent incident reported in the press. Trepov had visited a
prison and ordered the flogging of a political prisoner who had failed to
remove his hat in his presence. As well as pointing out that flogging in
general had been banned in Russia, except for prisoners and a few other
categories, and that this particular flogging was illegal because the victim
had not yet begun his sentence, defence counsel, despite the protests of the
prosecution, described Vera's past life. How, being vaguely associated

with various revolutionaries, she had spent periods in prison and exile. How, despite being cleared in court, she had still been subject to police supervision and exile. How she had developed a feeling of great sympathy for others who were in gaol for political reasons and how her sensitivities had been thus outraged by Trepov's illegal violence. Defence counsel was enabled to summon witnesses under the terms of the 1864 Reform, and presented to the court other political prisoners who had seen the flogging. The appearance of these young men, pale and worn from months of incarceration, but obviously men of good breeding and education, produced its due effect not only on the jury, but on the public, which burst into applause at several emotional speeches of the defence. The jury brought in a verdict of Not Guilty. The spectators, who included many persons of high birth, broke into prolonged cheering, and defence counsel was carried out on the shoulders of his admirers. The government never again risked an important political trial in the regular courts. The presiding judge could not be removed, but he lost any immediate chance of promotion, and the minister of justice was dismissed. Although most of St. Petersburg society was overjoyed, many had subsequent second thoughts. Among Russian émigrés after 1917 there were many who insisted on believing that, had there been no Vera Zasulich case, there would have been no revolution. As for Vera, she emigrated, became a marxist revolutionary, and helped edit, at the beginning of the century, revolutionary journals such as *Iskra*. Lenin admired her, but she died in 1919 a Menshevik. In the nineties, interestingly enough, she wrote several articles condemning assassination as a revolutionary tactic.

Military reform

It is arguable that, after serfdom, the heaviest millstone around the neck of Imperial Russia was the army. It consumed one-third of the government's income, but failed to provide the armed strength proportionate to this input. It might well be argued, too, that the huge Russian army was less a deterrent than an incentive to war. Increases of armed strength made to satisfy genuinely felt needs of defence all too often led to greater self-confidence in foreign policy, then to risk-taking, and then to wars in which the real losses outweighed the gains originally sought, and the gains themselves, if any, took the form of vulnerable territorial additions open to attack and therefore demanding additional defence expenditure. A study of nineteenth-century Russian arms provides a good example of that state of mind which regards the army, no matter how big, as too small. At one time the Russian ministry of war was content with merely the biggest army in Europe. Then it required an army equal to those of Austria and Germany combined. Finally it began to doubt whether even a two-power standard was enough, but the progression was broken by the First World War, in which Russian society and the Russian army devoured each other.

This does not mean that the war ministry was blindly pursuing its own interests. Its anxieties were justified, for defence of the long frontiers against more developed neighbours, and defence of the interior against possible rebellions, demanded more men and equipment than the empire was willing or able to provide. Lack of resources would become increasingly felt in the last tsarist decades. On the one hand, re-equipment became more expensive and was required more frequently as technology accelerated, and on the other, the ministry of finance became less willing to allocate to the army money that it reckoned could be used for more productive purposes. By the end of the century the military budget was about double that of France or Germany, but because the army was so big[4] the money spent per soldier was far less than that of the industrial powers.

The generally acknowledged failures of the Crimean War led to the military reforms of 1863–75, initiated by the war minister, Dmitri Milyutin. Apart from changing the conscription system, Milyutin reorganized the army's administration (so that the basic administrative unit became the military district), and put life into the moribund General Staff. Also, he phased out the old cadet corps that had provided a free, somewhat brutal, and certainly mediocre education for sons of the nobility entering the army. In their place he established military gymnasia providing a broad education, whose graduates proceeded to a military school where academic subjects were taught alongside military. Civilian teachers were appointed to these schools. A few of them, as well as the less prestigious junker schools for future officers, were opened to non-nobles. Henceforth education was to be a prerequisite for a commission; in the Crimean War less than a third of the officers had possessed a military education. Wider and better education and more opportunities for non-nobles were Milyutin's two aims, aims that were not philanthropic but absolutely necessary for an effective army.

In line with this emphasis on the intellect, he established a staff college with very high standards of both entry and work; officers successful in the difficult entrance exam might still fail to graduate because admission to the third and final year was limited to those who had done well in the first two. Graduates went on to accelerated promotion and in course of time

---

[4] At the turn of the century it numbered about one million men, almost double the German army. One reason for the large size of the peacetime army was that conscripts served longer than in France or Germany. Rightly or wrongly, it was felt that the Russian conscript was an ignoramus who needed several years to become a trained soldier.

occupied most of the key posts, including those in the war ministry. Milyutin also established three specialized officer schools of similarly high standard, for the artillery, engineers, and military lawyers. Although some of these reforms were diluted after Milyutin's departure, their spirit persisted (the military districts were retained right through the Soviet period as well). Although the Russian officer corps for the remainder of the tsarist period was numerically dominated by the unprivileged, unintellectual, underpaid officers of the numbered[5] infantry regiments, there was a sprinkling of highly professional officers who had a broader view of how an army should fit into society.

The abolition of serfdom, and to a lesser extent the growing railway network which facilitated mobilization and deployment, made a new conscription system desirable. During most of the sixties the conscription levy was around four per thousand eligible males, providing an annual intake of around 100,000, of whom four-fifths went to the infantry. The standard length of service had been reduced *de facto* to fifteen years' active service and ten years' 'leave'. Increasingly, soldiers were allowed to end their active service after from seven to thirteen years. By 1870, and especially after the triumph of the Prussian army over the French, others in addition to the war minister were concerned about the size and professionalism of the Russian army. In liberal, and even in some conservative circles, opinion moved in favour of a Prussian-style conscription system entailing, among other things, a shorter period of service and a conscription liability extended to all social classes. Milyutin had long hankered for such a change, and with this new support was able to introduce it despite opposition.

The essence of Milyutin's proposals was the extension of military liability to all social classes, which would raise the pool of eligible males by a small fraction; the registration each year of males reaching the age of twenty-one, of whom about one-quarter would be chosen by lot to serve; the period of military service to be set at fifteen years, of which only seven would normally be full-time active service; men doing their eight-year reserve stint would be subject to occasional calls to summer camps or refresher courses to maintain their effectiveness; only medical evidence could relieve a young man of his liability, but in practice deferments would be granted to students completing their studies, and exemptions granted to the only sons of widows, or other young men who could claim they were

[5] Numbered regiments were those that lacked one of the inspiring names accorded to regiments of ancient lineage or of distinguished battle record. Some of their officers were good and capable of independent thought; generalizations are perilous because there was among the officer class an enormous range of intellect and view. But with Milyutin's reforms the way was opened for a professionalization of the officer corps, despite the tsars' continuing power, copiously exercised, of appointing and promoting their protégés.

the sole support of their families. During the discussion stage of the proposals there was strong opposition, which all but defeated them. This was expressed most forcibly by Dmitri Tolstoy, the minister of education. This opposition centred on, and was largely provoked by, Milyutin's intentions in respect to officering and to the privileges to be offered to educated recruits. Milyutin realized that the educated would be trained quicker than the uneducated, and that their withdrawal from civilian life represented a larger social and economic loss to the nation. He therefore proposed reduced lengths of service for these recruits, pointing out that this would encourage young men to remain students as long as possible, thus adding to the intellectual capital of Russia. Those with university education, suggested Milyutin, need serve only six months, while those with a secondary education would serve eighteen months, and even graduates of district and of primary schools would have only, respectively, a three-year and four-year term. These concessions were paralleled by the arrangements envisaged for supplying the increased number of reserve officers which would be needed. This question, too, would be treated with reference to educational levels. A university graduate who volunteered before he was conscripted would pass a simple examination and become an officer, with only three month's active service. Those with secondary or district school education would have the same privilege, but serve one and two years respectively.

Opposition to the reform by the landed gentry, in these circumstances, could hardly have been a surprise. Hitherto, when the sons of the nobility entered the army they did so as volunteers, and provided the service with almost all its officers. Now it was proposed that twenty-one-year-old nobles who had not volunteered should be liable to conscription just like others. Not only this, but noble conscripts might have to live and work together with sons of peasants and workers. Moreover, because of the privileges granted to the educated, an increasing number of the army's officers (and especially reserve officers) would be of non-noble origin. Many merchants, too, were unhappy, being especially resentful of Milyutin's insistence that the hiring of substitute conscripts be banned. But despite all this opposition, which was expressed not only in open discussion but in the press, and by influential men in private discussion with the Tsar, the reform eventually won the royal assent in 1874, becoming law in 1875. Because it was such a great step towards the abolition of archaic class privileges, it ranks with the Emancipation and the transformation of justice as one of the three most significant reforms of the reign.

Serving as minister for seventeen years, Milyutin was able to see his reforms firmly established. The next tsar, Alexander III, promptly removed him but allowed most of the changes to remain in place. However, the military gymnasia were replaced by cadet corps, entry to which was again restricted virtually to nobles, and the use of civilian teachers in army schools, which Milyutin had favoured as a way of broadening officers' minds, was discontinued.

Education, censorship, and publishing

How to advance the state by educating the people, without educating the people to question the state? This is a dilemma not unknown elsewhere, but has often seemed more acute in Russia, especially during and after the reign of Alexander II.

For the universities the late fifties and early sixties were unhappy years. Due to Nicholas's virtual ban on foreign teachers, the low salaries, and the generally low status of the universities, the standard of instruction was poor, and many chairs were empty. The students still found themselves inadequately prepared by their gymnasiums for university work, and expressed their dissatisfactions by demonstrations and disorders. Their disorders, and their equally disliked criticism of the government, were only intensified after Alexander's first steps in increasing public liberties. The result was the appointment of a former admiral as a 'strong' minister of education, and of a Cossack general as head of the St. Petersburg educational district. In 1861 new and restrictive regulations were introduced. Student organizations and even unauthorized student gatherings were banned, impecunious students lost their privileges, including their exemption from fees and, presumably to help break the students' *esprit de corps*, student uniforms were forbidden. The students responded with large demonstrations of protest which, in the two capitals, were suppressed by police and troops.

In 1861 and 1862 it seemed to many that Russia was approaching a new crisis; dangerous situations seemed to be developing everywhere. In Poland, what was to become the Polish Rebellion was already manifesting itself; the putting into effect of the Emancipation Act was expected to ignite disorders all over Russia: the example of Garibaldi and other factors were encouraging would-be revolutionaries; and to all this was added discontent and disorder in the universities. The incarceration of 300 students in the Peter–Paul Fortress, and the beating-up and expulsion of hundreds more, did not satisfy those among the public who regarded the students as a dangerous, immoral, and unholy threat to Russian society. When in May of 1862 a succession of fires broke out in St. Petersburg, it was not long before some newspapers and some influential personages began to suggest that the fires were the work of resentful revolutionary students. But an investigating commission found nothing more conspiratorial than three students who had started one fire when in an almost unconscious state of intoxication. It would seem that the almost daily outbreaks of damaging conflagrations at that time were a consequence of a period of hot dry weather, the prevalence of wooden housing, and the absence of water for quelling fires in their initial stages. Similar fires had devastated part of the capital two years previously. On that occasion, however, they had been blamed on the Poles.

Alexander, disliking harsh measures, in 1863 approved a new set of university statutes. The planning of these, in which he had shown great interest, included consultation with the universities and their professors, and the dispatch of several of the latter to the better European universities to seek out useful ideas. The new statutes adopted the German practice of giving the universities autonomy in administration, and the French practice of the ministry of education prescribing the curriculum for all the universities, with annual examinations. University administration was placed in the hands of a council at each institution. Each of these university councils supervised teaching, degree awards, and had the right to censor the university's publications, thus freeing the latter from the general censorship. Rectors, deans and other high positions were filled by faculty elections. Student miscreants were tried by a court of three professors. Previously abolished chairs in philosophy and constitutional law were reinstated. Teaching salaries were raised, and stipends were made available to two-fifths of the students. But the Tsar insisted that those teachers who did not hold the degree stipulated for their particular rank should start working for it immediately. Despite the subsequent appointment of the conservative Dmitri Tolstoy as minister of education, the universities did not lose the advantages of the new statutes until the following reign. At the time of Alexander's death in 1881 there were eight universities. To the seven universities of St. Petersburg, Moscow, Kazan, Kiev, Vilna, Kharkov, and Dorpat had been added Odessa, and in Siberia the university of Tomsk was well on the way to establishment. In addition to new universities, in Alexander's reign seven more specialized institutions of higher learning were created.

The *zemstva* administered local primary schools through school boards, the membership of which, however, was heavily weighted in favour of the nobility, the clergy, and government officials. By about 1900 the church schools had been left behind both quantitatively and qualitatively. In 1915 there were 34,000 primary schools under the Holy Synod, but the ministry of education, with the *zemstva*, was supervising nearly 81,000, totalling six million pupils. In secondary education, a new code confirmed the division between the classical gymnasiums and the more vocational secondary schools, where no dead languages were taught but attention was paid to modern languages, science, and mathematics. The latter became known as real gymnasiums. Thanks to the government's interest in schooling there was a doubling of the number of pupils in the first decade of Alexander's reign, 800,000 being reached in 1865. Only the district schools failed to benefit in this period; it was decided to abolish this category, converting some to an improved type of primary school and others to 'pro-gymnasiums', providing gymnasium-type courses on a four-year cycle instead of the classical gymnasiums' eight-year curriculum.

A pistol shot which missed the Tsar in 1866 was fired by a former student of Kazan University. This supplied all the evidence needed by those who had long been eager to castigate educated young men as revolutionary, immoral, and the product of a misguided ministry of education. The first head to fall was that of the minister of education, who was replaced by Dmitri Tolstoy. The latter was already Over Procurator of the Holy Synod, so once again the two offices were held by the same man. Tolstoy believed that the spirit of revolution originated in the schools and universities, and especially in the science courses. He accordingly withdrew science from the schools, replacing it with larger doses of the classics. The real gymnasium courses were reduced to a six-year cycle; hitherto, like the classical gymnasium, they had offered an eight-year course. At the same time entry to universities was limited, more strictly than previously, to those who had graduated from the classical gymnasiums. This last restriction meant that fewer middle-class and more noble youths would attend universities, because the sons of merchants and artisans usually went to the real gymnasiums, which offered the technical and commercial subjects they needed. At the same time, difficult final examinations in the gymnasiums ensured that only those capable of absorbing and regurgitating an enormous quantity of facts and quotations would ever receive their leaving certificate. It became usual for only about one-third of those entering the gymnasiums to succeed in graduating, and it seems likely that this was a policy deliberately adopted to restrict university entry to those students who had kept their noses to the grindstone and thereby lost the dangerous habit of looking around them.

Tolstoy did not take serious action against the liberties of the universities, apart from transferring certain disciplinary functions from the universities to the police, a move which led to the renewal of student demonstrations in the seventies. He did, however, impose greater ministerial control over the primary schools. The school boards set up in 1864 were tending to be dominated by their *zemstvo* representatives, largely because the latter were more energetic than their colleagues. Tolstoy in the early seventies therefore transferred such decisions as teachers' appointments and the opening and closing of schools from the local school boards to inspectors from his own ministry. Thus by 1877, although the *zemstva* and town councils were providing about two-thirds of the funds for primary schools, the ministry had effective supervision. The ministry's inspectors, who were always too few to be as effective as Tolstoy had anticipated, were encouraged to be vigilant over such matters as the choice of books, the nature of the political and moral views conveyed by teachers, and the eating habits of the latter on fast days. However, because the inspectors were quite often competent in pedagogic matters, they did also bring positive benefits.

In the mid-sixties, the proportion of army recruits (almost entirely peasants) who were literate was about 7 per cent, and this rose to about 30 per cent by 1890. Inside the army, the ministry of war since the fifties had encouraged units to teach their men to read and write, and some officers gave not only their time but also their money to this task. By 1870 the army had a literacy rate much higher than that of the general population; about half the soldiers could read, and about a quarter could read and write. In the first twenty years after the 1874 reform, probably two to three million men were taught by the army to write and read. Thus the army remained Russia's greatest single educational institution. The ministry of war also attempted to mitigate the ruling by Tolstoy that only classical gymnasium graduates could continue to higher education. The ministry found that this meant that insufficient candidates came forward to train as army surgeons in its medical school. The minister, Milyutin, therefore waived the requirement. But Tolstoy, who was always glad of an opportunity to attack Milyutin, persuaded the Tsar to reprimand the latter for this. However, Milyutin's failure here did not prevent him offering medical training to female students.

There were already a few girls' schools, traditionally supervised by the empresses, and in 1870 some gymnasiums and pro-gymnasiums were established for girls, together with teacher-training courses. The university statutes of 1863 excluded women from universities, but public pressure persuaded most of the universities to offer extra courses on holidays and weekends for female students. However, it had already become a tradition for the more adventurous girls to go to foreign universities, and this continued until 1914.

The spread of education, the relaxation of censorship, and the increasing interest in public discussion created a growing demand for the written word. In 1855, 1,020 book titles were published, 1,836 in 1864, and 10,691 in 1894. The 1894 total was about equal to the output of new titles in the USA and Britain combined. The Imperial Library at St. Petersburg with its million titles ranked third in the world after the Bibliothèque Nationale and the British Museum, and the St. Petersburg Public Library had almost half a million volumes in addition. Periodicals flourished in the second half of the century. In 1855 there were about 140 periodicals in circulation. Of these about sixty were 'official'; they were published by one or other government department but often only part of their contents was related to that particular department. (Pirogov published several of his advanced educational articles in the navy's journal.) A similar proportion of the periodicals was scholarly or specialized journals, leaving less than twenty dealing in general terms with literary or current affairs. Periodicals dealing with current affairs, literature, and other general interests did not multiply under Alexander III; the total remained more or less constant, with the number of new ventures equalling the number of those periodicals which ceased publication. In 1894 Russia had eighty-nine newspapers and thirty-two general-interest 'thick' periodicals. In Alexander II's reign the practice (continued in the Soviet period) of government departments publishing their own newspapers for general distribution became widespread. Especially noteworthy among these was the *Russkii Invalid*, published by the ministry of war. This became especially popular among the public during the Polish Rebellion, because it was able to give the latest (and most reliable) news about the military situation. Milyutin used the paper not only to publicize his own strong anti-Polish and anti-Catholic sentiments, but also to popularize his views on the army reforms he was planning. Milyutin's possession of a newspaper, in which he could dispute the views of the conservative press, caused his political enemies to persuade the Tsar to issue an order compelling departmental newspapers to publish only 'official' items. This order robbed Milyutin of his most valued weapon, but it did not permanently affect the departmental newspapers.

One of the factors encouraging the public to read more books and periodicals after 1855 was the relaxation of the censorship. When Alexander succeeded his father, there was not so much a formal relaxation as a completely new atmosphere, in which newspapers and journals freely criticized those aspects of the government which had been proven shameful or ineffective during the Crimean War. However, even at this time there were certain topics which could not be mentioned. In 1860 censorship was removed from the ministry of education and later came into the purview of the ministry of the interior. The multitude of separate censorships, which in Nicholas's time had meant that a publication had to be approved by several offices, was almost eliminated, although the Church and the army insisted on maintaining their own separate right to censor material dealing with their own fields of interest. 'Preventive' censorship (the submission of publications before distribution) which enabled and encouraged censors to interfere in all kinds of details, was largely replaced by 'punitive' censorship, which simply involved the punishment of publishers and writers and editors if they broke the rules and published material of a type known to be forbidden. Under this system both the authorities and the publications knew, in theory, just how far they could go. But within two weeks of the 1865 law formalizing these concessions, an unsuspecting newspaper was served with an official warning for discussing a financial question; it was claimed that this article was against the interests of the state, for it might harm Russia's international credit. Soon, other newspapers received cautions, and their editors were aware that if they received too many of these they would become eligible for stronger measures. Later, after Valuev had been thwarted by the courts in his efforts to punish delinquent editors, he issued an instruction removing censorship cases from the provincial courts. In the succeeding years of mild reaction, further changes hampered the development of a healthy press. Some papers could be sold only to their established subscribers, some journals were returned to preventive censorship, and the minister of the interior could arbitrarily forbid the discussion of certain questions of state. In the reaction following the 1866 attempted assassination of the Tsar, Valuev even suppressed the well-established journal, *The Contemporary*. Nevertheless, for writers and publishers the reign of Alexander II was an interlude of freedom separating the repressive years of Nicholas I and Alexander III.

The arts

The reign of Alexander coincided almost exactly with what is called the golden age of Russian literature, the age of Turgenev, Dostoevsky, and Tolstoy. It was also the golden age of Russian realism, although that term is misleadingly broad; it might be more meaningful to say that writers preferred to write about their own country and their own time, and that they had a deep seriousness and sense of responsibility towards society. For the historian, their novels have great value in conveying the atmosphere of the time; they should be read, rather than read about. For their original readers, too, they were more than entertainment. Because Russians so often have been prevented by censorship from discussing issues openly, fiction has often been a unique medium for presenting unpleasant truths and original solutions. Turgenev's *Sportsman's Sketches* (1847), for example, presented portraits of Russian peasants and thereby suggested to its readers the novel truth that the peasants were real suffering individuals, not just insensible and indistinguishable components of a grey mass.

In other novels Turgenev dealt sympathetically but sadly with the young radicals. In *On the Eve* (1860), the only radical character is a Bulgarian, suggesting that Russia is not yet producing the energetic young men she needs. Then, in *Fathers and Sons* (1862), the Russian nihilist appears in Bazarov, who denies the worth of everything that cannot be justified scientifically, is unable always to practise as he preaches, and dies before achieving anything. Later, *Virgin Soil* (1877) portrays the idealism, naïvety, and pathos of the young men and women who 'go to the people' to educate and radicalize the masses.

Dostoevsky condemned Turgenev's sympathy for the radicals. He put his faith in Christian humility and the 'Russian soul'. His novels present a wide range of complex psychological types, and were of great interest to psychologists and philosophers; Freud and Nietzsche were but two who were influenced by them. It is not easy to decide which characteristics of Dostoevsky's heroes are specifically Russian, and which universal, but it is widely accepted, for example, that the three brothers in *The Brothers Karamazov* (1880) represent three salient Russian types. Ivan is an atheist intellectual who hankers for the west, even though he knows the west is alien. Dmitri exemplifies the extremism of the Russian character, which can shift in a flash from generosity to swinishness, from caution to reck-lessness, from kindness to cruelty. The third brother, Alyosha, a disciple of the local holy man, represents Russian love, humility, and self-sacrifice.

Tolstoy was revered by many as the greatest Russian ever. He was not simply a writer, but in his later decades a moralist and philosopher who influenced, among others, Gandhi. His condemnation of violence and wealth, of government repression and Church hypocrisy, brought him administrative pinpricks and excommunication. After his two best-known novels, *War and Peace* (1869) and *Anna Karenina* (1877), were completed, Tolstoy underwent a spiritual crisis. This affected his subsequent works, which tended to reflect whatever mental torment their author was passing through at the time. The novel *Resurrection* (1889), for example, dealt very harshly with the workings of the judicial system, and was written after Tolstoy discovered by experience that Alexander II's reforms meant that nobles like the Tolstoys could no longer influence verdicts in the local court. Again, *The Kreutzer Sonata* (1889), a diatribe against feminine sexu-ality, reflects Tolstoy's failure to adapt to monogamy. *War and Peace*, which was written between 1862 and 1868, is regarded as *the* Russian novel. Describing the events of 1812, it did much to restore confidence lost in the Crimean War. By depicting 1812 as a time when all Russians were com-rades with a single goal, it expressed the idea of Russian nationality without arrogance or chauvinism. Tolstoy, himself an old soldier, described the battles of 1812 with an absence of heroics and a lack of respect for

Napoleon; whereas the wise old Kutuzov realizes that history will take its course irrespective of what so-called great men may do, Napoleon imagines that he is controlling events, and thereby the destiny of the world.

Among writers less well known in the west, although available in translation, Goncharov, Leskov, Saltykov-Shchedrin (see p. 78) and Chernyshevsky are especially rewarding for historians. The hero of Goncharov's *Oblomov* (1859) is an extreme example, both of the 'superfluous man' and of Russian inertia; while he sits around in his dressing gown, apathetic and opportunity-wasting, his energetic friend (who, not by coincidence, is of German origin) gets things done. Leskov specialized in the holy, corrupt, comic, and superstitious lives of the provincial clergy. Chernyshevsky perhaps belongs more to the history of the revolutionaries than to the history of literature, for his novel, *What is to be Done?* became an inspiration for generations of revolutionary intellectuals. The son of a priest and educated at St. Petersburg University, Chernyshevsky became one of the editors of *The Contemporary*, the favourite journal of the radical intelligentsia. In this position, and in so far as the censorship permitted, he advanced his theory that most unhappiness in the world had economic causes, and that society could only be perfected through socialism. In the student disturbances of 1862 the authorities decided to arrest him as a precautionary measure. This precaution lasted two decades, and after his return from Siberia he was not in a condition to make much further contribution to Russian letters. However, in 1862, while in gaol, he wrote *What is to be Done?* This novel had an enormous public success, especially among the young, many of whom tried to model their lives after those of the heroes. The theme of the novel is the emancipation of women, as expressed by the heroine, whose initial marriage enables her to escape from grasping and unperceptive parents,[6] and who then marries a second time for love, the first husband having generously faked his own suicide. The heroine, by establishing humane but profitable seamstresses' co-operative workshops, shows how socialist ideals and female self-sufficiency are complementary.

Chernyshevsky, in his role as critic, did much to further the concept of critical realism as a standard by which literature should be judged. In this he was aided by his friend Dobroliubov, who is regarded as one of the most influential Russian critics, even though he died at the age of twenty-five. Like Chernyshevsky, Dobroliubov was the son of a priest and a contributor to *The Contemporary*. However, the influence of the radical critics of the Belinsky tradition was not always positive. For example, in the early nineteenth century there had flourished in Russia native novels of the *Tom*

---

[6] This feature later inspired many real-life 'fictitious marriages' of young women seeking freedom from parental control.

Jones genre, but after Belinsky's condemnation these fell rapidly out of fashion and were never revived. Thus Bulgarin's *Ivan Vyzhigin* was a best-seller in 1830 but forgotten by 1840; Bulgarin was a proponent of Official Nationality and this may have given Belinsky's criticism extra venom. Again, radical critics were inclined to invent a cause when running short of genuine issues. When the progressive educationist Pirogov, an opponent of corporal punishment, wrote an article recommending the limitation of birching to a few specific circumstances, Dobroliubov immediately attacked him as an advocate of birching. Corporal punishment, being applicable only to non-nobles, was an issue too much imbued with class distinction to be treated rationally by the radicals.

Although literature was reaching a wider audience, among the educated there were still loyal subjects of the Tsar who distrusted contemporary writers. The mathematician Sofia Kovalevskaya, whose father was a retired general living in a remote village, described a childhood experience of 1865 in her memoirs:

> Our father, as I have mentioned, regarded with great mistrust anything which originated from the literary world. Although he did give permission for my sister to make the acquaintance of Dostoevsky he did so with a shudder and inward trepidation.
> 'Remember that you are responsible, Liza,' he told our mother as we said good-bye on leaving our village. 'Dostoevsky is not from our kind of society. What do we know about him? Simply that he is a journalist and was once in gaol. That's a fine recommendation! What more is there to say? You must be on your guard with him.'[7]

In the theatre, foreign plays remained the most numerous, but Ostrovsky's work was popular. This playwright illuminated the naïvety and pettiness of the Russian middle class. That the characters he portrayed were types well-entrenched in Russian society is suggested by the popularity of his works in the USSR. Like the ballet, Russian theatre would not attain worldwide acclamation until the turn of the century. Until 1881, city theatres were state-owned, and there was a tendency to refuse the staging of truly original plays. In the absence of privately owned public theatres, the only other performances were in the private theatres of the greatest landowners. The actors, designers, musicians, and playwrights of these were often former serfs, a few of whom rose high in the theatrical world. However, until Ostrovsky founded various theatrical associations, the social status of the actor was very low in Russia.

During the reign of Alexander II, most Russians would have named Anton Rubinstein as their best-known musician. A child prodigy as a pianist,

---

[7] S. Kovalevskaya, *Vospominaniya i pisma* (1951), 103.

he had later written operas and done much to encourage Russian musicians by founding the St. Petersburg Conservatoire. One of his students was Tchaikovsky, composer of operas, ballets, and overtures which were acclaimed at home and abroad. Tchaikovsky died in the 1893 cholera, soon after completing the *Nutcracker* ballet. He frequently found his ideas in Russian folk music, although his works were really more European than Russian. It was the group of musicians known as the Young School (Balakirev, Cui, Borodin, Rimsky-Korsakov, and Musorgsky) which set out to create a specifically Russian music. By 1882 the eminent critic Stasov was able to explain how, after Glinka had shown the way, Russian music had become so different from European. He wrote that whereas in western Europe the old folk songs had been extinguished by 'European culture' and could be resurrected only by research, in Russia the folk song was still part of everyday life. Peasants, craftsmen and craftswomen, soldiers, all had their own working songs on their lips, and when they went to the big cities they took their songs with them. Moreover, almost all the important Russian musicians had either been born in the country, or had passed their youth there, and had thus been in daily contact with folk songs. Consequently, their early musical impressions had been decidedly national, not international. In addition, many musicians had visited the Caucasus and had brought back eastern elements which were hard to measure but certainly important. With all this, and the new Russian composers' refusal to accept blindly the values of 'universally-recognized authorities', there had developed, according to Stasov, not merely a Russian school, but a completely new musical system.

While Balakirev was the inspirer of the Young School, and Cui its publicist, it was Borodin, Rimsky-Korsakov, and Musorgsky who were most productive, although the latter's music was too unfamiliar to be widely appreciated at the time. For most of the new composers music was a part-time interest. Cui was a military engineer who wrote standard books on fortification. Balakirev was afflicted with religious mania and later became a railway station-master. Rimsky-Korsakov originally followed family tradition by becoming a naval officer. Borodin, best known later for his *Prince Igor*, was renowned in his time as a professor of chemistry who also helped to establish a medical school for women. Musicians were not immune to censorship; Rimsky-Korsakov's opera *Maid of Pskov* had to be changed because the original libretto referred to medieval Pskov's republican form of government, and the same composer discovered that Nicholas I's ruling that pre-Romanov tsars might be depicted in drama and tragedy did not apply to opera, because officials feared the unseemliness of a ditty-singing tsar appearing on stage.

5.   *From Bombs to Pogroms*

The Russo-Turkish War

THERE were no more honeymoons of tsar and people after the mid-sixties; for the next half-century revolutionaries and unnecessary wars wore down the state, while the state wore down its peoples. Like other Russian rulers, Alexander II found that relaxation and reform, after prolonged repressions, led not to contentment but to increasing demands for concessions which he had never been prepared to grant. This, and the attacks of revolutionaries, was presumably why his earlier reforming zeal seemed to fade. Yet compared with his successor, Alexander III, Alexander II at his worst was only mildly repressive. On the other hand, unlike his son, he damaged himself by becoming embroiled in war.

Fundamentally, it was not the Russo-Turkish War but the emergence of a united Germany that was the main event in Russia's foreign relations during Alexander's reign. Bismarck's work was to have as damaging an effect on Russia's position as it would have on France. Whereas Russia's relations with the German states had been successfully managed in the post-Napoleonic period, helped by royal marriages and common interests, there was now a completely new situation. For a time, cordiality between the Romanovs and the Hohenzollerns persuaded the former that the old relationships might continue. But the underlying reality, which emerged plainly in 1914, was quite different. With a new and militant power established in central Europe and determined to make its mark, an additional and usually unhelpful voice was heard as the great powers strove to accommodate peacefully the political and social upheavals of the time.

Bismarck was familiar with Russia, having been the Prussian minister in St. Petersburg. He had no great regard for the Russians and, like several of his successors, tried to encourage them to turn their attention towards expansion in the east; if kept busy in Asia, Russians would be less concerned with the Balkans, where Austrian ambition, British anxieties, Ottoman decline, and local nationalisms promised perilous changes. In fact, Russia no more needed encouragement in her military excursions into Central Asia than she did in her continuing pacification of the Caucasus. But despite these preoccupations she was unwilling to turn her back on the Balkans. Alexander was anxious to avoid trouble, yet even the Tsar-Autocrat had to heed the outcry from those of his subjects for whom the tribulations of Orthodox Christians under the Turks was a burning wrong. Among these subjects of the Tsar it was the Panslavists who were the most vocal, and they were influential not only in Russia but also in the Slavic lands of the Ottoman Empire. In 1875 a revolt started in Herzegovina and spread to Bosnia and Bulgaria. Despite British reluctance to intervene, the 'Bulgarian Atrocities' perpetrated by the Turks precipitated interference by the great powers. A European conference was summoned at Constantinople, but its decisions were rejected by the Turks, as were subsequent proposals by the powers. In 1877, Alexander, influenced more by Dmitri Milyutin than by the Panslavists, declared war on Turkey in defence of the Slavic peoples.

The war, fought mainly in what is now Bulgaria and Roumania, occurred while the Russian army was still in the period of transformation following Milyutin's reforms. Thus many of the deficiencies of the Crimean War reappeared. Only the engineers and the sailors distinguished themselves. The engineers brilliantly executed the initial crossing of the Danube, and made possible the eventual capture of the Turkish stronghold of Plevna. Bold young naval officers, including the future Admiral Makarov, commanded steam launches whose torpedoes defeated the Turkish navy. Early in 1878, under British pressure, Alexander signed an armistice which was followed by the Treaty of San Stefano. Alexander intended that a final settlement of the Balkan issues should be with the participation of other interested powers, but in this treaty he was able to put Russia into a good bargaining position. With his army threatening Constantinople, he extracted terms highly favourable to Russia, including the establishment of a large Bulgarian state which would be independent but under Russian influence. When Bismarck proposed a congress in Berlin to discuss a modified treaty, all the governments involved accepted. The result was the Treaty of Berlin (1878), which superseded the Treaty of San Stefano; the provisions of the latter were partly retained, but modified to meet the objections of those powers which felt that Russia had demanded too much (see map, p. 596). Because Britain had gone through the motions of preparing for war prior to the Congress, and because, among other things, the new Bulgaria was reduced in size and Britain received Cyprus, the Congress of Berlin was represented as a triumph of British diplomacy. Although the Tsar realized that the avoidance of large-scale war was more important than the possibility of increasing Russian influence in the Balkans, not all his subjects took the same view; the Panslavists were infuriated at what they regarded as Russia's humiliation at the Congress, and their agitation was one of the main factors in Alexander's loss of popularity at this time.

The revolutionaries

The informal circles of intellectuals of the late twenties and thirties had devoted themselves mainly to the idealistic philosophy then in fashion. At that time, questioning young men like Belinsky and Bakunin were buried in German metaphysics and in the study of Schelling and Hegel, placing the pursuit of truth and beauty before the problems of Russian society. But there were others, of whom Herzen was the outstanding representative, who were beginning to care about social problems, were acquainting themselves with the French socialist thinkers, and were adopting the view that, instead of the political revolution which had proved so disappointing in France and Poland, what Russia needed was a social revolution; if the economic advantages held by the property-owning class were eliminated, political privilege would automatically disappear. The intensification of the Westernizer versus Slavophil discussion in the forties also indicated a growing concern in intellectual circles about whether Russia should follow the path of industrial and liberal western society, or should build a unique society on the basis of her traditional institutions and concepts. After emigrating in 1847, Herzen began to accept that the Russian peasant commune might well be the factor enabling Russia to by-pass the capitalist phase of development. The commune, with its implication that the land belongs to those who collectively cultivate it, had prepared the people for the principles of socialism; hence the latter would be more easily accepted than in western Europe, where the capitalist mentality was well entrenched. Like many of his generation, Herzen did not exclude the possibility of the tsar himself introducing the needed reforms; the centuries-old acceptance of the autocrat as the agent of revolutionary change was slow to disappear.

When the long-repressed revolutionary movement emerged after the death of Nicholas, it was largely in the hands of students, or recent students. Alexander II had soon removed many of the previous restrictions on university entry, and this had led to an increase of student numbers, especially of students from poorer backgrounds. More than half the students relied on state financial help. Many were undernourished and diseased. Student co-operatives, organizing communal kitchens and libraries, emerged as a form of self-aid, while a student *esprit de corps* developed in reaction to poor teachers, absurd discipline, and the police actions which were the authorities' all-too-frequent response to complaints. In 1861 there were large-scale disturbances, and the government's response was a reduction of scholarships and a ban on student meetings. At St. Petersburg University the students retaliated by breaking into a locked lecture room to hold a protest meeting, marching through the city, and boycotting lectures. Several hundred were gaoled for a couple of months and the University was closed until 1863. In Moscow there were similar disorders and several injuries, inflicted by local inhabitants who had been persuaded by the police that the demonstrators were either young landowners demanding the retention of serfdom or, worse, were Poles. Student and peasant disturbances, with growing governmental repression, persuaded many that peaceful transformation was no longer likely. Those who, like Herzen, still shrank from a violent revolution, found themselves criticized as old-fashioned and ineffective. The younger generation increasingly gave its adherence to Chernyshevsky and his like-minded colleagues on the editorial board of *The Contemporary* who, within the limits of the censorship, were advocating the imposition of socialism by revolution if necessary. Chernyshevsky was well aware of the price of revolution but many of those whom he inspired were not; the futile violence advocated by some of his followers led to public alienation and his own imprisonment. He never again took an active part in the revolutionary movement, although his novel, *What is to be Done?* (see p. 104) inspired many subsequent generations of revolutionaries, including Lenin's.

The more realistic dissidents perceived that 'the people' did not yet want a revolution, and that the successful revolutionary must spend years, even decades, preparing people's minds. Notable among such thinkers in the sixties was Pisarev, who, apart from his aversion to revolution-at-any-price, had great faith in the scientific method as the solution to all problems. In fact the good society he envisaged was a kind of technocracy, with an educated élite providing the leadership, Pisarev was described by conservatives as a 'nihilist', a word which became popular among those seeking derogatory generalizations for those who were against tradition, against authority, and against hypocrisy. With the help of conservative journalists, 'nihilism' soon became associated in the public mind with young people who were alarmingly immoral—godless, free-loving, subversive, treasonous, indecent, dirty, and with menacing hairstyles:

According to popular opinion the Nihilists were a band of fanatical young men and women, mostly medical students, who had determined to turn the world upside down and to introduce a new kind of social order, founded on the most advanced principles of social equality and Communism. As a first step towards the great transformation they had reversed the traditional order of things in the matter of *coiffure*: the males allowed their hair to grow long, and the female adepts cut their hair short, adding occasionally the additional badge of blue spectacles...

This was the ridiculous side of the movement, but underneath the absurdities there was something serious. These young men and women, who were themselves terribly in earnest, were systematically hostile, not only to accepted convention-alities in the matter of dress, but to all manner of shams, hypocrisy, and cant... while ridiculing romanticism, they had romantic sentiment enough to make them sacrifice their time, their property, and sometimes even their life, to the attainment of an unrealizable ideal... I must say that, without at all sharing or sympathizing with their opinions, I could not help respecting them as honourable, upright, quixotic men and women who had made great sacrifices for their convictions...

In a satirical novel of the time a little girl is represented as coming to her mother and saying, 'Little Mamma! Maria Ivan'na, our new schoolmistress, says there is no God and no Tsar, and that it is wrong to marry!' Whether such incidents actually occurred in real life, as several friends assured me, I am not prepared to say, but certainly people believed that they might occur in their own families, and that was quite sufficient to produce alarm even in the ranks of the Liberals, to say nothing of the rapidly increasing army of the Reactionaries.[1]

The reading public, regaled with the real and imagined superficial char-acteristics of the nihilists, rarely noticed that these young people did not merely reject the old but sought a better alternative, even though they had not yet agreed on the latter. Certainly many of those who called themselves nihilists did so uncreatively out of a desire to be fashionably radical, but for the sincere dissidents, the misrepresentation of their views was a factor driving many of them to extreme forms of revolutionary activity.

Of the varied groups meeting in the sixties, Land and Liberty was not-able. It was very radical, and against reformism. Bakunin, who was a heroic figure for the young revolutionaries, gave his blessing to this organ-ization, although Herzen disapproved of it. Another revolutionary circle was the Committee of Russian Officers in Poland. The latter prepared a rising in Poland, hoping to persuade fellow-officers and soldiers not to fire on the rebels. But the Polish Rebellion of 1863 was premature. The troops remained loyal to the Tsar, and there was much bloodshed. Herzen reluct-antly gave his approval to the rising, but was probably not surprised when his *Kolokol* immediately lost readers; even Russian radicals were not im-mune to 'Great Russian chauvinism', especially when the Poles were in-volved. Like dissidents at other times and places, Herzen had to admit that 'the public is worse than the government and the journalists are worse than the public'.[2] Land and Liberty was crushed by the wave of arrests which followed the Polish Rebellion, but other revolutionary circles continued. These represented a variety of opinions, and inside each there was again a

[1] D. Mackenzie Wallace, *Russia* (Vintage, 1961), 449–452.
[2] Quoted in A. Yarmolinsky, *Road to Revolution* (Collier, 1962), 132.

difference of views. One circle, generally devoted to Chernyshevsky's socialism, harboured an extremist wing calling itself Hell, which attracted romantic young men anxious to become instant martyrs, and obsessed with all kinds of ill-thought-out schemes of violence. In 1866 one of them, Karakazov, a sickly youth believing that he was suffering from a progressive and incurable mental disease, sought to win a glorious place in history by murdering the Tsar. But his bullet flew wide of its august target. He was immediately arrested and found to be carrying a list of the members of the circle. One arrest led to another, and one circle led to others, including those of the moderates. The latter were now unable to carry out their plans for on-the-spot propaganda and study in the provinces; this delayed for some years the revolutionaries' discovery of what 'the people', on whose behalf they were acting, were really like.

Apart from intensified censorship, the banning of some periodicals, and the arrest of genuine or suspected revolutionaries, Karakazov's shot also led to closer supervision of higher education because he had himself once been a student. Student co-operatives were banned because, although recognized as an aid to poor students, they provided good places to exchange revolutionary opinions and leaflets. But police action inside the universities continued to radicalize students whose indignation overcame their reluctance to break the law.

Most newspapers blamed 'outside agitators' for student troubles, choosing to ignore the factors which made the students receptive to subversive ideas. One such agitator was Tkachev. Like many other revolutionary ideologists, he was of the 'penitent nobility'. He was a journalist and one of the first Russians to be interested by Marx, although his ideas came mainly from Chernyshevsky. He was as opposed to the moderate reformers as he was to the regime itself. For him, violent revolution was the only solution and revolutionaries, being entrusted with so high a task, were absolved from the bounds of conventional morality. He formed a group to radicalize the students, that is, to convert the widespread student grievances against their universities into a hostility towards the regime. After renewed student unrest in 1869 he was imprisoned, but soon escaped abroad.

One of Tkachev's admirers was Nechayev, a student of proletarian origin. It was probably he who presented the police with a list of students sympathetic to the radicals, hoping that the resulting arrests would convert the 'liberals' into real revolutionaries. Nechayev also fabricated and planted evidence that he had been arrested but had succeeded in escaping from the hitherto prisoner-tight Peter–Paul Fortress. Having with this and other tales made himself into a student hero, in 1869 he paid a visit to émigré revolutionaries in Switzerland and convinced Bakunin that he controlled thousands of revolutionary students. In return for this fictitious asset, he received a certificate signed by the great anarchist himself, declaring that Nechayev was a representative of an émigré organization controlled by Bakunin (equally fictitious, unknown to Nechayev). During his stay in Geneva, Nechayev published several leaflets calling for a destructive revolution. Some of these were smuggled into Russia, but others were sent through the mails in the hope that the addressees would be arrested and thereby radicalized.

When Nechayev returned to Russia, the prestige of Bakunin's alliance brought enough supporters to at last turn his fictitious organization into a real one. The ideology of the movement was expressed in the *Catechism of the Revolutionary*. This declared that a revolutionary should be totally dedicated, should not allow himself to be distracted by questions of survival or by noble feelings, should be absolutely vicious and selfish for the sake of the new benevolent society to come. The aim was to kill the intelligent and the influential, who might hamper the ruthless course of the revolution. However, hated or corrupt figures of the regime were to be spared, because their acts served to incite the people. Liberals were to be enticed into conspiracy by working on their consciences and then, once they had broken the law, blackmailed into doing the dirty work of the revolution. The *Catechism* drew the conclusion that since the masses would not revolt unless they were desperately miserable, and since they could be made happy only through revolution, it was the duty of the revolutionary to ensure long-term social happiness by intensifying short-term social misery. Nechayev's post-revolutionary society (ridiculed by Marx as 'barracks communism') was to be communistic, with a controlling central committee, and various compulsions: compulsory physical labour for all, including mothers, compulsory membership of a workers' organization, and compulsory utilization of communal dining halls and dormitories. Nechayev organized his membership into small cells which were unknown to each other. He insisted on the strictest secrecy and obedience. This enabled him to send on suicidal missions those members whom he distrusted, to set one member to spy on another, and to convince his handful of members that they belonged to a vast underground organization. In his dealings with the cells he claimed to be speaking as the representative of an all-powerful and highly secret central committee. This in reality had but one member, Nechayev himself.

When Nechayev was opposed by one of his doubting comrades, he had him murdered. The discovery of the body led to the discovery of the organization. Murder was not a political crime, so Nechayev's flight to

Switzerland in late 1869 ended in extradition and imprisonment for life. The trial of his comrades, who had not fled, and especially the reading of the *Catechism* in court, enormously damaged the whole revolutionary movement, even though Nechayev represented only an anarchistic fringe. Many who had been sympathetic to radical thought came to believe that all revolutionaries resembled these cold-blooded conspirators, whose only achievement had been the savage murder of one of their more scrupulous members. Dostoevsky's novel, *The Possessed*, based on the Nechayev episode, reinforced this disquiet.

The 1870s was the great decade for revolutionaries seeking a socialism based on the peasantry. These revolutionaries were called Populists (*Narodniks*), but later the term Populist was applied misleadingly, and often against their will, to all those from Herzen to the anarchists who sought a revolutionary change enabling Russia to escape the capitalist stage of development. The true Populists of the seventies idealized the traditional agricultural commune, and the traditional co-operative workshop (*artel*); many believed that these two institutions would provide a base on which economic development could be built without recourse to capitalism with its big factories, centralized control, unequal distribution of wealth, and reduction of the individual to a cog in the economic machine. Two ideologists of Populism were Mikhailovsky and Lavrov, both of noble birth and both journalists. Lavrov's *Historical Letters* of 1868 had added a new element to Populism by arguing that only the intellectual élite, united in a *party*, would be able to assure the people's welfare. It was, moreover, the intellectual's duty to serve the masses, for it was their labours which in effect had paid for his education. The new Populist circles, distrustful of Nechayev-type central committees, were uncoordinated. Wary of Nechayev's cold-blooded violence, they stressed a clean-hands policy. They were more interested in propaganda work among the workers and peasants. In 1874 and 1875 there was a spontaneous 'going to the people'. Perhaps as many as two or three thousand young men and women, dressed as workers and peasants, settled in the villages and industrial cities. The ever-hopeful Bakuninists anticipated that their arrival would ignite an instant rebellion, while the Lavrovites regarded it as the start of the long process of winning people's minds. But the results were disappointing for all. The peasants, perhaps recalling their proverb 'the egg does not teach the hen', were unconvinced and unimpressed by their young visitors.

Many of the young missionaries were arrested. The subsequent trials only strengthened the will both of the arrested and the survivors. Two notable trials were held in 1877. At the 'Trial of the Fifty', the idealism and the honesty shown in court by the defendants made a great impression on the public; the Russian Christian mind was not slow to see saintliness in the accused. The long prison sentences which were imposed gained the victims additional sympathy. At the 'Trial of the 193', involving almost 200 defendants (some of whom died in prison before the trial opened), the prosecution presented the scattered activities of the various individuals and circles as though they were all part of one gigantic conspiracy. This attempt to make the prisoners appear more dangerously subversive than they really were did not, apparently, impress the court, for sentences were light and there were many acquittals. Those acquitted, however, were immediately deported to Siberia by the so-called administrative procedure. Of the eighty condemned, twenty-eight were described as being of the nobility, seventeen were sons or daughters of priests, ten were middle class, five were children of government officials, five were peasants and three were foreigners.[3]

The failure of the 'going to the people', and the arrests, encouraged the extremists among the revolutionaries. They argued that the people were far from revolutionary and that government-encouraged capitalism with its ethic of private property and free enterprise was making the people ever less receptive to socialist ideas. It would be better to make the revolution first and win people's minds afterwards. Many of those who had not been arrested joined a resurrected Land and Liberty. This reverted to a strong central organizing committee, in reaction to the ineffectiveness and muddles of the post-Nechayev unorganized circles. Its programme (with which not all its members were in agreement) included the allocation of all land to the peasants and the abolition of the state apparatus, to be achieved by a revolution which would take place as soon as possible. The society's central organization possessed the two essential tools of the revolutionary, a secret press to print its leaflets and a section skilled in the forgery of passports and other documents. It also owned a racehorse.

With great caution, Land and Liberty formed cells in town and country. Its first big manifestation was in St. Petersburg, where a demonstration, organized by and on behalf of discontented workers, was taken over by radical students. There was a particularly violent speech by a student named Plekhanov, and then a procession formed, soon broken up by the police with the help of hooligans. Land and Liberty had a section devoted to violent action, whose task was the freeing of imprisoned members, the murder of informers or of key or despotic administrators. Among others, the head of the Third Section and a high official of the Kiev police were

---

[3] *Krasnyi arkhiv*, Vol. 30, 194–9.

killed, the former in broad daylight with the two assassins escaping with the aid of the society's racehorse. The government was alarmed, but in some quarters the revolutionaries' daring and success earned admiration. The government decreed that cases of political violence would be tried henceforth by military courts. Within the society there was a widening split between those who wished to develop the terroristic branch and those who did not. Attacks on some men could be justified as defensive measures against official illegality and brutality, but indiscriminate murders seemed likely to alienate the masses. Vera Zasulich was among those who opposed unrestricted violence, and so was Plekhanov. These differences came to a head when a would-be regicide appealed for assistance from the society. Several members of its central committee pointed out that attacks on the Tsar could only lead to mass arrests of the innocent, and would bring the society into disrepute since the masses, especially the peasants, still revered the monarch and believed simply that his good intentions towards them were being thwarted by the gentry in the administration. The society compromised, simply refusing to make available its racehorse. The attempt was made. All five shots missed, the assassin failed to poison himself as planned, was hung, and Land and Liberty was blamed. Many arrests followed.

Disagreement on the uses of terrorism in 1879 caused a formal though amicable break between those like Plekhanov, who wished to concentrate on propaganda, and those who were devoted to violence. The latter became the People's Will, while the former took the name of Black Repartition (referring to their proposed redistribution of the land). The People's Will had a strong executive committee, organizing a membership which was probably in the region of four or five hundred. It was probably the biggest of the nineteenth-century Populist organizations, but its members never agreed on a common ideology and tactics.[4] By this time the revolutionary movement included fewer gentry; the People's Will was largely composed of young men and women from the middle class or from the educated lower classes.

The declared aim of the People's Will was the destruction of the state, followed by the taking of power by the people and a redistribution of economic power on socialist lines. Only the people could fill the post-revolutionary vacuum because there did not exist any organized force in Russia which could usurp the leadership. The People's Will had no intention of becoming an élite governing party. Its chosen role was to ignite the revolution by a campaign of necessary but regrettable terrorism. The group became mistakenly obsessed

---

[4] 'Populist' is an accepted but misleading description of the People's Will, which was also strongly anarchistic.

with the supposed necessity of killing Alexander II, persuading itself that the murder of the Tsar would alone cause revolution. A plan to dynamite the royal train was adopted. Tunnels were dug under the rails, and dynamite placed in readiness. But of the three mines, one was laid under the wrong route, one failed to explode because the battery had been wrongly assembled, while the third was successfully detonated under the wrong train. A well-planned scheme to blow up a St. Petersburg bridge as the Tsar passed over it came to nothing because one of the pair entrusted with the detonation arrived too late, not having a watch. Yet another attempt in 1880 demonstrated the same courage, determination, and technical incompetence. Dynamite was secreted under the dining room of the Winter Palace, but the conspirators fired the charge before enough had been accumulated; some guards were killed but Alexander was unhurt.

The government, picturing hordes of revolutionaries busily tunnelling like moles all over Russia, was driven to unusual measures. Loris-Melikov, soon to be minister of the interior, initiated a programme of short sharp repression, to be followed by a new leniency. Some students were hanged merely for distributing leaflets, but Tolstoy, the much-disliked minister of education, was dismissed. Fact-finding missions were dispatched to the provinces and Loris-Melikov persuaded Alexander to agree to the establishment of a 'General Commission', including some members elected by the *zemstva* and city councils, as a consultative body. This commission would have fallen far short of a national assembly, but it would nevertheless have been a short step towards popular government. The Third Section was also abolished at this time, although its functions were transferred to a department of the ministry of the interior. Loris-Melikov improved its organization and tried to ensure that it interested itself only in genuinely dangerous persons (more than 31,000 citizens were by this time under surveillance). The apparent government concessions damaged the appeal of the People's Will, and the group was further weakened by the arrest of a conspirator who turned informer. A last, desperate almost, conspiracy to kill Alexander was therefore hurriedly devised. The attempt was to be made when the Tsar was on his way to review troops in St. Petersburg. More by luck than good management this attempt was successful. Two bombs were thrown and the second mortally wounded the Tsar (1881).

One of the bomb-throwers made a full confession, betraying his comrades. Five of the conspirators were hanged, including one woman, Sofia Perovskaya, who was the daughter of a former governor of St. Petersburg. The army mutiny and civil disorders which the assassination had been expected to ignite did not take place; soldiers and citizens resented the murder. Meanwhile a law (destined for a long life) was passed which made it possible for the ministry of the interior to declare states of emergency in provinces or regions. Among other things, this enabled civilians to be tried by military courts according to wartime regulations; that is, civilians could be tried and convicted on harsher principles than soldiers, who would still be tried under peacetime procedures.

Arrests weakened the People's Will, which never regained its previous strength, but neither the government nor its supporters realized how weak the People's Will had become; it was at this time that the short-lived Holy League, an unofficial counter-terrorist organization, was set up by a group of reactionaries intending to meet violence with violence. The weakened central committee of the People's Will, in view of the failure of its terrorism to spark a popular revolution, soon inclined towards the possibility of a revolution made by a small conspiratorial minority, which would impose a socialist system before handing over power to the people. Its supporters abroad opposed this change, accusing it of seeking power not for any cause, but for the sake of power itself. There was a split in the group, and it was further weakened by the presence on its central committee of a police informer. At times it sank to anti-semitism, welcoming the *pogroms* as a form of popular rebellion and condemning those few police forces which intervened against 'the people' to protect the Jews. Some young people, claiming to be the heirs of the People's Will, did attempt to bomb Alexander III in 1887. Due to lack of caution, they were arrested before their target appeared and five were executed, including the presumed ringleader Alexander Ulyanov, Lenin's elder brother.

The powerful Socialist Revolutionary party (see p. 152) eventually developed from the remnants of the People's Will, but the other wing of the Populists, 'Black Repartition', turned to marxism. The great age of Russian Populism was finished. Populism had more viewpoints and outstanding individuals than can be mentioned here. But typically a Populist was an educated man or woman attracted to radicalism while a student, who would join a circle and, during his lifetime as his views changed, proceed from one circle to another, often via prison. Thus circles which were almost unknown to anybody, or which due to arrests or dissension had a brief existence, could nevertheless be influential in moulding or changing the views of those who passed through them. Most Populists were against violence on principle. But the supposed need for an early revolution did persuade many to accept violence as a temporary necessity. Non-violence increasingly seemed to be a dead-end; opening the eyes of the ignorant masses was a slow process and, it seemed, would not be accomplished before the last propagandist died in gaol. Savage penalties imposed on young idealists whose only crime was to express their views in public predisposed more and more Populists to accept violence as a last resort. Violence was a reflection of weakness as was, essentially, the violence practised by the government. The terrorism of the revolutionaries appears understandable but counterproductive. The reason most frequently given for this conclusion is that Alexander was on the point of introducing the beginning of a constitution at the time he was assassinated. But this presupposes that the reforms would have developed in the way the optimists expected, which seems doubtful. However, terrorism produced several other negative results. It alienated that part of the public which accepted the criticisms made by the Populists but could not tolerate their methods. It was excessively expensive in terms of money (which was never plentiful) and also in terms of personnel; almost every terroristic act was followed by a wave of arrests, and it was the outstanding members who tended to be caught first. While achieving nothing in the long run, this expenditure of money and members held back the less dramatic but less unpromising propaganda work among the people.

Although in 1917 the heirs of the Populists, the Socialist Revolutionaries, failed to exploit their potential strength, it is wrong to belittle the movement simply because it never gained power. It was the Populists who made a start in developing the political consciousness of ordinary people. Moreover, their actions inspired, and their ideological discussions informed, later generations of revolutionaries, including the marxists. Above all, those Populists who distrusted western industrial society may have been right. As Peter the Great had discovered, and as subsequent tsarist and Soviet governments would discover, the Russian masses did not relish westernization, especially when the fruits of westernization were not immediately apparent. Yet western modes of production to be fully effective required western attitudes to life and work.[5] For underdeveloped countries the westernization of technique is relatively easy, but imposed westernization of culture is difficult and perilous because it threatens the soul of a nation.

Alexander III and his ministers

Because his reign seemed repressive and unimaginative, Alexander III is also regarded as repressive and unimaginative. This is adequate as a generalization but may be somewhat less than fair. As always, the execution of the tsar's will was coloured by the views and prejudices of the bureaucracy, while policies themselves were distorted by inter-ministerial (and inter-minister) wrangling. His suspicion of liberalism may have come largely

---

[5] See p. 316 for some concrete examples.

from his education, but he had, after all, seen how his father's reforms had been followed by terrorism. However, his intellect was far from scintillating, although this judgement has to take into account the alcoholic fog in which Alexander seems to have done most of his ruminating. Nobody denied his honesty, nor his loyalty to subordinates. His hatred of war aroused mixed feelings; it may have been at the root of Alexander's growing preference for the views of the finance ministry against those of the war ministry and therefore a factor in Russia's economic development. But war ministers did not see it that way. Alexander had actually served as a wartime officer. In the Russo-Turkish War he commanded 70,000 men in battle and knew what a battlefield really looked, sounded, and smelt like. Perhaps because of his experience, unlike other tsars he loathed military pomp and was adept at finding reasons to miss parades. One of his first acts, prompted by his adviser Pobedonostsev, was to reject the constitutional proposals which his father had been ready to introduce. This rejection, and Pobedonostsev's apparent dominance, was followed by the resignations of the more progressive Loris-Melikov and Dmitri Milyutin. The reign was notable for the persecution of national and religious minorities and the partial reversal of several promising reforms developed during the reign of Alexander II. However, Alexander III's administration has been credited with two successes: it kept Russia out of war, and it helped industrial development. The first achievement is perhaps over-praised; after all, Alexander only reigned thirteen years, and moreover he laid the foundations of the Russo-Japanese War. His achievement of a French alliance certainly changed the international situation, but not necessarily for the better. More sustainable is the economic achievement of Alexander's minister Bunge. As finance minister (1881–6) and chairman of the Committee of Ministers (1887–95), Bunge helped several industries by tariff protection and railway building, established the factory inspectorate, reduced peasants' redemption payments, established the Peasant Land Bank to help peasants buy additional land from the nobles, abolished poll-tax, and envisaged a universal income tax.

The finance minister from 1892 was Witte, one of tsarist Russia's most notable ministers. The son of an official and of Germanic ancestry, Witte had graduated from Odessa University and soon entered the administration of a then-private railway company. He appears to have attracted Alexander III's attention by indiscreetly warning other railway officials, despite the Tsar's displeasure, that their timetables for the imperial train were likely to break the imperial neck. In a subsequent derailment (1888), caused by excessive speed, Alexander was unhurt, and in 1892 Witte became minister of transport. The same year he was promoted to minister of finance. During his eleven years in this office he developed the expansionist economic policies favoured by Bunge. Large-scale railway construction, more protectionist tariffs, the securing of foreign capital, and high taxation of the peasantry were his chosen methods of fostering home industry. Alexander had great faith in his advice, and so had foreign investors after he succeeded in elevating the rouble to the Gold Standard. Nicholas II had less confidence in him, and dismissed him in 1903, although he felt obliged to rely on him as prime minister in the critical year of 1905. Bunge and Witte were Alexander's best advisers but unfortunately, outside economic affairs, the Tsar was most influenced by Pobedonostsev.

Pobedonostsev's published works on Russian law and acquaintance with the right people had earned him appointment as tutor to the heir in 1865. Earlier, he had helped in the preparations for the 1864 Judicial Reforms, but this was his last participation in a liberal endeavour; by 1873 he was condemning the jury system and had become a complete though intelligent reactionary. In the sixties he gained great influence over his pupil Alexander. The latter was far from brilliant and therefore tended to respect the judgement of those who appeared to speak with intellectual authority. Pobedonostsev began to fear that the future tsar was too inclined towards westernism and liberalism, but soon his prescribed reading changed Alexander's outlook. During the Russo-Turkish War, pupil and teacher became very close, so that long before the former became Alexander III, Pobedonostsev was his closest adviser. This was unfortunate for Russia because Pobedonostsev, although he had abandoned his erstwhile Panslavist fervour, remained reactionary and was inflexibly devoted to the official Orthodox Church. Since Pobedonostsev was not only tutor and adviser to Alexander III, but later to Nicholas II, he was able to ensure that just when Russia needed continuing reform, the next two tsars would be implacably against change and, like Pobedonostsev, devoted to the principles of Autocracy, Russianism, and Orthodoxy. One year before the assassination of Alexander II, Pobedonostsev was appointed Over Procurator of the Holy Synod. This was on the recommendation of Loris-Melikov, whose views were very different from those of Pobedonostsev. Loris-Melikov had calculated that this appointment would gain him the favour of conservative and religious circles which otherwise would have resisted the new set of reforms which were being prepared. He also believed that Pobedonostsev would be less dangerous in this position, but was proved wrong; the Over Procurator not only had influence in the Church (which in turn influenced the population), but also was concerned with such matters as education and social welfare. Moreover, Pobedonostsev enhanced the importance of his office by persuading the Tsar to give it

ministerial status, enabling him to participate in the Committee of Ministers. Pobedonostsev's earlier work in the Senate had taught him about the
inefficiency of the bureaucracy, and it was this experience which led him to
advocate government by a small body of well-informed and intelligent
men surrounding the Tsar. He had no sympathy for democracy, which he
termed 'the biggest lie of our time'. Pobedonostsev not only desired that all
citizens of the Empire should become Orthodox Christians but also
believed that the non-Orthodox must inevitably be disloyal. This attitude,
that anybody who is different is necessarily hostile, was demonstrated in
other actions, and was often a self-fulfilling allegation: Pobedonostsev
treated loyal non-conformists so badly that they did become hostile to
Russia, Orthodoxy and Autocracy. He died in 1907, having placed the
regime firmly on the rails which would lead to 1917. In his last decade he
was less influential for, in attacking the Lutherans of the Baltic provinces,
he aroused powerful and influential enemies who succeeded in reducing
the trust which Nicholas II felt for his former tutor.

The minorities

Non-Great-Russian minorities accounted for more than half of the
Empire's population.[6] They differed from the Great Russians not only in
geographical location, but in language and often in religion. To some
extent all had been subject to a degree of russification, but until the reign
of Alexander III they had, in the main, retained their privileges and
individuality. But after 1881 all this changed, and russification remained
the policy of the government up to 1917. This implied a change in the
ideology of the Empire; hitherto it had been sufficient for a non-Russian to
show loyalty to the autocrat, but now a recognition of the leading role of
the Great Russians was also required of loyal citizens. This change in
attitude was probably a combination of several factors. First there was the
old love of standardization on the part of the bureaucracy. The important
civil servants by the end of the century were still drawn mainly from the
nobility, but they tended to have less contact than their predecessors with
country life, with its more tolerant attitude to individualism; devotion to
official business had given an official shape to their minds. Then there were
the dignitaries of the Orthodox Church. These had always sought the
conversion of the non-Orthodox, both Christian and non-Christian, but in
Pobedonostsev they had found a powerful supporter. The war ministry,
too, was in favour of russification, partly in the interests of a good military-
style standardization, and partly because of the presumed security risk

---

[6]   55 per cent, according to the 1897 Census.

posed by the non-Russian borderland areas. By this time, too, many Slavophils had degenerated to a condition in which they no longer simply believed in the superiority of the Slavs and the Orthodox Church, but insisted that the Great Russians had a duty to impose their virtues on those brother Slavs who had not yet seen the light.

The Russian minorities could be divided into three groups: the mainly loyal, the mainly disloyal, and the Jews. The loyal minorities, those in which a majority of the population was in favour of the relationship with the Russians and of carrying out the obligations imposed by such a relationship, included the Finns, the Baltic Germans, and the Armenians. These nationalities, however, were treated just as insensitively as were the potentially disloyal Ukrainians and Tartars, and the actually disloyal Poles. Thus by 1917 the Finns in particular, the Armenians, and some of the Baltic Germans had been driven into opposition to St. Petersburg. In terms of security, russification only weakened the Empire.

In Poland, russification had intensified earlier than elsewhere, following the abortive 1863 revolt. The Warsaw educational district was absorbed into the Russian system, and in 1869 Warsaw University was closed, to re-appear as a genuine university only during the German occupation of 1915. Under Alexander III the Polish language was prohibited as a language of instruction in all institutions, including primary schools, except for Polish language and scripture courses. Only for a few months was this prohibition lifted, as a temporary concession after the 1905 disturbances in Poland. The state service was more and more reserved for Russians, although some Poles found insecure positions in the bureaucracy outside Poland. When the Warsaw–Vienna railway was nationalized, Polish executives and engineers were replaced by Russians, and the Polish railwaymen retained had to perform their duties, like announcing train departures, in Russian only, even though they themselves and perhaps all the passengers were unfamiliar with that language. With increasing industrialization and russification, Polish society was changing rapidly. Poles predominated in the professions and among the workers and peasants, but the bulk of the civil servants were Russian, while in commerce Jews and foreigners were more numerous than Poles. The old Polish landowning class still existed, but was not prospering. With rapid social change and urban growth there came a movement towards socialism, and this inspired a majority of the revolutionary groups seeking eventual independence from Russia. But there were other socialists who advocated continued ties with Russia. This split, together with the division of Poland between Russia, Austria, and Germany, was the main reason why there was a multiplicity of non-cooperating revolutionary groups in Poland. The revolutionaries achieved

nothing. Many were arrested and executed. Others, including the socialist
Pilsudski, were exiled to Siberia. But in 1914 Poles were still Poles. A
famous general expressed the dislike felt by an influential section of Russian society towards not only the Poles, but Finns and other 'privileged'
peoples of the Russian Empire:

I do not refer to those Poles who have begun to regard Russia as their Motherland, and the Russian language as their mother tongue; I refer to those Poles who
inside Russia talk loudly, demonstratively, in Polish, even in official relationships,
in buffets, and on railway platforms . . . Accepting this kind of Pole in the Russian
railway service and in judicial or other departments is a big mistake. We have already paid for our trust in such Poles, notably on the Transcaucasus Railway and
other lines in 1905.[7]

In the Ukraine the situation was somewhat similar to Poland, except
that the nationalist movement was much weaker; probably a majority of
the Ukrainian people were not greatly interested in the concept of an
independent Ukrainian nation. There had been an influx of Russian and
other non-Ukrainian people into this area, and many of them were in key
positions; the local officials, for example, were mainly Russian. On the
other hand repression and russification were less intense, repression being
directed only at the comparatively small intelligentsia, which included
most of the nationalist movement.

Although in Central Asia there was little overt russification, in the
Tartar areas of Russia the Orthodox Church carried on an intense and
mainly forcible conversion campaign. By the end of the century well over
100,000 Tartars had become Christian. However, a large number, perhaps
one-third, of these relapsed and, moreover, Moslem missionaries were
simultaneously and less obtrusively converting neighbouring Christian
peoples to Islam. Among the Crimean Tartars there also developed a strong
and mainly secular nationalist movement. This, devoted to the regenera-
tion and eventual union of the Turkic peoples, published its own newspaper and soon gained adherents among the Tartars in other parts of
Russia. In 1905 an All-Russia Moslem League was established. After the
1905 Rebellion Moslem members of the Dumas had a forum in which to
voice their complaints of the way Russian officials and Orthodox clergy
put pressure on the Tartars and other Moslems, and of the official encouragement of Russian settlement in Central Asia and traditional Tartar
areas, in many of which Russians had become a majority. But these
remonstrations had no result; by 1914 the Moslem leaders were looking to
Turkey as a source of inspiration, while the Moslem masses, who if left

    [7] A. Kuropatkin, *Rossiya dlya russkikh* (1910), III, 73.

alone would have been loyal subjects, were becoming more and more resentful of Russian domination.

The situation in Armenia was complex. The Armenian nation was divided by the Russo-Turkish frontier, and those Armenians inside the Russian Empire considered themselves lucky and did what they could to help their compatriots, who from time to time were massacred by the Turks. The Russian government in the early twentieth century was anxious to improve relations with Turkey, and was embarrassed by the anti-Turkish activities of its Armenian citizens. Accordingly it encouraged the Tartar neighbours of the Armenians to attack the latter, and for several years there were civil disturbances, sometimes engineered and usually encouraged by the Russian authorities, in which Tartars would beat up, loot, and kill their traditional Armenian enemies. It was only the appointment of a relatively wise governor, who realized that one day the Armenians might be needed in a new war against Turkey, that prevented this nation turning completely against the Russian regime by 1914. However, as in neighbouring Georgia, there were many revolutionaries among the townspeople.

In Georgia, too, fear of the Turks was a strong factor in the acceptance by the local population of Russian domination. Yet here again, the unholy alliance between the Russian administration, the Russian Church, and the landowning class transformed what might have been a loyal domain into a hostile and strongly revolutionary nation. The serfs of Georgia on various pretexts had not been truly emancipated in 1861, as had the Russian serfs. This naturally had led to discontent, which would manifest itself in the initial success of the Georgian rebels in 1905. The Georgian Orthodox Church was alienated by the claim of the Russian Orthodox Church to supervise its affairs. After Russian troops were called in by the Russian Orthodox to chastise the local clergy, there was an outbreak of ecclesiastical assassination, in which church dignitaries of both persuasions were the victims and the instigators. Although on the eve of the Great War the peasants received more land and administration became wiser, Georgia was one of the least loyal and most revolutionary parts of the Empire.

Finland, like Poland, was becoming an industrial nation in the last half of the century. When Finnish products began to compete in Russian markets, new arguments were provided for those Russians who resented the continued existence of so-called privileged minorities living under the Tsar's protection. Not only were tariff barriers raised against Finnish products but at the turn of the century, under the auspices of Governor Bobrikov, various standardizing and russianizing measures were introduced, despite the Finns' contention that, under the terms offered by Alexander I at the time of annexation, they were legally entitled to their privileges. Hitherto,

Finns had been virtually free from military service, but now they were compelled to serve on terms more onerous than those of the Russian conscripts. The Finnish post office, and later the railways, became part of the Russian system. Russian laws were given precedence over laws passed by the Finnish Diet. Russian officials had to be brought in to replace recalcitrant Finns. Russian became an official language of the administration. In 1903 Bobrikov suspended the Finnish constitution and in 1904 he was assassinated by a Finnish revolutionary. After the 1905 Rebellion the government was forced to make some concessions; the conscription law was rescinded and a new Diet established. The latter, in which the Social Democrats were the largest but not predominating party, was remarkable at the time because it was elected on a franchise which included female suffrage. But the new situation was not regarded as permanent by either the Finnish revolutionaries or the Russian nationalists. The Russian prime minister Stolypin, in particular, was determined to return Finland to what he considered its original and natural position, that of a Russian province. With the support of Russian nationalists and the unimpressive remnants of the Slavophil movement, and with the interesting slogan 'Russia for the Russians', the government in 1908 embarked on a new campaign to repress 'the separatists and traitors' of Finland. The Diet's powers were reduced, it was dissolved, re-elected, dissolved and re-elected again, then abolished. Russian police were introduced, partly to limit the refuge which Finland provided for Russian revolutionaries hard-pressed in their own country. By 1914 there were very few Finns who openly advocated maintenance of ties with Russia.

In the Baltic provinces, the Russian government again failed to win the support of the local population. Nicholas I and Alexander II had resisted the campaign waged by certain Slavophils to russianize these areas, but with the ascendancy of Pobedonostsev the russifiers had their opportunity. With the encouragement of Pobedonostsev, the Orthodox Church, helped by government funds, campaigned against the local Lutheran church. In Riga a huge Orthodox cathedral was erected, an object of resentment for most of the inhabitants. In the schools Russian replaced German, the University of Dorpat became the University of Yuriev (Yuriev being the Russian name of Dorpat) and its student body was no longer primarily German but mainly Russian. But while the German upper class was thus humiliated, the native lower classes were not appreciative, even though they disliked the Germans. For them it was a case of one alien dominating class replacing another. At this time native Estonians and Latvians were beginning to settle in the towns, and from this new class there emerged nationalist and revolutionary groups. After the shock of 1905 the pressure on the Germans was relaxed, for they had remained mainly loyal in that year. In neighbouring Lithuania the situation was less acute; there the Polish ruling class was not quite so obnoxious to the local inhabitants, and after the stern 'pacification' following the Lithuanians' participation in the 1863 Polish Rebellion, this area gave little trouble.

The Jews in Russia

When Alexander III became tsar there were about five million Jews in the Empire. They were officially regarded as an eccentric and undesirable part of the population. In 1835 new legislation had clarified the various laws and ordinances relating to them. The Pale, that area in which Jews were allowed to settle, was redefined; henceforth it consisted of Lithuania, Poland, the south-western provinces (including the Ukraine), and White Russia. In most of these areas Jews were not allowed to live in rural localities, and a few cities were also prohibited. In the Baltic provinces old settlers could remain but no Jews could enter as new settlers. Also, no Jews were permitted to settle along the western frontier. Other restrictions introduced or confirmed at this time were the prohibition against building synagogues close to Orthodox churches, on Jews employing Christian servants, and on the use of Hebrew in public documents. In the first part of Alexander II's reign, some concessions were made to the 'useful' Jews. Jewish merchants of the First Guild (those paying more than 1,000 roubles in taxes each year) were allowed to trade and reside anywhere in the Empire, university graduates had the same right and could henceforth enter government service, while incorporated artisans could obtain documents allowing them to work and live outside the Pale. But after the Polish Rebellion of 1863 (blamed in some quarters on the Jews), liberalization was halted. The rebellion intensified Russian nationalism and renewed anti-semitism followed naturally. Influential newspapers forgot their sympathy for the Jews, anti-semitic literature of both intellectual and obscene content appeared. One book, forecasting a Jewish take-over of the Empire and the enslavement of its Christian population, was printed at state expense and distributed to government offices. Many Jewish schools were closed. The reorganization of town government in 1870 limited the participation of Jewish citizens; no Jew could become mayor, and Jewish representation on town councils could nowhere exceed one-third of the total.

It was in the reigns of Alexander III and his son Nicholas II that the situation of the Jews changed from uncomfortable to unbearable. In those thirty-six years, officially sponsored anti-semitic hooliganism and brutality not only shocked the outside world, but brought forth the protests of foreign governments. The murder of Alexander II in 1881 was ascribed in some quarters to the Jews, and scarcely had the late Tsar expired before the first of a series of *pogroms* was launched against them. Essentially, a *pogrom* consisted of the assembly of a mob which would throng into the Jewish parts of a town, break into houses and shops, to loot, beat, rape, burn and frequently kill the inhabitants. Local police, and even sometimes the local troops, seemed reluctant to intervene except against those Jews who were successfully defending themselves. In the 1881 disturbances, the minister of the interior was still Loris-Melikov, who was not the kind of man to instigate this sort of action. Yet the 1881 *pogroms* were well organized, with bands of hooligans brought in by train, well-primed with alcohol and anti-semitic indoctrination. Local authorities knew of planned *pogroms* in advance, and made preparations. It would seem that the force behind these disturbances was the Holy League, consisting of extreme nationalists and anti-semites. Pobedonostsev was a supporter of this organization, and many high and middling officials were members. When Loris-Melikov was replaced by Ignatiev, a member of the Holy League, these 'spontaneous demonstrations of an outraged people' were intensified. However, it seems possible that the Tsar disapproved of this unseemly way of dealing with the Jews. Ignatiev was soon replaced by Dmitri Tolstoy at the ministry of the interior. Tolstoy, though disliking the Jews, certainly did not favour brutal civic disturbances, and for a time the *pogroms* ceased.

There were other ways to deal with the Jews, even after the dismissal of Ignatiev and the banning of the Holy League. Just before his departure, Ignatiev had issued what were called Temporary Regulations, which in fact lasted until 1917. Among the provisions of these was a ban on new Jewish settlers in all rural areas of the *Pale*, a ban on Jews either owning or managing land, buildings and farms outside the towns of the *Pale*, and a ban on Jewish trade on Christian holidays, including Sundays. Under cover of the latter regulation, as was no doubt anticipated, Jewish traders lost business to their Christian competitors, because they henceforth closed on both Christian and Jewish holidays. Many Jewish businesses had to be sold at giveaway prices in the countryside because they had become illegal, and many Jewish settlers were turned out of their homes. It sometimes happened that a Jew who had made a trip outside his own locality would on his return be defined as a 'new settler' and ejected; in 1905 this even happened to wounded Jewish soldiers returning from the Manchurian front. Those Jews of the upper category who resided outside the *Pale* were harassed, and the thousands of Jews who were illegal residents were expelled, even though hitherto their presence had been ignored. Finally, in 1891, the Governor-General of Moscow (Grand Duke Sergei) celebrated

Passover by issuing an Edict of Expulsion which announced the ejection of legal as well as illegal Jewish residents. This edict was itself of doubtful legality, for it revoked an 1865 law, but was signed by the Tsar on present-ation by the minister of the interior. Legal residents were given a few months grace to settle their affairs, offering bargain sales of possessions and businesses to Muscovite Christians, and glorious opportunities for the police to gather bribes in exchange for time extensions. For the illegal or semi-legal residents, execution of the order was immediate and brutal. Other measures taken during the reign of Alexander III were the limitation of Jewish university students to 10 per cent of the total enrolment in universities within the *Pale*, 5 per cent outside, and 3 per cent at Moscow and St. Petersburg Universities; parallel limitations on gymnasium entries; the limitation to 5 per cent of Jewish military surgeons in the army be-cause, as the official order alleged, of their bad effect on hygiene.

The Jewish reaction was mass emigration, especially to the USA and South America, and a strengthening of the Zionist movement. More im-portant, with the Jews forming an urban and oppressed community it was natural that they should be attracted to the socialist and revolutionary parties. Thanks to official policy, the Jews provided a strong flow of ideal recruits for the revolutionaries: intelligent types hardened by circumstance and having nothing to lose. In 1897 the Jews' own social democratic *Bund* (union) was formed.

Under Nicholas II there was no likelihood of improvement. Pobedonostsev remained the Tsar's spiritual adviser, and Nicholas had imbibed his tutor's anti-semitism. It is probably true that, whereas Alexander III merely strongly disapproved of Jews, Nicholas had a well-entrenched hatred of them. Sensing this, many provincial officials were encouraged to take actions which Nicholas would have found excessive. *Pogroms* began again on a large scale, and existing restrictions were tightened. As in most fields of Russian official life, the application of anti-semitic laws and policies was never absolute or complete; there were some officials, high and low, who were ashamed of the government's policy and would make exceptions wherever possible, and there were others who would make the same con-cessions for a bribe. Thus in reality there were usually Jews illegally resident outside the Pale, and Jewish students in excess of the legal propor-tion. Under Nicholas, however, such exceptions were rarer.

Pogroms, which typically took place as part of the Christian Easter celebrations, reached a new peak in the Kishinev outbreak of April 1903. The ground was laid for this by a local newspaper which for several weeks printed fantastic and frequently obscene anti-semitic stories. It was prob-ably sanctioned by Plehve, the minister of the interior who, though himself no great anti-semite, was anxious to please the Tsar. The army was slow to respond, possibly because the district commander was an avowed anti-semite but also because the police and army commanders were at logger-heads. There were about fifty deaths and hundreds of injuries in the two days of the outbreak. It caused an outcry not only in Britain and the USA, but in Russia itself, with Leo Tolstoy openly accusing the government of complicity. In 1905, when the war against Japan was going badly, there were fresh outbreaks, and these were intensified after the 1905 Rebellion, in which Jews took a prominent part. In October a *pogrom* was organized, with the assistance of the local police, at Odessa. Probably about 500 lives were lost in this, which lasted four days. Further outrages followed in later years, despite the efforts of many members of the Duma to investigate them. Moreover, there were mass executions of Jews by the army, during the 'pacification' of the Baltic states and Lithuania.

It was at this time that a new organization, similar to the old Holy League, was formed to unite anti-semites and nationalists for propaganda and *pogrom* work. This was the so-called Black Hundred, and it seems that the Tsar himself patronized this. It was the Black Hundred which estab-lished in 1905 the Union of the Russian People, a political organization in many ways a precursor of subsequent fascist parties and which was in-tended to be the overt instrument of the movement. In 1908 Nicholas re-ceived a delegation of the Union and agreed with a proposal to allow army chaplains and officers to join right-wing organizations; on this occasion Nicholas's much-condemned readiness to change his mind had positive results, for he soon backtracked in response to a war ministry presentation about the non-political status of officers. In fact, inside the army there was, as usual, a great variation of attitudes. On balance the war ministry, at least after 1905, favoured opening the officer corps to Jews, but the engin-eer generals were horrified by the idea of Jews or Poles[8] becoming officers, whereas the artillery strongly welcomed the proposal.

The reputation of the Empire abroad was badly damaged by its anti-semitism, especially in the United States. Reacting to the *pogroms* which followed the assassination of Alexander II, Congress passed a joint resolu-tion, nicely pointed:

To request His Imperial Majesty to exercise his august power . . . to protect the Jewish subjects from the violence of their enemies and to extend to them his protec-tion as the late lamented sovereign, his father, did over the Christians of Bulgaria at a time when said Christians had been the victims of a like persecution.[9]

---

[8] Nationalists and aggressive pan-slavists usually put Jews and Poles at the top of their list of undesirables. As for Polish Jews . . .

[9] *Congressional Record*, 47th Congress, HR Res. 151, 1647.

In 1911 the USA terminated the commercial treaty with Russia. The immediate cause of this was that foreign Jews, unlike other foreigners, had no clear right to visit and reside in Russia; thus there had been discrimination against Jewish US citizens. The termination caused a great stir in St. Petersburg. The administration explained that if American Jews were given new rights, then Jews of other nations would demand the same treatment (which would enable them to settle in Russia outside the *Pale*) This nightmare vision of the world's Jews clamouring to settle in Russia did not seem very convincing, except perhaps to right-wing members of the Duma, who accused the American press, 'almost entirely owned or controlled by Jews', of trying to stir up hatred against Russia.

In 1913, the Beilis Case persuaded many that the tsarist administration was incorrigible. Beilis, a young Jew, was accused of murdering a child in order to obtain Christian blood for one of those totally secret rituals which everyone knew about. Although the defendant was eventually acquitted both in trial and re-trial, the re-trial court implied in its judgement that Jews, unknown, had indeed committed the crime, and for a dark purpose. The bureaucracy's obsessive urge to have Beilis found guilty was demonstrated by pressure applied to lawyers and judges, harassment of newspapers reporting the case, and the ministry of justice's frantic search for an 'expert' who would testify that Jews did use Christian blood in certain rituals.

When the war started in 1914, some of the Cossack troops went into immediate action against Jews, sometimes alleging that they were German spies and sometimes for no stated reason. Acts of heroism by Jews in the Russian army tended to be uncelebrated.

6. *Russia in Asia*

Russia in Central Asia

RUSSIAN interest in Asia dates back to at least 1469, when Nikitin visited India and wrote an account of the wonders he encountered. In the next century an Englishman employed by the tsar visited Central Asia, and this was followed by the dispatch of emissaries to the various khanates of the region. Peter the Great sent expeditions to the Kazakh steppelands and to the khanate of Khiva. The latter expedition was instructed to steal the Amu-Darya river by diverting it into the Caspian Sea, but was massacred before it could achieve this. By 1800 the Kazakh nomads had acknowledged Russian sovereignty but this was hardly felt, even though Russian forts were maintained in the steppes. More alarming to the natives were the independent Cossacks who settled in the vicinity of those forts.

Alexander I decided to enforce his nominal rights over the Kazakhs. Russian military government with mainly Russian administrators was imposed. The Kazakhs were not allowed to grow crops, thus giving the Cossacks a monopoly in grain production. These measures, plus the burden of taxes, caused a number of revolts and an expansion of Russian territory as rebels were pursued into non-Russian lands. Throughout the century, campaign followed campaign as the Russians established a new frontier, built forts, pushed on to make those forts less vulnerable, and again established a new frontier. There were bigger campaigns in the reign of Alexander II, during which the last three major khanates were defeated. These conquests added big Moslem cities like Tashkent and Samarkand to the Russian Empire (see map, p. 597). The major part of this huge territory became the new Russian province of Turkestan, the defeated khans becoming vassals of the Tsar. The building of the Trans-Caspian Railway eastwards from the Caspian confirmed the Russian possession of yet more territory. As Russian influence neared the Himalayas, there was disquiet in London, which was not wholly unjustified.

Although it was the government's intention to interfere as little as possible with the lives of the original inhabitants, this could not be reconciled with the intended development of the new territories. In agriculture there was an upheaval after a new direct railway brought Moscow to within three weeks of Tashkent by freight train. This enabled existing cotton cultivation to expand rapidly, supplying the textile industries of European Russia. The region became dependent on outside sources for its grain but, on the whole, the shift was beneficial, especially after the government embarked on a big irrigation programme. Much more serious in its effect was the Russian immigration. To find land for peasants arriving from European Russia, the original inhabitants were dispossessed, often by military force (the official euphemism was that the land was 'surplus'; the original owners did not really need it). Expropriation became more and more common as immigration increased, especially after Stolypin in 1910 decided that the region was ideal for his programme to relieve land hunger in European Russia. Although it is probably true that the new settlers used the land more efficiently, this was little consolation for the dispossessed who, typically, moved to less desirable land or to the towns. It was this virtual expulsion of the natives by the Russians which was, and by some accounts still is, the prime grievance of the Moslems of Russian Central Asia. When in 1916 the government decided to kill a number of birds with one stone and began to conscript the Moslems for labour service, the resentment exploded. There was a big but little-reported rebellion in which many thousands of lives were lost; it was still in progress when the 1917 Revolution started.

The settlement of Siberia

Not long after Ivan the Terrible captured the Tartar city of Kazan in 1552, Russian freebooters acting in the Tsar's name began to penetrate beyond the Urals. The big lure was furs, but the prospect of adding territory in the east was also an incentive. The pioneers, who later included Cossacks and regular soldiers, used the rivers as far as possible, constructing wooden forts at key points along them. Local tribes sometimes resisted, but in the long run were subdued and subjected to tribute, usually in the form of so many skins per year, the sable being especially sought. Tyumen, later an important Siberian town, was the first permanent settlement, being founded in 1586. Yakutsk was reached in 1637, and two years later a band of Cossacks reached the sea. Regular settlers were not far behind although, in contrast to the settlement of the American west, there was a generous sprinkling of state employees among the new inhabitants. Fur traders predominated, but the tsars sent administrators and soldiers to guard the interests of the state. Later, the fur traders were joined by cultivators, peasants coming east to seek freedom and land. In the eighteenth century, Russia's explorers discovered the Bering Strait and established settlements in Alaska, Oregon, and California. Later, there were expeditions to Japan and to Hawaii. With the foundation of the Russian America Company it seemed that the Pacific might well become a Russian lake.

In general, the Russians refrained from turning southwards to annex territory in which the Chinese Empire had an interest. Russian penetration into the Amur Valley had earlier led to conflict between the two empires, regulated by the Treaty of Nerchinsk in 1689; in this the Russians agreed to leave and to recognize a frontier more to the north. But in the mid-nineteenth century, when China was weakened by the Opium War and when her territory was being divided by the powers into spheres of influence, Russia took advantage of the situation and forced on China a series of new treaties. The first of these, the Aigun 'Treaty of Friendship' in 1858 and the Peking Treaty of 1860, transferred extensive territories from China to Russia, including the northern shore of the Amur and the Maritime Province east of the Ussuri River. It was in this latter acquisition that Russia established her new naval base of Vladivostok. The new territory also meant that Russia henceforth had a frontier with Korea. In 1875 Russia acquired Sakhalin from an unwilling Japan.

Although Russian expansion in the east at this time was inspired by a desire for expansion as such, and a desire for military and commercial advantage, there were several nobler reasons which received more publicity. The Slavophils, and especially those who had progressed to Panslavism, emphasized the civilizing role which God had prescribed for the Russian people in the Orient. Others began to claim that Russia was indeed an Asian nation and therefore had much more moral right than the western powers to impose itself in Asia. A world-famous Russian professor of international law justified the breach of treaties with the assertion that, when dealing with uncivilized peoples, human rights could not be considered as having their usual force. The Russian advance was frequently referred to as the liberation of subject peoples from the Chinese. Under Alexander III Russian officials began to dream not only of Manchuria and Korea, but also an eventual conquest of the moribund Chinese Empire and even the annexation of India. The more level-headed, such as Witte, were more cautious but nevertheless favoured a strong policy in the east, largely because the latter might provide that mass market which Russian industry so obviously needed. Alexander's eastern policy had two prerequisites, a strong navy in the Pacific and a railway to supply Russian Far Eastern forces. These he set out to achieve.

Russian naval policy

In the eighties Russia was the fifth largest naval power in terms of battle-ships, but probably ranked lower in terms of effectiveness, for her battle-ships were small, her ports iced-up for several months each year, and her two fleets were separated. On the other hand, she led the world in torpedo craft. The main preoccupation of her navy was the protection of cities like St. Petersburg and Odessa from seaborne attack, and her myriads of small torpedo boats seemed a cheap way to achieve this. But although torpedo boats might defend the capital, they were of no account in an expansive foreign policy; it was battleships and bases which were needed. Just before his death Alexander II had sanctioned a new naval programme aimed at making Russia a real naval power. As approved by his successor in 1882, this programme covered twenty years and anticipated an expenditure of eighteen million pounds sterling (battleships at that time cost from half a million pounds apiece). By the late eighties new ironclads built under this programme were joining the navy, although their impact was diluted be-cause Russia, unlike the other powers, had to divide her ships between two fleets which could not be united; by treaty her ships could not move freely to or from the Black Sea.

The 1882 programme had stipulated that the hulls of the new ships should be built in Russia (engines continued to be imported, mainly from Scotland, and guns were usually Russian-made but of foreign design). Complete self-sufficiency in shipbuilding was never attained, but the ship-yards of St. Petersburg expanded and were kept busy. Russian-built ships cost about one-third more than imports, and took longer to build. The ships were enclosed in enormous barns so that work could continue in the winter, but a hull which was not launched in the autumn had to wait six months for the thaw; the cruiser *Avrora*, which fired a famous shot in the 1917 Revolution, took six years to build. In 1898 a follow-on construction programme reflected increasing tension in the Far East and envisaged an expenditure of £51 m. over the period 1898–1904; eight new battleships with attendant cruisers and destroyers were to be built so that Russia would remain the world's third naval power.

After the Russo-Japanese war it was often said that Russian warships were of inferior design and construction, that Russian officers were incom-petent, and that Russian sailors were dull. To some extent these criticisms could have been applied to any of the world's navies, and the Russian navy was not glaringly bad by the standards of that time. In some respects the Russian navy led the world; for example, in mine and torpedo warfare, in the design of armour-piercing shells, and in the application of oil fuel. In the adoption of the watertube boiler, Russia was second only to France. As for her officers, there were indeed very many bad ones and some were corrupt. The Sevastopol trial of 1900 revealed that high officers of the Black Sea fleet had been bribed by contractors to accept inferior supplies for their ships at superior prices, and this trial probably only revealed the tip of an iceberg. It is true also that there were many autocratic denizens of the quarterdeck whom a speck of dust would render apoplectic, but who were not in the least interested in accurate gunnery. But as in other navies, this type was slowly dying out. As for the sailors, these were mainly conscripts, and they had plenty of cause of dissatisfaction. They were bawled at rather than instructed, they were badly fed, during their seven-year active service they were not allowed to marry or to go home, and they had scant chance of promotion. Training was a slow process because the ships were activated only during the summer; ice prevented ship movements in winter, both in the Baltic base of Kronstadt and the Black Sea base of Sevastopol. Thus for half their service the crews lived ashore in barracks. Towards the end of the century ships of the Baltic fleet were detached to form a Mediterranean squadron, much to the disgust of the British, and it was this squadron, and the Pacific Squadron, which provided the best training for officers and men. The Pacific Squadron had grown from the former Siberian detachment, based on Vladivostok. The latter port was also iced up in the winter, but the ships went south each year on long cruises. Before relations with Japan deteriorated, the Russian navy had a base near Nagasaki and here for a few months each year the ships would anchor and their officers settle ashore with temporary Japanese wives.

The Pacific Squadron was maintained with ships sent out on rotation from the Baltic. When war became more likely in the east the Baltic freeze-up became a serious problem, because if war broke out in November reinforcing ships could not be dispatched until April. This was why a new ice-free port was started at Libau, in Lithuania, in 1893. However, by the time it was completed the Russian navy, prompted by Admiral Makarov, had already acquired its first icebreaker. Vladivostok was also developed, being provided with a battleship-size dry dock in 1897, one year before the ice-free base at Port Arthur was acquired. The latter was not quite so valuable a prize as the Russian government imagined. It was separated from Vladivostok by 1,500 miles of sea, much of which was Japanese home waters. In a war against Japan it would be exceedingly difficult to unite the Vladivostok and Port Arthur forces.

Siberia as a planned economy

The great period for Russian railway-building was the last three decades of the nineteenth century, and the Trans-Siberian Railway can be regarded as the culmination of this period. It ran from Chelyabinsk in the Urals to Vladivostok, and at Chelyabinsk connected with lines to European Russia. It was a state enterprise, and was started in 1892, construction being carried on from both ends and in the middle at the same time.

The transport ministry had been making proposals for a railway-based development of Siberia since the 1870s, but had been consistently opposed by the finance ministry. The latter's wish to be the dominant influence in railway construction, daggers-drawn relationships between the ministers of the two rival bureaucracies, and the finance ministry's distrust of any proposal that might increase state indebtedness, all contributed to delay in approving the line. As so often in Russian history, there was also a conflict of nightmares; some dreamed of a Yellow Peril threatening underpopulated Siberia, others of an economically developed Siberia feeling strong enough to follow the example of Britain's American colonies. In the end, those who thought that economic development might be followed by a Siberian independence movement decided that development based on a railway planned, controlled, and operated from St. Petersburg could be a safe option.

Witte, railwayman, finance minister, and born manipulator, was well placed to convert the idea into reality. Persuading the astonished Alexander III to appoint his callow heir Nicholas as chairman of Witte's Siberian Railway Committee was a clever move. It assured royal enthusiasm for the project during two reigns, it gave the young Nicholas useful experience of decision-making, and, as so often with Witte's dabbling in appointments, gave the latter a colleague whose will was conveniently weak.

Once approval was given, construction proceeded fast to make the most of the warm months. Witte's overriding aim was to create a fact as soon as possible and engineering considerations, accounting, and honesty had lower priority. In the feverish atmosphere he created, sections were built before they were properly surveyed, green timber was used for track and bridges, costs consistently overran estimates, and bribery, speculation, and misappropriation were widespread even by Russian standards.

But the line was built. So far as western Siberia was concerned it had great economic advantages, but its eastern sections were through difficult and unproductive territory. In fact its entire eastern half could be regarded as simply a strategic railway intended to supply Russian forces in the Far East and to confirm and extend Russia's interest in that part of the world. This political aspect was emphasized when it was decided to take the final sections through Chinese Manchuria rather than over the longer but all-Russian route along the Amur River. The Chinese government was in no position to resist Russian requests, and leased a strip of land across Manchuria on which the Russians could build their railway and maintain troops. This line was built by a Russian-controlled and subsidized private company, the Chinese Eastern Railway, which made enormous losses. However, the consequent drain on the Treasury was considered well worth while, for not only did the Manchurian routing of the railway cut several hundred miles from the distance to Vladivostok, but it also promised to be an excellent first step towards acquiring more territory from the Chinese Empire. By 1904 rail transport between Europe and Vladivostok was a reality, even though Lake Baikal for a time was crossed by ferry. After the Russo-Japanese War, in which the Chinese Eastern Railway was shown to be vulnerable, the Amur line was started, to provide an all-Russian route. This was finished during the First World War, in the expectation of one day 'having another go' at Japan. The Trans-Siberian Railway had an enormous political effect although, at the time, the world was most impressed with the passenger service. By 1912 there were regular arrangements for round-the-world tours using the line, and its 'International' train with marble-tiled bathrooms and grand piano was world-famous, even though it only averaged about twenty m.p.h.

The building of the railway was not the beginning of economic development in Siberia. For decades previously enterprising peasants had been moving eastwards. Rural overpopulation in European Russia, expressing itself in frequent famine, caused many villages to dispatch a 'scout' to look for land across the Urals. If the scout returned safely (and often he did not) villagers might move to the land he had inspected and found good. But moving hundreds of miles over tracks and waterways entailed a high casualty rate; only about four-fifths of the migrants survived the journey. The railway project, largely through the influence of Witte, was regarded as only the most important part of a plan to transform the economy of Siberia through government planning and participation. As feeders for the railway, rivers were made suitable for navigation. Peasant scouts were given low rail fares, and land settlement was made easy. Government medical and sanitation points reduced the casualty rate to about 1 per cent. Schools, churches, and prisons were built in anticipation of needs. The government provided agronomists and encouraged co-operatives. The incoming peasants responded both to official encouragement and to the free atmosphere of Siberia. Siberia was, and remained, the least controlled part of Russia; there had never been serfdom there, and government officials tended to be less repressive. It was natural that the settlers would be the more enterprising peasants of European Russia, but nevertheless the speed with which they adopted new techniques surprised many who were familiar with the inertia of the typical Russian peasant. In the first decade of the century there were several years in which immigrants into Siberia (mainly western Siberia) exceeded a quarter of a million. By 1910 the railway served about ten million inhabitants. Although grain was grown, the new lands specialized in high-value products; by 1914 half the meat consumed in Moscow and St. Petersburg came from Siberia, while a fleet of white-painted refrigerator-car trains plied between Siberia and the ports with butter for the markets of England and Germany. For the benefit of the export trade, arctic ports were developed, served by Siberia's great north-flowing rivers. Other projects were under way in 1914, like the Turkestan Siberia Railway and the Yakutsk Highway, both completed by the Soviet government.

Given the centralized control, the breakneck speed of construction, the ramshackle result, and Witte's concept of Siberia as a planned economy, it is legitimate to regard the Trans-Siberian Railway as a precursor, even a dress rehearsal, for Stalin's industrialization of the 1930s. Many similarities can be noted, including Witte's use of convict labour to speed construction and reduce costs. This device was enthusiastically developed under Stalin, although there was a significant difference: under Witte good work was rewarded, whereas under Stalin bad work was punished.

The Russo-Japanese War

The accession of Nicholas II coincided with the Chinese-Japanese War. The basic cause of this was Japan's desire to expand her territory, or at least her influence, at the expense of China. The field of battle was Korea, which China regarded as her own, and the result was a Chinese defeat. The victors imposed a hard treaty which included the payment by China of a war indemnity and the cession to Japan of the Manchurian territory around Port Arthur. None of the other great powers welcomed this strengthening of the Japanese position, for they had their own ambitions in China. At the suggestion of St. Petersburg, France, Germany, and Russia diplomatically forced Japan to return Port Arthur to China. At the same time, in a bid to buy Chinese goodwill, Russia raised a loan in France to enable China to pay off her war indemnity. It was at this time that China agreed to the building of Russia's Chinese Eastern Railway across Manchuria, thus extending Russian influence in that region.

China's faith in Russian friendship was misplaced. In 1898, with Nicholas's foreknowledge, Germany occupied Kiaochow and other powers demanded their own fair share. Russia demanded the most; she leased Port Arthur and its peninsula and built a railway southwards from the Chinese Eastern Railway to link the latter with her new acquisition.

Port Arthur, ice-free, became a Russian naval base. This caused great indignation in Japan, where the forced relinquishment of Port Arthur after the Chinese-Japanese War still rankled. More humiliated than Japan was China, and this showed itself in the Boxer Rebellion of 1900. When the European legations were besieged in Pekin it was the Russians, with their garrisons and ships close at hand in Port Arthur, who did most in the raising of the siege. It was Russian troops who first broke into the city, battering down the ancient gates with their artillery. In Manchuria, at this time, a war was fought between China and Russia. The Chinese Eastern Railway was attacked not merely by rebels but by regular troops. The city of Blagoveshchensk on the north shore of the Amur was bombarded by the Chinese, as were many Russian settlements along the route of the railway. Fighting was often savage, but the Russian army was better equipped and better trained than its opponent. Russia then used the presence of her armies in Manchuria to demand stiff peace terms, but with Japanese backing the Chinese resisted these. Finally, Russia agreed to withdraw her troops by the end of 1903. The victory over the Chinese army convinced most Russian officers that their army could beat any other oriental enemy, a dangerous conclusion.

With both Japan and Russia insisting on expansion at the expense of China, tension was inevitable. It was in Korea that the crisis arose. At first Russia and Japan managed to coexist uneasily in Korea, and Japan would have been willing to concede Russian supremacy in Manchuria in exchange for Japanese supremacy in Korea. But the Russian government seemed to want both, although in this connexion the term Russian government was, even more than usual, an imprecise term. At the time the crisis was developing neither the minister of finance (Witte) nor the minister of war (Kuropatkin) nor the foreign minister (Lamsdorff) wanted a conflict with Japan, though they certainly wanted to strengthen Russia's presence in the East. According to Kuropatkin, Plehve, the minister of the interior, avidly wanted 'a little victorious war', believing it would calm discontent at home.[1] More important, there was a group of Guards officers, admirals, and courtiers with access to Nicholas who were intent on an aggressive policy. Their motives differed, but some of them were concerned with one or other of the shady business enterprises with interests in Korea.

When in 1901 Japan sent a distinguished negotiator to St. Petersburg,

---

[1] Most likely, Plehve never actually said this but, equally likely, the anecdote expresses his thoughts. Theodore Roosevelt had used almost identical terms in his sponsorship of the Spanish-American War. Roosevelt's little war was a great step forward in a career which would bring him the presidency and a Nobel Peace Prize. Plehve's little war would bring him only a bomb. Problem: find the moral.

he languished in the capital making no progress. At the time it seemed to be a case of insulting prevarication, but in retrospect it seems likely that the conflict of views around Nicholas prevented any decisive response being made. Japan, impatient, then secured the Anglo-Japanese Alliance of 1902 which, among other things, would make it risky for France to assist her new friend Russia in the event of a Russo-Japanese conflict.

The Russian troops in Manchuria were not withdrawn as promised. Tension built up. To the surprise of Nicholas, Japan commenced hostilities prematurely in February 1904. Prematurely for Russia that is; for Japan it was a carefully timed attack. The line capacity of the Trans-Siberian Railway was still limited by the Baikal ferry crossing; Russia had seven battleships in the Pacific in 1904 but five new ones could be expected in 1905, and by February the weather was suitable for a Japanese landing in Korea.

Before Japan declared war she landed troops at Chemulpo (Inchon) in Korea, and her torpedo boats made a surprise night attack on the Russian Pacific squadron at Port Arthur. Some officers of the latter were on shore attending a ball given by their admiral's wife, the ships were lit, and there were no torpedo nets. Despite this, most of the torpedoes missed. Three Russian ships were damaged but none sunk. However, this was a serious blow to Russian morale and the next morning the main Japanese naval forces appeared on the horizon to block any sortie. Command of the sea was crucial, because Japan's expeditionary force depended on the sea route from the homeland. When Russia's only competent admiral, Makarov, took command, it seemed that the Russian squadron would take some damaging initiatives. Makarov took his dispirited ships to sea, practised them and occasionally exchanged shots with the Japanese, all in preparation for a subsequent decisive action. But Makarov was drowned when his flagship struck a mine outside the harbour, and his successors were timid characters. There was one occasion when Russia could have won the war in a day. This was when two of Japan's six battleships struck mines off Port Arthur and sank. But instead of issuing forth to finish off the demoralized Japanese squadron the Russian ships remained safely in harbour.

The minister of war, Kuropatkin, was appointed to command the Far Eastern land forces and, no doubt familiar with *War and Peace*, adopted a strategy of retreat. Since he was outnumbered, this had much to justify it but many, for reasons of officerly honour, proved reluctant to carry out his orders. Kuropatkin was further embarrassed by the earlier appointment by Nicholas of a Viceroy for the Far East, who could override Kuropatkin's orders, and frequently did so. The first big battle, at the Yalu, occurred when the Japanese army, moving northwards out of Korea, encountered the Russian army defending south Manchuria. The Russians were out-numbered by three to one, but their defeat astounded world opinion, which had not expected a European army to be beaten by orientals. In fact the defeat was unnecessary; if the Russian commanders had obeyed orders and withdrawn in good time Russian dignity would have been preserved. But so many officers insisted on fighting that when the retreat did begin it was disorganized; one Russian commander even retreated in the wrong direction. This Japanese success enabled her more easily to raise loans to continue the war, and had the opposite effect on Russia's credit; this was a 'fight now, pay later' kind of war. Also, inside Russia, discontent and angry humiliation developed, not the loyal patriotism on which Plehve had counted. It was not long before Port Arthur was besieged, isolating its 60,000-man garrison from Kuropatkin's main forces (at the beginning of the war Russia had only 100,000 men in the Far East, and the single-track Trans-Siberian Railway was delivering about 35,000 reinforcing troops each month). The Russian defences at Port Arthur were excellent, as were the engineering troops, who won great successes with their sapping and mining. But these advantages were wasted in the hands of the command-ing officer, Stoessel, a man of breath-taking incompetence. The Pacific Squadron, uneasily anchored in the besieged port, made one attempt to break out to Vladivostok but in the fleet action which followed an un-lucky shot killed its commander. The next in command panicked and the ships fled back to the comparative safety of the harbour they had just quit. Meanwhile the Baltic Squadron was dispatched to link up with the Port Arthur ships and thus form a fleet considerably stronger than that which the Japanese Admiral Togo could muster. The voyage of this squadron half-way across the world was an epic in itself. It had the use of no bases and few anchorages en route (and its ships needed to take coal every several days), its sailors were hastily recruited reservists, defaulters, or new conscripts, and it had a disproportionate number of incompetent officers. It was commanded by Admiral Rozhestvensky, a favourite of the Tsar. With its repair ship, colliers, and hospital ships, it was a forerunner of the Task Force concept used four decades later in another war against Japan.

Russian secret agents abroad had sent fanciful reports of Japanese torpedo boats lurking in the North Sea, so it was not surprising that when the squadron was crossing the Dogger Bank at night the unexpected appearance near the battleships of the cruiser *Avrora* was greeted with a hail of shells. Some British trawlers fishing the Bank were fired at during the confusion and this killing of innocent fishermen caused an inter-national crisis. Much of the British press did what it could to stir the public into demanding war with Russia, and Rozhestvensky did not help the cause of peace by blaming the trawlers for wilfully obstructing the Russian shells. However, the British government had no wish for war, and the matter went to international arbitration.

At the end of December 1904, when the Baltic Squadron was off Madagascar, Port Arthur surrendered. It could have been defended for several more weeks, but for reasons best known to himself Stoessel gave up the struggle. He did send a telegram to Nicholas, beginning 'Great Tsar, forgive me . . .', and he did, like the Japanese general commanding the siege, receive a military decoration from the Kaiser (for whom the war was a great excitement), but this did not save him from being indicted as a traitor after the war. With Port Arthur the Japanese acquired the scuttled remnant of the Russian Pacific Squadron, but nevertheless Rozhestvensky was ordered to continue with the Baltic Squadron to Vladivostok. To reach that port he had to pass through narrow Japanese-controlled waters, and in May 1905 he was met by Togo's experienced and faster fleet in the Tsushima Strait. Here the Russian squadron was annihilated. Meanwhile Kuropatkin was continuing his retreat northwards. By this time he had more men than his pursuers, but they were of low quality because the best troops were kept in European Russia in case of rebellion. At Mukden, his headquarters, he unwisely made a stand, and after a two-week battle was forced to retreat. The fall of Mukden, and Tsushima, made peace almost inevitable. The Tsar sent Witte to negotiate with the Japanese, under the auspices of President Roosevelt. In the resulting Treaty of Portsmouth, Witte succeeded in gaining moderate terms; Russia would not pay a war indemnity but agreed to withdraw from Port Arthur, southern Sakhalin, southern Manchuria, and to acknowledge Japanese supremacy in Korea (see map, p. 598).

This war had shaken the tsarist regime, and shocked the world. Russia had been regarded as a great power and Japan as a minor power; David had defeated his fellow-imperialist Goliath. The traditional comment is that this was the first full-scale war in which an oriental nation defeated a western, but since Japan's warships were built in England, her admirals trained in England, and her armies similarly built on the Prussian model, it is perhaps relevant to ask which of the two belligerents was western, and which oriental.

7. 1905

HISTORIANS seeking something good to say about Nicholas habitually point out that he was a good husband. This he was, but family happiness has never yet saved a dynasty. The lives of Nicholas and Alexandra were tragic because both had endearing qualities and both found themselves playing roles for which they were quite unfitted. Perhaps Nicholas deserves the greatest sympathy, for he had little choice but to rule whereas Alexandra consciously chose to meddle in politics, though with the best of intentions.

To be the son of Alexander III and the pupil of Pobedonostsev was a bad beginning. Nicholas had genuine charm and simplicity but was unable to overcome attitudes imbibed at an early age: belief in an absolute holy autocracy, chauvinism, anti-semitism, and a touch of militarism. Many instances have been pointed out of his political naïvety: his open approval of the extreme right-wing and demagogic Union of the Russian People: his taking of advice from his palace commandant and not from his prime minister in 1906, just when Russia was supposed to be making a new start in representative government; and his faith in holy men, of whom Rasputin was not the only example. His father, apparently, had little confidence in his intelligence, but nevertheless allowed him to participate in various committees to familiarize himself with his future duties. Chairmanship of the Trans-Siberian Railway Committee was one of these duties. He also toured India and Japan, unsuccessfully hunting tigers in the former and having his forehead sliced by an assassin's sword in the latter. This narrow escape is said to have been the source of his subsequent hostility to the Japanese, whom he called 'yellow monkeys'.

He acceded in 1894. His Moscow coronation was marred by the death of hundreds of common people massed for the ceremonial distribution of royal gifts; these deaths by crushing could have been avoided if only commonsense precautions had been taken by the authorities. Nevertheless, although big disappointments were suffered by those who had hoped that Alexander's death would mark the beginning of a more liberal era, in general the first years of the reign were not disastrous. This was partly because several of Alexander's ministers, including Witte, stayed in office and gave good advice. Later, as will be seen, Nicholas tended to appoint ministers who knew how to please him, and to take council with advisers who, at best, were talentless and, at worst, dishonest. Throughout the reign both the ministry and the court were riven by intrigues, intrigues which flourished on the Emperor's lack of will and reluctance to make the intellectual effort to get to the bottom of a situation.

The Hague Conference

Resentful after the Congress of Berlin, which had seemed to deprive her of the fruits of her 1878 victory over Turkey, Russia seemed to lose interest in European affairs. This perhaps was why Alexander III's reign had been peaceful. Apart from some intrigues in Bulgaria and Roumania, which included the kidnapping and murder of figures hostile to Russia, the government concentrated its attention on the East. Alexander disliked the Germans and his reign coincided with a loosening of the bonds which previously existed between the three monarchies of Russia, Austria, and Germany.[1] To avoid isolation, a mutually satisfactory alliance was concluded with France. Russia at this time benefited from French investment, so better relations were desirable on both economic and political grounds. There were military staff conversations, and the navies exchanged visits, Alexander standing respectfully as the revolutionary *Marseillaise* was played at Kronstadt.

Relations with Germany improved after Nicholas became Tsar. He had a fairly close, though not devoted, relationship with his kinsman Kaiser Wilhelm, with whom he corresponded on 'Dear Willy'—'Dear Nicky' terms. Wilhelm was anxious to turn Nicholas's attention towards Russia's civilizing mission among the inferior yellow races, and his telegram to Nicholas, 'The Admiral of the Atlantic greets the Admiral of the Pacific', was notorious for its blatant appeal to the Tsar's vanity. In 1905, when Nicholas was thoroughly embroiled in the Far East, Wilhelm induced him to sign a Russo-German treaty at a private meeting off Björkö in the Baltic. However, the remonstrations of his ministers and his reluctance to behave dishonourably towards France persuaded Nicholas to back out, and henceforth Willy and Nicky were less intimate.

An unusual initiative with permanent consequences came from St.

[1] He married a Danish princess, unlike his predecessors who had married Germans.

Petersburg in the beginning of Nicholas's reign. This was no less than a call
to the nations of the world to gather together and discuss a halt to the arms
race, and kindred subjects. The genesis of this move came when the
Russian General Staff realized that Austria was re-equipping with quick-
firing field artillery. Austria was Russia's potential enemy, but the Russian
economy could not afford new guns. Or, rather, the finance ministry
preferred to invest in railways than in guns, and could argue that the
former did more to strengthen the Empire.

With the encouragement of Witte, what started as a proposal for a
rearmament moratorium with Austria developed into a full-scale peace
conference at The Hague. Many ridiculed and resented the notion of
abolishing war, and cast aspersions on the Russian motives. In fact
Nicholas's proposal was for arms limitation rather than the abolition of
war, but despite this Kaiser Wilhelm condemned the idea because, he said,
it would mean the disbandment of ancient sacred regiments and would
place monarchs at the mercy of democrats and anarchists. Rudyard Kipling
gratified the always-strong Russophobic segment of British opinion by
penning some verses about how especially dangerous is the bear 'When he
veils the hate and cunning of his little swinish eyes'. Many governments,
including the British, sent men known to be warmongers as delegates to
the Conference. However, it was realized that some positive measures
should emerge from the Conference, which had raised great hopes among
the common people of Europe (that is, those who would do the fighting in
the next war). So a few agreements were made, of which the most progressive was a five-year ban on balloon warfare. More permanent than these
agreements was the general acceptance of arbitration as a means of settling
international disputes. One of the earlier cases to be thus passed to international judgement was the dispute between Britain and Russia after the
latter's Baltic fleet had fired on British trawlers in 1904. In this case, at
least, the possibility of arbitration made it easier to avoid war.

Marxism comes to Russia

The relative decline of Populism after the murder of Alexander II was
mainly due to exhaustion, repression, and a feeling that nothing had been
gained. There were also the attractions of a rival revolutionary movement,
that of the marxists. Marx's theories had been known and appreciated
since the forties by Russian radicals, but the Populists, devoted to the idea
that Russia, because of her backwardness, might skip the capitalist phase
of economic development, naturally could not accept Marx's declaration
that every society inevitably passes through that phase (Marx subsequently acknowledged that Russia might possibly escape capitalism). Nor

did early Russian revolutionaries approve of the post-capitalist society implied by Marx: Bakunin, for example, said that marxism would merely replace the capitalist with the bureaucrat. On the other hand, Marx's forecast of the post-revolutionary withering away of the state was attractive, or could be made attractive, to most Russians, so great was the alienation of the people from the state apparatus.

By the eighties it was obvious that, despite the wishful denials of Populists, capitalism was firmly entrenched in Russia. More and more intellectuals turned towards marxism for an explanation of society more in keeping with reality than Populism. The tsarist regime and its police had always been relatively lenient towards the marxists,[2] whom they regarded as a small group which not only did not advocate terrorism like the Populists, but might even weaken the latter movement. In 1872 the first volume of Marx's *Capital* in Russian translation passed the censor. Publication had been sponsored by Populists, and proved to be the first commercial success for the work.[3] Populists liked it because it portrayed the horrors of the capitalist system which they wished Russia to avoid. Slavophils liked it because it condemned western society. Even St. Petersburg industrialists liked it because it described, they said, the kind of factory system which their rivals, the Moscow industrialists, were trying to imitate. But although sales were good it took about ten years for the book's political significance to become plain.

According to Marx, production was society's main function, and social institutions reflected, with some distorting time-lags, the nature and ownership of society's means of production. In western Europe capitalism had replaced feudalism after commerce and large-scale production had created a social class more powerful than the nobility, whose land was no longer the dominant means of production. Under capitalism workers were dehumanized, and more and more exploited and impoverished. But growing monopoly, increasing industrial depression, and workers' discontent would eventually cause a collapse and a revolution in which the owners of the new dominant means of production (the labour of their own hands) would take power. After this inevitable proletarian revolution, existing institutions (political, judicial, economic, cultural) would be refashioned, because such institutions always reflected the requirements of the dominant class.

---

[2] Towards the end of the century many marxists (the 'legal marxists') operated on the basis of what the government would tolerate; for example, by confining their writing to permissible publications.

[3] Marx rather ungratefully ascribed the high sales to Russian intellectuals' notorious enthusiasm for any extremist fashion originating in the west.

By the eighties, with Plekhanov's allegiance transferred to marxism, Russian radicals were increasingly discussing *Capital*. Some became marxists, and passed on their opinions to some of the more thoughtful workers. But few working men had the time and inclination to master marxist theory, and there was a wide cultural gap between them and their instructors. The marxists had more success when, in St. Petersburg, they introduced an idea which one of their members, Martov, had borrowed from the Jewish socialists of Lithuania. Instead of devoting time to explaining the intricacies of marxism to a chosen few, Martov advocated offering help to the masses of the workers in the struggle for higher wages and better conditions, thus winning their trust and providing an opportunity to transmit a few of the most appealing postulates of marxism. Among the marxists of St. Petersburg there was strong opposition to this idea, because it implied that it was possible for the workers to improve their lot under capitalism. However, the idea was eventually adopted (Lenin, a friend of Martov, was one of those supporting it) and it did enable the Social Democrats to take off as a real political force. The marxists played a small but noticed role in the St. Petersburg strikes of 1895, 1896, and 1897, which extracted concessions from the industrialists and brought publicity and a few worker-members to the Social Democrats. At the end of 1895 the police at last took action against the marxists of St. Petersburg, many of whom were arrested and given light sentences of exile in Siberia. Thus in 1898, when the Russian Social Democratic Workers' Party was founded to unite the marxists, the main strength consisted of young activists like Lenin and Martov confined to Siberia, and a handful of veterans in Switzerland gathered around the revered figure of Plekhanov, one of the first Populists to turn to marxism.

Marxism because of its breadth attracted a great variety of adherents, each of whom seemed to find what he was looking for and tended to ignore other aspects of the ideology. There were Social Democrats who had abandoned the idealism of the earlier French and German socialists in favour of the more 'scientific' marxism. There were ex-Populists, often people whose main interest was revolution. There were those who had great faith in technology as a solution for all social problems. There were the born bureaucrats, drawn to a doctrine which seemed to promise a new, orderly, and well-organized society. And there were the ill-at-ease intellectuals, who idolized the 'pure' worker just as the Populists had honoured the primitive peasant. With such variety among its members it is not surprising that the history of Russian social democracy was largely a succession of doctrinal disputes and consequent splits and 'deviations'. Presumably the first marxist deviationist was Marx himself, who made substantial changes in his ideas during his life. A dangerous schism in the Russian party developed with the emergence of the view known as Economism. This advised the party to acknowledge that some of Marx's prognostications were apparently not being fulfilled, and to devote itself henceforth to obtaining better conditions for the workers while supporting the liberals' campaign for a constitution through which socialism might eventually be achieved. Lenin and his supporters bitterly resisted this deviation.

Lenin

Lenin, whose real name was Ulyanov, was born in 1870 in Simbirsk (now Ulyanovsk). His father, the son of a serf, had been a school teacher but had risen to the rank of schools inspector, an office which carried a title of hereditary nobility. His mother was the daughter of a doctor. Thus Lenin grew up in a cultivated, liberal environment. The death of his father and, soon afterwards, the execution of his brother (see p. 118) no doubt had their influence on the young Lenin, but did not affect his school work. He won the gold medal for the best graduate of his gymnasium and, highly recommended by the director of the latter (who was the father of the Kerensky whom Lenin was to displace in 1917), he proceeded to the University of Kazan to study law. However, it was not long before he was expelled, in company with forty-five fellow-students, for taking part in a demonstration. Because he was the brother of an executed terrorist, his several petitions for re-admission were refused. So for three years, from the age of eighteen, Lenin lived with his family at Samara, occupying himself with reading. It was apparently when he was nineteen that he embraced marxism; he had been a great admirer of the Populists and Chernyshevsky, but an acquaintance with Marx's *Capital* and a persuasive work by Plekhanov convinced him that only revolutionary socialism offered a genuine solution to Russia's inadequacies.

Not for the first or last time, Lenin's mother pulled strings on his behalf, and the ministry of education agreed that although he could not be allowed to attend any university, he would be permitted to take university examinations. Thus, through private study, he was able to pass the law finals of St. Petersburg University. After spending more time in Samara, he returned to the capital and joined a law firm in 1893. His employer, a liberal, was quite content for him to devote most of his energies to revolutionary activity.

In Samara Lenin had had experience of marxist discussion groups, and his legal training, combined with a naturally logical way of thinking and speaking, soon helped him to become a leading figure among the socialists in the capital. With many others he was arrested in 1895, spent fifteen months in gaol, and was then sent to Siberia for three years' 'free exile'. This sentence meant that he was confined to a certain area, but was free to move about and do what he liked there. His mother was again able to influence the authorities on his behalf, and he was sent to one of the warmer parts of Siberia, being allowed to travel there as an ordinary passenger, not under escort. During his exile he married Nadezhda Krupskaya, one of his socialist associates in St. Petersburg. He spent much of his time reading, carrying on correspondence with other socialists, both free and unfree, and writing.

After release in 1900 Lenin soon went abroad to carry on the struggle for what he considered the correct interpretation of marxism. He brought to the socialists a hitherto rare hardness in discussion. He could be scurrilous about his opponents. He would not compromise, would not admit that his ideological enemies might be partly right. His friends, like Martov, were only friends so long as their views coincided. And yet, although in politics Lenin seemed devious and unpleasant, there were some who found him an enjoyable companion in private. In his later years, Lenin suffered progressive arterio-sclerosis of the brain. When this became evident is unsure, but he appears to have consulted a Swiss specialist sometime before 1917. Apart from leading to strokes, this affliction can sometimes cause extreme changes of mood but how far, if at all, this affected Lenin's behaviour is unknown.

Revolutionaries and reformers

The Social Democratic Party was eventually cured of its Economism deviation, thanks largely to Lenin's persuasiveness. After his exile, Lenin emigrated in order to confer with the elders of Russian marxism and to help edit a new periodical. The latter, called *Iskra* (Spark), was smuggled into Russia and was intended to unite the marxists inside Russia, to encourage them to reject revisionism and to give them a sense of belonging to a big international organization. The six-man editorial board included Lenin and Martov as well as the veterans Plekhanov and Vera Zasulich.

After about 1895, marxism was in competition with a revived liberal movement and with the new Populism expressed by the Socialist Revolutionary Party. The liberals attracted those in favour of non-violent change while the Socialist Revolutionaries (who had a terrorist section) attracted those who believed that revolutionary goals should be centred on the peasantry rather than the workers. It was to re-assert the Social Democrats and to attack those members who, relying on Marx's predictions, were content to wait while history took its predetermined course, that Lenin produced his *What is to be Done?* (1902). This, distributed inside Russia by *Iskra*'s agents, expressed Lenin's idea of what the Russian Social Democrats should be and do.

Superficially, it was a one-sided and sharp attack on Economism, but really it marked the beginning of what was later to be called Marxism–Leninism. That is, it was a substantial revision of Marx, although its author took care to claim that it represented orthodox marxism. It admitted that the workers were not really capable of spontaneous socialist thought, because their horizon was limited to trade unionism, improved conditions, and higher wages. Thus, since the workers did not see where their real interests lay they had to be protected by a socialist party which would act on their behalf. This party could no longer be a collection of well-meaning amateurs, but had to be a tightly knit group of full-time, well-trained, devoted professionals, controlled by a strong central organization. It was this latter small group which would do the conspiratorial work of the revolution. Lenin was not against open organizations, like trade unions, for the masses, but these could only be of secondary importance. Terrorism was rejected. The organization of the party was to consist of a supreme organ abroad (the *Iskra* board) with a subordinate Central Committee inside Russia which would organize secret local committees throughout the country.

This did seem a possible path towards socialism. But the ordinary party member did not relish the proposed strong organization, with its implied stress on obedience; this was quite the reverse of the traditional free discussion which had hitherto preceded all actions and which was one of the most-valued features of the revolutionary movement. However, when in 1903 a party congress met in London, most delegates seemed willing to accept the ideas of *What is to be Done?* But perhaps because revolutionaries are by nature contentious and intellectuals disputatious, it was not long before the 1903 congress was riven with disagreement, which developed into dissension and animosity. The delegates of the Jewish socialist union (*Bund*), walked out, feeling that they had little in common with the white-handed radical intellectuals who knew nothing of the practical side of the Jewish workers' miserable lives. Then Lenin's proposal to reduce the *Iskra* board from six to three members aroused opposition. Martov opposed Lenin on this but was defeated by five votes. It was this vote, much more important as a symbol of division than the issue itself warranted, which resulted in Lenin's faction being termed the *Bolsheviki* (that is, 'those of the majority') and Martov's supporters the *Mensheviki* ('those of the minority'). Underlying the split lay a distrust of Lenin's personality and methods, and his uncompromising demands. Martov refused to co-operate with him. Those delegates who had come, furtively, from Russia had to return home and tell their appalled comrades that the movement was split. Martov persuaded Plekhanov to withdraw his support from Lenin. Lenin then resigned from *Iskra*, and thereafter resisted conciliatory moves to mend the Bolshevik–Menshevik split.

Among the Socialist Revolutionaries there was also a diversity of views; some of the members were inclined towards marxism, some had spent their entire revolutionary lives working among the peasants in the Populist tradition, and others were addicted to violence. The Socialist Revolutionaries never became a highly centralized and disciplined group as did the Bolsheviks, nor at first did they have a large membership. But in time, and especially after their participation in several peasant risings, they attracted much support among country people; in the nation-wide and relatively free election of 1917 they and their associates gathered a majority of the votes. In the early years of the century their terroristic organization gained them much publicity after a number of successful assassinations. Among their victims were two ministers of the interior in 1902 and 1904. The 1904 success, killing the unpopular Plehve, brought not only public renown but public acclaim.

Although it was not until 1905 that the Constitutional Democratic Party was formed, the liberals had been growing more active since the death of Alexander III. In Russia the term 'liberal' was avoided, perhaps because Russian liberalism embraced viewpoints as far apart as those of marxists who accepted Marx's interpretation of society but preferred non-revolutionary solutions, and those who wanted merely to temper autocracy with the ancient practice of the tsar taking council with his people through a consultative assembly. Preferring to call themselves the 'social movement', or even 'public opinion', Russian liberals were predominantly *zemstvo* members[4] who were impressed with their own effectiveness and wished to extend their sphere of influence, or paid specialists employed by the *zemstva*, or urban professionals.

When Alexander III died the liberals had great hopes of a future in which people's representatives (that is, themselves) would have some influence in the decisions of the government. In its loyal address to the new Tsar, the strongly liberal *zemstvo* of Tver Province even mentioned the need for public opinion to be expressed and heeded. Nicholas, under the influence of Pobedonostsev, responded with his own public opinion about *zemstvo* representatives 'intoxicated by senseless dreamings' about participation in government. 'Let it be known that I will maintain the principal of autocracy as strongly and as firmly as my late memorable father.'

[4] But by no means all *zemstva* were predominantly liberal. Some were strongly conservative.

This was not a good beginning for the liberals, and subsequent concessions never included the granting of real power. When *zemstvo* members' advice was needed in the agricultural committees set up to examine Russia's pressing rural problems, care was taken to see that they were not elected, but selected by the provincial governors. In such an atmosphere the more radical liberals, who were demanding not only moves towards constitutional government but also universal primary education and a higher legal status for the peasantry, began to turn towards illegal activities. One of their acts was the foundation of the Union of Liberation, an illegal, largely liberal, political organization. In 1904 the Union emerged from the underground and held a series of banquets which were advertised as celebrations of the fortieth anniversary of the 1864 law reform. Banquets were a form of public gathering permitted by the police, but at these particular celebrations speeches were made, and reported in the press, demanding such things as a constituent assembly, social justice, and better schools. Meanwhile those liberals for whom the Union of Liberation was too radical weathered the discouragements of Plehve, and were allowed in 1904 to hold a national congress of *zemstva*, but only in private.

Luckily for the government, three waves of rebellious dissidence had not coincided. From 1899 to 1902 the rebels had been the students, whose crowning hour had been the assassination of the minister of education. Then, in 1902, a poor harvest superimposed on existing land hunger set off a series of peasant attacks on landowners' estates, actions that were suppressed by troops whose purpose was as much to teach the peasants a lesson as to restore order. Then, in 1902–3 many industrial workers staged strikes. Meanwhile the government was split between repressors and reformers. Plehve believed in repression, Witte in reform, and Plehve prevailed. But, in the old tradition, widespread arrests of actual or suspected troublemakers were followed by a few concessions: the students were allowed to hold meetings so long as they were properly supervised by their professors, the peasants' debt arrears to the state were cancelled, workers injured at work were allowed pensions. This last measure was supported by Plehve, as also was the law enabling workers to elect 'elders' to negotiate with employers. Yet Plehve's interior ministry, with its officials placed all over the country, could often work against what it regarded as policies of appeasement, and its repressive measures did much to ensure that in 1904 the government was facing a revolutionary situation. The war against Japan was going badly, and the government was blamed for its handling of the armed forces. Many began to feel that the proved administrators of the *zemstva* organizations should be given more executive responsibility, for the official bureaucracy was obviously deficient. All this strengthened the cause of the liberals, and the government could hardly have failed to notice that, among the guests at the liberal 'banquets' being held to further the cause of a constitution, there was a sprinkling of army generals.

The Socialist Revolutionaries were active. Plehve was murdered and so, in 1905, was the equally disliked Grand Duke Sergei, the Tsar's uncle and governor of Moscow. In many localities the Socialist Revolutionaries were successfully persuading local peasants to expel the landlords and take over their land. To contain these threats, the war ministry felt obliged to keep the most reliable troops in European Russia and to send mainly reservists and recruits to fight the Japanese.

That the police had agents in all the revolutionary parties was no longer of great help, for while an agent could recommend the arrest of key conspirators he could do little to prevent popular manifestations. Moreover, the secret-police network was by this time so thick it was repeatedly tying itself into knots with its double agents, treble agents, and quadruple agents. Perhaps the most dramatic police scandal, which subsequently damaged both the regime and the Socialist Revolutionaries, was that involving the murder of Grand Duke Sergei. Azev, the leader of the Socialist Revolutionaries' terrorist organization, was himself a police agent. It was he who organized the murder of Plehve and several police officials, but there was an understanding between him and his official paymasters that he would prevent any attacks on the royal family. Obviously, if he was to play the part of a good revolutionary he would have to carry out some murders, and perhaps those who employed him had their own quarrels with some of the victims. However, it seems that he felt unable to refuse the revolutionaries' suggestion that Sergei should be killed. For some people, therefore, Sergei's death came as a double shock, but it was not until 1908 that Azev's activities were publicly denounced. By that year Azev had been five years in control of the Socialist Revolutionaries' terrorist section, and the revelation that he was a police agent took away much of its hard-won glamour.

Free trade unions were not permitted, and to divert the workers' desire for unions into safe channels the police, through its agents, had set up its own legal trade unions. The originator of this idea ('police socialism') appears to have been Zubatov, chief of the Moscow security police, who, in 1902, obtained permission to establish an association for engineering workers. With the help of mostly unsuspecting university professors and some former Social Democrats, this was a great success, and the idea spread to other industries and other cities. The membership, which was large, was regaled with lectures and community singing, but to maintain its support the union leaders had to produce clear gains in terms of wages and working conditions. Since most employers favoured this kind of union, for fear of something worse, some real concessions were negotiated. But it was not long before the unions felt obliged to take strike action, and the spectacle of police-organized strikes and demonstrations was too much for the administration, especially as foreign capitalists were beginning to drop hints that Russian industry was perhaps after all not a good investment. So police socialism, whose success for some time had alarmed the Social Democrats, came to an end. But not before its St. Petersburg affiliate had brought about that turning point in the history of the Romanovs known as 'Bloody Sunday'.

Bloody Sunday

In St. Petersburg an Orthodox priest, Gapon, had founded with police participation a union for industrial workers. Like many other such unions, it was penetrated by Social Democrats who used its gatherings for agitation. However, Gapon made great efforts to weed out the marxists (and also, as a loyal citizen and good Orthodox Christian, Jews). The strikes and demonstrations into which he led his members were probably not instigated by workers fired by socialist propaganda, but were embarked upon because Gapon was impressed by the misery of the working class and rather fancied himself in the role of saviour. In January 1905, after the news of the fall of Port Arthur reached the capital, discontent intensified among all classes. There were more workers' protests, and Gapon organized a Sunday march of the St. Petersburg workers to present a petition to the Tsar at the Winter Palace. In fact the Tsar was not in residence at the time, but the thousands of marchers had no opportunity to discover this, because before they reached the palace they were shot down by troops who had been brought to the capital in anticipation of trouble. How many were killed and wounded is unknown, for unofficial and official counts differed widely. The fact remained that a peaceful column of workers, singing hymns and the national anthem as it marched to present a petition to the sovereign, had been fired on. When a new governor of the capital was appointed in haste to sort out this crisis, his main initiatives were to arrange a deputation of 'good' workers to ask the Tsar's pardon for their misdemeanour, and to send many of the surviving demonstrators out of the capital. These expellees, scattered all over Russia, spread the news of the massacre and it was this which, on the one hand, led to a wave of sympathy strikes throughout the Empire, and on the other, discredited the traditional belief among the simple masses that all the evils they suffered could be remedied if only they could reach their 'little father', the Tsar, to tell him what was really happening. As for that other little father, Gapon, he denounced the Tsar and fled abroad to be lionized by European society, canvassed by the revolutionaries, and to write *The Story of My Life*. He eventually joined the Social Revolutionaries, who hanged him in 1906 on discovering that he still had contacts with the police. At one stage Lenin declared Gapon was a Social Democrat, because in 1905 great public prestige attached to the group which could claim Gapon's favour. And after all, Gapon had succeeded in doing something which the revolutionaries had long failed to do: he had aroused the workers *en masse*. That he had done this was probably because he had much of the reputation of the holy man, a class of person traditionally able to work on the emotions of simple Russians of all classes. Probably as a holy man he was only second-rate, for he was a great drinker and gambler, but with his holiness there was also a real sympathy for simple workers and, at first, an inspiring optimism.

The *Potemkin Mutiny*

Bloody Sunday was followed by a general strike in the capital, and an outbreak of protest strikes throughout the Empire as the news spread. Apart from the capital, most rebelliousness occurred in the non-Russian parts of the Empire. Disgust and discontent were not confined to the traditionally dissident; even the industrialists' association showed its disapproval by voting a sum of money to aid families whose breadwinners had been killed on Bloody Sunday. Early in February came the assassination of Grand Duke Sergei, and that same month the Tsar publicly conceded that some kind of elected consultative (but only consultative) assembly was desirable. At about the same time localized peasant revolts became more numerous, especially in the south. In the following weeks the liberals, expressing themselves through the *zemstva* or through professional associations, became more bold in their demands; that summer Nicholas spoke to a delegation of *zemstvo* figures, and a joint meeting of *zemstvo* and city council delegates was held in Moscow, despite a police prohibition.

Especially unnerving was the mutiny on the battleship *Potemkin* in June; for a regime which seemed unlikely to survive without the use of troops, this first substantial demonstration of disloyalty in the armed forces had great significance. The *Potemkin* was a fairly modern battleship of the Black Sea fleet, which after the recent loss of the Pacific and Baltic Squadrons was the only fleet still in being. As hostilities with Japan had revealed, there was a certain rottenness in the Russian navy, and part of it was in the officers. The majority of officers were not brutal and incompetent, but many were. Brutal treatment of seamen had been a traditional feature of all navies, but whereas in most navies a kinder atmosphere prevailed in the twentieth century, this was not always the case in Russian warships. Arbitrary corporal punishment was officially forbidden in the army and navy, but not all officers conformed. This is what one of the seamen who survived Tsushima thought of his officers:

These noblemen's sons, well cared-for and fragile, were capable only of decking themselves out in tunics with epaulettes. They would then stick their snouts in the air like a mangy horse being harnessed, and bravely scrape their heels on polished floors, or dance gracefully at balls, or get drunk, in these ways demoralising their subordinates. They didn't even know our names. Corporal punishment was forbidden on paper only, for decency's sake: the sailors were beaten for all kinds of reasons, and often. It was considered the natural order of things. There was no way of complaining . . . We were compelled to eat rotten biscuits and stinking decaying meat while our officers fatted themselves with the best food and drank the most expensive wines.[5]

The *Potemkin* was an unhappy ship, and there were no perils of war service to distract the men from their grievances and hatreds. So the crew, which included several revolutionary agitators, killed many of the officers, took control of the ship, and cruised around the Black Sea. Other ships were close to mutiny and it was thought unwise to order their crews to open fire on the errant battleship. At one point, later celebrated on film and canvas, the *Potemkin* steamed unscathed past the warships which were, theoretically, hunting her down. However, after bombarding Odessa and threatening other southern ports, she was compelled to steam off and seek asylum in Roumania. She had shaken the nerve of the regime, brought the navy ministry into even more disrepute, had excited the revolutionaries (who had at first thought she would ignite a full-scale revolution in South Russia), and had destroyed much of the Empire's remaining prestige in foreign capitals.

The strike and the Moscow Rising

Taking advantage of the government's confusion and indecision, trade unions and political parties were busily establishing themselves during the summer of 1905. The various professional organizations set up a co-ordinating body known as the Union of Unions. This was a third and radical liberal body, supplementing the Union of Liberation and the *zemstvo* group; its first chairman, Milyukov, was also a leader of the Union of Liberation. Only a few weeks passed before the Union of Liberation and the majority of the *zemstvo* group jointly founded the Constitutional Democratic Party (usually referred to as the Kadet Party). Its main demand was for a freely and fairly elected constituent assembly to sort out the Empire's political problems.

[5] A. Zaterty, *Za chuzhiye grekhi* (1907), 19.

In August a proposal for a consultative assembly had been published (the 'Bulygin proposal'), but by that time half-measures were no longer acceptable; almost all politically conscious citizens expected something more. A further government concession, the granting to the universities of that autonomy which the students had long sought, did bring to an end the students' strike. But now that the lecture rooms were open they provided almost the only place where meetings could be held without police permission, and it was not long before socialist students in St. Petersburg took advantage of this to hold anti-government meetings, attended in the evenings by the city's workers. General dissatisfaction culminated in the railway strike of October.

The railwaymen's union was effectively organized throughout most of the Empire, and, since the latter was dependent almost entirely on the railways for moving troops and feeding the cities, it was clear that the regime was now in really mortal danger. When strikes spread to other industries, when the peasant revolts seemed to be on the increase and when disturbances occurred among troops in transit from Manchuria, it was clear that extraordinary decisions were needed. Thus, after toying with the idea of a military dictatorship, Nicholas accepted Witte's advice and issued what later became known as the October Manifesto. This conceded the principles of freedom of speech, conscience, and association, freedom from unwarranted arrest, and accepted the calling of an assembly (*Duma*), which would be elected (though not by direct or equal voting). But the ministers would not be responsible to the Duma, and although it could block a law going into force, it would not have the right, alone, to enact legislation. Thus, although an improvement on the Bulygin proposal, it seemed inadequate to those parties which had been demanding a constituent assembly. Only those liberals who found the Kadet Party too radical rallied behind the Tsar's October Manifesto, calling themselves the Octobrist Party.

Just before the October Manifesto appeared, leading workers of St. Petersburg had established the St. Petersburg Council (*Soviet*) of Workers' Deputies. This was a body to co-ordinate the strikes and other activities of the various factories, each of which was to elect its own delegates. The Socialist Revolutionaries and the Bolshevik and Menshevik factions of the Social Democrats all realized the potential significance of this ultra-democratic workers' assembly and soon had their own delegates on its executive committee. There were similar soviets in other cities, and in many, including the capital, the soviets became virtually the local government for some weeks.

Although the political parties varied in their attitudes to political change, they were more united in their demand for civil rights. This probably reflected the attitude of ordinary people for whom, ultimately, civil rights was the great goal. The term 'personal inviolability' had become almost a slogan, not least among workers, and reflected longstanding resentment at the powerlessness of the ordinary person, both at the workplace and in society as a whole.

In general, committed revolutionaries played a small part in the 1905 upheaval. The Socialist Revolutionaries were more interested in the countryside, while the Social Democrats in exile were too busy with their own feuds to pay full attention to what was happening in Russia. Many of them no doubt also felt that there was no hope of the socialists taking power at this stage. Eventually some of the exiles returned to Russia to participate in events, but of them all only Trotsky won great distinction. Trotsky had met Lenin in 1902, during the latter's stay in London, and had won his respect as a great intellect and a great speaker. However, he had stayed with the Menshevik faction after the 1903 split and it was as a Menshevik that he became the leading figure of the St. Petersburg Soviet. His skill as an orator was unmatched by any of the other socialists. For Lenin and his friends the 1905 Rebellion was a rude awakening; the workers had revolted spontaneously and were conducting their affairs in their own way. Cultured Russian gentlemen like Lenin, skilled in fine arguments, seemed unable to find a way to arouse the proletariat so that it would follow their leadership along the true path to a socialist society. Only Trotsky, it seemed, had the oratorical skill to set his listeners on fire, and even he achieved a smaller response among the masses than had Father Gapon. Only the anarchists could congratulate themselves; spontaneous revolts, and soviets, seemed to confirm their belief in grass-roots democracy.

From October, Witte was virtually prime minister, being the chairman of the Council of Ministers, whose powers had been strengthened. His first task was the pacification of the country. Not only was there trouble in the cities, but there were mutinies among the troops returning home from the war and nationalist demonstrations in Poland, the Caucasus, and other non-Russian parts demanding more independence from St. Petersburg. At one stage the Trans-Siberian Railway was in the hands of rebellious troops and workers, and much of Transcaucasia fell from government control. To clear the Trans-Siberian Railway a trainload of loyal troops was dispatched from east and west under 'firm' officers. With frequent halts, to disarm mutineers and execute their leaders, the trains met half-way, and the railway with its vital telegraph line was declared re-opened for traffic. In the Baltic provinces, where armed bands of workers and peasants were fighting armed groups of the disliked German landowners, the pacification was brutal, many innocent suspects being hanged to set an example to others. How many hundreds or thousands of executions took place is not known, but it was certainly an unnecessarily large total.

In St. Petersburg, the Soviet called a general strike in November, but its indifferent success only encouraged Witte to dissolve the Soviet and arrest its leaders. But in Moscow a parallel strike developed into a full-scale rising which lasted almost two weeks and was savagely suppressed by loyal troops. There were also smaller mutinies in the naval bases of Kronstadt in the Baltic and Sevastopol on the Black Sea.

In early 1906, in the breathing space between the quietening of urban rebellion and the not unexpected surge of rural violence in 1906–7, the autocracy engaged in a purge of the faint-hearted and the recently dissident. Unreliable officers, and sometimes their units, were dispensed with. Newspapers and their editors were suppressed. Professionals of radical inclination lost their jobs in local government and were sometimes exiled. An international loan, raised with the help of French bankers, helped the government through this difficult period. Meanwhile, as the country seemed to become more stable, a new political life was being born as the promises of the October Manifesto became a temporary reality.

Russian government before and after 1905[6]

Autocracy, in theory, meant that all the power of the state was exercised by one person; the monarchy was absolute even though it had chosen to be ruled by law.[7] In practice, no tsar exercised his powers alone. He entrusted authority to men of his own choice and it was not always clear where the real power in Russia lay. As a generalization it might be said that the tsar could and did intervene in any matter he chose, but the day-to-day decisions, which were not always minor decisions, were made by the bureaucracy. Since the tsar had the final word, those persons who could influence him also had great power. Such persons are sometimes referred to as court influences, but not all of them were courtiers and not all courtiers had influence.

Until 1905 the bureaucracy was headed by the State *Soviet* (Council), whose members were nominated by the tsar. Legislative projects were handed down for study to the relevant ministry (or to a special commission) and were then returned for discussion by a general meeting of the Council. The opinion, often divided, of the Council was transmitted to the

---

[6] A useful description of the structure of Russian government is M. Szeftel's article in *Essays in Russian and Soviet History*, edited by J. S. Curtiss (1963), 105–19.

[7] In Finland the Russian tsar was still a constitutional monarch (but not in Poland after 1832).

tsar and he made his own decision, which became law. His verdict was not necessarily in accordance with the majority or even minority opinions, and moreover he could, independently of the Council, promulgate a manifesto or *ukaz* at will (some notable reforms were effected thus). In 1906 the State Council was transformed into an upper house to balance the new Duma. Its nominated members were supplemented by elected representatives of the towns, Church, guilds, universities, *zemstva*, and nobility. As was intended, it became a conservative though quasi-parliamentary body which considerably restrained the more liberal and energetic Duma; all proposals had to be passed by both the Duma and the State Council before being submitted to the Tsar for approval or disapproval.

Until 1905 the *Soviet* (Council) of Ministers was moribund, but there was a Committee of Ministers which discussed current questions involving several ministries. The four most weighty members of this were the ministers of the interior, finance, and war, and the Over Procurator of the Holy Synod. In the nineties there were ten ministries: foreign affairs, imperial court, war, navy, interior, education, transport, finance, agriculture and state domains, and justice, plus departments with ministerial status (state control, charities of the Empress Maria, state horsebreeding, and the Procuracy of the Holy Synod). Of these the ministry of war had by far the biggest budget: two-fifths of the total for all ministries, ten times more than the ministry of education and two hundred times more than the horse-breeders. By 1917 the ministry of agriculture had become a department, and a new department of health had been introduced.[8]

Neither before nor after 1905 were the ministers responsible to anyone but the tsar, and it was the tsar who chose them. Thus they were bound by no sense of ministerial solidarity. Vying for the favour of the tsar, they were often divided by jealousies and intrigues. The minister of the interior had perhaps the most influential office, for he controlled the police, censorship, and provincial governors. But the minister of finance could also make himself felt, for not only did he administer taxes, tariffs, and the vodka monopoly, but he could also set back the proposals of other ministers simply by saying no funds were available. Only the minister of war could sometimes count on getting funds over the opposition of the minister of finance; the military strength of the Empire was usually regarded by the tsars as their overriding priority. But no minister had total authority in

---

[8] For a study of the works and working of the ministries of finance, interior, and agriculture in the pre-war decade, see the article by G. L. Yaney in *Slavonic and East European Review*, Vol. XLIII (1964), 68–90. Ministers' competence varied, and there were some who were far from being the privileged and unperceptive intriguers that are sometimes portrayed as the norm. D. Lieven's *Russia's Rulers under the Old Regime* (1989) provides a fair picture.

his own sphere. That there were powerful figures in the tsar's entourage was well known, and strikingly confirmed when the Russo-Japanese War was provoked against the advice both of the minister of foreign affairs and the minister of war.

In 1906 the Committee of Ministers was abolished, its functions being divided between a revived Council of Ministers, the Duma, and the State Council. The Council of Ministers had been formally established in 1861, coexisting with the Committee of Ministers and the State Council; Alexander II did not favour his father's system of private chanceries. Under Alexander it consisted of ministers and nominated officials, chaired by the Tsar himself. It discussed project-laws and other measures, which might receive prompt royal assent or be sent to committee for further study. Through the Council passed Alexander's great reforms, but its functions ceased in 1882. Then, in October 1905, it was transformed into the supreme legislative and administrative body. Its chairman (prime minister) was selected by the Tsar from trusted officials. It gave preparatory study to projects which would later be debated by the Duma and State Council. However, the ministers of foreign affairs, war and finance frequently by-passed these channels by reporting to the Tsar privately. According to Article 87 of the *Fundamental Laws of the Empire*, promulgated in 1906, between sessions of the Duma or State Council proposed laws could be submitted directly to the Tsar for his approval. As it was difficult for the assemblies to undo such laws, this provision provided a loophole whereby the government could pass measures that would have been rejected by one or other of the houses. In the World War the Council's functions diminished, although its four special committees for defence, supply, transport, and fuel were important.

The supreme court after 1905 remained the Senate, which by 1914 had nine sections. It was not only a court of appeal, but was also the promulgator of imperial *ukazy*, the confirmer of titles of nobility, and the settler of landowners' boundary disputes.

Each of the ministries had its own offices in the provinces, and these offices would often act under direct orders from St. Petersburg without reference to the local governor. At the turn of the century there were seventy-eight provinces (*gubernias*), together with eighteen regions which, because of their remoteness or other special features, were considered unsuitable for division into provinces. A province was headed by a governor (*gubernator*), responsible for the observance of the laws of the land and directly answerable to the minister of the interior. His province was subdivided into districts and the latter into towns and cantons. Largely subject to the will of the governor were the provincial and local *zemstva* which, despite limitations[9] imposed in the reign of Alexander III, had considerable influence in economic, agricultural, and social matters. The towns were administered by the town councils, elected by the wealthier citizens; Moscow with over a million inhabitants had about 10,000 electors. The peasantry had its village commune (*mir*), and sent representatives to the *volost* (canton) assembly. Each village elected its elder, an office which was more a burden than an honour because its holder was personally liable for the conduct of his electorate. Each *volost* had a three-man magisterial bench to try petty crimes. Between 1889 and 1912 rural self-government was restricted by the supervision of 'land captains', appointed from the local nobility.

Bureaucracy and bureaucratic practice were (and remained) a pervasive and depressive feature of Russian life. The officials not only preferred to place administrative convenience before the interests of the individuals they allegedly were intended to serve, but in Russia they had exceptional opportunities to do so. This was partly because the ordinary citizen had no channels of effective complaint. The police were part of the bureaucracy, and in any case complaints against the bureaucracy were investigated exclusively by the bureaucracy. Ordinary Russians seemed to accept injustice from above as something which had always been and always would be. Moreover, the traditional Russian emphasis on the common good in preference to individual rights worked in the same direction; many would not find outrageous, for example, the arrest of ten men in the hope that one of them might be a criminal.

For many Russians the bureaucracy seemed an alien imposition, an internal colonialism almost. In the sense that public power and noble status were linked, the bureaucracy was behind the times. The pedigrees of the most exalted office-holders sometimes revealed imposing titles but no really relevant training for their responsibilities, although it is true that there were institutions like the Corps of Pages and the Institute of Jurisprudence to train the sons of the wealthiest nobles. Possibly the slavish relationships between upper and lower ranks in the government offices were merely a reflection of this feudalistic remnant, reinforced by the regulation that the higher officials could dismiss the lower with no cause given. Corruption and bribery were still normal. It was said that the low pay scales of public officials were a reason, and excuse, for this, but it was the worst-paid officials (abacus and copy clerks) who received the least in bribes. While this clerical proletariat was literally starving towards an

---

[9] Peasant representation in the *zemstva* had been limited, the provincial governor had been given the right of veto over the *zemstva*'s staff appointments, and the local bureaucracies continued to stifle spontaneous initiatives of the *zemstva*.

early death, the better-paid officials could enrich themselves with bribes, book-cooking, and plain theft; the higher the salary the higher the bribe. But nevertheless it was not the dishonest official who was the most harmful. It was the zealot, sitting behind his desk, ignorant of the real life outside, virtuously formulating new regulations or new schemes for the common good, who aroused the most resentment.

The Dumas and the parties

Witte, whom Nicholas was beginning to blame for the concessions made in 1905, was dismissed before the Duma met. His successor was Goremykin, whose only distinction, according to Witte, was his whiskers. The election results showed that the hope that the peasantry would choose conservative candidates was ill-founded; both town and country elected a preponderance of radicals. The Kadets and their allies won 179 seats. The Socialist Revolutionaries boycotted the elections as a party, but their sympathizers, thanks to rural support, were the second largest group in the Duma: they won ninety-four seats and called themselves the Labourists (*Trudoviki*). The Social Democrats had also decided not to participate in the elections, except in the Caucasus, where they knew they were strong: they elected eighteen members, mainly Mensheviks from Georgia. The Octobrists, near the centre of the political spectrum, won seventeen, while right-wing parties won fifteen. From the non-Russian parts of the Empire came strong groups of Polish and Ukrainian nationalists and weaker groupings from the Baltic provinces. There were also thirty Moslems, most of whom allied themselves with the Kadets.

Some half-hearted negotiations were started to persuade moderate party leaders to enter the government, but these produced no results, largely because such leaders had no intention of sitting side by side in the Council of Ministers with reactionary colleagues chosen by the Tsar. In the Duma intelligent debates were staged on some of the main problems of the Empire (land distribution, the rights of Jews and religious dissenters, the Polish question) but since the government gave only perfunctory attention to the opinion of the chamber these discussions had no immediate effect on policy. They did, however, have some effect on public opinion, because the debates were reported in the press. This, the First Duma, did not last long. Angered by a governmental announcement that compulsory redistribution of landowners' land was absolutely out of the question, which was not the Duma's opinion, the latter issued its own statement on the rural crisis. The government was able to describe this as a revolutionary and certainly an illegal action, and with this excuse troops were sent to occupy the chamber. The Duma was thus dissolved only two months after its first meeting.

Under Article 87, the ensuing period before the election of a new Duma provided an opportunity for the government to pass measures by decree. By this time Goremykin had been replaced as chairman of the Council of Ministers by the far more energetic and perceptive Stolypin. When the Kadet and Trudovik members of the dissolved First Duma crossed into Finland and signed a proclamation (the 'Vyborg Manifesto'), urging the Russian people to resist the government by refusing taxes and conscription, Stolypin retaliated by arresting them on their return. They were put on trial (automatically barring them from election to the new Duma) and were sentenced to short terms of imprisonment. In December 1905 Witte, dissatisfied with some army officers' softness toward disturbances, had obtained the tsar's support for a more trigger-happy policy, which the war ministry unwillingly passed on to its commanders. Regular military courts were trying hundreds of alleged civilian rioters but, because of their usually quite high standards of procedure, were taking more time and acquitting more accused than the government wanted. So in summer 1906 Stolypin and the interior ministry, despite the distaste of the war ministry, decided to introduce field courts martial. Great care was taken to appoint officer judges who had not been tainted by training as army lawyers, and in general the courts martial achieved the aim of fast trials and fast executions. They aroused great protest in the Duma.

Stolypin was himself the target of a Socialist Revolutionary bomb at this time, and throughout Russia there were assassinations, sporadic peasant revolts, and more naval mutinies at Sveaborg and Kronstadt. Not all these plots were the work of anarchists and Socialist Revolutionaries. By this time the extreme right-wing groups had their own terrorists, and one of these succeeded in killing a Kadet leader; the assassin had his death sentence commuted by the Tsar.

Distaste for 'Stolypin's neckties', the hundreds of hangings authorized by courts-martial, was one of the reasons the Octobrist leaders refused his offer of a place in the government. In February 1907 the Second Duma was elected; the Kadets, damaged by the arrest of so many candidates after the Vyborg Manifesto, won only ninety-two seats, while the Trudoviki won 101. The Social Democrats, who this time participated wholeheartedly, won sixty-five seats, and even the Socialist Revolutionaries won thirty-four although that party still claimed to be boycotting the election. On the other hand, while the right-of-centre Octobrists increased their seats to thirty-two, the extreme right-wing parties rose to sixty-three. The government was still reluctant to co-operate in any real way with the Duma, although Stolypin himself was perhaps more flexible than his colleagues. Right-wing confidants of the Tsar were horrified by the Duma's criticism of the way the Russian army was managed, while Stolypin himself was riled by the Duma's opposition to his land reform. The police soon came to the rescue of those clamouring for a dissolution, using a tactic which they would still favour half a century later. A document, in the form of an appeal to soldiers to mutiny, was obtained. This was then handed to a Social Democrat member of the Duma, who before he had time to read it, was arrested and accused, together with his Social Democrat fellow-members, of sedition. A similar action was taken against a Socialist Revolutionary. Stolypin believed the police evidence to be genuine, but the Duma refused to lift the socialist members' immunity without a thorough examination of the charges, and this provided an excuse for dissolution. Troops were brought into the capital in case of trouble, the Tsar issued a manifesto accusing the Duma of subversion, and it was announced that the next Duma would be elected under quite a different system.

The new electoral system was an infringement of the *Fundamental Laws* by which the Duma had been established in 1906. It gave great weight to the country gentry and to the urban rich, thus ensuring that the resulting chamber would be dominated by those in favour of the *status quo*. At the same time it contrived to reduce the influence of the nationalists from the non-Russian parts by a similar gerrymandering. Warsaw, for example, was to send an equal number of Polish and Russian members, even though Warsaw's Russian electorate was small. When the Third Duma met in late 1907 it had, not surprisingly, a preponderantly right-wing complexion. It was now the Octobrists who were the largest party, with 120 seats. To their right were 145 members of various affiliations, but to their left comparatively few; the Kadets were down to fifty-two seats and the socialist parties had been reduced to much below their level in the previous Duma.

Nevertheless an unrepresentative Duma was not necessarily an ineffective Duma. Although its members were predominantly of right-wing inclination, they were mostly able and sincere. The government was anxious by this time to show that it really did wish to co-operate with the Duma, and Nicholas and his personal advisers found the composition of the new chamber not entirely distasteful. Thus little by little the government attached more and more importance to gaining the Duma's approval for its measures. Ministers went to the Duma and were expected to give genuine answers to the criticisms, often searching, voiced by members. Stolypin's tampering with the electoral system had not affected the field of competence of the Duma, and the latter, especially through its discussion of the annual budget, discovered that few fields of inquiry were closed to it. In fact Duma committees were largely responsible for the improvements in the army and navy which occurred at that time; if the navy ministry and the war ministry had not been forced to respond to Duma criticism, the Russian armed forces would have been in a very bad state indeed by 1914. During its term the Third Duma also succeeded with two reform projects of its own. The justices of the peace, introduced under Alexander II and replaced by land captains under Alexander III were reinstated and the land captains abolished, and health and accident insurance programmes were established for industrial workers. This Duma served its full term to 1912. Towards the end its relations with the government deteriorated, due largely to Stolypin's inability to understand its rights and sensibilities; faced at one stage by difficulty in getting a measure passed by the upper chamber, Stolypin prorogued both chambers for three days, in which period he employed Article 87 to put his measure into effect. This action destroyed the trust which had been built up between the Duma and the ministers, and the leader of the Octobrists in the Duma, Guchkov, in protest resigned from his office of Duma president. It had been the mutual respect of Stolypin and Guchkov which had enabled this Duma, despite its bad beginning, to do better than its predecessors and to demonstrate to the people, as well as to Nicholas, that some kind of interaction between rulers and ruled was indeed workable.

The measure which Stolypin had passed into law with Article 87 was for the extension of the *zemstvo* system into the western borderlands. This had aroused intense dispute because Russian landowners in that region feared that excessive numbers of Poles and peasants would be elected. The electoral regulations did seek to minimize this danger, but in the course of the lengthy argument the Nationalist Party organized itself. Among its principles were loyalty to both the autocracy and the new representative institutions, financial help for the peasants, strong armed forces, support for the Orthodox Church and its educational institutions, the promotion of the Russians as the leading people of the Empire, and the impossibility of granting full citizenship rights to Jews. It was a well-organized party and Stolypin began to rely on it. It seemed likely to replace the Octobrists as the leading party, but it did less well in the election to the fourth Duma than it had hoped. That election, held in 1912, produced the final Duma, whose leaders would supervise the abdication of Nicholas in 1917. Of the 432 members, ninety-one were of the Nationalist Party, but they did not dominate the right because the Octobrists managed ninety-five and various other rightists sixty-three. But it was very much a right-leaning assembly and subject to successive bouts of manœuvring as the prime minister of the day strove to coax two or three parties into a supportive majority. The Centre Party had thirty-one seats and the Kadets fifty-three, but the left had only ten *Trudoviki* and fifteen Social Democrats. However, by 1914, after many disappointments, the various rightists were in no mood to give automatic support to the government.

Stolypin

Undoubtedly the outstanding Russian statesman of the last Romanov decade was Stolypin. He was a man of many enemies, and these enemies were to be found in all political camps. Like many others of unimpeachable integrity and definite views, he did not hesitate to take strong action, and it was probably this which created the hostility towards him. His field courts martial with their high-speed death sentences earned him the hatred of the revolutionaries. His abuse of Article 87 and his interference with the electoral process earned the dislike of the liberals. He caused offence among the minorities, especially among the Finns, whose liberties he curtailed. Above all, perhaps, he was hated by the right extremists, those who resented any dilution of autocracy and found offensive Stolypin's executive power.

Unlike so many other ministers, Stolypin did not rise through the ranks of the central administration, but first attracted public attention as governor of Saratov province. In this office he distinguished himself by personally, and at some risk, intervening in peasant disorders; instead of sending troops he sent himself, talked to the peasants, and avoided bloodshed. He was called to St. Petersburg as minister of the interior, and his elevation to chairman of the Council of Ministers soon followed. He could perhaps best be described as a progressive conservative. His actions were often repressive and uncompromising, but it should be remembered that he was contending not only with left-wing revolutionaries, but with extreme right-wing radicals also. Apart from the right-wing parties with strong representation in the Duma there also existed from 1905 the Union of the Russian People. This, which was intelligently led, aimed at appealing to the emotions of the masses and enlisting their support for a return to the traditional autocratic regime. It was anti-Jew and anti-intellectual, and participated actively in the *pogroms*. There were also those, often in close touch with Nicholas, who spent much of their time devising ways to abolish or emasculate the Duma, so that power could be returned to where it traditionally belonged. Compared to some of their schemes, Stolypin's tampering with the electoral system was mild indeed. Among the ambitious men seeking to replace Stolypin was Witte, embittered by his own dismissal in 1906 and not averse to consorting with the rightists if that would improve his chances.

Witte, however, never got back. But he wrote his memoirs and outlived Stolypin. The latter was bombed in 1907, but although his house was damaged, his daughter crippled, and about twenty-five persons killed, he emerged unhurt physically, though injured emotionally. In 1911 he attended a Kiev theatrical performance in the presence of the Tsar. During the interval, Nicholas wrote later to his mother:

we heard two noises . . . I thought a pair of opera glasses had fallen on somebody's head and ran back into the box to look . . . women shrieked, and right in front of me stood Stolypin in the stalls. Slowly he turned his face towards us and made the sign of the cross with his left hand in the air. Only at this point did I notice that he was very pale and that his right hand and uniform were bloodstained. He sat down quietly and started to unbutton his tunic.[10]

Stolypin died a few days later. His assassin was a romantic revolutionary acting mainly to satisfy his own needs. A police informer as well as a revolutionary, and finding in neither activity a cause to which he could belong or contemporaries who would respect him, he sought to win appreciation by a glorious deed. As an *Okhrana* agent, he had secured a pass into the theatre and got to within three paces of Stolypin.[11] His first shot ricocheted into the leg of a violinist sitting in the orchestra pit, but his second was fatal. His association with the police later led to rumours that the assassination had been arranged with the complicity of highly placed officials.

The Stolypin Reform

Lenin later described 1905 as a dress rehearsal for 1917. This was a dress rehearsal that demanded substantial rewriting of the plot, for the revolt took a course that surprised both the regime and the revolutionaries. Hitherto the latter had supposed future revolution to be on the lines of the European upheavals of 1848, but events had shown that the Russian workers could spontaneously organize themselves into soviets and that the peasants were not the inert conservative mass that had been supported.

The scattered peasant revolts of 1906–7 had taken many forms, beginning with invasion of private and state forests or grazing land, or refusal to pay taxes, and progressing to robbery of warehouses, arson, destructive attacks on the property of local landowners and often on the landowner families. Although landowners were the main target, government officials, and especially the police, were also attacked. Contrary to official descriptions, these risings were not co-ordinated with each other and were not instigated by a small minority or by outsiders. What typically happened was that the peasants of a *mir* (commune) decided that enough was enough, found their own leaders from among themselves, and deliberately and with

[10] *Krasnyi arkhiv*, Vol. 35 (1929), 210.
[11] *Slavic Review*, Vol. XXIV (1965), 314–21.

forethought set out to wreak their havoc. The richer among them were the keenest to participate, while the poorer tended to hang back. They had no revolutionary or even socialist goals, but they had a strong feeling for social justice. They were cruelly repressed. Many, including teenagers, were hung with virtually no trial.

This unexpected display by the peasants was noted, each in his own way, by Lenin and Stolypin, and each absorbed its lesson. Lenin, while continuing to underestimate the strength of the peasant *mir*, nevertheless began to think of a democratic dictatorship of not just workers, but workers and peasants. Stolypin was strengthened in his belief that the autocracy could not survive unless it solved the peasant problem.

The far-reaching and fundamental peasant reforms introduced piecemeal between 1906 and 1911 are called the Stolypin Reform, although they were worked out by a Danish agricultural expert and other government officials. Because Stolypin hoped that they would create from the 'best' peasants a class of prosperous smallholders with a stake in the *status quo*, the reforms were sometimes called a wager on the strong (or, more realistically perhaps, a wager on the sober). Instead of easing the land shortage by expropriating the landowners (as many Duma members demanded), the reforms promised a solution at the expense of the *mir*.

In the official view, the *mir* seemed harmful and, with the end of redemption payments, superfluous. It still imposed the traditional methods of the majority, and its strip system of land division by which a peasant landholding might be divided into thirty or more strips could never be efficient. It is true that since the Emancipation it was possible for peasants to withdraw from the *mir,* and to consolidate their strips, but all too often the *mir*'s opposition prevented such action. It is also true that most peasants wanted to keep the *mir*, partly because it protected them from the winds of change; it was only a minority which had the will and the ability to be independent. It was this minority of shrewd, perhaps selfish, farmers which the government wished to increase and encourage; the less enterprising would, it was thought, eventually either quit agriculture or begin to imitate their more advanced neighbours.

In the beginning, release of unused or underused land[12] for sale on easy terms to the poorer-than-average peasant was the most publicized feature of the legislation, but the planners were also hoping to spread better

---

[12] In 1905 in European Russia about 25 per cent of the land was privately owned, 35 per cent was peasants' strips, and about 40 per cent state-owned. Of the private land 62 per cent was owned by the nobility (as against 80 per cent in 1877), 15 per cent by merchants, and 15 per cent by peasants (6 per cent in 1877). See P. Khromov, *Ekonomicheskoye razvitiye Rossii* (1967), 495–6.

farming practice. The new legislation established a land settlement commission, whose officials were to confirm peasants in the ownership of the
strips which they cultivated at that time. Then, in the many communes
where there had been no complete land redistribution since Emancipation,
any householder wishing to convert ('consolidate') his strips into one
integrated landholding could request the survey officials to suitably rear-
range all the strips of the commune, whether or not his neighbours desired
this. In other communes a two-thirds majority vote could enforce consolidations for the whole village. The cherished hereditary household plot
of each family, which traditionally had not been subject to redistribution,
was not included in consolidation plans. It was hoped that eventually the
new peasant farmers would transfer their homes (which stood on or near
their household plots) to a site on their new consolidated land area, but
this was a slow process. The legislation included a prohibition of the sale of
peasant land to non-peasants, and a maximum allowable landholding: it
was not intended to create a few big landowners.[13]

The legislation, and especially its local application, was very much a
play-it-by-ear process, peasant reaction to the earlier measures affecting
the later decisions. After the first few years, consolidation on behalf of
individual peasants declined, but more and more peasants collectively
demanded village consolidation. Thus officials began to deal with villages
as collective units rather than with individuals; their task virtually became
village redevelopment.

Some poorer peasants sold their land as soon as their ownership was
confirmed, and then went to the towns in search of work. Many more
stayed on, eking out a meagre and often resentful existence; resentful
because often their familiar way of life and work was changed by land
rearrangements desired by their better-off neighbours. In this way the reforms added fuel to the already smouldering social tension in the countryside. But, given a few decades of peace, there might have developed a
prosperous and loyal peasantry. In the immediate pre-war years there were
indeed higher yields, increased use of machinery and fertilizers, and a
burgeoning of farmers' co-operatives. When peasants became soldiers in
1914 the reform had to stop, because the possibility of changes in the home
village was demoralizing for soldiers at the front. By that time about two
and a half million households (of an eligible total of about twelve million)
had had ownership of their strips confirmed and were thus outside the
authority of the *mir*. Of these about one-half had reached the second stage

---

[13] This section, and especially this paragraph, is somewhat simplified. For a fuller and better account see G. T. Robinson, *Rural Russia Under the Old Regime*.

of consolidating their holdings. In the wheat-growing south almost half the households had broken away from the *mir*.

One of the first consequences of the 1917 revolutions was a partial reversal of this process, with the resentful majority of a village forcing the independent minority to replace their land at the disposal of the *mir*. But this reversal seems to have been prevalent mainly in areas where extensive individual consolidations had taken place, or where outsiders had bought consolidated plots; village consolidations appear to have been reversed only rarely.

8. *On the Eve*

The population

ALTHOUGH as early as the thirteenth century the Tartars had organized a population count of Russia, it was not until 1897 that a really comprehensive census was undertaken, and even this was far from perfect. According to this 1897 census, the Empire contained 125 million inhabitants (excluding Finland, which had about 2.5 million). Both the birth-rate and the death-rate were higher than in most other parts of Europe, and the fourteen per thousand excess of births over deaths promised a fast population growth. What this increase amounted to by 1914 is disputed, but a conservative estimate for the 1914 population is 155 million,[1] of whom 125 million were in European Russia, thirteen million in Central Asia, ten million in Siberia and the Far East, and six million in Transcaucasia. The most densely populated part of the Empire was Poland, followed by the notoriously overpopulated wheatlands of the Ukraine (which had 150 persons per square mile in 1897). Six per cent of the Empire's territory (Poland, Ukraine, Lithuania, the Moscow region, the central agricultural region) contained two-fifths of the population. In 1897 15 per cent of the population was classified as urban,[2] but there were only nineteen cities of more than 100,000 inhabitants. St. Petersburg approached 1,250,000 and Moscow had recently reached the one million mark, while Warsaw, in third place, had 684,000. By 1914, thanks to high birth-rates and rapid migration to the towns, St. Petersburg had 2,118,000, Moscow 1,762,000, while Riga and Kiev had doubled their populations and passed the half-million mark. There were over half a million villages, averaging 200 inhabitants each in 1897. Urban returns indicate that by 1911 the towns of Russia (many of which were little larger than villages) contained almost two million residential buildings, of which a little more than half were

[1] Some reputable estimates go as high as 170 million. In any case, the Russian population was roughly one and a half times greater than the American, and more than treble the British.
[2] Compared with four-fifths in Britain and two-fifths in the USA.

wooden. Of the 1,082 communities classified as towns, 886 claimed to have some street lighting (usually kerosene, but seventy-four had electric and thirty-five gas lighting). 192 towns had piped water systems, and thirty-eight some kind of piped sewage. Fifty-five had tramways and 182 had telephone systems. Moscow's telephone system dated from as early as 1882; the city council of St. Petersburg took great pride in its Central Telephone Exchange, opened in 1905 soon after the local system had been taken over from Bell Telephone.

According to the 1897 census, there were ninety-two million Slavs in the Empire, of whom fifty-seven million were Great Russians, twenty-two million Ukrainians, six million Byelorussians, and eight million Poles. Among the other nationalities were five million Jews, about fifteen million Germans, and thirteen million Turkic and Tartar peoples. Seventy per cent of the population was classified as Orthodox (including Old Believers), 11 per cent as Mohammedan, and 9 per cent as Catholics. Of the Empire's males 0.2 per cent, and of females .01 per cent, had had some form of higher education. In Finland and the Baltic provinces the literacy rate was over 75 per cent, but in Russia proper much lower; only the Moscow and St. Petersburg regions exceeded 40 per cent, the rest of European Russia ranged from 10 to 40 per cent. Thanks partly to the growth of primary education after 1905, about 30 per cent of the population were literate by 1913, with a much bigger percentage for young urban males.

Seventy-seven per cent of the population in 1897 was classified as peasant, 10 per cent was 'middle class', and 0.5 per cent was of the Christian priesthood. The hereditary nobility amounted to 1 per cent, and non-hereditary nobles plus non-noble officials added another 0.5 per cent to this. Cossacks were 2.3 per cent, and foreigners 0.5 per cent. Emigration was small, but increased in the early twentieth century. In the first decade of the latter about 1.5 million emigrants left for the New World; nearly half of these were Jews, and one-quarter Poles. Seventy-five per cent of employed persons were engaged in agriculture. Nine per cent were in manufacturing and mining, and this increased to about 10 per cent by 1914, by which year about 1.5 per cent of the total population were non-agricultural workers, compared to 12 per cent in the USA.

Compared with the figures for the beginning of the nineteenth century (see p. 9), the most striking change is the absolute growth of the population and the growing importance of the non-Russian nationalities, reflecting a territorial expansion which had enlarged but not solidified the Empire.

With a pervasive bureaucracy there was a correspondingly large output of official statistics. These were of varying accuracy and relevance; two returns which throw some light on Russian society are the medical/mortality figures, and the annual state budget. According to the 1897 statistics, one-tenth of all Russians died of 'old age'. Infantile mortality was very high, but after this the most common cause of death was unhelpfully defined as 'convulsions', accounting for 14 per cent. The traditional scourge of the intelligentsia, tuberculosis, was not confined to that class, for it caused 10 per cent of all deaths. Cholera took 4 per cent, and strokes 5 per cent. The 'English disease' (rickets) took less than 0.5 per cent. Murder was responsible for almost 0.1 per cent, and accidents 2 per cent. Suicides at 1 per cent were low compared to more urbanized nations. These categories obscure the incidence of two causes of death which were causing much anxiety, vodka[3] and syphilis. In 1913 in Russian towns 1.8 per cent of the inhabitants were registered syphilitics. In the famous Moscow Foundlings Hospital there was a ward devoted to syphilitic babies, who were fed by specially recruited syphilitic wet-nurses.[4]

Until 1894 the government farmed out the right of selling and manufacturing alcoholic beverages, but in that year Witte introduced a state liquor monopoly. This was designed to reduce drunkenness and also to divert to the Treasury funds which had previously swelled the fortunes of the liquor merchants. Deaths attributable to alcohol did fall but, after the Russo-Japanese War dislocated the state budget, revenue needs took precedence over temperance. Higher sales were encouraged and temperance measures were half-hearted. One such measure was the regulation that liquor could not be consumed within fifty paces of the place of sale, presumably in the expectation that only the sober would find their way back for more. That the death-rate from alcohol was four or five times higher than in western Europe was largely because Russian imbibing was concentrated in a few drinking bouts, rather than spread evenly through the year. Drunkenness was especially widespread on holy days, which are generously distributed throughout the Orthodox calendar. In winter, a drunken sleep could mean a frozen death, unless the victim was picked up by one of the special police patrols organized in some districts. In 1908 an anti-alcohol exhibition was held for the first time in Russia, and there was a strong temperance movement in the Duma. Prohibition was achieved in 1914.

Whereas Russia in 1913 could take pride in her veterinary services, medical services were still inadequate, though improving. For several decades the *zemstva* (which, however, only existed in about two-thirds of the provinces) had organized rural medical services, and it is indicative of the advanced social consciousness of the Russian professional class that the ruling principle of these services was that a free medical service was a

[3] Convulsions?   [4] H. Troyat, *Daily Life in Russia* (1962), 103.

right, not a privilege or charity. The doctors who practised under the *zemstva* were a particular type, hardworking and idealistic. In the cities it was different. There the medical services were usually paid for and, apart from factory medical services, little was done for the poor. In all, there were about 25,000 doctors in 1913; more than ten times more, and better prepared, than a century earlier. Among the wealthy the belief persisted that German doctors were better, and few would admit to their friends that they had a Russian doctor.

In the section on Russian society in 1812 (see p. 14), the state budget was analysed. The figures given may be compared with the following, which are for 1910 (when the finances were back to normal after the upheavals of 1905). The state budget from 1901 to 1910 increased by about 50 per cent, on both the revenue and expenditure sides. Direct taxes accounted for only 8 per cent of income, whereas indirect amounted to 21 per cent.[5] Indirect taxes on sugar, matches, kerosene, tobacco, and cigarette paper were proportionately more burdensome for the poor, although as the range of taxed items widened the urban classes began to take a fairer share of the tax burden. Various internal duties accounted for another 6 per cent, but the biggest sources of income were state investment (29 per cent, including 22 per cent from state railway receipts) and 31 per cent from state monopolies. Of the latter, almost all was accounted for by the liquor monopoly which, unlike the state railways, had low operating costs. The liquor monopoly income, plus taxes on various beverages, accounted for 29 per cent of the state revenue in 1910. Compared with 1901, when the state liquor monopoly was still only partially in force, this income had doubled; even when the operating expenses were deducted it still amounted to 25 per cent of state revenue. On the other side of the budget, operating costs of the state railways accounted for 22 per cent of expenditure, the ministry of war for another 20 per cent, and the ministry of finance for 17 per cent. Interest on government loans had reached 16.5 per cent of the total expenses. The ministry of the interior (which besides security was responsible for a host of services: fire brigades, some roads, telegraphs and posts, map publishing, etc.) took 7 per cent, and the ministry of education 3 per cent. (The latter figure was only a part of the Empire's educational expenditure, for other organizations made their own contributions.)

The social classes

For the landowning nobility, the portents were not good. Long before the Emancipation many had been leading lives far in excess of their incomes.

---

[5] Personal income tax was not introduced in Russia until 1916, and even then was at a rather low graduated rate, which excluded half the population.

On the eve of Emancipation two-thirds of their property had already been mortgaged to government banks. Over the century, in effect, state funds had been diverted as mortgage loans to landowners who used them less for productive investment than for maintaining their standard of living. For many of these improvident gentry, Emancipation meant the paying-off of their mortgages through the indemnities which the government allotted for the land transferred by the nobles to the peasantry. But in the long term, Emancipation only made things worse for the average landowner. A few saved themselves by marrying into rich commercial families, while others did weather the storm and learned to farm their estates on commercial principles. But many had recourse to the Nobles Land Bank, founded in 1885 to advance mortgage loans, or sold their land to peasants and cut their links with the countryside. Whereas in the mid-seventies the gentry possessed about 200 million acres, by 1910 this had diminished to less than 140 million, of which about nine-tenths was rented out to peasant farmers. Although about two-thirds of the senior state offices were held by landowning nobles, this proportion was diminishing as educated non-landowners made successful careers in the bureaucracy. The landowning gentry was not at all homogeneous. It had, for example, a liberal component anxious to extend its role in local government, and an enterprising component that dabbled in industry and intellectual pursuits. But what might be called the traditional, or provincial, nobility was still very influential. It did not like change and did what it could to hinder progressive innovations like the *zemstva* and Stolypin's reforms.

Much of the country's new wealth, the industry and commerce that had developed since the freeing of the serfs, belonged not to the nobles but to a developing middle class which by 1914 exceeded two million people. This was small by European standards and its effectiveness was further diminished by its divisions. The Jews and foreigners, who were prominent in trade and industry, were certainly 'middle class' but were hardly of the Russian middle class. There was also a division between the commercial class on the one hand and the intellectuals on the other. Of the latter, the professionals were growing fast and probably amounted to a million workers by 1914, although only about 130,000 of those had higher education. Primary-school teachers and doctors multiplied especially fast, and may have doubled between 1900 and 1914. Both the creative intellectuals and the more numerous professionals tended to scorn the capitalist and the merchant. This is probably why the capitalists were ignored or treated negatively by Russian writers, even though many of their names were household words, and even though their works determined the shape of Russia's economic life.

The best-known industrialists of the nineteenth century were the Morozovs, whose four establishments employed 54,000 workers by 1914. The founder of their fortune was a serf born in 1770, Savva Morozov, who secured his landowner's permission to start a dyeing works on the estate, and made a fortune. He purchased his freedom in 1820, and died forty years later. His son Timofei was an innovator too. He imported foreign specialists, encouraged the domestic production of textile machinery, established scholarships for technicians wishing to study abroad, and invested in banks and railways. But his passion for efficiency drove him to extract the last ounce of production from each worker. He introduced a fining system which not only penalized obvious misdemeanours such as lateness, but any failure to achieve what Timofei considered was achievable. The very best worker could expect to pay back about 10 per cent of his wage in fines. Timofei was so ruthless towards his workers that he spent tearful hours before his icon, asking for forgiveness. However his prayers did not avert the famous Morozov strike of 1885, when his 8,000 workers protested against the fines. The strike was broken by armed force and its leaders imprisoned, but Timofei was never the same again, and neither was the Russian labour situation, for the strike encouraged other workers to resist their managements. Timofei's son, Savva, was deeply affected by these events, and when he succeeded his father his reaction took the form of improving working conditions, workers' housing, and medical services. He was also interested in the arts, financing the new and soon-celebrated Moscow Arts Theatre, much of whose stage equipment he designed himself. He became a friend of Chekhov and Gorki. The latter portrayed him in one of his works, and was bailed out of gaol by him in 1905. Savva, on Gorki's invitation, also contributed to the Social Democrats' funds, including the budget of Lenin's journal *Lskra*. But when in 1905 he proposed a plan for profit-sharing among his workers, his mother persuaded the board to dismiss him, and he shot himself.

Men like the Morozovs were exceptional, but they were the leaders of a whole class of capitalists which did much for Russia. If the breed disappeared in 1917, certainly the bricks and mortar of their works lived on. Often Jews or Old Believers, they were notable for their quiet lives; apart from their work and their families they had few interests apart from the arts, which they encouraged by their patronage of native talent. But despite their commonsense and enterprise, they did not understand that the transformation of Russian economic life which they were engineering was producing the social and political tension which in 1917 would engulf them.

By most standards, the status of women was at least as good in 1913 Russia as elsewhere. The revolutionary movements, which after all practised a natural sexual equality, had included female liberation in their aims and these ideals had spread among the educated classes. Fictitious marriages inspired by Chernyshevsky emphasized that, unlike western women, advanced Russian women were more interested in sexual freedom and careers than in voting and property rights. Many girls had gone abroad to study, and returned, hoping for a better Russia. By the turn of the century it seemed that their hopes might be justified. In 1908 the first all-Russia women's conference was held, at which it was said that although there was much to be done, the opportunities available to a woman outside the home were less restricted than in western Europe. There were already female teachers, doctors, and architects working in *zemstva* and town council organizations. In 1904 the first women's agricultural college had been opened. In 1905 university co-education was won. For those interested in the 'woman question', and for those actually working for sex equality in the 'women's movement', educational equality was regarded as a commanding height whose capture would eventually change the structure and attitude of society. But despite middle-class sympathy, despite literary and journalistic successes by women, the women's movement was less strong than it might have been. This was largely because the conventional radicals expected militant women to fight for the general cause rather than the female cause; once the regime was overthrown, they promised, women would get their rights. Those women who gave priority to female emancipation they castigated as 'bourgeois', or worse.

As for the peasants, the casual observer might have noticed little external change in the villages since 1861. There was still very little direct contact between the administration and the peasantry. Although many peasants had acquired extra land from bankrupt gentry or from poorer neighbours, there were others who were dissatisfied and receptive to revolutionary propaganda which they incompletely understood but often found convincing. The Stolypin reforms had done little to remove the tensions between landowners and peasants. On the other hand, tension between rich and poor peasants was by no means as great as marxists liked to believe. A characteristic of the period was the increasing number of peasants who became industrial workers, either in local enterprises or in the towns. Those who went to the urban factories usually maintained their ties with the village, often returning home to help with the harvest. Others, more independent, moved about Russia seeking temporary work; most of these would also go home at harvest time, taking with them whatever they had managed to save. The élite among them were the specialists, who often grouped themselves into a co-operative (*artel*) whose elected leader would seek short-term contracts in such trades as house-painting or stonemasonry.

Artels were also important in industry. They were formed by workers who capitalized themselves by paying an entrance fee. Because the members knew and trusted each other, and cherished the reputation of their group, the *artels* were noted for their reliability and good workmanship. In a sense an *artel* member was a privileged member of the proletariat, but he was found only in small-scale enterprises. The bulk of Russia's industrial workers worked in factories. These were often situated far from towns, and frequently were much larger than their western counterparts. Their owners were usually responsible for the housing of their workers, providing barracks near by. The barracks, though making little demand on the workers' pockets, were hopelessly overcrowded and insanitary, with each man having barely the space of his own bunk; with a two-shift system two workers might be expected to take turns with one bunk. Workers' families also inhabited the barracks. But on working days the men were too tired to notice discomfort, and on holidays too drunk. Moreover, conditions were much worse in the smaller enterprises, where workers and their families would live alongside their workbench in cramped, slimy, and stinking conditions unmatched in the most primitive village.

As industry developed, there appeared a small but growing nucleus of skilled workers. These tended to live outside the factory in private rooms, and gradually broke most of their ties with the villages. They lived in overcrowded conditions, but in several respects they were privileged. Especially at times of boom, enterprises had to make some effort to attract and keep them, so they enjoyed better wages and working conditions. They had a high literacy rate and were ready to listen to revolutionary propaganda. It was from their ranks that the Social Democrats drew much of their strength.

Although trade unions were not permitted (except, with many restrictions, after 1905), the existence of workers' mutual aid associations did foster some sense of solidarity among the proletariat. In the last fifty years of the tsarist regime, there were many strikes which, in part at least, led to government intervention to improve working conditions. The first law came in 1882, and limited the industrial employment of women and children. After the Morozov strike it was made illegal for an employer to benefit from workers' fines; the practice of fining continued but the proceeds went to a fund to help the workers themselves. In 1896, after the St. Petersburg textile workers' strike, the government imposed the 11½ hour working day (with ten hours on Saturday). By 1914 most enterprises worked a nine- or ten-hour day, which, in view of the ninety-eight Sundays and religious or statutory holidays each year, was not arduous.[6] But wages

---

[6] The industrious Dutch had only fifty-seven Sundays and holidays.

were low. Although strikes were illegal even after 1905, with instigators liable to imprisonment, they intensified in the prosperous years preceding the outbreak of war. The most notable strike was that at the Lena gold-fields in 1912. Originally in demand of better working conditions, it was transformed into a demonstration protesting against the arrest of its leaders. Troops were ordered to open fire, killing many workers. This massacre aroused angry reactions throughout Russia:

There has never been so much tension. People can be heard speaking of the government in the sharpest and most unbridled tones. Many say that the 'shooting' of the Lena workers recalls the 'shooting' of the workers at the Winter Palace of January 9 1905. Influenced by questions in the Duma and the speeches which they called forth there, public tension is increasing still more . . . It is a long time since even the extreme left has spoken in such a way, since there have been references in the Duma to 'the necessity of calling a Constituent Assembly and overthrow the present system by the united strength of the proletariat'.[7]

Large enterprises were held responsible for providing medical services, including hospitals and sometimes maternity homes, for workers and their families. The first workers' accident insurance scheme was organized, and in 1903 and 1912 was enhanced by new provisions, the most important of which acknowledged the employers' liability for work accidents, with no necessity for the victim to prove negligence. Many factories provided schools for the children of their workers. There were many ruthless employers, but some did more than the law required. Probably individual consciences were as important as the government's factory inspectors in setting standards.

In contrast to its attitude towards trade unions, the administration did little to hinder, and even encouraged, the co-operative movement which flourished after 1905. Producers' co-operatives in the form of *artels* were already part of Russian tradition; what was new was the sudden popularity of marketing and purchasing co-operatives. There was also a blossoming of the savings bank movement. By 1918 the co-operatives' membership was equivalent to about one-third of the total population.[8] The biggest co-operative retail store was Moscow's *Kooperatsiya*, which had 210,000 members. There was a co-operative wholesale union (*Tsentrosoyuz*), and in 1911 a People's Bank had been founded. The latter, the Moscow Narodny Bank, was 85 per cent owned by the co-operative movement. All this does not mean that Russia in 1914 was well on the road to socialism, but it does

---

[7] From a Moscow *Okhrana* agent's report, published in *Istoricheskii arkhiv* (1962), 1, 178–9.
[8] The 1914 figure would have been lower; consumer co-operatives approximately doubled their membership 1914–17.

suggest that Russians, and especially rural Russians, had not become as individualistic as some commentators assumed.

Internal security

Among the sections of the tsar's Private Chancery abolished by Alexander II was the Third Section, but after its elimination in 1880 its functions continued to be exercised in rather the same way under different names. Earlier, in 1871, its executive arm, the gendarmerie, had been entrusted with the investigation of anti-state activities and later (1878) with the right of search and arrest in factories. When the Third Section was abolished the gendarmerie became part of the new department of police under the ministry of the interior. The assassination of Alexander was followed in 1881 by the 'Decree Concerning Measures for the Protection of State Order and Social Tranquillity', which strengthened the gendarmerie and established the *Okhrana*.

While the ordinary police (dealing with minor crimes and disorderly behaviour) were regarded with some justified contempt by the ordinary Russian, the *Okhrana* soon gained a sinister reputation. It became a widespread secret political organization with the right to arrest any person it chose. In theory, arrestees had to be released within a month or placed on proper trial, but this did not always happen. Moreover, with the assent of the minister of the interior, suspects could be dealt with 'administratively', providing the sentence did not exceed five years of exile.

The *Okhrana* employed thousands of informers, both 'outsiders' and 'insiders'. The latter were those who were members of suspect groups and kept their superiors informed of what was happening. If it seemed that a given group was, or might become, a danger to the state, then its members were arrested and exiled. No doubt genuine revolutionaries, and terroristic conspiracies, were broken in this way, but so were many innocents, and non-violent dissident opinion was suppressed. The insiders were sometimes professionals who wormed their way into the confidence of those whom they would betray. Many, like Azev, actually planned and encouraged terroristic crimes so as to disarm suspicion. Others had been genuine conspirators who had been blackmailed or bribed to change sides, or who had undergone a real change of heart and were ready to spy on their friends. In 1914 three of the seven members of the Bolsheviks' key Central Committee in St. Petersburg were police informers. It was acknowledged that the insiders were often shady characters, but the outsiders were the pride of the organization. To ensure that only men of high character were employed in this side of the *Okhrana*, great pains were taken: Poles and Jews were excluded, recruits were sworn-in before an Orthodox priest. The outsiders were masters of disguise, were entrusted with the observation and tracking of suspects, and listening to the conversations of ordinary citizens. Many of them masqueraded as city cab drivers, for this occupation gave the best opportunity for eavesdropping. Others specialized in the opening, reading, and skilful resealing of suspects' correspondence, or in code-breaking.

Day-to-day control of the population was aided by the internal passports which citizens had to carry, and by the registration with the police of all travellers staying overnight outside their home districts. The janitors of dwelling houses kept lists of arrivals and departures which were sent to the local police. In towns the police kept a list of all the inhabitants' addresses (and by applying on a special form a citizen could obtain the address of any individual he was seeking). Scant attention was paid to individual rights. For example, on May Day 1912, men without collars were chased away from St. Petersburg's main streets, because this seemed the most convenient way to prevent a workers' demonstration.[9] Despite occasional outrages such as this, and the feeling that everyone was being watched, it is probably true that police repression was accepted by Russians as a necessary evil. Most citizens had been shocked by the murder of Alexander II: many regarded the revolutionaries as enemies of reform, and believed that violent protest only strengthened the position of the reactionaries.

Freedom of the press was one of the 1905 guarantees frequently evaded by the administration. It could happen that particular issues of a newspaper were impounded, but more frequently newspapers appeared with white spaces where material had been deleted. Arbitrary (and illegal) attacks on press freedom were most blatant in the provinces:

> The newspaper report concerning the small Kiev kopek-newspaper *Ogni* is arousing deep indignation. It has been fined 1,200 roubles each month and now the present editor, Madame Prokhasko, has been put under administrative arrest despite her illness. They wanted to make her keep quiet about three things: about the Jews, about the workers, and about the priesthood.[10]

The Russian talent for euphemism was well exploited. For example, when newspaper criticisms prompted the administration to ban mention of Rasputin, the term 'dark forces near the throne' was substituted. In 1913 there were about 1,000 newspapers published in the Empire (excluding Poland and Finland). Since the combined circulation of these was about three and a quarter million, it is evident that in Russia small circulation newspapers could survive, especially since one-third of the combined

---

[9] Six years later it was men who did wear collars and ties who were at risk in revolutionary Petrograd.

[10] *Vestnik Evropy* (1910), 11, 352.

figure was contributed by just three papers: the *Russkoye Slovo* of Moscow (750,000), the right-wing *Novoye Vremiya* of St. Petersburg (200,000) and the liberal intellectuals' paper, *Russkiya Vedomosti* (100,000). By contrast the St. Petersburg liberal paper *Rech'* sold only 17,000 copies.[11]

The economy

Russian output grew fast but unevenly after the end of the Crimean War. In terms of industrial production, there was a doubling of output between 1860 and 1880, and a doubling again over the following twelve years. The nineties were a decade of boom, thanks largely to the 1891 protective tariff and renewed railway-building sponsored by Witte. Despite a recession in 1894 there was a further doubling of production in the eight years 1892–1900. After 1900 there was a slower growth, but only 1905 produced an actual decrease. Overall economic growth (measured by net national product) averaged 5 per cent annually from 1909 to 1913, with large-scale industry growing by an annual 7 per cent and even the inefficient agricultural sector (favoured by a run of good weather) by around 3 per cent. On a per-head basis, overall growth would have been about 3.5 per cent, because of the rapid population increase, but that was still a fast rise. However, 1913 national income per head (a rough indication of prosperity) was still only one-fifth of Britain's and one-eighth of the USA's. In terms of production (and especially consumption) Russia was far behind the other great powers. In 1913, in absolute terms, Russian coal production was only one-tenth of Britain's and one-seventeenth of the United States'. Oil production, in which Russia occupied first place in the world in 1900, was only one-third that of the USA in 1913. In steel, Russia produced one-half the British output and one-eighth the American, in cotton textiles one-quarter and one-third respectively. The picture would only be marginally changed if Polish and Finnish output were included in these calculations.

The main industrial areas were the St. Petersburg and Moscow regions, Poland, and the Ukraine. The first two were primarily manufacturing, whereas the Ukraine had supplanted the Urals as the Empire's metallurgical base, using the first-rate coal of the Donets Basin and the iron ore of Krivoi Rog. Cartels, in which ostensibly rival companies joined to share contracts and fix prices, were strong in the coal, engineering, and textile industries. Factories tended to be large; labour productivity was so low that to produce the same output a Russian plant might be double the size of an equivalent American plant. Although there were many big factories, some well-equipped, small-scale and handicraft industry still provided a

[11] These figures are quoted in an article in *Slavic Review* (1963), 663–82, which also gives some examples of how the administration harrassed the press.

high proportion of the Empire's needs. By 1914 output classified as work-shop or artisan occupied about two-thirds of the industrial workers, although it accounted for only one-third of total production.

Witte, when minister of finance, tried with some success to solve the same problem faced by Stalin in the late twenties, how to bring backward Russia to the same industrial level as the more advanced nations. Taxing the peasants hard to raise money for state investment was one policy, but most of this tax revenue was spent on other things. Much more effective, because they produced profits and savings for investment, were the unequal terms of trade (low grain prices and high prices for manufactures) which transferred wealth from the peasants to the industrial towns. Witte's protective tariffs, discouraging low-priced imports, were part of this process, while his gold-based stabilization of the rouble encouraged foreigners to invest their capital in Russia. By 1913 foreign investors had provided Russian private industry with about one-third of its plant and equipment. Expressed differently, one-third of the capital of private companies was foreign-owned. Since the economy was developing quite rapidly, this still left wide opportunities for the Russian investor; although foreign investment was growing faster than domestic, the latter was increasing rapidly, aided by a favourable balance of trade after 1908 which the official statistics did not fully indicate. About one-third of foreign investment was French capital, which was especially strong in mining and metallurgy. Britain and Germany accounted for about one-fifth each, Belgium for about 5 per cent. The USA share of about 5 per cent included, notably, the Russian establishments of the International Harvester Corporation. Apart from direct foreign investment in companies, Russia also benefited from the sale of government bonds abroad. Witte was very successful in persuading the capitalists of Europe to subscribe to Russian government loans. By 1914 probably 45 per cent of the state debt was held abroad. But as the total of foreign investment grew, so did the problem of servicing it. By 1914 interest on foreign loans and investment equalled a quarter of export earnings. This was why balance of payments problems, as well as balance of budget problems, frequently dominated the deliberations of the government.

Foreign investment brought with it much-needed foreign technology. Although there was some home-grown technical innovation, designs and equipment obtained from the West were the usual basis of the new industries. When factory production of aircraft began in 1911 the designs were French, and this was still substantially the position in 1913, when 280 machines were produced by the three companies involved, although one of the latter, the Russo-Baltic railway car works which had diversified into automobiles and aircraft, was building Sikorsky's novel designs. But in

1917 Russian aircraft output of 1,900 units was less than a tenth of French. With automobiles the picture was similar, the French De Dion Bouton being built from 1900 and an Oldsmobile design (known as the *Duksmobil*) from 1904. World War I spurred the development of new car plants, one state-owned and the others private, which would form the basis of the subsequent Soviet automobile industry. Other advanced industries, like optical equipment, machine tools, and bearings, were painfully emerging but were at a low technical level. The optical industry was sponsored by the navy, which needed good rangefinders, and other defence needs were a spur to the government in its encouragement of foreign investors.

By 1914 Germany was the Empire's main trading partner, with Britain far behind in second place. Russia's need for German colliers to supply her naval squadron en route to Tsushima had been a lever enabling Germany to obtain a favourable trade treaty in 1904; the previous treaty, according to the Prussian landlords, had ruined German agriculture. In 1913 one-half of Russia's imports came from Germany, and only one-seventh from Britain. British consular officials complained that British firms would not supply on credit and would not modify their products to meet the customers' wishes. The Germans were more obliging, and of the major British exports only Scotch herrings and whisky seemed safe from German competition. Russia's main export was grain, for which there was a ready demand in the industrial nations of northwest Europe. Several of Russia's railways had been built simply to carry grain from the producing areas to the ports of the Baltic and Black Sea. However, Russian grain lost some of its attraction when grain from the Americas entered the world market. Luckily, the expansion of wheat production in the north Caucasus region enabled Russia to gain substitute markets in the Mediterranean nations, for the new wheatfields produced a grain ideal for spaghetti and macaroni.

In 1914 agriculture was still the weakest part of the Russian economy, although since the turn of the century it had been showing definite signs of progress; the 1913 harvest was the best ever. Grain production per head of population had risen appreciably over the previous decade, although not in the overpopulated central agricultural region. While most peasant farmers still used primitive methods, the formation of large and medium farms using modern knowledge and equipment was accelerating. In many areas small farmers were uniting themselves into producer, consumer, or credit co-operatives, and almost everywhere newly trained agronomists were at work. As both Witte and Stolypin realized, Russia's main economic problem was how to shift part of the agricultural population from the land to the factories. Rural overpopulation meant that there were too many mouths, and a surplus of hands, on the farms. Thus millions of peasants consumed more than they produced, relying on loans, charity, or casual work to tide them over the hungry months. A peasant who ate all, or more than, the food he produced was an economic liability: transferred to a factory the value of his work would be greater than the value of his consumption, and he would become an asset. But Witte's policy of taxing the peasant hard, and Stolypin's policy of helping the strong peasant squeeze out the weak, intensified rural discontent and rural hatreds.[12] Moreover, when the taxed-out or squeezed-out peasant moved to the insalubrious factory barracks, he became part of an ill-paid, unhealthy, unskilled and uneducated proletariat which was a social problem in itself.

The army

Although in the Russo-Japanese War the army had not suffered any crushing defeats, the very fact that it had surrendered territory aroused enormous and often wild criticism after the war. Really the performance of the army in Manchuria had been limited mainly by the supply problem: neither munitions nor men arrived at the front in sufficient quantities. Nevertheless, it was true that even the munitions and men which were available were not handled efficiently. Post-war reforms were therefore almost inevitable, especially as public opinion had a new way of expressing itself, through the Duma.

In the war ministry and among commanders there were many who had drawn their conclusions from the late war and were eager to make changes of organization and tactics, but they faced several handicaps. One of these was Nicholas, who regarded the army as his, loved the superficialities of military life, and took advice from officers of the élite regiments, officers who in many cases he had appointed himself from regiments unsullied by the recent war. In 1905 Nicholas placed the general staff directly under himself, so the war ministry often did not know what the staff was recommending. Nicholas believed that duelling was beneficial for *esprit de corps* (and failed to see that this much-vaunted *esprit* was only a euphemism for a caste system). Although during his reign only about thirty officers died from duelling, a larger number were discharged from the army by their regiments when they refused to duel, or staged a sham duel, after some alleged insult. He appointed and promoted incompetents and caused great damage by putting grand dukes (nephews, cousins, uncles) in high positions.

---

[12] Witte's policy as minister of finance meant that the peasant had to sell his grain immediately after harvest in order to pay his taxes. That is, to sell when prices were low. This boosted grain exports, but also meant that peasants were impoverished and, frequently, undernourished. Witte's fall from power had probably been accelerated by intrigues by the minister of the interior, alarmed at the discontent caused by this economic policy.

The tsar's distrust of the Duma and of reform in general was also a great handicap. Many officers wanted to co-operate with the Duma which, they saw, had a better grasp of military realities than the government. But one reforming war minister was dismissed largely because Nicholas distrusted his cordial relationship with Duma leaders. As for reform, the contrast between the high morale of the Japanese soldier and that of his Russian opponent had impressed on many high officers that only by creating a better society would it be possible to create a better soldier. This view was also unpalatable to many of those influencing the tsar.

Another handicap was the continuing lack of resources, made worse by the war. Lastly, there was the long-continuing controversy over the army's interior role. Continuously, but especially in the disturbed years after 1905, considerable numbers of troops were engaged in internal security. Most of these were on guard duty outside banks, prisons, or railway stations and were rarely called upon to open fire. But these units had to take their orders from the despised local police, whose deficiencies they were making up, and this was as bad for morale as their exposure to dissident influences. Most important, with so many troops engaged it was difficult to stage the field manœuvres that the war ministry realized were so essential for training. But despite these burdens, successive war ministers did introduce some useful changes.

To end justified complaints that staff officers frequently had little understanding of real life at the front, a rule was introduced making it obligatory for such officers to spend periods actually in command of units. Just before the First World War another blow was struck against incompetent higher officers. This took the form of a Supreme Control Commission, chaired by the minister, which would examine the competence of any general officer and, if necessary, retire him. How well this measure would have worked in the prevalent conditions of favouritism is questionable, but it at least showed an awareness of the problem of incompetent senior officers; other armies had the same problem, but did not yet know it.

Artillery had always been a strong point in the Russian army, but in the war against Japan it had not distinguished itself. This was because it was unused to indirect firing in close co-operation with the infantry, because it was ill-provided with weapons suitable for the Manchurian terrain, and because ammunition was not only scarce but also defective: a creeping barrage fired over the heads of the infantrymen was perilous, because of unreliable time fuses. These defects were remedied after the war, and rearmament by Germany and Austria caused the Duma in a closed session in 1913 to approve an increased investment in artillery. The war began before this could bear fruit, which meant that Russian divisions had significantly less artillery support than their opponents. Lack of gun-making capacity, and especially of gun-repair works, would be a serious handicap in the war. Such deficiencies, as well as the rather small stocks of ammunition, resulted more from financial stringency than lack of fore-sight.

The infantry was still equipped with the .299 inch rifle of 1891, with a 5-round magazine. This was a sound weapon when properly made and maintained. After 1905, the so-called Suvorovite reliance on the bayonet was discredited, and both officers and men spent more time on marksmanship. But in the Great War many of the older infantry officers still relied on the bayonet charge. The Russian bayonet was a fearsome four-edged blade which, when attached to the rifle, formed a weapon five and a half feet long. Machine guns had been used in the Russo-Japanese War, but only in small numbers. They had been treated as artillery rather than infantry weapons and their main advantage, local intensification of fire-power at short notice, was thereby lost. After the war more machine guns were issued, but their significance was never quite grasped before 1914, when it was realized that infantry units needed many more than the approved allocation.

The 1874 conscription system implied that the army was to be the nation armed, yet the soldier was still considered as a being apart from society; or rather, a being beneath society. Successive reformers and critics had pointed to the necessity of treating the soldier as an individual, of educating him and stimulating his initiative, but the army always found it easier to treat him like a sheep. Russian military law gave the lower ranks less rights than in other armies: as critics liked to point out, a soldier who defended his wife from violation by an officer thereby committed a crime. Nor could a soldier refuse to carry out an illegal order. When civilians addressed a soldier, they did so in the second person singular, as to a child or pet. If a soldier met a general in the street he had to stand to attention so long as that officer was within three paces of him. He was not allowed to ride on a private carriage, and on a public carriage was not allowed to sit inside. On the railways he was forbidden to enter the first and second class. On a steamship he had to occupy the lower deck in the bow. In the two capitals a soldier was not allowed to sit in the theatre stalls, nor lower than the third row of the balcony. He could not enter restaurants or cafés apart from third-class railway and steamer buffets.

The soldier lived on soup, tea, and black bread; which, according to a British war correspondent, was why he smelt like a horse. His pay was negligible. Yet he was loyal, and not dispirited. His term of active service had been reduced after 1905 to three years in the infantry and artillery, or four years in the other arms (five years in the navy), with a further fourteen or fifteen years in the reserve (and then a final five years in the *opolcheniye*, a kind of elderly territorial army). In 1914 the standing army was about 1,400,000 men, and mobilization produced almost four million more. During the war over fifteen million men were absorbed by the army, peak strength being reached in January 1917 (about 6,900,000). However, it was not easy to equip so large a force, especially as the Russian munitions supply partly depended on imports. Nor was it easy to officer such a large army. The 1874 reform had prescribed shorter periods of service for educated conscripts, which meant that the men who had become reserve officers in peacetime had served less than the two years regarded as the minimum required to train good officers. Another drawback of the 1874 scheme was the large numbers of exemptions; with nearly half of each age-group able to claim exemption, the 'Russian Steamroller' would soon become short of steam. By 1917 the proportion of over-forties in the army would be high, and minimum physical standards would be lower than those of the other belligerent armies. The high proportion of the population exempted from service is evident from the following approximations, indicating the number of men (in millions) called up for army service by the belligerents:

	Peacetime army	After initial mobilization	By end of war	Total population	Per cent called
Russia	1.4	5.3	15.3	180	8.8
France	0.8	3.8	7.9	39	19.9
Britain	0.2	0.6	5.7	45	12.7
Germany	0.8	3.8	14.0	68	20.5

Source: P. Lyashchenko, *Istoriya narodnogo khozyaistva SSSR* (1956), II, 613.

The navy

The Russo-Japanese War was painful for the army, but catastrophic for the navy. Of the three main pre-war squadrons, two had been destroyed ignobly and the surviving Black Sea Squadron was mutinous. The navy ministry was openly accused not only of inefficiency, but of gross corruption. The ministry and the Naval General Staff (founded 1907) wished to rebuild the fleet, but for several years they mishandled their case, failing to convince the public (and especially the Duma) that they were capable of producing a good return from any budgetary appropriations.

Like other nations, Russia had its naval lobby, but instead of one Navy League, as in Britain, the USA and elsewhere, she had two. The League for the Renewal of the Navy, which numbered two grand dukes among its leadership, was the advocate simply of a big navy. The Russian Naval Union, financed largely by industry, wanted a big navy, but built in Russia. These two organizations were in frequent opposition because the domestic shipyards had longer deliveries and higher costs than foreign companies. However, this weakening of the naval lobby was compensated by Nicholas's emotional attachment to its cause; one general lamented that the usually polite Nicholas would shout and thump the table whenever he heard criticism of his beloved fleet. The Duma's Defence Committee could be circumvented by appealing directly to the Tsar. This was done, and four Dreadnought-type battleships were laid down for the Baltic. They were to be built at home, although with technical help from a Scottish company. But opposition from the Duma was an inconvenience, and a threat to further developments, so its demands for the reform of the navy ministry and the appointment of a better navy minister were satisfied. The new minister, Admiral Grigorovich, was sympathetic to the Duma's criticism. The powers of the minister were strengthened so that he was no longer bound by the decisions of innumerable committees which had been established to control almost every detail of naval administration; the Chief of Naval Staff henceforth reported to him, and not directly to the Tsar. With the reduction of the role of committees and the introduction of one-man control, decisions became speedier and better co-ordinated. The Duma, mollified, approved a five-year plan for the navy, which envisaged the construction of four big battlecruisers for the Baltic and three battleships for the Black Sea, with appropriate additional investment in smaller ships and dockyards. A long-term naval programme was subsequently drawn up and approved. This specified the construction for the Baltic of two capital ships each year until 1931—by which time the Empire would be the world's third greatest naval power, with twenty-four battleships and twelve battlecruisers in that sea alone (the Baltic fleet was also the source of the Far East Squadron). In the Black Sea the aim was to construct a fleet one and a half times bigger than the combined navies of the three other Black Sea powers. Foreign participation was envisaged: some smaller ships, especially prototypes, would be built abroad, and the British Vickers and John Brown companies would help to reorganize the government shipyards on the Black Sea and Baltic respectively. Vickers were also to build a new ordnance works at Tsaritsyn. Attention was also paid to undersea operations. Russia was ahead of other countries in mine warfare: it had built the world's first successful minelaying submarine and in 1914 supplied mines to the British navy. Wireless was also well advanced, and a series of radio-direction stations on both sides of the Gulf of Finland enabled the navy to locate any vessels which broke radio silence. The *Novik* was so far in advance of other countries' destroyers that even in the 1990s some naval historians, unwilling to believe that tsarist Russia was capable of successful innovation, were still claiming that it was really built in Germany. By 1914, although the ambitious capital-ship programme was far from complete, the quality of the officers and the morale of the seamen were vastly superior to their 1905 condition.

When the war against Germany began, the commander of the Baltic fleet was von Essen. His cruiser division was commanded by von Schulz. The commander of the Black Sea fleet was Eberhard. Baltic Germans provided one-fifth of the navy's officers. After 1914 this would be the most common grievance of sailors, who believed or were persuaded that German-speaking officers naturally preferred a German victory.

Education

In 1914 there was still an imbalance between the developed university system and the rather inadequate primary and secondary schools. Nevertheless, elementary schooling had been greatly extended since the sixties by the work of the *zemstva*. By 1896 there were nearly 79,000 primary schools, compared with nearly 23,000 in 1880. These 79,000 schools were attended by about three million males and 850,000 females. 33,000 of them were the direct concern of the ministry of education, being mainly *zemstva* schools and Sunday schools (the latter, about 1,000 in total, were usually financed by benevolent citizens to teach basic subjects to adults). The Holy Synod supervised about 34,000 parish schools, and another 10,000 primary schools were the responsibility of the ministry of war. The typical (one-class) primary school taught religion, Church Slavonic, Russian, calligraphy, arithmetic, and singing, but there were superior town, district, and two-class schools where geography, history, drawing, and geometry were also offered. Secondary education at the turn of the century remained divided on class lines, with the gymnasiums providing an eight-year course concentrated on the classics and leading to the Attestation of Maturity. The latter enabled its possessor to enter a university or to obtain preferential treatment if entering state service. The real schools provided a six-year course of more practical subjects, and their graduates could, by taking an entrance examination, continue studying at a higher technical institution. Higher fees, and limitations on non-noble entry (with quotas for Jews) ensured that rather more than half the secondary students were of the nobility. Many sons and daughters of the richer non-noble classes were sent abroad for their education. In 1899 there were 191 gymnasiums, plus fifty-three pro-gymnasiums and 115 real schools. In addition there were very many secondary schools for girls, with about 130,000 pupils.

By 1914 there were 120,000 schools of all types, with eight million pupils (of whom seven million were in primary schools). In the gymnasiums the classics were beginning to lose their predominance and more practical subjects were increasingly favoured. Despite the efforts of the ministry of education, the lower classes were making headway in the gymnasiums; even in 1902 nearly 10 per cent of gymnasium students were from peasant families. Most of the one-class primary schools offered an extra, fourth, year, while most of the real schools had an extra, seventh, year to prepare students for higher technical education.

The peasant saying, 'Education is an ornament in good times and a refuge in bad', well expressed the attitudes of most Russians, but not of the ministry of education. Under the last Romanov, the history of Russian education is an excellent illustration of the gap between state and people. By 1914 education had undoubtedly progressed, but this was more a result of public energy than government action, even though the education budget was increasing much faster than total government expenditure.

Perhaps the most influential sector was the elementary education provided by schools founded by the *zemstva*. At the turn of the century, four-fifths of the funds of elementary education came from *zemstva* and town councils, yet the ministry of education controlled these schools, repressing initiatives uncovered by its inspectors, standardizing approved textbooks, controlling the smallest details of their teachers' working and private lives. The church schools, declining in quality and importance, were also supervised by the ministry.

Apart from the local councils, various enterprising bodies or individuals established schools, but all (except those established by other ministries) felt the mortifying hand of the ministry. By 1914 the *zemstva* were in theory not allowed to communicate with the teachers of the *zemstva* schools or to interfere in the education they provided, while the school buildings built out of *zemstva* funds were declared to be state property. When quota systems had denied most Jewish children an education, they began to go to private schools, but within a few years the quotas were applied to the latter too. Adult schools, another interest of the *zemstva*, soon felt the supervision of the ministry. Even private schools were not allowed to choose their own teachers. All teachers were underpaid, few had meaningful qualifications, most had lost enthusiasm, were subject to frequent transfers and obliged to follow to the letter the prescribed programmes and procedures. They could be dismissed for subscribing to journals of 'advanced' views. In 1913 a meeting of teachers in Yaroslavl to discuss two papers (on new tendencies in grammar and on self-expression in primary schools) was banned because it threatened 'to disturb public tranquillity'.

Many of the most damaging educational restrictions had been introduced under Alexander III, including one ironically referred to as 'the Regulation Concerning Children of Cooks'. Part of the latter (1887) was as follows:[13]

> ... The gymnasiums and pro-gymnasiums, therefore, shall be freed from the attendance of children of drivers, footmen, cooks, laundrymen, small traders and other persons similarly situated, whose children, with the exception perhaps of exceptionally gifted ones, should not be encouraged to abandon the social environment to which they belong.

In the pre-war decade the Duma, by voting more money for education than the ministry wanted, and by denouncing the ministry's attitude, helped to meet popular demand for more and better education. But it was not until the war and a change of minister that the government changed its course. In 1916 the ministry agreed that the post-war schools would not be differentiated according to social classes but would form a unified system with all students able to pass from one grade to the next. Moreover, lower schools would use the local language, and there would be compulsory education provided for all children by 1922.

In the final Romanov decades there was a steady increase in the number of specialized and technical institutions. This was especially marked outside the capital, many technological institutions being established in provincial cities. Also notable was the increase in agricultural colleges and, to a lesser degree, of commercial schools. Women had access to both agricultural and commercial instruction. Schools of art and of music were quite generously financed, and those of St. Petersburg and Moscow enjoyed international repute. Various ministries still had their own higher educational establishments; the ministries of war and commerce were pre-eminent in this respect but were not alone. Even the Department of Posts and Telegraphs of the ministry of the interior had its very modern Emperor Alexander III Electrotechnical Institute.

In 1899 there were still nine universities, but their enrolment had risen to 16,500 (excluding auditors) of which one-quarter was at Moscow University. The typical university had four faculties, of which the largest was Law and the smallest History–Philology; the other two were Medicine and Physic–Mathematics. Certain superior colleges, such as the three lycées, also existed and gave university-style courses in a limited range of subjects.

---

[13] Quoted in P. N. Ignatiev, and others. *Russian Schools and Universities in the World War* (Yale University, 1929), 31.

University autonomy had been restricted by the statute of 1884. In particular, rectors, deans, and professors were no longer appointed by the university councils. The university rector was appointed for four years by the minister of education and was subordinate to the curator of his educational district. Vacant chairs were advertised, and candidates investigated by the university council, but the latter could only make recommendations to the minister. The minister also appointed the university inspectors, who were charged with supervising discipline. Under Alexander III many professors were dismissed for alleged disloyalty, often after they had protested against the expulsion of dissident students.

For girls there was a limited opportunity for higher education before 1905. The St. Petersburg university-style courses for women continued, and had about 1,000 students, but similar courses in Moscow were banned in 1888 and reinstated only in 1900. Some provincial universities were also giving special courses for women. The pioneer medical school for women at St. Petersburg, which opened in 1872, had been closed ten years later, but reopened in 1897. Financed largely by *zemstva* contributions, it gave a five-year course and its graduates, idealists, tended to enter *zemstvo* service, devoting their lives to the rural medical services. But most ambitious girls if they had the means went to foreign, especially German universities. No doubt they were inspired by the example of Sofia Kovalevskaya, the mathematician. This talented woman, born in 1850, had shown signs of mathematical genius at the age of sixteen but, unable to enter the all-male Russian universities, graduated abroad. She was later appointed to a chair at Stockholm, thereby becoming, apparently, the world's first female professor.

The Russian student at the turn of the century was very different from his western contemporaries. He was young but not youthful. He did not seek outlets for boisterousness in sports because he was not boisterous. Rather was he gloomy and tense. All too often the future before him was a choice of becoming a cog in the bureaucratic machine or following his own inclinations and risking exile. It is true that the universities contained many students from the rich nobility, who resembled in some ways (and tried hard to resemble) the students of Oxford and Cambridge. But the Russian institutions were not the preserve of the well-to-do; most of their students were poor. These less wealthy students had entered university via the gymnasiums, where they had learned the classics by rote and practically nothing else. Until the reforms of the twentieth century the gymnasiums did not provide real education; they provided a valuable diploma. Even the classics were not taught with a view to understanding, but only with a view to repetition. Thus in the gymnasiums only the dull were content. The majority learned to despise school authorities, and at university it was a short step from this to despising all authority.

Although a greater proportion of students received financial assistance than in most other countries, the sums received were very small. The student without his own financial resources lived a cold and hungry life. He would probably share a room (and books) with four or five others, and on the coldest days would not attend lectures because he had no adequate clothes or footwear. He would talk endlessly about academic freedom, about Russia, and would probably learn more from reading and discussing the newspapers and journals than from his teachers. Student meetings were forbidden; porters and lodging-house keepers were required to inform the police of any student gatherings (which would then be broken up) and of students' habits, reading, friends, and movements. The university inspectors were hated by all. They could expel students at will. They could cancel or grant government financial assistance. They could forbid a student giving private lessons (an essential source of income for many). They could impose penalties for lateness, improper hairstyles, or untidiness. They spied on professors. Whereas under Alexander II the number of expulsions rarely exceeded 100 in any one year, under Alexander III they sometimes reached four figures. In general, the student unrest which intensified each year was the result of increasing repression and not vice versa, although the more revolutionary students and the more reactionary officials drew strength from each others' extremism; each needed the other to attract adherents from the moderate majority caught in the middle.

Student unrest, which had originally centred around university conditions, under Nicholas became more concerned with general social and political issues. A student council was organized at Moscow University in the late nineties, and this petitioned for the abolition of inspectors and the admission of women. Its leaders were promptly arrested but a new council was formed. There were affrays with the police and 660 students were expelled. At St. Petersburg in 1899 the police for the first time used whips to disperse students; thereupon, 13,000 students throughout Russia, enraged that they should be treated like peasants, went on strike. The universities had to close, and the government responded by allowing the organization of student clubs and by making an effort to improve student housing. But at the same time the number of inspectors was increased to an average of one per 150 students, students were requested to attend the university of their home district, and student eating and reading co-operatives were banned. More teachers were expelled, and about one-third of the striking students were refused re-admission. Following a brainwave that afflicted Witte, a new law allowed hundreds of students considered dissident to be drafted into the army. The war minister, Kuropatkin, thereupon took it upon himself to share a piece of his mind with Nicholas; he thought it dishonourable to treat the army as a penal colony and moreover, he darkly commented, the students were spreading bad ideas in the army. This last argument was compelling, and in 1901 Nicholas ordered the army to discharge the students.

Cossack whips were increasingly called upon to break up student demonstrations. Some students were killed. One expelled student murdered the minister of education in 1901 and literate public opinion, already shocked by police attacks on students, approved the assassination. In 1903 Warsaw students protested against russification. In 1904 the minister of the interior (Plehve) ordered the breaking-up of a meeting of professors from all over Russia, and some of its participants were exiled.

The 1905 crisis, in which university students played a leading role, resulted in certain concessions. Student organizations were again permitted, university councils and their rectors were given back their responsibility for university discipline and other matters. The emergence of open political parties in Russia led to open political associations in the universities. Hitherto the semi-legal or illegal left wing had been predominant. But with the formation of moderate and right-wing associations this predominance diminished, although it did not disappear.

One of the gains of 1905 was women's access to the previously men-only courses at university. Although, as auditors, they did not have all the rights of male students, the government did eventually allow them to take the state university examinations. By 1909 there were 640 of them. Diehard officials tried sporadically, with varying success, to re-exclude female students, and it was not until 1915 that the latter could feel secure. Male students, including those who previously had preached sexual equality, did not at first take kindly to female intrusion. One girl wrote:

At first there was embarrassment when we were working on a corpse; the male students regarded us negatively, not having matured sufficiently in a spiritual sense to the point where they could accept working alongside them women who retained feminine spirit and beauty. In time both we and they got used to it and the awkwardness disappeared.[14]

Another female student wrote:

I think our presence in the universities has softened the male students. Fewer resort to drunkenness . . . there is no bad language . . . competition forces the male students to work harder out of vanity, for fear that the women will do better in the examinations than them.[15]

[14] *Vestnik Evropy* (1912), 9, 376.   [15] Ibid. 375.

By 1910, mutually catalysing dissidence and right-wing pressures led Stolypin to new repressions in the universities, which he regarded as the main source of unrest. Not for the first or last time, a non-Russian was chosen to chastise respected Russian institutions; Kasso, a Bessarabian, was appointed minister of education. Using as a pretext student demonstrations (held to mark the death of Tolstoy), Kasso forbade all non-academic meetings in universities, and the police were empowered to enter universities to enforce this regulation without consulting the rector. There was a student strike in protest. The professors, who had mostly opposed the strike, were enraged by the often brutal activities of the police; some resigned, while others who merely protested were dismissed. Disturbances of one sort or another continued until 1914, and at least 6,000 students were expelled for various periods, some being exiled. Yet in 1914 the universities responded loyally to the Empire's danger. Students and professors ceased their protests and engaged in voluntary work until defeats and official mismanagement (and perhaps the extension of the call-up to students in 1916) turned this enthusiasm into apathy.

Not all was black during the pre-war years. State education was beginning to mean public education. Foreign observers were favourably impressed with the teaching and research in Russian universities and higher institutions. In 1914 there were thirty-nine institutions classified as higher, including ten[16] universities (Saratov University had been founded in 1909; Perm University would be opened in 1916). In the universities between 50 and 60 per cent of the students were of middle-class or noble origin, which suggests that in 1914 access to a university was by no means impossible for a talented youth of the lower classes (although in comparison with the population the number of places was small). Many poor families of the middle class, of the bankrupt nobility, of the skilled working class, and especially of the priesthood, impoverished themselves to support a son at university, hoping thus to raise themselves from their low estate. For some, the result of this sacrifice was a disappointment, because government offices and many commercial firms were becoming hesitant in employing former students from the poorer classes, who were increasingly regarded as being revolutionary or, if not revolutionary, bloody-minded.

Science and technology

Russian science by 1914 had enhanced its international reputation earned in the previous century. Pure mathematics and its applications in engineering

---

[16] This does not include the Shanyavski 'peoples' university' in Moscow, founded by a private benefactor in 1905 to provide low-cost, co-educational instruction, with no diploma required for entry. Nor does it include Helsinki University.

and other fields had always been a strongpoint of Russian scholarship. Although no Russian mathematician quite attained the fame of Loba-chevsky, there was a host of brilliant men, including Markov (theory of numbers and probability) and Bernstein (theory of functions). In biology Mechnikov was a leading figure, having earned his reputation in the study of infection and immunization; he worked mainly in France, directing the Pasteur Institute from 1895 and receiving a Nobel Prize in 1908. The physiologist Pavlov was popularly regarded as Russia's greatest scientist. The son of a priest, he spent much of his life at the Institute of Scientific Medicine at St. Petersburg, receiving a Nobel Prize for his work on digest-ive enzymes. His study of the conditioned reflex, using bells and salivating dogs, brought him renown among the general public. Mendeleyev, a Siber-ian who died in 1907, made a brilliant career in chemistry, evolving his Periodic Table and describing several new elements. Michurin was produc-ing an enormous range of new hybrid fruit trees with his grafting tech-nique, and an enormous range of controversial conclusions. Russians were recognized as pre-eminent in soil science and petroleum chemistry.

During the Stalin period of Russian history, many claims would be made that Russians had been the first to invent almost all the innovations of the previous century. Although these claims were unbalanced, and attracted thereby some ridicule, they were not always baseless. Russians had indeed invented or researched new machines and techniques, but all too often their experiments were abandoned because obtaining financial support from the government was a long, uncertain, and bureaucratic process. Among the technologies in which Russians had a claim to leadership were hydrodynamics, in which the work of Krylov is still basic; Krylov lived long enough to modify in 1904 the hulls of the battleships sent to Tsushima, and to receive a Stalin Prize in 1941. Popov had at least as good a claim as Marconi to distinction in the field of radio. Yablochkov, as early as 1875, invented and patented the world's first successful electric lamp, using the arc. The use of oil fuel in locomotives and ships was pio-neered in Russia, where residues from the Caucasian refineries were cheaply available.

Russian technology was particularly distinguished in aviation. Even before the internal combustion engine became available, a steam aero-plane was built by a Russian army officer; apparently it was too heavy to leave the ground, but its aerodynamics were very advanced. Later, Zhukovsky and Chaplygin at the Institute of Aerodynamics worked out such essential airflow problems as those of lift and wing loading, wing and propeller shape. At about the same time Tsiolkovsky, more visionary but rightly regarded as one of the fathers of space flight, was working on large rockets. He built a wind tunnel in 1897 and six years later produced his theoretical book, *The Investigation of Space by Rocket Devices*. In the Soviet period he would make further contributions to aviation and space flight; he forecast multi-stage rockets and space stations. In the actual design and production of aircraft Sikorsky was already distinguished. Thanks to him, Russia in 1914 had four-engined 400 h.p. aircraft capable of carrying sixteen passengers. Aviation aroused great interest in Russia, and a number of universities and technical institutes founded aero-clubs. The latter, being 'unofficial' organizations, soon aroused official suspicion:

> Bearing in mind that the student milieu is a particularly fertile soil for the development of extreme revolutionary ideas and that in these circumstances the activity of student aero-clubs could easily take an undesirable direction, the Deputy Minister of the Interior, commanding the special gendarme section, has graciously noted the necessity, in towns having institutions of higher learning, of establishing the closest surveillance over the persons and activities of student aero-clubs ...[17]

During the final Romanov decades scientific and exploratory expeditions were mounted more and more frequently. These went to Central Asia, Siberia, the Far North, and the Arctic, as well as to more familiar parts to search for minerals. In 1915 two icebreakers completed the first voyage by the Northern Sea Route from the Pacific westwards across the top of Russia.

But compared to other countries, scientific research was not well provided for. A handful of ministries, notably those of war and transport, set up their own research institutes, but such institutes were few. Higher education establishments, whose main function was teaching, provided few facilities. Much inventiveness was self-financed, or at the mercy of grants administered by the state-financed Imperial Academy of Sciences. Nevertheless, there was a flourishing of scholarly societies and journals. The non-academic public was encouraged to take an interest in scientific life by popular scientific societies, by new observatories, botanical gardens, museums, and public lectures. Meanwhile the growing educated class meant a growing demand for books and journals. Hitherto, Russian publications had small circulations and rather high prices, but from about the seventies this changed. In 1874 a French novel by Zola was printed in 7,000 copies, and this was considered the best-seller of that year (after the new *Conscription Regulations*, which sold no fewer than 50,000 copies but was exceptional). In the eighties, however, one publisher introduced cheap editions of Russian classics, printing at least 100,000 copies of each volume. Similarly, the 'thick' journals were being supplemented by the

[17] From a confidential circular sent in 1911 to local police and *Okhrana* authorities, published in *Istoricheskii arkhiv* (1961), 3, 286.

'thin'. Most popular of the latter was the illustrated weekly *Niva*, which flourished from 1870 to 1917. Vaguely liberal in tone and designed for 'family reading', it was more readable than the thick journals. In 1900 it had a circulation of 235,000. Among newspapers, the cheap 'kopek-newspapers' of the capitals had been imitated in the provinces.

The arts

By 1914 the writers of the great age of Russian literature were dead, and there were already harbingers, like Gorki, of a later generation of proletarian writers. Chekhov had been a link between the generations; influenced by his friend Tolstoy (whom he predeceased in 1904), he in turn influenced Gorki. The grandson of a serf, Chekhov qualified as a doctor after working his way through university, but soon devoted himself entirely to writing. He had grown up in a penurious middle-class family, and it was the middle class and the official world which predominated in his sketches, stories, and plays. He claimed that comedy was the essence of all his works, but his 'superfluous man' tended to become the melancholy man, leading an empty and repetitive life, dreaming of a more stimulating life but lacking the incentive to transform dream into reality. Chekhov's plays (*The Cherry Orchard*, *The Three Sisters*, and others) became standard repertory offerings both inside Russia and abroad. They were staged by the innovative Moscow Art Theatre, which had been founded in 1898 by Stanislavsky and Nemirovich-Danchenko. The performances were made memorable by the direction of the former; what became known as the Stanislavsky System was admirably suited to Chekhov's subdued style. There were no conventional histrionics, each actor was made aware of the importance of pauses, slight changes of tone, and complete naturalness. The stage success of Chekhov and Stanislavsky led to a brief popularity for Russian dramatists (including Gorki), but by 1914 it was foreign playwrights such as Bernard Shaw and Ibsen who were most fashionable. By that time Stanislavsky had been joined by younger inventive directors, of whom Meyerhold was the most notable.[18]

Maksim Gorki, who as a young orphan had wandered from place to place and job to job, achieved success with his short stories about lowly characters like those he had met in his wanderings. Outside Russia he became well known after the translation and staging of his play, *The Lower Depths*. This was set in a cheap boarding house inhabited by a collection of semi-human misfits, degenerates, and murderers, who were what they were

---

[18] Meyerhold continued to direct after 1917, but he and his wife disappeared one night in 1939, a few days after he had publicly described Socialist Realism as 'a pitiful and sterile something'.

because poverty had made them so. Gorki gave financial help to the Bolsheviks, but from 1906 was anti-Leninist. He criticized the Bolsheviks' seizure of power in 1917 but was later reconciled with the regime. Of the writers influenced by Gorki, Bunin was perhaps the most notable, although he had not yet published *The Gentleman from San Francisco* (1915), with its portrayal of cigar-smoking shapers of men's lives. In 1933, in emigration, he would become the first Russian to win a Nobel Prize for literature.

By the turn of the century critical realism was under attack by newer movements. The most concerted attack took the form of a symposium called *Vekhi* (1909), in which non-radical philosophers, critics, and politicians presented a new assessment of values. Some of the contributors, like Berdyaev and Struve, were former marxists (Berdyaev would soon become a well-known Orthodox philosopher). Others were simply admirers of Dostoevsky, or of the Christian idealist philosopher Vladimir Soloviev. Their ideas, vulgarized, tended to inspire and reinforce that obsession with the occult and the mystical which became noticeable in St. Petersburg society. By 1914 the Belinsky tradition was in a retreat which would continue until its resurrection in the thirties as the basis of Socialist Realism. In 1914, of the foremost writers only Gorki and perhaps Bunin and Kuprin represented this tradition (see p. 58). In poetry, N. Nekrasov's *Who can live well in Russia?* (1866) had probably approached the peak of critical realism with its exquisite portrayal of the seamy side of Russian life. In following decades there was a reaction leading to the emergence of Symbolists like Merezhkovsky and Blok, who in their turn were challenged by the Futurists (notably Mayakovsky) and other hopeful trend-setters. In prose, Belyi and Andreyev were prominent Symbolists, but were themselves challenged by the Neo-Realists like Aleksei Tolstoy. All these movements influenced Soviet literature of the twenties.

In painting, the second half of the nineteenth century had been marked by a conflict between different schools. In 1863 St. Petersburg art students refused to paint the subject chosen for their annual competition; they wanted to paint a real contemporary scene, not 'The Banquet of the Gods in Valhalla'. This preference accorded with the precepts of critical realism, emphasizing content rather than style. The students, helped by the industrialist and collector Tretyakov, formed their own 'Society of Circulating Exhibitions', which enjoyed great success, although the movement later ossified. These artists (the '*Peredvizhniki*') valued the realistic presentation of ideas and tended to minimize technique and artistic truth. They soon became over-didactic, but when more attention was paid to form and colour, as it was in Repin's works, realism was reinvigorated. Like other

Peredvizhniki, Repin was addicted to the story-telling picture, which he accomplished very well and thereby created paintings which are often used to illustrate history textbooks (Ivan the Terrible after murdering his son etc.). But he was versatile; he had worked with the traditional icon-painters in his youth and later produced some religious compositions, as well as portraits of notable Russians.

Although by the turn of the century realists like Repin were being overshadowed, in the eyes of the fashionable, by Russian impressionism, realism as such never disappeared from Russian art; it coexisted. Of the new impressionistic school Vrubel and the portraitist Serov were the most notable early examples. In 1898 the periodical, *Mir iskusstva* ('*World of Art*') was founded, and this name was attached to the movement of artists and critics who opposed utilitarian and realist art, and who advocated art-for-art's-sake. *Mir iskusstva* in its articles brought together modern west European trends and the traditions of old Russian art, especially of icon-painting. It also organized exhibitions for its members. Although the periodical ceased publication in 1904 the ideas of the movement lived on, influencing, among others, the Futurists. By 1914 St. Petersburg was considered the capital of the world of progressive art. The experimentalist Kandinsky was regarded as the first really abstract painter, and Expressionism was joined by Rayonnism, Suprematism, and Constructivism. The new styles were not to the taste of traditionalists and frequently invited ridicule, but a public certainly existed for advanced art.

In the nineteenth century ballet had flourished in Russia, but it was hardly specifically Russian, being strongly influenced by the French and Italians. But in the nineties Russian music was increasingly being used, and in 1909 the Ballets Russes was launched by the impresario Diaghilev. The success of this company abroad was based on previous performances of Russian music and opera which had attracted growing appreciation, aided by star attractions such as Chaliapin singing the title role in Musorgski's *Boris Godunov*. The Ballets Russes, which from 1911 to its disbandment in 1952 was permanently abroad, owed its success also to the masterful combination of several arts: choreography by Fokin, sets by new and original Russian artists, and star dancers like Nijinsky and Pavlova. Music was contributed by the innovative Stravinsky, whose pre-war *Firebird*, *Petrushka*, and *Rite of Spring* established the foundation of his subsequent reputation as the most important composer of the twentieth century.

In a later idiom, St. Petersburg by 1914 was a swinging city. In the arts Russia was no longer backward, no longer so many decades or centuries behind the west. In the theatre, poetry, music, and painting she was in front, even if many of her innovations had their roots in the west. Perhaps this was why the once-compelling question of Russia's place in the world seemed to lose its significance. It had become easier to accept that Russia was Russian; whether Russia was of the west or of the east or of neither seemed no longer a burning issue. A more compelling question in this last decade of Romanov rule was whether Russia was destined for a renaissance or for a revolution. For the alert and intelligent citizen of that time there were abundant signs of both.

Stability or instability?

Historians disagree on whether revolution was inevitable by mid-1914. Many regard 1905–14 as a period of stabilization and progress brought to a premature end at Sarajevo; in short, that if there had been no 1914 there might not have been a 1917. Soviet historians, on the other hand, regarded the Revolution as historically logical, as inevitable, and discerned a 're-volutionary upsurge' in the industrial unrest which began in 1912. They claimed that by August 1914 Russia was ripe for an imminent revolution, for which the Bolsheviks had begun to plan in 1913, and that the war in reality delayed this revolution until 1917.

Certainly, the first five years after 1905 were years of reaction and repression (that is, of stabilization). Many intellectuals, depressed by the defeat of 1905, or not relishing their memory of armed workers and peasants, abandoned radical causes. The working class relapsed into apathy, chastened by the failure after the first heady days of the rebellion. The urban middle classes seemed willing to work for reform within the limits set by the government; they too had been alarmed at what they considered to be the excesses of the workers and peasants in 1905, and had abandoned the struggle when the October Manifesto seemed to offer them a way out.

But after 1910 it seemed that the situation was changing in the towns.[19] There was a return to industrial growth, more spontaneous than that of the nineties. The industrial labour force in 1914 was about two and a half million strong, almost a third more than in 1910. This labour force included a new generation whose resentments were not tempered by any memories of 1905, and an influx of peasants squeezed off the land by agrarian reforms. When strikers at the Lena gold-fields were shot down in 1912, sympathy strikes were called throughout the Empire, and from then until 1914 strikes became ever more frequent, bitter, and confused in their objectives. The climax came in July 1914, when the St. Petersburg Bolsheviks instigated a

[19] Peasant disturbances had declined drastically in 1908–9, but by 1914 they, too, seemed to be on the upswing, although numbered in the hundreds rather than the thousands of 1905–7.

strike in protest against police repression of another local strike. In the working-class districts, barricade-building and violence recalled the events of 1905, but there was little sympathetic response from other sections of society, as there had been in 1905. The strike was finally suppressed less than a week before the outbreak of war.

This 1914 experience, added to memories of the 'desertion' by the middle class after October 1905, persuaded many politically conscious workers that a 1905-style co-operation between the workers and educated society was no longer feasible, and this would have its repercussions in 1917. At the time, what seemed more important than the gulf between the workers and 'public opinion' was the stalemated hostility between the latter and the bureaucracy, official Russia. Whereas 'unofficial' educated Russians had been striving to make the most of the concessions won in 1905, the regime was trying with some success to whittle away those concessions (for example, by tampering with the Duma, arresting leaders of 'legal' organizations, confiscating 'legal' publications). By 1914 former reformists were beginning to regard violence as the only means left to loosen a regime which seemed more and more intolerant, intolerable and, worse, untalented. This trend meant that the political parties were splitting at all possible seams. The Octobrists' left wing split away, the Kadets were uneasily divided into left, right, and centre, while the businessmen's new Progressist Party actually made overtures (neither accepted nor rejected) to the Bolsheviks. Had there been no war it seems likely that a realignment of parties would have occurred, with the emergence of a strong and 'respectable' movement prepared to support violent change.

The Beilis Case and the rise of Rasputin seemed symptoms of the increasing rottenness and incapacity of the state administration at a time when modernization of Russian society made the educated and professional classes all the more essential to the state. The autocratic Empire was desperately trying through modernization to remain a great power. Indeed, with Germany to the west and Japan to the east, the Empire could survive only as a great power. Yet modernization, which few Russians could envisage without an accompanying westernization, could only threaten internal stability in the short term. Modernization meant the rise of new classes, skilled workers and professionals who would use their new importance to demand political rights. Modernization meant squeezing peasants off the land and bringing them to already overcrowded cities where, cramped in their own stink, they formed a dissatisfied class of unskilled and underprivileged workers. Modernization meant westernization and the erosion of stabilizing traditions and values; how much resentment such an erosion caused cannot be measured but Peter the Great, the greatest westernizer of all, had certainly had cause to reckon with it. Modernization, as under Witte, meant a minimal standard of living for the majority, in order to save resources for investment.

Perhaps, if there had been no war, the most painful stages of change would have been passed, and some of the fruits of modernization enjoyed by the people. And perhaps not.[20] But, as 1905 demonstrated, the regime could always win the last trick so long as it could rely on the army. In July 1914 the forces of revolution were in dynamic equilibrium with the forces of stability, and the key stabilizing force was the Russian army. But after Sarajevo another army, the German, upset the balance.

[20] The stability or instability of Russian society in 1914 is discussed in articles by L. Haimson and others in *The Slavic Review*, Vol. 23, No. 4, 619–42, and Vol. 24, No. 1, 1–22, 47–56. See also the article by H. Rogger in *The Journal of Contemporary History* No. 3 (1966), 229–53. For the opinions of economic historians, see R. W. Davies (ed.), *From Tsarism to the New Economic Policy* (1990).

9. *The Empire's Last War*

THE aura of failure which, in many western eyes, seems to surround the foreign policy of the final Romanov century, is misleading. Probably it derives from memory of Russia's unsuccessful wars in the Crimea and Manchuria, but these wars were fought against enemies who did not threaten the most sensitive cares of the tsars: the maintenance of the Empire's frontiers and of an autocratic regime free of foreign tutelage. Despite geographic, cultural, economic and diplomatic difficulties, the Empire was not only able to maintain these essentials, but even to extend its territory. Like a good chess-player, Russia moved in to fill accessible power vacuums while showing no interest in attacking strong positions. The Empire's diplomacy usually compensated for the disparity between Russia's claims as a great power and her actual economic power. The foreign ministry, aware that economic weakness meant military weakness, never recommended, until 1914, moves which would bring the Empire into conflict with the great powers. At the same time the ministry fostered alliances with European powers, to ensure that Russia would have powerful friends if the worst should come to the worst. Meanwhile, even at the risk of social tension and distress, the government sought to create an economy capable of sustaining a major war in an age of ever-developing military technology. Some commentators, very plausibly, see a recurring pattern in these efforts: beginning with Peter the Great, if not earlier, military competition with other powers required the establishment of war industries, and this could only be achieved by a ruthless exploitation of the people. The need to drive the people hard, in the right direction and without deviations, required a strong centralized administration.

With the end of the Napoleonic wars, the expansion of Muscovy into territories held by weaker neighbours seemed, at last, to have reached a natural conclusion in northern and central Europe. The absorption of Poland meant that there was no longer a buffer state separating Russia from Prussia. Finland had been acquired, and St. Petersburg thereby made more defensible against naval attack. But Russia still had aspirations, although no definite plans, in south-eastern Europe. Access through the Straits was still a genuine issue, while Russian racial and religious obsessions with the Balkans meant that this was an area in which policy might not always be rational. In Asia, too, expansion could continue at the expense of weak or fragmented neighbours.

Throughout most of the nineteenth century the foundation of Russian foreign policy was friendship with Austria and Prussia. They were ideologically congenial, and as allies their location ensured that Russia's potential enemies (France and Britain) would have difficulty in striking overland at the vital parts of the Empire. But after Bismarck's successors neglected to renew the Reinsurance Treaty, Russia felt compelled to seek alternative friends; the 1894 alliance with France resulted. Britain, however, was still at the turn of the century regarded as a likely enemy, and this feeling was mutual. But while British newspapers and parliamentarians spoke knowingly of dark Russian designs, the Russian foreign ministry in reality was preoccupied with security, although admittedly the policy of the foreign ministry was not always the policy of the government. Especially in the Balkans, Russian agents did embark on all kinds of intrigues to win influence; such agents, if unsuccessful and exposed, could be disowned. Similarly, in Central Asia, campaigns were sometimes launched by medal-seeking generals without government authority; these campaigns might be condemned, and the generals recalled, but the conquered territories could be retained. Such methods, like the separate activities of the foreign ministry and the Comintern in Soviet times, sometimes resulted in embarrassment, as happened in the Balkans in 1913.

When the Russo-Japanese War ended, the French alliance seemed even more needed; attempts by Nicholas and the Kaiser in 1904 and at Björkö in 1905 to initiate a new treaty between their two empires had been frustrated, Britain's support for Japan was no longer an issue, and there was an understanding with Vienna over the Balkans situation. With French encouragement, some of the outstanding issues dividing Russia and Britain were settled in 1907; Persia was to be divided into two spheres of influence, Afghanistan was not to be annexed by Britain, Tibet was to remain Chinese. In 1908 King Edward VII visited the Russian Baltic port of Reval. By 1914 the Anglo-French understanding and the Franco-Russian alliance had merged into the Triple Entente. But although when war began Russia appeared to be on the strongest side, in retrospect it might seem that the Empire would have done better if the old alliances with Berlin and Vienna had, instead, been maintained. Whatever material advantages the

Triple Entente offered were outweighed by Germany's and Austria's con-
tiguity; the war presented right from the start the probability of strong
hostile armies marching on the Empire's heartland. The French army was
weaker than the German, while Britain's dreadnoughts, as critics said,
were of little use to Russia unless they could move on wheels.

Neither the earlier alliance with Berlin and Vienna, nor the later Entente
with Paris and London, furnished allies who would embroil themselves on
Russia's side in the Balkans. With the shrinkage of the Turkish Empire,
the consequent emergence of independent Balkan states, the simultaneous
ambition and instability of the Austro-Hungarian Empire, and continuing
Russian interest in the area, conflict was almost inevitable. In the 1908
'Annexation Crisis' Russia was openly humiliated. Her new foreign minister, Izvolsky, unwisely agreed with Vienna to support Austrian annexation
of Bosnia-Herzegovina (which Serbia regarded as Serbian) in exchange for
Austrian support for another Russian attempt to gain free passage
through the Straits; the great powers accepted Austria's gain but would
not countenance a change for the Straits. Germany threatened to support
Austria should a Russo-Austrian war develop from this situation. Conscious of military weakness, St. Petersburg was wise enough to refrain
from war, despite resentment at Germany's action and emotional links
with the Serbs. The Russian government's prestige fell further with the
Balkan wars of 1912–13. Russian semi-official agents, hopefully advising
the independent Balkan states to join forces against Austria, succeeded
only in uniting them against Turkey. Having won Macedonia from the
Turks, the coalition quarrelled over the spoils, with the result that Bulgaria, which had done most of the fighting and was in spirit closest to
Russia, came out badly.

Once again the Russian government wisely refrained from intervention,
but once again Russian public opinion had been aroused. The Balkans was
an area, perhaps the only area, in which foreign policy had to take account
of public opinion. That is, the Balkans was an area in which foreign policy
might be affected by irrational considerations; in 1908 and 1913 governmental rationality prevailed over public irrationality, but this did not
guarantee cool heads in the future. That Russia's 'mission' in the Balkans
was not simply a right-wing myth was demonstrated by the emergence of
the so-called Neo-Slav movement. Whereas Panslavism implied an eventual Russian-controlled federation of Slavic peoples, the Neo-Slavs envisaged truly independent Slavic nations in a free association. The Neo-Slavs
included many prominent liberals; conservatives were usually opposed to
the movement because it implied eventual independence for Poland and
the Ukraine.

Summer 1914

The causes of the First World War are still a matter for discussion, but certainly neither the Russian government nor Nicholas wanted this war. As in the 1930s, although Russia made blunders, her contribution to the world's catastrophe was far from being the main contribution.

In July 1914, using the murder at Sarajevo as a pretext and confident of German support, Vienna determined to crush once and for all troublesome, Slavic, Serbia. On 28 July Austrian troops commenced hostilities against Serbia. The great European war, that awesome contingency for which military staffs had long been planning, now seemed imminent. The German war plan (the 'Schlieffen Plan') envisaged an initial concentration of forces against France so as to drive the latter out of the war within the first few weeks, and then the transfer of the German troops to the Eastern Front to deal with Russia.

This exploited the well-known fact that, because of long distances and sparse railways, Russia's mobilization would need more time than those of the other powers. The Russian mobilization plans were very complex interlocking schedules, drawn up every few years at secret conferences. Each railway section received the part of the plan relevant to it in the form of a sealed packet, which was placed in an iron box to be hidden until the fateful day. The plan covered the first two weeks, and envisaged the suspension of normal railway services so that the railways would be completely devoted to military movements in those weeks. There were two variants of the plan; Plan G was for a war against Austria and Germany if Germany was the main enemy, Plan A was for a war against Austria and Germany if Austria was the main enemy. In 1914 a new plan to take account of increased line capacity was being worked out, but was not yet in force; thus in 1914 the railways had more capacity than the existing plan called for, which is one reason why the 1914 mobilization went so smoothly. During the initial two weeks it was planned to mobilize and transport about half the infantry, together with supporting arms. The remainder would follow according to circumstances (in the event, the last Siberian units reached the front in October).

Military planners (although not all railway operators) firmly believed that because each part of the mobilization plan was interlocked and co-ordinated with the other parts, once mobilization was started it could not be modified or halted without throwing the country's defences into chaos. Also, it was clear that if Russia mobilized, Germany would be compelled to mobilize too, because otherwise the Schlieffen Plan, on which her survival seemed to depend, would be inoperable. For these two reasons, mobilization was almost equivalent to pressing the button in the age of the nuclear deterrent, or to reaching for the personal deterrent in the age of the cowboy. For these two reasons, Russia's decision to mobilize on 30 July made war virtually certain.

The Tsar was well aware of all this. On 25 July, on the advice of his ministers, he consented to the call-up of reservists, the cancellation of soldiers' leaves, and to a partial mobilization, if need be, against Austria. He also suggested that the Austro-Serbian dispute be submitted to the Hague International Tribunal, a suggestion which does not appear to have been passed on by his foreign minister, Sazonov. On 28 July Sazonov announced the partial mobilization against Austria. It was only after this that Sazonov, the Tsar, and the ministers were informed by the Chief of Staff that partial mobilization was impossible. Both Plan G and Plan A envisaged war against Germany and Austria, not against one of the two. Russia's great deterrent was indivisible and therefore inflexible.[1] But by now Russia had publicly embarked on a 'policy of strength'. To retreat would be a crushing humiliation. So in the morning of 29 July the Tsar signed the order for general mobilization. That same evening, conscious of what this order meant, Nicholas cancelled it. The next morning, besieged by his military and diplomatic advisers, all urging that without general mobilization Russia would stand unprepared before disaster, Nicholas restored the mobilization order. The rest was ultimatums.

Military operations

The war minister, Sukhomlinov, was expecting to command the army, but instead it was the Tsar's uncle, Grand Duke Nikolai, who became C-in-C. The new C-in-C took as his Chief of Staff Yanushkevich, at forty-four the army's youngest general. Although a gifted quartermaster-general partly compensated for Yanushkevich's shortcomings, by late 1915 it was clear that the latter was a disaster. It was Yanushkevich who, imposing harsh regimes in areas occupied by the Russian army, dissolved the sympathy with which local populations regarded Russia's fight against the Teutonic threat. His murderous treatment of the Jews seemed likely to cause intolerable embarrassments abroad. So in September 1915 Nicholas transferred the Grand Duke and Yanushkevich to the Caucasian front and himself went as C-in-C to GHQ, the collection of railway cars sidetracked at a junction near the front. Nicholas's wish to be with his troops was laudable, and he had chosen a very competent Chief of Staff, but his absence from the capital meant that too much political responsibility would be placed on unreliable informants and advisers.

---

[1] When the Chief of Staff, Yanushkevich, was asked why he had not mentioned this disconcerting fact previously, he explained that he had held his post for only five months and had therefore been unacquainted with the mobilization plans. Only five months!

The Russian plan for the first weeks of war took account of the expected German strategy. The initially small German forces would be held by just one Russian army, and three of the other five armies would attack Austria, hoping to rout the latter's forces before the full strength of the German army could be transferred from France. But, to help the French, this plan was changed; two Russian armies advanced into eastern Prussia and won early successes, before the arrival of fresh German troops and generals led to a damaging defeat at the so-called battle of Tannenberg. The Russians had advanced before they were properly mobilized and this was later criticized, but the fact remains that nine German divisions were transferred to eastern Prussia just as the German thrust towards Paris reached its climax on the Marne. The German failure at the Marne put an end to German prospects of a quick victory. Various Russians at various times have argued that in both world wars their country saved the west from defeat. In the case of the First World War there is much to support this argument; both the Marne and Verdun were won with the aid of the Russian army.

Meanwhile, the Russian south-western armies successfully defended Poland against an Austrian offensive and then themselves captured large areas of Austrian Galicia. One fiery commander, disregarding instructions, even rampaged around the Hungarian plains; this was Kornilov, later famous in another connexion. He was a real cavalry officer, being described by his contemporaries as 'having the heart of a lion and the brain of a lamb'. German troops were sent to rescue Austria, and by early 1915 the Russian armies were in retreat on both the northern and south-western fronts. By the end of the summer they had been driven out of Galicia and had lost Poland and part of White Russia. The front then became more or less stabilized until 1917, running southwards from near Riga, through the Pripet marshes, to the Roumanian frontier. (See map, p. 595.)

By 1915 the Russian army was losing its professional sparkle. Losses had been heavy, and replacements were inexperienced and sometimes only semi-trained. The weapon and ammunition shortage was becoming catastrophic, Russian guns were sometimes limited to four shots a day or less. Trainees, and sometimes front-line reinforcements, had to share rifles. There was an almost total lack of barbed wire. Russia, like other belligerents, had not expected a long war and was less successful than others in overcoming production difficulties. Nevertheless the army, although it lost territory, was never destroyed. Not for the first or last time, its deficiencies were compensated by a lavish expenditure of its sturdy soldiers. During the first year of war it lost about four million men.[2] By 1915 it was facing

---

[2] Russian casualties for the entire war were about eight million, including 1.7 million dead and 2.4 million captured.

poison-gas attacks, but these new manifestations of German technological superiority neither terrified nor surprised the Russian soldier. After all, there was a well-known Russian proverb, 'it must have been a German who invented the monkey'.

War against Turkey began in October 1914, when Odessa was bombarded. Militarily, Turkey presented little threat, but henceforth Russia could receive supplies from the Allies only through Archangel (Murmansk until 1916 lacked a railway) or through Vladivostok. This was one reason why the Allies in 1915 embarked on the Dardanelles campaign. One cause of the failure of the latter was Russia's refusal to approve the participation of the Greek army in the venture. The Russian government had obtained British approval for a post-war settlement of the Straits question which would favour Russia, and it was hoped that the old Orthodox capital of Constantinople might be acquired. Greek participation seemed a potential threat to these hopes because Greece, too, had her ambitions.

In the winter of 1915–16 the Russian army began to recover from its mauling. There was time to train the conscripts properly and to build up ammunition stocks. Machine and field guns were more plentiful and rifles were being produced at the improved, though still insufficient, rate of 10,000 monthly. The Red Cross detachments organized by the Union of *Zemstva* found time to attend to the soldiers' recreational and morale needs as well as to medical matters. In February 1916, in response to French requests following the first German attacks on Verdun, the Russian western armies began advances which developed into a costly retreat, but what was a setback for the Russians was a gain for the French. After further urgent requests from Britain and France, GHQ adopted a plan for an offensive against Austria on the south-western front, to be followed by an even stronger thrust against the Germans by the western armies in Lithuania. This plan was submitted by the commander of the south-western armies, Brusilov, who then worked out its execution in meticulous detail and with an understanding of Russian logistic difficulties. As he himself wrote later, 'Knowing the limitation of our railway transport . . . I knew that while we were entraining and transporting one army corps, the Germans would manage to transport three or four'.[3] This meant that a Russian breakthrough might be blocked by fresh enemy troops before Russian reinforcements could be brought up to exploit the situation. For this reason Brusilov ordered each of the four armies of his front to prepare their own attacks; there would be four breakthroughs and no reserves.

---

[3] A. Brusilov, *A Soldier's Notebook* (Macmillan, 1930), 239.

On 4 June, as the siege of Verdun reached a climax and as the Italian army was reeling from Austrian attacks, the Brusilov Offensive[4] was launched. It was a crushing success. Great areas of territory were occupied. Hordes of prisoners were taken. The Austrian commander, Archduke Josef Ferdinand, was shelled in the middle of his birthday party. But what might have been a war-winning triumph remained only a great victory, because GHQ did precisely what Brusilov had warned against. Instead of starting the planned follow-up attack by its western armies just as the enemy was off-balance, it sent western troops to reinforce Brusilov. This left the German commanders free to send their own reinforcements to aid the Austrians, and to arrive there first. Nevertheless, the offensive, apart from being a great boost to Russian and foreign morale, forced the withdrawal of thirty-five German divisions from France. Verdun did not fall. Russian losses had been heavy, about half a million casualties. There was little possibility of another offensive on such a scale being launched again before many months of recuperation. There was also the question of morale after the offensive became a retreat. It seemed unlikely that the army and the public could accept many more hundreds of thousands of killings, maimings, gassings, and mental derangements.

There was another side effect of the Brusilov Offensive which seemed at first a great success but later proved catastrophic. Throughout the war the belligerents' diplomacy had concentrated on persuading, by threat or bribe, the remaining neutrals to join in on their side. The western Allies had lost this game in Turkey, and even in Slavic Bulgaria. But Roumania, always an expert fence-sitter, was still waiting to make absolutely sure which side would win before throwing in her lot with the victor. The Brusilov Offensive, coupled with some diplomatic action by the admiral commanding Russia's Danubian flotilla (who distributed two million roubles' worth of trinkets to the wives of influential Roumanians) finally won the day for the Allies. The almost immediate result was the rout of the Roumanian army by the Central Powers, the occupation of much of that nation by enemy forces (facilitating communication with Turkey), and the hasty dispatch of Russian units to help the Roumanians. In effect, Roumania's accession meant the extension of Russia's war front down to the Black Sea, a dilution of troops she could ill afford.

Naval operations

Thanks to the careful planning of the naval staff, the Russian navy was not caught unprepared in 1914 as it had been in 1904. The commander of each

---

[4] It was the only victory of the war to be named after its commander.

ship, having received a prearranged signal, unsealed his mobilization orders to learn his task, place of concentration, and details of the mine-laying plan. The latter was the basic element of the Baltic Fleet's activity. The entry to the Gulf of Finland (on which lay St. Petersburg and the Kronstadt naval base) was sealed off by eight lines of mines, 3,000 mines in total. Later in the year Russian minelayers went out at night to lay mines in enemy waters, especially in the approaches of Danzig, and these caused some serious losses. The German battlefleet, preoccupied with the British navy, never made any deep offensive sweeps into the Baltic. But smaller ships did, and also appeared as escorts to the ships supplying the German army as it advanced along the southern shore of the Baltic. Of the several German cruisers and destroyers lost in these operations the fate of the cruiser *Magdeburg* in 1914 was perhaps the most significant. This vessel ran aground in fog off a Baltic island, and was located by Russian radio direction stations. Russian cruisers were dispatched, and discovered that the *Magdeburg* had been abandoned. The German naval code book was found, and was sent to the British Admiralty, which made good use of it. In the Baltic both sides tended to regard their naval activities largely as support for land operations, but in the Black Sea initial Russian naval superiority was challenged by the entry of the ex-German battlecruiser *Goeben* and its accompanying cruiser, *Breslau*. This pair, though vulnerable to the newer Russian battleships (which on one occasion did damage the *Goeben*), could make damaging raids and escape by virtue of their higher speed. The situation was further complicated by the appearance of U-boats in the Black Sea. These, despite defensive net- and mine-laying, sank about one-quarter of the supply ships on which the Russian armies depended. When Kolchak took over the Black Sea command in 1916 the position improved. Kolchak abandoned defensive minelaying in favour of offensive. Night minelaying expeditions were made to block the Bosphorus and Varna, and shallow-draught minelayers were sent in to lay additional mines in already existing fields in case the enemy had already cleared the latter. In three months 2,000 mines were laid. From November 1916 few, if any, enemy ships could leave the Bosphorus, and Turkey was in the throes of a coal famine, for she depended on coastal shipping to connect her coalfields with her towns and industry. Thus by 1917 Russia had regained control of the Black Sea. A combined operation to capture the Dardanelles (and Constantinople) was being studied.

When the Allies began to ship supplies to Archangel, the White Sea acquired strategic importance. Warships from the Pacific Squadron were therefore sent to this new theatre. Japan, now an ally, sold back some of the ships which she had captured in 1904–5, and these were also dispatched to the Arctic. One of them, a battleship which had been scuttled at Port Arthur, went down for a second and last time in the Mediterranean, after striking a mine while on her way home.

Russia as an ally

There was a certain pro-German sentiment in Russia among some right-wing groups, but it was never as strong as the Allies feared. There was also a tradition of anti-British feeling, dating back probably to the mid-nineteenth century and fed by Britain's determination to keep Russia out of the eastern Mediterranean. In general, there was an underlying friendliness towards France and the USA, and equally towards Frenchmen and Americans. At various times in the war both France and Britain were criticized because, whenever their armies were in difficulties, they asked Russia to stage a diversionary offensive, but did nothing to help the Russian army when it had its own back to the wall. In the Russian army the officers of the old school (in effect, the senior officers) had more respect and understanding for their German counterparts than they had for the Allies, although the reserve officers, being younger, less militaristic, and more liberal, were just the opposite.

At the beginning of the war many prominent Britons and Russians openly wondered whether they had chosen the right allies. British liberals did not relish the idea of fighting alongside the most reactionary of the Great Powers, whose Cossack troops were already killing Russian Jews in the border areas, while Russian conservatives regretted that Russia should he fighting against the two empires which represented traditional monarchy. As the war became more arduous these feelings became muted; nevertheless the question of a 'separate peace' was the basic element in the diplomacy of this period. France and England feared that Russia, because of the influence of the so-called 'German Party' or because of the heavy losses she was sustaining, would make peace with Germany and enable the latter to exert all her strength against the west. Germany did make peace offers to Petrograd. The first appears to have been conveyed by one of the Empress's maids of honour, who lost her job in consequence. Nicholas, who had a developed, perhaps over-developed, sense of honour, had no intention of breaking his promises. But although German peace feelers failed, they did damage Russian morale. Sufficient information leaked out about them to support rumours which suggested that Russian officials were in touch with the Germans, thereby aggravating the suspicion that part of the government was in league with the enemy.

An apparently successful solution of the centuries-old Straits problem was not matched by a corresponding decision on Poland. Sazonov, the foreign minister, urged his government to promise an autonomous Poland and a united Poland (that is, the re-unification of Russian, Austrian, and Prussian Poland) in the post-war settlement. However, the suggestion was rejected; an autonomous Poland, even under the Russian crown, was too much for influential right-wing figures in Petrograd. Sazonov was replaced by Sturmer and the Central Powers offered the Poles what Russia had refused. The Polish independence movement did not, however, respond to the German offer. It concentrated its propaganda work in Paris; since the French were traditional friends of the Poles this agitation caused the Russian government the maximum of embarrassment. Less damaging, although more spectacular, was the anti-Russian Polish legion led by Pilsudski, sponsored by Austria and fighting on Austria's side. All the belligerents intrigued to exploit their enemies' weak points, especially national minorities whose nationalism might be turned, by skilful propaganda, against their governments. In addition, the Germans sought to foment industrial unrest in Russia. In this they were aided by Russian exiles, of whom the most valuable, versatile, and intelligent appears to have been Helphand (pseudonym Parvus), a Russian Jewish marxist with interests in politics, scholarship, and international trade. Through Helphand and others, funds were sent, via Scandinavia, to Russian revolutionaries organizing propaganda and strikes. During 1916 the strike movement in war industries became quite serious; how far German money assisted the 1917 Petrograd strikes which developed into the February Revolution is still unclear.

By 1916 the Russian need for material assistance and the Allied need for a staunch partner in the east led to the exchange of several delegations. As the Russian government became weaker and obviously more ineffective the western Allies began to apply, in a gentlemanly way, real pressure. Just three months before the February Revolution, during an inter-allied conference in Petrograd, Lord Milner indicated that further British munitions would not be forthcoming unless British officers were allowed to supervise their use by the Russian army. Furthermore, he hinted that the British government did not approve Nicholas's choice of ministers, and he praised the work of the *zemstva* voluntary organizations. The French had already asked for 400,000 Russian troops, and by 1917 about 60,000 had arrived, divided between the Western Front and Salonika. They learned of the February Revolution (from French newspapers rather than from their officers) and some demanded return to Russia. In April 1917 General Pétain refused to permit Russian units to go to the front until their soldiers' committees (allowed by the new Russian government) were disbanded. He complained that 'the introduction of committees into your army has encouraged several cases of indiscipline in our own, which is now demanding similar committees'.[5] Semi-mutinous Russian troops were attacked by French infantry and arrested. Some were shipped to forced labour in Africa, but others formed a legion to continue the fight against Germany.

The home front

When war was declared, the St. Petersburg students, who recently had been protesting against the government, once again broke the ban on demonstrations and marched on the German embassy. This, a new and barracks-like building, was sacked and its mass of external copper statuary toppled into the street. Some days later students toured the city with pots of paint, obliterating German street and shop names. Some humorist wrote to one of the capital's most Panslavic and anti-German newspapers, complaining that its title was set in Gothic type.[6] Not since 1812, it seemed, had the people seemed so united with their tsar. The war was seen as an attack by Germany on Holy Russia, rather than as a quarrel with Austria over Serbia. The Duma only needed one day to approve the war credits, the Social Democrats and the Trudoviki abstaining. Although both main factions of the Social Democrats opposed the war verbally, only the Bolsheviks urged Russians to fight their own government rather than the Germans (which was why, in November, the five remaining Bolshevik Duma members were arrested and exiled). Young and old volunteered for the army. The German-sounding Sankt-Peterburg became Petrograd. There were declarations and street demonstrations by workers and others in support of their tsar and country. And yet, impressive and frequent though the demonstrations were, they did not prove very much. As with all demonstrations, the majority who stayed at home were not noticed. There were some observers who quietly wondered how far the bureaucracy's traditional skill in organizing spontaneous demonstrations had been brought into play. Even the French ambassador wrote in his diary about groups of 'poor devils at each corner shouting hoorah! under the eyes of a policeman'. Certainly public opinion, the collective expressed view of journalists, officials, gentry, politicians, and other influential figures, was strongly for the war, and would probably never have forgiven Nicholas if he had not made a stand. But in Russia public opinion is not necessarily the opinion of the public.

There were over two million German-speaking people in the Empire, including many German and Austrian subjects. In Petrograd it was quite

---

[5] *Krasnyi arkhiv*, Vol. 44, 155.
[6] The Editor defended his paper by claiming that the London *Morning Post* used the same style.

normal to hear German spoken in the streets, for the capital had its own German community with its own shops and newspapers. The loyalty of citizens of German descent was not questioned by the government, but towards the end of 1914 German and Austrian subjects were expelled.[7] This was not enough for the extreme Panslavists. The popular and illiberal Petrograd newspaper *Novoye Vremiya* conducted a vicious campaign against the Baltic Germans, dredging up supposedly damaging facts (e.g., that von Zeppelin's wife was a Baltic German) to imply that they were disloyal. The government was carefully watching for pro-German sentiments in the Baltic provinces but did nothing drastic, although in some cities of the Empire the assembly of more than two German speakers was forbidden, and public use of the German language was banned. But after the defeats of 1915 there were lethal *pogroms* against 'German elements' in which, in Moscow at least, the governor and local priests participated.

Coinciding with the 1914 mobilization, the often-recommended prohibition of the sale and consumption of vodka and spirits was decreed. Although this was followed by increased sales of substitutes like methylated spirit and floor polish, astonished eye-witnesses reported that drunkenness suddenly disappeared (except in Archangel, where the crews of British freighters soon organized a black market in Scotch whisky). Prohibition, together with the prosperity which war brought to the villages, was considered the explanation of the wartime decline in the rural death-rate. In the towns there was a reduced crime rate, and higher productivity. That the Empire began the greatest war in its history by sacrificing its most valuable source of revenue was considered highly eccentric, but not without merit. An embarrassing consequence was that Russians were left with more money to spend on food and goods which were in short supply, thus exacerbating wartime inflation.[8] Although small-scale illegal distillation of spirits became popular in the villages, in general sobriety prevailed until the Revolution: sorrows could no longer be drowned in drink.

In 1914 many of the outstanding members of the Duma and of the *zemstva* went to the front and organized hospital services, for the war ministry had made few preparations for the enormous influx of wounded. In August 1914 the Tsar had given his approval for a Union of *zemstva* so that the various local *zemstva* could pool their resources and their

---

[7] In one Moscow district the police mixed up their lists, rounding up all the British residents and not interfering with the Germans until a detained Englishman politely suggested that a mistake might have been made.

[8] Perhaps this was why in 1941, when Hitler attacked, the gesture was not repeated; instead, the price of vodka was quintupled. But prohibition was an experience long remembered; as late as February 1970 the Soviet newspaper *Literaturnaya gazeta*, conducting a campaign against drunkenness, accorded the tsarist regime rare praise for this measure.

experience in order to make a really worthwhile contribution on a national scale. Soon after, the city councils formed a similar union with the same purpose. The *zemstva* not only fitted out hospitals and hospital trains, but they organized in their various localities new industries to provide army boots, tents, hospital supplies, and other items which were in quite inadequate supply. The government also set up relief organizations, while the Empress and her daughters enrolled as nurses and did not shirk the most gruesome of nurses' duties.

Another non-governmental organization was the War Industries Committee, established in 1915 to stimulate the production of munitions, its members including representatives from ministries, industry, and the *zemstva* and cities unions. Guchkov, the prominent Duma member, was its chairman. It was notable also in including ten workers' representatives. It did much to by-pass cumbersome bureaucratic channels, which is one reason it and similar organizations were disliked and often obstructed by officials but welcomed by the generals. More important in 1915 was the formation, with the Tsar's approval but with the misgivings of many of his ministers, of the National Defence Council, which included nominees from the more important ministries, from the War Industries Committee, and one each from the unions of *zemstva* and cities. Its associated councils for food, fuel, transport, and refugees included many nominees of the non-official organizations, and seemed to be bodies which would give the public representatives a real influence. The minister of the interior was unable to accept this dilution of the autocratic principle and resigned, being replaced by a more liberal and intelligent man who had attracted notice by his skill in breeding horses for the army. In June 1915 the war minister, Sukhomlinov, generally blamed for the munition shortages, was replaced by Polivanov. With the exception of just one or two ministers and of the prime minister, Goremykin, the Council of Ministers now consisted of reasonably capable men who were willing to co-operate with the Duma leaders.

The mood of the Duma was unfavourable to the government, but not irrevocably. The Kadet, Progressist, and Octobrist liberal parties combined to form the nucleus of a new grouping, the Progressive Bloc, which demanded a government having 'public confidence'. This would not have been too difficult to achieve at that time, only a few ministerial changes being necessary to achieve a government consisting of men having the trust of the Duma rather than being merely the Tsar's nominees. Some demands of the Duma were already being met. For example, the stream of Jewish refugees fleeing from the German and Russian armies made nonsense of the much-resented laws of Jewish settlement, and other parts of Russia were therefore opened to them (but not Moscow and Petrograd).

But one basic problem, that of the military zones, was not solved. Under war conditions the military were given complete control not only of the frontier area, but of the areas behind the frontiers, including Petrograd. In these areas they exercised civil control, did not allow entry to non-military persons without permission, and in various ways antagonized the inhabitants. The *zemstva*-organized medical services were among those with restricted entry, which was an obvious handicap in their work. Conflicts between civil and military authority were frequent and damaging to the war effort, and were usually the result of obstinate ignorance on the part of army officers. At one stage of the war, for example, there was a coal famine because empty railway cars being sent to the Donets mining area were held 'in case of need' by the military authorities through whose zone the railway passed; no empty cars south meant no loaded cars north, no loaded cars north meant no fuel, no fuel meant no factories operating, no factories meant no munitions. And such absurdities arose constantly; the ministry of war had little influence at GHQ.

Military reverses led to increasing dissatisfaction with the government. In particular, it seemed that the 'public organizations', like the War Industries Committee and the *zemstva* bodies, were much more capable of administering the war effort than the ministries. In other words, an alternative government was being born—and this process was reflected in the various demands of the Duma leaders, industrialists, city councils and *zemstva* for more authority. Liberals predominated in the 'public organizations' and sought to exploit their indispensability in the war effort as a lever to obtain a government 'responsible to public opinion'. By this they meant a government whose members would need to retain the approval of the Duma. No doubt most liberals (and Nicholas) felt that it was a case of now-or-never; if the liberals did not gain their objective during the war, they would be very vulnerable after it. In mid-1915 there was a majority of ministers who favoured the formation of a responsible government, but the Tsar and the prime minister (Goremykin) were unreceptive. When in September 1915 Nicholas left to take command at GHQ, against the advice of most of his ministers, it seemed that any hope of a responsible government had disappeared. Following the Tsar's decision, the more capable ministers resigned or were dismissed. Even Goremykin was replaced in early 1916. Henceforth, and until 1917, a dreary succession of nonentities would play musical chairs around the cabinet table, with the Empress and Rasputin calling the tune.

The Empress and Rasputin

Alexandra was in many respects a superb woman, even though she was fated to bring into public gaze her failings rather than her virtues. Nominally a German princess, by education and upbringing she had been essentially a part of the British royal family. She brought to Russia not only the haemophilic gene of her grandmother, Queen Victoria, but a sincere prudery, a deeply religious mind, and a repugnance for the rituals and empty pomp of court life. Being required by her marriage to adopt the Orthodox faith, she became more fervent than the born Orthodox. For someone like Alexandra, whose marriage was also a choice of profession, the Orthodox Church seemed to offer, apart from spiritual nourishment, the soundest way to understand the soul of the ordinary Russian. The Empress, like Nicholas, really did want to share the lives of the people, of the peasants. But the people never really accepted her, especially after 1914. Moreover, when she and Nicholas after about 1905 withdrew from their expected but vapid participation in court life, preferring to spend their spare time with each other, the Empress became unpopular with St. Petersburg society.

Rasputin became a political influence in about 1911, but it was not until later that this was generally realized. Prior to 1911 he had been an intimate of the royal family, but little more. When, in 1903, he arrived in St. Petersburg from his native Siberia, he was in his thirties, and already enjoyed the reputation of a holy man. His acquaintance with Nicholas and Alexandra began in 1905, a very bad year for the Imperial couple. There were the defeats of the Russo-Japanese War, the internal upheavals, and above all the cruel shock of discovering that the long-awaited, long-prayed-for, and long-despaired-of heir, who had finally appeared in 1904 to the accompaniment of a 300-gun salute, was haemophilic. Nicholas himself was an outdoor man, and the idea of his son leading a glass-case-and-cotton-wool existence must have pained him. In fact, though, the young Alexis was permitted to lead as normal a life as possible; some risks were taken and some serious crises thereby created. In 1907 the Tsarevitch seemed to be dying a prolonged and agonizing death after a minor fall, but he began to recover after Rasputin had been called in. Previously, miraculous cures of other sick or injured people by Rasputin had been reported. Only the most hostile of Rasputin's detractors have found it possible to find conventional explanations for each and every manifestation of these so-called miracles. In the case of Alexis, it has been plausibly suggested that Rasputin kept away the official doctors, whose repeated prying and prodding of the patient were precisely what a haemophilic must be spared. In the other cases, it is possible that the confidence inspired by Rasputin's presence was a saving factor. Nevertheless, it is still difficult to rule out the existence in Rasputin of powers, or properties, or senses, ordinarily unknown to man. As for his hypnotic power, this seems to have been a reality, but was not exceptionally strong. Apparently he once tried to hypnotize his enemy Stolypin, but failed.

Nicholas's faith in Rasputin was somewhat less uncritical than that of his wife, and he may have realized that not all the tales of the holy man's drinking and womanizing achievements were the product of jealous or envious rumour-mongers. Nevertheless, by 1914 Rasputin was firmly installed as the Imperial family's confidant, and through the Empress he could influence policy, although it is not true that Nicholas blindly followed Rasputin's advice; more often than not he ignored it. But when in 1915 Nicholas went to the front, Rasputin's influence was strengthened simply because the Empress had such magnified authority. The first major change, engineered by ambitious men who took great trouble to gain Rasputin's favour, was the appointment of Khvostov to the key office of minister of the interior. Khvostov's ambition and cunning far outstripped his talent, but the Empress found him a charming genius. *Khvost* means 'tail' in Russian, so it was not long before she began to refer to him as 'my tail' just as she referred to Rasputin as 'our friend'. This virtual personification of her anatomy became known, and doubtless there were those who soon found even more homely words for Khvostov.

Once Khvostov and Rasputin were safely installed as the Empress's advisers, the better ministers one by one were dismissed or resigned, being replaced by what the triumvirate liked to call 'our men'. 'Our men' all too often were those who knew how to flatter, how to propose actions they anticipated would be pleasing to the Empress, Rasputin, and Khvostov. The climax came in February 1916 with the replacement of Goremykin as prime minister by the even more incapable Sturmer. Some indication of the inner life, the network of intrigues (with each ambitious participant contriving to endear himself to Rasputin in private but to have no connexion with him in public), the corruption, the hosts of worthy and unworthy petitioners beating on Rasputin's door, the mismanagement of the inner life of the country and of the defence of the nation, can be gleaned from the pages of the official post-revolutionary investigation, which includes Russian-style soul-baring confessions by several of the most deeply involved offenders. Rasputin was finally murdered in 1916 by a group of conspirators of whom the young and rich Prince Yusupov (related to the Tsar by marriage), the Tsar's young cousin, Dmitri Pavlovich, and the right-wing Duma member Purishkevich were the most important. The plot was successful, although almost every move was bungled. The assassins were regarded by the public as heroes who had rid the country of an evil influence and probable German spy. The government merely exiled them to their country estates. Although they had acted to save the monarch's reputation, they probably damaged the government; the prime minister who had been appointed to replace Sturmer a few weeks earlier was more capable than the latter, but was dismissed in the aftermath of the murder.

The facts and rumours of Rasputin's influence aroused great popular resentment against the regime. Yet Rasputin may well have been a man of much goodwill, who failed to make Russia a better place only because he lacked the education and experience to see through those who, protesting friendship, were merely using him. There seems little doubt that Rasputin had a horror of war, a real understanding that the Christian phrases about the brotherhood of man are inconsistent with sending millions of men to their deaths for the sake of national honour. It is claimed that he helped to dissuade Nicholas from war in 1909 and 1912, and he did his best to avoid the 1914 war, foreseeing its results for the Romanovs and for Russia. During the war, when hatred of the Germans was whipped up to a peak and when talk of a separate peace was regarded as treason, Rasputin nevertheless urged an end to hostilities. He used to wander around villages on foot, meeting the maimed returned from the front, and the widows of those who would not return, and he brought his stories right into the Imperial drawing rooms. War to the Russian royal family had never been a big thrill, as it was for the journalists, and Rasputin made it impossible to forget that war had nothing in common with those stirring peacetime parades. In 1916, apparently, Rasputin urged that the Duma should be reconvened, against the advice of Khvostov. He also suggested that Nicholas should break precedents and address the Duma; this was done, and the Tsar made a good impression, even referring to the members as 'representatives of the people'. It was Rasputin who, realizing that standing from wintry dawn to dusk outside a breadless bakery could turn the meekest housewife into a flaming revolutionary, urged that priority be given to food trains.

The last months of the Empire witnessed the Empress, aided by incompetent and intriguing denizens of the court and ministries, attempting to guide affairs in Petrograd and telegraphing all kinds of admonitions and advice to Nicholas at the front. 'Be an Emperor. Be an Ivan the Terrible . . . Send Milyukov, Guchkov, and Polivanov to Siberia.' To the population at large, 'that German woman' seemed to be the source of all Nicholas's troubles. Perhaps the peasants' proverb summed up the situation: 'It's a sad home where the cow instructs the bull'.

10. *1917*

The February Revolution[1]

IT was only to be expected that after two years of war and sacrifice, with no apparent result, Russians would be beginning to ask themselves whether their country was being properly led. This question had been asked by men of knowledge or influence ever since the war started, but during 1916 lack of confidence in the government spread to the people as a whole. 'That German woman', the Empress, was suspected of sympathy towards the enemy, and when it was realized that she was, in effect, at the helm in Petrograd while her husband was at GHQ, popular alarm grew. The influence of Rasputin, which was common knowledge, was equally resented. The feeling that there were many in the government who wanted the Germans to win, or who were in German pay, gained sustenance from memories of the alleged chaos in the ministry of war in 1914, blamed on the war minister, Sukhomlinov. The latter seemed so incompetent that many believed he was a German agent. His protégé Colonel Myasoyedov was executed as a spy in 1915, arousing further public misgivings, even though the trial and conviction resulted more from personal animosities and paranoia than from any real evidence of treason. In February 1916 the appointment of Sturmer as prime minister in place of Goremykin aroused fresh suspicion; not only was he dishonest and incompetent, but he had a German name. There were a number of occasions when Russian attacks at the front had been met by withering resistance, and it seemed not only to the uninformed soldiers but also to their officers that the Russian plans had been betrayed to the enemy. What is more likely is that Russian radio messages were too often uncoded, and that counter-intelligence failed to prevent information leakage from the capital, where so many

---

[1] Russia changed from the Julian to the Gregorian (western) calendar on 14 February 1928, which became 1 February of the new style. This is why the February Revolution may also be described as the March Revolution, and why the revolution occurring in November was celebrated as the October Revolution.

highly placed personages and their wives ignored the warnings against careless talk. In retrospect it would seem that the main source of the rumours of treason in high places were liberal politicians, many of whom beneath their veneer of western parliamentarianism were just as dishonest, ambitious, wishful-thinking, and uncompromising as their political rivals. Desperately anxious to so weaken the monarchy that Nicholas would feel forced to grant them greater influence through some kind of responsible government, before the end of the war ruined their chances, the liberals appear to have changed their tactics after 1915; hitherto they had merely spread doubts about the government's competence to win the war, not about its willingness. Of all the influences which, in turning public opinion against Nicholas, prepared the ground for the Revolution, the liberals were the most effective. At the same time, thanks to their contacts, through the 'public organizations', with the front line, they strove to influence the generals who, in the last resort, would regard military victory as more important than the survival of autocracy. But they operated cautiously, remembering 1905 and the dangers of a revolution that might run out of their control.

Although workers were beginning to heed anti-war agitators, the strikes in key industries were largely a result of the superior bargaining position of workers that resulted from growing labour shortages. Most Russians did not condemn the war as such, only the way it was being prosecuted. Partly influenced by anti-German propaganda, but mainly impelled by the belief that this war had not been sought by St. Petersburg but had been imposed by the Central Powers, Russians intended to continue the war until the defeat of Germany. But by the end of 1916 almost all the feasible age-groups had been conscripted, and a stream of gassed or maimed soldiers was returning to the towns and villages, not to speak of the long lists of dead which were posted in public places, to be scanned daily by those with relatives at the front.

The drafting of more and more peasants was not the cause of the food shortages which developed in 1916 and 1917. The Russian countryside was still overpopulated and in most regions could afford to shed young men, and even horses. The process could not continue indefinitely, and there was some fall in farm output as agriculture became the almost exclusive province of women, old men, and war wounded, but the cessation of grain exports and vodka distillation compensated for the production loss. Overall there was enough food for everybody. The urban food shortages which are held to be the immediate cause of the February Revolution were not the result of insufficient supplies, but of inefficient wholesale and retail distribution.

Distribution troubles were partly caused by the failure of the railway system to meet the demands of war. This failure was not so much the failure of the railways themselves, but of the way they were administered. In fact, during the war railway construction proceeded at a rapid pace.[2] However, rolling stock was lacking, because railway works had been transferred to munitions production or had lost skilled workers to the army. A crucial factor in the transport failure was the division of the railway network into two administrations; about one-third of the mileage, the railways of the western region, was placed under military administration, and the civilian administration of the remaining lines was expected to co-operate with the former. This it did, and in a short time the western railways had accumulated masses of rolling stock which they were unwilling to relinquish but unable to utilize efficiently. In these circumstances it was hardly surprising that the railways were unable to cope with the change of traffic flows caused by the war. Food trains for the cities, which had a low priority, became fewer and fewer, resulting in reduced stocks. It was the bread shortages in Petrograd which, justifiably, caused the political police the most worry. Their agents could feel the strength of the indignation of those women who queued all day at the bakeries only to be told that there would be no bread.

Massed in long queues before the Petrograd bread shops and then transformed by frustration into an indignant and unruly mob that grew into a crowd big enough to frighten the police into violent action, these women willy-nilly became the catalyst for a social upheaval that would last for decades. Within hours their protest had the support of demonstrations by the more militant Petrograd factory workers.

Nicholas seemed unconscious of the seriousness of popular unrest. To him it was just one more God-sent storm to be weathered. Towards the end of February the Duma was convened and its first session was marked by a speech by the leader of the Trudovik socialist group, Kerensky. He went so far as to assert that only the removal of Nicholas—by force if necessary—could save the Empire. There was a demonstration in the capital, with officers joining with students in singing revolutionary songs. Nicholas, from GHQ, ordered the commander of the Petrograd garrison to put down the disturbance, and orders were issued to shoot rioters.

What made this situation different from previous protests was that many of the soldiers, and some of the officers, were refusing to shoot down their fellow-countrymen. The whole basis of the autocratic system

---

[2] Among the many new lines was the Murmansk Railway, finished in 1916, which together with the widening of the narrow-gauge Archangel line promised to reduce the enormous dumps of strategic imports which had accumulated at those two ports.

was the ability of the autocrat, as a last resort, to set his army against those who challenged his authority; Nicholas was losing that ability in Petrograd, where the soldiers were mainly new and unsettled conscripts or reservists in temporary postings. Rodzianko, President of the Duma, wired Nicholas that Petrograd was descending into chaos; there was a food and fuel crisis, and shooting on the streets. He asked Nicholas to form a new and responsible government. The Tsar responded by dissolving the Duma. Duma members, however, remained in the capital and met informally on 27 February. On this day the streets were crowded with strikers, demonstrators, and students, with soldiers openly consorting with the protesters. A Petrograd Soviet of Workers' Deputies, modelled on that of 1905, was set up by socialist intellectuals; its first chairman was the Georgian Chkheidze, leader of the Duma Mensheviks, and its vice-chairman was Kerensky. Soldiers and workers invaded the prisons and released political prisoners as the various factories elected delegates to the Soviet, which met that evening. When representatives began to arrive from the regiments of the capital, announcing that their units had decided to join the revolution, it seemed clear that the regime would be unable to call on immediate military support. This feeling was reinforced when even the crack Semeonov Guards mutinied. To accommodate the regiments' delegates, the Soviet was renamed Soviet of Workers' and Soldiers' Deputies. A proclamation drawn up by the Soviet was published the next morning in the first issue of its own newspaper, *Izvestiya*. This proclamation announced the formation of the Soviet, appealed for the maintenance of order, and demanded the election of a constituent assembly which would decide how the new democratic Russia would be governed.

The Soviet operated very informally, yet it had great power, even though it did not demand responsibility. In the Petrograd area it could determine which industrial work should continue and which should be strike-bound. Its soldier-members could to a large extent approve or veto the use of armed force. Without the approval of the Soviet the trains might not run, electricity and other services could not continue. Yet it did not pretend to be the government. It was the Duma leaders who began to fulfil that function; they at least had been elected, and represented the whole country, and included men well known for their organizing ability.

As the politicians in Petrograd hurried to and from urgent meetings, trying to agree on what to do, special trains began to move, necessarily passing through junctions that might be controlled by garrisons of changeable disposition. Train movements were organized by the transport ministry in Petrograd, headed by managers who were mainly in favour of the revolution. With its own telecommunications, this ministry was in a good position not only to control movements but also to question its officials about the state of affairs in the country outside the capital;

'How are things in Gatchina?'
'Twenty thousand loyal troops here.'
'What do you mean by loyal?'
'Not revolutionary.'
'Get it, once and for all, that they are rioters. Loyal means those on the people's side. So, Gatchina is in the hands of rioters? Continue'.[3]

Interest shifted to the railways as soon as Nicholas decided to return to his palace at Tsarskoye Selo, outside Petrograd. Hitherto, at GHQ, he had not received a true account of what was happening and, when told of the army mutinies, merely ordered fresh troops under General Ivanov to go to the capital to restore order. The approach of the imperial train put new pressure on Rodzianko and his associates. When it was reported on the main line 100 miles south of Petrograd, Rodzianko ordered that it be stopped, without specifying how. The joint efforts of local railwaymen, who put one of the royal engines out of action, of the local railway manager who helped send the train off, and of the imperial staff who could not think of any better idea, resulted in its going back the way it had come. But, when next reported, the imperial train was proceeding west, towards Pskov, where it was feared it might join with friendly troops. It was slowed down by various expedients, like placing stationary freight trains in front of it, but meanwhile another railborne threat appeared in the form of General Ivanov who, under the pretext of an exhibition of captured trophies being staged at Tsarkoye Selo, had managed to secure clear passage for three trainloads of reliable troops to that town. From there he could join with more troops at Gatchina, and advance on Petrograd.

Railwaymen on the spot (some of whom he executed), and managers in the ministry, together kept him under control. His advance north was frustrated by the removal and despatch to Petrograd of those vital track components, switch frogs, and his excursion ended when his train was despatched with only enough water to allow the locomotive to get halfway to the next watering point.

Meanwhile another railway drama was played with a succession of special trains ordered by Rodzianko to take him to meet the tsar. Holding these trains ready and cancelling other train services to give them a clear run took longer than expected, because Rodzianko kept delaying his departure and the imperial train's movements were unpredictable. Eventually, after three main lines from Petrograd had been successively paralysed

[3] Yu. V. Lomonosov, *Vospominaniya o Martovskoi Revolyutsii* (Stockholm, 1921), 42.

by this situation, a train carrying not Rodzianko but Guchkov was guided down the line to Pskov, where Nicholas's train had finally arrived. Guchkov and another Duma member formed a delegation charged with bringing Nicholas's abdication document back to Petrograd.

The tsar had already been persuaded by his generals to abdicate, but had decided not to transfer the burden to his son Alexis. He named his brother Mikhail as his successor, but Mikhail, on learning from the Duma leaders that the Soviet opposed the continuation of the Romanov dynasty, refused the succession.

The Provisional Government and the Soviet

Before the abdication, the leaders of the Duma, accepting the Tsar's order for dissolution but unwilling to disperse, had formed a temporary committee of members drawn from all the parties except the Bolsheviks (whose deputies were in exile) and the extreme right. It soon appointed commissars to replace the Tsar's ministers and arrested most of the latter; only the trusted navy minister Grigorovich remained in office. Members of the police were also arrested, some at their own request to save themselves from a worse fate. Meanwhile the Moscow garrison mutinied, leaving that city in the hands of the revolutionaries. Outside Petrograd the revolution spread almost bloodlessly; whereas in the capital there had been more than a thousand casualties in the disturbances, elsewhere the transfer of power took place almost by mutual consent. A major exception was the Baltic Fleet, where mutineers murdered many officers.

The Petrograd Soviet agreed, on certain conditions, to support a provisional government which the Duma's Temporary Committee was endeavouring to establish.[4] The new cabinet was headed by Prince Lvov, who with the aid of the liberal press had made a good but exaggerated impression on public opinion as head of the Union of *Zemstva*. The most energetic minister was Milyukov, leader of the Kadets, who was entrusted with foreign affairs. The Octobrist Guchkov became minister of war, and Kerensky minister of justice. Kerensky, whose acceptance of the post was against the wishes of many of the leaders of the Soviet, was the only minister to be also a member of the Soviet.

With successive reshuffles that gave moderate socialists more influence, the Provisional Government lasted more than seven months. This in itself was quite an achievement, for it had little power and faced enormous

---

[4] The available evidence, suggesting that the self-appointed Provisional Government consisted largely of men who, well before February 1917, were linked in a conspiratorial semi-masonic secret society aimed against the autocracy, and that a *coup d'état* had been planned for spring 1917 by Guchkov and others, is presented in G. Katkov's *Russia 1917* (1967).

problems. The Soviet's Order No. I (see p. 236) seemed to have deprived the government of an effective army. The old police had by general consent been disbanded, but the militia which was to replace them never became an effective force. The Soviet, because it controlled the workers' organizations, could deny vital services if it so chose; thus the measures taken by the Provisional Government needed the acquiescence of the Soviet leaders if they were to be effective. The Provisional Government, co-opted from members of a Duma elected on a narrow franchise and consisting of gentlemen favouring a western-style parliamentary democracy, could hardly claim to be a popular government, even though it was popularly accepted for the time being.

Meanwhile, Russia's problems did not disappear with the abdication. Rather did their solution become more urgent as public expectations rose and were transformed into spontaneous and unsanctioned actions. The central problem was, of course, the war. During 1917 public opinion gradually became less enthusiastic about continuing the war. The Kadet leaders, who, because the old conservative parties had disappeared, were now regarded as right-wing, wished to continue the war until victory, so as to qualify for the anticipated territorial gains (notably Constantinople and Galicia) and because they believed that the people had overthrown the Tsar primarily because he was failing to win the war. Most of the socialists, including the bulk of the Soviet leaders, accepted that Russia must fight on, but simply in order to protect the revolution; peace should be made as soon as possible on the basis of no annexations and no war indemnities. Most of the Bolshevik leaders regarded the war as an imperialist phenomenon and believed it could be ended by calling on the working class of the belligerent nations to force their governments to make peace. It was Milyukov's promise to the Allies to maintain the existing understandings on the prosecution of the war which finally impelled the Soviet to oppose the Provisional Government in May, a collision which resulted in the first re-shuffle of the cabinet (Milyukov and Guchkov resigned, Kerensky became minister of war, and five other socialists joined the government in a bid to associate the Soviet more closely with the administration). In July Kerensky became prime minister.

The war made almost inevitable the end of the Provisional Government. To keep the revolution under control would have been near-impossible in any case, with the sudden release of the enormous social pressures accumulated by centuries of autocracy. To fight the war and conduct the revolution simultaneously was a hopeless endeavour. Yet if the government had decided to end the war on unfavourable terms at this time it would probably have been overthrown, because too many Russians would have rejected such a defeat. Pride, patriotism, and the lure of territorial gain still had their effect, while most socialists believed that surrender to the Germans would mean the Kaiser would triumph over the Allies and then be free to send his armies to suppress the revolution. The pressures of the revolution followed four main channels. There was the disintegration of the army. Then there was the disintegration of the Empire as the non-Russian nationalities demanded their long-sought autonomy and received a sympathetic hearing. The peasantry was preoccupied with taking for itself the fields of the gentry. The workers were striving to protect their jobs and their wages, and above all to assert their human dignity.

The first decree of the Provisional Government, drawn up just before the abdication, set the tone for the new regime. It was composed with the participation of the Soviet leaders; both the cabinet and the Soviet agreed that political and personal freedom should have first priority. The decree introduced an amnesty for political, military, and religious prisoners. It completely abolished the death penalty. It established freedom of the press (although hardly for the reactionary press), freedom of speech, the right to strike and to organize trade unions. Social or religious or national discrimination was declared illegal, a measure which benefited mainly but not exclusively the Jews. It abolished the existing police organization. It accorded to soldiers the same rights as civilians except in the front line. In response to pressure from soldier-members of the Soviet, it agreed that the Petrograd regiments which had participated in the revolution would not be sent to the front. And it promised to arrange for elections, by universal suffrage, of a Constituent Assembly, whose members would determine Russia's future form of government. There was thus some justification for Lenin's remark that in the summer of 1917 Russia was the freest country in the world.

However, one result of these upheavals was that the Provisional Government was disarmed. The disappearance of the old governors and their experienced administrators (a disappearance resulting more from spontaneous local actions than from government policy), and the disintegration of the police meant that a government intent on establishing a rule of law to replace tsarist arbitrariness had no means of enforcing its laws.

Although differences of nationality never became the dominant issue of the revolution (except perhaps in Latvia where a native Latvian working class and peasantry confronted a mainly Germanic middle class), it was only natural that the various nationalisms uneasily contained in the Empire would make their own contribution to the instabilities of revolution. Probably it would have been best to make concessions to local demands for autonomy but, as in so many other fields, the moderate socialists and a section of the liberal parties that would have favoured such a compromise were checked by the Kadet leadership. The latter's reluctance to grant independence was partly emotional but also partly based on reluctance to offend the army officers, who were still thought capable of overthrowing the revolution. As it was, granting independence to Poland, which was under German occupation, seemed no great loss and the Kadets agreed to this. The case of Finland, however, was postponed until after the Constituent Assembly had been elected; some autonomy had been conceded but there was a demand for complete independence and the evacuation of Russian troops. In the Ukraine, where national sentiment had been released by the revolution, agreement might have been reached if the Kadets had not carried their objections as far as precipitating the first of the cabinet reorganizations.

In the early months after the revolution there was a honeymoon period between different sections of society which was particularly evident in industry, where managers and factory-owners, quite pleased with the end of tsarist mismanagement, were willing to satisfy the requests of their workforces. Wages rose, overseers who had humiliated or terrorized workers were dismissed at the request of the latter, an eight-hour working day was agreed, and, above all, workers' committees were formed in the factories. These committees, which the Provisional Government approved, gave workers' representatives an increasing say in the conduct of work, but originally their main concern was to keep the factories going at a time when shortage of materials and, sometimes, lack of demand were threatening closures. Later in the year, when it appeared that factory-owners were ceasing production simply to avoid losses at a time of inflation and economic crisis, the committees became more interventionist, giving rise to the phenomenon known as workers' control, with the workers' committees closely supervising the management.

Although the government did establish a state monopoly in the grain trade and took power to requisition grain at fixed prices, its agents hardly made use of their powers, partly because most of them were opposed to coercive measures. The long-awaited share-out of the large estates among peasants was postponed until the Constituent Assembly was in being. The Kadets were sincere in their belief that this was too important a matter to be hurried but it placed them, and the government they dominated, in the situation of delaying a transformation that was impatiently awaited. Spontaneous take-overs of estates by local peasants, usually acting on the principle of fair shares for all, became ever more widespread.

In its first days the Petrograd Soviet was a very informal body, with a membership fluctuating between 2,000 and 3,000 as new delegates dropped in and old delegates dropped out.[5] In the beginning the regiments had a disproportionate number of seats but soon equality was imposed, with one delegate per 2,000 workers or soldiers. Most of the Soviet's decisions were taken by its executive committee, which itself had a smaller nucleus of twenty-four key members who met separately to discuss basic issues. All the socialist parties were allocated seats in the executive committee, although at first the Mensheviks and Bolsheviks were represented by secondary figures because their leaders had not yet returned from exile. It was a Menshevik exile, the Georgian Tseretelli, who on his return became the most dominant personality of the Soviet and succeeded through logic and oratory in imposing some kind of order and direction to its discussions. It was largely Tseretelli's persuasion which in May coaxed an unwilling Soviet to allow six of its members to become ministers in the Provisional Government.

Soviets were established more or less spontaneously in the provinces in the month following the revolution. Like the Petrograd Soviet, they could limit both economic and military activity in their locality; any attempt to defeat the revolution could be neutralized by a cessation of railway and telegraphic services, and perhaps demonstrations by the local garrisons. In April there was an All-Russia Conference of Soviets in Petrograd, and henceforth the Petrograd and the provincial soviets maintained a closer co-ordination. Moreover, by admitting representatives from the provincial soviets into the Petrograd Soviet, the latter became almost a national organization.

That real power lay with the Soviet and not with the Provisional Government became more and more obvious. This implies that the causes of the 'failure' of the February Revolution should be sought in the Soviet rather than in the Provisional Government. In the Soviet, the Socialist Revolutionaries had a strong majority and in addition enjoyed the co-operation of the Mensheviks. They had massive popular support and their leader Chernov was trusted even by his opponents. But Chernov never emerged as a strong leader, perhaps because the different factions in his party were too unwilling to compromise. Moreover, in the early months of the revolution the Socialist Revolutionary–Menshevik *bloc* failed to obtain what it, the people, and the revolution needed; that is, an end to the war. It did dispatch delegations and appeals abroad, seeking a 'just peace without annexations or indemnities', but not only were these frustrated

[5] Most regarded their delegates as 'elders', for the election of elders was one of the village customs which had been brought to the factories from the countryside. The dual leadership of Soviet and government might also be regarded as traditional, in the sense that both before and after 1917 there were other examples of executive bodies supervised by parallel 'watchdog' organizations.

by the belligerent governments, but even the socialist leaders of France, Germany, and Britain were only lukewarm in their support. The hatreds of war defeated the Russian appeals to humanity and commonsense. Having failed to obtain peace, the non-Bolshevik socialist leaders seemed to lose their zest; in May they had forced the resignation of Milyukov because he advocated an energetic war effort, but in June they accepted the generals' advice to stage another offensive at the front. Another factor inhibiting the Soviet leaders was that the disastrous falling away of middle-class support towards the end of the 1905 Rebellion had convinced them that the 1917 Revolution should not in any circumstances become too radical. Whereas Lenin had concluded that revolutionaries should be prepared to act without middle-class support, the Mensheviks and Socialist Revolutionaries in 1917 were reluctant to arouse the enmity of the Kadets. Moreover, for marxists the February Revolution was the bourgeois revolution which Marx had said would be followed by a bourgeois government. Thus the existence of the Provisional Government, even though it lacked the power to govern, was necessary for the ideological peace of mind of many revolutionaries. For these reasons, when in July the Provisional Government seemed at the mercy of street demonstrations, and the demonstrators urged the Soviet to take power in accordance with the anarchist-inspired and Bolshevik-sponsored slogan 'All Power to the Soviets', the Soviet refused.

The army in 1917

Accounts differ about the spirit of the Russian soldiers in 1917, although all agree that the morale of the front-line troops remained much steadier than that of the rear garrisons. Similarly, the navy's small ships, frequently operating in dangerous waters, had steadier crews than the battleships, which had remained month after month in harbour. But front-line servicemen were depressed by the rumours of treason in the capital, of ministries dominated by the Empress and Rasputin. In March 1917 censorship ensured that only incomplete accounts reached the troops about the end of the Romanov dynasty; not for the last time, many Russians learned of great events through foreign broadcasts, in this case placards hoisted above German trenches, announcing the abdication of Nicholas. The abdication seemed to raise the question of whether the war might soon end, and whether the landowners' land would be redistributed. Natural reluctance to become the final casualty of the war, and rumours that back home the peasants were already taking over the land, caused many a soldier to desert. However, it was not until the summer that the desertion rate became alarmingly high.

The desperate world war which had made possible the revolution also provided the worst possible conditions in which to carry it through. The Soviet in particular, and supporters of the Provisional Government in general, feared that officers would use the army to restore the monarchy. This fear was largely a result of their being convinced by their own propaganda, for the army officers with few exceptions had lost their faith in the monarchy months earlier. Even in 1914 a large proportion of the officers had been liberal to the extent of preferring a constitutional form of government. However, the revolutionaries' fear of the army, the only barrier between them and the German Empire, which if it broke into Russia would assuredly reassert the monarchical principle, did pose a fundamental problem.

The chosen remedy was to subordinate the officers to the men, and to instil political vigilance in the latter. Manifestations of this policy included the famous Order No.1, the soldiers' councils, the commissars, and visits from agitators and speechmakers. The Petrograd Soviet's Order No. 1, and its subsequent amplifications, removed the traditional authority of officers over men. It ordered units to elect their own soldier-representatives to form councils (soviets), and it was these soviets which would approve orders. Officers would, of course, be retained for the sake of their technical and leadership training, but would be responsible to their soviet. The Declaration of the Rights of Soldiers soon followed. This removed some of the humiliations to which the private soldier had hitherto been subjected, and went somewhat further by forbidding the employment by officers of orderlies, making saluting voluntary, and outlawing disciplinary punishments imposed by officers. Meanwhile, in accordance with the new freedom of speech introduced in the country, speechmakers and agitators of varied points of view were allowed to visit the front and address the soldiers. Those who opposed the war advocated fraternization between the German and Russian front-line troops. This did take place, but it was usually in the form of implicit 'if you don't bother us we won't bother you' understandings. The German troops were still the Kaiser's troops, subject to strict military discipline, and seemed disappointingly uninterested in revolutionary propaganda.

The dissolution of the officers' authority could not fail to break the army eventually, but it was not a fast process. At the front the situation differed from unit to unit. Many officers were insulted and some were killed, usually because they had made themselves unpopular or, more rarely, because the soldiers, inflamed by a visiting orator or a resident revolutionary, were carried away by a sudden and short-lived blood-lust. But most unpopular officers were merely asked to leave, and in many units, especially those in which there had been good relations between officers and men, there was no violence. The soldiers' councils, although they might spend hours arguing, made administrative decisions which were wise and well thought-out. Frequently, too, the officers would be respectfully consulted. However, many officers could not face the breakdown of all the accustomed forms, and tended to find new postings in rear administrations. Drill and field training were neglected, and it was obvious to the front-line officers that, though their men would resist attacks by the enemy, not all would agree to themselves attack. But patriotism among soldiers was still strong. In the capital, especially in the newspapers, there was great talk of the wonderful fighting spirit of the army under the new regime, and the anti-German fervour which had been deliberately fostered during the war was still at a high pitch. To this aggressive spirit on the part of those Russians who were safely in the rear were added French appeals for a new Russian offensive, and the belief of the new war minister, Kerensky, that a successful offensive would act like a tonic on morale at home, and thus strengthen the government. To boost the morale of the front-line troops and counteract the influence of anti-war and anti-government propagandists, Kerensky sent out to the units his ministry's own propagandists, called commissars. These men were also intended to mediate between the soldiers' councils and the remaining officers. The war ministry at the same time was having moderate success in regularizing and controlling the proliferating mass of soldiers' soviets and committees. Kerensky made tours of the front, making those fiery speeches in which he excelled and inspiring his listeners with a temporary thirst for offensive action against the German Empire. Old-school officers contemptuously referred to their war minister as the 'Persuader-in-Chief'.

In the middle of June, just as the Petrograd garrison was demonstrating against the continuation of the war, the Russian troops at the front went over the top. The ground had been well prepared by an intense artillery barrage and the Austrians were soon in flight. General Kornilov, in particular, made a wide and dangerous breakthrough. Yet even at this stage many units refused to go into battle. The death penalty had been abolished in the army; no longer was it possible to drive soldiers into an attack at gunpoint. The most effective troops were the Czechs, those former soldiers of the piebald Austro-Hungarian army who had amicably allowed themselves to be taken prisoner by their fellow-Slavs, and then volunteered to fight against Austria for an expected independent Czechoslovakia after the war. Also distinguished were the so-called shock units, consisting of officers only.

The initial successes did provoke some enthusiasm at home. Streets which on one day were thronged by anti-war demonstrators were the next day filled with enthusiastic warmongers parading icon-style portraits of Kerensky. But as soon as German troops were sent to help Austria, the Russian offensive collapsed and turned into a rout. Henceforth the Russian army was incapable of offensive action, unwilling to exert itself, but still able to put up some resistance to an enemy advance. Soldiers who had hitherto elected Mensheviks or Social Revolutionaries to their committees did not forget that these two parties had agreed to the unwanted and unrewarded offensive.

The Bolsheviks

That the Bolsheviks played so minor a role in the early weeks of the revolution was partly because their leaders were dispersed in exile, and partly because they had little support outside the working-class districts of the big cities. The years since 1905 had not been prosperous for any of the Social Democrat factions, even though on the eve of the war there had been signs of a recovery. Membership had fallen drastically, especially among older supporters. Intellectuals, in particular, had deserted the Social Democrats. This meant that, while there was a higher proportion of proletarians, there were fewer competent agitators, polemicists and writers. The average member was now in his mid-twenties, and deplored the factional struggles which seemed to him a result of irrelevant émigré wranglings. In 1914 there were no fewer than six recognizable Social Democrat factions.

In the repressions following 1905, the Bolshevik underground was demoralized by defeat and ideological wrangling. It was the Mensheviks who seemed to recover from defeat most readily. In the relatively peaceful labour situation which existed up to 1912, the Mensheviks fostered the development of legal workers' organizations: trade unions, insurance societies, night schools, co-operatives. From these, it was hoped, would grow an experienced workers' intelligentsia; leadership would thus grow out of the labour movement itself, rather than be supplied by middle-class intellectuals. Some progress was made despite governmental harassment of even legal workers' organizations,[6] but after 1912 it was Bolsheviks, not Mensheviks, who tended to be elected to leading positions in these organizations. Mensheviks and Bolsheviks co-operated in the elections to the Fourth Duma in 1912; the Bolsheviks won six seats, only one fewer than the Mensheviks. Meanwhile, the economic revival brought more workers into the labour force, especially into areas where the Bolsheviks were strong; particularly the engineering industry and the factories of St.

---

[6] The *Okhrana*, still regarding the Bolsheviks as useful splitters of the revolutionary movement, preferred to arrest Mensheviks, especially effective or popular Mensheviks.

Petersburg. On the other hand, the Bolsheviks faced serious problems. By 1914 most of their best-known intellectuals (Lunacharsky, Bogdanov, Gorki, and others) had quarrelled with Lenin's tactics and deserted the party. The violent bank robberies and other 'expropriations' made by the Bolsheviks to raise funds not available from an unsympathetic public also damaged their reputation. So did the revelation in 1914 that the leader of the Bolsheviks in the Duma, Malinovsky, had long been a police informer. Also, while simple uncompromising Bolshevik slogans attracted the younger or most reckless workers, it was not certain that the Bolshevik leadership could control these new adherents; when the St. Petersburg Bolshevik Party Committee called off the strike of July 1914, the Bolshevik rank-and-file ignored the instruction. The outbreak of war further damaged the Bolshevik cause, at least in the first year. Holding true to their earlier promise not to support imperialist wars, the Bolsheviks found themselves opposing the Russian war effort in a period of hysterical patriotism.

When in 1917 the new freedom of the press allowed *Pravda* to recommence publication, it was Molotov[7] who became editor. This was a key position, because *Pravda* was the most important link between the Bolshevik leaders and the ordinary members. It was *Pravda* which indicated what the correct attitude on current problems should be (that is, the 'party line'). Molotov was in his mid-twenties, had been a Bolshevik since 1906, and was the most senior member still at liberty of the Russian Bureau of the Central Committee. Under his editorship *Pravda*, contrary to popular feeling at the time, advocated resistance to the Provisional Government, termination of the war, and immediate distribution of the landowners' estates to the peasants. But it was not long before Molotov was replaced by a trio, including Stalin and Kamenev, of more senior Bolsheviks recently released from Siberia. Under this new direction the party line was reversed. The new editors, believing that the Provisional Government was the bourgeois government which, in Marx's forecast, would rule after the bourgeois revolution, advocated support of the government. Like the other socialists, they believed that it was in danger of overthrow by a counter-revolution on the part of the reactionaries. There were still, after all, many generals still in office, and it was not yet realized that most of these officers had little effective command of their men.

---

[7] His real name was Skryabin. Bolshevik and Menshevik leaders often adopted pseudonyms. Usually these were intended to conceal their identities from the authorities, but after the revolution the pseudonyms were retained, partly because they were more familiar to the public, partly out of pride, and sometimes because they sounded Russian although their owners were non-Russians. Other pseudonyms included Stalin (Dzhugashvili), Zinoviev (Radomyslsky), Kamenev (Rosenfeldt), Trotsky (Bronstein), Kirov (Kostrikov), Martov (Tsederbaum), Kaganovich (Kagan).

Pravda's line infuriated Lenin. During the war Lenin had lived in Switzerland, occupying himself by organizing international anti-war meetings of left-wing socialists. He had broken with many of his former associates and his closest colleague was Zinoviev. He now strove to find a way to return to Russia to take personal command of his party. This was not easy, because to reach Russia from Switzerland he had either to pass through Germany or Austria, which were at war with Russia, or through one of the Allied powers which, aware that he opposed Russia's continued participation in the war, would be unlikely to facilitate his passage. (Trotsky, returning to Russia from New York, was arrested by the Allies in Halifax for this reason, and was only released after the Provisional Government had applied pressure in London.)

Until he could leave Switzerland, Lenin attempted to direct the party *in absentia*. The first of his *Letters from Afar* was printed in *Pravda* in mid-March. In this he attributed the February Revolution to the machinations of Britain and France, which had heard that Nicholas intended to make a separate peace with Germany and therefore determined to overthrow him. Rather less wild was his assertion that the Provisional Government was continuing the war so that the Allied powers, Russia included, could enjoy territorial gains at the expense of the Central Powers. But although his letters were discussed they did not change the policies of the Bolshevik leadership inside Russia. Despite Lenin's condemnation, Stalin and his colleagues still advocated support of the Provisional Government, the continuance of the war, and the merging of the Bolsheviks with the Mensheviks' left-wing.

By this stage of the war the direction of German policy was in the hands of generals such as Hindenburg and Ludendorff. Intent at all costs on preserving their professional reputations (that is, to avoid obvious military defeat), they received sympathetically the suggestion that Germany should facilitate the return of émigré revolutionaries. The German Chief of Staff (Hoffmann) wrote later that Germany had just as much right to attack Russia with Lenin as with poison gas. Thus the expedient of sending Lenin and other émigrés to a Baltic port in a sealed (that is, extra-territorial) railway car was quickly approved. Like other returning exiles, Lenin was met at the Finland Station in Petrograd by a welcoming delegation led on this occasion by the Menshevik Chkheidze. He responded coldly to the latter's speech of welcome and made it clear that he had no intention of co-operating with the other socialists. Then he met the Bolshevik leaders and assailed them for their timidity. Not all were convinced, and Lenin was himself attacked by several of his colleagues. On the following day, when Lenin at a meeting of all Social Democrats refused to countenance a merging of the different factions into one party, he was again attacked by fellow-Bolsheviks, who accused him of fomenting a civil war with his allegations that the other socialists were in fact betrayers of socialism. At the same time Lenin's reputation among the urban masses was deteriorating, especially when it became public knowledge that he had returned to Russia with the assistance of the hated Germans. On the other hand, Lenin acquired a valuable ally when Trotsky joined the Bolsheviks.

The Mensheviks and Social Revolutionaries had agreed to join the government at a time when the honeymoon between potentially conflicting forces was still apparent. Moreover, they regarded their coalition partners, the Kadets, as essential propitiators of the officer corps. But almost as soon as the coalition government was formed the economy took a further turn for the worse. Rapid inflation prompted workers to demand wage increases that the industrialists were unwilling and sometimes unable to grant. The honeymoon was over. The government's efforts to create a civil society in which concepts of contract, private property, and trespass would be a major part, in which decisions would be taken deliberately and at great length, had coincided with a period in which the population was demanding fast action on major issues: the war, the land, the economy. With the prospect of a Constituent Assembly receding (for the Kadets were now holding back the organization of an election because they feared its result) and with the new-found confidence of the various workers', soldiers', and peasants' committees, it seemed increasingly clear that the Soviet was quite capable of taking over the government and doing what needed to be done. The Provisional Government seemed to have become merely the protector of a status quo that was acceptable to only a minor part of the population.

This change of mood was reflected in elections to committees. The Bolsheviks, whose arguments began to match most closely the actual situation and who had consistently opposed the government, were the main beneficiaries. The Socialist Revolutionary party split, with the Left Socialist Revolutionaries, indignant at the failure to settle the land question, taking their own independent path. In the various local committees, where Bolsheviks (often contrary to the instructions of their leadership) did co-operate with other parties, they tended now to find common cause with the Left Socialist Revolutionaries.

Gradually Bolshevik influence increased. Opinions differ as to the intentions of the Bolsheviks in this period, and especially their relationship to the armed anti-government demonstrations of the summer. Some historians assert that the party intended to convert the popular demonstrations of June and July into riots in which the government could be overthrown. Others believe that the Bolsheviks, far from encouraging violence and extremism, were a moderating influence on the demonstrators, who tended to be more radical and impulsive than the party. The truth is that the Bolsheviks had several policies. At the top, Lenin was frequently opposed by his colleagues, while at the bottom the party members active in committees tended to act according to their own appreciation of the local situation, of which they had a more accurate understanding than the central committee. Lenin, who feared that a successful coup in Petrograd would be suppressed by forces outside the capital, preferred to wait until the government and other socialists had lost more support, while lesser Bolsheviks, in closer contact with the mood of the streets, favoured an insurrection. Lenin's *April Thesis*, published after his return and advocating that the Soviet (in which he hoped sooner or later to have a majority) should take power, was gradually winning acceptance within the party, but some members felt the party might lose some of its support to the anarchists, who were less restrained than the Bolsheviks.

At the All-Russia Congress of Soviets held in June, Kerensky was able to ridicule Lenin's assertion that the country's problems could be solved by arresting a hundred capitalists and by the Soviet overthrowing the government. Yet the audience, largely workers and soldiers and sailors, evidently found Lenin's ideas more to its taste.

In June the Bolsheviks called for street demonstrations in favour of their programme, which by this time included such slogans as 'All Power to the Soviets' and 'Bread, Peace, and Freedom'. Apparently it was intended that pro-Bolshevik army units would take part, carrying arms. Chkheidze warned the All-Russia Congress of Soviets that the Bolsheviks were planning an insurrection, and many delegates spent the night visiting factories and barracks to dissuade intending participants. This caused the party to cancel the demonstration at the last minute. Stalin was among those who opposed cancellation, but he was outvoted in the Central Committee. Despite the widespread belief that the Bolsheviks had only narrowly failed to take power by force, they were not arrested. They merely lost prestige for a few weeks.

After the chastening experience of June, the news which Bolshevik leaders received in July of an impending uprising was probably unwelcome. The unrest was caused by the Kerensky military offensive in June, which had aroused great resentment among the Petrograd soldiers and the Kronstadt sailors after its initial successes against the Austrians degenerated into a rout. The sailors, the most militant of the armed supporters of the revolution, were regarded as staunch upholders of the Bolsheviks. If the Bolsheviks failed to lead this uprising they would inevitably lose much support among the soldiers and sailors. Yet an uprising still seemed premature. The original instigators of the rising were unknown, and could have been German agents. The Provisional Government, apparently, could command loyal troops from outside the capital. The other socialist parties would be opposed to a coup, as in June, and after all it was the Socialist Revolutionaries who had most support in the country and in the soviets. Lenin was away and could not be consulted conveniently by the Bolshevik leaders. Moreover, when the time came to make a final decision, Kamenev and Zinoviev were absent. So it was Stalin who, consulted by the Kronstadt leaders, obliquely approved the dispatch of 20,000 armed sailors to the capital. However, when it became clear that the Provisional Government was making careful preparations to squash the rising, the party's Central Committee decided that, after all, it would not take command of the demonstrators. As in June, *Pravda* appeared on the day with a blank space where the proclamation announcing the party's sponsorship of the demonstration had been hastily removed. But nobody remembered, or dared, to warn the sailors of the changed circumstances. They marched into the capital according to plan, listened to a fierily non-committal harangue by Lenin, who told them they were beautiful, and then marched off to the Tauride Palace, seat of the Soviet and of the old Duma. As they marched they became more disorderly, the capital's population became excited, and shots were fired. There was looting, and well-dressed individuals were beaten up, killed or taken into custody. Chernov, the Socialist Revolutionary leader who came out to address the sailors, was attacked and seized, to be rescued by Trotsky, whose never-failing oratory convinced even the unruly sailors that they were helping nobody by arresting stray individuals. After this, the sailors reacted to the anticlimax by disappearing. They were replaced at the Tauride Palace by a pro-Bolshevik regiment which had been marching to their aid. The soldiers did not seem to have a clear idea of what they were supposed to do and there were no Bolsheviks around to guide them. They were thus easily persuaded by a Menshevik leader (who himself did not know quite what was happening) that they had been summoned to guard the palace. And thus it was that the 176th Regiment, which in the morning had left its barracks to overthrow the government, in the afternoon vigilantly stood on guard outside the Tauride Palace, symbol and seat of the status quo. Here it blocked the third wave of pro-Bolshevik assailants, this time the armed workers of the Putilov factory. Only a few of these could penetrate into the palace; one worker made a short speech, urging the unenthusiastic Soviet to take power, before sheepishly picking up his rifle and following his comrades home.

Although Bolsheviks and their historians later wrote nostalgically of the heroic 'July Days', the truth is that the party's activity at this juncture produced a shambles. Yet undoubtedly the Bolsheviks were in a difficult situation. In retrospect, it seems that had the party taken the lead it might indeed have won power (the Provisional Government was defenceless on this day and could have been arrested without any resistance). But although power might have been won it probably would not have been kept. Obviously, it would have been better if the Bolsheviks had not at first encouraged the rising, but this was not Lenin's doing. Nevertheless, the Provisional Government took advantage of the failure of the rising to issue warrants for the arrest of the leading Bolsheviks. It also released what was claimed to be evidence that Lenin was a German agent. Although the more sophisticated realized that this evidence was at least partly fabricated, to the ordinary revolutionary masses it appeared convincing, especially as they remembered how the Germans had helped Lenin to return to Russia. He became highly unpopular as a result. In later years Soviet historians took great pains to deny not only that Lenin was a German agent, but also that he accepted money from Germany. However, this last allegation was perhaps the best-founded element in the accusations levelled against him, and the balance of evidence suggests that his party did indeed benefit from German funds at this time. But in the circumstances this does not seem as immoral as both detractors and defenders seem to assume. After all, revolutionaries need money, and the Bolsheviks merely took it wherever they could get it.

After the July fiasco Lenin, against much resistance, persuaded his colleagues to drop the 'All Power to the Soviets!' slogan, on the ground that the Soviet, under Socialist Revolutionary and Menshevik leadership, had supported what he termed the 'counter-revolution'. This was one of those occasions when the refusal of lower Bolsheviks to obey instructions saved the party from the consequences of its ill judgement, and some weeks later this powerful slogan, which local Bolsheviks had continued to use, would be reinstated.

At this low point in his fortunes Lenin sought refuge from the arrest which he believed was threatening him. For two weeks a rural hut was his shelter and then, disguised as a locomotive fireman, he rode over the Russo-Finnish border on a locomotive. He then took up residence in the home of the Helsinki Chief of Police, a Bolshevik sympathizer, waiting for better days.

The Kornilov affair

The Bolsheviks, in the aftermath of the July 'rising', strove to increase their influence in the factory committees, which were increasingly important.

By August the Bolsheviks were considerably more influential in the Petrograd factories than the Mensheviks, but the latter were strong in the provinces, while the Socialist Revolutionaries still had the allegiance of the bulk of the politically conscious peasants. At the end of July Kerensky succeeded Lvov as prime minister, and his government, though it contained more socialists than non-socialists, was moderate in its approach. Some Bolsheviks were arrested, including Trotsky and Kamenev. The death penalty was restored at the front in response to General Kornilov's demand for measures to halt the alarming desertion rate, as soldiers left their posts to participate in the share-out of land in their native villages. Citizens were forbidden to keep weapons, and some of the most troublesome regiments were disbanded. Nevertheless, many conservatives and moderates began to look for a new leader, someone who would restore order and legality, by dictatorial means if necessary. When Kornilov succeeded Brusilov as C-in-C, it seemed that perhaps such a leader was in sight.

Kerensky appointed Kornilov under the influence of the former Socialist Revolutionary terrorist Savinkov, who was now the trusted administrator of the war ministry. But although Kornilov and Kerensky were broadly in agreement on what should be done first, namely that the Bolsheviks should be quelled and public order restored, their personal philosophies differed. Kornilov was killed by a shell during the early weeks of the Civil War and most information about him comes from his enemies and critics, but it seems that he had little political sense and in 1917 was influenced by his adjutant and other officers. He gave an impression of unreliability and untrustworthiness, which may have only reflected the hesitancies of an honest but unsophisticated mind. Like other officers, he had a low opinion of Kerensky, whom he regarded as a windbag lacking the strength to take the decisive action which Russia needed.

Kornilov's attempted coup has defied satisfactory analysis; even the bare facts are difficult to establish because of the false trails laid by participants and their supporters wishing to divert the blame on to others. For most Russians at that time, the Kornilov affair was simply what happened in the last week of August, when the 3rd Cavalry Corps moved towards Petrograd under the orders of Kornilov, with the aim of replacing the Provisional Government by a military dictatorship.[8] The main controversy concerns the degree of Kerensky's complicity: how far he encouraged Kornilov, how far he was deceived by Kornilov, and vice versa.[9] Probably both Kornilov

[8] It was probably intended to form a collective dictatorship including Kornilov, Kerensky, and Savinkov.

[9] Apart from his own memoirs, strong evidence for Kerensky's innocence may be found in A. Ascher's article in *Russian Review*, No. 4 (1953), 239–43. At the other extreme,

and Kerensky began to think about military intervention after the disturbances of July, and entered into what turned out to be a very ambiguous understanding. In August the Germans captured Riga, and Kornilov requested that troops in the Petrograd region be placed under his direct command. Kerensky wished to exclude the Petrograd garrison from Kornilov's command, but asked Kornilov to send him a cavalry corps to defend the government against anticipated attacks by the Bolsheviks and their supporters. Kornilov, it seems, had already made his own plans for a march on Petrograd, ostensibly to defend the government from a Bolshevik rising conveniently forecast for September, and he had grounds for believing that Kerensky approved of such a move. Hence Kerensky's request for a cavalry corps was not unexpected. But when Kerensky heard that Kornilov was moving other troops (or perhaps when he heard rumours that Kornilov's friends were planning to murder the prime minister) he ordered Kornilov to resign and report to the capital. Kornilov, with the support of several influential generals, then sent his troops towards Petrograd and issued a proclamation saying that he was acting to save the Russian people from becoming slaves of the Germans, that he was himself the son of a Cossack peasant with no political ambitions, and that he would support the decisions of the forthcoming Constituent Assembly. However, his offensive fizzled out when his already unenthusiastic troops were further demoralized by agitators sent out from Petrograd, and when the railway workers, on the instructions of the Soviet, refused to transport his supplies and reinforcements. The non-Bolshevik socialists rallied to the support of the Provisional Government, while the Bolsheviks used the crisis to extract their arrested leaders from gaol and to obtain the approval by the Soviet's Committee Against Counter-revolution of an armed workers' militia to defend the revolution. In this way the already existing armed Bolshevik supporters (the 'Red Guard'), who helped to defend Petrograd against Kornilov, received the Soviet's recognition.

The Kornilov coup was suppressed with little bloodshed. But after it was all over soldiers and sailors, infuriated by what they were convinced was essentially an officers' plot, began to turn on officers who were still serving with their units. Hundreds of army and naval officers were murdered, often in brutal circumstances. Yet the Kornilov affair had demonstrated

---

I. Strakhovsky's article in *The Slavonic and East European Review* (1955), 372–95, asserts that Kerensky tricked Kornilov into sending troops to Petrograd. J. L. Munk's 1987 book (see Bibliography) uses an extremely wide range of sources but nevertheless does not provide enough evidence for a clear-cut verdict on Kerensky's role. Probably the question will never be resolved, although it seems likely that Kerensky, a lawyer, whatever his contacts with Kornilov may have been, took great care to avoid any provable, as opposed to moral, complicity.

that the once-feared generals had no real power to move against the revolution, or even to defend themselves. The 'loyal' units, quite impressive on paper, were composed of soldiers who would not fight.

The Bolshevik Revolution

Analysis of the results of city council elections held during the summer of 1917 suggests that the Kornilov affair was not the cause of that recovery of the Bolsheviks' strength and prestige which became marked in September and October, except in so far as its failure demoralized right-wing forces. The Bolsheviks' popularity was already increasing before the July disturbances brought them into temporary disrepute. With workers and soldiers becoming ever more assertive and frustrated in their expectations, that party which was closest to their bitterness was bound to attract favour. Anarchists, gratified by the Bolsheviks' regard for workers' factory committees, which they themselves advocated, supported Lenin's party until after October, when it became clear that the Bolsheviks believed in strong government. How far anarchist support helped Lenin is difficult to judge because, being an attitude more than an organization, the strength of anarchism in 1917 seems indeterminable. In mid-September two events showed how far the Bolsheviks had progressed. For the first time, the Petrograd Soviet passed a resolution proposed by its Bolshevik faction. In re-elections to the soldiers' section of the Soviet, hitherto dominated by the Socialist Revolutionaries, the Bolsheviks gained nearly half of the votes.

The government in the meantime fixed elections to the long-awaited and long-postponed Constituent Assembly for November 25. To bridge the gap until its convening, Kerensky organized a 'Pre-Parliament' to fulfil the temporary role of popular assembly. Lenin, still in Finland, sent a furious letter to the Bolshevik leaders in Petrograd when he learned that they were participating in these arrangements. The Central Committee, surprised but not submissive, quietly agreed to burn this letter. Nevertheless Lenin continued to bombard his lieutenants with demands for a forcible seizure of power, meanwhile writing a pamphlet on what he considered to be the real question, *Can the Bolsheviks Keep State Power?*

Lenin's decision to press for an immediate seizure of power represented a change of programme, and it was not easy to persuade the party to accept it. The arguments which he used may be summarized: the party was now capable of obtaining majorities in the Petrograd and Moscow Soviets (in early October, Trotsky was elected chairman of the Petrograd Soviet), thus the early Bolshevik slogan of 'All power to the Soviets' was paying off; Kerensky, whom Lenin described as a 'Kornilovite, Stolypinite, and Bonapartist', might well surrender Petrograd to the advancing Germans simply because the Bolsheviks' strength lay in the capital; to wait for the Constituent Assembly or for the next All-Russia Congress of Soviets (scheduled for late October) would be purposeless and indeed harmful, for the Bolsheviks would be outnumbered in these bodies; the Bolsheviks had at their disposal more armed strength than any of their opponents and the few army units which remained loyal to the government could be neutralized by skilful agitators; once having acquired power, the Bolsheviks could retain it because their first acts would be to legalize the seizure of private land by the peasants and to promise an end to the war; these two policies would automatically assure the allegiance of the soldiers; but the promise of peace would lose its effectiveness if the Allies and Germany made peace first, or if Kerensky, out of spite against the Bolsheviks, himself negotiated peace.

The Central Committee of the party in Petrograd forbade Lenin to return from Finland. He tendered his resignation, and under this threat the Bolsheviks did walk out of the Pre-Parliament, Trotsky alleging that the bourgeois parties were determined to block the election of the Constituent Assembly. In the villages the Bolsheviks were seeking an alliance with the dissatisfied left wing of the Socialist Revolutionaries. This would soon be in formal alliance with the Bolsheviks, broadening the appeal of the latter because in the countryside, where Bolshevism had not been strong, the Bolsheviks could now claim connexions with the Socialist Revolutionaries. Lenin meanwhile returned in disguise to Petrograd, and at a crucial meeting of the party Central Committee on 10 October persuaded his colleagues to seize power before the election of the Constituent Assembly. There were varying accounts of this meeting, the official Soviet history claiming that the members received Lenin's proposal enthusiastically, only Zinoviev and Kamenev opposing. But it is more likely that most opposed it at first, and that only after hours of wearying argument did Lenin win a small majority; knowledge that lower Bolshevik organizations were in favour of taking power helped to change minds.

Organizing the insurrection was mainly the work of Trotsky. His instrument was the Military Revolutionary Committee. This had been set up by the Petrograd Soviet to organize the forces defending the revolution and, since the Mensheviks and right Socialist Revolutionaries refused to participate, was controlled by Trotsky and his Bolsheviks. Its use by the Bolsheviks meant that the approaching coup would not take the outward form of the party taking power and then handing it to the Soviet, as Lenin had envisaged, but of the Bolsheviks leading a Soviet organization, the MRC, in the take-over. This, which was Trotsky's concept, would make it harder to accuse the Bolsheviks of seizing power unilaterally. The MRC on October 23 appointed its own commissars to the various Petrograd army units, with instructions that orders not countersigned by these commissars were to be ignored. In a sense this was the start of the Bolshevik insurrection, for it was an open challenge to the Provisional Government. On 24 October Lenin wrote to his Central Committee, explaining why it was necessary to act that same evening rather than await the uncertain votes of the All-Russia Congress of Soviets which was to begin its meetings on the morrow. He added that 'the people' had the right to make historical decisions by force rather than by vote.

On 24 October Kerensky revealed to the Pre-Parliament that he had evidence of a planned Bolshevik insurrection, and asked for members' support of strong action against the party. However, the Mensheviks argued that the majority of Bolshevik rank and file were opposed to an armed seizure of power, but would become more militant in reaction to the strong measures which Kerensky proposed. After a long discussion the Pre-Parliament voted for the Menshevik resolution and against Kerensky. As things turned out, at this point the Bolshevik conspiracy could have been nipped in the bud by a few companies of reliable troops. In the Petrograd Soviet, opposition to the Bolsheviks grew as their intentions became clearer, and *Izvestiya*, the newspaper of the All-Russia Central Committee of the Soviets, declared that if the Bolsheviks did succeed in seizing power against the will of the other socialist parties the result could only be civil war.

During the night of 24–5 October Trotsky's Red Guard detachments occupied without bloodshed the central telephone exchange, railway stations, the central post office, and other key installations. The Winter Palace, where the Provisional Government was in emergency session, was threatened by the guns of cruiser *Avrora* and of the Peter–Paul Fortress across the river. Red Guards, Bolshevik soldiers, and Baltic Fleet sailors surrounded the Winter Palace and requested the government to surrender. The ultimatum was rejected and, with some sporadic shooting and scuffling, that part of the government's guard which had not melted away in the darkness was overcome in the night of 26 October. The ministers were led off to the Peter–Paul Fortress. Kerensky, however, was not among them, for he had left earlier to seek loyal troops outside the capital.

Kerensky's quest was forlorn, not only because few soldiers were willing to fight for his government, but because those that were willing were led by officers who themselves were not. Not only the more reactionary officers, but many others, had been so incensed by what they considered to be Kerensky's betrayal of Kornilov that they refused to lift a finger to help him. He did, however, find some support among the Cossacks of General Krasnov, and these troops succeeded in capturing Tsarskoye Selo. But here they stopped, and were approached by revolutionary agitators. Discussions between revolutionary envoys and the Cossacks took place. Kerensky was placed under guard by Krasnov for his own protection, while revolutionary sailors also took up their own guard duty. Much of this mutual escorting and guarding took place in the same building, with the local revolutionary leaders and Krasnov's staff occupying different floors; it was not quite clear who had captured whom and who was protecting whom. When it appeared that the Cossacks were about to accept the sailors' offer to capture and surrender Lenin to them in exchange for Kerensky, Krasnov evidently decided that Kerensky should be allowed to escape. A seaman guarding Kerensky's room was tied up and stripped, and the prime minister slipped out dressed as a Baltic Fleet sailor. He passed along the streets just as revolutionary and Cossack search parties were rushing out in search of him. He later began an academic career in the USA, where he died in 1970.

In Moscow, where sectional animosities were more moderate than in Petrograd,[10] the Bolsheviks had won a small majority in city elections and were well placed to seize power. Neither they nor their opponents, on hearing the news from Petrograd, showed much enthusiasm for armed conflict, but small groups of extremists on both sides managed to give an impression of heavy fighting, until a truce was followed by the Bolshevik assumption of power. In the army, most divisions did not welcome the Bolsheviks' coup. The soldiers' soviets were in general not pro-Bolshevik, and while the soldiers were not prepared to fight for the Provisional Government, they were not willing to exert themselves for the Bolsheviks either. The General Staff, led by the Chief of Staff Dukhonin, refused to obey Lenin's order to negotiate a cease-fire at the front. Red Guards were thereupon dispatched to GHQ. The subsequent murder of Dukhonin was one of those innumerable incidents in which extremist or violent individuals exceeded the intentions of Bolshevik leaders.

It may be easy to list reasons why it was the Bolsheviks who succeeded in taking power, but it is harder to list them in order of importance. The insuperable problems faced by their rivals were certainly factors. Each party had its own quite valid reasons for its policies, but circumstances developed in such a way as to make the Bolsheviks' concepts seem most relevant. The Socialist Revolutionaries, who had enormous electoral support, were handicapped by what they saw as the need to conciliate their coalition partners the Kadets, and they were unable to get the prompt

---

[10] The revolution followed different courses in different places, and it is only natural that research has been concentrated on Petrograd, but this situation is changing. Apart from the books mentioned in the Bibliography for this chapter, there is D. J. Raleigh's article about 1917 Tsaritsyn in *Slavic Review*, No. 40 (1981), 194–209

land redistribution that had been the centrepiece of their programme. The Mensheviks believed that government intervention was necessary to solve the economic crisis, but could not persuade their partners. They, too, saw a need to keep the Kadets on the side of the revolution. The Kadets, like the other parties, had a strong left wing, but on the whole they were devoted to that kind of civil society sometimes termed 'bourgeois', in which property rights were seen as an essential part of freedom. They, too, had good reasons for what they did (and for what they stopped others doing) and it was not irrational to suppose that the presence of their party in the Provisional Government would placate the property-owning classes and make a counter-revolution less likely.

But the coalition of Kadets and moderate socialists could not achieve what ordinary people saw as urgent tasks: ending the war, redistributing the land, providing a decent living standard for the workers.

It was the Bolsheviks who hammered away at these failures. It was the Bolsheviks who (unlike the Mensheviks) asserted that the working classes were quite capable of running the country and should do so through their Soviet. It was the Bolsheviks whose doctrine of the class struggle seemed to be validated by the increasing 'them-and-us' split between the government and most of the population.

Additionally, the Bolsheviks had the advantage that their membership was strongest in Petrograd; that is, in the centre of a very centralized state. More perhaps than their rivals, they may have been more understanding of the people on the streets. They were also less scrupulous, or at least their leadership was. Just hours before the coup, Stalin and Trotsky were telling their own party members attending the congress of soviets that the Bolsheviks had no intention of staging a rising.

Certainly, after their successful coup the Bolsheviks were regarded by their fellow socialists, and even by some of their own membership, as dishonest power-seekers. For decades afterwards the Bolshevik seizure of power was portrayed as a cynical act, orchestrated by Lenin and Trotsky, that was intended to put the Bolsheviks in a position to assume dictatorial power.

But it was not quite like that. In the minds of Lenin and his colleagues the events following February had confirmed not only the soundness of their ideology but also the capacity of the working population to organize its own state on a basis of rationality, justice, and fairness. In a sense they were guilty not of cynicism but of utopianism. In staging the October coup the Bolshevik leadership had pushed revolutionaries in at the deep end, not with the intention of drowning them but in the sublime expectation that they could swim.

11.   *The Civil War*

The Bolsheviks in power

WHEN an opposition takes power, whether by revolution or by election, it often fails to practise what it preached; the realities of governing prevail over old theories or slogans. The Bolsheviks did not escape this transformation, which they found as disconcerting as did their competitors and friends. In the months following October they abandoned many of the aims which had been professed by Russian revolutionaries, including themselves, for the previous century and they reintroduced, often in a more repressive form, long-reviled tsarist practices which had been abolished after the February Revolution.

Their enemies, then and subsequently, had strong grounds for claiming that there never was an October Revolution, only an October Counter-revolution. On the other hand, a detailed study of the early months, with a blow-by-blow account of the crises and threats which daily threatened the new regime, can only evoke sympathy for the Bolsheviks, forced by circumstances to choose between losing power (and probably their lives) or abandoning at least temporarily their ideals. Once in power, ideals and illusions which had once sustained them were abandoned one by one. Some Bolsheviks were quicker than others to accept the necessities of power (which was why there were splits and disagreements) and some had fewer illusions to begin with, but the Communist Party[1] which emerged from the Civil War was morally very different from the party which had taken power in 1917. In this period there were few, if any, who had a clear idea of what was happening; it was a period of continual jumping from a greater evil to a lesser, as measures to solve one problem raised new problems elsewhere. The first priority throughout was retention of power. It is true that in the early days even Lenin had his doubts about whether his regime could survive more than a week or two, but he believed that if power was retained

---

[1] At Lenin's urging, in 1918 the Bolshevik Party was renamed the Communist Party.

the sacrifices of principle made in keeping that power could be recovered at a later date. This meant that when Lenin died he bequeathed overwhelming problems to his successors; he did live long enough to persuade his party in 1921 to make the change of course known as the New Economic Policy, but there remained other dangerous tendencies. The period following October 1917 was a period when the Bolsheviks were driven to pile contradictions on top of paradoxes, and all too often temporary expedients were later transformed into basic and eternal principles.

The main issues and events of 1917–21 are dealt with in the following sections. It should be remembered, however, that the Bolsheviks could not in this neat way lay out their difficulties. For them, it was not possible to deal with one set of problems while leaving aside the others. Problems assailed them from all sides and were interconnected.

The first steps

In October Trotsky had persuaded Lenin of the importance of securing, at least nominally, some evidence of support from the All-Russia Congress of Soviets, whose opening the Bolshevik coup had been timed to forestall. The Congress, though it represented only workers and soldiers, had at least been elected. Thus on October 26 Trotsky went to the Congress to announce the capture of the Winter Palace. The Bolsheviks were outnumbered in the Congress but could count on the support of the left wing of the Socialist Revolutionaries, a combination which gave them a small majority. The moderate Socialist Revolutionaries and the Mensheviks walked out in protest at the Bolsheviks' violent seizure of power; it was on this occasion that Trotsky derided the anti-Bolshevik socialists with his 'Go to the garbage bin of history !' taunt.

With a majority assured, the Bolsheviks could obtain a favourable vote and thus 'legitimacy' for their new government and its policies. The soviets stood high in the estimate of the workers, soldiers, and Bolshevik rank-and-file, who looked forward to a *Soviet*, rather than a *Bolshevik*, regime. Lenin obtained the Congress's approval for his first two decrees, which were designed to capture mass support (especially from the peasantry, who so far did not favour the Bolsheviks) by promising what the masses wanted, land and peace. The Decree on Peace called for an immediate truce and a just peace, and could be interpreted as an appeal to foreign peoples over the heads of governments. The Decree on Land sanctioned what was already happening, the take-over by peasants of private land, but specified that the distribution should be arranged by village soviets.

The Decree on Peace had no influence on the other warring nations, as might have been expected. The Decree on Land was contrary to the

Bolsheviks' agricultural theories, as it split the land into smaller average allotments and strengthened the 'petty bourgeois' proprietary instincts of the peasantry. But in order to retain power the Bolsheviks in this and other cases were obliged to forget their theories and move with the tide of mass demands. Also, this land policy was virtually the Socialist Revolutionaries' policy and helped to propitiate the Left Socialist Revolutionaries.

The Congress of Soviets also approved the new government ('Council of People's Commissars') and, having thus conferred a degree of legitimacy on the new regime, was disbanded, still in the belief that the government was its own *Soviet* government.[2] Perhaps to maintain this supposition, most of the new ministers ('People's Commissars') were not leading lights, but secondary figures, of the Bolshevik party. Lenin was prime minister ('Chairman of the Council of People's Commissars'), Trotsky had foreign affairs, Stalin the nationalities, but Lunacharsky, who had only recently rejoined the Bolsheviks, was entrusted with education, while the key commissariat of the interior fell to Rykov, who in 1910 had broken with Lenin and returned to the party only to become an advocate of conciliating the Mensheviks. Initially the Left Socialist Revolutionaries were also represented in the government.

Many Bolsheviks, including Kamenev, Zinoviev, and Rykov, urged a coalition of the Bolsheviks with other socialist parties. After all, they argued, the Bolsheviks were only a small fraction of the revolutionary parties. Lenin resisted this plea, even though a majority of his colleagues were against him. However, he did renew the alliance with the Left Socialist Revolutionaries and the latter broke with the moderate wing of their party. Lenin's main objection to a coalition was that it would mean compromise, and that Bolshevik policies would not be carried out. In protest at his refusal, and the implication that minority rule would be imposed on Russia despite earlier advocacy of the democratic principle, Kamenev, Zinoviev, and Rykov resigned temporarily from the party. Other resignations followed the abolition of press freedom, one of the most cherished gains of the February Revolution. The relevant decree was passed in November and meant the suppression of many socialist as well as right-wing papers. Lenin, recalling how the Bolsheviks had made great use of the press in their climb to power, had no intention of leaving this weapon available to the anti-Bolshevik groups.

The most dramatic reversal in practice of policies the Bolsheviks had

---

[2] The Council of People's Commissars was nominally answerable to the Congress's Central Executive Committee, which remained in being. The latter now had a Bolshevik majority and Sverdlov as its chairman. The Central Executive Committee and Soviet Congresses continued to meet until the introduction of the Supreme Soviet in 1936.

earlier advocated was the treatment of the Constituent Assembly. Before October they had repeatedly embarrassed the Provisional Government by accusing it of postponing the election of the Constituent Assembly, which would decide the nature of the future Russian democracy. At the time of taking power, elections had already been arranged for the Assembly and Trotsky advised Lenin that to annul the arrangements would arouse a dangerous reaction. Thus the election was allowed to take place with little interference. The result was what Lenin had feared, a majority for the Socialist Revolutionaries (370 out of 707 seats),[3] 175 seats for the Bolsheviks and forty for the Left Socialist Revolutionaries (the Mensheviks and Kadets did worse with sixteen and seventeen seats, and the Kadets were never allowed to take their seats). Before the Assembly met in January 1918, the Socialist Revolutionaries spent their time devising the political programme which they would place before the members. The Bolsheviks devoted their energy to agitation work, seeking to discredit the Assembly. However, workers and soldiers gave few signs of shaken faith in the Assembly, so Lenin transferred politically reliable Latvian infantry to the capital. Despite interference, the Assembly duly met, preceded by the dispersal by bullets of a street demonstration staged to welcome it. The Bolshevik delegates walked out after failing to get their resolutions passed, and on the second day Bolshevik troops barred entry and the government ordered its dissolution. At the same time bands of sailors and other hooligans murdered two Kadet leaders in hospital.

A new constitution, confirming the supremacy of the Soviet, formalized the end of the Constituent Assembly. Members of the other parties were described as counter-revolutionary. There was little outcry in the country as a whole but, although Lenin's uncompromising firmness had won the day, it helped to make civil war inevitable. The Socialist Revolutionaries could claim that it was they, not the Bolsheviks, who had popular support. Of the eighteen anti-Bolshevik governments which developed in 1918 in Russia proper, several, including the Samara and the North Russian governments, were headed by Socialist Revolutionaries who had been elected to the Assembly.

The CHEKA

For many, the most chilling evidence of Lenin's ruthless and uncompromising rejection of calm and conciliation was the CHEKA. Probably

---

[3] These included non-Russian Socialist Revolutionaries, and certain nominal allies. It is doubtful whether the Socialist Revolutionary Party would have been able to assemble an absolute majority. With Bolsheviks holding majorities in key urban soviets, the Socialist Revolutionaries in any case would have hardly been able to govern.

influenced by his interpretation of French history, Lenin had well before 1917 envisaged the use of terror in the post-revolutionary period. Thus in December 1917 was set up the All-Russian Extraordinary Commission for Fighting Counter-Revolution and Sabotage (whose abbreviation was CHEKA). Its head was Dzerzhinski, a Polish communist who had been released from Siberian exile by the February Revolution. Lenin often complained that Russians were 'too soft', and it may well have been this which influenced him in this appointment. But Dzerzhinski had other qualities too; he was reputed to be incorruptible and devoted to the cause.

The CHEKA established its permanent headquarters in the offices of an erstwhile insurance company in Lubyanka Street, Moscow. In subsequent decades 'The Lubyanka' would be the end of the road for thousands of victims, executions being carried out in its basement or courtyard. But it was not simply a prison and place of execution, it was a complex system of offices and departments administering the ever-widening bureaucratic empire known as 'state security'. In 1918 there were CHEKA detachments in all localities under Bolshevik control. The CHEKA was instructed to act according to its 'revolutionary conscience' in protecting the Revolution. In practice, it arrested and sometimes shot arbitrarily those whom its operatives considered dangerous. Anybody who looked like, or was denounced as, a 'bourgeois element' was in danger:

> Do not demand incriminating evidence to prove that the prisoner has opposed the Soviet government by force or by words. Your first duty is to ask him to which class he belongs, what are his origins, his education, his occupation. These questions should decide the fate of the prisoner.[4]

In the summer of 1918 the CHEKA's arrests changed from a retail to a wholesale operation. Instead of individuals, whole sectors of the community were dealt with. The stimulus for this launching of mass Terror were the activities of the Left Socialist Revolutionaries. As the Bolsheviks' grip became firmer, Lenin had been less inclined to compromise with his allies, and the latter had been particularly incensed by the re-establishment of the death penalty and by the peace treaty with Germany. Their representatives in the Council of People's Commissars resigned, leaving an all-Bolshevik government. However, their members continued to occupy posts in the CHEKA.

In July two Left Socialist Revolutionaries of the CHEKA applied to see the newly appointed German ambassador, on CHEKA business. In the presence of the German military attaché, one of these CHEKA officials fired five shots almost point-blank at the ambassador. All the bullets

---

[4] *Pravda*, 25 December 1918, printing the advice of a leading CHEKA official.

missed, whereupon the second assassin threw a bomb, whose blast felled the military attaché who was just rising after throwing himself flat on the floor. A lucky shot from the second assassin finally killed the ambassador as the latter ran off. Concurrently, the Left Socialist Revolutionaries participated in anti-Bolshevik risings in many towns; in Yaroslavl the rebels succeeded in gaining control for several days, and in Moscow the rebels, led by a veteran female terrorist, captured the telephone exchange. But the revolts were mastered and the period of mass executions began. Not only Left Socialist Revolutionaries, but former officers, prosperous farmers, some workers, priests, lawyers, doctors, and members of pre-revolutionary governments were among those shot. Others were sent to prisons or prison camps. There was still sporadic resistance, however; the head of the Petrograd CHEKA was murdered and Lenin was injured in another point-blank revolver incident. The attacker, a woman with a revolutionary past and defective eyesight, was promptly alleged to be a Socialist Revolutionary and executed. These two incidents on the same late-August day gave extra zest to the CHEKA and Red Army detachments engaged in the mass slaughter of citizens considered to look suspicious.[5]

It was at this time that the CHEKA, aware that British diplomats were engaged in anti-Bolshevik plots, scorned diplomatic immunity and despatched an armed detachment to invade the British embassy. In the resulting shoot-out a British naval officer defending the grand staircase (probably to win time in which documents could be burned) was killed, resulting in an Anglo-Russian diplomatic commotion that was eventually settled by an exchange of Britons arrested in Russia for Bolsheviks arrested in Britain.

The CHEKA was distasteful to many, probably most, Bolsheviks, and came into frequent conflict with local soviets. There was an attempt (repeated in the 1960s) to present the CHEKA as a glorious and virtuous institution; Lenin referred to it in terms reminiscent of Benckendorff's praise of the rather more innocuous Third Section. In fact the CHEKA was deplorable in so far as it introduced the principle of killing people, not because of what they had done, but because of what they were (or even because of what their parents were). It is true that its victims were numerically only a minute fraction of the innocent lives thrown away in the Great War but, as with the Great War, the tragedy was measured in ideals as well as lives. CHEKA operatives saw things differently. In an article

---

[5] Indicative of the rag-bag composition of the CHEKA was the appointment in due course of another head of its Petrograd office, none other than the Latvian who had killed three policemen in the 1911 London drama known as the Sidney Street Siege. He later rose even higher in the OGPU, but met his end in Stalin's purge.

celebrating the tenth anniversary of the founding of the CHEKA, the former head of its Moscow branch reminisced:

There were centres of counter-revolutionary organizations all over Russia, and all counter-revolutionary conspiratorial threads came together in Moscow . . . at the same time there was a marked development in Moscow of activity by speculators and criminal bandits . . . the fact that we discovered the secret conspiratorial threads, and the counter-revolutionary bandit and speculation organizations was not thanks to some Sherlock Holmes sitting in the *Cheka*, but was due to the fact that the *Cheka* was a revolutionary organ of struggle for the defence of the revolution and was closely coupled to the party and the working class.

The writer went on to discuss the highlight of his career, the investigation of an explosion in late 1919 at the headquarters of the Moscow party committee, which had at first been blamed on White agents:

. . . workers and Red Army travellers on the train were talking about the explosion and expressing their indignation at this work of the Whites, those betrayers of the revolution. A young woman travelling in the same car broke into the conversation and said that maybe the explosion had been carried out not by Whites, but by genuine revolutionaries and defenders of the people. This seemed suspicious, and the passengers detained her and handed her over to the *Cheka* at the next station. It turned out that this girl belonged to the anarchist group *Nabat* . . . on her person was found a letter from a leader of the group in which he vaguely wrote to a friend of similar views that the explosion at the Moscow committee was carried out by a group of 'underground anarchists' . . . the Moscow *Cheka* in consequence was able to quickly uncover and liquidate the entire band . . .[5]

In 1922 the CHEKA became the GPU (a section of the NKVD), by which time large-scale Terror had ceased.

The end of Nicholas

After his abdication Nicholas had stayed at his palace at Tsarskoye Selo while the Provisional Government decided what to do with him. At first it was intended to send the royal family to England, via Murmansk, but this plan was never attempted. For their own safety the royal couple and their children were then sent to Tobolsk in Siberia, but when the Bolsheviks took power they were transferred to Ekaterinburg, in the Urals. Here they lived, under guard, in the house of a merchant. Other members of the royal family were kept near Perm, also in the Urals.

It seems that Trotsky had visions of putting Nicholas on trial, with himself winning renown in the role of public prosecutor. But evidently others in the party had different ideas. The continued existence of the new regime was threatened by the survival of, not only Nicholas, but of any possible heir; an anti-Bolshevik movement with a royal heir as its figure-head would

[5] *Izvestiya*, 18 December 1927.

have a strong claim to legitimacy. The wish to put an end to the danger must have been strengthened by Bolshevik leaders' interpretation of the French Revolution. In the summer of 1918 the Civil War was not going well, and it seemed that the Czechs would soon capture Ekaterinburg and Perm. Although there was adequate time to remove the royal family it would appear that the decision was taken to kill all its members, using the Czech advance as a pretext.

The eleven victims at Ekaterinburg were the Tsar and his family, together with their doctor, cook, valet, and housemaid. Elsewhere, at the same time, the other detained grand dukes and their families were killed. The official announcement of the execution of Nicholas declared that the Empress and the children had been 'sent to a safe place'. This deception was undertaken because public opinion would have found it difficult to reconcile the Bolsheviks' humanitarian ideals with the killing of women and children. Moreover, the government at the time believed that it was on the brink of war with Germany; to announce the execution of the Empress (a German princess) would only have increased this danger.

The execution was a macabre and bungled affair, with several of the victims requiring extra shots to finish them off. The disposal of the bodies had presented two irreconcilable problems. From their knowledge of Russian history it must have seemed inevitable to the Bolshevik leaders that, following the death of Nicholas and his heirs, there would appear pretenders claiming to be Nicholas or Alexis or a daughter or a grand duke, miraculously escaped from execution. But to prove that they were really dead by exhibiting the bodies would have risked the creation of a whole new set of holy relics, with the backward masses revering real or faked bones of 'Nicholas the Martyr' and his family.

In the main the disposal of the bodies was successful. The Whites did disinter some oddments, but these did not make satisfactory relics. Pretenders did appear, and continued to appear for decades afterwards. But they embarrassed mainly the Whites and, later, the émigrés. The first pretender appears to have been an eighteen-year-old telegraphist in a remote village in Kolchak territory. He dressed himself in a sailor's uniform and claimed to be the Tsarevich Alexis. He sent a telegram to Kolchak's forces asking for a bodyguard to protect him from the Bolsheviks, and meanwhile enjoyed the favours and feasts offered him by the villagers. The bodyguard was sent, but took him to gaol.

The Red, White, Green, and other armies

The Soviet government was in desperate need of an effective and loyal army, first to fight off the Germans and later to defend itself against the Whites

and foreign intervention. The old army, on the verge of complete disintegration, formed the basis of the 'Workers' and Peasants' Red Army', founded
in early 1918. That discipline and some degree of professionalism were restored was largely due to the energy and persuasive oratory of Trotsky,
who at critical periods could usually rely on Lenin's support (Lenin concentrated on economic and political problems, leaving Trotsky to handle
the Civil War). As Commissar for War from 1918, Trotsky visited the
fronts in his special train, ordering executions for failures, promotions for
successes, arranging supplies, haranguing the troops, encouraging the
faint-hearted, and carrying through against opposition a number of radical measures which determined the subsequent form of the Red Army.

Conscription, abolished in 1917, was reintroduced, bringing back into
service thousands of men of the old army. Because 'bourgeois elements'
could not be trusted with weapons, conscripts of this description were organized into unarmed rear-service battalions. Trotsky offered commissions
to former NCOs of the tsarist army, and opened schools to train promising young soldiers as 'commanders' ('officer', like 'minister', was by now a
derogatory term). More significantly, since the Bolsheviks could not supply from their own adherents sufficient qualified men to direct their forces,
Trotsky, against bitter opposition from party members, re-established
senior tsarist officers as 'military specialists'. Since numerous officers had
joined the Whites, while others had White sympathies, many members
doubted the reliability of those who joined the Reds. For this reason, each
'military specialist' was supervised by a political commissar, which meant
that units were managed by the dual leadership of commander and commissar. By the end of the Civil War about four-fifths of the Red Army's
commanders were former officers. While it is true that some deserted
(partly because they were often treated with hostility by Bolshevik colleagues) their collective contribution to the Red victory was great, and
probably decisive.

The Red Army's political commissars were officially established in
April 1918, although they had been preceded by the commissars sent to
the front by Kerensky in 1917. They were reliable party members whose
task was to encourage (and watch) the loyalty of officers and men, to
boost morale and efficiency, and to explain the policies of the party and
government. The 1918 decree emphasized that a prime function of the
commissar was to ensure that the Red Army did not become independent
of the Soviet government (that is, hatch any military conspiracies). To
enhance the commissar's power, only orders with his countersignature
could be considered as valid (this seems to have been rigorously applied;
one of the causes of the Red Army's débâcle in Poland in 1920 was the

refusal of one Red commander, Budyenny, to obey an order signed by Tukhachevsky, a former tsarist lieutenant, but not by Tukhachevsky's commissar). The best of the commissars did much to raise the fighting efficiency of the units to which they were attached, while the worst did much to lower the effectiveness of the commanders whom they were supposed to supervise. Some commissars fancied themselves as tacticians, tried to supplant the nominal commanders, and developed 'revolutionary' theories of warfare. One of the important roles of the former tsarist generals was to discourage such theories at the higher levels. When necessary, Trotsky supported them in this, which was one reason why many Bolshevik military leaders detested him. A Red Army unit's fighting efficiency could usually be gauged by the proportion of party members and of workers in it. Units with more than one-fifth of workers were regarded as crack troops, while those with more than 95 per cent peasants were of little use. The Red sailors and the Red Cossacks had the most fighting spirit, but this was devalued by their volatility, disobedience and general unruliness. Supplies were usually short, and sometimes non-existent. Some battles were fought barefoot, some petered out because of weapon shortages. Supplies and weapons that did arrive were often looted. There was an enormous desertion rate, especially of peasants who had gone home in 1917, only to be re-conscripted in 1918. Trotsky reduced, but did not eliminate, this drain by his re-introduction of the death penalty for desertion. The most reliable Red troops, especially in the early and less brutal stages, were Latvians and Central Asians, who had no compunction about killing Russians.

After the end of the Civil War several writers who had served with the Red Army began to record their impressions, in fictional or documentary form. It is these writings which show the ordinary men and women fighting for the Bolsheviks as they really were; not as clean-cut heroes with the correct political ideas, but as a heterogeneous collection of characters, each with his own blemishes. An illuminating example of the documentary approach in Civil War literature is Serafimovich's *The Iron Flood*. It is based on a real incident, a Red army making an epic march out of encirclement. Its hero, Kozhukh, is a thinly disguised version of the celebrated real-life commander Kovtiukh, who was a Bolshevik hero in the twenties, although purged in the thirties. The hero's past, as described in the novel, is not untypical of those once-alienated young men who distinguished themselves in the Civil War. Kozhukh had been a non-Cossack settler in the Cossack lands, and therefore has a background of poverty and humiliation. In the Great War his bravery earns him a place in an officer training school, but he is so mocked and despised by the socially superior instructors and fellow-cadets that he fails his examinations. Eventually, after two more attempts, he gains his officer's epaulettes, but his fellow-officers look down on him while the soldiers, who previously had admired him, no longer quite trust him. When the Revolution comes the ordinary people, to whom Kozhukh feels he belongs, begin to kill the officers and his hard-won epaulettes become dangerous. For his own safety he tears them off and returns home disguised as an ordinary soldier. But soon

the powerful hate of officers with which he had been filled now seemed trivial beside his feelings for the unlimited class struggle. The officers were simply pathetic lackeys of the landlords and bourgeoisie.

He determines to prove himself by work and sacrifice for the party. The story of *The Iron Flood* is how he imposes through strength of character some kind of order and battleworthiness on the wild and unruly Red army which is entrusted to him. Kozhukh's warriors consist of three elements. There are the infantry and artillery, who are an undisciplined mob of peas-ant soldiers demobilized from the Tsar's army, plus a few who have joined the Reds after the Revolution. They are from the surrounding local Cos-sack territory and are mainly former hired peasant labourers who have been long trodden down by their Cossack landowning superiors. For them the Revolution has opened up the chance of overthrowing their social su-periors and overcoming their poverty. The second element is the Cossack cavalry. Like most Cossacks who fought for the Reds, they tend to be of the poorer families, but nevertheless are smart and full of pride. Thirdly there are the Red sailors; these fight savagely, but far from being 'the pride and joy of the Revolution' (as Trotsky described the Red sailors) they are little better than land-going pirates. They tease and provoke the unruly peasant soldiers, they start rumours against the commander, they con-sider themselves an élite and will not submit to orders unless the latter are backed up by a machine gun. The turbulence of the foot soldiers is re-corded early in the book. Democratically assembled to discuss their tactics, they curse and shout down their commanders, killing one. Later, they fight fierce battles against each other as each tries to reach a vital bridge first. They have a weakness for strong drink. They are cruel, but although they shoot their prisoners—men, women, and children—they do not mutilate them as do the Whites. After a battle they insist that a priest be summoned to give their fallen comrades a proper funeral with all the trimmings: cros-ses, incense, and fervent intonations. And it is these men, dishevelled, bed-raggled, hungry, and despairing, who beat the Whites and thereby make history.

Babel's sketches published under the title Red Cavalry are also illumin-ating, with each story telling of an episode in the life of Budyenny's renowned cavalry corps in the Polish campaign. The author's Jewish background and his own unpleasant experiences when serving in this unit probably explain why his stories emphasize the unnecessary savagery practised by both sides, and the discrepancy between the communism as promised and the communism as practised. Taken alone, these stories perhaps reveal only one side of the truth, but as such they are useful as correctives of the later glamorized versions. With his unflattering allusions to artificial legendary heroes like Budyenny and Voroshilov, it is hardly surprising that Babel perished in the purges of the thirties. Among the memorable characters of *Red Cavalry* there is the former swineherd who returns to his village as a high Red commander. Encountering his hated former master he does not shoot him, but stamps and tramples him to death because 'shooting only kills a man . . . you never get at the soul'. There is the unlucky soldier who escapes after five years in a German prisoner-of-war camp, crosses Germany and Lithuania, and when almost within sight of his home and wife, is conscripted into the Red Army. There is the ignorant and savage warrior who, though not really understanding what the Revolution is about, uses the new terminology and practices to justify his own conduct. After murdering a woman, he reports, 'I took my loyal rifle down from the wall and washed away that stain from the surface of the Workers' Land'. Then there is the regimental washerwoman, the mistress of the *Red Trooper*'s correspondent, whose boring revolutionary monologues drive her into the bed of the regimental cook. Finally there is the narrator himself, the unhappy Jewish intellectual whose heart is in the cause but not in the fighting. Accused by his fellow-soldiers of being a 'milk-drinker' and 'God-worshipper', he soldiers on, 'begging fate to grant me the simplest of abilities, the ability to kill my fellow-men'.

Other themes, like the contradiction between some of the peasant leaders' desires for farming freedom and the reality of the Bolsheviks' intentions for the peasantry, occur over and over again in the fiction about this period. One theme is the effect of the war on those who fought it, how young idealistic men from the towns became of necessity hardened killers, how a commander of twenty after a few months would look as though he were forty. There was a recognition too that the Revolution had not put an end to the scoundrels of tsarist times. The latter might skilfully adopt Red language, fight for the Reds, and yet remain scoundrels. Several writers highlighted the dull stupidity of the 'liberated' peasants, the farce of local elections, and the unprincipled demagogy of many Bolsheviks. The devoted revolutionary is another familiar character. One such is the heroine of Lavrenev's *The Forty-First*, who falls in love with a captured White lieutenant whom she is escorting. When White forces approach she shoots him to prevent his escape; in the 1970s this story was still highly praised as an illustration of good revolutionary morals.

The Red Army was frequently troubled by peasant rebellions in its rear, but the White Army suffered even more from these, as well as from urban disturbances fostered by underground communists and Socialist Revolutionaries. The White Army was much smaller than the Red and no better supplied, but it had a surplus of officers, many of whom agreed to serve as ordinary soldiers in the Volunteer Army which was formed in the south in early 1918. Later the Whites resorted to conscription, when reliance on Cossacks to provide the rank-and-file proved mistaken owing to the propensity of Cossacks to change sides according to where they considered their immediate interests lay. However, White conscripts, like Red, were prone to desert. Until Wrangel took over the southern Whites, their army was even more chaotic than the Red Army, and many of their officers set bad examples of drunkenness, intrigue, looting, and violence, which were usually unchecked. In the east, there were several anti-Bolshevik armies in 1918. There was that of the Omsk government, a White regime controlling great areas of Siberia and ruled by a reactionary government under the nominal leadership of Admiral Kolchak. The latter had been a popular and efficient tsarist admiral, but was now reduced to the role of figure-head as 'Supreme Ruler' of this regime. There was another anti-Bolshevik government at Samara, composed largely of Socialist Revolutionaries who had been elected to the Constituent Assembly. The Samara government expired as a result of military defeats by the Reds and intrigues and repressions by the Omsk government.[6] The anti-Bolshevik movement in the east was encouraged in early 1918 by the revolt of the Czechoslovak Legion. The latter had been formed from disaffected Czech and Slovak soldiers of the Austrian army who had allowed themselves to be taken prisoner by the tsarist army. The original intention had been to use them on the Eastern Front, but the Revolution prevented this. In 1918, at the request of the western allies, they were being shipped to France via Vladivostok. At a time when they were distributed along the length of the Trans-Siberian Railway in troop trains, some of them were confronted with a Bolshevik order to hand in their arms. Their resistance was so spirited that they seized control of the railway and then campaigned against the Bolsheviks in conjunction with the Whites.[7] In the Far East, in Kolchak's rear, there was Semeonov's Japanese-supported regime. Nominally a White, Semeonov

---

[6] In the later stages of the Civil War the surviving Socialist Revolutionaries and Mensheviks tended to support the Bolsheviks, as the lesser of two evils.

[7] According to some accounts, this coup was prearranged, and the French were involved.

was little better than a terrorist, but his savage little empire lasted until the Japanese withdrawal.

In the far north there was a small White army around Archangel, co-existing with British, French, and US forces there, while in the Baltic lands west of Petrograd there was the White army of General Yudenich. The Allied troops at Archangel and Murmansk had been sent there, with Russian acquiescence, to protect munitions shipments which had accumulated at those ports in 1916 and 1917; a German thrust towards Murmansk seemed quite possible. In March 1918 further British troops were sent to Archangel and the same year the British entered the Caucasus to protect the oil region from possible Turkish occupation. When the World War ended in November 1918 several influential voices favoured the transformation of these precautionary troop movements into an active intervention to suppress the Bolsheviks. In Britain, Churchill and Milner were the main advocates of this, but Lloyd George, fearing disaffection among war-weary troops and workers, was opposed. The French, mindful of the thousands of small investors who seemed to have lost their savings in Russia, were more anti-Bolshevik than the British. Foch proposed a plan for a multi-national crusade against Bolshevism, but this plan was rejected by the Supreme Allied Council in March 1919. President Wilson was for mediation, and in general US troops were committed to Russia more to keep an eye on the other interventionists than to suppress the Bolsheviks. Churchill and Foch could argue that Bolshevism was threatening to spread through Europe; the 1918–19 revolution in Germany, which before it was suppressed established soviet governments in Bavaria and several cities, was plainly aided by the Russians (notably by Lenin's representative, the Bolshevik propagandist Radek). Moreover, in early 1919 Bela Kun engineered his short-lived Red revolution in Hungary. For Churchill and Foch the idea of quarantining Bolshevik Russia behind a 'cordon sanitaire' of nations like Poland and Roumania seemed insufficient. But after the rejection of Foch's plan the half-hearted build-up of foreign forces in Russia halted. At the end of 1918 there were only about 15,000 Allied troops in north Russia, probably 17,000 Japanese troops around Vladivostok (accompanied by several thousand US troops sent to forestall a permanent Japanese annexation), French and British warships in the Black Sea, substantial French forces at Odessa, British warships in the Baltic ostensibly protecting Latvia, Lithuania, and Estonia from Bolsheviks and German 'volunteers', and small British detachments in the Caucasus and Turkestan.

In general, therefore, the western intervention was feeble and unenthusiastic. Allied soldiers were war-weary, and repelled by the cruelties of their Russian allies and enemies. In North Russia the British troops, including Royal Marines, even went as far as mutiny.

I came back from the patrol thinking that this so-called war was a fantastic charade, far removed from real soldiering. My illusion was rudely shattered by a talk I had with a young officer who had been serving with the partisans.

'I commanded the partisans who retook Tivdia,' he said.

'That must have been exciting.'

'Exciting hell!—it was ghastly. You see, when the Bolos took Tivdia they killed everyone they could find—all the old people, women and children. I had a number of men from Tivdia with me—they told the others. So when we retook the village, they began to kill all the Reds. I did my damnedest to stop them—quite useless. They nearly killed me too. So I went away into the forest for about half an hour. When I came back it was all over. I couldn't really blame my men—they thought they were exacting justice for the murder of their parents, wives, and children.'

. . . I was with a Marine officer when he was selecting men for a patrol. The men fell in in a half-hearted manner. They were badly dressed, and some were unshaven and dirty. To my astonishment they began to answer the officer back. 'I can't go sir, I've got a sore toe!' 'I can't go sir—me stummick's bad!' And so on.[8]

In early 1918 the Allies would have helped the Bolshevik government if the latter had been willing to continue the war against Germany (and at one stage the Bolsheviks were indicating that they might indeed accept help), but the encouragement of communist revolution in Europe, the murder of the Tsar (a cousin of the British King and the object of much sympathy after his abdication), the nationalization without compensation of foreign-owned enterprises, the Red Terror, and various hostile acts and speeches, discouraged those who advocated acceptance of the Bolsheviks and encouraged the interventionists.

The French contingents left in 1919, the British in 1919 and 1920. The Japanese stayed until 1922, when British and US pressure persuaded them to leave. The direct military contribution of the intervention was negligible; a few skirmishes were fought against the Reds, and a few communists executed. Western governments (and the Poles and the Finns) were especially reluctant to give full military support to the Whites after the latter had refused to recognize the new states (like Poland and Finland) created from the nations of the old Russian Empire. However, western military supplies were a great help to the Whites (and often to the Reds, who at times relied on arms captured from the Whites).

Apart from the armies of the Reds, Whites, and interventionists there was a great variety of lesser armed forces fighting at certain times and places. Among these were the Greens, consisting mainly of deserters from other

---

[8] From an unpublished memoir by Lt. W. G. Irvine-Fortescue, Royal Engineers, describing experiences in North Russia in the late summer of 1919.

armies and fighting both the Reds and Whites according to circumstances. Then there were the semi-independent peasant armies, which usually fought on the side of the Bolsheviks and owed their military efficiency, if any, to their chosen leaders, several of whom were remarkable men; Chapayev was the most famous of the latter, a simple man capable of inspiring his unruly and illiterate soldiers to heights of endurance and heroism. There were also bands of anarchists, the most important of which was Makhno's army, which successfully fought Reds, Whites, and Germans. After the Civil War the Bolsheviks quelled these peasant and anarchist forces, but not before, in 1920–1, Green uprisings around Tambov and the Volga gathered sizeable support. Makhno escaped with his life across the frontier, but Antonov, leader of the Tambov revolt, died fighting.

The Civil War campaigns

The Civil War was fought mainly in the east and south, although at one stage the north-western front became critical. The Bolsheviks managed to hold the central region (including Moscow and Petrograd) but their constantly expanding or contracting territory was smaller in area than that of their opponents (which was one reason why foreign governments were unwilling to recognize the Bolshevik government). Campaigns tended to be fought along railway routes, which sometimes made the armoured train equal the cavalry as a decisive arm. Because Russian railways mainly radiated from Moscow and Petrograd, the Bolsheviks enjoyed interior and centralized lines of communication, enabling them to shift troops from one front to another at short notice.

Although in the Don Cossack country the Civil War dates from late 1917, it was not until the summer of 1918 that the Whites assembled major forces in the south and east. In the south, under General Denikin, they gained control in the Don and Kuban regions and advanced towards the Volga, with the eventual aim of linking up with Kolchak's Siberian forces. By the summer of 1918 they were besieging Tsaritsyn, through which passed grain supplies for the Bolshevik cities. The Reds determined to hold Tsaritsyn at all costs, and Stalin was sent there as the party's supreme representative. Among the defenders of the city who collaborated with Stalin were Voroshilov, son of a railwayman and a former party secretary, who commanded the defending army, and Ordzhonikidze, a Georgian who was political commissar of Voroshilov's army. Both these had previously worked with Stalin, and their close relationship with him was cemented by this siege. Also at Tsaritsyn, and working with Stalin, was Budyenny, commanding what was later to be the most celebrated of the Red cavalry units. These four combined against several of Trotsky's initiatives, and intrigued against the former tsarist officers admitted to the Red Army by Trotsky. But their energy and decisiveness were largely responsible for the failure of the White siege. In 1925, to commemorate Stalin's role, Tsaritsyn was re-named Stalingrad, the first major manifestation of what would later be called Stalin's 'cult of the individual'.

Despite the failure at Tsaritsyn, Denikin's army staged another offens-ive in 1919. This was loosely co-ordinated with attacks mounted from other anti-Bolshevik fronts: there was to be a joint Franco-Ukrainian of-fensive in the southern Ukraine, Kolchak was to advance towards the north-west, to link with White forces around Archangel, and General Yudenich's White Army in the Baltic states was to advance on Petrograd. But while Denikin's offensive was spectacularly successful, coming to within 200 miles of Moscow, the other sectors were disappointing. Yudenich was easily defeated by the determined Red Guard of Petrograd. Kolchak's ad-vance was crippled by internal quarrels, by the apathy of the Czechs, by partisans in the rear aroused by the reactionary policies of the White Omsk government, by revolts staged by Socialist Revolutionaries, and by strong Red counter-attacks led by Frunze, Kuibyshev, and Tukhachevsky. All these factors turned Kolchak's advance into a long and hopeless retreat, Kolchak being captured and shot in 1920. In the Ukraine, the planned Franco-Ukrainian offensive came to naught when Paris, alarmed by com-munist-inspired mutinies in its warships off Sevastopol, ordered its forces home, leaving the way open for the declaration of a Soviet Ukrainian Republic.

The defeat of Denikin was delayed because Trotsky's plan was opposed by Stalin and others. Eventually, after Lenin had backed Trotsky, the plan was put into effect with a startling sweep by Budyenny's cavalry through Denikin's rear. Henceforth the White Army was in retreat, finally evacu-ating the Crimea (and Russia) at the end of 1920. By that time Denikin had been succeeded by Wrangel, whose better political sense came too late to save the White cause. Meanwhile, since 1919, the Bolsheviks had been fighting a new enemy, the Poles. Dissatisfied with their eastern frontier (the Curzon Line) as proposed by the western Allies, the Poles hoped to take advantage of Russia's disarray to annex territory which had once been part of the Polish Empire. At first their troops, led by Pilsudski, were victorious, capturing Kiev in May 1920. But there could have been noth-ing more effective than a Polish invasion in arousing Russian patriotism. Many opponents of the Bolsheviks, including the popular General Brusilov, changed their allegiance and rallied round the government. The Poles were forced back to the Curzon Line and Lenin, against Trotsky's advice, decided to push on to Warsaw, hoping to establish a Soviet government in

Poland and thus make physical contact with Germany, whose masses were still believed to be on the verge of revolution. This, the first clear attempt to spread the Revolution by force, failed when the Red Army was defeated by Polish troops advised by the French General Weygand. The Red defeat might have been avoided if Tukhachevsky's advanced army had been properly supported by the forces under Egorov, Budyenny, and Stalin. The dilatoriness of this trio was later ascribed to jealousy, but was probably a result of confusion. The result of the defeat was that in 1921 the Treaty of Riga, ending this war, allotted to Poland considerable White Russian and Ukrainian territory which the USSR did not regain until 1939.

The Russian emigration

Before 1917 Russian émigrés consisted of disaffected intellectuals, working for (or at least hoping for) a revolution, and concentrated in such cities as Geneva, Paris, and London, and of peasants and Jews who had settled in the west, especially in the Americas, and who had no intention of returning. Ten years later the picture had changed completely. The pre-1917 intellectuals had gone home (although many of them, alarmed or disappointed, soon returned), and there had been a new flow of refugees after the defeat of the White armies.

When Wrangel abandoned the Crimea he was accompanied by about 150,000 refugees. These were settled in temporary camps in Turkey. About 60,000 of them were soldiers and, expecting a Bolshevik collapse, an effort was made to keep this army in being. However, it soon dispersed, although the Russian Imperial Navy continued to exist for some years, anchored off Bizerta and training annual intakes of cadets. Several of the Slavic states of eastern Europe aided the refugees, while many Russians settled in Paris, Berlin, and the western hemisphere. In addition, there were sizeable Russian communities in Manchuria, composed largely of refugees who had arrived after the defeat of Kolchak: many of these moved to Australia and elsewhere when the communists attained power in China in 1949. During the twenties many dissidents, intellectuals in particular, were allowed or compelled by the Soviet government to emigrate legally.[9] Refugees continued to arrive in the thirties, and during and after the Second World War there was a new wave, of a rather different type.

Although much émigré publishing was done in Berlin, Paris was the political centre of the refugees. Here, in various organizations, members of the old political parties continued their previous and often sterile disputes.

[9] The number of Russians who emigrated as a consequence of the Revolution is unknown; certainly there were several hundred thousand and one estimate, apparently well-based, goes as high as one million.

The Grand Duke Cyril Vladimirovich was proclaimed Tsar Cyril I by émigré monarchists. Of more concern to the Bolsheviks was the émigrés' Union of Servicemen, a White veterans' association which could conceivably reform into a new anti-Soviet army. In the Russian tradition it was soon infiltrated by agents of the Soviet government; many of the most vociferously anti-Bolshevik officials of this and other émigré organizations were, it seems, in the pay of Moscow. Two chiefs of the Union of Servicemen were kidnapped and removed to the USSR in 1930 and 1937. The story of the Russian émigré organizations and their conflicts with the Soviet government is still obscure, but is certainly fantastic. The picture is both enlivened and distorted by the activities of various fringe organizations. Not the least eccentric of these was the Young Russia Movement, whose slogan was 'For Tsar and Soviets', and whose leadership appears to have included Soviet agents.

The bulk of the émigrés settled down quietly throughout the world, often in their own communities. These communities began with a few families, which would contrive to build a church, then a school, and then a meeting hall. In France in the late thirties there were nearly seventy Russian schools. In Paris there were several thousand Russian taxi drivers, and Russian was almost an official language at the Renault works.

The emigration was a great, though unmeasurable, loss to the USSR, because it contained a disproportionate number of professionals and intellectuals. Emigration and Red Terror were partly responsible for that chronic problem of the Soviet economy, shortage of managerial talent. Many of Russia's most useful scholars and scientists were among the émigrés, and later occupied prominent positions in western universities and western industry. They included, to mention only a few: Sikorsky, who had developed four-engined airliners for Russia and would develop the helicopter for the USA; Struve, who made revolutionary discoveries in astronomy; Zvorykin, later to be regarded as the inventor of modern television and of the iconoscope; and Vinogradsky, the world-famous microbiologist. With this élite there were hundreds of other eminent names, of professors, engineers, researchers. At the Pasteur Institute, much frequented by Russian scientists before 1917, a virtual colony of émigré biologists developed. At times Russian émigré biology seemed more productive and creative than Soviet biology.

In the arts there was a similar picture, although several men of talent, unable to create when cut off from their native soil, returned to Russia and were generously received by the Soviet government. Among the repatriates were the proletarian writer Gorki and the composer Prokoviev. While Lenin was alive it was possible for distinguished figures to obtain permission to reside abroad legally, and many took advantage of this. Among writers who made a definite break with the USSR was Bunin. In music Russia lost S. Rachmaninov and Stravinsky, as well as Chaliapin. Among artists Chagall was perhaps the most prominent loss; he had been appointed director of an important art academy in the euphoric days following October, but had caused some consternation among party critics by celebrating the first anniversary of the Revolution with a portrayal of green cows and horses capering in the sky. He had then lost his job because, it was said, he was unrevolutionary. As for Repin, he went to Finland to paint icons.

Muscovy and the outside world

For much of the Civil War period the Bolshevik state was reduced to little more than the old Muscovy, as former subject nations broke away and hostile armies invaded peripheral territory. After October 1917 there were three basic problems in external policy. These were Russia's still continuing war against the Central Powers, the urge towards independence of non-Russian nations of the former Russian Empire, and the unconscionable slowness of the expected world revolution to develop in Europe. These three issues, like all issues which faced the Bolsheviks, were interconnected, but will be treated separately here.

The early Decree on Peace was widely disseminated at home and abroad, but its proposals of a just peace without annexations raised little enthusiasm in belligerent capitals. The western Allies tried without success to persuade the new Russian government to remain in the war. Lenin at this time expected, and preferred, a German victory; he believed Germany was on the point of revolution and a strong revolutionary Germany was better than a weak revolutionary Germany. The publication by the Bolsheviks of the secret treaties of the tsarist government, including a 1915 agreement between the Allies concerning the partition of a defeated Turkey, caused embarrassment and further resentment in London and Paris.

In early December a one-month truce was negotiated on the Eastern Front, followed by peace negotiations at Brest-Litovsk. The Central Powers demanded as their prize Poland and the southern Baltic provinces, but when an anti-Bolshevik Ukrainian delegation appeared at Brest-Litovsk to demand independence for its nation, it became clear that the Ukraine would also be lost to Russia; and the Ukraine was the source of grain as well as four-fifths of Russia's coal and metal production.

Although the Bolsheviks' declared policy was to allow non-Russian nationalities to secede if they wished, and the Central Powers were demanding no more than the sacrifice of the biggest of these nations, few Russians and few Bolsheviks could face the prospect of accepting the terms offered. But the Russian army by this time was, as Lenin said, not even capable of making a retreat. Although Lenin clearly realized that for the sake of peace any German demand, except a demand to change the government, would be acceptable, his colleagues insisted on rejecting the peace terms. Finally Trotsky was allowed to return to Brest and carry out his own plan, but Lenin extracted a promise from him that if he failed he would support Lenin's proposal to accept the peace terms. Trotsky's plan proved to be one of his more notable fatuities. He declared to the astounded German and Austrian delegation that their conditions were unacceptable and that his government had adopted a policy of 'neither peace nor war'. This idea of neither fighting nor surrendering made a fine theatrical stir, but the German response was to reopen hostilities, and by the end of February German forces were occupying the Baltic provinces, much of the Ukraine, parts of the north Caucasus and the Crimea. Petrograd was in danger. A socialist and nationalist government was established in the Ukraine under German auspices. Yet Lenin was still unable to convince a majority of his Politburo colleagues that peace with Germany was worthwhile at any price. Some suggested accepting western assistance, others like Bukharin proposed a picturesque 'fight to the last man'. Eventually Lenin was able to get his own way, but by this time the Central Powers' demands had stiffened: all the Baltic provinces, the Ukraine, Finland, and certain territory on the Russo-Turkish border were to be abandoned, and an unfavourable trade treaty to be signed with Germany. The resulting Treaty of Brest-Litovsk was signed in March 1918, the Bolshevik signatory being Sokolnikov because other more prominent Bolshevik leaders refused to attach their names to it. Lenin intended to denounce the treaty at the first opportune moment. He believed that the Germans might still renew hostilities, which was why Russia's capital was moved from Petrograd to the less vulnerable Moscow in March. When Germany was defeated in November the Bolsheviks declared the Treaty of Brest-Litovsk null and void.

The magnitude of the problem posed by the different nationalities of the former Empire was little realized at first. When the Bolsheviks took power they were confident that their intention to allow the non-Russian nations to secede if they wished would not raise great difficulties. There had been various independence movements afoot since the February Revolution, but the Provisional Government had done little to satisfy them. When Stalin, who some years previously had made a study of the nationalities problem and was himself a non-Russian, was appointed Commissar of Nationalities, one of his early acts was to grant independence to Finland (November 1917). The independence of Poland was also accepted by the

Bolsheviks, but they had optimistic expectations that the seceded nations, most of which had significant Bolshevik parties, would eventually return to the Russian fold in one way or another. In Finland the local Bolsheviks, supported initially by Russian troops who were still stationed there, staged a rising in January 1918 which developed into a civil war in which the anti-Reds, led by a former tsarist general, Mannerheim, and with German support, emerged victorious, subsequently inflicting various cruelties on their defeated enemies. In Poland Pilsudski, once an unwilling resident of Siberia and no friend of Russia, became Head of State. The Ukraine, which during 1917 had established a quasi-autonomous status for itself, after the Bolshevik Revolution declared itself to be the Ukrainian People's Republic. It demanded that Ukrainians in the Russian army be released to form the Ukrainian army.[10] The Bolsheviks responded by creating their own Ukrainian government, whose forces threatened to conquer the entire territory. It was at this point that the 'legitimate' government appealed to the Germans at Brest-Litovsk. It was thus clear that the Bolshevik acceptance of secession for the nationalities could, in the case of the Ukraine at least, create a threat to the Russian government. So in early 1918 Stalin qualified the earlier declaration; he reserved the right of secession for the 'working masses' of a given nation. In effect this meant that if the Bolshevik leadership considered secession was not conceived by and for the working-class cause, it would not be granted. But during 1918, sometimes under direct or indirect foreign protection, nationalities of the Russian Empire in Europe began to create their own states. However, with the exception of Finland, Poland, Estonia, Lithuania, and Latvia, the new republics were short-lived. As early as 1919 new Bolshevik regimes were imposed in White Russia and the Ukraine. In 1920 the independence of Azerbaizhan was brought to an end by a Bolshevik rising, and Armenia was forcibly dismembered by Turkey and Russia. Georgia, however, was recognized by the Bolsheviks as independent in that same year. It had a Menshevik government which enjoyed considerable support both at home and among socialists abroad. However, on Stalin's initiative, the Red Army invaded and conquered Georgia in 1921.

Perhaps the biggest disappointment endured by the Bolsheviks in their early years was the failure of the 'world revolution' to materialize. According to marxist theory, the initial triumph of communism in Russia was premature in so far as the theory prescribed that the proletariat would rise first in the most advanced capitalist countries, not in the most backward. Moreover, socialist society could be built only in prosperous conditions.

---

[10] Such a release could only cause chaos in the Russian army, and seemed a threat to Bolshevik power.

Trotsky, among others, had solved this theoretical problem by regarding the Bolshevik Revolution as a trigger which would detonate 'the permanent revolution', a series of revolutions in the more advanced countries; the victorious proletarians of the latter would then provide communist Russia with the economic aid which she needed. In October 1917 the Bolsheviks expected an immediate spread of their revolution, in the first place to Germany, which was economically advanced and whose armed forces were under great strain. In the first year of the Bolshevik regime hopes were maintained, but gradually the Bolsheviks resigned themselves to the possibility of a long wait. But it was not until the twenties that the theory of permanent revolution was finally discredited.

To catalyse the world revolution, the Third International (Comintern) was established in Moscow in 1919, with Zinoviev as its chairman. The Comintern was to link and co-ordinate the efforts of all communist parties in their efforts to spread the revolution. It was not long, however, before it became a means of putting the interests of 'the first socialist state' before the interests of the individual parties. This was not unfair or illogical, since the survival of Bolshevik Russia was evidently crucial to the communist cause in general, but it was applied rigidly and selfishly in later years. The Comintern through its agents and other resources did its mediocre best to stimulate revolution in those early years. 1919 had been disappointing. Spontaneous risings had had initial success in Bavaria and Hungary but had been soon suppressed (although the Bavarian Soviet Republic lasted two months). In 1923 the Comintern attempted another rising in Germany. This achieved an enormous failure; the thousands of armed proletarians whom Zinoviev believed to be on the march in Germany simply did not exist, and the German communists did not even produce a general strike. The ultimate beneficiary of this attempt was Hitler, who would owe his rise to power very largely on his promises to fight the Bolsheviks. Zinoviev's prestige was damaged even further when he instigated a similarly abysmal attempt at revolution in Estonia, to be started by Red Army men in plain clothes.

The Comintern did little good for the Red cause. It failed to make revolutions, and its machinations gained support for right-wing governments and fascist movements abroad. In Italy, Bulgaria, and Germany its directives to the local communists to struggle against the other socialists, sometimes in alliance with fascism, was a crucial factor enabling the extreme right to defeat the left in those countries. It embarrassed the commissariat of foreign affairs because foreigners would not accept that it had no connexion with Soviet foreign policy; in the thirties the distrust which it had sown was one of the factors discouraging a common front of the west and Russia against fascism. And it discouraged the initiatives of foreign communist parties, while making them vulnerable to accusations of putting the interests of Moscow before those of their own peoples.

The party

By the end of the Civil War, the party's organization had taken the forms which would prevail over the following decades. By 1921 there were about 730,000 members.[11] Although at times of intensified recruitment in the Civil War and in the twenties and thirties entry standards were lowered, in general members were carefully selected. It was not a mass party, but an élite which, though rooted in the masses, would nevertheless lead the latter. Membership was a privilege and could be withdrawn; thousands of members were expelled for drunkenness, apathy, and other faults. The quality most sought by the party was obedience; the leadership's decisions were only valid so long as the membership could be relied on to carry them out without questioning or foot-dragging. Democratic Centralism, which was the concept on which the party was based, implied this, but also offered ordinary members the chance to influence the policies which would be handed down to them. Such influence was exercised by the party organizations, in which every member had a voice, and which elected delegates and sent resolutions to the higher organizations. The lowest party organization was the cell, which could be formed wherever a minimum of three members was located in a given unit of production or institution (for example, a workshop or a warship). The cell members would be represented in the next highest organization (a town or district committee). The latter would be represented in the next highest organization in the same way. The top of the pyramid was the Party Congress, which at this period met annually. To carry on the day-to-day work of the party, the Congress selected a tenth of its members to form the Central Committee. In the critical post-revolutionary years the Central Committee proved too large for making quick decisions and this meant greater influence for its political bureau (Politburo). The latter, for most of the Civil War period, consisted of only five members (of whom two were always Lenin and Trotsky). Since the Central Committee rarely objected to the decisions of its Politburo, the latter (or its majority) was the effective ruling body.

Parallel with the party organizations were the government organizations. The central government came to consist of the Council of People's Commissars headed by its chairman (prime minister). The governmental

---

[11] On the eve of the February Revolution membership had probably been around 20,000. This grew to between 100,000 and 400,000 (according to whose estimates are believed) by October.

administration, like the party, had its subordinate provincial, district, and village organizations. Both local and central administrations were answerable to elected soviets, the lowliest (and often illusory) body being the village soviet. The party's control of the governmental administration was secured by the dual membership of individuals in party and governmental institutions. In the higher government organs there was 100 per cent party membership: key administrators would be members of key party organs at the same level (for example, the 'prime minister', Lenin, was a member of the Politburo).

One of the main functions of the party was therefore the provision of reliable administrators ('leading cadres') for governmental and non-governmental bodies at all levels, ranging from People's Commissars to newspaper editors to factory managers. The new administrators would take their instructors from the party, would be responsible to the party, and would conduct affairs in conformity with the party's priorities and aspirations. Other members, primarily the rank-and-file, were supposed to verify the fulfilment of the party's directives in their own locality, and to 'mobilize' the non-party masses by means of example, exhortation, persuasion, and propaganda. As time passed, the differing functions and the differing capabilities of members expressed itself in the informal division of the party into several categories. First there were the full-time paid party organizers, who collectively made up the *apparat*. The secretaries of the various party organizations were the most prominent among these. These were the men who selected members for various posts and tasks and who were responsible to the superior party bodies for the carrying out of the party's wishes in their own area. Whether they were the party's General Secretary in Moscow, or local party secretaries in the districts, they were the key figures in their particular spheres. A man who was appointed party secretary had moved a long way up the ladder; later he might find he had a long way to fall.

This party bureaucracy amounted to about 8 per cent of the party in the thirties. The next most influential group were those members who occupied administrative and governmental posts. Much of the 'white-collar' element of the party was included in this group. Finally there was the rank-and-file, in which the working class and peasant membership seemed to concentrate (partly because, when workers and peasants were promoted to administrative posts, they became classified as 'white collar' in the statistics). In proportion to its numbers in society, the white-collar category was over-represented in the party; it was about 30 per cent of the total in 1917, 70 per cent in 1941. This was partly because such people had most need to join the party (to hold or obtain administrative jobs), knew people who would sponsor their admission, had the time to devote to party work, were less liable to resign from the party, and possessed the skills the party needed in its effort to run the country.

From time to time there were purges of the membership. These were started during the Civil War to rid the party of 'radishes' (red outside but white inside) who had joined not from conviction but for personal advantage. In the early purges (which involved calling in party cards and re-issuing them after due appraisal), shameful personal behaviour (notably drunkenness), indiscipline, and non-participation in party activities were the most frequent causes of expulsion. Many members also left voluntarily, either because they were disillusioned, or found the party's demands on their time too burdensome. The first of the really major purges was in 1921–2, when no less than a third of the membership was eliminated, bringing the total down to less than half a million.

The role of party members in the Civil War was as stiffeners of morale, leaders of detachments, organizers, and administrators; members were mobilized and sent to whichever sector of the front or link of the economy seemed to be critical. As always, war with its succession of crises and urgent requirements necessitated authoritarian central direction; reasoning why was a luxury in wartime, doing and dying was the role of the communist. Thus it became accepted practice for the party *apparat* to direct particular members to particular tasks, to appoint and dismiss, without discussion or appeal. The working of the party became less democratic and more bureaucratic, while certain questionable practices, like sending contrarious members to distant posts, developed unchecked.

War Communism

The period of the Civil War coincided very closely with the period of 'War Communism', a term used to describe the economic and social climate produced by the interaction of rigorous government policies with the confusion, chaos, and anarchy of post-revolutionary Russia. Frequently, the policies of the Bolsheviks bore little resemblance to their earlier intentions; it was a case of riding on the tide or perishing. However, there were many Bolsheviks who persuaded themselves with varying degrees of willingness that the policies adopted out of necessity were in fact truly communist. Party members varied in their economic views, and the same members might at different times hold diametrically opposite opinions. Lenin himself changed course frequently and succeeded not only in retaining power, but also, in 1921, in persuading the party to completely change its economic outlook.

The Decree on Land, which broke up private landholdings and distributed them to the peasants, was followed (still in November 1917) by the Decree on Workers' Control. The latter gave additional powers to the already-existing workers' committees, which before October had been established in the factories. At this time the trade unions (where Bolshevik influence was still weak) were not considered a suitable medium of industrial control, which is why the workers' committees (which were independent of the unions) were favoured. However the committees were by no means subordinate to the party and tended to run their factories for their own benefit. They made life difficult for the factory managements, no doubt they protected the enterprises from possible sabotage by disaffected managers and owners, and they probably had an educational value for those who participated in them, but that was all. The committees were later merged into the trade unions, after the latter had been taken under firmer control by the party.

The problem of the trade unions was not finally solved until the twenties. Essentially, the unions in 1917 wanted to run their own industries in co-operation with the government, whereas the party (or at least Lenin and Trotsky) felt that the unions' role should be merely the application of the party's policy. Until March 1918 the railwaymen's union succeeded in running the railway network independently, but with its subjugation by the Bolsheviks in that month the first stage of union opposition to the party was over. Trotsky later introduced martial law on the railways, and proposed the similar militarization of other industries, but the opposition he aroused prevented further moves in this direction.

Lenin had initially expected to proceed very cautiously in the take-over of industry and commerce, co-operating at first with the capitalists and their managers. But, as in agriculture, events forced his hand. A strike by the State Bank (in effect a refusal to issue any funds to the Bolshevik government) led to an immediate take-over and the nationalization of this and all banks. In December 1917 the Supreme Economic Council was established to supervise the economy and to operate nationalized enterprises. It was still hoped that nationalization would be initially limited to a few key industries (the 'commanding heights' on which other industries were dependent: fuel, transport, banking, foreign trade, etc.), but local soviets all over Russia were already 'nationalizing' on their own initiative the enterprises in their areas. In February foreign debts were cancelled.

War Communism is reckoned to have begun in mid-1918 with the Decree on Nationalization, making all large-scale enterprises liable to nationalization without compensation. In the following three years there was wholesale nationalization, grain requisitioning, extreme inflation and the virtual disappearance of a money economy, a chaotic decline of industry, rationing, hunger, and disease, a decline of urban population, a gradual subordination of the unions to the government, and a Civil War which demanded the dispatch of all available human and material assets to the fronts.

Of these features grain requisitioning was the most important. Even without the Decree on Land there would have been a food shortage, but in 1918 the Bolsheviks made things worse. Deliveries to the towns fell as peasants waited for the state to offer fairer prices for their grain. The government responded by sending armed detachments of workers or of the CHEKA to the villages, with instructions to confiscate grain stocks beyond the personal needs of peasant families. At the same time the opportunity was taken to 'fan the class war' in the villages by establishing 'committees of the village poor', whose task it was to spy out the hidden grain stocks of the richer peasants. This naturally led to animosity and violence, but since it was a crime to 'speculate', and the holding of grain stocks was considered evidence of speculation, the peasants found that all forces were against them. The richer peasants were the most productive peasants; when their surpluses were thus confiscated they naturally reduced their sowing areas so as to produce less.

In the towns there was a rationing system for food and other necessities. Rationing was discriminatory; workers and soldiers received most, the bourgeoisie least. At times the ration, even for workers, was well below starvation level but could be supplemented by the black market. The latter was illegal, but usually tolerated. Whether a black marketeer was shot or made a handsome profit depended on luck and the time and place of his operations. Private trade in necessities was forbidden, but since the state trading organizations and co-operatives were chaotic and incapable of feeding the citizens it was the black marketeer, the 'speculator', who kept people alive. The 'bagmen' who would bring to the towns grain they had purchased from peasant hoarders made a big profit on resale, but were liable to be shot if caught by a CHEKA man in a bad mood. This was the period when the once-prosperous would go down to the black market with their paintings, china, clothing, even grand pianos, which they would exchange for a sack of flour or basket of eggs.

The constant movement of lousy troops, the absence of soap and hot water and medical supplies, combined with malnutrition, meant that millions of Russians died in the Civil War from diseases, of which typhus was the most lethal. Disease, battle, rebellion, and repression caused about 10 million deaths, of which only a tenth were military. Townspeople fled to the countryside, where they believed starvation was less likely; the number of workers fell from two and a half to one and a quarter million. In 1921

the gross output of industry was one-fifth of the 1913 production, and in
some key sectors the decline was even more catastrophic; while coal production had fallen only from 29 million to 9 million tons, sugar had
dropped from 1,300,000 tons to 50,000 and steel from 4,300,000 tons to
200,000. Small wonder that from 1917 to 1921 the prevalent attitude towards the Bolshevik government changed from apathy to resentment.
And yet there were many party members who relished the almost total
breakdown of Russian society. For them, this was communism.

Among these enthusiasts were those who saw in inflation a welcome 'inevitable dying-out of money', an institution which they considered 'bourgeois'. The economist Preobrazhenski described the money-printing press
as a 'machine gun which has attacked the bourgeois structure in the rear,
through its monetary system'. By October 1920 the rouble stood at one
per cent of its 1917 value and would decline even faster in subsequent
months; in May 1922, for example, railway fares were one million times
higher than in June 1917, and in the following November four million
times higher. In industry, money ceased to be a meaningful medium of exchange because inter-enterprise transactions became merely book-keeping
transactions and labour and materials were more and more paid for in
kind, either with an enterprise's own products or by items such as food or
clothing made available by the government. In early 1921 more than nine-
tenths of wages were paid in kind. In addition, services, like transport, were
made free services (in many towns the trams had ceased running, but they
were free). In the spring of 1919 another decision on nationalization specified that all enterprises employing more than ten workers were to be
nationalized (even 'left communists' like Bukharin rejected the idea of
nationalizing the smallest enterprises). But again the process followed its
own localized courses, irrespective of what Lenin or Trotsky or Bukharin
intended. According to one source over 30,000 enterprises were nationalized by 1920, including many (like windmills) which employed only one
worker. How the Supreme Economic Council could find able and reliable
communists to supervise these enterprises was apparently not considered
by the more ardent nationalizers, for whom the nationalization process
was simply taking a few armed men and declaring a given enterprise or
workshop or mill to be the property of 'the people'.

In 1920, with the critical period of the Civil War over, there was a continuation of the same ruthless and rigorous atmosphere. Lenin, unusually
late in recognizing the inevitable, discouraged those who recommended
moderation in economic life. Proliferating peasant revolts he blamed on
the Socialist Revolutionaries. Declining sowing areas he proposed to counter with a plan for each peasant, specifying how much land should be

planted. The overloading and confusion of the Supreme Economic Council was met by making it subordinate to the Council of Labour and Defence, of which Lenin was chairman. 'Communist Saturdays', the voluntary labour of workers on their day off, were spoken of as the way to
tackle post-war restoration. But in the countryside peasant revolts were
becoming widespread and threatening. There was no longer the need to
support the Reds simply because they were a lesser evil than the Whites, so
the savage resentment aroused by grain requisitioning was no longer
constrained. By the end of 1920 the Civil War had merged into a peasant
rebellion.

Lenin seems to have decided to reverse course in early February 1921,
accepting the need to replace grain requisitioning with a system which
would increase food production and mitigate the animosity of the peasant
masses. To persuade his party of the need for this 'New Economic Policy'
was a formidable prospect; that Lenin achieved it so quickly was due to
peasant risings, strikes, and especially the Kronstadt revolt of late February, which shook the party more than the Whites had ever done.

The Kronstadt sailors were the traditional heroes of the Revolution.
Although by this time the Baltic sailors of 1917 had been diluted by new
recruits, this had not affected the esteem and regard which they received
from the party. Second only perhaps to the Baltic sailors were the workers
of Petrograd, although here again the workers of 1921 were not the same
as the workers of 1917. In early 1921 the Petrograd workers were demonstrating against the Bolsheviks on several grounds; economic privations,
Trotsky's so-called Labour Army (in reality, organized strike-breakers
sent to discontented factories), the fixing in the Bolsheviks' favour of
elections to soviets and trade union organizations, the presence of armed
communist detachments in the factories, and the arrests and executions
carried out by the CHEKA (which did not spare the workers). These complaints were distorted by the press. A communist later wrote:

The truth seeped through little by little, past the smokescreen put out by the
Press, which was positively berserk with lies. And this was our Press, the Press of
our revolution, the first Socialist Press, and hence the first incorruptible and un-
biased Press in the world! Before now it had employed a certain amount of demagogy, which was, however, passionately sincere, and some violent tactics towards its
adversaries. That might be fair enough and at any rate was understandable. Now it
lied systematically.[12]

The seamen of Kronstadt noticed glaring differences between what the
newspapers said about the Petrograd disturbances and what their sailors'

[12] V. Serge, *Memoirs of a Revolutionary* (Oxford, 1963), 126.

representatives reported from the capital. They noticed that the party and the press were misrepresenting the workers' demands and concealing the repressive actions which were being taken. The Kronstadt sailors in a succession of meetings thereupon made demands on the Bolsheviks in the form of resolutions. They demanded new elections to the soviets with a secret ballot and other measures to prevent the Bolsheviks rigging the elections. They demanded freedom of speech and of the press for all of the left wing, freedom of assembly, liberation of left-wing political prisoners and a re-examination of the cases against other political prisoners, freedom to bring food into the towns from the countryside, abolition of extra rations for privileged persons, withdrawal of armed guards from the factories, and other lesser liberties.

Party spokesmen were shouted down, since they refused to concede these demands. Trotsky delivered a menacing ultimatum, which was rejected. Tukhachevsky was summoned to capture the island of Kronstadt. The first assault across the ice failed, largely because the attacking troops sympathized with the rebels, and two weeks elapsed before more reliable troops, stiffened with communists from the concurrent Party Congress, could be launched for a second attempt. This eventually succeeded after heavy losses. Street fighting in Kronstadt was transformed into a virtual massacre of the sailors.

The revolt was passed off, and sixty years later was still passed off, as a White conspiracy aimed at the restoration of the monarchy. In fact, as Lenin said, 'it illuminated reality like a flash of lightning'. Whether or not Lenin realized its full implication is not clear. If the demands of the rebels are examined it is evident that what they were demanding, and what the Bolsheviks would not concede, was virtually what most Bolsheviks and their supporters had believed they were fighting for in 1917. Nothing could have been more revealing of the gap between the aspirations of the Bolsheviks in 1917 and their intentions in 1921. In the intervening four years the Bolsheviks had given the retention of power overriding priority in their struggle against all kinds of perils. In their own terms they had emerged victorious, but in terms of ideals, of ambitions, of compassion, of all the things which make a revolution worth while, they were no longer the same people. The Communist Party of 1921 was not the Bolshevik Party of 1917.

When Lenin spoke of Kronstadt as 'illuminating reality' the reality to which he referred was ostensibly the reality of economic policy. But he may have suspected another reality, that in the Civil War the Bolsheviks had been defeated.

12. *Disputes and Decisions*

Famine

FOR Russians, hunger was not a new experience. There had been especially serious famines in 1833, 1840, 1867, 1873, 1891, and 1911. That of 1891 had been the most lethal, but was exceeded by the famine of 1921–2. With the area under oats and summer wheat at less than three-fifths, and under winter rye at four-fifths, the 1917 extent, it could hardly have been otherwise. Signs of an impending crisis were evident in 1918; deaths from hunger were rare, but deaths from malnutrition were rising. Some figures for Petrograd are indicative.[1]

	City Population (million)	Births per thousand of population	Deaths per thousand of population
1914	2.2	25	21
1917	2.5	18	25
1918	1.5	15	44
1919	0.8	15.5	81.5
1920	0.6	12	uncertain, between 90 and 120

There was widespread drought in 1920 and 1921. As food became short the older and weaker began to die. There was an increase of orphans and of physically defective infants. Crime grew, new criminal careers typically beginning with theft of food. Such thefts might progress to armed attacks by groups on such life-or-death objectives as granaries or potato fields. The towns emptied as their populations left to seek food in the countryside, while at the same time starving countryfolk thronged the railway stations as they sought to reach some rumoured area of plenty. The railways were already barely functioning; the few passenger trains which were running

---

[1] L.A. and L.M. Vasilievskii, *Kniga o golode* (1922), 64–5.

were crammed with the starving, the weak being pushed off to make room for the strong at each station. Those without strength or hope huddled for days and weeks on the station platforms, quite silent, occasionally picking off each other's lice as they starved to death.

In such times there could be no morality. Even party officials entrusted with food distribution sometimes gave short rations for their own profit. Cannibalism appeared, and so did body-snatching:

> Sometimes insensate mothers and fathers feed their children human meat as a last resort. Sometimes a starving family eats the body of one of its junior members. Sometimes a father, seeing no other way, cuts the throat of a neighbour's child and brings it to his children as 'mutton' (his own poignant term). Sometimes parents at night seize part of a body from the cemetery and feed it to their children.[2]

These observations were written by two doctors working in one of the worst famine areas, the Ufa region. They mentioned another case:

> A Tartar killed a thirteen-year old girl, a relative, who had come to visit him, by hitting her over the head with a log. He not only ate her, but also cut off from her several pounds of fat, which he sold at the market.[3]

In the villages, where there was no grain and no seed, where the emaciated horses and bone-dry cows were being eaten, there seemed to be no hope unless the promises of government help on the way, made by the local party men, were miraculously kept. But few by this stage had much faith in party promises. The government appealed to the outside world for food and medical aid. Many charitable organizations responded, and others were set up for the purpose. The work of Herbert Hoover's American aid project, of the Quakers and other religious groups, and of Nansen's organization, together with exertions by the government, partially coped with the disaster. At first there were difficulties because the authorities did not wish potentially subversive westerners to be at large in the countryside, while the foreign organizations, fearful that their supplies might be distributed only to known supporters of the regime, insisted on keeping distribution in their own hands. Eventually a compromise was reached, but throughout the crisis there were occasional arrests of relief workers in Russia, especially of those Russians employed by the various agencies.

This famine probably took about five million lives.

The New Economic Policy (NEP)

The first indication that Lenin was willing to abandon the economic practices of War Communism had come in February 1921, when he accepted the idea of a tax-in-kind to replace grain requisitions. With a tax-in-kind

---

[2] L.A. and L.M. Vasilievskii, *Kniga o golode* (1922), 81–2.   [3] Ibid. 178.

fixed in advance, the peasant would know that he could dispose of any surplus over the tax in his own most profitable way, and would therefore increase his production and his sown area. Such a change was long overdue. If it had occurred a year earlier both the peasant revolts and the famines would have been moderated. But the Bolsheviks seemed unwilling to give peasants what they most wanted and needed, a feeling that something was their own. Even the feeling that their crops were their own had been taken from the peasants by the requisitioning policy.

The Party Congress, shaken by the Kronstadt revolt, did agree to this change, which became even more radical when the tax-in-kind for the various food products was fixed well below the previous requisitioning targets. This meant that the peasantry would certainly produce a marketable surplus and, since the state was not in a position to organize a marketing and distribution system, the return of private trade had to be accepted. Once the private trader (soon known as the *nepman*) was admitted in one sector, it was not long before he began to dominate all retail trade; the peasant with money in his boot wanted somewhere to spend it, and neither the state nor the co-operative movement could organize adequate retail distribution.

In the changed atmosphere, and with the critical industrial situation, the readmission of private enterprise into industry was also accepted, although Lenin needed all his powers of persuasion to convince his party of this. While taking care to retain in state ownership the 'commanding heights' of the economy, small-scale manufacturing was largely returned to private management. By 1924, while the state still owned and managed 98 per cent of large-scale industry, small-scale factories were about four-fifths privately run, and one-fifth co-operative. Since the state and party lacked enough talented administrators to run all enterprises efficiently, placing the majority under private management was a wise move from the economic point of view, though distasteful to the party.

1921 was a year of great industrial crisis. There were mutually exacerbating fuel, food, and railway crises, causing many enterprises to close. Radical measures in that year to increase industrial productivity created additional short-term chaos. Hitherto, enterprises had been subordinate to one or other of the departments of the Supreme Economic Council, and their task was to produce rather than to cover their costs. Money hardly entered their calculations; they received allocations of raw materials from the Supreme Economic Council, which in turn allocated their output. Wages were paid in food rations, clothing, and services. In 1921 this high-cost, low-output, and bureaucratic system was changed. Enterprises were reorganized and grouped into trusts, which had a high degree of autonomy, and were expected to observe conventional accounting procedures. Materials were to be paid for out of income, and so were wages; free rations, and rationing, were to be eliminated. The State Bank was to provide credit, and in 1922 a new rouble was introduced to stabilize the currency. To improve standards of management further, and to acquire advanced plant, foreign entrepreneurs were invited to participate in Russian industry. Few were willing, but foreign trade increased, and a commercial agreement was made with Britain in 1921.

The 'scissors crisis' of 1923, so called because two divergent trends resembled scissors when plotted on a graph, was less serious than it seemed at the time. It was essentially a marked disharmony between food prices (that is, the peasants' income), and the prices of industrial products (the peasants' expenditure). At its worst, industrial prices were nearly three times higher than pre-war, whereas food prices were slightly lower. This problem caused further discontent among the peasantry, and a diminution of the market for manufactured goods, before it was overcome.

The private entrepreneur, both in trade and industry, performed essential tasks which official organizations were unable to handle. He made a handsome profit in doing so, and the conspicuous luxury in which some *nepmany* indulged was one of several features of NEP which irritated the more sensitive party members. By 1923 *nepmany* handled three-quarters of all retail trade. Not only were they able to get goods from producer to consumer faster than state or co-operative organizations, they were able to do so more cheaply because their operations were less bureaucratic. Co-operatives, for example, marked up their prices for commodities like sugar or cloth by about 100 per cent over the ex-factory price; the *nepmany*, who dealt with state-produced goods as well as private, could operate profitably on much narrower margins. However, the various types of marketing, retailing and production co-operatives did flourish in this period. Production co-operatives included several forms of collective farm which were voluntary and, often, very productive. Co-operatives had become popular in tsarist times, and by the end of NEP about half the peasant households belonged to them. They seemed to appeal to the peasantry especially, and were a way of reducing costs and improving supply without recourse to coercion. Until 1926 the trade of the *nepmany* rose absolutely, although it fell proportionately after 1923 as the state, through the newly formed people's commissariat of trade, made efforts to compete. In general, the first three or four years of NEP were the heyday of the *nepman*, but also a period in which the government and party succeeded in extricating themselves from the self-defeating economic policies of War Communism. By 1926 in most products the economy had regained the

1913 output level. The NEP environment with its combination of market and planning had worked quite well, especially when it is remembered that NEP really had barely three years (1925–7) in which it was impaired neither by hunger nor by grain requisitioning. On the other hand, regaining 1913 levels by 1926 meant that the economy was still thirteen years behind, and much of the advance had been obtained simply by putting back into service disused and abandoned plant and equipment.

The party

During the Civil War the most valued party members had been those who best fulfilled urgent tasks, if necessary by holding a bayonet at their fellow-countrymen's throats. But under NEP many of the more hardened Bolsheviks found that their rough-and-ready methods were no longer appreciated by party organizers who now worked in neat offices with neat typists and neat rows of rubber stamps. At the same time, the authority which party organizers had acquired over members did not disappear, even though the practice of party bureaux directing unquestioning members was incompatible with the pre-revolutionary concept of the party; 'Democratic Centralism' had become all centre with no democracy. Meanwhile, those members appointed to administrative posts tended to lose contact with ordinary party members and ordinary people. When there was a conflict, administrative convenience usually prevailed. When Lenin in his final years railed against 'inner-party bureaucracy' it was these tendencies that he had in mind.

Nevertheless Lenin attacked groups which criticized what they regarded as the deterioration of their party. Prominent among these groups were the so-called Left Communists, who had regarded such decisions as the peace with Germany and the employment of ex-tsarist officers as threats to the party's purity. There was the Workers' Opposition which grouped members who believed that the workers were not receiving their just reward from the revolution they had made, and that non-worker elements were too influential inside the party. Then there was the group for Democratic Centralism, which demanded more genuine democracy in the party. It was to muzzle movements such as these that the Politburo, while making some concessions, in 1921 introduced a ban on 'factions' in the party. This meant that, although a member might oppose a proposal, he was liable to expulsion if he tried to join with others in opposing it after it had been adopted as policy. This ban effectively ended real discussion of many critical issues, but was justified by the leadership on the grounds that the party was still in danger and could not risk splits. Since the other left-wing, non-Bolshevik,

parties were about to be finally eliminated[4] this meant there was no longer
a tolerated source of organized criticism of current policies. The ban on
factions (in effect a ban on one member joining with one or more others to
express dissent) would later help Stalin to overcome his critics piecemeal,
but those leaders who later suffered from it voted for it at the time.

Another, more basic, threat to the party was the disappearance of its ostensible *raison d'être*, the proletariat it was supposed to lead. Not only had
the Revolution occurred in a nation lacking the developed capitalistic society which Marx had envisaged, but the small proletariat had disappeared
during the Civil War. True, there were urban workers, but few of them
were the experienced and politically conscious men of 1917. The latter had
been killed while fighting for or against the Bolsheviks in the Civil War, or
had become Bolshevik officials and army officers, or had left the factories
in favour of the countryside. The factory workers of the early twenties were
largely ex-peasants, ill-educated, ill-disciplined, and not particularly interested in the party. Thus the Bolsheviks, who had regarded themselves as
the vanguard of the proletariat, found themselves in the van with nothing
to guard. This is what Lenin implied when he surprised his followers by
saying that the workers were uncultured in terms of education and behaviour, and that the first task was to raise them to at least the level of bourgeois culture. This is what he meant when he opposed the admission of
too many additional workers into the party.

The end of Lenin

From late 1921 to his death in January 1924, Lenin suffered a series of
major and minor strokes.[5] Some deprived him temporarily of the ability
to write or speak, while that of March 1923 made him permanently speechless. Far from withdrawing into inactivity during these painful two years
in which haemorrhage succeeded haemorrhage, Lenin, so far as he was
able, devoted himself to combating dangerous tendencies in the party. Possibly, convalescences gave him the opportunity to ponder more deeply the
problems of his party. In early 1922 it appears that he was not as greatly
alarmed as later. He had approved the ban on factions and the appointment of Stalin to the new position of General Secretary (that is, chief secretary) of the party. It was perhaps these two moves more than any others
which laid the foundations for the misfortunes which were to befall the
party in later decades.

[4] There was a trial in 1922, followed by death sentences, of surviving Socialist Revolutionary leaders. Many SRs and Mensheviks had already joined the Bolsheviks. Among the ex-
Mensheviks were Lenin's Commissar for Foreign Affairs Chicherin (an aristocrat of ancient
lineage), and Vyshinsky, who would attain high office in the thirties.

[5] An account of these months is presented in M. Lewin, *Lenin's Last Struggle* (1968), on
which this section is partly based.

Lenin had never attempted to dictate to the Politburo, relying on persuasion and persistence. However, he was less persuasive *in absentia*. A serious difference, which probably caused Lenin's misgivings about Stalin, arose over Georgia. The Georgian communists did not relish Moscow's suggestion that Georgia, Armenia, and Azerbaizhan should be amalgamated. But the Politburo's representative in Georgia, Ordzhonikidze, and his fellow-Georgian Stalin (still Commissar for Nationalities) nevertheless tried to impose amalgamation. Also, Stalin's proposal for a Russian Federation in which nations like Georgia and the Ukraine would be constituent 'autonomous republics' was unwelcome both to the national communist parties and to Lenin. In the Politburo, Stalin condemned Lenin's counterproposals, accusing his absent leader of 'national liberalism'. But when it became evident that the Politburo majority supported Lenin, Stalin backed down.

In Lenin's scheme, the Russian Federation was not governed by the Russian Republic's government, but by a Union (i.e. federal) government, making the Russian Republic the equal of the other national republics. Because Georgia, while welcoming this, still opposed the amalgamation of Georgia, Armenia, and Azerbaizhan, Stalin and Ordzhonikidze conducted a Georgian-style vendetta against the leaders of the Georgian Communist Party. What was probably the turning point in Lenin's attitude came when he heard that Ordzhonikidze had struck a Georgian communist leader; Lenin's own appointee, in other words, had behaved like one of the very worst tsarist governors. Henceforth Lenin was determined to solve the nationalities problem without recourse to 'Muscovite chauvinism', and to cleanse the party leadership of its high-handed and bureaucratic characters. In December 1922 he asked Trotsky to form a 'counter-bureaucratic' bloc.

Despite his stroke of December 13, Lenin began a thorough examination of the Georgian affair. He worked through his wife and secretaries (one of whom was Stalin's wife), writing and telephoning when he was able; he no longer trusted the information supplied by Stalin. The latter was alarmed at the increasingly intimate correspondence passing between Lenin and Trotsky, and telephoned Krupskaya to arrange a meeting between himself and the invalid. Krupskaya refused to allow such a visit, and Stalin showered her with reprimands, threats, and crude abuse.

After another stroke on December 23, Lenin was allowed to dictate only for five minutes each day, and that is how in that last week of December the various notes known as Lenin's 'testament' were written. Lenin wished, before it was too late, to divert the party from its bureaucratism and authoritarianism. Although he appeared close to death, he refrained from suggesting who should succeed him, but he did offer some guiding comments. Most quoted is his comment on Stalin: 'Comrade Stalin, having become General Secretary, has concentrated unlimited authority in his hands, and I am not sure whether he will always be capable of using that authority with sufficient caution.'[6] Then followed an appreciation of Trotsky's pre-eminence in terms of sheer ability, coupled with a warning of his excessive self-confidence and high-handedness. After this there was an ambiguous reference to Kamenev and Zinoviev, simply mentioning that they had opposed the October uprising but should not be condemned for this. Lastly, Lenin envisaged a bright future for the young pair Bukharin and Pyatakov. The comment on Stalin was not as damaging as it might seem, because by mentioning Stalin before Trotsky it acknowledged that Stalin was now pre-eminent. Zinoviev and Kamenev, who fancied themselves as Lenin's immediate colleagues, were relegated to a passing mention. Lenin probably had reached the sad conclusion that there was no one person fit to succeed him; until younger aspirants matured, the best hope lay in an unlikely co-operation of Trotsky and Stalin, with the party keeping a stern eye on both. Lenin must have realized that as General Secretary Stalin had amassed so much personal leverage that, irrespective of ability, he had much greater power than the other leaders. Presumably he also feared that Stalin's great and growing power would prevent a dual Trotsky–Stalin leadership on equal terms after his death.

This problem, the imbalance caused by Stalin's power, Lenin tackled two weeks later in a postscript to his 'testament'. In the meantime he had been investigating the Georgian affair; probably the more he learned of this the more he distrusted Stalin. Hence the hardened attitude expressed in this postscript. He now proposed the dismissal of Stalin from the General Secretaryship, replacing him by a man 'more patient, more loyal, more courteous, and more considerate of his comrades, less capricious'. Lenin also dictated five newspaper articles which, among other things, castigated the operations of the Workers' and Peasants' Inspectorate,[7] headed by Stalin.

In early March Lenin's secretaries presented him with their conclusions on the Georgian affair, confirming his earlier misgivings. As part of his 'testament' he had in December written that Ordzhonikidze and Stalin had acted like bullies, aided by Dzerzhinski, who had shown that intense Russian chauvinism so typical of russianized non-Russians, and that all three should be condemned by the party. Now, conscious that his days were numbered, he asked Trotsky to defend the Georgians before the Central Committee against the persecutions of Stalin and others. About the same time he wrote to Stalin demanding an apology for the insults which the

[6] V. Lenin, *Sochineniya*, 4th Ed., Vol. 36, 544.
[7] This organization (*Rabkrin*) existed from 1919 to 1934 and was intended to send investigators to root out arbitrary and 'bureaucratic' practices in the government administration.

latter had directed at Krupskaya. The next day he had a severe stroke. By March 10 he was half-paralysed and speechless; his political activity was finished. In his last active days he had done what he could to reduce Stalin, to overcome party bureaucracy, and to fight 'Great Russian chauvinism'. As things turned out, he failed. Lenin was only fifty-four when he died. Stalin would live another three decades, to the age of seventy-three. Lenin's relationship with Stalin had generally been warm; although, like others, he probably underestimated Stalin's intelligence, he appreciated that he was a man with a mind of his own. Even at this tense period he did not seek to exclude Stalin from the top leadership, and in any case it is arguable that his exceptionally bitter anger at Stalin's treatment of Krupskaya may have been partly a result of his illness. Eye-witnesses said that on Lenin's death Stalin collapsed into tears and this is believable, given Stalin's apparent admiration for Lenin and the circumstance that the latter's death prevented the reconciliation that could otherwise have been expected.

Stalin

Born in Georgia in 1879, Iosif Vissarionovich Djugashvili later adopted the name Stalin as a revolutionary pseudonym. There is much of his childhood and youth which has remained unknown, or has been obscured by invention. His father was violent, and his mother pious. He attended a local church school and then went to train for the priesthood at the Orthodox Seminary in Tbilisi. At school he seems to have impressed his teachers, and thrown his weight around among his fellow-pupils. His record at the Seminary was also good, at first. As his later career demonstrated, he had all the makings of a successful Orthodox churchman and would no doubt have gone far if his mother's pious intentions had not been frustrated. While at the Seminary Stalin became interested in revolutionaries and their ideas. His sympathy towards them became known to his teachers, his academic work deteriorated. He failed to attend the penultimate examinations and this, almost automatically, led to his expulsion. He emerged as a mixed-up teenager, seeking a job and closer contact with the revolutionaries. By this time his basic characteristics were entrenched. He remained a Georgian even though he had received a Russian education. His priestly education later seemed to be reflected in his outward humility, and in the style of his writings and argumentation, which suggested that he might well have become a convincing preacher. Stalin's character is still very much a mystery, although several biographers have tackled it (see Bibliography).

By his early twenties he was well known among local Social Democrats. He took some part in the strike movement in the Caucasus and attended party conferences abroad, including the 1907 London conference. He was also one of the organizers of armed 'expropriations' (including the notorious 1907 Tbilisi banknote robbery) which simultaneously financed and discredited the Bolshevik faction. During the pre-war decade he was arrested and exiled from time to time, but except in the final case escaped. In 1913 he was in Vienna, writing a theoretical treatise, at the request of Lenin, about the nationalities problem. He then returned to Russia, was arrested, and sent to Siberia, where he stayed until liberated by the February Revolution. Until Lenin's return he supported Kamenev's policy of co-operation with the other socialist parties, but then became a loyal adherent of Lenin's policies. After October he was appointed People's Commissar for Nationalities; being himself a member of one of the national groups of the former Russian Empire he was a natural choice for this post. During the Civil War he was also a military commissar and clashed with Trotsky on several matters. From 1919 he was additionally in charge of the Workers' and Peasants' Inspectorate, which gave him a right to interfere in the operations of all government departments. He was closely associated with the party's organization bureau (*Orgburo*), which allocated and recalled members to and from key posts. Then, in 1922, the Politburo appointed him to the new position of party General Secretary.

Party leaders, well-versed in European history, had always been vigilantly on guard against a Bonaparte emerging from their ranks. But while watching for Corsicans they overlooked the Georgian in the woodpile. They were pleased by Stalin's assumption of the drudgery which his new office implied; while he was labouring over his files they could devote themselves to higher things. The new duties inevitably led, however, to great influence inside the party. With two associates, Molotov and Kuibyshev, as assistant secretaries, Stalin appointed and dismissed party organizers (enabling him gradually to place congenial men in key posts), and prepared the agenda and supplied information for Politburo meetings.

In the disputes which split the Politburo after Lenin's departure, the rival factions discovered that Stalin was a required ally because, among other things, he had by this time been able to install many of his protégés in the Central Committee; in other words, he could deliver the votes. Trotsky may have called him the 'most eminent mediocrity in the party', but in the twenties it was votes, not intellects, which counted. And in any case Stalin may not have been all that mediocre. Despite their refined intellects, men like Zinoviev and Kamenev habitually backed the wrong horses. Surrounded as he was by highly-developed minds which clouded and distorted every problem with all kinds of complexities, Stalin's simplicity must sometimes have seemed like genius.

Stalin and the succession

After Lenin died in 1924, the body was brought to Moscow. Like a saint of the Russian Orthodox Church, it was embalmed and glass-cased, then put on permanent exhibition in a red marble mausoleum. Subsequently, the locomotive of the funeral train was laid to rest in a temple-like structure in Moscow, to be revered by guided tourists. Thus sanctification of Lenin, and all things (but not persons) connected with Lenin, had begun almost before the body was cold. In the funeral rituals Stalin stood out as the first disciple of the late leader, and soon began to use the term 'Leninism' as a slogan to justify his own arguments. 'Leninism' began to denote orthodoxy, the 'correct' party line as laid down in the words of Lenin. Trotsky was certainly a man whose intelligence matched that of Lenin, but he lacked the ability to lower himself into the drudgery of politics. Moreover, he did not have Lenin's prestige in the party, and hence had less power of persuasion. He excelled as the commentator, the critic, the orator, the executor of policies, and as such had been an ideal complement to Lenin. With Lenin gone, Trotsky lost his most important role.

The term 'struggle for power' is misleading when applied to the party disputes of the twenties. Issues of policy were deeply felt and usually transcended personal discords. For the most part, the intrigues and manœuvres of the contestants were motivated not so much by desire to get to the top as by the desire to keep rivals away from the top. Although Stalin seemed to win every trick, it is unlikely that he followed a long-term plan. He did not need to, he could stand back and watch his rivals dig their own graves, occasionally offering his spade to one or other of them.

Trotsky lost his opportunity when, contrary to Lenin's wishes, he did not attack Stalin on the Georgian question. This was the penultimate occasion when he could have opposed the General Secretary with Lenin's prestige behind him. The last chance was Lenin's 'testament', but this was neutralized with Trotsky's acquiescence; when in May 1924 the Central Committee was acquainted with Lenin's criticism of Stalin, it was proposed that since Stalin had since improved, there was no need to carry out Lenin's wishes in this matter. This was agreed, and it was also decided to keep the 'testament' secret.[8] Thus another damaging weapon against Stalin had been voluntarily sheathed, and could not be bared again without defying the decision of the Central Committee.

While Lenin was dying a triumvirate of Stalin, Zinoviev, and Kamenev had provided the party's leadership, and had already fired the opening

---

[8] It was published by the *New York Times* in 1926, but was not revealed in the USSR until after Stalin's death.

salvos against Trotsky. The alliance of these three was essentially a means to prevent Trotsky gaining a majority in the Politburo, and thereby becoming *de facto* leader of the party. Trotsky's arrogance and conceit made him very unpopular in certain sections of the party: the *apparat* tended to dislike him, partly because he was an upstart ex-Menshevik, but largely because he attacked the bureaucratization of the party and because the intellectuals of his own generation could not forgive him his arrogant brilliance. Nor did the new generation of workers favour Trotsky. On the other hand, students and recent students, government workers, and much of the Red Army, respected him. The nature of Trotsky's support was perhaps why there was a decision to expand the party by admitting new working-class members, for whom admission standards were lowered. For the most part these were ignorant and docile characters, willing to vote the way the local party organizers wished (and the local party organizers were more and more Stalin's men). Thus the party had ignored Lenin's warning that the working class was still too 'uncultured' to provide many useful members. Meanwhile, purges of the existing membership tended to discriminate against members known to be supporters of Trotsky.

By 1925 party membership was just over one million. The new members were easily controlled by the party organizers; many workers were glad to be admitted because unemployment was rising and party membership often helped to obtain, or retain a job. Others found themselves on committees or taken into full-time party work. Contrary to the party's rules, the new members were allowed to vote in the selection of resolutions and delegates to be sent to the 13th Party Congress in 1924. When that Congress opened in Moscow, it was largely composed of delegates who would turn a deaf, if not uncomprehending, ear to Trotsky's oratory.

The policy issue on which Trotsky and the triumvirate were opposed at the Congress was the contradiction between NEP and the 'permanent revolution' as propounded by Trotsky. But there was little genuine debate as at previous congresses; instead, there was mass applause, mass condemnation, and predetermined votes as the well-instructed Stalinist delegates went into action. Trotsky's arguments were defeated by non-argumentative means and he was unwilling to split the party by forming an oppositional *bloc*. Nor did he seek to take belated advantage of Lenin's 'testament'. Later, Trotsky was to declare that 'a man can be right only with the party'. This reluctance to split the party was one of the basic reasons for his fall. After his defeat at this Congress his hands were tied; in 1921 he had warmly approved the ban on factions and now this ban could be used against him if he sought to organize opposition. However, he did not accept Zinoviev's demand to recant publicly his past errors. And in October he published

Lessons of October, a pamphlet on party democracy which bitterly criticized Kamenev and Zinoviev.

With Trotsky's withdrawal from active opposition, Stalin began to diverge from Zinoviev and Kamenev. In the preceding controversies he had remained in the background, allowing his two allies a free field in their disputes with Trotsky: the wrangles thus tended to lower the public reputation of Zinoviev, Kamenev, and Trotsky, but not of Stalin. At this time NEP and 'socialism in one country' were complementary. Bukharin was a proponent of NEP, and Stalin was a champion of 'socialism in one country' (the concept[9] directly opposed to Trotsky's 'Permanent Revolution'). Hence there was emerging a new alliance between Bukharin and Stalin, both of whom advocated peasant prosperity and, following from this, more peasants in the party. But in Leningrad and the north-west, the local party organizers were still largely Zinoviev's protégés, and ignored the summons to foster peasant recruitment. Meanwhile the Zinovievites prepared to argue for a reversal of the party's pro-peasant recruitment drive at the forthcoming 14th Congress in late 1925. But by this time the press was largely a controlled press, and one feature of a controlled press is the ease with which it can promote the uncorrectable smear. For example, one of Zinoviev's supporters had advocated that 90 per cent of the party should be workers and *Pravda* chose to interpret this as a ludicrous suggestion that 90 per cent of the workers should be party members. In ways similar to this, the other arguments of the Zinovievites were distorted, and at the 14th Congress Zinoviev and Kamenev were defeated when they opposed Stalin's new industrialization plan and when they proposed a vote of no-confidence in Stalin. Many of Zinoviev's and Kamenev's supporters did not dare to vote for their patrons.[10]

Consolidating his victory, Stalin sent Kirov to undermine Zinoviev's position as Leningrad party secretary. Kirov succeeded so well that in 1927 he was himself elected in Zinoviev's place. Kamenev and Zinoviev now sought an alliance with their old enemy Trotsky, and in 1926 all three unfruitfully criticized party policy before the Central Committee, pointing to the soft line towards the richer peasants, the growing bureaucracy, and failures abroad. Following this, Zinoviev was excluded from the Politburo.[11] Kamenev lost his position as Commissar for Foreign Trade, being replaced by the Armenian Mikoyan. Trotsky had already been unprotestingly

[9] The theory of 'socialism in one country' held that it was indeed possible for Russia to build a socialist society without waiting for more advanced countries' revolutions to take place.

[10] By this time the GPU was intervening, at the lower levels, in party quarrels.

[11] Until 1925 this top decision-making party body consisted of Stalin, Trotsky, Bukharin, Kamenev, Rykov, Tomsky, and Zinoviev, but in that year Stalin added three of his adherents, Kalinin, Molotov, and Voroshilov.

deprived of his key (and potent) position of Commissar for War in January 1925. Nevertheless the opposition continued to oppose, sometimes even visiting party cells to agitate among the grass-roots. The *apparat* responded with 'spontaneous' interruptions of speeches, and other short-term measures. Then, in October 1926, Trotsky and Kamenev were expelled from the Politburo, and Zinoviev lost his chairmanship of the Comintern. But the leadership's failures abroad during 1927, especially the massacre of the Chinese communists, again aroused the opposition. Trotsky even hinted that if, as seemed likely, Russia was again attacked by foreign powers, he would ask for dictatorial powers and direct the war effort.

Trotsky and Zinoviev were thereupon expelled from the Central Committee and, after some of their supporters had attempted to organize street demonstrations, they were expelled from the party. Other pressures later resulted in the expulsion of about seventy-five of their leading supporters, and the suicide of others. At the 15th Party Congress in late 1927, appeals by both 'left' and 'right' spokesmen to give the accused a hearing were shouted down by the majority, Stalin's 'centre'. Complete confession and recantation were demanded. Eventually Kamenev and Zinoviev did recant, enabling them to be readmitted to party activity for a few more pathetic years. Trotsky refused to recant. One night in 1928 he was bundled by the GPU into a train for Central Asia, still wearing his pyjamas. At first his exile was fairly comfortable, and he maintained contact with some of his supporters. However, when Stalin adopted an industrialization programme very similar to his own, many of his adherents transferred their loyalties to Stalin. Perhaps because of this, Stalin felt strong enough in 1929 to expel Trotsky from the USSR. From then until 1940, when an agent of Stalin murdered him at his Mexican home, Trotsky with other Bolshevik émigrés carried on a propaganda campaign against Stalinism.

After thus defeating the 'left' opposition with the aid of the 'right', Stalin was ready to turn against his former allies. A conflict impended as soon as Stalin decided that a hard line should be taken with the peasantry.

Agriculture under NEP

One essential reason why the Bolsheviks retained power after 1917, was their disarming of likely opposition from the peasant masses by means of land reform. This land reform was perhaps little more than acquiescence in the peasants' own spontaneous take-over of the land of rich peasants and landowners, but was nonetheless politically effective. But, as so often, what was politically or ideologically sound was economically disastrous; the 'retreat' of NEP was largely an acknowledgement that ideology and politics lose their priority when the masses are starving.

The expropriations of 1917–20 meant that average landholdings grew smaller as the larger holdings were divided up.[12] In that period the number of holdings increased by about one half. Among those expropriated were many of those who had taken advantage of the Stolypin reforms and launched themselves as independent private farmers. The *mir* once more became powerful, while the strip system and three-field rotation became more common. While the strengthening of the *mir* had a negative effect on productivity, more serious was the decline in marketability caused by the shrinkage of the average landholding. The poorest peasants produced no marketable food, consuming not only all they grew but often using income from other sources to buy additional food, whereas the pre-revolutionary rich peasants and landlords had marketed almost all their grain.

Thus after 1917 not only did production fall, but the food which was produced tended to be eaten by the peasants rather than sold. Expressed differently, there was a larger number of landholdings which could do no more than support those who worked on them. Demobilization of soldiers and the exodus from the towns had meant more mouths in the villages to be fed from the same total land area. It was largely to remedy this situation, virtually an industrial revolution in reverse, that NEP was introduced. As such it was very successful. The peasants who were willing and able to respond to the financial inducements allowed by NEP increased their production, and such increase was marketed.[13] Once the famine of 1921–2 was over, it seemed that there would be enough food for all and for export too. This would permit re-urbanization and re-industrialization. The party's dilemma in this situation was that the more the peasants prospered, the greater the ideological threat they seemed to present. The peasantry still represented 'petty bourgeois' attitudes, and it vastly outnumbered the proletariat which, led by the party, was supposed to form the dictatorship of Russia. To many it seemed that any step to encourage

[12] By 1919 97 per cent of the arable land was held by individual peasants, with the remainder farmed by communes, artels, state, or collective organizations. While the proportion of landless peasants had fallen from 11 per cent in 1917 to 6 per cent by late 1919, and the proportion of horseless peasants from 29 to 18 per cent, the proportion of landholdings larger than twenty-two acres had dropped from 8 to 3 per cent. About four-fifths of peasant households had land areas of less than eleven acres. The proportion of households with more than one horse fell from 16 per cent in 1917 to 8 per cent in 1920 (Yu. Polyakov, *Perekhod k Nepu i sovietskoye krestyanstvo* (1967), 98, 103, 120.

[13] According to figures given by Stalin in 1928 and quoted by M. Dobb in *Russian Economic Development since the Revolution* (1928), 423, total grain production in 1913 and 1926–7 was eighty million and seventy-six million tons respectively. But whereas in 1913 the poorer and middle peasants produced 50 per cent of the grain (with rich peasants producing 38 and landowners 12 per cent), in the year 1926–7 they produced 85 per cent. The amount of grain placed on the home or export market was ten million tons in 1926–7, compared with twenty-one million in 1913.

the peasantry to produce more was a step which weakened socialism. The more the peasant exerted himself in response to the government's plea for more production, the more he prospered and developed bourgeois attitudes. Hence the disputes within the party on the correct attitude towards the peasants. Hence, too, the contradictory nature of the party's pronouncements, with exhortations to the peasants to prosper, and warnings of the fate awaiting rich peasants.

Lenin, who had long preached that the Revolution could only survive on the foundation of a firm and friendly alliance of workers and peasants, had in his last years advocated the encouragement of peasant co-operatives and state-aided agricultural mechanization. He had hoped that this would eventually incline the peasants towards socialist attitudes and away from their bourgeois tendencies. The process would be long, but Lenin cautioned against coercion. The great debate which, intertwined with the struggle between factions of the leadership, dominated the party for the half-dozen years following the death of Lenin, was concerned above all with the problem of how to have productive agriculture without a prosperous 'bourgeois' peasantry. For without productive agriculture industrialization was impossible, and without industrialization there could be no socialism, it was thought.

The industrialization debate

NEP had been accepted by the party as only a temporary retreat from its principles and intentions; following this breathing space there would be another economic offensive and further social reconstruction. The question of how long NEP would continue had never been settled, and from about 1925 a growing number of members favoured an early termination of the policy. This was partly because the question of 'where do we go from here?' became more acute at that time: pre-war industrial production was almost regained by 1926 and further increases could no longer be obtained merely by restoring existing plant.

Nor was it only a question of when. The most bitter dispute in the party was over the question of how. What came to be known as the Left Opposition (Trotsky and his supporters, joined after 1925 by Kamenev and Zinoviev) believed that NEP was a rotten compromise and was too soft towards the rich peasants. What was needed was rapid industrialization, for only thus would Russia become proletarianized and be ready for socialism. In order to raise capital for industrialization, the Left Opposition recommended a squeeze on the peasants, who would be required to sell their products cheaply while buying manufactured goods dearly. Trotsky's theory of Permanent Revolution was quite reconcilable with this industrialization, for the latter would be much more rapid after Germany and other industrial nations had undergone their own revolutions, enabling the proletariat of these more advanced nations to give economic aid to Russia. The so-called moderates (Bukharin, Rykov, Tomsky, and, at first, Stalin) ridiculed the high rates of industrialization advocated by the left. They considered that there should be a slow but steady industrialization. Industry would concentrate on consumer goods, and the availability of the latter would encourage the peasants to produce more; more grain meant more industrialization because it would permit growth of urban labour and of export earnings.

The conflict between these two views concerned means more than ends. Certain basic premises were accepted by all: the party's retention of power; the need to industrialize; the need to prevent *nepmany* profiting from the shortages and confusion which industrialization would entail; the need to absorb the increasing unemployment caused by efficiency drives in industry; the desirability of exploiting the stronger position which the party and government had won over the previous four or five years. By 1927 there were additional reasons for industrialization; there was a genuine fear of war following setbacks in foreign policy, and the policy of maintaining low prices with goods in short supply was simply encouraging *nepmany* to buy cheap and sell dear. In general therefore, the various anti-*nepmany* and industrial measures adopted between 1925 and 1928 had the approval of the whole party. These measures included railway tariff surcharges on 'private' freight, increased taxation of private activities, and the more stringent application of penalties for so-called speculation and hoarding.

Despite the shortage of funds, industrial investment was doubled in the year 1926–7. In that year were started some of the projects which later became famous as examples of economic achievement: the Dnieper hydro-electric scheme, the Stalingrad Tractor Plant, and the last link of the Turkestan–Siberia Railway. Then, in 1927, the Council of People's Commissars called for a national plan of industrialization: the planned economy was about to emerge.

The State Planning Commission (*Gosplan*) had existed since 1921, and some experience of nation-wide planning had been gained in, 'Goelro', a 1920 ten-year plan for electricity production. *Gosplan*, staffed mainly by non-communist economists and statisticians, had at first merely produced sets of control figures. These were forecasts of what the various branches of industry could be expected to produce in a given period. They served as guidelines for economic decisions but were not targets; except for one or two key products, the trusts planned their own outputs and inputs. Later, as statistical services improved, *Gosplan* pioneered the formulation of 'national economic balances'. The latter were quantified analyses of the interconnexions between different branches of industry so that, for example, a statistical forecast could be made of the changes in the forestry industry which would be required for a doubling of the size of newspapers. Such balances (on which the five-year plans would be based) could only be imperfect, because accurate statistics were not always available, and they could only be incomplete, because only the key branches of the economy could be covered by the limited number of clerks and statisticians available. Nevertheless, they were a great step forward in non-capitalist enterprise.

Such were the difficulties encountered in collating and formulating the First Five-Year Plan, a book-size document, that it was presented to the 16th Party Conference only in spring 1929, even though it covered the period October 1928 to September 1933. It was presented in two variants, a standard version and an optimum version with somewhat higher targets. The latter was chosen. Here are the approximate figures for three key industries:

	Coal (million tons)	Oil (million tons)	Pig iron (million tons)
Actual annual output 1927/28	35	12	3
Planned annual output 1932/33	75	22	10
Actual annual output 1932	64	21	6

In reality both variants were over-optimistic. In existing circumstances the target of doubling industrial production over five years seemed impossible; there was simply not enough investment capital available. There was an emphasis on the output of means of production (that is, products which would not be consumed but used to produce additional output): fuel, cement, electricity, metals, timber. Grain was to be exported in exchange for machine tools. These salient aspects made the plan irreconcilable with the views of the 'moderates'. However, Stalin had already politically routed the Trotskyites and could now make final his break with the Bukharinites. As for experts who condemned the plan as too optimistic, these were intimidated by the Shakhty show trial, which convicted several 'bourgeois' technicians of 'sabotaging' a mining enterprise. The road now seemed clear for Stalin's own revolution. This, which Stalin termed 'the intensification of the class struggle', would be first felt in the villages.

Collectivization

Many defenders and detractors of Stalin assume that the mass collectivization of peasants which began in late 1929 was the result of a considered decision. Those who accuse Stalin of Machiavellism suggested that he had chosen collectivization as a solution to Soviet economic problems several years before 1929, but had kept quiet until he had disposed of his rivals. Others explain that investment capital had to be squeezed out of the peasantry, and that collectivization made it easier to procure grain at rock-bottom prices, released labour for the new factories, and by permitting large-scale production made possible increased grain production. However, it seems most likely that mass collectivization resulted from a hasty decision taken at the last moment.

Ever since 1917 there had been a tense expectation each autumn as Moscow received from the provinces accounts of how much grain had been marketed or procured. Fear of famine had perhaps receded during NEP, but the availability of grain for the towns and export was crucial. Under NEP food production had made a rapid recovery, exceeding the pre-war level in 1925. There was plenty of scope for further increase; for example, locusts, rats, and other pests were destroying, according to one Soviet economist, one-third of the potential grain supply, and in 1927 there were five million hopelessly inefficient wooden ploughs still in use.

From the mid-twenties the private grain trader, who often paid the peasant double the state's price for grain, was increasingly restricted. Thus state and co-operative grain-purchasing organizations were in a stronger position, and could progressively lower their procurement prices. In 1924 the peasants' tax-in-kind had been replaced by a money tax, so in order to pay his taxes, as grain prices fell, the peasant would sell increasing amounts of grain. Or at least that was the expectation. In practice, this situation might initially have increased the grain marketed by the peasants, but in time economic reality and human nature triumphed; with grain prices falling and meat prices rising, peasants fed their grain to livestock, and those peasants who could afford to wait kept their surplus grain in the expectation of an increase in the state's purchasing price. At the end of 1927 incoming statistics showed that the grain procurements might be only three-quarters of those of the previous year.

Bukharin and others did advocate an increase in grain prices. For them, War Communism had shown the impossibility of coercing the peasantry. For others, however, War Communism was more an example to be exceeded. Many party members regarded longstanding economic realities simply as remnants of bourgeois thinking; the party which had stormed the Winter Palace was surely capable of overthrowing old economic concepts. So instead of substantially raising grain prices, Stalin went to western Siberia with a retinue which included police officials. Some of Stalin's trusted colleagues went to other grain areas. Using the Criminal Code's article on hoarding and speculation, and backed by police, it was possible to assert that any peasant with stocks of grain had broken the law, and that his grain was therefore liable to confiscation. Despite the soul-searching of local party members and officials, a thorough and sometimes violent programme of grain confiscation was carried out on these lines. These tactics, virtually a return to the forced requisitioning of War Communism, did bring forth needed grain, but also broke the alliance of peasantry and proletariat which Lenin had been so anxious to foster, and which had been delicately recomposed during NEP. Conciliation of the peasantry, as advocated by Bukharin, was no longer practical. However, in early 1928 the 'moderates' had not been eliminated from the party and their criticisms induced Stalin to promise that his extraordinary measures would not be repeated. But the same methods were used the following year.

Partly because of the weather and partly because of a reduction in sown area, the 1928 harvest was poor. Bread rationing was reintroduced. The 1929 harvest was good, yet by August 1929 grain procurements were causing anxiety. The several government and co-operative procuring agencies were unco-ordinated, and there was corruption as well as bad management among their officials. The latter were not as adept at handling grain consignments as had been the private traders (who were finally eliminated in 1929). Peasants saw, or heard, how the grain which had been forced from them was left to rot in unprotected storage. The few state and collective farms were as reluctant as the independent peasants to deliver their grain; in 1929 some farms were even 'decollectivized' as a punishment for this recalcitrance. Some local party officials complained that after requisitioning no grain was left for local consumption or even for seed. By October there was extensive though unorganized peasant violence which might conceivably, given leadership, have been transformed into a new Pugachov rebellion. At this point *Pravda* began to hint about mass collectivization.

Hitherto the party had accepted only a gradual increase of *kolkhozy* (collective, co-operative, or communal farms) and of *sovkhozy* (state farms with wage-earning peasants). In 1928 about 3 per cent of the acreage was farmed by these organizations. The Five-Year Plan envisaged that up to 20 per cent of agricultural output would come from *kolkhozy* or *sovkhozy* by 1933. Collectivization was to be voluntary but the supply of tractors and combines to collectives was expected to prove a great inducement to join. The party, including Stalin, had accepted that a faster rate of collectivization was out of the question. Agricultural experts and rural party administrators were too few, tractors and machinery were still scarce.

Thus large-scale collectivization was regarded as impractical for the time being. Yet early in November 1929, just as Bukharin lost his seat in the Politburo, Stalin announced the decision to begin mass collectivization immediately. In December he declared the intention 'to liquidate the kulaks as a class'. In reality there was no such thing as a kulak class. In tsarist times *kulak* had referred to those rich peasants who lent money or services at extortionate rates to their poorer neighbours. When Stalin spoke of kulaks in 1929 he meant the richer peasants. These kulaks were hardly a class; they were an integral part of the villages, having family ties with poorer neighbours. They often set an example of good agricultural technique, they often owned machinery (including tractors) which they hired out at reasonable rates, they were usually respected by their neighbours, and more than others they responded to official encouragements to grow and sell more grain. During the forced procurements of 1928 and 1929 they had been hard pressed. Evidently seeing which way the wind was blowing, many had reduced their operations so as to merge into the mass of 'middle peasants' (the press hinted that this 'selfdekulakization' was some kind of conspiracy). In many localities, their land and implements had been confiscated because of alleged speculation, but in autumn 1929 the most serious action which the party Central Committee was prepared to take against them 'as a class' was to exclude them from collective farms.

What happened in the three months between Stalin's December announcement and his statement in March 1930 that 58 per cent of peasant households had been collectivized was ghastly. Party officials and members, often unwillingly, obeyed the instruction to 'fan the class war' in the villages. Poor peasants were invited to rob the richer. Of the so-called kulaks, some were sent to concentration camps and their families deported, others were merely deported to inhospitable regions. Some, lucky or regarded as innocuous, were allowed to stay in their district and were allocated land considered too poor to be worth collectivizing. This last group were subsequently eliminated by the imposition of impossible grain-delivery quotas, followed by deportation for failure to deliver. Peasants who resisted collectivization were classed as kulaks, or 'ideological kulaks', or 'subkulaks', and treated in the same way. At least a million families, or about six million people, were transported or expelled from their home villages as kulaks. A 1988 estimate was as high as one-eighth of the twenty-five million peasant families. Calculation is hampered by the circumstance that the number of those who set out was more than those who arrived. The conditions of the transportation were not, as was later said, an anticipation of Hitler's Final Solution; they set a standard of depravity that Hitler never quite attained:

The old party member E. M. Landau in 1930 met one of these batches in Siberia. In the depth of winter a big group of kulaks with their families were being taken on carts 300 kilometres into the backwoods of the region. The children were shouting and crying from hunger. One of the peasants, who could no longer stand the cries of a baby sucking the dry breast of its mother, seized the infant from his wife's arms and smashed its head against a tree.[14]

The fundamental idiocy of the campaign is indicated by the 58 per cent collectivization claimed in March. To explain how such a massive rural reconstruction could be carried out in a few weeks at the height of the Russian winter must surely have strained the wits of the most flexible propagandist. What typically happened was that party or government activists, with police or military support, would persuade or force peasants to sign a register signifying their demand for collectivization. Then the party organization would duly report another village collectivized. Stock, implements, and buildings taken from the 'kulaks' usually formed the basis of the new collective farms.

By March in many localities the peasants were still in a state of rebellion, and so were some party members. Since the spring sowing could not be postponed, the breakneck speed of collectivization was slackened. Stalin blamed local officials for so-called excesses. Making them look like fools, he accused them of being 'giddy with success':

... by 20 February 1930 we had over-fulfilled the five year plan for collectivization by more than 100 per cent . . . but successes have their dark side, especially when they are achieved with relative 'ease'—'unexpectedly' as it were. Such successes sometimes induce a spirit of conceit and vanity . . . people not infrequently become intoxicated by this kind of success . . . Can we assert that the voluntary principle and the principle of taking local peculiarities into account are not violated in some areas? No, unfortunately we cannot say that . . . we know that in a number of areas of Turkestan there have been already attempts to 'catch up and overtake' the advanced areas of the USSR by the threat of using armed force, by the threat that peasants who are not yet prepared to join the collective farms will be deprived of irrigation water and of manufactured goods . . . Is it not clear that the authors of these distortions, imagining themselves to be 'Lefts', are really serving Right opportunism? . . . One such over-zealous 'socializer' even goes so far as to issue an order to an *artel* including the following instructions: 'all poultry of all households are to be registered within three days' . . . to say nothing of those revolutionaries (pardon the expression!) who *begin* the work of organizing *artels* by removing the church bells. Just think, removing church bells—how very revolutionary![15]

Thus, just as in tsarist times, the peasants were led to believe that their misery was due to the officials interposed between them and their 'little father' at the top. When Stalin announced that those peasants who so wished could quit the collectives, there was an immediate exodus. By June 1930 only 24 per cent of peasants were collectivized. However, a new drive, coercive but less hasty, brought 98 per cent of agricultural land into collective or state farms by 1941. The village commune, which in the twenties

---

[14] *Novyi mir*, No. 3 (1988), 18, quoting the historian R. Medvedev.
[15] *Pravda*, 2 March 1930.

tended to be much more influential than the village soviet, was abolished by decree in 1930.

A natural consequence of the upheaval was the deaths of millions of peasants in the rural famine of 1932–3. This famine, which may have equalled that of 1921–2, was not admitted and there was therefore no appeal for foreign aid, despite the agricultural glut which the capitalist world was enduring at that time. Not only the peasants' winter supply, but also sometimes seed grain, was requisitioned. The resultant famine was very much man-made, and affected the Ukraine in particular. How far it was deliberate, as opposed to merely irresponsible, is still debated. What is certain, and symptomatic, is that to discourage the starving peasants from stealing their own grain, intended for the towns or for export, the death penalty was extended to 'pilfering'.

At the height of the collectivization campaign many peasants slaughtered their cattle, rather than see them taken and collectivized. For those cattle which were collectivized, fate was often crueller: they froze to death because there were no large barns for them. Slaughter of horses meant that the shortage of farm tractive power became even more acute. By 1932 the cattle and pig population was half that of 1928, and the sheep population two-thirds. Urban communists sent to supervise the new collectives were ignorant of agriculture. Food production dropped abruptly and recovered very slowly; on the eve of the Second World War production may have even been lower than on the eve of the First World War.[16] For three decades after 1929 the Russian diet remained deficient in protein.

According to Churchill, Stalin privately admitted that the years of forced collectivization and famine had been the most frightening of his life. And well they might have been; many party members, as well as Stalin's wife Allilueva, committed suicide in this period. The why and the how of the 1930 collectivization still needs research, but it would seem that it was simply an emergency measure against peasants rebelling, violently and non-violently, against the injustice and wastefulness of forced procurements. Paradoxically, the uproar in the countryside strengthened Stalin's position in the party. Even those who suspected the truth realized that Stalin was the leader most capable of mastering a peasant uprising.

Despite the elimination of the most productive peasant farmers, collectivization was regarded as having at least enabled agriculture to supply the capital and labour required for industrialization. But even this is not certain. It is true that procuring grain from collectives was relatively easy, but

[16] The uncertainty of this assertion is due to the inadequacies of tsarist as well as Soviet grain statistics.

the total grain available was reduced. It is true that peasants left the farms to work in industry, but this was simply because industrialization and rural poverty made it advantageous for them to do so.[17] Collectivization did not raise labour productivity. It did eliminate rural unemployment since the unemployed were absorbed into the collectives, but collectivized peasants did not work so hard as the uncollectivized ones. It seems likely, therefore, that collective farms were able to stand the initial loss of workers to the towns, not because they economized on labour, but because there had been a labour surplus before collectivization. In the twenties, Russian agriculture was undercapitalized, overpopulated, and had no easy way of increasing the arable land available. Until tractors and machinery were plentiful, collective farming in itself could solve none of these problems. And despite crash programmes and much talk of 'tractorization', there would remain an insufficiency of farm tractive power for several decades.

The choice facing the party in 1929 was not simply the choice between Stalin's mass collectivization and Bukharin's appeasement of the peasants. The circumstances allowed of other solutions. The twenties had shown that the individual peasant receiving a fair price for his products could be highly taxed, and that so long as he was not driven to desperation he was not a threat to the regime. Co-operatives (which collectivization effectively eliminated) had shown their potential. The twenties had also suggested that the individual peasant could be highly productive if provided with the unspectacular tools of efficient small-scale agriculture. Perhaps, to a revolutionary party, tractors and big fields had greater emotional appeal than fertilizers and mousetraps, but the thirties would not have been so hungry if investment had been made less in tractors and more in fertilizers and pest control, and if the premature shift from small-scale to large-scale farming had been postponed.

The collective farm

Collective farms, varying from simple co-operatives to establishments of 100 per cent communal ownership, had been set up on a small and experimental scale well before 1929. As confirmed by the Model Collective Farm Charter of 1935, the post-collectivization form of *kolkhoz* was the so-called *artel*. This was not regarded as a completely socialist form of production, but at least it was not capitalistic. Members of a *kolkhoz* pooled their implements and livestock in order to make production a communal task.

---

[17] In some years they left in such embarrassingly large numbers that measures were taken to restrict their movement. When, in 1932, the old tsarist internal passports were revived, they were issued only to urban-dwellers. The peasant had to apply for official documentary permission to move from his village.

¹ They were granted the use of the land, though not its ultimate ownership. Their main task was the cultivation of the collective land, but each household was allowed to keep its own private plot of up to one acre, and could keep privately a cow, a pig, four sheep, and unlimited fowl. Moreover, the private animals could be pastured on collective land.

A typical *kolkhoz* consisted of from 50 to 100 households, was generally rather decrepit-looking with few, if any, new or even painted buildings. Its chairman was unlikely to know much about farming, and was usually newly-appointed, for this office had a high turnover, as each incumbent was dismissed by the local party secretary for failure to reach one or other of the production targets. The latter were frequently fixed at an impossible level so as to squeeze the maximum effort from the peasants. Although nominally organized democratically, with the members meeting in an assembly, in reality decisions were made by the farm chairman. Additional supervision was exercised by the management of the local machine and tractor station (MTS). The MTS were established to make the best use of the scarce tractors and farm machinery. They kept, manned, and maintained these machines, hiring them out to the surrounding collective farms.

Collective farmers were credited with 'workdays' in exchange for their labour on the collective fields. The workday value varied according to the quality of the particular kind of work,[18] so that it was possible to earn more than one workday in a working day. Peasants received no wage, but at the end of the agricultural year the profits of the farm were divided among the peasants in proportion to the workdays credited. Payments were also made in produce (usually grain) according to the same principle. In Stalin's lifetime the cash received by the peasant was negligible or non-existent; agricultural prices were deliberately kept low, so that very few farms made any profit. At the same time, prices of products bought by the peasants were allowed to rise steeply (cloth by up to ten times, sugar by six times).

The first priority of the collective farm was to meet its procurement quota of grain or other products. This delivery to the state was at very low prices; the state sold it in the towns at higher, but still low, prices (thus providing cheap food). If the state quotas were met peasants could sell the surplus on the free market. The latter, in its legal and typical form, was a few stalls in a nearby town where peasant women purveyed food to urban-dwellers. The main significance of this market, which was a bastion of free enterprise in a socialized economy, was that peasants could sell there the products from their own private plot and livestock. Food was short, and

[18] In the nineteenth century the French observer Le Play had noticed a similar workday scheme applied by landowners in southern Russia.

products like meat, eggs, butter, honey, fruit, and vegetables could fetch a good price. Thus it was more profitable for the peasant to work his own small private economy than to work on the collective fields. Even though from 1939 each able-bodied peasant was obliged to contribute a minimum number of workdays to the collective, he still worked more enthusiastically on his own plot.

13. *The Thirties*

Industrialization

THE incredibly high demands of the First Five-Year Plan were met in some quarters with enthusiasm, in others with pessimism, and in yet others with apathy. Among the apathetic were no doubt the majority of those peasants who, to escape the miseries of collectivized agriculture, went to the towns to work in the new industries. Thanks to their influx the industrial labour force doubled during the plan, as against an expected increase of about one quarter. Among the pessimists were some economists, as well as managers faced with targets which they knew were unfulfillable. Those who voiced their doubts were soon discredited; some were convicted of 'sabotage' or 'wrecking' while others simply disappeared. The enthusiasts included probably the majority of the party; that is, the party's outward enthusiasm was, or became, genuine. The transformation of the USSR into a great industrial power was indeed something to get excited about. Many workers, and especially the young, were similarly inspired by the great task. Those workers and young people who in the next few years would volunteer to work on distant projects under arduous conditions really did believe in the worth of what they were doing and were prepared to make sacrifices for its achievement. If industrialization was to really get going, the discouragement of the pessimists and the encouragement of the enthusiasts was probably essential. But it was taken too far; if some of the voices urging moderation had been heeded, the industrialization drive might have been accompanied by less inefficiency, fewer disasters, and less chaos. Moreover, enthusiasm soon turned to over-enthusiasm; by the end of 1929 it was already decided to complete the programme of the First Five-Year Plan in four years. Even then, targets were raised in succeeding years.

At the end of 1932 Stalin declared that the plan had been fulfilled or over-fulfilled in its main sectors. In reality, most branches of industry had under-fulfilled their targets, but nevertheless almost all had achieved remarkably large increases of production. Electric power production, for example, had almost trebled, but its target had been much higher. Similarly, coal and iron ore both doubled their output. Steel production achieved only a one-third increase, compared with a planned increase of two and a half times. The chemical industry did badly, which implied a shortage of artificial fertilizers (but by this time Stalin was persuaded that fertilizers were over-rated—see p. 381). The railways had been deliberately starved of resources; a few lines had been built or doubletracked, but main reliance had been placed on the utilization of unused capacity. It was in consumer goods that the shortfalls were most marked. Targets for these had been comparatively low from the start, and even these were not fulfilled. Woollen textiles actually declined during the plan, instead of trebling as intended. Small-scale handicraft industry, once important for supplying consumer goods, had practically disappeared. The urban housing situation, which had been bad in 1928, was abysmal by 1932.

In the coal and metallurgical industries the bulk of the investment was in the old region of the Don Basin, but a decision was made to create a second iron and steel base east of the Urals. This was the Urals–Kuznetsk Basin Combine. The ores of Magnitogorsk in the Urals and the coal of the Kuzbas (1,250 miles to the east) were to be exploited by new furnaces in both locations, with trains conveying coal westwards and ore eastwards. Artificially low rail tariffs disguised the fundamental inefficiency of this scheme. Even so, it was probably justified, for the need of vastly increased steel capacity, and the strategic desirability of locating such an industry far from the frontiers, outweighed conventional profit-and-loss considerations.

In general, efficiency took second place. There was much investment in high-cost projects, and so much emphasis was laid on target fulfilment in terms of gross output that efficiency of production was mainly ignored. A manager was more likely to lose his job for non-fulfilment of plan than for compelling his workers to work more than the legal hours, or relaxing safety precautions, or even for poor quality of output. Managers acquired greater responsibility in this period. On the one hand the individual enterprise was made the basic unit of management (the former functions of the trusts and the Supreme Economic Council were largely taken over in 1932 by four ministries: the people's commissariats of heavy industry, light industry, timber and food . At the same time 'one-man management' was re-established; the enterprise party organization and the trade union branch lost their power over the manager. (But local party secretaries, or party troubleshooters sent from Moscow, could and did interfere.)

The waste, chaos, confusion, and mismanagement of these years of break-neck industrialization were enormous. There were many instances of expensive plant being ruined by untrained workers. To a large extent the blame for such breakdowns was laid on 'wreckers' and 'saboteurs' who were taken to court and usually convicted. It was at these show trials that men like Vyshinsky gained the experience in stage-management which they would utilize in the political trials of the late thirties. Typically the victims were the old bourgeois specialists; those technically educated men of the pre-1917 generation who had continued their professions under the new regime. At the Metrovick Trial, British specialists were involved.[1]

The Second Five-Year Plan (1933–7) was also ambitious, but in its first year of operation was rewritten. This change was occasioned by the realization that things could not go on in the same way; a limit had been reached in what the economy could do and what the people could take. Living conditions were by this time horrifying, initial enthusiasms of the First Plan had worn off, and the population had become too apathetic to respond to any further coercion. Despite police and party precautions, there had been street demonstrations in several towns in 1932, following a reduction of food rations. There was a feeling in the party that Stalin had again overdone things. So the Second Plan was modified. The Great Leap Forward had been leapt and henceforth consolidation, the improvement of efficiency and technique, and better living standards were to be emphasized. For three years things did get better. Together with increases in most fields of production there was a perceptible improvement in living standards, projects uncompleted in the First Plan began to contribute to the economy, new mining projects were opened in Central Asia and a start made in developing a second oil area in the Urals–Volga region.

But from 1937 growth rates slackened. In the high-priority iron and steel industry, output actually declined in 1938. This may partly have been due to the dislocations caused by the increased emphasis on armaments production, but the main cause was almost certainly the purges which were then taking place. Not only were thousands of key technicians and managers removed to labour camps, where there was little scope for their talents, but those who inherited their jobs took care to avoid making decisions whenever possible. The Third Five-Year Plan (1938–42) was curtailed by the war. It envisaged a doubling of production and, like the Second, promised an increase in consumer goods production which did not materialize in full. It also witnessed an abrupt shift to military production; by 1940 armaments approached one-third of total industrial production. During

---

[1] Many foreign specialists were employed in Soviet industry at this period, some as consultants and others as employees of foreign companies supplying equipment or building factories for the USSR. The Metrovick Trial took place just as the USSR was becoming less dependent on such foreign help. The British subjects found guilty were later released.

the first years of this plan there were signs of strain; there was a fuel crisis, caused largely by the failure of the oil industry to meet its not especially high goals, and there was a severe labour shortage. However, the total productive capacity of the USSR was strengthened by the territorial acquisitions of 1939–40. Interestingly, the planned economy as it expanded was not without its booms and troughs. There were two periods of very fast growth (1928–30 and 1934–6) and two of slow growth. Over-investment in the first three years seems to have been responsible for the hesitant growth of the following period (in 1930 there was an absolute decline of production and productivity for some months). However, the effects of collectivization and purges, as well as the destabilizing shift to war production in the late thirties, were very influential.

Statistics of this period are very unreliable and would be misleading even if they were not. One difficulty is that output figures do not reflect quality of product: in these years quality in terms of design or specification usually improved, but quality of production often declined. For example, Soviet steel output began to include higher quality steels that previously had not been produced, but which were very necessary for new engineering products, yet at the same time rails produced by the same steel industry had an increasingly high breakage rate.

Although American technology was favoured, if not revered, there were a few instances when home-grown technology produced very superior results. Synthetic rubber, the celebrated T34 tank of World War 2, and long-distance electricity transmission were instances of this. But most technology was imported and, because of the obsessional reluctance to interrupt production flows to change designs, the imported models remained in production while foreign industries advanced to new improvements. For example, when the automobile factory at Gorki was organized by Ford engineers, the existing American motor truck design was used and this remained in production after Ford had produced far better designs in the USA and elsewhere. Moreover, the very superior Ford v-8 engine was introduced in America just as the Gorki plant was getting into its stride, and it was not adopted for Soviet production. Also, new technology was concentrated on a few favoured sectors. Some industries, like construction and the railways, had a very small share of this particular cake; the railways' dieselization programme, which was in advance of the rest of the world, was ended by Kaganovich in the mid-thirties.

Thus the Soviet lag in technology that attracted so much comment in the 1980s had its roots in the 1930s. All the same, despite the failures, despite (or because of) the savage drop in real wages since 1928 and the decline of food consumption per head over the same period, by 1941 the main aim of

Stalin's policy of rapid industrialization had been achieved. The USSR, though politically demoralized, was one of the world's great industrial powers.

The planned economy

Fundamentally, the system of economic planning which evolved during the twenties and thirties was designed to do two things; to co-ordinate the activities of the various branches of production, and to make optimum choices between alternative methods, techniques, investments, and other economic strategies. In the classical capitalist economy these goals were attained, more or less, by the adjustment of supply and demand through the price medium. In the USSR the aim was to replace financial regulators with a system of economic administration which would itself decide how resources should be allocated, what should be produced and how, where, and when.

By the end of the thirties almost all state enterprises were subordinated to a people's commissariat (ministry) specializing in one or another branch of industry.[2] Plans were evolved for various periods. The Five-Year Plans, which received the most publicity, were perspective plans for the national economy which could be modified during their term; they laid down the general direction. There were also one-year and quarterly plans which had a more operational nature, were more detailed, and which individual enterprises observed very closely. The Five-Year Plans were legislative acts, so that failure to meet a plan's target could be treated as a criminal offence. Bonuses were payable to those enterprises which over-fulfilled the plan. In theory enterprises had a say in the formulation of the plan, for draft plans were submitted to scrutiny by the enterprises and by workers' meetings before being formally promulgated. This gave an opportunity for alterations suggested 'from below', although in the Stalin period such suggestions took the form of 'spontaneous' demands that the enterprise in question be set even higher targets. Detailed plans were worked out by each ministry for its own enterprises on the basis of the general targets set for that industry. *Gosplan* was the co-ordinator of the plans, and the intermediary between the industries and the party. It was the party which decided the general economic strategy and set targets for key industries, and it was the party's representatives who checked on the fulfilment of the plans and who could

---

[2] By 1941 the Council of People's Commissars had expanded to 27 industrial and 9 'traditional' ministries, and 6 chairmen of key committees. The industrial commissariats ranged from heavy industry to fisheries. By 1947 new industrial ministries brought the total to 60. Under Khruschev there was a short-lived reduction followed by an increase. In the late 1980s an amalgamation of ministries reduced them from 55 to 37.

intervene in critical sectors and override local management. (A high-level example of this was the Politburo's dispatch in 1935 of Kaganovich to take command of the railways when industrialization seemed to be threatened by a new transport crisis.) A disadvantage of the system was its demand for paperwork. In practice, much of the feverish activity in planning organs was nothing but paperwork; as always in Russia, there was a wide divergence between what was intended to occur, what was said to occur, and what did occur. The essential reality of the Soviet planned economy was that the party, acting through *Gosplan*, imposed priorities for the key industries and was in a position to ensure that the priorities were observed. The economy and its problems were less complex than they would be twenty years later. Thus the system worked reasonably well in the thirties, was admirably suited to wartime with its ruthless fixing of priorities, but was unsuitable in later years.

Personal predilections of Stalin sometimes occasioned serious errors. He eliminated 'pessimistic' statisticians and economists, replacing them with those who would present the figures he wanted. In the absence of voices pointing out errors in good time, there was a tendency for mistakes to be big mistakes. Relative neglect of the oil industry and over-reliance on coal was one mistake. So was the investment in inland waterways at a time when the railways could have made more productive use of capital. Two contradictory policies sometimes coexisted, as with machine tools, where the policy of concentrating on the mass production of a few basic types (mainly designed in tsarist days) conflicted with the policy of producing small runs of highly specialized tools. There was serious over-investment in the mechanical engineering industries, which meant that new plant was under-utilized. But the capitalist economies made big mistakes too; at least the USSR avoided the cult of the automobile. Above all, Stalin's system got things done, and in Russia this is always a rather special achievement.

Labour

There had never been a deep-rooted trade union tradition in tsarist Russia, so the subordination of the Soviet trade unions to the needs of the government (as opposed to the needs of the workers) was not perhaps surprising. During the thirties Stalin actually accused trade union leaders of 'trade-unionism', but long before then it was clear that workers' organizations would not be allowed to obstruct the government.

After the Revolution, Bolshevik trade unionists tended to put the workers before the party, and Lenin in 1920 was still trying to persuade them that it was not the role of the workers to provide management. At that time many enterprises had a workers' representative at the top, with specialists (that is, members of the old managerial or technical staff) to guide him. Others had a specialist manager, supervised by one or more commissars representing the workers. During the NEP the '*troika*' system became common, with management consisting of a specialist (usually 'bourgeois'), a trade unionist, and a party representative. All these combinations attempted to utilize the experience of the old managers and the political vigilance of the new class, but they all led to confusion, or at least inefficiency, and Stalin was right to re-introduce one-man management.

Trotsky in 1920 advocated the militarization of labour to meet the crisis of that time. Such a subjection of workers to martial law did occur, notably on the railways, but was not generally accepted. In the twenties, trade unionist Bolsheviks like Tomsky were in a difficult situation; they felt the privations of the workers deeply, yet could not allow labour movements to hinder the party's policies. Thus although there were strikes in protest against low wages and poor conditions, these did not usually have union backing. For the union leaders, production was already the priority, although they were consulted on matters of welfare, and although workers did participate in factory consultative councils (where they did little, but gained experience of managerial problems). In the thirties the trade unions became completely docile. Many of their officials suffered in the purges, and there was a shameful neglect of industrial safety and working conditions.

During the twenties there was considerable unemployment, amounting to one and a half million in 1929. But unemployment was fully absorbed by the demands of the First Five-Year Plan. The number of workers doubled to twenty-three million by 1932. The eight-hour day for industrial workers had been introduced in 1917, and in 1939 there was a short-lived and partial seven-hour day. But in 1940 a reduction of wage-rates was accompanied by a reinstatement of the eight-hour day. Compulsory overtime was significant. Total working hours, however, could be adjusted by other means: by 1940 national holidays had been reduced to seven,[3] and the working week was also changed. Many industries worked non-stop and individual workers had different rest days (making it difficult for couples to have the same day off). The abolition of Sunday as a day of rest gave additional scope (as well as disorganizing church attendance). In 1939 workers were allowed to rest every sixth day (this gave a five-day working week, but because of the 'abolition' of Sundays was not the same as the five-day week proposed in other countries). But in 1940 there was a reversion to a

---

[3] These holidays were New Year's Day (which served as a substitute for Christmas), 1 and 2 May, plus Lenin Day (22 January), October Revolution Anniversary (7 and 8 November), and Constitution Day (5 December).

rest every seventh day, and Sunday was re-established as the general rest-day.

Women workers made a come-back from their low percentage in the 1920s. In 1914 they had been about 30 per cent of the workers in large-scale industry, and about 40 per cent by 1917, but the subsequent decline of industry meant that only in the mid-thirties did the proportion regain the 1917 level. But then it rose rapidly; women were valued because many were already urban-dwellers so did not require housing, and married women tended to change jobs less frequently than men. They began to enter industries formerly considered unsuitable; while continuing to predominate in textiles, for example, by 1935 they also accounted for almost a quarter of the coal industry's labour force.

However, most of the new workers recruited in the thirties were peasants. There was an enormous influx in the First Plan and this raised many problems. Despite emergency measures it was impossible to train them properly, so that much inefficiency, as well as accidents to people and machinery, resulted. The peasant was unused to factory discipline. By tradition he tended to slacken his effort as soon as his earnings covered his necessities; after a certain point he preferred leisure to money, an attitude inappropriate to modern industry. He was used to working hard and long at certain seasons and taking things easy at other times, and this attitude, far from being eradicated, was transferred to industry; as late as the eighties the party was condemning '*stormovik*' methods (slack work in the first part of a planning period followed by a feverish effort to reach the production target at the eleventh hour). The new worker did not always realize that work could go on when it rained, or that punctuality was essential, or that a recalcitrant machine could not be cured by a hammer or a smear of grease. In these years it was quite typical for workers to change their jobs four or five times a year, making it even more difficult to train them.[4] After the peasants, the next most important source of new labour was women, and in these years educated females took over much of general medicine and school teaching, while the less educated became labourers or factory workers.

Wages were usually piece-rate, to provide incentive. In the thirties the difference between the highest and the lowest rates of pay was very much widened to provide yet more incentive (in 1934 rationing was abolished

---

[4] It was for such reasons, and because of managerial inexperience, that the early projects were so inefficient. The Stalingrad tractor plant, for example, was finished several months ahead of schedule by its American constructors but it needed another three years to reach its planned output. The American-built Gorki automobile works, approved in 1929, began production in 1932 but then stopped because of component shortages. Up to World War 2 it never reached its planned output. See *Slavic Review* (1990) No. 2, 200–12.

and prices allowed to rise). There were also psychological incentives, such as the award of honours to outstanding workers or teams. In the Second Plan labour productivity improved, partly because training programmes were taking effect. There was also the Stakhanovite Movement. Stakhanov was a Donbas miner who produced several times the normal tonnage of coal per manshift, using more intelligent work organization. His example was widely publicized and others invited to emulate him. Thus there appeared in all branches of the economy men who vastly exceeded the norm and were duly rewarded with red carpets, cash prizes, trips to Moscow, and medals. Once these men had proved it could be done, their exceptional output was treated as the norm for all. That is, the base piece-work rate was fixed at the new output. Since there was often a good deal of chicanery in the making of a Stakhanovite (he might be given the best tools and assistants and materials), the Stakhanovite Movement soon attracted intense but unacknowledged unpopularity, but it was not until the fifties that its shortcomings were acknowledged. However, despite its injustice and its blatant exploitation of man by man, it did emphasize that existing plant was capable of greater output, and it was used to demonstrate the alleged conservatism of managements. Many managers who realized that Stakhanovism was doing more harm than good in their enterprises or industries were purged, and it is arguable that purges were essential for the Stakhanovite Movement.

During the Second and Third plans there was increasing control of the working force. At the same time, extra financial incentive was provided by the 'voluntary' purchase by workers of state bonds (equalling, on average, two weeks' pay per year). Absenteeism, which previously was punishable merely by dismissal (and the consequent loss of welfare benefits such as factory housing), in 1940 became a crime: second offences brought a gaol sentence, and twenty minutes lateness was counted as absence. Nobody was allowed to change jobs except in exceptional circumstances. School-leavers were drafted to certain key jobs where there was a labour shortage (those who were drafted to the railways were trained on short narrow-gauge 'children's railways' set up in public parks). Earlier, labour books had been issued, to be carried by all workers; these listed an individual's jobs, misdemeanours, and qualifications. Like a report card, unfavourable entries could have serious repercussions. Most of these measures remained in force until the fifties.

The party and the purges

In 1928 the differences between Stalin and the 'moderates', especially Bukharin, Tomsky, and Rykov, came to a head. Although the dispute was not publicized, it is apparent that Bukharin not only concluded that Stalin was no longer in sympathy with his ideas, but that he was totally unscrupulous. Unwisely, Bukharin turned to his former enemy Kamenev for support. This not only gave Stalin a new accusation to level at him, but also disconcerted Bukharin's fellow-moderates, who had long been struggling against Kamenev's 'left'. By this time Bukharin and Stalin differed not only on economic policy, but also on foreign policy. Stalin insisted that the Communist International (of which Bukharin was the chairman) should mobilize the communist parties of Europe against the non-communist left, whereas Bukharin believed that European communists should be fighting the emergent fascist movement in alliance with the other socialist parties. In January 1929, Bukharin published an article in *Pravda* in which he recalled Lenin's exhortation to the party to move from the political struggle, which had been won, to a policy of non-violent persuasion and co-operation between worker and peasant. Since Stalin was at this time already suggesting the 'rekindling of the class struggle' it was clear against whom the article was directed.

In April 1929 Stalin attacked the moderates before the Central Committee, accusing them of aiding the counter-revolution by defending the kulaks, and of consorting with the already condemned 'leftists' of the Kamenev group. The moderate leaders were duly reprimanded. In summer 1929, as soon as his industrialization policy had been approved by the 16th Party Conference, Stalin felt strong enough to pursue his former allies further; Tomsky was replaced by the Stalinist Shvernik as head of the trade union organization, and in November that year Bukharin was obliged to relinquish his membership of the Politburo. Rykov, the most innocuous of the trio, was not ejected until the following year from his premiership (which he had held ever since he had succeeded Lenin in the post). In late 1929 the three attempted to restore their position in the party by accepting the condemnation of the Central Committee. However, the latter condemned this acceptance as insufficiently humble, because the trio had not completely admitted the error of their ways. The three thereupon presented an amended version in which they fully acknowledged their sins and promised to fight against future deviations from the party's line. Thus there was no opposition a month later when Stalin announced his intention 'to liquidate the kulaks as a class'. As for the dispersed leftists, many made their peace when they realized that Stalin in his new industrialization policy was in fact adopting their own proposals. Even Trotsky, in exile, could not condemn Stalin unreservedly. Meanwhile, a new purge of the party took place in 1929 and 1930. This was especially severe in the rural areas, where many party members had shrunk from their collectivizing tasks. Moderates were again badly affected by this series of expulsions, which removed a tenth of the membership. Moreover, fear of being branded as a 'rightist' discouraged members from criticizing the new policies of the party.

In mid-1931, Stalin began to transform the party into a primarily white-collar organization. Hitherto white-collar workers, although by this time regarded as part of the intelligentsia, had not enjoyed great prestige, for it was the working class which was the pride and joy of the party; traditionally, non-manual work had been regarded as a refuge of the bourgeois-minded. But with the five-year plans the manager and the administrator became key figures, and it was desirable to associate them more closely with the party. Managers who were members would, among other things, be more likely to understand and apply the wishes of the party. Moreover, Stalin argued, the old dependence on bourgeois specialists was becoming a thing of the past as more and more workers or sons of workers were taking over managerial positions. Hence there was a recruiting drive among the intelligentsia, the eventual aim being to ensure that most managers, and perhaps all top managers and administrators, should be party members. This aim was in the main achieved, although it meant that over succeeding decades more and more white-collar employees joined the party to further their own promotion prospects, rather than for reasons of deep political conviction.

In early 1933 party recruitment was stopped for three years while the party underwent the first stages of its most serious purge. Throughout the half-century after 1917 there was a tendency for the party to increase its membership at times of crisis. The Civil War was one such crisis, the new revolution of 1929–32 was another. When a crisis was over, the need for broad support was diminished and the party reduced its ranks, striving by means of the purge technique to dispense with its least valuable members: the drunkards, the moral degenerates, the self-seekers, the unenthusiastic. The purge of 1933–5 can partly be explained in this light, especially as a disproportionate number of the expellees were those who had been recruited in preceding mass-membership campaigns (during which admission standards had been lowered). However, there was a definite attempt to use this purge as a means of expelling members suspected of critical views towards the party line as laid down by Stalin. The exhortation to purge 'enemies and deceivers' as well as other degenerates meant that the party leadership was determined to weed out of the lower ranks of the party those members who might one day support Stalin's rivals. Including those members who voluntarily withdrew from the party, this purge reduced membership by no less than one-third. Before it was completed, it was overtaken by a new and bloody purge which followed the murder of Kirov in 1934.

The party's unpopularity in 1933 even exceeded its unpopularity of a decade earlier. The violence, death, destruction, and officially sanctioned robbery of collectivization had turned the peasantry into such enemies of the regime that the murder of rural communists was quite common. Possibly, by 1933 the party was equally disliked by the town workers; the enthusiasms of 1929 had been dissipated by hunger, privation, overcrowding, and regimentation by party bosses. Stalin, and men of his type, flourished in such times just as they had flourished during War Communism; at times of confusion and peril such men were needed for the party to survive.

For some time, it seems, some party members had been discussing the possibility of moderating the breakneck pace of industrialization, giving the masses more food and clothing and living space, and replacing Stalin by a less unbalanced leader. Led by M. Ryutin, they drew up a 200-page alternative party programme which, among other things, criticized Stalin's power-hunger. Not many party members read this, but Stalin did, for informers were very active. The leaders were sent into exile for fifteen years. There seems little doubt from the evidence of subsequent émigrés, and later revelations by Khrushchev, that Stalin wished to execute these dissidents (hitherto, disgraced members suffered a more-or-less comfortable exile, living in distant parts under police supervision, as in tsarist times). It also seems that Stalin's wish to treat party opponents in the way non-party opponents had been treated in the past, that is, to unleash terror tactics against former comrades, was resisted by his fellow-Politburo members. Of the nine full members of the Politburo, only Molotov and Kaganovich were sufficiently devoted to Stalin to support him on this. The others, willing to support Stalin in most things, were either reluctant (Voroshilov and Kalinin) or entirely opposed (Kirov, Kossior, Ordzhonikidze, Kuibyshev, and Rudzutak). This analysis is supported by the fact that none of the five last-named survived the upheavals of the next few years. Nor did Ryutin. He was secretly tried in 1937 and shot. Of his immediate family, all but one daughter were subsequently killed.

It may have been Kirov who was the most moderate of the Politburo members at this time, and it would have been Kirov who was regarded by many as a suitable replacement for Stalin. He was popular, he was handsome, and above all he was a Russian. At the 17th Party Congress of 1934 he appears to have received as much applause as Stalin himself, an ominous distinction. At this Congress there were signs that Stalin read the portents and was prepared to hasten more slowly. The targets for the Second

Five-Year Plan were indeed more modest than those of the First; so-called former oppositionists (including Bukharin, Zinoviev, Kamenev) were allowed to address the Congress, and the new Central Committee elected by the Congress included men who had opposed Stalin in the past. Even Bukharin, Tomsky, and Rykov were elected as candidate members. The new Central Committee elected a new Politburo whose nine members included only two totally loyal Stalinists (Molotov and Kaganovich), and three who might well oppose Stalin (Ordzhonikidze, Kirov, Kossior). The new Party Secretariat had three assistant secretaries under the General Secretary (Stalin). They were the two Stalinists, Kaganovich and Zhdanov, and Kirov.

In December 1934 Kirov was shot in his Leningrad party headquarters by a young communist. There are a number of circumstances, including the death of a key witness in a faked car accident and allegations by Khrushchev in 1956, that suggest Stalin himself was behind this crime. It certainly offered him the way out of a difficult situation, and he had the recent example of Hitler's killing of Brownshirt leaders to inspire him. The crime, which shocked and alarmed the party, was at first blamed on foreign powers, then on the Zinovievites, then on the Trotskyites. It was followed immediately by that campaign of terror for which Stalin had evidently been hankering. A decree was issued which specified that persons accused of 'preparing terroristic acts' should be investigated immediately and that execution should follow directly after conviction; there would be no appeal and no rights of defence. This was in effect a *carte blanche* for mass judicial murder (or, as Khrushchev expressed it more delicately in 1956, 'it became the basis for mass acts which abused socialist legality').

In the executions which followed it was non-communists who suffered most. But former members, and members who had once supported certain opposition factions, were arrested and deported. In 1935 the deputy procurator, Vyshinsky, an unscrupulous lawyer and devoted Stalinist, announced the forthcoming trial of Kamenev, Zinoviev, and some of their supporters on charges of organizing a secret conspiracy. The trial was in secret and the accused were imprisoned. This, the first imprisonment as criminals of party figures, seems to have aroused protests inside the party. Meanwhile, reliable Stalinists took control of the key organizations; Yezhov became head of the party's Control Commission,[5] Zhdanov succeeded Kirov as head of the Leningrad party organization, while Khrushchev moved from the Ukraine to lead the Moscow party organization. Poskrebyshev, of whom little is known but who became a key figure, was head of Stalin's personal

[5] This, one of the Central Committee's most important organs, supervised party discipline.

secretariat. Vyshinsky was soon to become Chief Procurator. Beria, a Georgian who was the ostensible author of a history of the Caucasian Bolsheviks which grotesquely exaggerated the role of Stalin in the pre-revolutionary years, became the leading party figure in Georgia.

A new purge had been launched in the party in 1935, before the previous purge had run its course. Local organizations were ordered to 'unmask' Trotskyites and other enemies of the people. But in 1935 Malenkov (another Stalinist, who with Yezhov was entrusted with the current party purge) complained that there were 'liberals' in the party organizations who were 'unmasking too few criminals'. In 1936 the re-issue of party cards was made the occasion for yet another purge.

In mid-1936 began the so-called 'Great Purge'. Party organizations received a letter from the Central Committee saying that there were still at large too many 'Trotskyite–Zinovievite monsters . . . enemies of the people . . . spies, provocators, diversionists, whiteguards, kulaks', and ordering their unmasking, no matter how well they were camouflaged. This was the signal for a mass orgy of accusations, denunciations, confessions, and deportations. The records of all members were scrutinized for dangerous tendencies. One comrade might have given a testimonial ten years previously to a member since convicted of Trotskyism. Another might have refrained from the current fashion of denouncing one's colleagues. Another's wife's aunt might have emigrated from Russia in 1918. Another might have approved concessions to the peasants in 1925. Their fate was the same; they were 'unmasked' by one or another of their colleagues, invited to confess before a mass meeting, were rarely found not guilty, lost their jobs, were usually deported to work camps of low survivability, and their families and associates were next to be 'unmasked'. Not only were party members treated thus, but others also, varying from former party members (a very vulnerable group) to confused simple people like the peasant woman mentioned in the *Smolensk Archives*,[6] who was discovered to have a portrait of Trotsky hanging among her icons.

In August 1936, sixteen former 'left-oppositionists', including Zinoviev and Kamenev, were tried in public, accused of organizing a terroristic centre which had murdered Kirov and prepared to murder Stalin and others. All but one confessed the accuracy of these charges, were accordingly found guilty, and were shot. During the trial, dominated by Vyshinsky, as chief

---

[6] In 1941 the German army captured the records of the Smolensk party organization, covering the years 1917–38. They were later acquired by the US army and a selection, with commentary, was published: M. Fainsod, *Smolensk under Soviet Rule* (1958). Usually referred to as the *Smolensk Archives*, these have provided historians with a wealth of information about inter-war Russia.

prosecutor, confessions and questions implicated other former 'leftists', as well as Bukharin, Tomsky, and Rykov of the so-called right. Vyshinsky ordered an investigation of the latter three, and newspapers published resolutions said to have been passed at mass meetings of workers, demanding death sentences. Tomsky committed suicide.

Evidently the spectacle of 'Old Bolshevik' leaders like Zinoviev dying from the executioner's bullet aroused some misgivings among Stalin's associates. Probably Ordzhonikidze led the opposition to similar reprisals against Bukharin and Rykov. The investigation ordered by Vyshinsky was cut short and Bukharin and Rykov were declared clear of the charges. Nevertheless, in early 1937 a new batch of former 'leftists' faced charges at a second big show trial. In the meantime Yezhov had replaced Yagoda as head of the People's Commissariat of the Interior (NKVD), which by this time had absorbed the functions of the former OGPU. Yagoda had apparently been too scrupulous; his dismissal was followed by that of his subordinates.

The second show trial included Radek and Pyatakov among the accused. There were seventeen in all, accused of conspiring with Germany and Japan to divide the USSR between those two powers. Pyatakov (who had been a deputy commissar of heavy industry) was also accused of wrecking and sabotage; he was a convenient scapegoat for the current shortcomings of the industrialization programme. From the official transcript[7] of the trial, it would seem that Vyshinsky was his usual self:

This trial has uncovered and demonstrated the stupid obstinacy, the reptilian coldbloodedness, the cold calculation of professional criminals, shown by the Trotskyist bandits in their struggle against the USSR . . . Beginning by forming an anti-party faction, they moved to ever-sharper methods of struggle against the party and became, after expulsion from the party, the main mouthpiece of all anti-soviet groups and trends, transforming themselves into a fascist vanguard operating directly on the directives of foreign intelligence services. The liaisons the Trotskyists had established with the Gestapo and the fascists were exposed at the trial of the Trotskyist–Zinovievist centre last year. The present trial has gone even further . . .

The confessions of the accused again implicated Bukharin and the moderates as well as Tukhachevsky, the Red Army C-in-C. Thirteen of the accused were executed, and four were deported to camps which they did not survive. Radek was one of these latter four, and probably received this charitable sentence in recompense for the artistic confession he produced:

. . . The question has been raised whether we were tortured while being investigated. I have to say that it was not I who was tortured, but it was I who tortured the investigators and made them do a lot of useless work . . .

[7] Lengthy extracts from this transcript are included in T. Riha, *Readings in Russian Civilisation* (Chicago University Press, 1964).

I have to make one more confession. Having confessed my guilt and revealed the organization, I obstinately refused to testify about Bukharin. I knew that Bukharin was in just as hopeless a situation as I was because we were guilty of the same thing, essentially if not legally. But we are close friends . . .

By this time there seemed little hope of resisting Stalin's apparent thirst for blood. The judiciary was safely in the hands of Vyshinsky, the NKVD in those of Yezhov, and the army appeared to be quiescent. There were arrests of thousands of lesser men, including 70 per cent of the Central Committee and more than half (1,108 members) of the 17th Party Congress, few of whom survived. Meanwhile, the army was dealt with. In 1937, Tukhachevsky and several other Red Army generals were arrested and shot. They were accused of spying for Japan and Germany and of planning to establish a right-wing Trotskyite counter-revolutionary whiteguardist regime in Moscow. The execution of Tukhachevsky, whose Civil War reputation far outshone the manufactured military reputations of Stalin and Voroshilov, must have brought personal as well as political satisfaction to the latter two; Voroshilov is said to have presided at a secret trial which condemned Tukhachevsky and the other generals. Among other things, Budyenny accused them of 'wrecking' by advocating the replacement of cavalry by tanks. Tukhachevsky's brothers and sisters were arrested, and most of them killed. Wives and children of the other generals were incarcerated, but most were shot in 1941 in the orgy of preventive executions that occurred when the German army seemed likely to overrun some of the prison camps. These arrests were followed by others, and by the end of 1938 about 35,000 Red Army officers had been purged, including 80 per cent of the colonels, 90 per cent of the generals, 100 per cent of the deputy-commissars for war. This brought better promotion prospects for the survivors, but for the more thoughtful officers this was not necessarily a blessing. Marshal Zhukov, in a part of his memoirs which was withheld from publication until 1991, wrote of 1937:

Frankly, in a way I was glad I was not promoted, because at the time there was a particularly active hunt going on at the higher levels on the part of the state security organs. No sooner did you succeed in getting a high appointment than you were taken under arrest as an 'enemy of the people'.[8]

The leadership of the Young Communist League (*Komsomol*) was next to be purged, and this movement was reorganized. Then, in March 1938, came the third of the big show trials, with Bukharin, Rykov, and Yagoda among the twenty-one accused. Sabotage, anti-Stalin conspiracy, espionage for Germany and Japan were the main charges. In addition Yagoda was accused of poisoning Maksim Gorki and Kuibyshev, when he had been

[8] *Gudok*, 5 July 1991, 4.

in charge of the NKVD.[9] Bukharin was also charged with plotting to murder Lenin in 1918. All but one of the accused confessed. The exception was Krestinsky, who in court revoked his confession, which he claimed had been obtained through torture. But, after a night with the NKVD interrogators, he revoked his revocation the next day, and was executed along with Bukharin, Rykov, Yagoda, and most of the others.

Apart from the leading figures thus eliminated, millions of lesser and non-party persons were shot or died in the NKVD's camps. Managers and administrators, army officers, Civil War veterans, one-time Stalinists, foreign communists (including the entire leadership of the Polish Communist Party, living in exile in Russia, and the Hungarian communist, Bela Kun), Russians who had returned from service in the Spanish Civil War, ex-Mensheviks and ex-Socialist Revolutionaries, former members of *Gosplan*, and associates of Kirov were particularly affected. But as the wave of denunciations spread so did the variety of victims. Workers were in no way spared. On the railways, for example, locomotive men were shot both for driving their trains at less than the maximum possible speed ('sabotage' of the plan) and for attaining maximum possible speeds ('wrecking', because it caused extra wear and fuel consumption). Some persons denounced to settle old scores, some to prove their vigilance and virtue, a few in the hope that they would inherit the apartment or job of the victim, but most because they were 'invited'. Once a denunciation was made there was little the victim could do, and his family and friends automatically became suspect. Even Ordzhonikidze (who committed suicide soon after) was unable to save his subordinate Pyatakov. No defence was possible:

Polish rabbit: Why have you fled to Poland?
Russian rabbit: Stalin is preparing a bear hunt.
Polish rabbit: But you are not a bear.
Russian rabbit: No, but I can't prove it![10]

The total of those who died in consequence of the purge has been variously estimated at between one and ten million; in 1990 the KGB reported that 786,098 had been executed for counter-revolutionary or anti-state crimes between 1930 and 1953, but this figure excludes those who died in captivity and those who were executed under other classifications. If the purge had continued accelerating past 1938, it would eventually have made every Russian a prisoner. It was not unknown for a prisoner to encounter his recent interrogator or accuser in the same camp. Some intended victims

---

[9] This accusation gave some plausibility to the rumour that Gorki and Kuibyshev had been poisoned on Stalin's orders after they had protested against the first wave of executions.

[10] Subversive, anti-Soviet, jokes can rarely be pinned down to a source, but many came from the general direction of Poland.

living at obscure addresses were saved because the official sent to arrest them was himself arrested before he could find them.

But in 1938, with the administration and industry disorganized, with nervous breakdowns and heart attacks becoming a mass phenomenon, as citizens listened apprehensively in the small hours for the dreaded knock on the door which would mean immediate and probably eternal separation from their families, Stalin called a halt. He blamed Yezhov and Yezhov's subordinates for the excesses. Beria replaced Yezhov, and the latter disappeared. The pace of arrests slackened (but did not cease until after 1953), and a few inmates of camps were released. So thoroughly had the old party been liquidated that, of the 1939 membership, four-fifths had joined since 1930. A new recruitment drive was begun, directed mainly towards the white-collar intelligentsia. By 1941 the party had about four million members.

Much about the purges remains uncertain. At the time, many commentators outside Russia believed that the show trials were genuine. The repellent truth tended to be voiced mainly by conservatives and anti-Soviet observers. However, in 1956 Khrushchev indicated that the allegations of the anti-Soviet commentators were indeed true and many details were revealed after 1985. Millions of innocents had been condemned. Physical and mental torture had been used to obtain confessions. Many signed confessions because they believed it was for the good of the party, or because their families were threatened, or because they were isolated for months, beaten up, promised merciful treatment if they co-operated. Some went to their deaths believing that 'an unliquidated counter-revolutionary centre', unknown to Stalin, was at large in the NKVD and extracting false confessions. Many who did not confess were quietly shot.

The NKVD itself lost about 20,000 operatives in the purge, of whom some were punished for reluctance to carry out orders. Some victims were induced to sign confessions implicating leaders who, in fact, were never touched. These were held 'in case of need' and would have been sufficient to incriminate, among others, Zhdanov and Kaganovich. The élite among the victims might find themselves tortured in Beria's office, with the minister himself taking a hand from time to time. Families of those executed were told that the accused had been sentenced to 'prison without right of correspondence'. Close relatives would spend days waiting outside prisons and offices for news or to hand over food parcels, and for the most part were ignored or insulted. Anna Akhmatova wrote a very moving poem, *Requiem*, about these vigils, which was breathed around until, three decades later, it could be published.

Some of those sentenced wrote to party leaders asking for a reinvestigation or reprieve. They did not receive a reply but their letters were filed away, to be unearthed by later generations. In 1953 the recipient of many of these despairing letters, Beria, would be writing to Khrushchev with the same plea, and with the same result.

The 1936 Constitution

From the early days of Russian marxism, Marx's doctrines had been adjusted from time to time to suit Russian realities. Lenin's innovations, which produced what would be known as Marxism–Leninism, related more to the struggle for power than to the post-revolutionary society. He had asserted (and in 1917 proved) that a proletarian revolution could occur in a primarily peasant society, if the peasantry was regarded as an ally. He had adopted the Populist Lavrov's concept of the small professionalized party, and had proposed that such a party could capture the state bureaucratic apparatus and, through that apparatus, carry out a social revolution. Lenin had also made Democratic Centralism the basis of party organization, thus combining the democratic discussion traditional in radical circles with the centralized authoritarian system traditional in bureaucratic circles.

After 1917 there had been other modifications in Russian marxist doctrines, some of them introduced by Stalin; hence until 1953 the term Marxism–Leninism–Stalinism was in frequent use. Among ideas sponsored in Stalin's time were those that propounded that socialism could be 'built in one country'; that the 'Law of Industrialization' meant that economic planning would create the industrial base on which socialism could be built; that class conflict intensified *after* the Revolution (which conveniently explained the violence of the early thirties); and that the state would not automatically wither away, but would be needed to supervise the economy and to guard against internal enemies and 'capitalist encirclement'. Stalin also reiterated that before proceeding to Marx's final stage of communism, where the ruling principle would be 'From each according to his capacity, to each according to his needs', the preliminary stage of socialism had to be attained ('From each according to his capacity, to each according to his work'). In 1936 Stalin declared that the USSR, hitherto 'on the road to socialism', had duly reached socialism. The Stalin Constitution was to mark this achievement.[11]

Despite the purges, it would seem that Stalin in the late thirties was intent on stabilizing Russian life; in fact the purges, among other things, took out of the party those who were revolutionaries at heart. The model

[11] Two decades later Stalin's successor, Khrushchev, would announce that the growing strength of the 'socialist camp' had put an end to capitalist encirclement, and that the necessary industrial base had been created. Hence the USSR had entered 'the road to communism'.

charter for the collective farms which confirmed the status of private plots, the re-introduction of Russian history as a school subject, concessions to the Church, social changes such as limitations on divorce and fewer limitations on inheritance, and a partial return to a genuine rule of law, were other signs of stabilization, and so was the new Constitution.

The first Soviet Constitution had been that of 1918, which was acknowledged to be a temporary document, and was adopted because some formal statement was required and because a constitution was what revolutionaries had been demanding during the preceding century. The 1924 Constitution was more significant, for it formalized the creation of the federal Union of Soviet Socialist Republics, in which the national republics were subordinated in most matters to the central commissariats in Moscow. The 1936 Constitution was largely drafted by Bukharin and Radek; this was their last important service to the party before their arrest. It became known as the Stalin Constitution and as such was propagandized throughout the world. In its provisions it seemed to be the most progressive constitution ever devised, but in reality the articles guaranteeing various rights and freedoms were quite meaningless, because the Politburo or the NKVD could override any legal obstacle.

According to the 1936 Constitution the USSR was a federation of Soviet republics.[12] The union (that is, federal) government in Moscow monopolized such matters as defence and foreign policy, but in other cases the commissariats were not 'all-union', but 'union-republican'; that is, the federal commissariats acted through similarly titled commissariats of the republic governments. In a few fields the republics had complete jurisdiction (primary education was one such field). There was rarely conflict between the union government and the republics because party leaders controlled both. Moreover, the union government had control over the republican budgets, and all-union laws could override republican laws. Apart from the republics, there were autonomous republics, and the smaller autonomous regions and areas, to accommodate nationalities too small to justify a union republic. The Russian Republic (Russian Soviet Federative Socialist Republic, or RSFSR) had as many as fourteen autonomous republics and several autonomous regions, including vast areas of the north and pockets of Tartars, Moslems, and other peoples left high and dry by successive advances of the Russian Empire. These four categories of national division, and the encouragement therein of national cultures (which might be 'national in

---

[12] At the time these were Russia, Ukraine, Byelorussia (White Russia), Georgia, Armenia, Azerbaizhan, Kazakhstan, Kirgizia, Uzbekistan, Turkmenistan, Tadzhikistan. In 1939–40 they were joined by Latvia, Estonia, Lithuania, Moldavia, and Karelo-Finland. (The last-named was absorbed by the Russian Republic in 1956.)

form' provided they were 'socialist in content') did go some way towards maintaining the independent existence of the various minorities; in particular, local languages had official status. This administrative division of the old Russian Empire was largely Stalin's doing, and was one way of preserving that empire and restraining nationalistic impulses. But it depended, ultimately, on force. Frontiers delineating the Central Asian republics frequently had little correspondence with the ethnic boundaries. The various autonomous territories in reality possessed little autonomy, and their peoples often resented the rule of the union republics in which they were situated. According to the Constitution, a union republic had the right to secede from the Soviet Union (although in 1951 party leaders in Georgia were executed on the grounds that they were planning secession).

The exclusive right to make all-union laws was vested in the Supreme Soviet of the USSR. One of the several ways in which the 1936 Constitution resembled that of the USA was the structure of this body; it had two houses, the Soviet of the Union with members elected by electoral districts (one member per 300,000 people), and the Soviet of Nationalities (twenty-five members per union republic, eleven per autonomous republic, five per autonomous region, one per national area). The Supreme Soviet was to meet twice each year; the meetings lasted only a few days, during which the elected members were acquainted with the government's policies and gave their approval to whatever measures they were summoned to approve. It was thus not really a legislative body in the western sense, but it gave its members, and those who elected them and heard their reports, some sense of participation. Also, members did not need to give up their regular employment since sessions were so short. The quadrennial elections were not competitive, only one candidate being nominated for each electoral district. In practice, the aim at elections was to obtain for each candidate as near 100 per cent of the votes as was physically possible, thus demonstrating the mass support of the electorate. From the Supreme Soviet was elected the Presidium, the chairman of which fulfilled the functions of president of the USSR but had little real power. Also from the Supreme Soviet was elected the more important Council of People's Commissars, the chairman of which continued to be the equivalent of a western prime minister. In the union republics, government was similarly organized, but the supreme soviets had only one house.

Article 126 implied that the party was the real ruling force, that is, it 'forms the nucleus of all the public and state organizations of the working people'. That 125 other articles preceded this declaration hardly concealed that this was indeed the basic and distinguishing fact of the Soviet system of government.

There were several resemblances, perhaps interesting more than significant, between the Soviet and tsarist systems of government. For example, just as under the tsars there were, apart from the formal channels, many other ways of introducing laws (by decrees or manifestos or even by the tsar scrawling 'So Be It' on the proposal of a minister), so in the USSR people's commissariats and other bodies could issue their own orders, which were not laws but had the force of law. Again, people's commissars, like tsarist ministers, were heads of departments and belonged more to the bureaucracy than to politics. In some cases a minister might occupy his position for decades. Just as Kankrin served as Minister of Finance for twenty-one years so did the Soviet Minister for Transport, Beshchev, serve from 1948 to 1977.

Chapter One of the Constitution laid down the fundamental concepts on which the Union of Soviet Socialist Republics was based. Among the more important were: The USSR 'is a socialist state of workers and peasants'; 'The political foundation of the USSR is the Soviet of Working Peoples' Deputies, which grew and became strong as a result of the overthrow of the power of the landlords and capitalists and the conquest of the dictatorship of the proletariat'; 'All power in the USSR belongs to the working people of town and country as represented by the Soviets of Working Peoples' Deputies'; 'The economic foundation of the USSR is the socialist system of economy and the socialist ownership of the instruments and means of production, firmly established as a result of the liquidation of the capitalist system of economy, the abolition of private ownership of the instruments and means of production, and the elimination of the exploitation of man by man'; 'Work in the USSR is a duty and a matter of honour for every able-bodied citizen, in accordance with the principle: "He who does not work, neither shall he eat." '

Some of these declarations seemed somewhat optimistic; formally or theoretically the working people may have held all state power through the soviets, but in reality this proposition could hardly be sustained. If 'exploitation of man by man' was defined as a consequence of some men privately owning the means of production while others owned only their own labour, it was true that exploitation had ceased, but in fact there were many other possible forms of exploitation.

Contrary to popular impression, the USSR was not claimed to be a classless society. Stalin, introducing the Constitution, said only that the old conflicting classes had been abolished, leaving the workers and the peasants. The latter formed two mutually amicable classes and therefore, said Stalin, there was no need for a multi-party system, because political parties represented conflicting classes. As for the intelligentsia, Stalin described this as a stratum, not a class, and as a working-class intelligentsia rather than the old bourgeois intelligentsia. This explanation of the new class structure contained elements of self-deception, although undoubtedly the situation in 1936 was different from that in 1916 (see table, p. 601). In the last decade of the tsarist regime the class structure had been in a confused state of change. There were the old official 'estates' (nobles, priests, peasants, and others) which, even with the addition of distinctions like 'honoured citizens', could hardly accommodate the ever-growing number of those who did not fit into the old categories. Cutting across the official and mainly hereditary divisions were the new unofficial but very real differences of economic status. Moreover, noble status was becoming ever less exclusive; the universities and officer-training schools in particular provided a ladder enabling men of peasant or petty bourgeois origin to climb into the nobility. In 1917 the existing class system had been abolished, but this did not mean the end of class distinctions. Except during War Communism and the first two years of the five-year plans, egalitarianism was rejected. In 1931 Stalin came out against equality; industrialization demanded wide differentiation of incomes, in order to provide incentives. In the USSR the gap between the highest and lowest incomes became very wide indeed. The new intelligentsia which Stalin fostered in the thirties tended to enjoy high salaries, although these were matched by a few of the very best industrial workers. In time the highly paid and influential 'white-collar' stratum came to resemble in everything except in name a privileged class. It was not quite self-perpetuating like the old hereditary nobility, but certainly, bar accidents, its children had a much better than average chance of themselves attaining official, managerial, or technical positions, together with the privileges these jobs entailed.

Justice

The quest for stability reflected in the Constitution was also a feature of the judicial changes of the late thirties. The new general theory of Soviet law was laid down by Vyshinsky in his *Law of the Soviet State*,[13] a turgid work whose crudities camouflaged its underlying conservative principles. While describing other countries' laws as 'inhuman and bestial', Vyshinsky rejected the 'putrid, vaporous' theories of revolutionary Soviet legal theorists of the twenties. His book prescribed a law which was depoliticized except in those cases where political factors were considered important; the concept that all law and all cases are inherently political was condemned.

---

[13] The English edition was published in 1948. The original Russian edition (1938) was titled *Soviet State Law*.

Perhaps central to the Vyshinsky theory was the resulting proposition that there should be a genuine due process of law in all cases, except where violence was considered necessary. However obscure and unconvincing the theory, in practice it meant some real changes. There was stricter adherence to the law and to the correct procedures. The Soviet 'doctrine of analogy' was severely limited: this doctrine had meant that acts which were not crimes according to the laws could often be punished as crimes if a court considered them nefarious. Personal guilt in a crime became necessary for punishment; in other words, close relatives or friends of a convicted criminal could no longer be punished with him. These improvements did not apply to cases defined as political, and at this period the NKVD investigators usually succeeded in fabricating a political crime for anyone whom they decided should be eliminated. Moreover, judges were expected to follow their 'Bolshevik consciousness'.

The courts of law were headed by the Supreme Court of the USSR, whose chairman was a top party official rather than a top lawyer. The republics also had their own supreme courts. Then there were *oblast'* courts[14] and the People's Courts (courts of first instance). The 'bourgeois' jury system had long been abolished, and cases were decided and sentences handed down by a judge, assisted by two lay assessors. Judges and lay assessors were elected (by the corresponding soviet, or, in the case of People's Courts, by the local population), but in reality the appropriate party organization was most influential in their selection. Judges could be recalled before the expiry of their term if they were considered unsatisfactory. They were not required to have legal training. The procuracy (abolished in 1918 but reinstated in 1922) became highly centralized, with the Procurator-General (Vyshinsky) appointing and supervising republic and district procurators. The procuracy was mainly concerned with its role as state prosecutor, its role as supervisor of the judicial system being largely taken over by the Commissariat of Justice, which existed from 1938 to 1956.

The Church

Lenin's pre-1917 attitude towards the Church included a belief that the state should permit each citizen to follow his professed faith, but should not allocate public funds to any religious activity. At the same time the Bolshevik Party should wage a propaganda struggle for people's minds, to convince them that religion was indeed an opium. For the Church, the October Revolution was a disaster, because during the Provisional Government it

---

[14] The *oblast'* was the Soviet equivalent of the tsarist province. The district (*raion*) was a subdivision of an *oblast'* or of a city.

had been preparing to reassert itself. In people's minds the Church had sunk even lower during the final tsarist years when, it was believed, the Synod was dominated by Rasputin. After the February Revolution the Church saw an opportunity to break away from state control without sacrificing the privileges which co-operation with the state had obtained. Among other activities, it finally triumphed over Peter the Great by re-establishing the office of Patriarch. The first incumbent was Tikhon, after an election in which he did not receive the most votes. On the other hand, the Provisional Government did end legal discrimination against the minor religions and weakened the hold of the Church on education.

The Bolshevik Revolution meant that a small atheistic party would attempt to rule a devoutly Christian republic. This contradiction was at first as great an embarrassment for the party as for the Church, and the contradiction was transformed into conflict within weeks. Lenin probably foresaw that the Orthodox Church, if left alone, would sooner or later become an inspirational centre of anti-Bolshevik movements and that in a civil war the Church, with its influence over the rural masses, might well tip the scales against the party. The first priority was therefore the destruction of the Church as an organization, but not the destruction of Russian Christianity (which in the short term was out of the question). A decree issued in February 1918 disestablished the Church and confirmed the equality of all religious faiths before the law. Disestablishment was accompanied by such measures as elimination of references to a citizen's beliefs in official documents. 'Religious associations' (of which the Orthodox Church was one) had the right to conduct their ceremonies but henceforth could not punish, or extract fees from, their adherents. What really hurt was the depriving of all religious associations of the status of a juridical person. This meant they could not own property, and the decree provided for the nationalization of church land and buildings: believers would lease back their churches from the state. Later, believers were organized into local religious associations (consisting of at least twenty members), and it was these which arranged the lease-back and hired 'servants of the cult' (that is, priests). Religious instruction of children was banned, and conferences of clergy could be held only with official permission. The 1918 Constitution introduced further restrictions; the clergy were disenfranchised and classified among the 'non-toiling' (which entailed high taxation).

Strictly speaking, the conflict between party and Church had been started by the latter for, in January 1918, Tikhon publicly laid his patriarchal curse on the government: 'Come to your senses, ye madmen, and cease your bloody doings!' But the anti-Church measures of 1918 and 1919, the Red

Terror being applied against the Church, and the failure of the Whites, persuaded Tikhon in 1919 to call on his clergy to accept the regime.

The next crisis came with the famine of 1922. The Soviet government had appealed for foreign aid, and at the same time requested the Church to hand over valuables to be sold for famine relief. The Church might have contributed some of its treasures but hesitated, partly because of the problem posed by consecrated items. Tikhon's instruction to his priests to resist premature demands for their valuables was easily presented as proof that the Church still thought more of wealth than welfare. When émigré Orthodox priests appealed to foreigners *not* to contribute to Russian famine relief because this would help the Bolsheviks, the impression of clerical selfishness was strengthened. Some priests and believers were killed in violent demonstrations which occurred at some of the churches when valuables were confiscated. In general, however, congregations, as in 1918 and 1919, did not especially resent the chastisement of their priests. Some priests, including the Metropolitan of Petrograd, were executed for counter-revolutionary activities and in 1922 Tikhon himself was gaoled.

At this point a group of priests less unsympathetic to the Bolsheviks took over the leadership, calling themselves the Living Church. They were more co-operative, and replaced bishops who were openly hostile to them or to the regime. The latter helped by arresting priests who opposed them. Patriarch Tikhon was deposed by the Living Church and his state trial was fixed for the spring of 1923. However, he signed a confession, and publicly repented his anti-Bolshevik past. This earned his release and he immediately reasserted himself as head of the Church: many who had adhered to the Living Church transferred their support back to Tikhon. The Living Church continued to exist, much weakened, and occasionally the Soviet government played off one Church against the other. When Tikhon died in 1925 his testament recommended believers to support the Bolsheviks. Nevertheless, his successor did not take office until 1927, because all candidates were arrested. Metropolitan Sergius was finally released from gaol, after promising good conduct, and permitted to head the Church, although his installation as Patriarch did not take place until 1943.

Although there was frequently a difference between practice and theory, throughout the Soviet period the official attitude towards the Church had much to recommend it; the individual was allowed to find what comfort he could in the religion of his choice, but the Church as an organization was denied temporal power. Lenin, while despising the religions, nevertheless felt that freedom of belief should be guaranteed. In fact he did not consider religious belief a bar to party membership: in the twenties it was not unknown for members in Central Asia to take their prayer mats to party meetings. Individuals might in effect be denied the full practice of their faith because their church might be closed, or their local priest might be imprisoned, but such actions did not restrict their freedom of belief, and of private observance. The Church as an organization was not treated so tolerantly as its individual adherents: it lost legal title to its property, many monasteries were converted to barracks or hospitals, its priests were sometimes persecuted, and the 1936 Constitution, while restoring civil rights to priests, confirmed the illegality of religious propaganda, while permitting anti-religious propaganda.

The party, while allowing the state to tolerate religious belief, was determined to eventually eliminate such 'harmful superstitions' by means of propaganda. One of the most successful propaganda onslaughts took place soon after the Revolution, when the silver-and-glass cases containing the relics of saints were publicly opened in the presence of Church, press, party, and believers' representatives. In some cases the long-revered bones were found to be fabrications of wax or plaster: films of the disinterments were shown throughout the republic and proved a very persuasive anti-religious weapon. In 1925 there was founded the Godless League: at first this was a crude and farcical organization, whose young militants smashed church windows and vandalized cemeteries more to satisfy their own psychological needs than for the anti-religious enlightenment on whose behalf they claimed to be acting. The Godless League organized meetings in the villages but the audiences consisted largely of devout believers (sometimes including the village priest) who came because they wanted to show how obliging they were. Anti-religious lectures were given, and anti-religious books and journals published. One of the latter, *Science and Life*, survived as a popular magazine for decades. Like many others, it sought to show how science was making nonsense of traditional religious beliefs, and its popular-style scientific articles were good. If its atheistic articles were somewhat primitive, illustrated with caricatures of black spiky-tailed devils, this was only a reflection of the primitive nature of the Church's own teaching, with emphasis on ignorance and superstition rather than its earlier spirituality. Over the years the Godless League abandoned its cruder and more violent activities, concentrating on pure propaganda work. One of its enterprises was trips above the clouds for village folk, using the big passenger aircraft which Tupolev and others had designed. The object was to demonstrate that there was no God and no heaven up there, but the project backfired when a high-altitude aircraft crashed in flames.

Godless propaganda was primarily directed at the peasants, and a great effort was made to associate the priests with reaction: it was the priests who liked to see the peasants get drunk in the village *traktir*, it was the priests who opposed modern science and who opposed collectivization because it threatened their hold on the peasants. In a handbook for Godless agitators,[15] riddles were recommended as one effective form of propaganda:

> With an 'i' it drinks up people's money
> With an 'o' it helps work the land
> And this machine is so strong
> That it destroys the power of the priest

> (Answer: *traktir* / *traktor*)

Quizzes were also useful:

Q.   How do you reply to a priest who says 'your communism is just another religion'?
A.   All religions involve belief in the supernatural. Communism does not.
Q.   How did Karl Marx describe christianity?
A.   As the Executive Committee of the bourgeoisie.
Q.   Who said 'the best religion is the stupidest'?
A.   Pope Alexander VI.
Q.   In which country is the church separated from the state only on paper but in reality is in union with state power?
A.   America.
Q.   Which well-known imperialists are sectarians?
A.   Lloyd George, Rockefeller, Coolidge.

The influence of the Church in the countryside was obviously of great relevance in the government's struggle with the peasantry. In the circumstances, the Church escaped relatively lightly from the turmoil of 1930–3. However, in the early thirties there was a spate of church closures, and the Godless League flourished (its peak was probably in 1932, when it had about five million members). After the collectivization drive had been brought to a triumphal conclusion, Church and state coexisted more peacefully, even though anti-religious propaganda continued. This set the stage for the wartime reconciliation. The Godless League was finally disbanded during the war.

[15] S. Glyazer and N. Kopievskii, *Dosug bezbozhnika* (1930).

14. *The Great Patriotic War*

Foreign policy between the wars

THE New Economic Policy had been accompanied by a realization that improved relations with other powers were desirable, in order to preserve the peace which Russia so badly needed, and to attract foreign economic and technical assistance. Diplomatic recognition of the new Russia was a first step, because foreign businessmen were reluctant to trade with, or extend credit to, a nation which their own government did not recognize. (American businessmen were an exception; they made private commercial agreements with the USSR long before the USA belatedly recognized the latter in 1933.) Western governments were hesitant to recognize the USSR. All, and especially the USA, were periodically affected by 'red scares' agitating public opinion. The British government was additionally alienated by communist anti-colonial propaganda which was disseminated by Comintern agents in Britain and the Empire, while French governments were never allowed to forget the thousands of French investors who had lost their capital after 1917.

A trade agreement with Britain in 1921 implied *de facto* recognition, and about the same time Moscow began to cultivate good relations with Germany. At this time Germany and Russia were the black sheep of the European community, so a *rapprochement* between them seemed only natural. Because arms limitations had been imposed on Germany, her General Staff was glad to take advantage of a secret arrangement for military co-operation (see p. 342). On the diplomatic level, Britain and France were disagreeably surprised in 1922 when Russia and Germany signed the Treaty of Rapallo, which re-established relations, renounced financial claims, and envisaged economic co-operation. For Russia, this was the first *de jure* recognition by a European power. Relations with Germany were good following this agreement, but later became uneasy. Partly the deterioration was caused by the dissonance between the People's Commissariat of Foreign Affairs and the activities of the Communist International. The former, like its tsarist predecessor, was doing its best to promote Russia's interests within an existing world order, whereas the latter stood for the destruction of that order.

In 1924 the new Labour government in Britain recognized the USSR *de jure* and a new trade treaty was drafted. The principal obstacle to the latter, the payment of compensation for British property nationalized by the Bolsheviks, seemed about to be by-passed. (In 1922 the Soviet government had agreed in principle to negotiate the settlement of such foreign debts.) However, in October 1924, the Conservatives won a British general election which had largely been fought on the issue of the Labour government's alleged softness towards Russia. Just before polling, Conservative newspapers published a letter signed by Zinoviev, apparently sent by the Comintern to the British Communist Party, in which revolutionary activity inside the British army and in Ireland was suggested. Fears of Communism, exacerbated by this so-called 'Zinoviev letter', helped the Conservatives to win, and they refused ratification of the Anglo-Russian trade treaty. Subsequent anti-Soviet actions of the Conservative government were partly provoked by the Comintern's encouragement of British workers in the 1926 General Strike. The British government's rupture of diplomatic relations in 1927, however, was hardly warranted. When in 1929 a Labour government restored relations it was in a sense too late, for the actions of the Conservatives had been taken just in time for Stalin to use them as arguments against the conciliatory foreign policy recommended by Bukharin and Rykov.

In Asia, despite treaties with Turkey, Iran, and Afghanistan, the picture was clouded by events in China. Because the Soviet government believed that it was worthwhile supporting 'national-bourgeois' revolutions in countries seeking to free themselves from foreign domination, aid had been given to the Kuomintang revolutionaries of southern China. Among the Kuomintang officers sent to Moscow for training had been Chiang Kai-shek, who by 1925 was leading the Kuomintang. Although Trotsky and others opposed support of the Kuomintang, preferring to channel Russian aid to the Chinese Communists, Stalin insisted that the latter should ally themselves with Chiang Kai-shek. But after the communists had helped Chiang Kai-shek to win his 1926 victories over the Peking government, they were attacked by the Kuomintang and, for the most part, killed. Only a remnant eventually reached safety in western China and were reformed into a viable force by Mao Tse-tung and others.

Soviet foreign policy of the thirties, because it culminated in the Nazi–Soviet Pact of 1939, has not been favourably regarded in the west. But the Soviet government was far from being the most blameworthy in the events leading to war, even though it is true that Soviet policy helped the rise of

Hitler. The succession of Comintern-inspired and abortive revolutions in Germany after the First World War did much to inspire that fear of communism which Hitler exploited. Furthermore, the instructions (originating from Stalin) to the strong German Communist Party, demanding that it struggle not against the Nazis but the Social Democrats, fatally split the left in Germany during those critical years in which Hitler finally reached the chancellorship. After Hitler came to power the Russo-German military arrangements were finally terminated. Stalin, learning from his mistakes, instructed the Comintern to ensure that the French Communist Party allied with other left-wing parties in a 'Popular Front' to struggle against emergent fascism in France. In 1934 the USSR joined the League of Nations and her foreign minister, Litvinov, was active among those seeking 'collective security' against fascism. Unfortunately, the events of 1936–8 suggested that with France and Britain pursuing policies of weakness, the League of Nations would remain ineffective.

The Spanish Civil War was an embarrassment to Moscow. A fascist victory might have led to a fascist coup in France, but a victory of the Republicans, with their strong communist element, might have driven the French to seek an anti-communist alliance with Hitler. But if the USSR was to intervene, it could only have supported the left, and this is what happened after a long delay. First the Comintern arranged arms supplies to the Republicans, then organized the International Brigades. Moscow persuaded the Spanish left not to be too radical in its aspirations (that is, to respect foreign investments, and private property). The USSR sent arms and men to Spain, but could not match the scale of German and Italian intervention. Although Russian support was appreciated by the Spanish Republicans and their international supporters, the USSR lost prestige not because the Nationalists won but because of the activities of the NKVD elements which accompanied Soviet aid to Spain. Partly because of a wish to dominate the Republican cause, and partly in order to damage the non-Stalinist left (such as the émigré Trotskyists and anarchists) who were participating in the International Brigades, all kinds of intrigues, secret trials, murders, and arrests were perpetrated by the Soviet security services, and not all could be kept secret.

With Hitler rebuilding the German forces and openly talking of his intention of annexing the Ukraine, and the Anti-Comintern Pact signed by Germany and Japan in 1936, the USSR was faced with the prospect of a war on two fronts without effective allies. There was an undeclared war with Japan from 1938, beginning with Japanese probing attacks on the Manchuria–Russia border, and developing into localized hostilities which were hard-fought but left the frontiers as before. It was at this difficult time that Hitler annexed Austria and made demands on Czechoslovakia. Among the several treaties which the USSR had made in previous years was a 1935 tripartite pact in which Moscow promised to assist Czechoslovakia if the latter was attacked, provided that France did likewise. Despite Polish non-co-operation, which meant that to help Czechoslovakia the Red Army would probably have needed to force a passage across Poland, the USSR might well have been willing to meet her obligations under this agreement, but France (with Britain) shrank from a war against Germany. Reasons for this reluctance were lack of confidence in the Red Army following the purges, a disinclination to go to war for a small distant country, and perhaps a feeling among some conservative politicians that German expansion eastwards was not a bad thing. (Soviet historians gave precedence to the latter reason.) Thus the Munich agreement of 1938 was not only a betrayal of Czechoslovakia, but in a sense of Russia too. Probably it was at this time that Stalin began to visualize his own Munich, a bargain with Germany. He still preferred an alliance with Britain and France but these two powers, though less uncongenial, seemed unenthusiastic and unreliable. He probably did not expect the western powers to fulfil Britain's guarantee of the Polish frontiers in the event of a German attack.

In April 1939 Hitler omitted the customary denunciation of Russia from a foreign affairs speech. Stalin responded by replacing the pro-western Litvinov with Molotov. In August Ribbentrop arrived in Moscow. It was clear that a German invasion of Poland was imminent, and the best way of securing a few more peaceful years seemed to be an alliance with Hitler. The ten-year Non-Aggression Pact which resulted from Ribbentrop's visit came as a great shock to the west, although not to the western governments. It also came as a shock to the communist parties of the west; once more they were to damage their own prospects by supporting Soviet foreign policy. Probably it came as a shock to the Russian people too, but they accepted the view that only thus could the German threat be diverted from Russia. The shocked might have been shattered had they known of the secret protocol of the Pact. This divided Poland into Russian and German sectors, and allowed the USSR to regard Finland, Estonia, Latvia, and Bessarabia as her own sphere (Lithuania was later added).

Two and a half weeks after Hitler's invasion of Poland, after the Polish army had been shattered, the Red Army invaded eastern Poland and advanced to a line previously agreed between Germany and Russia. When Ribbentrop revisited Moscow in the same month, September 1939, it was agreed that Poland would be partitioned between the two victors, and cease to exist as a state. Having done what he could to secure his western approaches. Stalin turned to the defence of Leningrad. He induced the governments of Latvia, Estonia, and Lithuania to permit Russian bases on their territory and then, in 1940, he engineered a pretext to occupy these Baltic states. Their leaders were deported to concentration camps by the NKVD together with thousands of others suspected of being anti-Soviet or potentially anti-Soviet. Another independent state, Finland, was within shelling distances of Leningrad. Stalin tried at first to safeguard his military position here by negotiation. In exchange for a withdrawal of the Finnish frontier back from the existing line near Leningrad, the grant of bases on Finnish territory at the entrance to the Gulf of Finland and at Petsamo, and some minor concessions, the USSR offered Finland an area of Russian territory in a less valuable region but of double the size. After agonized negotiations the Finnish government refused, largely because it feared that agreement would lead only to further Soviet demands. In November 1939 the Red Air Force bombed Helsinki and the Red Army crossed into Finland. A new People's Government for Finland had already been collected from Finnish communists resident in Russia; it was never installed in Helsinki as intended but was stabled in a small town on the Finnish side of the Frontier. The Red Army in the first month of the campaign was tactically defeated time and again by the much smaller but more versatile Finnish forces. It was only after Finland had exhausted her reserves that she was obliged to negotiate a treaty by which she lost rather more than the territory originally requested by the Soviet Union, including the city of Vyborg. In this campaign the USSR lost enormous prestige, almost provoked hostilities with Britain and France, convinced Hitler that the Red Army was worthless, and ensured that when Germany did attack, Finland would be Hitler's ally. In the meantime the League of Nations expelled the USSR from membership.

In 1940, while Hitler was occupied with the conquest of France, the USSR annexed Bessarabia and adjoining northern Bukovina. The latter had not been allotted to the Russian sphere of influence, and Stalin's action appears to have annoyed Hitler. For this and other reasons Russo-German relations became uneasy. In December 1940, Hitler ordered preparations to be made for invading Russia in May 1941. In the nick of time, it seemed, Stalin achieved the signature of the Japanese-Soviet Neutrality Pact in April 1941.

The Soviet armed forces

After Trotsky's departure from the War Commissariat in 1925, the army was reduced to under 600,000 men, with a strong cavalry element. Discipline was tightened. Smart drill, well-kept uniforms, and a General Staff were three reversions to old army practices. The new soldiers were conscripts from the cities, and the poorer peasants. Rich peasants and 'bourgeois elements' were conscripted into non-military and arduous labour battalions.

In the late twenties, after Stalin's old crony Voroshilov became War Commissar, Russo-German military co-operation reached its peak. Among the achievements of this co-operation were the joint Russo-German tank training school at Kazan, a poison-gas training centre, a joint pilots' school, and a reorganization of the Soviet armaments industry. Russian officers attended German war colleges and German officers participated in Soviet military manœuvres (incidentally familiarizing themselves with the border regions, where Russian manœuvres were traditionally held). The termination of this co-operation in 1933 was regretted by both armies. However, by that time the five-year plans were ensuring that the USSR would soon be well supplied with armaments. The new tractor plants at Stalingrad and Kharkov would be easily adapted for tank production should the need arise to supplement the existing works. The tension caused by the rise of Hitler, together with uneasiness in the Far East, prompted an expansion of the Red Army, which exceeded one and a quarter million men by 1935. However, there was much that was still imperfect. The peasants who provided most of the infantry were alienated from the regime (and from the officers, who were almost entirely from the towns), and were difficult to train. The exclusion of men of 'bourgeois' origin from the army meant that there was a shortage of young men capable of mastering the theories of military engineering and artillery; all too often officers were men whose main claim to preferment was their proletarian background. This situation was remedied by making all classes of young men liable to conscription into the Red Army.

In 1934 the higher direction of defence was entrusted to the Commissar of Defence and his eleven specialist deputies. In 1935 officers' ranks were re-established, including the rank of marshal for the top five commanders. This was the start of a process which would culminate in the restoration of officers' epaulettes, the old symbol of tsarist militarism. In effect, a truly professional officer corps was being re-established. The revolutionary Red Army's tradition of badges of rank being worn only in operations, of commanders eating with the men, of the absence of saluting, was being replaced by conventional officer status and authority. By the mid-forties a harsh officer was regarded as a good officer; friendliness between officers and men was condemned.

In the late thirties most officers were mediocre. The old military specialists were disappearing, like their civilian counterparts, the 'bourgeois' specialists, in industry. The majority of the senior officers were Civil War veterans, many of whom could not see why the next war should not be fought in the same way as the last, or were men who had been appointed for reasons of political rather than military merit. Nevertheless, there was a nucleus of far-sighted high and intermediate officers whose anticipations of the next war were very close to reality. Tukhachevsky was the best known of these. It was he who largely wrote the new Field Regulations, which foresaw the use of massed tank formations, a high degree of co-operation between infantry, armour, artillery, and air power, and the use of motorized rather than foot-slogging infantry. There was also an emphasis on the use of parachute troops. The world's first parachute troops, apparently, had been Russian; in 1931 exercises Russian infantry, wearing American parachutes, clung to the wings of German planes and dropped off one by one.

Although the Red Army purge of 1937–8 may have rid Stalin of the only group capable of ousting him, it certainly set back the progress of the Red Army. Of the higher officers, those spared were mainly Stalin's old associates of the south-western front during the Civil War. For the most part, they were unfitted to apply the advanced theories adopted by their predecessors. In 1939, just as Hitler was about to demonstrate his *panzers* to the world, the new Soviet military leadership abandoned Tukhachevsky's concept of massed tank operations and reverted to the more familiar deployment of tanks in small numbers as infantry support.

The main reasons for the poor showing in the war against Finland were the lack of winter training, the mediocrity of the officers, and the disappearance of that close inter-arm co-ordination which the Tukhachevsky school had so valued. Time and again in this campaign masses of Russian infantry were sent against strongpoints which the artillery had failed to damage in the preparatory barrage. Repeatedly the artillery missed its targets, because there was no spotting service provided by the air force. Sometimes Russian tanks supporting the infantry would be picked off in turn by just one Finnish anti-tank gun. Almost invariably officers refused to depart from the regulations, or from their orders, to meet an unexpected situation. This lack of initiative was almost certainly an after-effect of the purge; no officer dared to be daring.

In addition to their fear of chastisement from above, the officers had difficult relationships with their men following the purges. Soldiers only with some reluctance obeyed orders from superiors who, even if they had escaped the purges yesterday, might tomorrow be declared enemies of the people. This mistrust, as well as resentment aroused by the technical incompetence of many officers, was probably aggravated rather than moderated by the free and easy (or, in some opinions, slovenly) relationships between officers and men that had become the fashion.

The poor performance of the Red Army in the Finnish campaign, added to the confidential reports sent in by NKVD and army political commissars during the 1939 campaign in Poland, caused great anxiety in the party's central committee and the defence commissariat. Timoshenko replaced Voroshilov as defence commissar and was charged with putting things right. A number of old officer privileges were restored and officers were required to re-establish a proper hierarchical gap between themselves and their men. Harsher discipline was introduced. Among other things, this allowed officers to shoot soldiers for refusing to obey an order in peacetime as well as in war. The inability of troops to carry out simple routine functions, like digging a trench or crossing a stream, in the early stages of the Finnish war was noted, and the performance of proper training programmes became a priority. Some changes were pushed to absurd lengths; for example, the Red Army's deficiencies in snow warfare were reflected in the institution of new winter training procedures so harsh that many soldiers died. And however hard Timoshenko might labour to put things right, much was irremediable because so many of the shortcomings reflected the realities of Soviet society. The contrast between the Finns and the Red Army in terms of fighting spirit and competence was just as noticeable as the difference between the Russian and Japanese soldiers in 1904–5, and in both wars demonstrated the weaknesses of Russian society. Timoshenko and his colleagues could not change Soviet society. They could not put an end to the NKVD's activity in the army, so destructive of morale, nor could they create a society that every soldier would fight for. The panics that so often overcame Soviet frontline units were not caused by character defects but resulted largely from the cult of secrecy so treasured by the NKVD. The habit of treating any item of information as a state secret meant that units were not told what to expect. Quite often, neither the soldiers nor their officers were told where the enemy was, or in what strength; such information was restricted to the higher officers who issued the orders to the unit. In such conditions panic and an inability to react to circumstances were quite understandable.

Successful field officers of the Finnish war were brought to the Defence Commissariat. The new Chief of the General Staff was Zhukov, who in 1939 had beaten the Japanese at the frontier battle of Khalkin Gol. Not least, the concept of mass tank formations was restored. Despite these measures, the year's breathing space before Germany attacked was largely misused, because Stalin rejected the possibility of a German attack so soon. The Navy Commissar later wrote:[1]

---

[1] *Oktyabr*, No. 11 (1965), 148.

In my opinion the great authority of I. V. Stalin played a dual role in military matters. On the one hand everybody believed firmly that Stalin had better knowledge and, when the time came, would take necessary measures. Secondly, this belief discouraged those close to him from having their own opinion, and expressing it directly and decisively.

There was much confusion in the Defence Commissariat, with urgent decisions being repeatedly postponed. Sometimes the generals could not agree about priorities, sometimes there was time-wasting interference by Stalin's protégés or representatives. It was apparently for resisting such interference that in June 1941 the Commissar of the Armaments Industry was arrested.[2]

Several generals were purged on the eve of the war. In some cases this may have been to encourage the others but at least one of the victims, the air force commander, paid for an indiscretion; reproachfully, he had told Stalin that he was losing too many pilots because they were forced to fly in unsafe aircraft. Many other generals were executed after the invasion, in some cases because they had obeyed orders and not made adequate preparations to meet an attack. Yet others were executed after the war for allowing themselves to be captured. On the whole, with a few glorified exceptions, it was not a good war for generals.

A continuing problem, unique to the Red Army, was the role of the political commissar. In the late twenties, because so many commanders were party members, the commissars were no longer required to countersign orders of the commanders except in the case of major orders or decisions. In 1934 one-man leadership was further strengthened when commanders were given complete authority both in military and political matters. The commissars were renamed 'political guides' and henceforth were merely to assist commanders in the political education of their men, and advise them on questions of morale and discipline. The army purge did not spare the political directorate of the Red Army. The head of this directorate, Gamarnik, was one of the first victims (like many others, he committed suicide when faced with arrest). At the same time political commissars were restored to their former authority; probably Stalin wished to forestall the resentment aroused in the army by the activities of the NKVD. The dual command of units which was thus re-established was one of the causes of the poor leadership demonstrated in the Finnish campaign. So in 1940 the pre-1937 system was restored, with the commissar again named 'political guide' and subordinated to the unit commander. During and after the war there would be more changes; there was no system which could at once guarantee the party *apparat*'s control over commanders yet

---

[2] He was one of the lucky ones who were released and reinstated when the war started.

at the same time allow commanders the freedom of command which they needed to perform their tasks.

The air force and navy were considered primarily as adjuncts to the army. When the war started in 1941, most Soviet aircraft were of old design. The standard fighter was slower than the German bombers. As with tanks and guns, the changeover to advanced designs, with its inevitable short-term disruption of production, had been too long delayed. The Soviet aircraft industry was capable of doing more than had hitherto been demanded of it, even though some of its best designers, including Tupolev, had been arrested.[3]

The reconstruction of the navy had been slow. The defeat of the Kronstadt rebels had not rid the fleet of its indiscipline and resentment. Moreover, the surviving ships had been in poor condition. Until the late thirties, when Kuznetsov was appointed People's Commissar of the Navy, a purely coast defence role was envisaged. The Russo-German co-operation before 1933 had brought blueprints and advice on submarine building, and by the mid-thirties a substantial underwater fleet had been created, intended for the coastal waters of the Baltic and Black seas. Then, in 1938, a new navy was planned. Most admirals would have liked aircraft carriers, especially for the new Far Eastern Fleet, but Stalin preferred the more traditional battleships and cruisers:

In their interventions, members of the government often emphasized that the project for one ship or another had been approved by I. V. Stalin personally. This was to imply that such a project was not open to discussion.[4]

The navy remained without aircraft carriers. Some of the cruisers were completed, but the battleships were destined to be destroyed in the shipyards to avoid capture. The Red Navy played a small role in the war, never quite recovering from the loss of ships and bases in 1941. However, towards the end of the war it distinguished itself in a number of combined operations. Its submarines became a serious threat to German sea communications.

June 1941

'Operation Barbarossa' began 22 June 1941, having been postponed for one month because of Hitler's difficulties in the Balkans. The catastrophic Soviet losses of the ensuing days and weeks suggested that Stalin had been taken absolutely by surprise. The truth was much more complex but, decades after the event, was still not fully clear.

---

[3] Individuals with especially valuable talents were sometimes allowed to continue their work as members of incarcerated design teams.

[4] Admiral Kuznetsov, in *Oktyabr*, No. 9 (1965), 175.

The Nazi–Soviet Pact could hardly have been regarded by the Soviet leadership as anything but a precaution which would remain effective only so long as Hitler was engaged in western Europe. The USSR loyally fulfilled her obligations under this agreement. Strategic materials were shipped to Germany. Murmansk was made available to German ships. Communist parties were persuaded to hinder the war efforts of those governments at war with Germany. Even German communists, sheltering in Russia from Nazi persecution, called on German workers to support Hitler's war effort. At first, Germany also carried out her obligations; German experts aided Soviet naval shipyards, a Soviet mission was allowed to purchase specimens of modern German aircraft.

According to some accounts, Hitler's decision in late 1940 to invade Russia in 1941 was known to Soviet intelligence within two weeks. In any case, indications were not long lacking. At the new Russo-German frontier in what was once Poland, the German guards who had previously saluted the appearance of Russian officers no longer did so, confining themselves to derogatory gestures. In February, a sympathetic German printer brought to the Soviet embassy in Berlin a new Russian phrase-book which he had been ordered to print in large numbers; the book included phrases like 'Are you a communist?' and 'Hands up or I'll shoot!' German reconnaissance aircraft made ever-more frequent appearances over Soviet territory. How this information was presented to Stalin is uncertain, but since the Nazi–Soviet Pact was concurrently being praised as one of Stalin's great achievements, and since Stalin openly rejected the possibility of German treachery, it is quite likely that the reports he saw discreetly minimized what was happening. In a private letter Hitler assured Stalin 'in confidence' that the German troops concentrated in Poland were there to preserve them from British bombing raids, and Stalin believed him. Zhdanov, the party leader entrusted with naval and military affairs, was not suited by character or ability for his role as Stalin's military adviser. In particular, he does not appear to have questioned Stalin's conviction that Germany would never fight on two fronts and that the English Channel was already one such 'front'. Stalin seems to have believed that Hitler would turn east only after the defeat of Britain, unless there were successful 'provocations'. It was this fear of provocations, of anti-Russian German officers on their own initiative beginning hostilities which would be impossible to stop, that seems to have been mainly responsible for the lack of preparations behind the frontier. Individual officers who, aware of the danger, might have tried to take precautions, would have done so at their own great risk, for they would have been opposing the official line; their political officers, or the NKVD operatives, would hardly ignore such 'alarmist' moves. While this equation of vigilance with 'alarmism' handicapped the military, the constant reiteration of how right Stalin had been in signing the Nazi–Soviet Pact prevented any psychological preparation of the population against a possible German attack.

In early summer there were more signs of danger. Warnings by western governments could be plausibly dismissed as efforts to embroil the USSR in war against Hitler. But German troop concentrations were not so easily explained, nor were increasing incursions into Soviet airspace by German aircraft. Stalin responded by placatory measures. Delivery to Germany of raw materials was speeded up, Soviet diplomats assured Berlin of Russian loyalty, and on June 14 TASS[5] issued its notorious communiqué on Russo-German relations. This message, given the widest possible publicity, stated that the recent dispatch of German troops '. . . to the eastern and north-eastern regions of Germany must be presumed to be in connection with motives quite independent of Soviet–German relations', and that '. . . in Soviet opinion, rumours of Germany's intention to break the pact and attack the USSR are baseless'. This communiqué has been described as the 'final tranquillizer' administered to the Red Army; after this authoritative statement it was virtually impossible for any Soviet commander to do anything to meet the threat. Thus, years after other world leaders had realized the futility of appeasement, Stalin had emerged as the biggest appeaser of them all. But the desperate lengths to which appeasement was taken do suggest that Stalin was aware of the danger. If so, the invasion found him both unsurprised and unprepared.

The abrupt departure of all German ships from Soviet ports, the arrival on the Soviet side of the frontier of at least one talkative German deserter, and other indications, persuaded Stalin to call an emergency meeting of defence officials on the afternoon of June 21. Telegrams were then sent to units near the frontier, warning of a growing threat but urging restraint in the face of provocations. Many units did not receive these telegrams until it was too late. Others replied by asking whether they should fire, if fired upon; to this they received no satisfactory answer.

The invasion began at 4 a.m., preceded by air attacks on certain towns. Radio announcements that the USSR was at war came only at noon. From the memoirs of those who were there, it would appear that as dawn broke on June 22 the same scene, with variations, took place wherever officers met: against a background of flame and smoke from Soviet airfields, fuel and ammunition dumps, amid bodies and shattered buildings, Soviet

---

[5] Telegraphic Agency of the Soviet Union, founded 1925 as the sole Soviet news agency.

officers with voices raised over the din of German dive-bombers and exploding shells turned to each other and asked, 'Are we at war?'

The frontier guards of the NKVD also seemed to be unprepared. One detachment later sent in a report which may profitably be read between the lines:

> ... Exactly 0400 Moscow Time 22 6 41 the Germans began to bombard the town of Taurog ... the first shells destroyed the fuel stock, all autotransport, and food supplies ... the documents of the detachment were loaded on to two vehicles and sent to Shanlyai. The Battalion Commander in person took away, by car, party documents, registration cards, blank forms, party cards ... [6]

The course of the war

Because Soviet military theory was still based on the doctrine of the immediate offensive, many Red army units and supply dumps were within easy range of German artillery, and were destroyed in the first hours. The Red Air Force was shattered, most of its losses being aircraft destroyed on the ground. Against the advice of his general staff, Stalin had placed the main weight of the Red Army to cover the Ukraine rather than the centre, and this proved mistaken. The German offensive was three-pronged: towards Leningrad, towards Moscow, and towards the Ukraine and southwest. Although the objective of destroying the entire Red Army was not achieved (because German intelligence was weak, and had not realized that a Russian redeployment had started in 1941), the Soviet forces were soon in disarray, suffering enormous losses. Several Red Army generals were shot for retreating, and others committed suicide to avoid a similar fate. Unlike the Patriarch Sergius, who immediately issued a patriotic proclamation, Stalin was silent and appeared to lose his grip of affairs in the first few days, but in early July finally made a broadcast in which his appeal for a total war effort was based more on patriotic than ideological themes; he even addressed his listeners as 'brothers and sisters, dear fellow-countrymen'. Meanwhile the traditional *stavka* (GHQ) was reinstated. This was located in Moscow and consisted at first of four generals (Voroshilov, Budyenny, Shaposhnikov, and Zhukov) and two party leaders (Stalin and Molotov). Despite the general collapse and at times headlong retreat, Hitler did not succeed in his object of capturing Moscow and Leningrad. The drive on Moscow was delayed by a very strong defence of Smolensk, and by Hitler's order to his armour to halt awhile outside the capital. When an assault was launched it was too late, although some German units reached the suburbs. In Moscow there had been a short panic, especially after the ministries were evacuated. Crowds besieged the

[6] *Istoricheskii arkhiv* No. 3 (1961), 78–9.

railway stations and there was some anti-semitic activity by optimistic Nazi sympathizers. The NKVD execution squads, ordered by Beria to deal with political prisoners, worked overtime (that is, they killed during day-light as well as in the customary night-time hours). Some government de-partments and treasures were moved out and a proclamation, never issued, and concealed for fifty years, was prepared for the evacuation of the cap-ital by other state bodies.

One night, in strictest secrecy, the body of V. I. Lenin was taken out from the Mausoleum and sent under strong guard in a special railway car to Kuibyshev.

There was one point in this proclamation that Stalin wanted nobody to hear about, especially when it became clear that Moscow was holding. It said that Com-rade Stalin was to go into evacuation as soon as the proclamation was published.[7]

When it became clear that Moscow was holding out, and that Stalin was still there, the Muscovites settled down to the struggle.

Meanwhile, in the north, Leningrad was soon besieged; Voroshilov's handling of the northern forces had not been in keeping with his inflated reputation and he was preparing to abandon Leningrad when Zhukov ar-rived to take things in hand. However, despite a gruesome siege of twenty-eight months, during which about 700,000 of the population starved or froze to death, Leningrad, like Moscow, never fell into German hands. The German south-western offensive was spectacularly successful. In just two pincer movements, a million prisoners were taken; Odessa was cap-tured and also much of the Crimea. By the end of 1941 the western part of European Russia was occupied.

Although one of the stated reasons for creating the Urals–Kuznetsk steel combine had been the desirability of shifting industry away from vul-nerable regions, little had been done to relocate arms industries before the war. Almost all the aircraft industry, for example, was in areas that would be overrun by the Germans. A relocation would have conflicted with the ruling military doctrine that a future war would be short and offensive. This doctrine meant not only that preparations for the air defence of industry had not been made, but also that plans for evacuating industry were not developed. However, in the short time available the railways and industry worked wonders in evacuating whole factories to the east. Some were taken into Siberia and Central Asia, but most were set down, usually on unprepared sites, in the Urals and Volga regions. Over 1,500 large-scale enterprises were said to have been moved in this way. Once set down, it took months to get them into production, because the necessary com-ponents, raw materials, and workers had to be obtained. Despite a cata-clysmic cut in civilian production it took time for the war industries to get

<hr>

[7] V. Karpov in *Gudok*, 19 July 1991, 3.

going. 1942 was the worst year, with arms and munitions production falling far short of requirements.

However, the German situation in late 1941 was not easy. The Wehrmacht was facing ever-stronger counter-attacks as the Red Army received fresh troops, and it was ill-equipped for winter; its tank engine cylinders cracked in the cold, its army boots, tight and steel-nailed, proved disastrously successful heat conductors (at one stage it suffered a thousand frostbite casualties daily), and its supply routes were long, slow, and subject to partisan attack.

Despite his generals' caution, Hitler decided to mount new offensives in the summer of 1942. The main target was to be the Caucasian oilfields, but it was also intended to finally capture Leningrad. Moscow was not considered a prime target. The Wehrmacht did advance through Rostov, capture Sevastopol, and occupy the north Caucasus. The loss of the Crimea and the débâcle of the Kerch Peninsula were disgraceful episodes that subsequent histories glossed over. The Red Army collapse here was partly because of interference by the feared army commissar who was monitoring proceedings, but displayed other symptoms of deep-rooted incompetence, including a cavalry charge against tanks.

But the German army did not capture the main Caucasian oil region. It might have been more successful if Hitler had not diverted 300,000 men to capture Stalingrad. This city, though of strategic significance, was not all-important, but both Hitler and Stalin chose to regard it as such (it was, after all, 'Stalin's City'). An impressive array of Soviet political and military talent was sent to the city: Vassilievsky, the new Chief of the General Staff; Zhukov, just appointed a deputy defence commissar in recognition of recently-won distinction; Chuikov, commander of the city's garrison; Malenkov, Stalin's personal representative; and Khrushchev, now a senior military commissar, who had retreated with the Red Army from the Ukraine. While a deliberately small holding-force defended the city, street by street, house by house, and room by room, big Russian reserves were assembled. As the winter started, these reserves, commanded by Rokossovsky, Yeremenko, and Vatutin, routed Italian and Roumanian forces covering the German rear. Hitler refused to allow his commander, Paulus, to withdraw. Goering was unable to keep his promise of a supply airlift. Relief forces failed to break through. Winter became bitter. In February 1943 Paulus and his army surrendered. It was a great Russian victory, especially psychologically. Coming soon after Alamein, it confirmed that the Germans could be beaten; henceforth the Russians were sure that they would win the war. To regard Stalingrad as the turning point of the war in Europe is therefore justified.

1943 was a year in which both sides had successes and failures, but the German army was well back from its 1941 positions. The battle of the Kursk Salient was the first time a German offensive had been defeated on its own start line. Hitler still insisted on rigid defence lines; the German army would have suffered less if he had sanctioned an elastic and mobile defence. In 1944 the big Soviet offensives began, and the Germans there-after never regained the initiative. In this year ('The Year of the Ten Vic-tories') Leningrad was relieved, Sevastopol and the Crimea were regained, the Finns were pushed back in Karelia, the Vistula was reached in Poland, German divisions were cut off in the Baltic states, and the Red Army en-tered Hungary and Yugoslavia. Finland and Roumania ceased hostilities, and Bulgaria (which had declared war against Britain but not against the USSR) was invaded. In January 1945 began the drive towards Berlin, which was captured in May, thereby bringing the war in Europe to a close. By previous agreement, three months later the Red Army attacked Japanese forces in Manchuria, capturing a large part of the region before (and after) Japan's surrender.

The Red Army at war

By 1941, in terms of quantity of men, weapons, and reserves, the Red Army was the world's biggest. Qualitatively it was not so outstanding. Hitler, ex-pecting the Soviet railways to fail in wartime, and influenced by the poor showing of the Red Army in Finland, was not deterred by the numerical disparity. He could even have allocated more forces to the invasion if he had so chosen. As it was, he committed only 182 divisions against about 200 Russian divisions, and about 3,200 tanks against the Russians' 20,000. After 1941 this disparity grew as the USSR's enormous manpower reser-ves were mobilized and new production lines were opened; in its final of-fensive against Germany in 1945, the Red Army disposed of more than five million men, and could mass 300 guns per kilometre of front in key of-fensive sectors.

As in previous Russian wars, defects of leadership were compensated by the sacrifice of masses of infantrymen. Some German eye-witnesses re-ported how tight formations of Red soldiers, primed with vodka, would march shoulder to shoulder against strongpoints, cheering and singing until they were cut down by machine guns. Right up to the end of the war the casualty rate remained very high. During the war, Red Army men killed or missing amounted to between seven and ten million, compared to German Eastern Front losses of about half that number (precise figures are not available for either side). Some hints as to why Soviet casualties were unnecessarily high are provided by several Russian war novels. In two prize-winning novels about Stalingrad, Simonov's *Days and Nights* (1944), and Nekrasov's *In the Trenches of Stalingrad* (1948) there appear, as subsidiary characters, officers who order one suicidal attack after another (both receiving their due reward, lethal shrapnel in one case, posting to a lethal penal battalion in the other). In a post-Stalin novel, *Men are not born Soldiers* (1963), Simonov portrays mediocre life-squandering officers who owe their positions to generals who themselves are mediocre and owe their appointments to Stalin, who prefers mediocrities. There is also an incident where a commander is removed because his plan of attack, although likely to gain a bloodless victory, would not capture a key objective in time for the Red Army Day celebrations. (Kazakevich's short story *By Light of Day*, published in the same period, harped on the same point: 'Listen, Colonel. You see Height 61.5? You will capture it tomorrow morning. If you take it you will be . . . a Hero of the Soviet Union. If you don't you'll be shot.')

The rule that only written orders were valid caused many costly delays until 1942, when oral orders were allowed for units at battalion level and below. The purges had not been forgotten, even though some of the surviving victims (including the subsequently distinguished General Rokossovsky) had been released. Thus there was usually a strict adherence to orders. Many a key bridge, requiring just the push of a button to demolish it, was captured intact by the Germans because the officer in charge had not received orders to destroy it (often because the next superior officer was awaiting permission from his own superior officer). In 1942 there was another attempt to solve the political commissar problem; since effective command was now all-important, the commissars were reduced to 'deputy commanders for political affairs'. As in the Civil War, these men varied in character; some did resemble the near-perfect heroes of war novels, but others were interfering, paranoid, and sometimes cowardly.

Many wartime novels sought to instil confidence in the military commissars. For example, Grossman's *The People Immortal* (1943) seemed designed to counter two tendencies, the tendency of military men to distrust or belittle their commissars, and the apathy with which many Russians seemed to regard the Germans in the early part of the war. The hero of this novel, Bogarev, is a military commissar and one of those faultless characters so often encountered in Russian literature of the period of Socialist Realism. He is a teacher, critic, and father to his men. When demoralized stragglers are addressed by him their shoulders become squarer, their faces calmer, and their eyes wiser, they decide to collect their precious scraps of tobacco and present them to Bogarev, who refuses twice but accepts the third time with tears in his eyes and a lump in his throat. Later, Bogarev incisively criticizes the unit's commander, a 'front-line man' who (it is implied) has little respect for commissars. Bogarev's comments turn out to be justified when the commander's attack fails. Bogarev reduces to the ranks an officer who openly admires German efficiency, and threatens to have him shot. His motivating force is love for his fellow-countrymen and hatred of the Germans: 'I shall devote all the power of brain and spirit to arousing hatred and vengeance! . . . We must learn to hate, or we shall not win'. In a subsequent novel Grossman again has a commissar hero, this time a stirring character who goes into the attack waving an automatic in one hand and his party card in the other.

The common soldier tended to be of great endurance and stolidity. Individuals at times of isolation often demonstrated a certain cunning and initiative but on the whole the soldiers fought bravely and intelligently only when well-led. In the final stages of the war, when the Red Army advanced into Europe, tales were spread of how Russian soldiers relieved the local population of their watches, and how no female between eight and eighty was safe. Much the same, perhaps more, might have been said about other victorious armies, and the Red Army, despite four years of barbarous war, was certainly not the worst of the belligerents.

When the war started the Soviet arms industry had only just changed over to new models, but the new weapons, though few, were often exceptionally good; the T.34 was probably the most successful tank of the Second World War. But the Tukhachevsky principle of using tanks as a separate arm, *en masse*, and using tanks to fight tanks, had not really been grasped by the generation of officers which rose to high positions during the purge. The tsarist tradition of high-quality artillery had been continued in the Red Army, but arrests had deprived this arm of many skilled officers. There was also a shortage of good gunners. This was perhaps why during the war there was a great reliance on mortars of various sizes, and why indirect artillery fire was less used than in other armies. In the latter part of the war, large numbers of caterpillar-tracked, armoured, self-propelled guns appeared, and gave the Red Army much-needed mobile artillery support. Also, there was the 'Katyusha', a multiple rocket projector mounted on a truck, which could saturate the enemy positions with its pattern of missiles. It was very effective and, being simple, was ideal for mass production. Mass production was essential, for Soviet strategy and tactics were based on a prodigious expenditure of lives and machines. The average expectation of life of a newly built tank or aircraft was about three months. A somewhat longer life was enjoyed by horses, which, because of the absence of trucks, were allocated to infantry divisions on the scale of one horse for every five men.

When Hitler invaded Russia, Britain assured the latter of full support, but this could not be immediately translated into action (however, it was gratefully received, because Britain's attitude might have been different). When in December 1941 the USA entered the war, this not only relieved the apprehension that Japan might turn against the USSR, but also secured preferential access to US industry. But transport difficulties limited this latter advantage, even though there was an Anglo-Russian occupation of Iran to provide at least one route for supplies (the Arctic sea route was also used, but entailed heavy losses). At first deliveries were almost negligible, but in 1943–4 a peak was reached, and in those years Allied deliveries were probably equivalent to the output of seven million Soviet workers. Over the war as a whole about one-sixth of Soviet aircraft were imported. Supplies of some commodities, including aviation fuel, telephone wire, and quality metals, were at times crucial. The Red Army's sweep into Nazi-occupied Europe was accomplished by soldiers wearing American boots, riding in American trucks, and feeding on American Spam. The British contribution was much smaller than the American, although Britain was expensively involved in the transportation of the Allied supplies.

The Red Army was not the only Soviet army. There were also the ground forces of the NKVD. At the beginning of the war these may have approached 200,000 troops, with their own armoured formations. The NKVD, apart from handling internal security, fire brigades, prison services, map publishing and other services, was by this time a great industrial–military complex. It ran its own industrial enterprises with its forced labour army, and it maintained security with its own military army. Among the sections of the latter were the frontier guards, who formed Russia's first line of defence; it was the NKVD, not the Red Army, which watched the frontiers. Inside the Red Army there were both open and covert NKVD elements. The covert element was made up of informers in the guise of officers and men whose task it was to report any signs of disaffection (often imagined rather than real). Among the overt detachments was SMERSH (a Russian acronym meaning 'death to spies'), whose main activity in the war was the shooting of Soviet troops. It was SMERSH units, standing with sub-machine guns behind Red Army units, which made it safer to advance than to retreat. In general, Red Army officers and men regarded the NKVD with impotent resentment and fear, but it was not until after 1953 that they would be able to reveal their feelings. It was the NKVD which regarded troops straggling back out of German encirclement as traitors. It was the NKVD which arrested the gifted artillery officer and future writer Solzhenitsyn, who had made some ironic references to 'the man with a moustache'. It was the NKVD which, later, applied

Stalin's 1942 instruction that any Red Army man who allowed himself to be taken prisoner was to be considered a traitor.

Another incentive were the penal battalions, which were made up of officers and men who had behaved badly, or who were regarded by the NKVD as suspect. The penal battalions were used for sacrificial enterprises; it was not unknown for them to be marched through minefields to clear a way for assault troops. Later in the war, the tsarist distinction of Guards units was re-established. Divisions which had distinguished themselves and were of high quality were granted this élite status. They received double pay, better equipment, and were rarely squandered in hopeless attacks.

Russians at war

The war began on a Sunday. Horrified citizens, beset by rumours and hearing little from official sources, gathered together to discuss the news or proceeded to their place of work to ask their bosses or party secretaries what was happening. This spontaneous move to the factory or collective for information and instruction implied much about Soviet society, but what was worrying to the authorities were the messages being received via local party and NKVD sources about the state of public morale in those first hours of war. Sharp criticisms were being voiced by ordinary people, it seemed. These ordinary people in fact were probably of two types. There were the straightforward, unsophisticated characters who believed that people arrested for anti-state activities in the past really had been guilty, and therefore did not realize the peril into which they put themselves by saying openly that the party, the government, and Stalin himself had made a mess of things. Then there were those who for years had been seething with impotent fury, who hated the communist party and its works, and at this time of peril and confusion felt they could express themselves openly. The common theme of critics was that the pro-German shift of the recent past had been stupid, and that Stalin was responsible for it. There was a feeling that the party had brought the country to this pass and it could not expect ordinary people to risk their lives to save the situation. There was also the feeling, frequently expressed, that the oncoming Nazis would make short shrift of Jews and communists, which would be no bad thing. Already, faith in the Red Army's ability to crush the Germans had been replaced by pessimism. In 1939 such faith had been widespread, fed by constant propaganda about Soviet military and industrial might, but the successes of the Germans in 1940 had made a great psychological impact.

Several measures were taken to counter this unpatriotic wave. In the first days there were arrests, and genuinely spontaneous meetings of workers were gradually replaced by organized spontaneous meetings at which only the proper sentiments were expressed. Passing on information that was contrary to that offered by the official channels became a capital offence. Nevertheless, it took some months for the Soviet population to place itself full-heartedly behind the leadership. Most people supported the government, but public opinion was mixed, if not mixed up. There were great scenes of despair and drunkenness at reservists' assembly points, but on the other hand, like Britain in 1914, thousands of citizens clamoured to volunteer for service, anxious to join up in time for the storming of Berlin.

It was the German failure to capture Moscow in late 1941 that solidified public opinion. Even though right from the first week the authorities had wisely described the conflict as a patriotic war, the patriotic response had not been total. But at Moscow the Red Army finally demonstrated that it might after all be able to stop the Germans. Equally important, the Red Army at this time actually recaptured lost territory. Such territory was small, but was large enough to reveal that it was not just Communists and Jews who faced extinction by the Nazis. For the first time, what Nazi occupation really meant became clear to all. When the Germans had first approached Moscow there had been disorder in the streets; some government offices and officials had begun to evacuate themselves; common citizens were fleeing, and others took the opportunity to loot and attack Jews. But that was the trough of public morale. Henceforth the Russian response to invasion was tough and solid. In the face of Nazi barbarity even the most resentful Russians could forget the past and give their full support to Stalin and the party.

In the non-Russian borderlands there was a different situation. In lands occupied by the Red Army in 1939 or 1940 there was naturally little support for Moscow. In the Ukraine, where the memory of the imposed collectivization and famine was still strong, and to a lesser extent in White Russia, feelings were potent enough to impel inhabitants on to the streets to welcome the German invaders. Perhaps if Hitler had promised to abolish collectivization the peasants of the Ukraine, and of Russia too, might have risen in a final and triumphant rebellion against the state. Hitler, however, chose to regard the Slavs as an inferior race, to be exploited until hard labour and hunger caused them to disappear; collective farms seemed an excellent system for this exploitation, and it was not until the tide turned against the Nazis that a few experiments in de-collectivization were started.

In the unoccupied zones life was extremely hard. There was a rationing system which, as previously, was discriminatory. However, the discrimination was no longer on a class basis, but varied according to employment. Bread became sacred, enormous care being taken to see that people got their daily ration, ranging (in 1943) from 4,418 calories for coal-miners to 780 calories for non-working adults. Other rationed foods were often unobtainable and never enough. People had to rely on unofficial sources: factory allotments, private gardens, collective farm markets, and barter; but slow starvation was the fate of millions. The only sections of the population that were guaranteed adequate food supply were frontline troops and some manual workers in vital heavy industries. Labour was completely mobilized, including pensioners and adolescents. Workers could be sent anywhere, and holidays were abolished. Deaths from cold, malnutrition, and overstrain were common. Including deaths from enemy action, probably about fifteen million Soviet civilians died because of the war. With military killed-and-missing at between seven and ten million, this suggests that more than one in ten of the population died during those four years. Many, if not most, of the five million or so who returned alive from German captivity appear to have gone straight to labour camps.

Thus Soviet press reports of the physical sacrifices made by ordinary Russians were not exaggerated. Some press campaigns, though, were unconvincing, as in the case of the drive ostensibly designed to raise funds for weapons but actually intended to absorb the public's spending power. Letters to Stalin like the following began to be printed in the papers:

Dear Iosif Vissarionovich,
In response to your historic report and order of the day, I am subscribing all my savings—155,000 roubles—to buy a tank . . . May the tracks of this tank mercilessly crush the German Fascist invaders.

LOKTYEV, Evgenii Ivanovich
Kolkhoz beekeeper[8]

Of real significance was the reconciliation with the Church. There had been signs of this before the war, but after June 1941 the Church's influence as a patriotic force was of vital importance, especially as in some occupied areas local priests were encouraging their flocks to take a pro-Nazi and anti-Soviet attitude. By 1942 there was a tacit understanding between Church and state that their differences were to be forgotten in the common struggle against the foreigner. This alliance seemed to be cemented when Patriarch Sergius published a message to Stalin in *Pravda*, '. . . I cordially and devoutly greet in your person the God-chosen leader of our military

---

[8] *Izvestiya*, 26 December 1942. This tank would carry a plate: 'Donated to the Red Army by Beekeeper Loktyev'. Public voluntary subscription for weapons was not new to Russia. After the Russo-Japanese War several patriotic citizens had bought ships for the navy. Prince Sheremetiev, for example, gave £201,000 and was rewarded, not entirely tactfully, when one of the 'Fish' class submarines was named *Sheremetiev*. The Sheremetievs were reputed to be tsarist Russia's biggest landowners; perhaps Loktyev was the USSR's biggest beekeeper.

and cultural forces. . .'. Additional spiritual reinforcements were dispatched by the Mufti of the Moslems '. . . May Allah help you to bring to a victorious end your work of freeing the oppressed peoples. Amen.' Then, after a discreet interval, the president of the Moscow Jewish community sent his own fiery encouragement to Stalin: '. . . the Almighty has prepared for the Fascist horde the inglorious and shameful destruction suffered by all the Pharaohs, Amalekites and Ammonites . . .' The support which these messages symbolized were a real asset in sustaining the morale of the Soviet people.[9]

The role of the partisans, small in the beginning of the war, grew later. They flourished especially in the woodlands of White Russia and the Ukraine, where huge tracts of country remained in their control. They were composed largely of Red Army men cut off in the retreat, party members who had been deliberately left behind or parachuted in later, and local inhabitants who joined to avoid deportation or as a reaction to German reprisals in areas subject to partisan activity. Probably many local inhabitants resented the partisans as much as the Germans did, because it is the aim of such guerrillas to prevent any compromise between locals and occupiers. Among some non-Russian nationalities there was a certain sympathy with the Germans. In Lithuania there was an anti-Russian rebellion on the eve of the German invasion. A Cossack unit was formed by the German army and, in the Ukraine, General Vatutin was one of many killed by anti-Soviet partisans. Nevertheless, the deportation *en masse*, under lethal conditions, of the Volga Germans, Crimean Tartars, and other smaller nationalities was hardly justified. As so often in Russian history, people suffered not for what they had done but for what the security organs suspected they might conceivably be thinking of doing.

Nazi ideology ruined the prospects of the anti-Soviet Russian army which was formed from prisoners of war. This army could have been a million or more strong and, if well-armed, might have proved decisive on the Eastern Front. The few units of anti-Soviet Russian troops which did go into action proved very successful. The leader of this army was one of the most popular and successful of the Red Army generals, Vlasov, who decided to make common cause with the Germans after he was captured. But Hitler could not relish the prospect of a Russian army winning successes over Stalin which the racially superior Wehrmacht had failed to win, so the majority of Vlasov's units were employed in non-combatant roles. In 1945 the Allies, in 'Operation Keelhaul', rounded up and handed back

[9] *Pravda*, 9, 12, and 16 November 1942.

to the USSR those 'Vlasovites' who fell into their hands. Vlasov was publicly hanged on Red Square.

No doubt one of the reasons why so many Russian prisoners of war volunteered for Vlasov's army was that the alternatives were less attractive. Branded as traitors at home because they had allowed themselves to be taken prisoner, they had poor prospects should the USSR win the war. On the other hand, being 'racially inferior', they were not granted the conditions enjoyed by other Allied soldiers in German captivity (Hitler claimed that this was justified because Russia had never signed the Geneva Convention). Over two million Red Army men died in captivity. In addition, about three million Russian civilians were deported to German labour camps, where they toiled until they dropped. Jews and communists suffered disproportionately, since it was the German practice to execute them immediately. Some communist prisoners escaped by concealing their party membership, but usually there was somebody who would denounce them. Similarly, massacres of the Jews were not always unwelcome in the Ukraine and White Russia, where the old anti-semitism lingered on. The worst massacres were at Babi Yar, outside Kiev, where at least 100,000 Jews were shot.

Russia and the Allies

Wartime co-operation between the USSR and her allies was marred by friction. In particular, Stalin in 1942 and 1943 railed against the absence of a Second Front. The Soviet press waged a campaign against idle British generals, and the idea was spread that the Americans were willing but the British were not. But Stalin did not see the enormous risks involved in a seaborne invasion. Moreover, Allied forces in Africa already held down significant German forces, and the mere threat of a Normandy landing prevented Hitler concentrating his troops against Russia. Also, Allied bombing of Germany obliged the Luftwaffe to allocate most of its fighters to home defence, enabling the Red Air Force to gain supremacy for the Soviet offensives of 1944–5. Nevertheless, although Stalin did not understand that the west could not wage war like he did, could not sacrifice masses of men simply to gain quick victories, it is also true that the western Allies failed to understand the underlying causes of Russian resentment. There were memories of the First World War, when costly Russian offensives had been launched to take the pressure off the Western Front, and there was an enormous difference between the war being fought in Russia and the war in western Europe. Whereas the latter was national and political, fought with a certain restraint, the Russo-German war was a quasi-racial war, fought with extreme savagery. The sacrifices of the Soviet

Union were enormously and horribly greater than those of her allies. Hitler made a deliberate distinction between his plans for the Russians, and his intentions towards the Anglo-Saxons.

A particularly contentious issue was the fate of Poland. Some Polish prisoners of war from the 1939 campaign, released from Soviet camps, were organized in a new Polish army under General Anders to fight against the Germans on the Eastern Front. However, most of them, including Anders, were anti-Russian, so after some strained discussion between London and Moscow they were allowed to join the Polish forces in Britain. About 15,000 Polish officers and men captured by the Russians had disappeared, and in 1943 German propaganda broadcasts reported the discovery of mass graves of Polish officers at Katyn. Despite a subsequent denial by a Soviet commission of inquiry, it was widely believed that they had been executed by the Russians. That the Soviet investigators were headed by Vyshinsky, well known for falsehood, tended to throw doubt on their published findings; the German investigating commission had included neutral experts. However, until the war was over most western newspapers supported the Soviet view; Allied unity was all-important. It was only four decades later, under the Gorbachev regime, that Soviet responsibility for this crime was confirmed. Apart from the Katyn victims thousands of other Poles, civilians and soldiers, appear to have perished in Russia at the same period.

The Katyn affair led to a breach between the Polish government-in-exile (in London) and the Soviet government. The latter assembled from Polish communists a rival government, which, despite British objections, was installed by the Red Army when it advanced into Poland. The London Poles lost strength when the Warsaw Resistance, which they supported, launched an ill-advised rising as the Red Army approached the city. The Red Army did not attack Warsaw when expected, and the Germans had time to suppress the Resistance. Contrary to its earlier intentions, the British government acquiesced in the new Polish frontiers demanded by Russia; Eastern Poland (annexed in 1939) was to remain in the USSR but Poland's western frontier would be moved westwards to the line of the Oder and Neisse rivers. Although this latter demarcation was regarded by the western Allies as provisional, the deportation of the Upper Silesian Germans from the area, and post-war circumstances, made it permanent. Thus the Second World War, which had started on behalf of Poland, ended with Poland's relocation and her eventual subjection to a pro-Soviet government. But in view of traditional Polish dislike of Russia, and Poland's own inter-war record, there was something to be said for Stalin's solution of the Polish problem. At that time the peace of Europe was perhaps best safeguarded by a government in Warsaw responsive to Soviet requirements, though this was not appreciated by the long-suffering Poles.

Soviet relations with her western Allies improved after 1943. The Comintern, which the war had made largely irrelevant, was dissolved in 1943, a gesture which the west chose to regard as placatory. More important, foreign communist parties after June 1941 were instructed to back the war effort of the Allies. When France and Italy were liberated the local communist parties made no attempt to seize power, even though they had great political strength, a fine record in the Resistance, and a stock of arms. Stalin, Roosevelt, and Churchill conferred at Teheran in 1943 and Yalta in 1945. At these meetings Stalin was able sometimes to play off the Americans against the British. This, plus his frequent intransigence, meant that more concessions were made to the USSR than by the USSR. At Yalta, however, Stalin's demand for a seat at the proposed United Nations Assembly for each of the constituent Soviet republics was turned down, although seats were allocated to the Ukraine and White Russia as well as to the USSR; the latter was thus the only state to have three UN votes. Stalin probably did not welcome Roosevelt's conception of the UN; he would have preferred a world run by Britain, the USA, and the USSR. This was why he ensured that the veto powers of the 'Big Five' would be extensive.

Together with the 1945 Potsdam meeting, these conferences outlined the post-war territorial changes. For Russia, the main gains were confirmation of her acquisitions of 1939–40, together with part of East Prussia (Königsberg becoming Kaliningrad) and, in the Far East, the former Japanese parts of Sakhalin and the Kurile Islands.

15. *Consolidation or Ossification?*

Post-war reaction

Despite the suffering, the war years were in one sense easier years because, as in 1812, the state and the people grew closer. Russians could identify themselves with their government, their party, and their Stalin in the common struggle. At the end of the war there was a more relaxed atmosphere, which Russians hoped would continue. Instead, there was a return to the old ways. Unlike most of the other ex-belligerents, the USSR turned its back on change and returned to the thirties. Even in the summer of 1945 the Soviet President (Kalinin) was announcing that the defeat of Hitler simply meant that only the most immediately dangerous enemies of the USSR had been dealt with. The threat of foreign attack was once more emphasized to justify the hard line at home.

The western influences that had penetrated during the war were one of the prime objects of attack. 'Soviet patriotism' was propagandized at the same time as western books, films, music (especially jazz), and technical or social achievements were vilified. In a 1947 admonition to Soviet writers, Zhdanov expressed himself in terms worthy of Nicholas I's publicists:

> Is it appropriate for Soviet patriots like us, representatives of progressive Soviet culture, to take the role of admirers or disciples of bourgeois culture? Our literature reflects a society which is on a higher level than any bourgeois-democratic society, a culture which is obviously superior to bourgeois culture and therefore, it need hardly be said, has a right to teach to others the new, universal, morals. Where can one find another people like ours, or a country like ours? Where can one find such wonderful human qualities . . . ?

Information about the outside world, restricted in the thirties, was even more distorted after 1946, and domestic information was only marginally better. Censorship was more intolerant and more rigorously applied than in tsarist times, and this rigour (though less of the intolerance) persisted after Stalin. There had never been any mention of the 1932 famine in the Soviet press[1]. Post-war encyclopedias contained no entry for Trotsky and in 1954, after Beria had been shot, subscribers to the *Great Soviet Encyclopedia* received neatly tailored pages about the Bering Strait which they were requested to insert in the space previously allotted to Beria. The censorship, whose existence was not publicized, effectively blocked the publication not only of heretical views but also of any facts which might possibly cast doubt on official ideology or official information. Newspaper editors had regular meetings with officials, in order to plan future news. Newspapers were censored twice, before printing and before distribution. Possibly this exhaustive scrutiny explains why Soviet newspapers were so admirably free of misprints.

The kind of propaganda which was inflicted on the Russian people was also inflicted on the outside world, through local communist parties or associations set up and financed either by Soviet agencies or by communist sympathizers. However, in conditions where there were several competing sources of information this propaganda probably made more enemies than friends. There was something ludicrous, for example, in the claim that Britain was planning war against the USSR at the very time when the British government was permitting the export to Russia of jet aero engines, of which the USSR had little experience. The 'Stockholm Peace Appeal', launched to obtain millions of signatures to a petition directed mainly against warmongering, seemed similarly inept, especially as it originated in the nation with the world's largest standing army.

Stalin was 66 in 1945, and he retained the two key posts of head of government (which he had assumed in place of Molotov in May 1941) and party Secretary. His desire to run the USSR in the old ways was expressed in the post-war composition of the Politburo, which was basically the same as in 1939 (both the 1939 and 1948 Politburos contained Stalin, Molotov, Voroshilov, Kaganovich, Mikoyan, Andreyev, and Khrushchev. Two 1939 members, Kalinin and Zhdanov, died in 1946 and 1948, while Malenkov, Beria, Voznesensky, and Bulganin joined after 1939). In the early forties, Zhdanov and Malenkov seemed to be Stalin's favourites. Zhdanov, a petty intellectual, was the guardian of ideological purity. Malenkov had risen rapidly since his first appointment to the *apparat* in 1925.

It seems that Malenkov, Zhdanov, and Stalin formed the same kind of eternal triangle as Golitsyn, Arakcheyev, and Tsar Alexander I; there was personal jealousy between Malenkov and Zhdanov, and Stalin was aware of it. When Zhdanov died in 1948 there was a purge of his associates. About 200 were purged and the affair became known as the 'Leningrad Affair'

---

[1] Even under Khrushchev, Russian calamities (for example, air crashes) were not mentioned unless foreigners were involved. Foreign disasters received good coverage, however.

because the victims were current or past officials of the Leningrad party organization. Among the executed was Voznesensky, whose demise removed a figure whose economic views were too rational for comfort, and Kuznetsov. The latter was First Secretary of the Leningrad party organization, had distinguished himself in the siege of Leningrad, and was said to be somewhat restrained in his public praise of Stalin. Nevertheless Stalin had appointed him to supervise the MVD[2] and security organizations, and this could hardly have failed to arouse the jealousy of Beria who, with Malenkov, engineered the Leningrad Affair. A few of Zhdanov's Leningrad protégés, including Kosygin, were spared.

It was in the wake of the Leningrad Affair that Khrushchev was recalled to Moscow; possibly Stalin felt a new counterweight to Malenkov was needed. At the 19th party congress in 1952 a nice balance of power was implied in the choice of Malenkov to present the Central Committee's main report, and of Khrushchev to present the new party Rules. This congress was the first for thirteen years; the party had lost its pre-eminence in the thirties, having become simply a tool of Stalin. It had grown enormously during the war because large numbers of servicemen had been enrolled with little check on their qualifications; the 1940 membership had been around four million, but this had grown to six million in 1945, even though wartime losses had been very heavy. At the time of the 19th congress three-quarters of the membership were under forty-five years of age. After the war the party was less a vanguard of change than an instrument of administration. Party professionals in a locality were responsible for coordinating economic activity, helping managers do their job. But it was quite common for them to interfere in management, which in principle was deprecated. During the war the party had become more centralized, and continued to be an auxiliary of the government rather than an independent force. Because of its huge wartime intake, many of its officials were inexperienced and lacked confidence; the blind imposition of central directives came naturally to them. Most had little feeling for the old revolutionary traditions, little knowledge of the outside world, but a great regard for the regime which had educated them and found white-collar jobs for them. In the post-war years there was a curtailment of recruitment, with stricter entry tests, and many party organizations which had become cliques during the war were purged. In these years some real headway was at last made in strengthening the party in the collective farms, while at the same time there was a drastic and intended fall in army membership.

[2] In 1946 the people's commissariats were renamed ministries. Hence the NKVD became MVD.

The 1952 congress was followed by the initial stages of what seemed to be a new massive purge. Possibly Stalin realized that his principal lieutenants were ageing men, out of touch with the new generation of the administrative and technical élite. Khrushchev's subsequent indication that Stalin was planning the removal of Molotov, Malenkov, and Mikoyan, among others, suggests that a new purge, once started, would have spread to all ranks of the party organization. In January 1953 it was announced that nine doctors (of whom seven were Jewish) had been accused of working for a US Jewish organization and of killing Zhdanov and other high Soviet leaders whom they had treated. The Minister of State Security, Ignatiev, was told (according to Khrushchev) that he would be shortened by a head if he did not obtain confessions from the doctors. The confessions were duly obtained (although two of the doctors died in the process) but Stalin died before executions could take place. The surviving doctors were then released, the 'Doctors' Plot' was declared a fabrication, certain MVD officials were executed, and the doctor (a part-time MVD informer) who had been awarded the Order of Lenin for her vigilance in first denouncing the doctors, handed back her decoration.

Post-war reconstruction

Even allowing for the fact that, when the rubble was cleared away, many 'completely destroyed' structures were revealed as partly intact, the physical damage caused by the Germans was enormous. Apart from the normal destruction of war, there was the Russian 'scorched earth' policy of 1941, and the thorough 'scorched earth' of the retreating Germans after 1943. When the war ended, at least twenty-five million Russians were homeless. Long lengths of railway track had been torn up. Dams, bridges and factories had been wrecked and livestock destroyed.

The Fourth Five-Year Plan (1946–50) was designed to restore the Soviet economy to the pre-war level; Stalin promised at least two more hard five-year plans to follow. In fact the economy recovered very rapidly, pre-war standards in industry (but not agriculture) being largely reached after three years. The main credit for this belonged to the unbelievably hard work and unbelievably harsh privations of the Soviet people. The labour of at least two million prisoners of war, reparations from Germany, Finland, Roumania, Hungary and Manchuria, one-sided trade agreements with the people's democracies, deliveries of some key items by UN agencies, Britain, and Sweden, and the advantages, in situations of scarcity, of strong central planning, also made substantial contributions.

This achievement was marred somewhat, especially in the Fifth Plan, by the resources devoted to the 'grandiose Stalin construction projects'.

Among these was the expensive Volga–Don Canal, which had very little traffic but many statues of Stalin. The enormous hydro-electric schemes, which converted long lengths of the Volga into artificial lakes, were also unwise in so far as they tied up great quantities of labour and material in projects which would take years to become productive.

The wartime relaxation of control over the farms had, among other things, meant that much collective land, implements, and stock had found its way into the private economy of the peasants. The party was even more weak in the countryside than previously. Many farm chairmen abused their positions. There was a shortage of tractors and horses, which meant that women were sometimes harnessed to the ploughs. The more able-bodied men had tended to move to the towns before the war, and many of those who had stayed had been later killed at the front. It was possible to find villages entirely populated by widows and children (and it was still possible in 1950). The poor harvest of 1946 resulted in a partial famine in 1947, accompanied by rioting in some localities.

Khrushchev, who after the dismissal of Andreyev fancied himself as the party's agricultural expert, proposed the amalgamation of adjacent farms to form units which would be more easily controlled and which would be big enough to maintain party cells. This was done; by the end of 1952 the previous quarter-million collectives had been merged into about 100,000 larger units. However, Khrushchev's advocacy of even bigger concentrations, 'agrotowns', was rejected. During this period peasant income was negligible. Strong measures were taken against misappropriation of farm property in 1946. Stalin tried to impose the 'Travopolye' rotation (see p. 381) and an additional burden was another of Stalin's grandiose transformations: the planting of extensive belts of trees in semi-arid regions, in order to improve the climate of the USSR. This scheme failed because most of the trees died from lack of moisture.

Russia and the world

When the war ended the Red Army was the world's most powerful, and it occupied most of central and eastern Europe. On the other hand, although Stalin publicly belittled the significance of the atomic bomb, the US monopoly of that weapon set limits to Soviet foreign policy; in a sense, the maintenance of a huge peacetime army, poised on the frontiers of western Europe, was Moscow's counter-deterrent. Outside the Soviet orbit Russia had earned great respect and popularity during the war. In Britain a Labour government was anxious to fulfil its election promise that 'left can speak to left'. But in the USA the sympathetic Roosevelt died in 1945 and was replaced by Truman, whose experience as a Missouri politician had not predisposed him towards favouring the communists; one of his first acts was to suspend Lend-Lease to Russia. Nevertheless, it seems doubtful that the so-called Cold War would have been avoided by a different US president; Stalin was already too distrustful. The Cold War began with mutual distrust, and continued with genuine differences which increased this distrust, causing each side to take measures which were followed by counter-measures and counter-counter-measures.

The gradual establishment of Stalinist peoples' democracies in central and eastern Europe was one cause of dissension between the former allies. The process which had started with Poland during the war was repeated in the cases of Hungary, Albania, Bulgaria, Yugoslavia and Roumania. Finland and Czechoslovakia were spared. Indeed, Finland was treated in the way which the west had envisaged for all of Russia's neighbours; there was an independent and freely-elected government which regarded friendly relations with the USSR as a first priority. In Czechoslovakia the Communist Party was able to establish itself as an important partner in the government by virtue of its genuine electoral support; in 1946 it received more than one-third of the votes. One people's democracy which failed was that of the Soviet zone of Iran. Northern Iran, occupied by the USSR at the same time as southern Iran was occupied by the British, was due to be evacuated after the war. The USSR was at first reluctant to abandon this outpost in the Middle East, in which a 'people's government' had been installed. But the Red Army was finally withdrawn in 1946, and the 'people's government' abandoned its people and retired to the USSR.

Another early cause of inter-allied friction was reparations. As was perhaps natural for a state emerging from the ruin of war, the Soviet Union was determined to transfer to the USSR German plant (and some key personnel) located in the Soviet zone of occupation. Russia also demanded a share of the industry of the Ruhr, as well as a share in the administration of that region. This claim was rejected by the western Allies, perhaps recalling the mistake of reparations after the First World War, and was one of the earliest causes of subsequent disagreement on the fate of Germany. Russia retaliated by refusing to sign an Austrian peace treaty. In Manchuria, the Red Army succeeded in stripping much of the local industry before that region was handed back to the Chinese.

The western press was beginning to talk of Soviet espionage, but its readers were unaware that western intelligence services were themselves engaged in anti-Soviet activities. The CIA was busy supporting the armed nationalists in the Ukraine, while British intelligence was shipping anti-Soviet emigrants back into the Baltic republics where, it was imagined, they would form the nucleus of an anti-Soviet rising. Neither the Americans nor the British were a match for the Soviet security organizations; in fact the British were hardly a match for anyone, with the amateurishness in which they took such pride verging on the inane. As a result, hundreds of brave Ukrainians and Lithuanians were sacrificed. 1946 witnessed Churchill's Fulton speech, warning America of dark Soviet intentions, and the first steps towards the long-term division of Germany; the British and American occupation zones were amalgamated and, together with the French zone, later became the West German Republic. At the same time the German Socialist Party in the Soviet zone was coerced into merger with the Communist Party to form the Socialist Unity Party, which later formed the Stalinist government of the German Democratic Republic. Over the years there were attempts to reach agreement on the reunification of Germany, although it is doubtful whether any government, apart from the US and West German, genuinely wanted reunification. Stalin's unsuccessful attempt to blockade the western sector of Berlin in 1948 was an incautious attempt to force Britain, France and the USA out of Berlin.

The Marshall Plan of 1947 was an anti-communist measure in so far as its motivation was the American wish to extend help to European economies struggling with post-war conditions, and thus discourage the spread of communism, which was believed to occur in conditions of social distress. The USSR delegation to the initial talks staged a walk-out, led by Molotov, and Soviet pressure prevented Czechoslovakia's participation. In the same year a new uncompromising Soviet line in foreign policy was presented by Zhdanov, who stated that the world was irrevocably split into two camps. To replace the Comintern, the Communist Information Bureau (Cominform) was established to co-ordinate the policies of the main European communist parties. In France and Italy the strong local parties were instructed to begin a campaign of strikes, demonstrations, and sabotage. When the latter caused casualties the communists lost much of their popularity in those two countries, and their electoral position worsened.

1948, with its deepening of the German crisis, also saw a transformation of the 'socialist camp'. The Soviet treatment of the people's democracies had not been as sympathetic as their communist governments had expected. The Soviet ministry of trade had taken over certain industrial enterprises, whose labour and materials were used solely to manufacture items for the USSR and it imposed commercial agreements in which Soviet exports were priced high and Soviet imports priced low. This reduction of the people's democracies to a colonial status was accompanied by close political and MVD supervision. Their governments were compelled to introduce socialism strictly on the Russian model: 'there is only one road to socialism, the Soviet road'. In reality, the Russian way was unsuited to these countries, if only because they were in many ways more sophisticated than the USSR.

In February 1948 a coup placed the Czech communists in absolute power. A few weeks later the popular non-communist leader Masaryk was found dead beneath a high window. In 1951–2 many agents of the coup, stalwart communists like Slansky and Clementis, were tried on charges of spying for Britain and Israel, and were executed. These and other arrests and executions in the people's democracies were occasioned by the defection of Tito and Yugoslavia in 1948; potential 'Titoists' elsewhere were liquidated as a precaution. Unlike other people's democracies, Yugoslavia was isolated from the Red Army, had a popular leader who had not depended on Soviet support to gain or maintain power, and was thus able and willing to resist Soviet interference. After the parties and governments of Russia and Yugoslavia had exchanged accusations of spying on each other, the Cominform expelled the Yugoslav party. Tito, in the vituperative language which for years had been favoured by Soviet propagandists, was called 'a capitalist hyena' and his government 'terroristic, shameful, and quite Turkish'. With strong support from his own people and party, and some help from the west, Tito, to Stalin's disgust, survived and provided a dangerous example of a non-Russian approach to marxist socialism.

In the Far East the communists finally overcame the Kuomintang and set up the Chinese People's Republic in 1949. Stalin had neither expected nor hoped for this success and had done little to help the Chinese communists. However, after 1949 Soviet economic and technical help was given to the new Peking government, although the Soviet technicians included the usual complement of MVD men.

In general the foreign policy of Stalin's last years was dismal. At the United Nations Vyshinsky (who was appointed Foreign Minister in 1949) specialized in negative vituperation until his insalubrious career ended with a heart attack and interment beneath the Kremlin wall. His conduct had earned the resentment of smaller nations which had placed great hope in the UN. Goodwill had also been lost elsewhere. The west had formed an armed anti-Soviet alliance, NATO, two of whose member-nations (Norway and Turkey) bordered the USSR and thus outflanked the new line of people's democracies which formed a buffer zone between the USSR and the west. In the people's democracies, the friendly post-war governments and often sympathetic people had been replaced by fawning governments and resentful people. Tito was having some success in showing that the Russian road to socialism was a cul-de-sac. East Germans and Red Army men were still deserting in large numbers to the west.

Population

According to the 1926 census, the population of the USSR was 147 million, and growing at the rate of three million annually. The 1937 census result was suppressed, and its compilers purged. A new and less reliable census in 1939 produced a figure of 171 million. The growth rate had fallen partly because of several million unnatural deaths but largely because of a fall in the birth-rate. The rural population had fallen from 82 to 67 per cent and urban families had a birth-rate even lower than usual because of the housing shortage. Nevertheless, in 1939 the population was a young population, which was a great advantage in the war years. The war brought great losses, and also the acquisition of new peoples in the annexed territories. There was a good deal of what euphemistically was called relocation but in practical terms was the uprooting of whole communities. From the new, formerly Polish, territories many Ukrainians and Byelorussians were shifted east, while new Russian and Ukrainian settlers were brought in from the east, some from as far away as Siberia: they were presumed to be more reliable inhabitants for a vulnerable area. Some of the nationalities moved during the war were allowed home, but not the Crimean Tartars, who were still regarded as traitors and many of whom were settled in the ostensibly Jewish autonomous region of Birobidzhan. In order to russify the Baltic republics, the heavy loss of natives by war and deportation was made up by the settlement of Russians; in the late 1940s Estonia received 180,000 Russians, an influential number because its pre-war population had been little more than one million. In Latvia, Russians accounted for a quarter of the population by 1959, compared to about 12 per cent in the 1930s. Most of the Russian intake to the Baltic republics came willingly, but this was not always the case with the half-million peasants drafted to the former German territory of Kaliningrad (Königsberg), to Eastern Siberia, and to Sakhalin, although the settlers were chosen from the more overcrowded lands of European Russia and, in the end, were probably better off for the change. In newly acquired territories, 'sovietization' was also undertaken, culminating in collectivization and deportation of so-called kulaks. In the case of the Baltic states, the Western Ukraine, and Western Byelorussia, as well as most of Moldavia, this collectivization was imposed in 1949.[3]

After the war the population soon recovered; those who had died from

---

[3] Collectivization was also imposed in the peoples' democracies. Whether it should be regarded as a seal of approval, a *pièce de résistance* or a *coup de grâce* is perhaps a matter of taste. But there was something obsessive about the importance Moscow attached to this change, almost as though, by repeating the process of 1930, collectivization could be proved right.

the privations of war were primarily the old and weak and there was therefore a drastic decline in the death-rate in the immediate postwar years. Thus, although the birth-rate continued to fall, the population reached about 209 million in 1959, and 242 million in 1970. After 1963 the urban population outnumbered the rural (for fuller population statistics, see pp. 599–602).

Throughout the Soviet period, policy on divorce, marriage, and abortion was determined partly by social and moral attitudes, partly by demographic needs. The introduction of civil marriage after the Revolution had made both marriage and divorce cheap and easy, but these advantages were seriously offset by the number of hastily contracted marriages which broke up, leaving children more or less abandoned (between 1920 and 1927, which admittedly includes the famine years, about two million children were abandoned by their parents, and many died from cold and hunger). In 1926 abortion was legalized to reduce the number of unwanted children, and this caused a fall in the birth-rate. In 1936, to halt a further and drastic fall in the birth-rate, measures were taken to 'strengthen the family'. Divorce became expensive and difficult. Abortion was forbidden except where the mother's health was in serious danger. Financial allowances were granted for large families. The war resulted in a further fall in the birth-rate, a shortage of marriageable men and a distressing number of young widows. In 1944 a new decree was issued; distinctions were introduced for fertile mothers (those who reached ten children became 'Mother-Heroines'), allowances were improved for large families, special financial and other help was granted to unmarried mothers and extra taxes were levied on bachelors, spinsters, and childless couples. The birth-rate did rise, and in the fifties averaged twenty-five per thousand, but began to fall noticeably in the sixties. In 1955 abortion on request was re-legalized with negligible effect on the birth-rate, although in the sixties abortions probably outnumbered births. In the towns, housing problems may have affected family size; even the housing achievements of the Khrushchev era were largely in terms of small-size apartments. Policy on birth control seemed indecisive; the right of a woman to choose the size of her family was unquestioned, yet incentives continued for large families and disincentives for small. In the late sixties the Supreme Soviet on average conferred 9,000 'mother-heroine' titles each year. Special allowances for unmarried mothers continued. In the early seventies the contraceptive pill was, and would remain, unavailable.

According to the 1959 census, two-thirds of females over fourteen years old were gainfully employed, ranging from one-tenth of the 14–15 age group to four-fifths of the 20–39 group. Although the official retiring age for women was fifty-five (for men it was sixty), one-third of the women working on their household plots. Partly because about 55 per cent of agricultural workers were female, about four-fifths of Soviet female workers were unskilled and therefore low-paid.

By 1948 over eight million soldiers had been demobilized, yet labour still remained short. In 1945 Russian prisoners of war and other displaced persons were returned home, typically being met at the frontier by brass bands before appearing before NKVD commissions that allowed some to go home but sent the others, as 'unreliable elements', to labour camps. There were also German prisoners, the majority of whom were made to work in harsh conditions until they died. Enemy prisoners, former Russian POWs, civilian repatriates, and the civilian criminal and political prisoners collectively made up the convict labour force and may have amounted to ten million people. To recruit free workers for unskilled work in arduous locations the recruitment organization *Orgnabor*, which had been useful in the 1930s for signing up peasants, offered contracts and found many takers among demobilized soldiers in the collective farms. There was also conscript labour, a continuation of the compulsory labour service introduced during the war; such conscripts were deployed especially in the newly acquired territories.

One problem in the post-Stalin period was the uneven distribution of population. While the cities of European Russia were overpopulated[4] the continuing priority placed on development of Asiatic Russia demanded an influx of new settlers. Yet in the fifties and sixties more people emigrated from, than immigrated to, Siberia; not only involuntary inhabitants in labour camps, freed by the death of Stalin, but also recent immigrants tended to return to European Russia, which they considered a more attractive place to live in.

Living standards

During the NEP period living standards had risen slowly, but probably faster than mere statistics indicated, because welfare services were not fully reflected in the figures. After 1928 living standards fell, and remained low, with troughs of privation in 1933, the war, and 1947. Various means were adopted for extracting the maximum effort from the people with the minimum satisfaction of their needs. In the First Five-Year Plan there was inflation, and in 1931 the Turnover Tax was introduced. This, essentially a form of value-added tax, was a device for absorbing spending power, and became the main source of taxation revenue; as in tsarist Russia, personal

---

[4] By 1979 Moscow had 8.0 million inhabitants and Leningrad 4.6. Eight other cities had more than one million. Permission to settle in the bigger cities was not easily obtained, and could be withdrawn.

income tax was negligible in Soviet Russia. Retail trade, like the industrial system as a whole, did not have goods seeking a buyer, but always the reverse; this is one reason why the professional salesman was absent from the scene, although not the tolerated but often shady character known as a 'fixer' or procurer. Shortages meant that the consumer had to 'take it or leave it', (a situation later described as the 'imposition of compulsory products'). Factory managers often found that the best or only way of fulfilling their plan was to supply poor-quality products. Rationing was ended in 1934, but there was a concurrent reduction in communal feeding. However, for a time consumer goods became less scarce and there was a consequent narrowing of the gap between wages and prices. From 1938 to 1941 there seems to have been little or no improvement in living standards over 1937. The effect of the war was cataclysmic. There were some Russians who did well (peasants who were able to get astronomical prices for those products which they could market in the towns, and many factory workers). But since there was little to buy, those who enjoyed high money incomes could only save and hope. In terms of what a wage-earner could actually buy with his money, 1945 standards were around 40 per cent of 1940, which had been a barely tolerable year. 1946 and 1947 witnessed a repetition of the conditions of the First Five-Year Plan, but in 1947 there were radical changes followed by a slow improvement. Wartime rationing was abolished and, to end inflation and to eliminate large personal savings, the currency was reformed. By 1952, the 1940 standard of living had been reached by the average worker, although he was working more hours (ten to twelve hours and six days a week) than he was in 1940.

The inadequate urban infrastructure was probably felt as much as shortages of goods. Inadequate transport meant that for many workers the day included hours of uncomfortable travel to and from work. The deliberate neglect of 'unproductive' services such as shops meant that everyday necessities like bread or vegetables were acquired by long queuing. Since, in order to make both ends meet, it was usual for both husband and wife to work, there was an important role for the grandmother, '*Babushka*' would look after the children, queue for food, and keep the household going while the married couple would earn the family income. The really black spot in Stalinist social policy was housing. Little provision was made for the vastly increased urban population. In the mid-thirties, only about 6 per cent of households in Moscow had more than one room, one-quarter shared a room with one or more other households, one-quarter of the households (mainly one-person) lived in dormitories, and about 5 per cent had neither room nor dormitory, living in a bathroom, kitchen, corridor, or hallway. The war made this situation considerably worse, and it was not until a housing drive started after Stalin's death that inroads were made on the backlog. What sometimes shocked even sympathetic western observers was that while Russians were abysmally and miserably housed, great prestige projects pre-empted valuable building resources. Before the war there was the Moscow underground railway, in which every station was an underground palace. After the war there were great skyscraper buildings, sometimes providing flats but more usually containing state institutions. But housing was cheap, few families spending more than about 8 per cent of their income on rent. Also, the Soviet equivalent of Cubs and Brownies, the Pioneers, with their daily programmes and holiday camps, took pressure off big families living in cramped quarters.

While strikes were unthinkable, and trade union economic demands nonexistent, the unions did perform a role in their administration of various welfare services. The local trade union branch would, in the biggest enterprises at least, provide sports facilities, meeting halls, film shows, and other cultural services. In addition, it might negotiate with management over questions of factory amenities. It maintained its own co-operative store and sometimes its own hospital. Also, it might operate in one of the resorts its own sanitorium and holiday centre (often a confiscated pre-1917 palace). Every worker was entitled to two weeks holiday with pay, although when labour discipline was tightened this became dependent on good behaviour. Some workers went on cheap holidays subsidized by their union. However, such accommodation covered only a fraction of those who would have liked to make use of it, and the selection process of applicants was yet another incentive for workers to become 'deserving'. Sick pay was also administered by the union.[5] Expulsion from a trade union could therefore be a serious matter; with union membership went the right to work in that particular industry, and a host of welfare services.

As in education, Soviet medical services had a pre-revolutionary foundation on which to work, but this does not detract from the achievement, especially as the number of doctors lost between 1914 and 1920 was disproportionately great. Just as education was designed to be available to all, so were medical services planned to benefit the entire population. Compulsory vaccination programmes were carried out, and in 1921 and 1970 cholera outbreaks were contained by ruthless quarantine and mass vaccination. From 1928 to 1940 the number of doctors increased from about 70,000 to 155,000; there had been 23,000 in 1913. By 1958 there were 362,000 and in 1967 this rose to one doctor for every 450 people, a better rate than in the USA. In terms of hospital beds, facilities rose from about 207,000 in 1912

---

[5] Unemployment pay was abolished when unemployment was officially declared nonexistent in 1930.

to 247,000 in 1928, 791,000 in 1939, 1,533,000 in 1958, and 2,567,000 in 1969. These figures do not include sanatoria, which provided about 300,000 beds by 1958. The health service emphasized preventive medicine; for example, all sanitary inspectors were doctors. The service was and remained authoritarian. Patients had little choice of treatment; they did what the doctor told them, even if this meant accepting vaccinations or operations they did not want, and they waited hours and even days for attention. In some ways this was the best way to run a health service, the wastage of frivolous demands and hypochondria being largely eliminated. On the other hand, there was a disdainful neglect of psychological and nervous complaints. Expansion of health services was made possible by the intake of women training to become doctors or *feldshers* (trained medical assistants), encouraged by the Bolshevik resolution to give equal professional opportunities to females. In 1970 about 70 per cent of doctors were female (compared with 10 per cent in 1913). Training of Soviet doctors (six years) was perhaps less thorough than in other countries, and the pharmaceutical industry was backward. Apart from a few special clinics reserved for top people, there was also a small private practice; although doctors were attached to hospitals and clinics they were allowed to treat private patients, their fees being rather highly taxed. After the twenties, all patients, private or otherwise, paid for their medicines. The last year of Stalin's life was especially difficult for the medical profession, overworked in any case. The 'Doctors' Plot' meant that vicious allegations about 'assassins in white coats' were repeatedly purveyed by the press and propagandists, so that medicine became a high-risk profession, especially for Jews. The MVD was eager to arrest doctors, who knew that they might be denounced by any patient dissatisfied with his treatment.

Education

Before 1917, the Duma had made plans for universal education by 1922, but this programme had doubtful prospects. After the Bolshevik victory a reconstruction of education was regarded as essential. Lunacharsky was appointed Commissar for Education in 1917, and supervised all schools and institutes except those operated by other ministries. In 1918 the church schools were taken over by local soviets. From 1917 to about 1931 educational policy was ostensibly revolutionary; old principles were overthrown and new theories applied. In 1919 the 8th Party Congress laid down the principles on which communist education should be based. These included free and compulsory education up to the age of seventeen (this was not achieved because of teacher and building shortages, although from 1927 it was applied up to the age of twelve). The basic type of school was the 'polytechnic' (a form of comprehensive school which would eliminate class divisions in education). Although both Lunacharsky and Krupskaya (who took a great interest in Soviet education) strongly favoured the polytechnic principle, others were reluctant to jettison the high quality nine-year schools which had been developed from the tsarist schools. This disagreement continued until, in the thirties, separate technical schools came back into favour.

One important measure was the establishment of 'workers' faculties' (*Rabfaks*). These were intended to bring workers up to the level at which they could enter higher education. Many workers volunteered for these courses which, though they were of variable quality and had a high wastage, did limit the lowering of academic standards caused by the policy of making higher education especially accessible to workers and peasants. Many party and government leaders of later decades, including Khrushchev, were *Rabfak* products. The *Rabfaks* survived until the forties, by which time they had been largely superseded by correspondence schools.

Another important side of educational policy was the energetic campaign against illiteracy. Although rather more success was claimed for this than was actually justified, and although the foundations for universal literacy had been laid in tsarist times, the effort and the achievement were great. The Red Army was perhaps the most effective force in the campaign, all illiterate recruits attending classes as part of their service. There was also a Literacy League, with its periodical *Down with Illiteracy!* By 1939 illiteracy was almost entirely confined to the elderly. According to the census of that year, of those aged between nine and forty-nine, 94 per cent in the towns and 86 per cent in the villages were literate (by 1959 these had increased to 99 and 98 per cent respectively).

In the twenties there was a great interest in foreign educational theory, and much was applied in Soviet schools; especially John Dewey's 'progressive' education with pupils engaging in projects rather than formal learning, teachers less authoritarian, and examinations discontinued. There was also a stronger trend towards polytechnics, where the students could mix labour experience with formal learning. The universities remained partly proletarianized as workers and peasants gained admission at the expense of children of 'bourgeois' parents. Much of this was reversed from about 1931, as the five-year plans and collectivization reached their climax. Lunacharsky was dismissed, and several educational theorists and psychologists were purged. Foreign educational theorists were condemned. Secondary education almost came to a standstill in the year 1931–2, and when it recovered there was a partial reversion to tsarist practices. Teachers were enjoined to discipline their pupils. The old examinations and marking systems were re-established. New standardized textbooks were introduced, so that pupils could learn, among other things, that Stalin was a genius. The influence of Zhdanov, who fancied himself as the party's cultural expert after the departure of Lunacharsky, was believed to be responsible for the more reactionary of the new measures. Nevertheless, while school education became less lively, pre-school education took the opposite course; in the nurseries and kindergartens, fairy stories and dolls once more became popular.

Because of the social upheavals, there was an alarming increase of juvenile delinquency in the thirties, with violence and vandalism especially noticeable in the cities. In 1935 the age of criminal responsibility was therefore lowered to twelve (ten in some cases) so that troublesome children could be treated as criminals. This not only made possible the imposition of savage sentences on children, but also provided an additional means of getting at their parents.

In 1932 the official requirement (often circumvented) that universities should take two-thirds of their students from the working class and peasantry was dropped. This meant that the children of administrators had a better chance of entry, and also that academic standards rose.[6] Working-class education also suffered in 1940, when fees were introduced for higher education and for the final three years of secondary education (after 1934 education was compulsory for the four primary years and the first three secondary years offered by 'seven-year schools'; the final three years provided by 'ten-year schools' were voluntary. Fees meant that these final three years were attended largely by children of the white-collar workers). But there were extensive opportunities for part-time, adult, and correspondence study, and many took advantage of these.

Efforts made during the war to preserve education could only be partly successful, due to the heavy toll of teachers and buildings. Among the measures taken during the war was the extension of military training from the peacetime 6 per cent to 11 per cent of the total secondary course. Partly because of this (girls were taught more nursing and less warfare than boys) separate education for boys and girls was re-established (and lasted until 1954, although never fully applied). For educating the sons of servicemen killed in action, many 'Suvorov' and 'Nakhimov' boarding schools were founded, their pupils being themselves trained for service careers. In 1943 there was a whole series of reforms. Educational theory was again in favour, and the Academy of Pedagogical Sciences was founded. The lower age for compulsory schooling was lowered from eight to seven. New evening

---

[6] After the mid-thirties children of the former bourgeoisie were no longer formally denied entry.

schools were established for young workers and peasants whose education had been cut short by the war. Twenty rules were evolved for pupils' behaviour, and these had to be learned by heart.[7] In 1944 examinations were fixed; they would occur at the end of the fourth, seventh, and tenth grades. The old school-leaving certificate ('attestation of maturity') was restored.

Recovery was fast in the post-war years. There remained a great shortage of school space, and many schools worked a two- or three-shift system. In time, the low wartime birthrate helped to mitigate this problem. Teachers, usually female in secondary and elementary schools,[8] varied in quality, but few could be lazy. In the non-Russian parts, the official requirement that Russians should learn the local language and the locals learn Russian was, apparently, often circumvented by the Russians. (In any case, even with formal equality of languages, the local language tended to be displaced, since Russian was virtually essential for those aspiring towards higher education or towards wider job opportunities; after all, Russian was the *lingua franca* of the USSR.)

The Fifth Five-Year Plan envisaged compulsory ten-year education, instead of seven-year, for all in the towns by 1955, and for all country children by 1960. In 1952 the polytechnic principle, which had been abandoned in the thirties, once more became accepted. However, the death of Stalin and the educational reforms of Khrushchev changed these plans (see p. 417).

Science and technology

By the end of the Civil War, much of Russia's intellectual and scientific talent had died or emigrated. A new Soviet science had to be created from the remnants of the old. In 1925 the old Imperial Academy of Sciences was transformed into the Academy of Sciences of the USSR, and placed in direct touch with the government. The Academy of Sciences, with the academies of science of the separate republics, was largely responsible for the organization of scientific research in the USSR. It defined tasks (with a view to the government's requirements), and allocated tasks and funds to selected research institutions or research teams. Membership of the Academy was highly prized; there were only a hundred or so full members, and membership brought great prestige and reward. Until about 1935 Soviet

---

[7] The first rule was: 'It is the duty of each school child to acquire knowledge persistently so as to become an educated and cultured citizen and to be of the most possible service to his country.' Others bade pupils to respect their teachers, 'greeting them with a polite bow', and obeying their instructions without question.

[8] By the early seventies more than two-thirds of the school teachers (but only one-quarter of secondary school heads) were women.

scientists enjoyed an increasing reputation in the outside world, and there was considerable scientific interchange. Foreign scientists visited the USSR to lecture or to share in research, and Soviet scientists visited the west. Some Russian scientific journals were printed in English or German to facilitate this interchange. In 1935, Kapitsa, a Soviet physicist working at Cambridge, did not return from a visit to the USSR, and this coincided with the end of the close ties between Russian and foreign scientists. Science in the USSR, like other fields of intellectual life, was feeling the tightening control of men like Zhdanov.

Soviet science suffered badly in the purge. For example, the world-famous Pulkovo Observatory was crippled by the arrest in 1937 of most of its astronomers, of whom several died in captivity.[9] At a more technical level, the device of arresting complete design teams (as happened in the aircraft and locomotive industries, among others) preserved skills and inflated the self-importance of the NKVD (which administered the captive design offices). But Soviet science and technology had much to its credit. In fact the five-year plans would have been unrealizable but for the flow of new technologists from the institutes of higher education. On the other hand, the international reputation, as well as the contribution, of Soviet science was undermined by some of the more eccentric of Stalin's scientific notions. The most notorious instance was the case of Lysenko. Lysenko, of Ukrainian peasant origin, was a biologist and agronomist who propounded a new revolutionary theory of genetics which was greatly to the liking of a party which still claimed to be revolutionary. Building on Michurin's achievements in the breeding of new strains of plants, he decided to reject 'conventional' theories of heredity. For Lysenko, chromosomes were not necessarily relevant; heritable changes could be achieved by subjecting plants to changes of environment. His experiments, in which wheat subjected to low temperatures allegedly produced seed grain which could be planted in the colder zones of the USSR, was of great interest to a party committed to the transformation both of nature and of the Soviet Union. In 1938 he was appointed head of the Academy of Agricultural Sciences. Those who disagreed with his theories were execrated and removed from their posts, sometimes with the help of the NKVD. Among Lysenko's victims was the founder of the Academy, Vavilov. Vavilov was a world-renowned geneticist who, despite Lysenko, upheld the relevance of the chromosome. Because of this, and because of the 'western' nature of his views, he was one of those arrested; he died in captivity in 1942. In 1948 the Lysenko controversy, muted during the war, was resurrected. This time the

---

[9] Like other such instances, this process seems to have entailed a blend of NKVD arbitrariness and professional jealousies among the scientists. See *Slavic Review*, No. 1 (1990), 100–17.

Central Committee of the party solemnly declared that Lysenko's theory of heredity was marxist and therefore true. Such a declaration invited foreign ridicule, but was the signal for the emergence of Lysenkos in other branches of Soviet science. In line with Zhdanov's cultural and intellectual offensive, scientists who believed in the validity of 'western bourgeois' theories were hounded, while scientists claiming to have developed revolutionary Soviet theories were elevated into high positions. It was not until the death of Stalin that Soviet scientists were free to openly pursue their former fruitful courses. Lysenko was then denounced by Khrushchev; he was accused of falsifying his experimental results, and also of giving diplomas to worthless students whom he happened to like. But in 1958 he made a partial and temporary return to favour, several of his scientific enemies losing their jobs.

Another scientist who appeared to gratify Stalin, the russified Celtic American Vilyams (ancestral name Williams), also had a deleterious effect on agriculture, though probably not a great effect on Soviet science. A party member since 1928, Vilyams developed the system of *Travopolye*: the use of grasses in a system of crop rotation. This system could, it was claimed, be applied in any soil conditions. Reliance on this theory, which was not baseless but was taken to extremes, was one of the reasons why artificial fertilizers received such a low priority in the five-year plans.

When greater freedom and initiative were permitted, after 1953, it was not long before Soviet scientists and technologists demonstrated genuine achievements. Evidently the preparation of a new generation of scientists had not been unduly held back in the repressive years. Also, it was in the last years of Stalin that the USSR developed the uranium and hydrogen bombs, as well as the family of rockets which later would launch the first *sputniks*. Until 1945 nuclear research had not received great priority. It is true that this field was pursued from about 1930 in Leningrad at the Radium Institute and the Physical Technical Institute, that there was a cyclotron in action by 1937, and that by 1941 prominent Soviet nuclear physicists such as Kapitsa and Kurchatov were well aware of the potentialities of nuclear fission. But when the extensive Soviet espionage organization in North America obtained information about the Anglo-Canadian-American atomic programmes, its significance does not seem to have been recognized. After the atomic bombs had been exploded over Japan, Stalin publicly minimized the significance of the new weapon, just as a decade later Mao Tse-tung would do. However, there was a crash programme, supervised by the MVD, to make a Soviet atomic device. The latter was first detonated in 1949, to the consternation of the western press, which had been misled by its own stories of Soviet technical incompetence. The contribution of German scientists acquired in 1945, and of Soviet espion-age, to this achievement is impossible to evaluate. It was probably exag-gerated by western commentators, but presumably helped Soviet scientists to avoid lines of research found fruitless by their western counterparts. In 1953 a thermonuclear device was exploded, and the first hydrogen bomb, successfully dropped in 1955, came a year before the first American one. A dubious distinction perhaps, but proving that when sufficient resources were allocated Soviet scientists could deliver the goods.

Literature and the arts

The arts did not flourish during the years of revolution and civil war. In lit-erature, there was a shortage of paper and of writers. Only poetry made headway, for it could express the spirit of the times while requiring a minimum of paper. Two celebrated poets of the Revolution, with little in common except their premature deaths, were Blok and Mayakovsky.

Once called 'the last of the penitent nobles', Blok had already estab-lished his poetic reputation by 1917. He had long felt the coming of the Revolution, which he knew would be distasteful to him but which he ac-knowledged to be justified historically and spiritually. His verse, though highly innovative, had its roots in classical Russian poetry. But his themes were quite new, and were familiar to the pre-war urban intellectuals and later to the new Soviet working class. After 1917 his everyday themes, and his acceptance of the Revolution, meant that Blok more than any other poet was able to interest and even enthuse the proletarian masses.

Mayakovsky was revolutionary from his childhood, and had joined the Bolsheviks while still an adolescent. The most celebrated of the pre-war Futurists, by temperament and style he felt absolutely at home in revolu-tionary Russia. Devoting himself to its cause, he expressed the feelings of the people in revolt, without lowering himself or his talent. His poetry was novel both in form and content. Of his several poetic tributes to the Re-volution, *150,000,000* became best known. The 150 million are the Soviet people, the hero of the poem. This people is opposed by one person, Pres-ident Wilson. The poem is a partisan portrayal of the conflict between cap-italism and socialism, an essay in anti-Americanism and an affirmation of polarization (there are two extremes, red and white, and nothing in be-tween). Later, particularly after the end of War Communism, Mayakovsky seemed to grow disenchanted with the Bolsheviks, resenting in particular their philistinism and their reincarnation of the old bureaucracy. In *The Bathhouse* (1930) he bitterly and satirically portrayed a government depart-ment headed by a communist official named Pobedonosikov, 'a living piece of socialism' who spends his virtuous and ideologically pure life composing speeches on revolution, signing documents, and applying rubber stamps. Although Mayakovsky earned the active dislike of officials, there remained many old Bolsheviks who regarded him as their own poet; his suicide in 1930 was a great shock for the party. After his death he was enshrined as the poet of the Revolution, but editions of his works omitted his later, stinging, poems.

In the early twenties the spirit of new freedom, which pervaded many sectors of Russian life, encouraged writers to experiment with lively new ideas. Provided a writer was not blatantly anti-revolutionary he was free to write and publish what he wished; he was not forced to follow any dictates from the party, as he would be in the following decades, although he might be subjected to humiliating criticism. Not many of the pre-war giants of Russian literature were still writing in the twenties and this, together with a growing literacy and the government's encouragement of literature, provided a healthy demand for the work of new writers. Starting in about 1922, new novels began to appear as young writers returned from their service with the Red Army or with the partisans, ready to give their experience a fictional form. The Civil War phase of the young Soviet literature culminated in 1929 with *And Quiet Flows the Don*, a long novel worthy of comparison with the great Russian novels of the nineteenth century. Basically it is a novel about the impact of the Great War, the Revolution, and the Civil War on the life of the Don Cossacks. The main character joins the Red Army for a while, before his distaste for the cruelty of the Whites is joined by an equally strong distaste for the cruelty of the Reds (he finally joins the Greens). The action takes place over a wide range of time and place, and the plot contains secondary characters and themes, together with real-life personalities undisguised by fictitious names. In all this it resembles *War and Peace*. The author portrays the Whites and Reds with commendable impartiality, but some changes were made in the later editions. It was with this book that Sholokhov established a reputation which his subsequent productions hardly maintained; later rumours that much of *And Quiet Flows the Don* originated from a manuscript acquired during the Civil War by Sholokhov from a captured White officer, a writer, remain unproven.

Not all writers during the twenties occupied themselves with Civil War subjects, and there was much experimentation as new, revolutionary, writers were encouraged to show what they could do. Although writers directly opposed to the regime were not published, not all of the new generation were committed to communism. Those who were thus committed were classified by the critics as 'proletarian writers' while those who merely accepted the Revolution were called 'fellow-travellers'. Some of the

'fellow-travellers' were influenced by Zamyatin. The latter, already established as a writer before the Revolution, in the twenties began to imply that
communism had an inhumane side; his novel *We*, which foreshadowed
Orwell's *Nineteen Eighty-Four*, was one of the first Soviet novels to achieve
world renown while being banned at home. But while the regime refused to
publish *We*, it tolerated the satirical works of Il'f and Petrov, who poked
fun at the New Soviet Man. Especially popular among Russians were this
pair's *The Twelve Chairs* and *The Golden Calf*, which portrayed the con-
ventionalized eccentricities of the twenties as people habituated themselves
to the new revolutionary standards: the compulsive sloganeering ('Brass
Bands: the Path to Collective Creativity'), the street renaming ('Lena Massacre Street'), the compromises between tradition and revolution ('Co-
operative Saviour Square'), the boring formal speeches by party men and
officials on all possible occasions, the former noblemen quietly working as
bureaucrats in government offices, the 'Moscow Bun Artel' which baked no
buns but speculated in clothing.

Among the émigré writers who reconciled themselves to the new regime
and returned were Aleksei Tolstoy and Gorki. Tolstoy in the thirties turned
to adulation of Stalin in his *Bread*, but he also wrote a notable trilogy describing the agonies of the intelligentsia between 1914 and 1921 (*Road to
Calvary*). Gorki, who had emigrated in 1921, returned in 1928 and was proclaimed in the thirties as the model whom aspiring socialist writers should
imitate.

In the late twenties, Russian writers came under severe pressure. The
'fellow travellers' fell out of favour, and the proletarian writers were elevated to a position in which they could dictate literary policy through their
Association of Proletarian Writers ('RAPP'). But this and other associations were abolished in 1932, and replaced by the Writers' Union. This became the sole professional organization of writers and contained within
itself a party organization to ensure, among other things, that writers conformed to the wishes of the party. In a sense this was a further confirmation of the importance which the party and Stalin attached to literature.
The writer, said Stalin, was 'the engineer of men's souls'. His task was to
produce fictional examples of the New Soviet Man which the party was creating, and thus give his readers a guide to correct behaviour. In practice,
over the decades, the Writers' Union served to repress all talent which was
not submissive (expulsion from the Union could mean that the victim
would no longer be published). At its first conference in 1934, the Union
was addressed by Zhdanov, who introduced the doctrine of Socialist Realism as the only pattern to which writers could work. Socialist Realism was
a term whose meaning varied over the years but, officially, it was defined

as the depiction of revolutionary reality, with a view to the re-education of the population in the spirit of socialism. In conforming to these dictates, the quality of literature fell. All too often it was a case of the survival of the unfittest; there was a flourishing of mediocre writers, while the genuinely creative tended to be suppressed. The low quality of contemporary literature, combined with growing literacy, was responsible for the enormous demand by readers for the old classics of Russian literature, which were reprinted in millions of copies.

The so-called five-year-plan novel became prominent in the thirties. The style of this had been set in 1925 by Gladkov's *Cement*; the object was to show how a certain sector of the economy fulfilled or overfulfilled its plan, despite wreckers, saboteurs, pessimists, and other perils. The new literary hero was the peasant who, by intelligent use of manure, doubled the potato crop despite the machinations of the local priest, the bus driver who by careful driving reduced his fuel consumption, or the factory worker who overcame all kinds of obstacles and produced rounder and shinier ball bearings. None of these novels was outstanding, but as propaganda to raise morale and production they were useful.

About a thousand members of the Writers' Union served at the front during the Second World War and about one-fifth of them were killed. Most were newspaper correspondents and many took advantage of their situation to collect material for novels which would be written in calmer years. During the war, Soviet writers benefited from the relaxed ideological atmosphere and from the renewal of cultural contacts with other countries. This relaxation came to an abrupt end in 1946, when Zhdanov opened a new campaign against 'cosmopolitanism' (interest in things foreign) and 'apoliticism' and 'objectivism' (failure to commit work absolutely to the current party line). Zhdanov singled out especially the humorist Zoshchenko and the veteran poetess Akhmatova. Akhmatova, who persisted in writing lyrical poetry rather than political poetry, was described as poisonous, half-way between a prostitute and a nun. As for Zoshchenko, Zhdanov said,

... If you bother to read his *The Adventures of a Monkey* closely you will discover that ... the monkey can make the filthy, poisonous, and anti-Soviet judgment that life in the zoo is better than life outside, that you can breathe more freely in a cage than among Soviet people. Morally and politically, how much lower can you get?

These denunciations were followed by a period of repression which lasted until 1953 in all the arts and intellectual pursuits. Mediocrities flourished; their works elevated all things Russian, denounced all things western, and included admiring references to Stalin. Features of this period were the condemnation as putrid and lecherous of almost all foreign contemporary novelists, and the re-issue of Soviet novels with new excisions and, sometimes, additional paragraphs elevating Stalin's role in the events portrayed. Among the books treated in this way was Fadayev's *The Young Guard* (1945), which was printed in millions of copies and received a Stalin Prize before the party critics had second thoughts. This novel, based on fact, told how teenage boys and girls formed a partisan unit in Krasnodon and, after many brave exploits, were arrested and shot. The very spontaneity of this group implied that the local party organization had made no preparations for the city's occupation by the Germans. Moreover the author's depiction of the loss of Krasnodon gave a poor impression of the Red Army. In 1947 the author prepared a revised edition in which the Red Army did better, but the critics were still not satisfied. Eventually a revised revised edition appeared, in which the Krasnodon party played a much bigger role and in which new passages in praise of the Red Army and of Stalin were incorporated. One writer who fell foul of Zhdanov's call for vigilance was Kazakevich, who restored himself to favour with two novels (*Spring on the Oder*, *House on the Square*) which even the most paranoid party hack could hardly find wanting. These novels have the same hero, Lubentsov, who is broad-shouldered with friendly, intelligent, and humorous blue eyes which seem to say 'I love you all because we are all from the Soviet Union and doing the same thing'. He is a professional soldier and party member with impeccable social origin; his father was a lumberjack and his mother a peasant (and, as if this were not enough, he has never worn a tie in his life). He is brave, loved by his subordinates and respected by his superiors. He turns down a safe HQ posting because he wants to share the common dangers of the front line. The only characters who criticize him are plainly bad characters. One of the latter, however, seems to utter a perfect description of the Stalinist literary hero. 'Lubentsov,' says this low type, 'walks around as though he is an icon.'

The party's long-standing ambition to offer everyone access to the printed word meant that books were cheap and that by 1959 there were about 135,000 libraries holding 800 million volumes (both these figures are about ten times greater than in 1913). The biggest reference library was the Lenin Library in Moscow (nineteen million titles), developed from an 1862 foundation. In Leningrad there was the Saltykov-Schedrin Library (twelve million titles), based on the former Imperial Library, and the Library of the Academy of Sciences, founded in 1775 and possessing twelve million titles. At 64,000 the 1958 total of book titles published was more than double the 1913 figure. There were over 10,000 newspapers published in 1958; most of these were very minor, but they had a combined circulation of fifty-nine million. The four main newspapers, edited in Moscow but circulating throughout the USSR, were *Pravda* (the party's paper), *Izvestiya* (the organ of the government), *Komsomolskaya Pravda* (organ of the Communist Youth League) and *Trud* (published by the Central Council of Trade Unions).[10] Newspaper editors were carefully chosen; they were men whose presentation and ideological interpretation of the news could be relied on. Under Stalin, and after, Soviet newspapers tended to exhort rather than inform, but perceptive readers could read between the lines. News was as far as possible planned in advance; for example, news of Khrushchev's death in 1971 was delayed, to avert a demonstrative funeral. A sure sign of unexpected big news was the delayed appearance, or even non-appearance, of newspapers, while editors sought official guidance.

The first decades of the Soviet regime coincided with the development of the cinema as a medium potentially more powerful than the written word. Lenin regarded the cinema as the most important of the arts and, rather optimistically, recommended that films should be informative 'like the best of our Soviet newspapers', imbued with the party's ideas, and entertaining. As in literature, the blending of party requirements with art was not always successful. But film-making and film-showing were generously aided by the government, and achieved notable results. Russian film-making on a regular basis had started in 1907. By 1917 there were about one thousand cinemas; despite illiteracy, which limited the value of subtitles, large audiences seem to have been found. Many notable feature films were made, usually taking the form of dramatizations of one or other of the classics of Russian literature. The first feature cartoon film, *The Grasshopper and the Ant*, appeared in 1913. When the Civil War ended most of the old directors and actors had disappeared, although several later returned to the USSR. The cinema industry was subordinated to the Commissariat of Education at first, but in 1929 was made directly subordinate to the Council of People's Commissars. From 1946 to 1953 there was a cinema ministry, but films then became the province of the Ministry of Culture. As in literature, there was a good deal of experimentation. The exploitation of montage in particular was studied in Soviet studios. The thirties were difficult for Soviet film-makers because the onset of Stalinism coincided with the changeover to sound films. A number of experimenters were removed, although their influence lived on in their pupils, of whom Pudovkin, Dovzhenko, and Eisenstein became best known. These three had already achieved fame with, respectively, *Mother*, *Earth*, and *Battleship Potemkin*, which inspired, among others, the Italian realism of the forties. From the early thirties to the death of Stalin, the Soviet film industry was

[10] By 1967 *Izvestiya* had the largest circulation, nearly 9 million.

artistically limited by outside pressures. But despite this, good work was done during the Stalin years. Many film-makers who fell into disfavour became teachers in film courses, and the 'diploma' films which their pupils made were a far cry from the turgid studio productions made for public screening. Thus, when there was a cultural relaxation after 1953 the new generation of film-makers was well prepared. Soon, notably sensitive films were appearing; some of these (*The Cranes are Flying, Ballad of a Soldier*) made a great impression abroad. By 1960 there were 59,000 permanent cinemas in the USSR. In 1940 fifty-four feature films and 198 shorts were made, but after the war only 'tried and trusted' directors were allowed to make films, and the latter were in any case often banned. Thus in 1952 only five feature films were made, rising under Khrushchev to 145 in 1959.

Painting and sculpture went through a similar sequence to the other arts. Experimentation during the twenties (Kandinsky was even appointed director of the new Department of Fine Arts), was followed by the imposition of Socialist Realism. In painting, the latter term implied a rejection of abstract art; portraiture predominated, being the most convenient *genre* for combining objective realism with adulation. There was a steady output of photographically detailed pictures, like the enormous painting entitled *Stalin and Voroshilov in the Kremlin*. Other paintings portrayed stirring events in the economy (*The Milkmaids, A Factory in the Urals*, etc.). Many painters, like writers, created original works for their own private satisfaction or for exhibition in better times; after the death of Stalin a number of abstract works emerged from attics and cellars. Under Khrushchev abstract art did not have official approval, but it was allowed to exist. Khrushchev did visit an exhibition of abstract art, but let his opinion be known in a choice sentence referring to what donkeys might do with their tails. Sculpture under Stalin likewise did not flourish. There was a boom in busts, but busts of Stalin, with few exceptions, were production-line rather than artistic creations.

Stalin's last years were architecture's worst years. Russian architecture had not been especially noteworthy in the decades preceding 1917. In the later nineteenth century there had been a neo-classical revival, which produced many graceless banks and railway stations but also some pleasant country houses. There was also an effort, favoured by Slavophils, to revive old Russian styles; Gothic architecture had never come to Russia, and in place of the Gothic Revival of the west there was the Russian Revival, few of whose structures were aesthetically very pleasing (the redbrick Historical Museum on Red Square is an example). From 1917 until the mid-thirties there was intensive (and sometimes hare-brained) innovation, with Moscow seeming to become the centre of the world's most progressive architecture.

Architecture was to be revolutionary and international; past forms were rejected in favour of the forms of the so-called machine age. A theatre was built at Rostov in the shape of a tractor, the glass wall was introduced to a land of climatic extremes, Corbusier designed a new Moscow ministry. But from the thirties Socialist Realism was applied to architecture (but not so uncompromisingly or bloodily as in other arts). Neo-classical forms were extolled and imitated, heavy ornamentation, high ceilings, and grandiose 'monolithic' façades became popular. In general, Stalinist architecture was ponderous, ostentatious, inconvenient, and sometimes badly built. On the other hand Soviet urban planning, only to a certain extent building on tsarist foundations, achieved much. It is true that some of the new wide streets of replanned Moscow were dull and uninspiring, but the 'parks of culture and rest', which were laid out as places of relaxation and entertainment in the big cities, were a valued asset for local populations.

Music also suffered from the perversions of the thirties and forties. However, composers and instrumentalists were honoured and rewarded, and the extension of musical opportunity to all sectors of the population meant that talent was discovered which otherwise might have been neglected. Of the Soviet composers, Khachaturyan, Prokoviev, and Shostakovich attained the most fame outside Russia, but there were many others whose talents were only appreciated at home. The Armenian Khachaturyan graduated from the Moscow Conservatoire in 1934 and soon became known by his original rhythms which, like his other works, often incorporated themes from Armenian folklore. Prokoviev, already well-established, returned to Russia in 1933, finishing his ballet *Romeo and Juliet* in 1936. Dmitri Shostakovich, son of a St. Petersburg chemical engineer, wrote his first composition at the age of eleven. His opera, *Lady Macbeth of Mtsensk*, was condemned in lurid terms by *Pravda* in 1936, and he was in disgrace until the war; it was said that he might have met a sad fate had not Aleksei Tolstoy interceded with Stalin on his behalf. After the war he was again banned, but was 'rehabilitated' in 1956. His music was characterized by great individuality, sometimes bordering on the sensational.

Addressing Soviet musicians in 1948, Zhdanov defined what Soviet music should do:

> There are two very responsible tasks facing Soviet composers. Firstly to develop and to perfect Soviet music. Secondly to protect Soviet music from infiltration by elements of bourgeois corruption. We should not forget that, as in all other fields, the USSR is the true protector of mankind's musical culture, a wall guarding human civilization and human culture from bourgeois decay . . .[11]

[11] Zhdanov's various pronouncements on the arts are available in English in: A. Zhdanov, *Literature, Philosophy and Music* (1950).

Fifteen years later Soviet musicians were still facing 'responsible tasks', but somehow Khrushchev seemed less ominous than Zhdanov:

In the spiritual life of our nation, in ideological work, music has a great and important role. It therefore seems necessary to make some judgments about the trend in music . . . In brief, we are for melodious music that has meaning, stirs people's spirits and inspires powerful sensations . . . Who is there who does not know the *Internationale*? For how many years have we been singing this song? It has become the working class international anthem. How it inspires revolutionary thoughts and feelings, elevating people and mobilizing them against the foes of the workers! When I listen to the music of Glinka rapturous tears invariably come into my eyes . . . But there is some music that gives one a bellyache.[12]

The nationalities

By 1970 about 53 per cent of the Soviet population was Great Russian, and the non-Great Russian population was on average younger. It seemed that within a few decades the Russians would be outnumbered, as indeed they had been before 1914. After 1917 there had been an attempt to dismantle the old Empire, but in such a way as not to endanger either the new Bolshevik republic or, subsequently, the party's predominance. The original and well publicized Bolshevik ideal of freedom for the non-Russian peoples was probably sincere in 1917, but was spoiled by the eagerness with which the beneficiaries made use of it, often endangering the Soviet state. By the very nature of the old Russian Empire, which had not expanded overseas but overland, the non-Russian peoples were located on the strategically sensitive periphery. Hence, after the first flash of idealism, Moscow's policy was changed to maintaining control over these areas while giving them as much independence as seemed safe.

But after the mid-1930s Stalin's policy was to russify the political institutions of the nationalities. The purge trials of 1938 made victims of many so-called 'bourgeois nationalists' among the leaders of the national communist parties. There was a diffusion of Russian bureaucrats into the key posts of the national republics, although this was frequently disguised by having a native in the ostensibly senior position, and a Russian in the actually more powerful position of deputy. But by the time Stalin died there had been created young national élites, russianized, qualified and loyal enough to occupy important posts. In time it was hoped that the lower strata of the national populations would themselves become russianized, adopting Russian language and attitudes for their own advantage. In this transition the question of language was vital. In one of his last theoretical works (1950), Stalin had condemned the 'revolutionary' theories of the

---

[12] *Pravda*, 10 March 1963.

linguist Marr. Marr in the thirties had propounded that a revolutionary new socialist system would develop a revolutionary new language. In rejecting this, Stalin suggested that the new socialist system would use the language of its strongest member, Russia. The compulsory study of Russian at school in the peoples' democracies was justified by this; compulsory Russian was already taught in the various national republics of the USSR.

According to the 1959 census, there were 114 million Great Russians in the USSR, many of whom lived in the non-Russian republics. The second largest nationality, the Ukrainians, amounted to thirty-seven million, although the population of the Ukraine was only three-quarters Ukrainian (17 per cent was Russian). The third nationality, White Russian, numbered eight million. Altogether, by 1959 there were twenty-two nationalities with populations of one million or more, plus a host of smaller groups. Three of these twenty-two (Jews, Tadzhiks, Mordvinians) had decreased since 1939. Kazakhstan by 1959 was the most diluted of the national republics, with the natives in a minority (they constituted 30 per cent, with Russians 43 and Ukrainians 8 per cent). The Kirgizians also were a minority in their own republic. Russians were widespread; only in White Russia, Armenia, and Lithuania did they amount to less than a tenth of the population. This Russian presence greatly facilitated the process of russianization. Intermarriage also tended to be a strong russianizing factor. But not always. Russian workers who migrated to the culturally advanced Baltic republics tended to become assimilated themselves, or at least their children did.

Of the major nationalities, the Jews were exceptional although it was true that three others (Poles, Germans, Moldavians) also might look to 'home' states outside the USSR. Unlike these three, however, the Jews were widely distributed throughout the Union. In the thirties the difficult task of creating a national republic for the Soviet Jews had been tackled, an area near Khabarovsk in the Far East being delineated as the Jewish Autonomous Oblast, with its capital at Birobidzhan. This did not attract many Jewish migrants because of its remoteness and the arduous life which it offered to the first settlers. But it is probably untrue that it was intended to fail; in the difficult conditions of that time resources could not be spared to make it a more attractive proposition. During the war there were enormous Jewish losses in the occupied zones. In the post-war period the creation of Israel apparently raised suspicions in Stalin's mind that the Soviet Jews might respect Tel Aviv more than Moscow. Hence there was a campaign against Zionism. Some Jewish leaders were executed, and the cultural freedoms which they had previously been allowed ceased to exist; Yiddish publishing, theatres, and schools were abolished. After Stalin's death there was a slight relaxation, although it would seem that Khrushchev was not without a streak of anti-semitism. The press gave considerable publicity to certain Jewish 'speculators' who were tried and executed in the sixties. However, taking the Soviet period as a whole, there was no definite intention to encourage anti-semitism. The Nazi occupation of regions, which under the tsar had been endemically anti-semitic, caused a reactivation, and post-war circumstances permitted this to linger. But official policy was usually to distinguish between 'Zionism', which was attacked, and the Jew, who was not. The 'Doctors' Plot' of Stalin and some of the acts of Khrushchev and his successors, could be considered as temporary aberrations of this policy. The situation of the Jews was exacerbated by Middle East conflicts; although the USSR had approved the creation of Israel, by the mid-fifties she had close relationships with Egypt and other Arab states. But in the 1970s, largely as a gesture to the outside world, the authorities eased (without making easy) the emigration procedures for Jews. This was followed by a quite substantial flow of emigrants. Similar concessions were made to citizens of German origin.

16. *The Khrushchev Revival*

The end of Stalin

ACCORDING to Khrushchev, the stroke which killed Stalin occurred in his country *dacha* near Moscow, on a Sunday in February 1953. He had had a late night, entertaining his closest colleagues at one of his frequent film-and-drinking parties. When he failed to stir on Sunday morning the security men, reluctant to approach him without summons, sent in an aged maidservant, who reported that Stalin was lying on the floor. The MVD men summoned up enough courage to lift him off the floor, and called the Politburo leaders.[1] The latter arrived, decided it would not be a good idea to let their eyes fall on the leader in his unseemly state, and went home. Late on Sunday night there was renewed alarm, and Malenkov, Khrushchev, Beria, Bulganin, Voroshilov, and Kaganovich drove out to the *dacha*. Doctors were summoned and the leading specialist was clearly disinclined to touch Stalin, no doubt wondering if this was to be a new chapter of the 'Doctors' Plot'. Stalin was partly paralysed, and speechless, and within a few days he was dead.

His unnerved successors had already allowed news of the illness to be reported to the population, although the communiqué for some reason reported that it had occurred in the Kremlin. A few minutes after his death, according to both Khrushchev and Stalin's daughter, Beria drove off with a sinister smile on his face as the remaining members of the Politburo assembled to decide what to do.[2] The latter discussed funeral arrangements,

---

[1] From 1952 to 1965 what was essentially the Politburo was called the Presidium of the party's Central Committee. For simplicity, the term Politburo has been retained for these years.
[2] Subsequent rumours that Beria had arranged Stalin's death seem improbable, even though he had the means and may have believed he was next on Stalin's shopping list. An article by one of the specialists (*Literaturnaya gazeta* 1 March 1989) says that the autopsy revealed a long-standing cerebral sclerosis. The parallel with Lenin is clear, but the degree, if any, to which this brain damage contributed to the weakening of Stalin's inhibitions is not. Stalin's personal doctor had recently advised him that rest was essential. (This advice, highly

and divided offices among themselves. This done, it was thought safe to permit an announcement of Stalin's demise. Apparently some discussion was devoted to the question of precisely how and when the news should be broken; evidently there were fears that some kind of popular explosion might ensue and the communiqué, when it appeared, included some unusual appeals to the population to resist panic and confusion. Internal security troops appear to have been placed at strategic points in the cities, but the absence of obvious upheaval is explicable less by the presence of troops than by the shattering effect the news had on a people long habituated to living under the one true god. The most dramatic occurrence was the loss of control over crowds pouring into the centre of Moscow to pay the last respects. In a small-scale re-enactment of the catastrophe which had accompanied Nicholas II's coronation, lack of imagination on the part of the police resulted in loyal citizens being crushed to death.

To Stalin's successors fell the task of finding a new course, directed away from the cruel absurdities of the Stalinist years, without discrediting themselves in the process. But although the Politburo leaders agreed that things could not go on as before, their unity did not extend much further than that. Not for the first time in Russian history, a relaxation of pent-up tension was seen to be both perilous and urgent, and there were conflicting views as to the speed and manner of this transformation. Added to this were conflicts between personalities. Stalin had not selected his closest subordinates with a view to their forming a closely-knit band of brothers, and this meant that the inevitable struggle for power would not be purely a matter of conflicting policies. In this struggle it was not long before Khrushchev emerged as the winner.

Khrushchev

1894, the year in which Russia's last tsar came to the throne, was also the year in which, with somewhat less ceremony, Nikita Khrushchev was born to an impoverished peasant family in a thatched hut at Kalinovka, in the grain belt of southern Russia. At the age of fifteen he abandoned rural life and went to the mining town of Yuzovka to seek a better fortune. By 1914 he had made some progress as a fitter, and was responsible for the operation of a pithead elevator, a position which appears to have gained him exemption from military service. He joined the Bolshevik party in 1918, served as a Red Army commissar during the Civil War, and then returned

---

resented by Stalin, and ignored, may have encouraged him to act against the medical profession by means of the 'Doctors' Plot'.) A commonsense explanation for the lack of haste in attending to Stalin is that when last seen by his colleagues he was drunk, and the symptoms would have been easily mistaken for a hangover.

to Yuzovka as an assistant manager. In the early twenties, his first wife having died during the famine, he studied at a technical institute, where he became a party representative. Soon he was a district party secretary and stayed with the Ukrainian Party *apparat* until his appointment in 1931 as party secretary of two Moscow districts. Within four years he was party secretary for Moscow and a candidate member of the Politburo. During the next three years he was largely responsible for the purging of the Moscow region and in 1938, having won Stalin's confidence, was transferred to the Ukraine to scourge the party there. In 1939 he became a full member of the Politburo, and during the Second World War played a worthy role as an army political officer. At the end of the war he was both party secretary and chairman of the council of ministers of the Ukraine. His was an especially important responsibility, because Ukrainian nationalists, separatists, and anti-Soviet partisans had thrived during the German occupation. Like every other public figure who wished to survive, he was ever eager to praise his leader:

All our successes we owe to the great Bolshevik party, to the experienced guidance of our beloved leader and teacher Comrade Stalin (*stormy applause*). Millions of workers in all countries of the world see how the Soviet Union is successfully carrying out the great socialist ideas, the ideas of Marx–Engels–Lenin–Stalin.[3]

Khrushchev was a man of great vitality, and under him the Ukrainian party flourished; unlike the All-Union Central Committee, the Ukrainian Central Committee met often and regularly. He was soon recalled to Moscow where agriculture became his main interest.

The leadership after Stalin

In the first redistribution of portfolios made at the death of Stalin it was Malenkov who became chairman of the Council of Ministers, a post which he expected to hold concurrently with his party secretaryship. This elevation of Malenkov was attained with the support of Beria, who achieved his own aim of becoming the minister of a new ministry of the interior (MVD) which was to absorb the previous ministry of state security; although under Stalin Beria had been in charge of these security ministries, he had not been their minister. Voroshilov replaced the dull protégé of Stalin, Shvernik, as 'President' of the USSR. Molotov, Kaganovich, Bulganin, and Beria became deputy chairmen of the Council of Ministers, while Khrushchev received no ministerial appointment but wielded great power inside the party secretariat and in the Politburo.

---

[3] From a report of proceedings at the congress of the Ukrainian communist party, in *Bolshevik*, No. 3 (1949), 7.

It seemed that Malenkov and Beria were working hand in hand, but the situation was fluid. Evidently everyone felt that Beria was the most powerful figure, a view shared by Beria himself. Beria not only controlled the MVD with its industries, troops, and informers, but he had developed self-confidence during Stalin's time. He had long had the habit of disparaging Stalin in private (being in charge of security and its informers, he was presumably the only citizen who could do this with impunity). He had been closer to Stalin than other leaders.

Khrushchev remarked that when Beria and Stalin clashed, it was not an execution affair, just a lovers' quarrel; Georgians quarrelled to amuse themselves and would make up in the end.

Beria seemed not only all-powerful, but sinister too. It seems safe to assume that his colleagues, in view of his unsavoury past, regarded him as not only a menace to the USSR but as a threat to their own lives. Possibly the demotion of Malenkov, achieved just two weeks after Stalin's death, was the result of a concentrated effort to weaken the presumed Malenkov–Beria ascendancy. Malenkov kept his chairmanship of the Council of Ministers but his party secretaryship was transferred to Khrushchev. Since under Stalin it had been the Council of Ministers which had wielded the most influence, with the role of the party downgraded, this change at the time was probably not seen as giving Khrushchev an extraordinary accession of power. But since others besides Khrushchev realized that one of the first tasks of the post-Stalin leadership was to restore the party to its previous eminence, the post did have great potential, of which Khrushchev made full use. The concept of 'collective leadership', introduced to describe a regime which would no longer be dominated by one man and in which the party and government would work hand in hand, was taken very seriously by Khrushchev. Malenkov's prime-ministerial decisions would need the approval of his colleagues, and Khrushchev's opinion was increasingly first among equals, for his was the voice of the party.

The new leadership was evidently inclined towards a relaxation in all fields of Soviet life. Malenkov was especially forthright in this; he even went so far as to admit that atomic war would be catastrophic for all mankind (but he was soon persuaded by his colleagues to backtrack on this rather crucial issue. He then said that atomic war would be catastrophic for the capitalist world, a prophecy which raised fewer awkward questions). The scanty evidence suggests that Khrushchev at this stage was noticeably less 'liberal' than Malenkov, and was not conspicuous in his support for the production of more consumer goods and for measures to improve the lot of the peasantry. Meanwhile, a start was made in releasing political prisoners. Some of the labour camps were closed and their inmates freed. It was not long before those who feared that a release of tension could be catastrophic began to receive apparent confirmation. When the expectations of relaxations in East Germany and Poland were disappointed there were strikes and demonstrations in those two peoples' democracies. At a particularly arduous Arctic labour camp, at Vorkuta, the prisoners actually went on strike for better conditions. This outbreak was led by a Pole, and was overcome when the MVD troops opened fire on the protesters during negotiations.

It is often assumed that in these early weeks Beria represented the forces wishing to maintain a tyrannous atmosphere. One source of this belief is Khrushchev's subsequent reminiscences. Beria did not have a chance to compile his own memoirs, for he was shot in 1953, and his execution was cleverly used in the delicate manœuvres aimed at what was later to be known as 'destalinization'. In fact, as the head of an organization which had great opportunities for evaluating public opinion not only in the USSR but also in the peoples' democracies, Beria was probably more aware than his colleagues of the urgent need for a retreat from repression and rigidity. And if it is true that Beria and Malenkov were aligned in these early weeks, then it can hardly be asserted that Beria was not in favour of Malenkov's first attempts at relaxation.

It is quite possible, therefore, that the arrest of Beria was due not so much to what he intended to do as to what his colleagues realized he had the power to do. Khrushchev appears to have been a leading figure in the delicate probing of the Politburo members, aimed at securing their support for an organized united front against Beria. Apparently Malenkov was the hardest to persuade, Kaganovich agreed as soon as he realized that the conspirators had a majority, while Voroshilov welcomed measures against Beria but was slow to reveal his hatred of the latter, fearing betrayal. Molotov seems to have been the first conspirator to advocate 'extreme measures' against Beria, rather than mere dismissal. In Khrushchev's subsequent account, Beria was denounced by his colleagues at a Kremlin meeting and was then arrested at pistol-point by six generals who had been secreted in an adjoining room.

In July 1953, a week after Beria's arrest, a plenary session of the party's Central Committee took place. This was only briefly reported in the press despite (or, rather, because of) its great significance. What was contained in Malenkov's report to this plenum was not related, nor was the resolution which the plenum passed after hearing and discussing this report. Knowledge of the resolution was carefully restricted to selected party officials throughout the USSR and to the highest officials of foreign communist parties. It is through the latter that details later leaked to the west. Ordinary Russians had to be content with the uninformative communiqué printed in the newspapers, while party members received a little more information from their superiors. The substance of the resolution was that there was much that was wrong in the USSR. Industry was backward. Agriculture was pitiful, with entire rural districts abandoned. The party had unjustifiably been put into the background, had been unable to participate in decision-making because of the emergence of a 'personality cult' in the party. But instead of directly accusing Stalin for all this, the resolutions heaped all the denunciations on Beria, whose MVD had dominated, it was said, both the party and government, and enabled Beria to damage the party, ruin the collective farms policy, distort Soviet policy in eastern Europe, and pervert relationships with the non-Russian nationalities of the Soviet Union.

Thus the leadership had eliminated Beria in a way that suggested that the MVD was now under control, and at the same time gave some explanation for the recent deviations from policies inherited almost as holy writ from the Stalin period. In the following weeks the press printed editorials that were obviously inspired by the change of outlook contained in the plenum's resolution. In December it was announced that Beria had been executed, together with some of his closest associates in the security services. Three decades later more details were forthcoming: there had been a five-day secret trial of Beria and six of his colleagues, resulting in executions based on fifty volumes of testimony.

Acquiescence for a change of course had thereby been obtained, even though the use of persuasive mass terror had been voluntarily relinquished. This was quite a landmark in Soviet political development. However, there was still an eminent skeleton in the Kremlin cupboard: open repudiation of Stalin had not been attempted. Such a repudiation would have threatened disarray, uproar, and even perhaps revolt. Not only had the population at large been taught to worship Stalin and all his works, but the party and government officials (that is, the entire administration of the USSR) owed their positions to adherence to Stalin's policies and concepts. A premature attempt to wrench Stalin from the hearts and minds of such people would have seemed to be an attack on their souls, and an attack which might well have generated desperate resistance. It was not until 1956 that a big move could be made against the Stalin myths. By that year Khrushchev had established himself as leader of both party and government.

From the start, Khrushchev as party secretary began to place his own nominees in key positions; many of them were former colleagues from the Moscow and Ukrainian organizations. At the same time he was reasserting the influence of the party over the administration. At this period there seemed to be a marked division of the party into those who regarded themselves as administrators who happened to be party members, and those who saw themselves primarily as party members having the duty of participating in administration. In general the latter tended to support Khrushchev, and the former Malenkov, in the various policy disputes of 1953 and 1954. Among the most important disagreements were, apparently, the government's intention of shifting resources from heavy to light industry (which Khrushchev opposed at this time), and the policy of ploughing up the 'virgin lands' to solve the food problem. Malenkov seemed unenthusiastic about the latter policy, which was Khrushchev's own scheme and which was executed by party and, especially, Komsomol volunteers, rather than directly by the government.

By early 1955 Khrushchev and his followers were able to compel Malenkov to resign. The latter's position was weak because many of those who favoured him in general had been antagonized by particular policies; Molotov and Kaganovich probably resented the diversion of resources from heavy to light industry, and other relaxations. Molotov favoured a continuation of the hard line in foreign policy, especially towards Tito. Reasons given for Malenkov's relegation from prime minister to minister for power stations included his alleged mismanagement of industry and agriculture, but in private he was blamed for his part in the Leningrad Affair.

The new prime minister was Bulganin, a man whom Khrushchev could usually dominate. However, the latter's position was by no means secure, especially after his 1956 denunciation of Stalin, and his over-energetic innovations elsewhere, had made new enemies. In 1957, while he and Bulganin were making one of their frequent foreign visits, colleagues conspired to demand his resignation. When the two tourists arrived back by train from Finland they were greeted by their fellow-leaders with the usual bouquets, but at the following meeting of the Politburo (see p. 393) Khrushchev was attacked and found himself in a minority. However, he insisted that the eleven-member Politburo did not have the right to decide his future; that was the right of the much bigger Central Committee. Assisted by an airlift arranged by the ministry of defence, Khrushchev was able to assemble a majority in this latter body. His opponents (Malenkov, Molotov, and Kaganovich) were out-voted and labelled 'the anti-party group'. They were expelled from the Central Committee and rusticated to minor and remote jobs. Soon after, Khrushchev felt strong enough to dismiss Zhukov, who had been minister of defence since 1955.

Zhukov was popularly regarded as the outstanding Soviet war leader, and enjoyed great and uncontrived prestige. His US equivalent, Eisenhower, had shown that such a man was in a good position to achieve the greatest political triumphs. His demotion was therefore more than a matter of putting the army back in its place. Still, the army undoubtedly had been deprived of its most powerful spokesman, and with the 'anti-party group' shattered, and the MVD firmly under the control of the party, it was not difficult for Khrushchev to make the final move. In March 1958 Bulganin, accused of supporting the 'anti-party group' in 1957, was dismissed. Khrushchev took over his office, thus combining once more the party secretary and the prime minister in one person. Apart from the elimination of Beria, which had been a collective move, Khrushchev in his rise to power had not killed any of his competitors. This, and subsequent events, seemed to confirm that there was an implicit understanding among Soviet leaders that Stalinist bloodbaths should not be repeated.

As the following sections will show, Khrushchev transformed all aspects of Soviet life, even though many of his innovations failed and he was dismissed in 1964. His successful destruction of the Stalin myths just three years after the dictator's death resembled Alexander's abolition of serfdom, in that it opened the way to a whole series of long-needed changes. Stalin's brand of totalitarianism had been much more total than others, but Khrushchev was able to bring about an almost bloodless relaxation, although he made many enemies in the process. Many of his enemies were those possessed of the traditional bureaucratic attitudes. Khrushchev was not at all of this cast. He was a man who was willing to respond to a new idea with 'why not?' rather than 'whose idea is it?'.

Khrushchev's 'secret' speech

Khrushchev's anti-Stalin speech to the delegates of the 20th Party Conference (1956) was gradually made known to party organizations both at home and overseas, so that all communists could be acquainted with it. The authenticity of the text published in western newspapers was not denied by Moscow.[4] However, western commentators tended to forget their usual caution; as would later be the case with Khrushchev's accusations against China, his strictures about Stalin were usually accepted as the whole truth and nothing but the truth. In retrospect, his speech seems well-lubricated with exaggerations (like the claim that Stalin used a globe to plan the Red Army's campaigns).

Even before 1956 the worst features of Stalinism were being checked. After Stalin's death the MVD had been brought under party control and there had been a new insistence on 'socialist legality', consumer-goods industries had been helped, the ponderosities of Stalinist architecture had

---

[4] The text of the speech was also published in T.H. Rigby's *The Stalin Dictatorship* (1968) and B. Wolfe's *Khrushchev and Stalin's Ghost* (1956).

been condemned, relations with Yugoslavia had been restored, the Kremlin was opened to the public, many labour-camp inmates had returned to normal life, foreign tourists were allowed into the USSR, some critical novels had been published, and leaders (especially Khrushchev) had begun to visit foreign parts and to actually talk with ordinary people in various parts of the Union. At the Conference itself, Khrushchev's revelations were preceded by speeches by Mikoyan and others in which the late-lamented dictator was not shown the customary respect. In particular, liquidated Bolsheviks, whose names had been unmentionable, were spoken of in respectful tones. The tendentious party history was condemned. The bloody dissolution of the Polish communist party in 1938, the post-war imprisonment of Gomulka, and the execution of the Hungarian revolutionary leader Bela Kun were among many acts which were now held against Stalin.

Among the matters included in Khrushchev's address was Lenin's 'testament', which was read to the delegates together with Lenin's last letters condemning Stalin ('commotion in the hall' was duly reported at this point). Then Khrushchev, while condemning Trotsky, Zinoviev, and Bukharin, expressed doubts on whether their executions had been necessary. He pointed out that anybody who disagreed with Stalin 'was doomed to . . . moral and physical annihilation'. Using material taken from the MVD archives, Khrushchev read out some of the last appeals sent by condemned Bolsheviks to Stalin and never delivered; well-known revolutionaries had written that false confessions had been tortured out of them, or that they believed that an anti-party group was at work in the NKVD, and that they were the victims of it. Stalin's role in the war was then condemned; the catastrophes of 1941, which earlier had been referred to as masterful tactical retreats, were directly blamed on Stalin's refusal to heed warnings and to make strategic retreats at the right time. The 'Personality Cult' was Khrushchev's term for describing the unquestioning adulation which Stalin had invited. The Stalin Prizes, which were intended to rival Nobel prizes, and the naming of innumerable towns, institutions, collective farms, and streets after Stalin, were among the practices condemned (subsequently Stalingrad was renamed Volgograd). It became a rule that leaders names could not be used for such purposes during their lifetimes; Voroshilovgrad once more became Lugansk, Molotov once more became Perm, and so on.

For anyone who had not lived under Stalinism the devastating psychological impact of Khrushchev's revelations was difficult to grasp. For a quarter-century the party and the population had been taught to regard Stalin almost as a god. On any question, whether it was scientific or political or cultural, Stalin's opinion was the correct opinion; unquestioned omnipotence begat unquestionable omniscience. Right from childhood the

Soviet citizen had learned to associate Stalin with all that was right and correct, and to regard his defeated critics as one or other of the zoological hybrids mentioned in party histories; fascist hyenas, capitalist running-dogs, white-guard reptiles. All kinds of sacrifices had been demanded, and obtained, of the people in the name of Stalin; many had sacrificed the urgings of their better nature and committed shameful deeds for Stalin. The 'Personality Cult' had meant that portraits and busts of Stalin were to be seen everywhere; not only on walls and in parks but at street corners, on railway locomotives and trams, on barn doors. Books, articles, and radio programmes on any kind of subject were prefaced with some kind of obeis-ance to the great man in the Kremlin. 'Long live Stalin' and 'Glory to Stalin' had been favourite slogans decorating all possible sites. And now the successor and former comrade of Stalin, in the presence of other for-mer comrades, had catalogued the lies and tragedies of the Stalin era.

Among those who must have been disconcerted by 'destalinization' were old Stalinists like Molotov and Kaganovich, who would have disagreed mainly on policies, and those like Malenkov who probably disagreed both personally and politically with Khrushchev. All these were aware how cun-ningly Khrushchev had constructed his speech so as to hint at their com-plicity in the crimes of the Stalin era while keeping clear of any insalubrious incidents in his own career. Among the lesser party members, there were, no doubt, many who feared that their activities in the purges might be investigated, while others, equally shattered, realized that they had closed their eyes or sacrificed their principles for no real end. There were suicides, while in Georgia, Stalin's homeland, students rioted against his dethrone-ment. The 1956 speech had been addressed to party members and referred mainly to the damage that Stalin had done to the party. Intelligent non-party citizens realized what had happened, and even the unintelligent could note the consequences, but it was not until 1961 that a truly public wave of anti-Stalinism was unleashed by Khrushchev at the twenty-second party congress. His speech, which acknowledged that ordinary Russians had suffered too, was published, and for symbolic emphasis Stalin's em-balmed body, which had hitherto lain in a glass case beside Lenin's, was removed and buried beneath the Kremlin wall alongside Dzerzhinski. Khrushchev's successors later allowed the grave to be marked by a bust.

The relegation of Khrushchev

Khrushchev's successful attack on the Stalinist myths in 1956, his chastise-ment of the 'anti-party group' in 1957, and the combination in his own person of party secretary and prime minister in 1958, did not enable him to institute his own dictatorship even if he had wanted to. The top leadership of the party worked on democratic principles in so far as Khrushchev depended on a majority of votes. But it was not until 1964 that Khrushchev's rivals and critics, aided by apparent setbacks to his policies, were able to engineer his downfall.

In October 1964 Khrushchev left Moscow for a Black Sea holiday. Two of his supporters who controlled the key news services (the head of the state radio, and the editor of *Pravda*) were also out of Moscow, although Khrushchev's son-in-law, whom he had appointed editor of *Izvestiya*, remained in the capital. Taking advantage of these circumstances, Khrushchev's critics called a meeting of the Politburo, which decided to initiate a long-desired change of leadership and then summoned Khrushchev to appear before it. At this second meeting he was condemned, and on the same day at a Central Committee plenary meeting resolutions were passed whereby Brezhnev became first secretary of the party and Kosygin chairman of the Council of Ministers. It was officially announced that Khrushchev had retired because of declining health. Since *Izvestiya* was suppressed on that particular day, while *Pravda* and the radio were carrying the official statement, Khrushchev had no chance of resistance. He went quietly into retirement with a personal state pension. Although most communists abroad made it clear that they had liked Khrushchev's policies, most publicly accepted the reasons given for his retirement. But there were some who expressed regret that after nearly half a century, and after a decade's freedom from Stalin and Beria, the Soviet regime still seemed incapable of changing its leader in an open, honest fashion.

Khrushchev had broken with the past, but while he had exposed basic problems, he left to his successors the task of finding lasting solutions. Some contemporaries, especially outside Russia, tended to deride Khrushchev. He was a man who came from a simple non-intellectual environment and, unlike intellectuals, was able to mix confidently with ordinary people. He was a sharp-witted polemicist (as his press-conferences with western journalists showed), but he used simple language, frequently making his point with references to the Old Testament. His enemies accused him of buffoonery, saying that people were simply laughing at him, but this is an accusation often levelled at those in authority who refuse to take themselves too seriously. His frequent overriding of the bureaucracy, a characteristic of those whose contribution to society is the ability to get things moving, must have made enemies and cooled the enthusiasm of supporters. Poor agricultural performance, which was vital since so many other improvements depended on it, was probably the most important single factor in emboldening his rivals. On 17 October 1964 *Pravda* hinted at the real reasons for his departure in a long editorial which did not actually mention Khrushchev and pretended to be about the communist concept of leadership:

The Leninist party is the enemy of subjectivism and drifting in communist construction, of harebrained scheme-making, of half-baked conclusions and hasty decisions and actions taken without regard to realities. Bragging and phrasemongering, bossiness, reluctance to take account of scientific achievement and practical experience are alien to it . . . It is only on the Leninist principle of collective leadership that it is possible to direct, and develop, the increasing creative initiative of the party . . .

Khrushchev had no chance of replying to these aspersions. Or, at least, that is what his successors confidently expected. But the former leader had not lost his craftiness. He confided his own account of his political life to a tape recorder, and the tapes were secreted out of the USSR to the west, where they were translated and published. These, Khrushchev's memoirs, are as fascinating and as slanted as any memoirs of a retired statesman.

Agriculture

Khrushchev rather fancied himself as an agricultural expert, and throughout his ascendancy intervened in most aspects of agricultural policy, readily replacing his ministers of agriculture and reducing the ministry of agriculture to little more than a research establishment. Agriculture, and especially the circumstances of the collective farms, was perhaps the sector of Soviet life in which glowing description diverged most markedly from grim reality. Although Khrushchev, when it suited him, did not hesitate to call a spade a spade, much of the new criticism of life down on the farm came not from him, but from Soviet fiction. In fact it seems to have been the writer Ovechkin who first drew public attention to a few home truths about Soviet farming.

Although Ovechkin adhered to the convention that criticism of officials was permissible, but criticism of the system never permissible, he was certainly bold, for his first critical sketch appeared in Stalin's time, in 1952. This, *Day-by-day in the District*, was followed during Khrushchev's time by a series of similar documentary sketches in which the role in agriculture of the district party secretary was critically examined. One of the most memorable of Ovechkin's characters is Borzov, a first secretary of a district party committee and an archetype of the bullying careerist who knows how to give an outward impression of devotion and efficiency while actually engaged in a life of mindless imposition of central directives on to local circumstances, composition of window-dressing reports about the non-existent successes of farms under his supervision, and harrying of peasants who, in the end, always seem to find ways of achieving failure. Borzov's foil, and Ovechkin's hero, is Martynov, another party district official who realizes that the peasants must be treated more generously and given material incentives, if they are to put their energies into the collective farm.

Khrushchev's stormy entry into the agricultural scene encouraged other writers to follow Ovechkin's example. Perhaps the best-informed was Troepolski, a professional agronomist. His *Notes of an Agronomist*, structured like Turgenev's *Sportsman's Sketches*, in which the narrator travels around not so much villages as collective farms, attacks by heavy implication the party hacks of the district committees who hinder the work of the farms by issuing directive after directive, directives based on the directives which the committees themselves receive from Moscow, and which all too often are in conflict with local circumstances or the weather. The way in which the district secretaries, themselves subject to dismissal if the farms under their supervision fail to meet their targets, appoint and dismiss collective farm chairmen on the same principle, is mocked in the character of one Prokhor, who is nicknamed Prokhor XVII because he is his farm's seventeenth chairman. Prokhor has had a succession of responsible jobs; he has made a mess of all of them but survives because of the patronage of a higher party official, the chairman of the regional party executive committee. In addition, Prokhor owes his survival to his aptitude at playing safe, and to his obsequiousness towards those who might make or break his career.

As writers complained from below, Khrushchev acted from above. During his regime, and especially in the first half, he had many successes, but nevertheless shortcomings on the farms were almost certainly a major reason for his dismissal. He had a good appreciation of what was wrong, but his reforms were all too often taken to extremes, or had adverse side effects. Towards the end of his career, when the earlier agricultural successes were overtaken by new misfortunes, he made so many changes and reorganizations that agricultural administrators became hopelessly confused.

Some of the twists and turns were forced upon Khrushchev by the need to placate or outmanœuvre his critics. Just as Stalin had exaggerated the supporting opinion of a section of party activists to justify his collectivization drive, so Khrushchev relied heavily on a few voluntary or semi-voluntary supporters among the local party committees. A bizarre sequence occurred when Khrushchev introduced impossibly high growth rates for meat production. Opposed by almost all who were familiar with the condition of agriculture, he could point to the success of one of his protégés, the party secretary of the Ryazan region, who was putting on the market vastly increased supplies of meat. In the first year of this great Ryazan campaign, it appears that almost every available animal on the Ryazan farms was butchered to produce these impressive statistics. In the following year, to avoid a scandal, Ryazan quietly bought up the required numbers of cattle outside the region. But the whole fiasco was soon uncovered, to the embarrassment of Khrushchev and of the Ryazan party committee, whose secretary committed suicide.

Khrushchev's main changes involved organization, incentives, and choice of foodstuffs for production. The ministry of agriculture was gradually reduced from a centralized authority over the farms to a mere consultative and advisory body. In its place, local party organizations were given greater opportunity to supervise, although many of their members, being reliable urban party administrators transferred to the countryside, were not really fitted to increased responsibilities. There was also a continuing trend towards farm mergers, making the collectives fewer but larger; by 1967 the number of collective farms had declined to 36,187, with each on average comprising 418 households, while state farms, which on average were more than double the size of the collectives, had risen to 12,773 (this process continued after Khrushchev, so that by 1978 the corresponding figures were 26,700, 495, and 20,484). State farms increased partly because new ones were used to develop the virgin lands, and partly because some collectives were converted to state farms (to the dismay of their peasants, who found that state farmers' private plots and livestock were minimal). Also noteworthy was the disbanding of the Machine and Tractor Stations. There had always been a conflict between these and the farms because while farms wanted to use the MTS service as little as possible to save expense, the MTS wanted to provide as much service as possible and hence extract higher payment-in-kind. In 1958 the MTS were abolished, and their equipment purchased by the farms they used to serve. The standards of maintenance, never very high, deteriorated. Even though tractors were worked rather intensively, this did not fully account for their short life. In 1969, according to official statistics, tractor production rose to 441,700, but the number of tractors possessed by state and collective farms was only 1,704,000 – four years' production at the current rate. (In 1978 the ratio had hardly improved, the corresponding figures being 576,000 and 2,297,000.)

In a speech to the Central Committee in 1953 Khrushchev admitted that agricultural production under Stalin had been inferior to that of the last tsarist years in many respects; this had been concealed by statistical sleight-of-hand. Incentives for peasants to work and for farms to invest was a first priority. Thus the prices paid for state procurements were increased, and some procurement quotas were reduced (leaving farms more surplus produce, which they could sell at higher prices). Other moves were promised to connect more farms with the electricity grid (most farms were without electricity, although some had their own diesel generators), and the reduction (and later abolition) of the taxes and state delivery quotas which had been imposed on the peasants' private plots. A 1953 concession which reveals how far exploitation of the peasantry had been carried in Stalin's time was that those peasants who did not possess animals were no longer required to deliver a quota of meat to the state. On the other hand, measures were taken to increase the time spent by peasants on collective work, and delinquents could be punished by a reduction of their private plot. Over the years, as party secretaries and farm chairmen endeavoured to win praise by squeezing the last ounce of effort from their peasants, this meant that despite higher state procurement prices (and hence higher incomes from collective labour) the peasants felt that they were worse off because they could no longer spend so much time on their much more profitable private production. Also, after the first few years, Khrushchev seemed to become alarmed at the size of the private agricultural sector. In particular he staged a campaign against private cows, and local parties responded by persuading many peasants 'voluntarily' to transfer their cows to the collective farms. This resulted in discontented peasants and, judging from milk production figures, discontented cows.

Khrushchev did not spare himself. He spent much of his time in the countryside, conferring with party secretaries, cajoling farm chairmen, making promises to the peasants in the kind of earthy language they could understand. This in itself was a great advance, not only for the USSR but for post-Petrine Russia; for the first time there was a genuine interchange between tsar and people. But the results in agriculture were disappointing. The basic difficulty was that what Khrushchev said to the peasants in order to shake them from apathy was taken by local party organizations as justification for excesses. Thus when Khrushchev condemned the *Travopolye* crop rotation system, party secretaries urged the local farms to plough up their grassland, even though grass might have been the best crop at particular times and places. The year after Khrushchev had said a few words in favour of legumes, there were extensive areas of Russia where grain had been displaced by beans and clover. Khrushchev was especially passionate in his advocacy of maize cultivation; with the virgin lands under wheat, the old ploughlands of European Russia could profitably turn from wheat to maize, with its high tonnage per hectare and its suitability as fodder. But again the intention was carried to excess, many farms unsuitable for maize being persuaded or coerced into transferring to this crop. After Khrushchev's visit to the USA a new use for maize was urged: the cornflake was introduced to Russia, and a people long habituated to buckwheat porridge discovered shop windows laden with cornflake boxes. At first, unwilling to squander this luxury of the western world, citizens contented themselves with breakfasting on a few flakes sprinkled over a bowl of milk.

Khrushchev's failure to remedy many of the longstanding ills of the countryside found literary expression in Abramov's short story, *The New Life*, published in 1963 by the 'thick' journal *Neva*. The between-the-lines implication of this tale was that woes persisted not despite Khrushchev, but sometimes because of him. The hero of this story is Mysovski, an age-ing party official and collective farm chairman who finds himself in the characteristic no-win situation in which peasants refuse to work enthusias-tically, or at all, to fulfil the inept directives received from the local district committee. The story revolves around one particular directive, that pre-paration of fodder (maize, no doubt!) should proceed parallel with hay-making. The farm assembly had decided that in view of the dry weather all hands should be used for hay-making, as fodder preparation was less dependent on the weather. In other words, the farm's decision to make hay while the sun shone conflicted with the instructions from above, and the district committee was not going to ignore this disobedience. Mysovski receives the first warning over the telephone, '. . . Perhaps the district committee will make an exception, but you really should be aware of the political line in this matter.' The second warning is less gentle, '. . . How do you expect me to interpret your obstinacy? Sabotage? Or uncomprehend-ing pigheadedness about the basic economic problem?' Then comes the dis-trict committee's reprimand, in the form of a Resolution:

For his political underrating of fodder as the foundation of collective farm cattle-raising, it is resolved to severely reprimand A. E. Mysovski, chairman of the 'New Life' collective farm . . . Comrade Mysovski is obliged within five days to liquidate the intolerable delay by the 'New Life' collective farm in the storage of green fodder.

Mysovski's ambulations about the collective, trying to persuade reluctant peasants to turn out for some real work, forms the bulk of the story and provides the opportunity for the author to relate a series of case studies which are only superficially fictional. There are, for example, the women who prefer to brave the chilling dampness of the woods to gather mush-rooms than spend their days in the collective fields. After all, said one, they could sell the mushrooms to the local co-operative and thereby have a few kopeks in their hands, whereas the whole summer she had toiled in the fields and had so far received no remuneration. And with so much hay about, it was disgraceful that however hard they worked they couldn't afford to buy their own cow. The cow question gets several airings in this tale, as possession of a cow made all the difference to a peasant family. One peasant, asked if he will turn out for the special 'Work Sunday' fixed by Mysovski to catch up with the haymaking, replies that he probably will not; if he had a cow to feed he might have thought the effort worth while. Mysovski reflects:

The cow problem again! And in a farm virtually smothered with pasture . . . at least a half of the peasants did not have their own cow. Fantastic! But there was a very simple explanation. For his work-day a peasant would get ten per cent of the collective hay he gathered . . . So a peasant had to gather enough hay for at least eight or nine cows in order to look after his own . . . Each farm chairman in one way or another tried to find ways around this system, but at that point a district prosecutor or the district committee secretary would intervene with threats, 'How dare you! Anti-government practice! Encouragement of private enterprise!'

The virgin lands, on which Khrushchev had staked his reputation, turned out to be an achievement concealed within a failure. The achievement was that land under wheat increased to sixty-seven million hectares, compared with thirty-nine million in 1950. For the first years the production of these lands justified the investment (of machinery, buildings, roads, railways, and labour). But Khrushchev, as usual, was not content to leave success alone. The programme was expanded, the land was worked intensively, and wheat was not alternated with other crops. It was not long before the warnings, by Soviet as well as western specialists, of future land erosion and infertility were shown to be justified. Erosion and exhaustion, combined with bad weather, suggested that the virgin lands had been merely yet another exercise in futility. But this was not so; farmed intelligently the lands were capable in an average year of making a great contribution to food supplies. But bad weather in both old and new agricultural regions led to a very bad harvest in 1963. There was a food shortage, and the USSR, which at the time was also supplying Cuba with grain, was forced to import grain from other countries, notably from the USA and Canada. The spectacle of four decades of Soviet agriculture culminating in food shortages and imports from the capitalist world was a sad blow to the prestige of the USSR and of Khrushchev himself. It probably accelerated the move to oust Khrushchev; the good harvest of 1964 came too late to save him. As might be expected, the first result of grain shortage was a reduction of fodder available for livestock, which led to renewed meat shortages. The pig population, as always, was the most vulnerable, and fell sharply from seventy million to forty million, a loss which was only made good after ten years.

The economy

The death of Stalin, and especially his posthumous fall from favour in 1956, opened the way for a whole series of reforms in all aspects of Soviet life. Changes which had long been necessary had been held up either because Stalin was against them, or because those who knew what was wrong did not dare to voice their opinions. Many of the reforms which took place under Khrushchev were minor, and did not originate from him. But the more important changes were usually carried out through his initiative and energy. Some were fundamental and long-lasting, but others were merely the product of his apparent passion for changing everything (or meddling, as his critics subsequently called it).

In the economy, there was a renewed emphasis on consumer goods; evidently Khrushchev's earlier opposition to Malenkov's wish to make more goods available in the stores had been prompted only by political motives. In time, not only larger quantities, but also a greater range of items became available to the Soviet citizen. Although the wage increases initiated by Khrushchev benefited mainly the lowest-paid, there were also price reductions which benefited all. Pensions became more meaningful, and for the first time small pensions were granted to peasants. In 1958 compulsory voluntary subscriptions to state loans were abolished, although interest and redemption for existing loans also ceased (in 1971, at the 24th Party Conference, Brezhnev promised amid prolonged applause that all such loans would be repaid by 1990). The worker's lot was also improved by the gradual introduction of the seven-hour day (with six hours on Saturdays; but by the early seventies the transition to a five-day week was well under way). Factory trade union committees were given more responsibilities. The 'bachelors' tax was restricted to males, and the tax on childless couples removed. Small quantities of imported goods found their way into Soviet shops and usually were sold within minutes. However, living standards remained abysmal, especially in the lesser industrial cities. In 1962 workers at Novocherkassk rioted in protest against shortages and increased food prices. Twenty were killed during the suppression, and a few more executed later. News of this bloody event, and of others at different times and places, was successfully concealed by a censorship and suppressive apparatus that had lost little of its effectiveness.

The targets of the Sixth Five-Year Plan (1956–60) being over-optimistic, this Plan was abandoned after two years and replaced by a seven-year plan (1959–65) which was itself subsequently replaced by the Seventh Five-Year Plan (1961–5). Khrushchev's insistence on shifting priorities from the traditional favourites of the planners (such as coal and steel) to modern industries which had been neglected in Stalin's time (in particular the chemical industry, especially its plastics and fertilizer sectors) brought benefits to the consumer, to agriculture, and to the economy in general. But Khrushchev's exuberant slogan 'Catch up and overtake the USA in *per capita* output by 1970', although widely publicized in the early sixties, was rash indeed. By 1970 the gap between the USA and the USSR had certainly narrowed, but the Soviet growth rate, hitherto very fast, was declining. It seems probable that 1963, with its poor harvest, produced a growth rate lower than that of the USA. In the sixties, heavy spending on advanced armaments and on the space programme held back other sectors of the economy. In particular, the bold housing programme which had earned Khrushchev the gratitude of millions of urban Russians had lost momentum by 1964.

In Khrushchev's early years there was new confidence in Soviet technological progress. There was large-scale railway electrification and dieselization; one of the accusations levelled by Khrushchev against Kaganovich in 1957 was that he was too fond of reactionary steam locomotives. In the air, the Aeroflot corporation was expanded in order to progressively relieve the railways of their role as the major long-distance passenger carrier. As early as 1956 it was flying the Tupolev-104 jet aircraft, and its fares were being lowered, in some cases to a level below those of the railways. In 1959 the world's first civil nuclear-powered ship, the icebreaker *Lenin*, was completed. Many of the products of advanced Soviet technology were proudly exhibited to the world; the USSR mounted impressive displays at both the Brussels and Montreal world fairs in 1958 and 1967, among others. However, the most effective demonstration of Soviet technical competence was the launching of the earth's first artificial satellite (*Sputnik*) in 1957. Although there had been several announcements of the intention to achieve this feat, when it happened the western world, misled by its own press, was startled. The alarm stemmed both from the realization that the Russian success was based on advanced high-power rockets, and from the prickly question of how a nation previously depicted as technically backward, oppressed, and crude, could have achieved such sophistication. Fortunately, though not quite accurately, western opinion concluded that the answer lay in the great attention paid to education in the USSR. Thus *Sputnik* not only resulted in great technological prestige for the USSR, but a more generous provision for education in the budgets of most western nations. Educationalists, following in the path of generals and industrialists, discovered that the best way to obtain funds was to relate their needs to what Russia was doing.

'Socialist legality'

The retreat from Stalinist terror and arbitrariness towards what was called socialist legality began with the early release of those accused in the 'Doctors' Plot'. Almost all the surviving inhabitants of the work camps were steadily rehabilitated and sent home, including even surviving members of

Vlasov's anti-Soviet army. A few highly-placed victims who had died in captivity or had been executed were posthumously rehabilitated; this was of little benefit to themselves, but it did mean a pension and a return to respectability for their families. Political terror disappeared; although there was no cast-iron guarantee that it would not be reintroduced, there could be little doubt that the party was determined to prevent a recurrence of the excesses of Stalin's day. The three-man Special Boards of the MVD, which since 1934 had the power to dispatch suspects to camps without trial, were abolished. The security service was removed from the MVD and placed under a Committee of State Security (KGB) which was headed by Shelepin, a young man who had risen in the party as leader of the Komsomol organization. The Procuracy, the foundation of the judicial system, was reformed; among other things it was empowered to supervise all criminal investigations made by the KGB, and its officials could be punished if they closed their eyes to malpractices in prisons and camps. Anti-state crimes (this term replaced 'counter-revolutionary crimes') could no longer be tried in secret, and the military courts, hitherto widely used in political cases, were limited to espionage and crimes committed by servicemen. Relatives of those servicemen who deserted to the west could no longer be punished for the desertion. Vyshinsky's doctrine that confessions were sufficient evidence for a conviction was repudiated, and so was his doctrine that in counter-revolutionary cases the accused is guilty unless he proves himself innocent. 'Terrorist acts' no longer included such misdemeanours as punching a party secretary's nose, but were confined to severe bodily injury to state or party officials, with a political motive. The doctrine of analogy was finally eliminated. After an acquittal the accused was no longer subject to a review of his case at any time; such a review had to be initiated within one year of the first trial. Penalties were reduced for many crimes. The labour camps were officially abolished, being replaced by labour colonies; these were usually the same institutions but with better conditions. Some criminal offences were abolished (abortion, absence from work, leaving a job without permission). Another step forward was the progressive declarations of invalidity extended to the hundreds of thousands of laws, decrees, and edicts issued in Stalin's time, still theoretically in force even though obsolete. Also noteworthy was the higher status assumed by jurists, who since 1917 had not been held in high esteem. They never attained their pre-revolutionary influence, but they were consulted when judicial changes were contemplated.

Moderation of the rigours of the law was followed by an increase in crime. This in turn led to a partial return to harsher measures in 1961. The death penalty, which had been reinstated in 1950, was extended from serious cases of espionage, treason, 'wrecking', aggravated murder, terrorist acts, and banditry to large-scale theft or embezzlement of state or social property, counterfeiting, 'speculation in foreign currency', aggravated rape, murder of police or auxiliaries on duty, and serious and repeated bribe-taking.[5] For at least one of these crimes, currency speculation, the new penalty was applied retroactively, past offenders already serving their sentences being shot (a special decree of the Presidium of the Supreme Soviet in July 1961 authorized this unusual step). Bribery was widespread in the USSR and its classification as a grave crime did not mean that a minor bribe would result in a death sentence or even imprisonment. It all depended on the circumstances; a person convicted of, say, accepting bribes from a German businessman would be in grave danger of execution. Executions for black market offences were quite rare and selective, although an ingenious Ukrainian who in the 1970s laid a pipeline from a distillery to his own premises and sold the alcohol on the black market received a death sentence. He had done three dangerous things: stolen state property on a large scale, dealt in a socially-sensitive commodity, and made an enormous profit for himself.

A retrograde step was the 'Law Against Parasites'. This was directed against persons 'evading socially useful work' and could be applied without the usual guarantees of the criminal law; in fact general meetings of a social organization (the workers of a factory, inhabitants of an apartment block, etc.) could impose the penalty of two to five years' internal exile (with possible confiscation of property) on one of their number, provided the decision was confirmed by the town soviet. In the first year of its operation, 2,000 'parasites' were exiled from Moscow alone. This law, and the stiffer penalties against hooligans, were largely directed at the growing number of dissatisfied young people who indulged in various kinds of delinquencies. In some cases the advantage of popular participation in justice was counterbalanced by the citizens' willingness, sometimes prompted, to hit out at nonconformists. There was a case of a young very nonconformist poet, who was exiled as a 'parasite', it being adjudged that he could not be a 'real' poet because he had no document to prove it. The 'Parasites Law', which had antecedents in communal custom of tsarist times, was soon withdrawn in many of the republics.

The trial of Daniel and Sinyavsky in 1966 marked a step backward, in that they were denied certain rights officially granted to the accused, and

---

[5] The death penalty was abolished in Russia in 1754, 1917, 1918, 1919, and 1947, but only the short-lived 1917 abolition was totally effective (notably, it did not exclude sentences passed by military courts). From 1932 the death penalty (known as 'the highest form of social defence') was applied to theft of state property and political crimes.

in the abuse (not for the first or last time) of the law against 'agitation and propaganda directed against the Soviet system'. Daniel and Sinyavsky had published abroad, under pseudonyms, works which because of alleged anti-Sovietism were not allowed publication at home. There was no law against this, so they were accused of anti-Soviet propaganda. The trial was preceded by newspaper articles in which the accused were regarded as unquestionably guilty. Their right of defence was curtailed by interruptions from the judge and the apparently hand-picked audience of hostile spectators. Thus the prosecution was able to present anti-Soviet statements by fictional characters in the novels as words actually voiced by the accused. The latter were sent to labour colonies.

But despite the occasional step backward, in the sixties and seventies there seemed little reason to doubt that the post-1953 law reforms had been a sincere and definite step forward. Certainly there were complaints, not unfounded, of police repression. But repression, like freedom, is a relative term and, as Alexander II discovered, it is when freedom is extended at the expense of repression that complaints of repression become loudest. Under Stalin, political intercourse, even between consenting adults in private, was perilous. Under Khrushchev and his successors individual Russians could safely criticize their government, provided they did not seek a large audience, or join together to form anything which might be described as an 'organization'.

The arts

After Stalin died, one of the most popular 'thick' literary journals[6] published an article suggesting that the true test of a literary work was sincerity, not conformity to officially imposed stereotypes. There was much opposition to this from those for whom 'party-mindedness' remained the key index of a work's value. They argued that if a writer is 'ideologically incorrect', or has 'alien attitudes', his sincerity only increases the harmful effect he has on his readers; sincerity is therefore dangerous and harmful. The struggle between the 'liberals' and the 'conservatives', veiled in most other aspects of Soviet life, was clearly evident in literary circles throughout the late fifties and sixties. During that period there was an initial move towards greater freedom, especially after Khrushchev's destalinization speech, then a few scandals, followed by the reimposition of stricter

---

[6] *Novyi mir*, No. 12 (1953). *Novyi mir* after Stalin's death was the most adventurous and 'liberal' of the literary journals; *One day in the Life of Ivan Denisovich* and *Not by Bread Alone*, among others, were first published in it. Its editor was the poet A. Tvardovski. After the departure of Khrushchev this journal's output was progressively restricted and its editor and board replaced by less liberal men.

controls. The latter, distasteful though they were, tended to set limits to the new freedom rather than reimpose the old restrictions.

By 1954 novels were appearing which quietly drew attention to the evils of the Stalinist way of life. For example, V. Nekrasov's *Home Town* showed how returning servicemen were disappointed at what they found back home. Ehrenburg's *Thaw* gave its name to the initial period of post-Stalin relaxation; in Russian, 'thaw' suggests not simply a melting of ice but the spontaneous renewal of life as the grip of winter breaks up. *Thaw* referred casually, though unexpectedly to the Soviet reader, to such things as the talented artists who either starve or paint murals of collectivized cows or shock-workers, and the local Jewish doctor terrified by press accounts of the 'Doctors' Plot'. It portrayed a rank-and-file Stalinist, Ivan Vasilievich Zhuravlev, a factory manager who cares more about plan fulfilment than the health of his workers:

... the factory was in excellent order. There had not been a single breakdown for six years. True, the Deputy Minister had told Ivan Vasilievich that he had spent illegally the funds intended for building living quarters, but Zhuravlev had decided that this was just for form's sake: 'the Ministry, like me, is interested above all in output'. Naturally, he had hastened to assure the Deputy Minister that all the workers had accommodation and that there was nothing catastrophically bad ... In town people were saying, 'Zhuravlev's going up in the world'. It was not surprising that Zhuravlev was now having his portrait painted ...

From the mid-fifties some condemned authors were rehabilitated posthumously and their works republished. Anna Akhmatova, whose poems had been condemned by Zhdanov, was once again praised. A wider range of foreign authors were published in Russian editions. There was some resistance from officials of the Writers' Union, and the head of the latter, Fadayev, committed suicide in 1956 (rather unchivalrously, his death was ascribed to alcoholism).

Poetry, which under Stalin had been little more than rhymed information, also reasserted itself. The nature of Stalinism itself, and why people had tolerated it, was one of its concerns. P. Antokolski ended one 1956 poem with

> He who has died we hate
> Less than our silence.

while Tvardovski treated the same theme with

> And who was there who did not praise him in his presence,
> Did not glorify him – just find such a one!

and in his '1945' Boris Slutski referred to the Stalinist habit of rebuilding people's homes last

From all the stones crunching underfoot
Were built first palaces, and then homes.

It was the young poet Yevtushenko who attracted most popular enthusiasm, both by his printed poems and by his public appearances at poetry-
reading performances. With his anti-Stalinist approach he became almost
an official poet for Khrushchev, although it was an uneasy relationship
and he was sometimes in semi-disgrace. Yevtushenko, and a very few other
poets, made frequent poetry-reading visits to the west, where they were received with enthusiasm.

One of the first writers to dispense with Stalinist literary conventions
and thereby create a best-seller was Dudintsev, whose *Not by Bread Alone*
(1956) showed how a talented, honest, and potentially valuable individual
was held back by an entrenched clique of bureaucrats who opposed innovation as a threat to their vested interests, and even managed to get the
hero sentenced to prison camp. Solzhenitsyn's *One Day in the Life of Ivan
Denisovich* (1962), apparently published on Khrushchev's instructions after
the censors had rejected it, was a short novel bringing home with powerful
understatement the miseries of daily life in a labour camp (of which the
author had several years' first-hand knowledge). A best-seller, it helped
Khrushchev's campaign against the spirit of Stalinism; it was novels like
Solzhenitsyn's which made Russians realize the enormity of the abuses perpetrated by Stalin and the MVD. Ironically, the work which caused most
embarrassment was not particularly dangerous, until it had been made so
by the antics of the censors. Pasternak's *Doctor Zhivago* (published abroad
in 1957), while certainly presenting an un-Soviet though not especially
anti-Soviet view of the Russian Revolution would never have attracted
such widespread attention had not the censors belatedly cancelled its
publication in the USSR after the author had already arranged publication of an Italian edition. The Italian publisher refused to abandon the contract, which means that what was possibly the greatest Russian novel of
the twentieth century was a best-seller abroad while banned in its country
of origin. It was well known that Pasternak was a man of great literary sens-
ibility who had refused to lower his standards during the Stalinist years.
Thus when, a sick man, he was forced to refuse the Nobel Prize and condemned by the Writers' Union, foreign communist intellectuals were
among those who protested. Yet Khrushchev had not, apparently, been
consulted about the ban.

Education

The 1958 education reform had been anticipated for several years by criticisms levelled at the existing system. Khrushchev, himself a self-made

man with little formal education, was not well-disposed to those who wished to escape physical work through academic success. The intelligentsia was the main beneficiary of superior education; as elsewhere, it made all kinds of efforts to get its children up the educational ladder leading to white-collar work and high social status.

Apart from his desire to restrict the development of the intelligentsia as a class, Khrushchev had other reasons for his reforms. As the economy became larger and more complex, there was emerging a shortage of skilled and semi-skilled workers. Reductions in the army could not bridge this gap, but changes in the educational system might. Educated young people who had failed to get into university were unfitted by their education and aspirations to enter industry. The universities themselves were turning out similar misfits (described by one critic as like stuffed fish: you could not tell what kind of stuffing they had, but you knew they could not swim). In other words, the educational system was turning out too many over-educated and too few partly-educated students.

The 1958 reform abandoned the earlier intention to provide ten-year compulsory education for all. Before 1958, ten-year schools existed in some towns but most pupils attended seven-year schools, leaving at the end of the then-compulsory seven years. Only those with ambitions (or ambitious parents) went to, or remained in, the ten-year school for the final three voluntary years leading to the 'Attestation of Maturity' certificate and, sometimes, university. After 1958 the compulsory course became eight years (from seven to fifteen). After these compulsory years, most students were expected to abandon academic studies and either go directly to work or attend other schools for practical and technical training. Those who went to work would be able to complete the optional part of secondary education by attending schools part-time. Those who wished to proceed to higher education had first to attend a new revised ten-year school, where there would be an extra year added to the existing voluntary three (Khrushchev had already abolished the school fees imposed by Stalin). In these four years industrial or farm labour would be combined with normal subjects. This would put an end to the 'divorce from life and work' of those who underwent advanced academic training. It was envisaged that before entering an institute of higher education, new students would have done at least two years of 'productive labour' which would make them better citizens and probably better graduates; it would also cut down the pressure on university places, since many aspirants would lose their ambitions, or their prospects in the entrance exams, during their production experience.

Khrushchev was unable to get all these changes actually put into practice.

In 1964 the extra year of the ten-year schools' optional secondary course
was dropped, and 'productive labour' training was expected to take place
more and more in the schools' own workshops and gardens. In the later
sixties, Khrushchev's successors laid down that in the future there would
be compulsory three-year primary and five-year secondary courses, with
an optional two-year extension, and then, in 1973, the school-leaving age
was raised from fifteen to seventeen. As Khrushchev discovered, many of
those who should have supported the principle of classless schools, and
equal opportunity for all, preferred a system which would separate an élite
(their own children) from the others. Thus at the end of the seventies much
was still as it had been before 1958. There were increasing numbers of academically educated graduates for whom good jobs were too few. Occasional press complaints suggested that there was also a good deal of bribery,
corruption, string-pulling, and pressurizing as influential parents strove to
ensure that their own children would receive favourable attention from
teachers, examiners, and entrance boards.

An innovation under Khrushchev was the secondary co-educational
boarding schools. These allowed pupils to spend much more time on 'useful' subjects, provided better opportunity for close pupil-teacher relationships, and, it was said, taught them how to live with their neighbours. They
were a failure, and were progressively closed. They had tried to accomplish
two inconsistent aims: to provide a good educative environment for socially
unfortunate children (typically children of one-parent families), and at the
same time to constitute an example-setting academic enterprise. Moreover, many of their advantages were obtained at less cost by the increasing
numbers of schools offering the 'extended day'. Pupils stayed at these into
the evenings, following planned but informal activities. The question of
whether gifted children should be sent to special schools was exhaustively
debated. A basic tradition of Soviet education was that schools were to be
comprehensive; children were not to be divided between schools on the
basis of ability. Even within schools there was no 'streaming'. That there
did exist schools for the artistically talented (like the Kirov School of
Ballet in Leningrad) was not considered a contradiction, as these were very
special cases. In time, however, initial experimental schools for children
exceptionally gifted in mathematics and languages were multiplied.

An important feature of Khrushchev's campaign to bring the educated
into closer touch with life was his stress on the expansion of part-time and
correspondence courses, which permitted work and study in various combinations. This particularly affected higher education (although citizens
also had the opportunity to attend evening secondary-school classes in
order to complete their secondary education). By 1964 there were about

1,708,000 correspondence and 569,000 evening students in higher education, compared with 1,584,000 in full-time regular courses (although the full-timers usually completed their courses faster). Correspondence students were treated more generously than their counterparts in the west, being given time off work in order to follow short courses or consult their tutors. By 1969 there were 794 institutes of higher learning with nearly 4,500,000 students. The forty universities were outnumbered by other institutions, which included technical institutes, agricultural institutes, more than eighty medical schools, teacher-training institutes and others. New higher-education institutes had been established in subjects previously neglected. In 1965 the management school appeared in the USSR, and other in-stitutes began to pursue modern techniques like the application of mathe-matical methods in economic planning (the related field of computers had been deliberately neglected in Stalin's time, and efforts were being made to catch up with the west in computer design and use).

As in the secondary schools, the higher education teaching process was largely the ingestion of facts and their successful evacuation at examina-tion time. Unlike western universities there was little emphasis on problem solving. It was held, perhaps rightly, that it was better to learn how to solve problems later, on the job. University students were required to devote a tenth or more of their lecture hours (which averaged 1,000 hours annually for five years) to political knowledge (Marxism–Leninism, Dialectical Ma-terialism, etc.). Although this subject was examined it appeared to arouse no great enthusiasm among students, partly because of natural cynicism and partly because of unimaginative presentation (e.g. 'It is vital for all Soviet citizens to understand the class struggle . . . In the Soviet Union there is no class struggle'). Cynicism was unsurprising in a generation which recalled that in 1956, throughout the Soviet Union's secondary-school system, the examinations in final-year history (History of the Soviet Union) were abruptly cancelled because Khrushchev had made obsolete what was being taught. The same generation would also have noticed the difficulties of their history teachers in the fifties and sixties, when it was impossible to foresee what, tomorrow, would happen to yesterday.

Except for a few students with rich parents, all were eligible for grants. The average grant was meagre but could be varied upwards or downwards according to the student's academic performance. Poor performance could entail loss of grant until an improvement was recorded. Graduates were required to spend the first few years of work in a job and place to which they were directed in accordance with national needs. Many pulled strings to escape this obligation and, just as the best tsarist cadets were allowed to choose their regiment, so the top graduates were allowed to choose their place of work. It was the mediocre student with uninfluential parents who would find himself directed to his first job in some arduous region; to make sure he arrived his diploma was dispatched to his future place of work. In the sixties Soviet students apparently did not share their western counterparts' interest in the illicit enjoyment of hallucinatory drugs. On the other hand, one-third of the students at the University of Vilno were willing to admit in a survey that they listened to foreign broadcasts. Possibly the latter, supplying the pleasure of nonconformism and an expansion of mental horizons, provided a similar but cheaper stimulus. The USSR did not escape student unrest in the sixties, but this unrest was expressed less demonstratively than in the west. Because open dissent had been so long non-existent, when it did emerge it could be effective even in mild forms. On occasion, Soviet students openly disputed with lecturers purveying official truths, and this was quite shocking for traditionalists.

The armed forces

After the death of Stalin the generals had great public prestige, and seemed relatively untainted by Stalinism. Even though Zhukov, like other successful generals, had been given a secondary and remote posting after the war, he was rightly regarded by Russians as the architect of victory. Indeed, he may have been the best general of the Second World War. It would be several decades before his reputation could be impartially evaluated; in his own lifetime the history of his battles was rewritten more than once to fit political requirements.

In the mid-fifties the generals were in a strong position and their acquiescence, at least, was required by the new leaders. Zhukov became Minister of Defence. But after the defeat of the 'anti-party conspiracy', Khrushchev could dispense with active army support. In October 1957 *Pravda* appeared with a front-page article celebrating Zhukov's return from a successful visit to the Balkans, while the back page of the same newspaper carried a small mention of his dismissal as Minister of Defence.

In the four years preceding Zhukov's dismissal the army officers had firmly reasserted themselves. The war's history had been revised so that Stalin was no longer portrayed as the great strategist and tactician, with the generals merely his executives. More important, although the long-suppressed desire of the officers to avenge the purge of the thirties was not gratified, their wish to reduce the role of the army's political officers was partly satisfied. Among other reliefs, professional army officers were no longer obliged to attend political lectures. After Zhukov's fall from grace, he was accused of hindering the party's work in the army and the political commissars regained some of their lost authority. Zhukov was also accused of 'Bonapartism', and new war histories ascribed to him much of the responsibility for the disasters of 1941. Khrushchev gradually appointed to the higher defence positions men whom he had known in the Stalingrad campaign, men whom he felt he could trust. However, these officers sometimes refrained from public approval of certain of Khrushchev's moves, an unmistakable sign of disagreement. This disagreement seems to have centred on Khrushchev's reductions of defence expenditure.

In Stalin's later years, military technology had stagnated. Stalin even seemed reluctant to acknowledge that the atomic bomb had changed the military situation. In the mid-fifties Khrushchev was able to win the acceptance by the more influential generals of a reduction of the army, in exchange for investment in new military technology. It seemed that Khrushchev would achieve a reduction in defence spending while increasing defensive capacity; rockets would be substituted for regiments and submarines for cruisers. However, in 1960 Khrushchev embarked on a new reduction of the armed forces, from the existing 3.6 million men to 2.4 million, the last figure being approximately half the 1953 strength. This attempt to demonstrate the sincerity of the policy of 'peaceful coexistence' with the west, and to divert military spending to civilian, did not go smoothly. Although demobilized soldiers found places in the economy, thousands of prematurely retired officers were less easy to accommodate. Some found lowly clerical or manual work, but their loss of status and prospects was shattering. It was this, with the humiliation in Cuba in 1962, and hints of further cuts, which ensured that there would be no military support for Khrushchev when his own retirement was demanded in 1964.

The peoples' democracies

Outside the Soviet Union, communists who for years had dismissed as capitalist lies the very allegations which Khrushchev confirmed in 1956, were in an unenviable situation. Some resigned, some lost faith in their leaders. This sudden lack of self-confidence was one of the factors in the 1956 revolts in Poland and Hungary. Other factors were the dissolution of the Cominform in April, and the joint declaration by the Soviet and Yugoslav communist parties that the 'road to socialism' could be different for different countries. When the workers of Poznan rebelled, the Polish communist party expelled the most prominent Stalinists from their central committee and, apparently without consulting Moscow, appointed Gomulka as First Secretary. The Red Army and Baltic Fleet staged ominous movements, but Gomulka was able to obtain a compromise agreement by which internal policy would be relaxed, Moscow's 'viceroy' in Warsaw,

Marshal Rokossovsky,[7] would be withdrawn, but Poland would maintain the unquestioned supremacy of the communist party and would stay in the Warsaw Pact. The latter, Moscow's answer to NATO, co-ordinated the armed forces of the Soviet bloc in Europe.

Hardly was the Polish crisis eased when a far more serious situation arose in Hungary. When Stalin was denounced in 1956, and when the news came of Poland's successful revolt, the Hungarian workers and intellectuals who had been criticizing the regime demanded not only concessions, but a radical change. In October the moderate, formerly imprisoned, communist Nagy became leader, and for a time the demands of the dissidents were met: more contacts with the west, release of political prisoners, a freer press and radio. But when Nagy agreed to take Hungary out of the Warsaw Pact the Red Army took action. During the next few, confused, days, there was considerable street fighting as both the Hungarian army and civilians resisted the Russians. Some Red Army men, shocked to find themselves fighting not capitalists, but workers, refused to open fire. Hungarian resistance, which cost about 20,000 lives, came to an end after the Red Army arrested the leading Hungarian generals, having invited them into its lines on the pretext of opening negotiations. About 200,000 Hungarians fled to the west. Nagy was executed in 1958.

The spectacle of the Red Army suppressing a genuine people's revolt against oppression caused yet another shock to the communist world. There were more defections from communist parties. Tito's condemnation of the Russians reopened a breach which was only just closing. Inside the USSR, most of the population seemed satisfied with the explanation that some Hungarian workers and party members had allowed themselves to be used by capitalist or West German counter-revolutionary conspirators, but even in conditions of strict censorship there were other Russians who suspected what had happened and were uneasy. Looked at retrospectively, the suppression of the Hungarian revolt was a sign that there were definite limits to the relaxation which Moscow would allow in the people's democracies. They would not be allowed to move much further in the direction of greater political freedom than the Soviet Union itself, and they would not be allowed to endanger the system of communist buffer states which were thought to facilitate Russia's defence. More fundamentally, the Hungarian crisis brought into the open the forty-year-old dilemma of the

---

[7] Red Army General Rokossovsky had been appointed Poland's Minister of Defence, deputy Prime Minister, and member of the Polish Politburo in 1949 in order to keep an eye on the government and party. Although Rokossovsky was the son of a Polish locomotive driver, he became to the Poles a symbol of Russian domination. Hence the popular demand for his dismissal.

USSR's two roles: the role of a nation building socialism and the role of a leader and instigator of world revolution. Stalin had temporarily hidden this problem by putting Russia first, which meant that communists abroad were often sacrificed to Russia's national interests. This, until the emergence of communist China, could be justified by the proposition that, in the final analysis, the victory of communism could only be assured through the USSR; what was good for the Soviet Union was good for the world. But after 1953 foreign communists were increasingly unwilling to put Russia first.

The suppression of the Hungarian revolt meant the end of open anti-Sovietism in the peoples' democracies, with the exception of Albania (which did not accept destalinization and condemned Moscow in terms worthy of Vyshinsky). However Moscow's increasing need for support in the dispute with China meant that some concessions might be obtained. Roumania, especially, took great advantage of this. It was the Roumanians who took the lead in questioning Soviet policy in Comecon. This organization, founded to co-ordinate the communist economies, took on new life after the death of Stalin. Genuine co-operation to mutual advantage was stressed. However, Comecon's plans ran into difficulties. The idea was that each nation should concentrate on producing for the whole bloc those items which it produced best. But it seemed to some, and especially the Roumanians (who complained that they were scheduled to remain unindustrialized, exporting raw materials and receiving finished goods in return), that the smaller countries were still being exploited. In 1963 the Roumanians asserted that they had a right to plan their own economy in their own way, and made commercial agreements not only with western Europe, but also with China and Yugoslavia. In addition, Roumania was offered and accepted credits from the USA. These economic contacts were followed by diplomatic ones; Roumania opened diplomatic relations with that *bête noire* of the communist world, Western Germany.

By 1964 almost all communist parties had asserted, in one way or another, their right to reach communism by their own path. In effect, they implied that communism did not mean russianism. Moscow was no longer the Third Rome. The leader of the Italian communist party, Togliatti, summed up the new concept in the term 'polycentrism'; there was no longer a world centre of communism in Moscow, but as many centres as there were parties. Meanwhile, as will be related in the next chapter, China was asserting itself quite vigorously against Moscow; Khrushchev was not at all to the taste of the Chinese leadership.

Foreign affairs

In the post-Stalin decade a relaxation of international tension was initiated by the Soviet government. Lenin's term 'peaceful coexistence' was resurrected to describe the new attitude; it did not imply friendship with the capitalist world, but admitted the possibility of compromise and contact until such time as the capitalist countries in one way or another would turn to socialism. There were several reasons for this relaxation; the barrenness of Stalin's hostile isolationism, a realization, openly acknowledged by Khrushchev, that nuclear war was too horrible to be thinkable, the economic burden of arms spending, and the desirability of learning from the west, either by imitation or by entering into commercial and technical agreements.

The new attitudes were soon transformed into deeds. At Geneva in 1954 the USSR helped to negotiate an end to the Korean and Indo-Chinese wars. In 1955 the USSR agreed to sign the long-delayed peace treaty with Austria, by which the Red Army finally agreed to quit its zone of occupation in return for the guaranteed neutrality of Austria. The post-war Russian bases in Finland were closed. Khrushchev visited many parts of the world, including India and Britain, and in 1959 toured the USA. Other contacts were fostered. BBC Russian language broadcasts were no longer jammed, from 1954 foreign tourists in increasing numbers visited the USSR and somewhat smaller numbers of Soviet citizens visited the west. The Cominform was dissolved in 1956. Selected foreign films were shown in Soviet cinemas. More trade agreements were made with capitalist countries, although foreign trade remained small. Student exchanges began.

At government level there were 'summit' conferences and foreign ministers' meetings. Sometimes there were setbacks to the *détente*. After the Hungarian crisis the reconciliation with Tito which, despite Molotov, had been very much on Tito's terms, was shattered for a few years. Washington was reluctant to respond to Khrushchev's conciliatory policy. In 1960 a summit conference came to an early bad end when Khrushchev stormed out after President Eisenhower had refused to apologize following the shooting down, well inside Russia, of a US photographic reconnaissance aircraft. Eisenhower's successor, Kennedy, had little understanding of the Russian situation at first and his repeated assertion, which Moscow knew to be untrue, that the USSR was taking first place in the missile race, seemed to contain a threat. In 1962 there was the Cuban crisis. Khrushchev had hoped to improve Russia's strategic situation (or at least, bargaining situation) by installing nuclear missiles in Cuba. However, President Kennedy, while leaving room for a dignified Soviet withdrawal, made it clear that the USA would use force to prevent the completion of the installation. Wisely, Khrushchev withdrew his missiles. Although he had clearly met with a setback it was only in high party and government circles that this was realized; the Soviet people, unlike the Cuban, were not told the full story. The problem of West Berlin, which Khrushchev described as 'a fishbone in the gullet', remained unsolved. Undoubtedly the western presence in this enclave inside East Germany was a grave embarrassment to the latter, only partly ameliorated by the erection in 1961 of the Berlin Wall to cut off more thoroughly the east from the west. Nevertheless, and despite the West German Chancellor Adenauer's hostility to the USSR, an effort was made in 1964 towards better relations with West Germany. This was unwelcome to the East German leader Walter Ulbricht, and also to many Russians. Whether Khrushchev's fall was accelerated by the alarm caused by his overtures to Bonn is not known, but probable. In general, Khrushchev's foreign policy (which he appears to have devised himself, merely using his foreign minister, Gromyko, as an aide) was not unsuccessful. The USSR became party to a number of international agreements, ranging from the termination of territorial claims in Antarctica to the Nuclear Test Ban Treaty. After the Cuban crisis Khrushchev and Kennedy exchanged long and private letters on common problems, and this probably did much to moderate tensions. Also to this period belongs the 'Hot Line', a permanent direct telephone link between the US President and the Soviet leader. This, too, was expected to act as a safety valve at times of mounting international pressure.

By the sixties it was evident that foreign affairs were much more complex than they had been in the early days of Soviet power. In Lenin's day it was customary to divide the world into the Soviet Union, the hostile capitalist world, and the colonial dependencies, and the general line for the USSR to take had been fairly clear. By the sixties the communist camp had grown, the capitalist diminished, and there was a host of newly-independent nations which were neither capitalist nor socialist. With the ex-colonial countries and those countries still struggling for independence, the difficult choice facing the Soviet government was whether to support indigenous communist parties which had little chance of gaining mass support, or the new nationalist governments which had power but were often suppressing local communists. Khrushchev and his successors tended to support the newly established nationalist governments with economic, technical, and sometimes military aid, so as to gain friends and influence in the new nations. This policy gave an opening for Chinese accusations that Moscow was putting Soviet aspirations as a world power before the needs of world revolution (China, and many Russians too, resented Soviet help to the new nations; they could both have used these resources themselves). Another drawback of the policy was that the expected returns did not always materialize. It is true that in 1956 Soviet aid to Egypt provoked the west into an inept self-induced crisis which culminated in the Anglo-French invasion of the Canal Zone and an accelerated loss of western influence in the Middle East, but there were no comparable successes elsewhere. Even the transformation of Castro's Cuba into a new member of the communist camp brought a new, unpredictable, leader to communist councils and also a fresh drain on Soviet economic resources. The USSR's reputation suffered when carefully cultivated leaders like Nkrumah of Ghana were overthrown by their own people. Russian-built steelworks in India supplied cheap steel as raw material for the capitalist sector of the Indian economy. Credits and armaments were given to Sukarno's Indonesia but Sukarno first aligned himself with Peking and was then violently replaced by a pro-western government. One of the criticisms voiced against Khrushchev in 1964 was that, on a visit to see the Soviet Aswan Dam project, he had conferred on President Nasser the Order of Lenin at the very time when the Egyptian leader was imprisoning local communists.

17. *The Brezhnev Regime*

Political life

AFTER the departure of Khrushchev, the union in one person of the party secretary and the prime minister was studiously avoided by the 'collective leadership' of Brezhnev and Kosygin. But when in 1971 the 4,963 delegates of the 24th Party Conference (irreverently described by western journalists as the 'world's biggest rubber stamp') met to approve Brezhnev's report on the work of the party, it seemed clear that Brezhnev had become at least first among equals. However, the concept of collective leadership still seemed strong. In their policies the post-1964 leaders were pragmatic rather than sensational, and preferred to let sleeping dogs lie. Their regime was characterized in the west as dull and conservative; this was perhaps an unfair judgement, although as the years passed Brezhnev did resemble more and more the headmaster of an authoritarian boarding-school.

The willing abandonment of government by terrorism after the death of Stalin had not only sweetened the lives of many citizens, but also entailed a new style of politics. Khrushchev's rise and fall had been a function of his ability to gain and hold the support of his immediate colleagues. The latter had personal ambitions, but also represented certain sectional interests. Despite, therefore, the unique role of the Communist Party in a one-party state, and the continuation of such characteristics as tight censorship and secrecy, there was a political life with a genuine interplay of interests. Evidently some interest groups were more powerful than others, and there were occasional moves to cut them down to size. Khrushchev in his early years of power seems to have been opposed by the officialdom of both the ministry of foreign affairs and of the MVD, and (as he later said in his memoirs) the military interest was capable of bringing extraordinary pressure on the government and party leadership. It is notable that, after the ousting of Molotov, the foreign minister did not have full membership of the Politburo until the elevation of Gromyko in 1973. Similarly it was only in the same year that the military gained a seat in the Politburo, with

Marshal Grechko's appointment as defence minister; after the latter's death, moreover, the new minister, Ustinov, although retaining a seat in the Politburo, was of civilian as much as military background. The power of the MVD had been reduced both before and after the arrest of Beria; a determination to prevent further terrorism in the name of security had been revealed by the removal of internal security from the MVD to a new commission, the KGB, which was headed by successive high party officials. It appears that the KGB for some years opposed the policy of relaxed foreign relationships, until in 1967 its director, Shelepin, was replaced. Andropov, a later and more reliable director, became a member of the Politburo in 1973.

The basic preoccupation of the Brezhnev regime was the need to allocate scarce economic resources between urgent claimants; a choice had to be made between those claimants and ways found to increase the resources available. More specifically, there was a great need to invest more in agriculture. Increased agricultural production would mean an enhanced standard of living (and, after all, the party's claim to its leading role depended very largely on its promise to raise living standards). It would also reduce the expenditure of foreign exchange on the import of grain; such foreign exchange was required for the purchase of western technology with which to modernize Soviet industry. But the traditional claimant of priority for investment was the defence interest, the interest which Khrushchev had described as the 'steel-eaters'. The essence of the Brezhnev 'line', at least until the late 1970s, was a limitation of the share of resources devoted to defence and a correspondingly relaxed foreign policy.

This policy had its critics, and it is possible to distinguish those who were most for, and those who were most against. Podgorny, who had been appointed 'president' in 1965, was so aware of the need for *détente* that in a major speech at Riga in 1973 his portrayal of what a third world war would really mean was so disturbing that it was omitted from the newspaper reports. Kosygin, whose background was in light industry and who regarded the party as essentially an organization whose first priority was the public welfare, held similar opinions; in 1974, when western economic difficulties led more ideologically-inclined colleagues to speculate about the prospect for revolutionary outbursts in the west, he warned that an immediate weakening of the west was not necessarily to the Soviet Union's advantage. But while Kosygin and others were asserting that increased arms expenditure did nothing to reduce the risk of war, Marshal Grechko and his colleagues were making speeches about the need to prepare strong military forces to forestall the stratagems of the imperialists. However, with the approval by the 1971 Party Conference of Brezhnev's policy of 'peaceful coexistence' and its confirmation at the 1976 Conference, it seemed that the Brezhnev policy was firmly installed.

An underlying theme of these years was the question of a possible 're-stalinization'. By 1966 official anti-stalinism was plainly ended; the trial of the two writers Daniel and Sinyavski, and the castigation of the historian Nekrich (who had written an account of June 1941 which was critical of Stalin) emphasized this.

There were many who thought that the condemnation of Stalin had gone too far. Party officials were among those who hankered for the good old days in which they had risen to the top, and had carried out their organizing duties without the slightest need to take people's feelings into account. The age-group old enough to have climbed to responsible positions under Stalin but too young to have experienced the mass purges of the 1930s was especially inclined to view Stalinism with something more than innocent nostalgia. The Brezhnev regime seemed to take the pressure of the 'neo-stalinist' wing of the party more seriously than the 'liberal' wing but, in general, succeeded in avoiding real, as opposed to token, moves back to the old techniques. In 1969 the ninetieth anniversary of Stalin's birth provided a pretext to prepare a long article and picture on the subject, to be published in most newspapers. But misgivings expressed by, among others, foreign communist leaders, persuaded the Politburo to change its mind. A similar sequence had occurred in 1966, when rumours of Stalin's imminent official rehabilitation caused not only foreign communists but also leading Soviet intellectuals to make successful protests to the party leaders. It may be surmised that most members of the Politburo regarded the Stalin question as a hot potato which was best left to cool in peace. In the Politburo, Shelepin appears to have been the centre of 'neo-stalinism', but he was gradually deprived of his offices, starting in 1965 and ending with his exit from the Politburo in 1975. In 1976 that reliable barometer of the political atmosphere, the *Great Soviet Encyclopedia*, reduced Stalin's entry to four columns.

Destalinization could never be unambiguous so long as a majority of the senior party officials (including, of course, the Politburo) were products of the Stalinist regime. The Politburo was essentially a group of old men; by 1980 its leading members were septuagenarians, and only Romanov, representing the Leningrad party organization, was under sixty. Several were in poor health; Kosygin had spent a period away from work, while in the late 1970s Brezhnev on trips abroad was seen to be a very ill and stumbling man who confined his participation in negotiations to the reading of prepared statements. His physical handicaps were concealed at home, but commentators abroad wondered how far he was really in control of Soviet affairs. Yet in summer 1980, when the Federal German chancellor visited Moscow after a period of extraordinary tension and strain, Brezhnev during the playing of national anthems was seen to be standing erect without any visible means of support, a living testimony to Soviet medical science.

In 1976 there were signs of a 'personality cult' enveloping Brezhnev. His experience in the war, when he was political commissar to one of the armies, was presented as a factor in the Soviet victory. He was also accorded the rank of Marshal of the Soviet Union. Possibly this assumption of the supreme rank gave him much-needed authority in dealing with the military interest; about the same time the defence minister, Ustinov also took this rank. Meanwhile Brezhnev became Hero of the Soviet Union for the second time and received his fifth Order of Lenin. In the press he began to be described as 'The Leader'. Soon his multi-volume memoirs began to appear, were serialized in several periodicals, and printed as large-edition books; for this effort he was duly awarded the top literary prize. In 1977 he took the office of Chairman of the Presidium of the Supreme Soviet, and thereby combined the two offices of party leader and head of state. Podgorny, the outgoing head of state, was virtually dismissed; he had been in disagreement with Brezhnev at this time. Brezhnev however, did not take over the prime ministership, as had his two predecessors Stalin and Khrushchev. Since his health was poor, moreover, he appointed a deputy to perform most of the routine duties of head of state.

By 1977 party membership was approaching sixteen million. Growth, however, had slowed down. Presumably, continued rapid expansion would have detracted somewhat from the image of the party as a small vanguard. Already one-third of those citizens with higher education were members. Because of the reduced intake, the average age of members was increasing. Whereas the average party member merely turned up at meetings of the party cell and had a very small role, the party members holding *Nomenklatura* posts (party and government posts important enough to be filled under close party supervision) composed an influential and privileged group.

A new constitution was presented and adopted in 1977, no fewer than sixteen years after Khrushchev had first mentioned its imminence. It was based on the old 1936 text. However, there were some significant differences. Thus Article 1 described the USSR as a socialist state of 'the whole people' instead of 'workers and peasants'. Moreover, it recognized the intelligentsia as not a mere 'stratum' but as a group of equal standing with the worker and peasant classes. The USSR was described as a 'developed socialist society', a stage leading to the eventual communist society. Evidently Khrushchev's reckless announcement of impending 'full communism' was not to be taken seriously. In this new constitution the 'leading and guiding role' of the Communist Party was clearly asserted, and as early as Article 6. However there was no mention of the party's Politburo, the leading decision-making body. 'Democratic centralism' received constitutional recognition at last. The interval between elections to the Supreme Soviet was increased from four to five years (paralleling a previous change in the party rules which made a similar increase to the interval between party congresses). The constituent union republics were no longer granted the rather meaningless right to maintain their own armed forces, but their right to secede from the USSR was maintained. More important, the eventual 'merging' of the various nationalities into one great Soviet nation was no longer mentioned. New articles guaranteed free health services, cheap housing, and public participation in decision-making. Environmental protection received a mention, strengthening the hands of those who were arguing that this was a very important matter. In line with the policy of *détente*, an article was added about the peaceful aims of foreign policy. This, however, was balanced by another new article stressing the importance of the 'Defence of the Socialist Fatherland'.

At the end of 1980 Brezhnev was still soldiering on, under great strain. Soviet troops were under fire in Afghanistan. Reagan's election as the next US President promised new anxieties. Kosygin had died (the one-time locomotive fireman Tikhonov was his successor as prime minister). Above all, in Poland the workers and ordinary party members, by strikes and demonstrations, had humiliated the corrupt and incompetent party hierarchy and established really free trade unions. There was a clear possibility that the Polish example might spread, but the consequences which could follow an intervention by the Red Army were almost as unattractive. Meanwhile, the censorship and intensified jamming of foreign broadcasts kept the Soviet population ill-informed about the events in Poland and Brezhnev's decrepitude.

Agriculture

Khrushchev's successors adopted a less hectic approach towards agriculture, but were fully aware that it was the most obvious weak link in the Soviet economy, and a sector where ideology was hard to reconcile with economics. Ministers of agriculture, although restored to their previous importance, fell from office at a rate which was very rapid in Soviet terms. Their fall was associated with their scapegoat role in years of poor harvests, even though grain production was more a matter of the weather than of ministerial competence. On the whole though, bad harvest years registered outputs which were considerably higher than the bad years of previous decades, while good years tended to be record-breaking years. In this sense agriculture in the Brezhnev years made good progress, even though the most obvious ways to exploit 'hidden reserves' had been used up by Khrushchev.

Notable ingredients of Brezhnev's success (and it is accurate to personalize this success, because Brezhnev clearly was the leading figure in agricultural policies) included the restoration of the old organizational system with the ministry acting through the state organizations in the rural areas, and with supervision by the local party organizations. The latter were still far from satisfactory; their personnel was largely of urban types whose efforts to get things moving on the farms recalled the Chinese saying about how a dog sets about catching a mouse. But it was better to have a stable though imperfect chain of command than a system constantly in the throes of upheaval. On the same principle, the Khrushchev-style campaigns, which aimed at rapid results in such matters as maize and meat production and even in the latest brainwaves of Lysenko, were abandoned for a more steady approach. However, although the new leadership promised an end to constantly changing quotas for the compulsory procurements by the state, it soon relapsed in the face of supply shortages.

Nevertheless the peasantry benefited enormously from the new leadership's realization that increased food production depended largely on incentives. The procurement prices paid by the state for agricultural products rose markedly. This was especially notable in the case of meat, and as the retail prices were kept low, the state subsidy which made up the difference grew correspondingly (by the early 1970s meat wholesale prices were little more than half the procurement prices; this added up to a state subsidy which was enormous even by West European standards). Higher procurement prices helped to finance the decision that peasants should be better remunerated. Higher incomes benefited both state and collective peasants, but the latter were particularly gratified by the replacement in 1966 of the work-day system. Henceforth, instead of waiting to the end of the year, hoping that the farm would earn a surplus to finance the cashing-in of their work-day units, they would receive a small regular wage, to be supplemented by an annual bonus if the farm did well. An unprofitable farm would be obliged to pay at least the wage, borrowing from the bank if necessary. Meanwhile, discouragement of private-plot production ceased, so the private husbandries of the peasants began to make an even greater contribution to the Soviet diet (they provided one-third of egg and meat supplies in 1978). With rural incomes increasing somewhat faster than urban, and with the urban economy contributing investment funds for agriculture, by 1980 it could hardly be said that the Soviet economy relied on the exploitation of the peasantry. The improvement of the peasant's status was symbolized in 1974, when it was announced that peasants would be issued with internal passports. These, essential for travelling within the USSR, had previously been issued routinely only to townspeople.

With little scope for increasing the cultivated acreage, and with Khrushchev having reaped the gains to be made by ending the most damaging absurdities of the Stalin years, the Brezhnev leadership had to rely on more intensive cultivation to produce the extra grain so badly needed by the Soviet economy. True, grain production was no longer a matter of famine-avoidance, but the average Soviet diet was still low in protein. Meat and milk production, in particular, were dependent on increased supplies of fodder. Moreover, in the 1960s the building up of adequate stocks to avoid the catastrophic consequences of bad harvests like that of 1963 was still an urgent matter. Khrushchev himself had realized the need to make greater use of artificial fertilizers. He had secured a quite remarkable increase of production, but the fertilizers were poorly utilized, either because lack of all-weather roads meant that they were delivered to farms too late in the season, or because the farms lacked the skill and equipment to apply them properly. Fertilizer production increased still further after Khrushchev's departure, and this was a field in which the import of western technology had a great and plainly beneficial role. Distribution and use were improved, and it can hardly be doubted that fertilizers were the main factor in the increase of agricultural production in the 1970s.

If investment in industries supplying agriculture is added to investment in the farms themselves, annual agricultural investment by 1980 was in the region of a quarter of the USSR's total investment. This was an enormous proportion compared to other countries (the corresponding US proportion was less than 5 per cent). But there were signs that increasing amounts of capital were required to secure the same rate of growth (that is, the capital–output ratio was rising). Moreover, about a quarter of the Soviet workforce was still employed on the land. Neither the collective farm nor the state farm seemed to provide a framework in which peasants would give of their best. Sometimes it seemed that the farms were too large for efficient management even if efficient managers had been available. Peasants who acquired skills still preferred to move to work in the town, leaving the older and unskilled peasants on the farms. This meant that new equipment was badly utilized and frequently allowed to fall into disrepair. Indeed, it seems likely that much of the bright new modern technology led to increased rather than decreased costs. The improvement-that-worsens is of course not unknown in the west, but was probably more of a menace in Soviet conditions. For example, if milking machines might break down and could not be repaired by the local staff, or if electricity supply was unreliable, farms still had to maintain an emergency staff of milkmaids. Cows, unlike peasants, could not be kept waiting.

Despite advances in production, therefore, Soviet agriculture performed poorly in terms of labour productivity and yield per acre. How far the Soviet system could remedy these defects without a radical change in the concept of collective and state farms was one of those questions which seemed to demand solution in the 1980s; a new compromise between ideology and economics (more accurately, between ideology and human nature) was needed.

Grain Production (million tonnes)

1953	83	1960	126	1967	148	1974	195
1954	86	1961	131	1968	170	1975	140
1955	104	1962	140	1969	162	1976	224
1956	125	1963	108	1970	187	1977	196
1957	103	1964	152	1971	181	1978	235
1958	135	1965	121	1972	168	1979	179
1959	120	1966	171	1973	222	1980	189

Industry

In the Ninth Five-Year Plan (1971–5) there was for the first time a faster rate of growth of the consumer-goods industries than of the capital-goods industries. There was also a new housing programme (as before, concentrating on apartment blocks) which would contribute 560 million square metres of new floor-space during the quinquennium. However, not all these good intentions could be realized. In this Plan and in the Tenth Five-Year Plan (1976–80) there were renewed manifestations of worrying tendencies. The slowdown in the growth rate continued. In 1979, which was an exceptionally unfavourable year, industrial growth was only 3.4 per cent, compared to the planned 5.7 per cent. For 1980 a modest growth of 4.5 per cent was prescribed by *Gosplan*. By the standards of other countries these were respectable rates, but far slower than had been hoped and far slower than the rates of previous decades. Also, 1979 witnessed actual declines in some outputs, including coal, steel, and timber as well as certain consumer items.

Falling growth rates was one reason why in the sixties and seventies there were continuing debates on how to modify the Soviet economic system in order to meet new problems. Growth seemed to be held back by a sharp decline in the return on investment; to secure the same additional output an ever-increasing amount of capital had to be found. Resources were not being used efficiently, largely because the methods of the thirties were not suited to the sixties. The task of the thirties, massive increases in the production of a few bulk commodities, had, except in agriculture, been achieved. But the economy was still using yesterday's methods and yesterday's investment to make yesterday's products, which were being replaced in other advanced economies by new products, more complex and often less suited to centralized planning.

In the Soviet Union the increasing number of new enterprises and of products which they supplied to each other entailed a geometric increase in the inter-relationships between enterprises and between industries. So many were these inter-relationships that they could not all be taken into consideration by the planners; one academician foresaw that within a decade the entire labour force would need to be employed in planning if plans were to remain workable. In any case the plans were impossible to fulfil precisely, partly because the industrial ministries in Moscow were out of touch with the real situation in the enterprises they controlled throughout the USSR. In 1957 Khrushchev introduced a radical reform to bring planning more into line with local conditions. He eliminated most of the central industrial ministries and divided the USSR into 105 economic regions, each with its own economic council (*sovnarkhoz*) to plan and supervise its affairs. However, this raised as many problems as it solved, and in any case was probably motivated in part by the knowledge that the bureaucrats in the dissolved ministries tended to be Malenkov's supporters, whereas the local party leaders who gained importance through their participation in the *sovnarkhoz* would appreciate that Khrushchev was their true friend. In 1965 the *sovnarkhozy* were abolished and industrial ministries re-established, bringing the total of ministries by 1972 to fifty-nine.

But reversion to the old systems made a reform of the planning system even more urgent. Not only were there problems of plan formulation, but also of plan execution. Enterprises were judged, and received bonuses, on their performance in relation to the output target which the ministries had set. This meant that managers were reluctant to overfulfil this target for fear that it would be raised the following year. They were equally reluctant to indulge in innovation because for them there was no real gain to outweigh the trouble and risk. Moreover, they tended to understate, to their respective ministries, the productive capacity of their enterprises. Also, since gross output by weight was the main indicator of success or failure, products were deliberately made heavy and little trouble was taken to fit the product to suit its ultimate user. Producers were interested in production, not in sales. Thus when improved economic conditions enabled customers to become choosy, shops found themselves burdened with masses of unsaleable goods.

In the sixties a number of Soviet economists suggested that enterprises should be set a reduced number of targets; bonuses should be related to profitability, not output, and fixed not year by year but over an extended period. The profitability indicator would reflect both productive efficiency and volume of sales. There was discussion, too, directed towards what western economists termed the irrationalities of the Soviet system. (Such irrationalities produced notorious phenomena such as Caucasian peasants finding it profitable to commute by normal air service to Moscow, taking as their luggage allowance a sack of lemons, lemons in Moscow being unnaturally expensive and air fares unnaturally cheap.)

Both for ideological and practical reasons, only some of the suggested improvements could be accepted. In the late sixties some consumer-goods enterprises were freed from output targets and their bonuses fixed according to the fulfilment of a sales plan. In other enterprises the number of targets was reduced and the volume of sales targets emphasized. Managers were given greater freedom in decisions relating to the work-force. Charges for the use of capital were introduced. But the centralized allocation of supplies continued, and prices remained fixed at unnatural levels.

Thus Soviet managements by the early seventies had not received as much freedom as had been advocated. Nor did the managers themselves, raised in the Stalin years, always want responsibility: as Brezhnev remarked, they feared innovation 'like the Devil fears incense'. Some, more willing, made initial mistakes which immediately were followed by a return of party or central intervention. There was also ideological opposition to 'capitalist' concepts (like the price mechanism), and this opposition was strengthened in 1968 by the events in Czechoslovakia where 'liberal' economists were prominent in the unwelcome movement to build a socialist society blatantly different from the Soviet prototype.

Possibly, given time, this managerial reform would have produced the results which Kosygin and others had hoped. Managers would have learned to take decisions instead of avoiding them, while local government and party functionaries might, just might, have learned not to interfere with factory management. But stability in managerial arrangements was lacking throughout the sixties and seventies. It was generally agreed that initiative was discouraged, and that central guidance was too often misguidance, but it was less easy to agree on remedies. There was a succession of alterations in the chain of command between Moscow and factory, but it seemed that each change brought its own undesirable side-effects. In the 1970s the introduction of 'production associations' signalled the end of Kosygin's effort to give enterprise managements more freedom. In these, factories making identical or interrelated products were grouped together, with many quite important decision-making rights being vested in the associations.

In 1979 yet another change altered the key indices used to judge an enterprise's performance. The introduction of these indices, which were quite complex, implied a reversion to stronger central control. Whether they could solve continuing problems seemed doubtful. There were certain features of the planned economy which had not worked out in practice as well as had been hoped; fifty years of five-year plans had shown that the irrational free-market system could be replaced by the planned economy, but they had not shown that the planned economy was necessarily more rational than the free market. Possibly the difficulties of the Soviet planned economy were fundamental. Possibly the assumption that the future could be planned was baseless. Possibly what the planners tried to do was to impose their view of what ought to happen on a future which rarely, if ever, conforms to human prediction. Certainly, each and every five-year plan had been more or less radically amended during its course (but the 'failure' of a five-year plan did not necessarily imply a failure of the economy).

One impediment was informational. Central planners, in order to replace the regulating function of the free market, needed to obtain and process vast quantities of data. Such data were likely to be unreliable in quality and indigestible in quantity. Central decisions would therefore be made on a basis of partial ignorance. At one time it was thought that the introduction of computers would end this particular frustration, but this appears to have been a vain hope. Quite apart from the fact that a computer was even less likely than a bureaucrat to change its mind, its information input was dependent on human competence and integrity; it could not, for example, cope with factory managers, who, to be on the safe side, would inflate their requirements of raw materials for a given level of production.

The centralized system did less than it should for co-ordination, because the various departments in Moscow were reluctant, or unable, to break down the barriers between them. All too often, for example, the eventual user of a piece of equipment had little say in its specification. For years the railway ministry was demanding high-capacity freightcars, but the ministry supervising the railway rolling-stock factories continued to supply old types, being unwilling to disturb its routines by changing production lines from an undesirable to a desirable design of car. This kind of situation was repeated with daily, ubiquitous, frequency, and in total constituted a considerable economic wastage. Administrators at the centre knew about these cases, but the very system of which they were the paid operators frustrated their efforts to improve things.

As Khrushchev discovered with his *sovnarkhozy*, moves away from a centrally-directed economy were likely to encounter resistance, or at least foot-dragging. Too many party and industrial administrators liked centralization. Party officials, whether they worked as *apparatchiki* in party organs or as government administrators, liked the importance they enjoyed as part of the chain of command: any move towards using mechanisms like rational pricing to regulate the economy could only reduce that importance. The military and a few other key sectors liked centralization because it simplified their priority access to scarce products or resources.

Brezhnev himself declared to the 25th party conference in 1976:

The Central Committee opposes hurried ill-thought-out reorganizations of the managerial structure and of established ways of running the economy. As the saying goes, one should measure the cloth not seven times, but eight or ten times, before cutting it. But once we have grasped that the existing economic mechanism has become too limiting for a growing economy, then we must resolutely improve it.

Thus the Soviet leadership was well aware of the problem. It was also fairly 'liberal' in its receptivity towards proposed changes. Various experiments in the peoples' democracies to solve similar problems, which often took the form of a partial breakaway from strict centralization, were regarded not as threats to ideological purity but as interesting and perhaps instructive endeavours. Nevertheless, these problems could be described as self-imposed, for over the decades since 1917 a conscious choice had been made to dispense with the economic mechanisms associated with capitalism. In the 1970s, however, the USSR was also facing problems which were independent of economic policy. Because of birthrate patterns, the growth in the supply of labour was slackening. This meant that labour productivity assumed an even greater importance, but Soviet workers seemed slow to improve their performance; industries which reported great increases of output per worker were those which had installed more modern equipment, and moreover that equipment was less productive than it might have been with a more spirited labour force. By 1980 it seemed likely that the working population of the Russian Republic would actually fall, and in this Republic the level of skill was high, compared to the level in Central Asia, where the growth of the labour force was expected to remain rapid.

At the beginning of the 1980s the main economic problem, therefore, was the achievement of policies or transformations that would lead to more, and better-quality, production, with more economical expenditure of materials and human talent. Such changes would be partly technological, but also managerial and political. Enough resources needed to be allotted to internal consumption to avoid popular unrest, and to defence to maintain the balance of strength with the west. Ideally, too, the growth rate would be high enough to maintain (at least) the relationship of economic strength between the USSR and the USA. The last two requirements would be influenced by western economic performance, and the difficulties of the western economies therefore made Soviet economic problems less serious.

In the longer term, the USSR seemed to have several advantages, not least of which was its possession of great raw material resources. The discovery and exploitation of Western Siberian oil was a major project of the 1970s, and the rise of world oil prices came at a fortunate time for, together with a rise in the value of Soviet gold production, it signified valuable exports just when Soviet overseas expenditure was uncomfortably high. In the short term, the inaccessibility of raw materials was a handicap. Four-fifths of the Soviet energy resources lay east of the Urals, whereas four-fifths of energy consumption was west of that line. It was not surprising, then, that in 1976–80 one-third of Soviet investment was allocated to Siberia, and US and Japanese co-operation was sought in developing some of the biggest projects. The Baikal–Amur Railway, linking Siberia with the Pacific, and laid north of the Trans-Siberian Railway through mountainous and seismic terrain, was expected to be finished in the early 1980s, and would rank as one of the great railway projects of the century, even though its critics said it was built at the wrong time and in the wrong place.

Technology

The gradual fall of Soviet industry's growth rate, from about 12 per cent per annum in the mid-1950s to 4 per cent in the late 1970s, led to increased interest in technical progress. Growth was held back by restricted capital investment, the reduced return from what investment there was, and a smaller increase of the labour supply. Improved technology seemed the best means of compensating for these deficiencies. In the early 1960s the State Committee for Science and Technology was set up to plan, administer and direct expenditure on research and development. One of its main tasks was the study of western technology, with a view to acquiring some of the latest techniques for application in the USSR. Although the Soviet system was better adapted than western systems for the central direction of research, in practice this advantage was outweighed by the cumbersome channels of communication between organizations, by the overload of information which made it impossible for central offices to separate the important from the unimportant, and various other features of the administrative structure which tended to stifle initiative. In general, the level of Soviet technology was lower than that of advanced western countries, and the rate of technological advance was slow.

There were exceptions. The defence industry was very much a pace-setter. It enjoyed priorities, it was less subject to administrative interference, and could devote all its energies to obtaining the best possible products. It had first call on scientific talent, and its performance was creditable in so far as despite Soviet backwardness in certain vital techniques (in integrated circuits, for example) it found the resourcefulness to create weapons that matched those built by the technically better-endowed US arms industries. Sometimes there was a 'spin-off' to the civilian economy; when factories producing weapons devoted part of their output to civilian products the latter were usually of superior quality. Managers who transferred from the defence industries to other, civilian, branches tended to enliven those branches. Apart from defence, there were other high-priority sectors, like the space industry, where performance was good. Also, a few of the basic industries were successful at devising or applying new processes.

Although efforts were made to stimulate Soviet invention (and the no less important diffusion throughout the economy of useful innovations), both the Khrushchev and Brezhnev regimes accepted that the large-scale acquisition of western technology was well worth while. It did require hard currency, but it avoided the duplication in the USSR of research that had already been done elsewhere, and moreover promised a short-cut to advanced technology. The USSR in 1965 accepted international conventions on licensing and patenting, and began to purchase rights to selected inventions and techniques. Western firms were invited to tender for the supply to the USSR of complete plants embodying the latest production technology. Several chemical plants were acquired in this way, as well as a Fiat-built automobile plant. The Kama Automobile Plant, designed to manufacture motor trucks, was similarly dependent on western techniques. When the extraction of West Siberian oil became urgent, western oilfield technology was imported on a large scale. A few consumer industries also benefited; to satisfy, at least in part, the thirst for western-style consumer goods, Soviet Pepsi-Cola and Soviet jeans appeared on the market. In a few cases it was western capital as well as technology that was sought. This happened in certain very large projects involving the extraction of gas, oil, and coal in Siberia, where long negotiations were entrained with Japanese and US interests.

As previously, in a few high-priority fields Soviet technology was a pacesetter. The Soviet supersonic airliner, the Tupolev-144, resembled the Anglo-French Concorde not only in design but in the circumstance that it had been built largely for the sake of vanity. Its prototype was proudly exhibited at the Paris Air Show of 1973, where it crashed. Still, in 1976 Aeroflot was able to claim that the TU-144 had made the world's first commercial supersonic flight, having stolen a lead on the Concorde by going into service initially as a freight carrier. It did later go into passenger service between Moscow and Central Asia, but was soon withdrawn.

Although it was Americans who first walked on the moon, it was probably Soviet space science which in the sixties pursued the broader range of achievement. In 1961 Gagarin became the first human to fly in space. Khrushchev had a sharp appreciation of the publicity value of Soviet cosmonautics, and his urge to follow each success with another meant that for a time steady progress was sacrificed for showy exploits. A two-man flight was riskily achieved by cramming two cosmonauts in a capsule really only big enough for one. Earlier, in 1963, Tereshkova became the first female cosmonaut. However, whereas the American space effort seemed to slacken once a human landing on the moon had been achieved, the Soviet effort went ahead steadily. By the late 1970s about a hundred space vehicles were launched each year. Most of these were modest, being of the *Kosmos* series, intended for studying the near-earth expanses. The *Interkosmos* series, started in 1969, involved co-operation with scientists from the peoples' democracies and included manned ventures in which one member of the crew was an East European astronaut, trained in the USSR. From 1968 the 6½-ton *Soyuz* spacecraft were available. In 1970 one of these, *Soyuz-9*, spent eighteen days in space with its two-man crew. In 1971 came the *Salyut* manned long-life research orbital stations, one of which studied the moon in that year. In 1971, too, a *Salyut* vehicle exchanged crews with *Soyuz-10* and *Soyuz-11*, but this landmark was attended by a fatal accident, when the three men in *Soyuz-11* died during descent. 1975 was notable for a joint US–USSR space-docking venture, using *Soyuz-19* and an American *Apollo* craft. This event, a high-water mark of US–USSR *détente*, was also the first Soviet space mission to be shown live on Soviet television. Meanwhile, beginning in 1967, a series of Soviet unmanned spacecraft investigated Venus, *Venus-9* and *Venus-10* going into orbit around that planet in 1975. In general, while Soviet rocketry was good, instrumentation was unsophisticated by American standards. This illustrated a continuing factor in the Soviet economy: that although in certain fields the USSR achieved great success, this was the result of giving chosen fields absolute priority. And when some enjoyed priority, the less-favoured branches were kept behind. This was why, in Khrushchev's time, the first Soviet supermarkets used abacuses and not cash registers.

In another high-technology and priority sector, nuclear energy, the Soviet Union was well advanced. In 1954, near Moscow, what was claimed to be the world's first nuclear power station (using a water-graphite reactor) had entered service. Later policy was to build nuclear power stations in European Russia, which had an energy deficit, unlike Siberia. By

1979 nine large stations were in use. Meanwhile the nuclear icebreaker *Lenin* had been joined by the larger and improved *Arktika* and *Sibir*; the former broke its way through to the North Pole in 1977. In that problematic but potentially revolutionary technology, thermo-nuclear power, Soviet scientists played an important role. In 1975 the Kurchatov Institute of Atomic Energy in Moscow opened its experimental *Tokamak-10* system, and it was not long before a twelve-mile accelerator-accumulator ring system was projected for construction near Moscow. In this technology there was a good deal of international co-operation, to which the Soviet contribution was significant. This reflected the circumstance that in some fields (high-power electricity transmission was one) the Soviet Union did occupy a leading place. In fact, the flurry of licence and patent exchanges of the 1960s and 1970s was not a one-way flow, a few Soviet inventions being acquired by western firms.

In pursuing new technologies the Soviet Union, like other countries, sometimes allowed progress to proceed faster than was really safe. One catastrophic result of this haste occurred in 1958, when there was a nuclear accident in the South Urals, owing to improper storage of nuclear wastes. Despite the large number of casualties and the obligatory depopulation of a huge area, this catastrophe was successfully concealed from the Soviet public at large. From the western public too; in what was probably not a conspiracy of silence but may have been a silence of mutual consent, this event was not reported in the west, although it seems unlikely that government scientists were unaware of it for long. (Another case of international professional solidarity was the reluctance of western psychiatrists to condemn the treatments imposed on political prisoners by Soviet psychiatrists, a reluctance explicable by the fact that similar treatments were used by prison psychiatrists in several western countries.) There was much less reticence in 1979, when a large-scale and fatal outbreak of anthrax occurred in Sverdlovsk. On this occasion it was claimed that the USSR was pursuing experiments in germ warfare that were contrary to international agreements. Evidence advanced by the western press for this was the rapidity and scale of the outbreak (untypical of a natural outbreak), the existence of what was believed to be a germ-warfare experimental establishment at Sverdlovsk, and the unconvincing Soviet explanation that it was only a small and natural outbreak.

The peoples' democracies

Czechoslovakia, the youngest of the European peoples' democracies, was late in rejecting Stalinism. But in the late sixties the Czechoslovak Communist Party under Dubcek, while continuing to be a loyal member of the

Warsaw Pact, sought broader political and economic contacts with the west. The Czech economy was freed from many of the old rigidities of the planning system; a genuine free press and radio appeared, and the security police lost most of its powers. During this process the Soviet government voiced its apprehension, and in 1968, after Soviet–Czech meetings had proved unrewarding, the Red Army, supported by units of some of the other peoples' democracies, entered Czechoslovakia. By order of the Prague government and party, armed resistance was not offered, but it was several days before all forms of non-violent resistance, such as clandestine anti-Soviet radio broadcasts, could be quelled. In the end, the Red Army's presence permitted the establishment of a new government and a new party leadership which, while not Stalinist, was pro-Russian.

The Russian intervention in fraternal Czechoslovakia, whose communist party had merely been trying to create, it said, 'socialism with a human face', was a greater shock to the communist parties of the world than the Hungarian rebellion of 1956. Although the relaxation of censorship had allowed many Czech writers to criticize the Soviet Union, there had been no anti-Russian violence as in Hungary. What prompted the USSR to put an end to the Czechs' policy of intervening in their own internal affairs was the likelihood that Dubcek and his colleagues would lose control of events. While the Soviet government would tolerate economic changes which seemed to move away from the Soviet model, political changes were another matter. In particular, the concept of a ruling communist party losing its monopoly of political activity was highly unwelcome; it not only set a dangerous example but also implied a weakening of Moscow's influence over the policies of East European governments. Czechoslovakia was, after all, one of the buffer states between the USSR and the hostile west.

But the intervention in Czechoslovakia by the Red Army and the armies of other Warsaw Pact countries did not for long disturb the trend towards *détente*. Even the so-called 'Brezhnev Doctrine' that socialist countries had a clear right and duty to intervene in any country of the Soviet bloc to prevent a reversion to 'capitalism' did not seem to cause prolonged indignation in the west. However, the doctrine was certainly unwelcome to communist parties both within and without the communist bloc; it meant that they, too, had a limited freedom of action.

In the long run the Soviet leadership sought a closer integration of the peoples' democracies with the USSR. In the Warsaw Pact this had to a large degree been accomplished in the military field, but it was less easy elsewhere. The Comecon organization secured a degree of co-ordination in industrial matters, with one or two members of the bloc supplying the entire requirement for certain products. But this did not go as far as Moscow desired. But integration was not helped by, for example, the barbed wire, minefields, and Alsatian dogs that sealed the frontiers between the USSR and its fraternal allies. The weeks required for obtaining a visa to cross that frontier were a barrier to close business relationships, as was the insistence that all transactions and proposals, however minor, had to go through the slow-moving and suspicious central ministries in Moscow. In any case, the peoples' democracies had their reservations about close integration, with Roumania remaining the staunchest adherent to national independence. Soviet economic policy had long lost its exploitative tendency. In fact, Soviet oil supplied by the 'Friendship' pipeline was sold at prices below the world market level. The USSR, indeed, had a vested interest in the healthy survival of the different communist governments and realized that nothing could endanger this survival as much as reduced standards of living. To some extent, and in different ways, the USSR, far from exploiting its friends, actually made economic and financial concessions to them. This was especially the case with Cuba, whose economy depended on Soviet support.

Also notable was the unobtrusive refusal of the Warsaw Pact countries to extend their alliance to cover Asia, a Soviet proposal which would have involved them militarily in the Soviet–Chinese quarrel. Here again Roumania took a lead. To an extent greater than in the other peoples' democracies, popular support for the Roumanian government depended to a large degree on how far it resisted Soviet pressures.

In the Brezhnev period flourishing 'Eurocommunism' continued to be a threat to the Soviet leadership of the communist movement. The Spanish and Italian parties in particular took up positions which the Soviet Party could not accept. Their acknowledgement that a communist party might gain power (and by implication lose it) by electoral process was unpalatable. The French party was also attracted by this idea. The dispute about whether communist parties should plan to obtain power by force came to a head in 1975 when West European parties, and especially the French, Italian, and Spanish leaders, were irritated by Soviet newspaper articles emphasizing that indeed they should. There was opposition, too, to the 'proletarian internationalism' espoused by Brezhnev, which implied that the USSR was still the leader. In 1976 the Soviet Union organized a Moscow 'summit' of European communist leaders, but was unable to persuade them to endorse a declaration reasserting the USSR's leading role. The spokesmen of the Soviet Communist Party attacked Eurocommunism, and it was stalwartly defended by the Spanish leader and others. So stalwartly that several important non-Soviet speeches were unreported in the Soviet press; the picture they presented was in too great a conflict with the picture habitually presented to the Soviet population. The failure of the somewhat Stalinist communist party of Portugal to make much headway during the upheavals in Portugal of the 1970s gave added force to the 'Eurocommunist' argument.

The USSR's relations with the European peoples' democracies were among the interests complicated by the dispute with China, which had come to a head in the 1960s. In its struggle for power the Chinese Communist Party had been substantially aided by the USSR, despite Stalin's mistaken alliance with the Kuomintang. But Chinese communist policy under Mao Tse-tung was never blindly subservient to Moscow; at times it chose to go its own way. After Mao's victory in 1949 the USSR gave great economic, military, and technical help to China, but, especially after Khrushchev's assumption of power, this help diminished. 'Destalinization' embarrassed Beijing. Open dispute at first took the form of Beijing condemning Tito, regarded as a Russian protégé, for his 'revisionism', while Moscow berated Albania (China's friend) for 'dogmatism'. Long angry letters followed. The fundamental issues, not always expressed in the dispute, were ideological, economic, strategic, personal, and sometimes even racial. On the personal level, the dispute was hottest when Khrushchev was in power. In one polemical exchange, Mao described Khrushchev as a laughing-stock, 'a Bible-reading and psalm-singing buffoon'. Khrushchev, never at a loss for homely invective, responded by describing Mao as 'a worn-out rubber boot which one can only put in the corner of a room to be admired'. The post-Khrushchev leadership evidently hoped that the breach with China might be repaired. But by 1966 the situation was even worse than before. In September of that year Moscow roundly condemned Chinese foreign policy, accusing Beijing of trying to foment a war between the USA and the USSR (both sides of the dispute accused each other from time to time of consorting with the USA, thereby betraying their nervousness at this possibility). In early 1967 Chinese students studying in Russia mounted a violent demonstration in Red Square. In Beijing the Soviet embassy was besieged for several days by masses of hostile demonstrators. Each government began large-scale expulsions of the other's nationals. Mao was accused of racialism, among other things. In 1969 there were serious armed clashes, with fatalities, on disputed parts of the Russo-Chinese border (correctly described as the world's longest and most ill-defined frontier). Photographs of these events were published in Soviet newspapers, together with allegations of Chinese atrocities. The novelist Simonov, revisiting the scenes of his novel of the Russo-Japanese clashes in the thirties, wrote a belligerent newspaper article designed to appeal to Russian national feelings. There were reminders of how the Tartars had devastated ancient Rus and how it was the Slavs who had protected Europe from the depredations of oriental invaders. By this time communist parties through-out the non-communist world were split into pro-Soviet and pro-Chinese factions.

The long-delayed reconciliation between the USA and China began dramatically in 1971. In the following years China began to assert itself in other ways, becoming an active member of the United Nations Organiza-tion in replacement of the expelled Nationalist China government. At times China seemed to be seeking allies in Europe, including Eastern Europe, but although this perhaps gave the communist governments of the peoples' democracies some extra bargaining power in relation to the USSR, China was not in a position to replace the Soviet Union as 'protector of last re-sort' for those countries. Moreover, the change of Chinese policies after the death of Mao put an end to the friendship with Albania.

Although there were long periods when the Soviet government gave as good as it got in the war of vituperation, it did make efforts from time to time to heal the breach. After the death of Mao, in 1976, Moscow made evident efforts towards reconciliation, but with scant success. On the other hand, both sides to the dispute strove from time to time to conduct their hostile relationship in a more civilized manner, and this resulted in such things as an agreement on navigation rights on the Ussuri River and other practical matters. On one occasion the USSR even apologized for an incur-sion of Soviet troops into Chinese territory. Fresh animosity was aroused in 1979 when the USSR's protégé, Vietnam, invaded a Chinese protégé, Cam-puchea (Cambodia); this was followed by a major but temporary Chinese punitive advance into Vietnam. But despite everything, some kind of recon-ciliation between the two powers was not unthinkable, for reasons of mutual advantage.

Foreign policy

Khrushchev's successors continued his foreign policy, although with more caution. In 1965 Russia emerged in the new role of peacemaker, when the Indo-Pakistani war was resolved at Tashkent by a conference under the chairmanship of Kosygin. The latter also visited the USA and Britain, and appeared to make sincere efforts to help bring the American war in Vietnam to some sort of compromise conclusion. Although in the late 1960s Soviet armed forces were again growing (an increase that must have been initi-ated in the last Khrushchev years), the early 1970s were years of unprece-dentedly eased relations with the west, and particularly with the USA. In 1972 President Nixon visited Moscow and the following year Brezhnev visited the USA. Several agreements were signed. Although the agreement to restrict anti-ballistic missiles to a certain extent re-channelled research and funds into other weapons, it certainly simplified the nuclear situation. The nuclear accidents agreement had a peacemaking function, and so did an agreement on preventing 'incidents' on and over the high seas. Other arms agreements followed; these were less likely to reduce the arms race than was claimed, but the discussions which preceded them gave each side a valuable insight into the other's anxieties, capabilities, and preoccupations. As forecast to the 1971 Party Congress by Brezhnev in a speech in favour of his 'peace programme', trade and technology was an important aspect of *détente*. In a 1972 trade agreement the USA even granted Most Favoured Nation trade rights and offered generous financial credits to the USSR. The latter began to settle the Lend-Lease debts of the Second World War period (whose non-repayment had always been a sore point among Americans and was a useful weapon for anti-Soviet propagandists). However, after Congress had reduced the amount of credit to be made available, and had insisted that certain concessions should not come into force unless the USSR issued emigration visas to thousands of Soviet Jews, Moscow abrogated this agreement in 1975.

Although trade continued, this setback may well have been the point at which Soviet critics of Brezhnev's *détente* policy began to gather their forces. Until 1980 relations did remain eased, but there was less optimism about the future. In a sense the Soviet conception of peaceful coexistence (which rejected war between the great powers, accepted co-operation for mutual advantage, but did not offer any easing of 'ideological' struggle), made a genuine long-term settlement difficult. President Carter in his first year of office emphasized the shortcomings of the USSR in the matter of human rights. Among other things, he wrote a supportive letter to the distinguished Soviet dissident Sakharov. In this way he too was asserting that coexistence did not mean ideological coexistence, but this acceptance of the Soviet interpretation did not please Moscow, and may be presumed to have made more difficult the task of those Soviet leaders favouring continued relaxation. The appointment of Brzezinski as the President's National Security Adviser must also have been alarming. Of Polish ancestry, Brzezinski had made some kind of an academic reputation by a series of publications which dealt in unfriendly terms with the USSR and the people's democracies. The developing friendliness between the USA and China also aroused nervousness; although the USA did not offer weapons to the Chinese armed forces, the statements at various times of both British and American defence officials during visits to China must have confirmed the gloomy Soviet suspicion that a sinister collusion between the west and China might emerge. Of all strategic nightmares, this must surely have been the most dread. Soviet apprehension and mistrust could hardly fail to have been aroused by the campaign, conducted in 1979 by Washington and the American press, about Soviet 'combat troops' in Cuba. Soviet military advisers had long been helping the Cuban forces, but for reasons which appear to have been related to domestic political needs Washington put up a display of manful disgruntlement about this alleged infringement of previous US–Soviet understanding. But no convincing evidence was produced to support the US allegations, and the affair was allowed to die of exposure.

An achievement of the drive for *détente* was the Helsinki Agreement of 1975. Since both Soviet and American anxieties were aroused by one or other of the provisions of this agreement, it is probably fair to regard it as both effective and balanced. The two powers were not the only signatories; since it largely concerned Europe, other European governments, east and west, also took part. In the west its main provision, the settlement of European frontiers, was sometimes attacked as a 'sell-out'. This provision at last confirmed the post-1945 frontiers. In other words, it conferred the status of permanence on such territorial entities as the German Democratic Republic and Poland. This did strengthen the position of the governments involved, but to that extent they became less dependent on the diplomatic and military strength of the USSR; in other words, it could be argued (and was) that this provision would ultimately weaken the hold of the USSR over some of the peoples' democracies. In exchange for agreeing on this territorial matter, the west secured various undertakings from the USSR. Among these was the latter's agreement to respect a number of individual human rights treasured in the west. It was said, not without justification, that the Soviet Union would be able to ignore the human rights promises it made. On the other hand, the setting up in the USSR of a dissident group devoted to 'monitoring' how far the Soviet authorities were treating their citizens with the respect for individual rights promised at Helsinki demonstrated that to some extent at least the provisions had made a mark. Moreover, the stipulation of the agreement that there should be periodical reviews by the signatories of how far its provisions were being observed seemed to some observers to provide a regular opportunity for washing the Soviet Union's dirty linen before a worldwide audience.

Détente in Europe had been helped by the *Ostpolitik* of the West German Chancellor Brandt. As mayor of West Berlin, Brandt had been reviled in the most scurrilous terms by both East German and Soviet commentators during the successive Berlin crises. But when he became Chancellor he initiated a policy designed to mend West German relationships with eastern Europe and the USSR. Aided by this diplomacy Germany became an important, almost essential, trading partner of the peoples' democracies, and also exported advanced-technology products to the USSR. The relationship between the two Germanies became markedly less absurd, and German–Polish relations, in particular, grew warmer. The USSR's position in all this was ambiguous; while welcoming Brandt's contribution to *détente* it made clear that closer German ties with the peoples' democracies were not entirely welcome. Nevertheless, when Brandt departed (he resigned after it was revealed that one of his closest aides was an East German spy) it seemed more of a loss than a gain for Soviet policies.

Khrushchev's interest in the 'third world' was maintained by his successors (the continuation through both regimes of the veteran Gromyko as foreign minister both helped and confirmed the essential continuity of foreign policy). Trade agreements, military assistance, and 'treaties of friendship and co-operation' were the typical stages of Soviet involvement with countries in the developing world. Such involvement, although not to the west's advantage, was not always quite so conclusive as was assumed. A nation might still reject the Soviet connection when it felt strong enough to do so. A notable example of this was President Sadat's 1972 'invitation' to the USSR to withdraw the military advisers who had played a considerable role in strengthening the Egyptian armed forces. In general, the USSR continued to support the Arab cause in the Palestine dispute, although when real crises developed it seemed to play a restraining rather than an exacerbating role. It appeared to resent its exclusion from the peace-making processes initiated by the Nixon and Carter presidencies, and so long as it was thus excluded seemed unlikely to use its influence to persuade its Middle Eastern friends to make concessions.

In the 1970s Africa continued to attract Soviet interest. A marxist regime defeated other revolutionary movements in Angola with the help of Soviet advice and the arrival of Cuban troops. However, subsequent Soviet influence in the new government was not especially strong. The sea route to the Far East was probably one reason for Soviet interest in East Africa. The other side of the Gulf of Aden seemed to be secure to the extent that the government of the South Yemen (formerly Aden) was marxist and closely aligned with the Soviet Union. At first Somalia was the beneficiary of Soviet interest, and the Red Navy at one stage had base facilities both in Somalia and South Yemen. But when the Soviet Union threw its weight behind the new marxist regime in Ethiopia, which was soon fighting a war against Somalia, the latter rejected its Russian alliance.

The Ethiopian regime was not well regarded in Africa. It was as characteristic of the USSR as of the USA that idealistic or moral considerations tended to be ignored in the choice of allies. The USSR applauded the Amin regime in Uganda, supplying jet fighters and describing British credit withdrawal as 'blackmail'. However, it was adept enough to withdraw its military advisers two months before Amin's fall. That fall was evidently not expected to be as rapid or irrevocable as it turned out to be, judging from the circumstance that *Pravda* waited two weeks before reporting it.

In Africa a power game was being played, and often Soviet diplomacy and influence was fighting on two fronts, against both the west and China; the latter, regarding itself as part of the third world, seemed sometimes to obtain a good deal of leverage even though its economic and military aid did not match those of the superpowers. But preoccupation with American or Chinese rivals sometimes seemed to lead to Soviet disregard of another power, that of Africa itself. Africans realized only too well what was going on and frequently took advantage of great-power rivalry to obtain what they needed without compromising themselves for the future. When in 1980 Zimbabwe celebrated independence, its government went out of its way to show that it felt no indebtedness to the USSR or to the peoples' democracies.

The Afghanistan crisis which occurred in late 1979 was several years in the making. That nation of 20 million Moslems had been the scene of Soviet–US peaceful competition, but by 1979, after several bloody episodes, a revolutionary government was in power and enjoying Soviet support. When this government aroused violent popular resistance the USSR arranged a coup and brought in a new leader, Karmal. Soviet troops entered Afghanistan at the same time to support the new government, and were soon fighting an arduous and far from glorious guerrilla campaign against what sometimes seemed to be the entire nation.

This was a Soviet advance into territory that was not regarded by the international community as part of the Russian sphere. The apparent weakness of US diplomacy, still undermined by the complexes generated by the unsuccessful Vietnam War and additionally hurt by more recent anti-American events in Iran, was both an encouragement for the Soviet action and a spur for the sharp US response. The consequent interruption of US–Soviet commercial relations, and withdrawal of US and other countries' athletes from the Olympic Games (held at Moscow in 1980) were symptoms of the renewed international tension. Although nervousness about the USSR's southern borderlands, with their Moslem populations, was suggested as a reason for the Soviet action, the main stimulus was the Politburo's unwillingness to accept that a marxist pro-Soviet regime could be overthrown by its own people. The Politburo did not make its decision easily, and it turned out to be a bad decision.

In any case the drive for *détente* had been slackening before this crisis.

For this deterioration it would be unfair to blame just one of the parties. Both governments faced a task which was so delicate, so dependent on an intimate understanding of the other side's position, that it may well have been a near-impossible undertaking from the start. Relaxation, by definition, meant dropping one's guard by graduated stages, and humans, with their ingenuity prone to create and magnify all kinds of anxieties, lack a natural ritual for this process. In both Washington and Moscow there were powerful interests which opposed guard-dropping, usually from quite genuine fears but occasionally from motives of short-term personal and political advantage. Moscow and Washington tried but failed in the 1960s and 1970s to halt the arms race, and in 1980 there were even signs of a reappearance of the cold war psychosis. However, in those two decades a whole succession of crises had been 'defused' in one way or another, even though there were always voices which would describe 'defusing' as 'appeasement'. With all their grotesque armaments, the leaders of the two great powers still rejected the feasibility of all-out nuclear war. They evidently realized that they were the only men who could lose the world in an afternoon.

The armed forces

By about 1970 the USSR had achieved parity with the USA in numbers of inter-continental ballistic missiles. This point reached, it was evidently felt that meaningful arms limitation talks might begin. The Strategic Arms Limitations Talks (SALT) had a disturbed history. The first SALT agreement between the USA and the USSR was in 1972, and marked the abandonment of proposed anti-missile installations as well as the imposition of certain limits on numbers of offensive missiles. The second SALT agreement was heralded by a meeting of Brezhnev and President Ford in 1974 at Vladivostok; after lengthy and very difficult discussions it had been found possible to fix the number of inter-continental missiles allowed to each of the two powers. For one reason or another the confirmation of this second SALT agreement was delayed year after year, the final stumbling block being the reluctance of the US Senate to approve it. In the interim, the two powers agreed to stick to their agreed limitations in the hope that the agreement would eventually be confirmed. In general, SALT did not restrict the powers building the numbers of missiles they wished to build, but it probably did enable them to avoid building more than they had intended. That is, it did not put an end to the arms race in missiles, but helped to keep it under control.

In 1967 the USSR introduced a new conscription law, to replace the 1939 law and its various modifications. Among its provisions was the shortening of the period of service by one year. Henceforth eighteen-year-olds would enter the army and air force for two years, or the navy for three, while graduates of higher education would serve just one year as officers (those who during their studies had participated in their institutions' officer-training units became second lieutenants in the reserve and did not serve in the active forces). Thus traces of the 1874 army reform, with its exemptions and discriminations, lingered on. Although all were liable to service, many exemptions were made, because otherwise the forces would have been uneconomically large. Conscription was selective, with the Council of Ministers deciding each year on the size of the call-up. There were general exemptions for young men with two or more children, or with aged dependent parents, or who worked in certain occupations or were studying certain subjects. Local draft boards were supposed to organize send-off celebrations for departing conscripts.

The Red Navy benefited disproportionately from the increase of expenditure on conventional weapons after 1965. Within a few years ships of advanced technology, carrying various types of guided missile, appeared. In ship-to-ship missiles, at least, the USSR seemed to have a lead, and its smaller missile-carrying ships in particular caused western naval staff to re-think their priorities. In the 1970s, too, the Red Navy acquired its first aircraft-carriers. These were not quite as large as the American carriers, being designed to carry only helicopters and short-take-off aircraft, but they were nevertheless a notable acquisition. These carriers, and the other new vessels as well, gave officers and men much-needed experience in seagoing operations; apart from long cruises in foreign waters, the Red Navy was able to indulge in very extensive fleet exercises. Meanwhile in 1972 the Commander-in-Chief, Admiral Gorshkov, published what might be called a new doctrine of Soviet naval power. This doctrine was somewhat reminiscent of the European 'blue-water school' of naval thought in Edwardian times, with its emphasis on the value of a seagoing navy for showing the flag, extending and protecting interests abroad, making discreet and finely graduated threats of force, countering enemy naval movements and, finally, adding a new and decisive element to the waging of a full-scale war. A Soviet naval squadron was permanently stationed in the Mediterranean, and a smaller one in the Indian Ocean. Soviet 'naval diplomacy' really began in 1967, although before then there had been several visits by ships to foreign ports. The basic squadron was the missile-armed anti-aircraft-carrier force, designed to counter the American carrier-centred task force. At times of tension it became the Soviet custom to shadow each US task force with its own anti-carrier force. During the Angolan civil war such a Soviet force was dispatched to the South Atlantic to match a US task force which in fact was never sent. Meanwhile, missile-carrying submarines continued to play their role as part of the Soviet Union's nuclear warfare strategy.

The arts

The publication of *One Day in the Life of Ivan Denisovich* was something of a high-water mark in literary freedom. Khrushchev in his last months seemed to take a less tolerant view of artistic freedom. His successors were even more cautious. Brezhnev and his colleagues, in this sphere as in others, did not welcome anybody rocking the Soviet boat. Literature could, if not closely controlled, set up dangerous movements of opinion. Executed by the bureaucratic petty intelligentsia installed in the key offices of the Writers' Union, the new policy meant that really outstanding critical fiction was not published, and writers who published abroad without permission lost their membership of the Union (and hence their official status as writers). In the early eighties Soviet writers still lacked that most important of all freedoms, the freedom to state the obvious.

Solzhenitsyn, by the late sixties, was published abroad but not at home. His *Cancer Ward* was essentially a novel about people's souls in the years between Stalin's death and Khrushchev's 1956 speech. The swinish side of Stalinist Russia received a full but low-key portrayal; the political exiles in Central Asia, the arrest of doctors with no arrangements made for the further treatment of their patients, the endless queueing for rubber stamps which enabled the recipient to queue for another rubber stamp, the appointment of mediocrities to responsible positions, the shattered lives not only of political prisoners but also of those who, in order to remain free, turned traitor to themselves and denounced their colleagues or voted at mass meetings for exemplary punishment. There was a sensitive portrayal of a member of the new communist bourgeoisie, the official Rusanov, who had a nice new car and a nice new apartment and a nice family which knew which strings to pull to get what it wanted. Although the author did not imply that all officials were like Rusanov, the type was easily recognizable. Rusanov was a stereotypical Stalinist, a man who loved The People but despised his fellow-humans, a man who knew that on certain questions a definite opinion had been established and therefore discussion was no longer permissible. He was a man who had denounced many in his time and was terrified when the government began to release political prisoners. The non-celebration of the second anniversary of Stalin's death, and the dismissal of the Supreme Court's judges, were to him ominous signs that the world in which he had made himself so much at home was about to break up.

Solzhenitsyn was expelled from the Writers' Union in 1969, and then in

1974 was banished from the USSR. His long experience of the Soviet literary establishment and the censorship is recounted in his *The Oak and the Calf* (1980). Other literary figures who either defected, or emigrated voluntarily or not-so-voluntarily, included V. Nekrasov, A. Sinyavsky, and I. Brodsky. It remained to be seen whether, cut off from their native soil, such writers would be able to continue with their creative work. Solzhenitsyn evidently came west with a good deal of work to finish. His multivolume *The Gulag Archipelago*, just one of his post-expulsion publications, became a best-seller; in the USSR it was duly described by prominent members of the Writers' Union as a filthy anti-Soviet perversion, although all it did was to add horrifying detail to the revelations made about Stalinist labour camps by Khrushchev himself. In exile, Solzhenitsyn seemed to set himself up as a latter-day Tolstoy, making didactic moralizing forays not only against the Soviet system but against those in the west who seemed to be too tolerant, or unaware, of the Soviet menace. His ultra-Russian, ultra-Orthodox Christian line seemed sometimes to irritate dissident Russians and émigrés.

A feature of the delicate path between freedom for dissemination of ideas and avoiding dangerous movements of popular opinion was the publication of a few bold literary and other works in very small editions. This meant that, as in the west (but for different reasons), it could be said that the smaller the number of copies printed, the more worth reading was the publication. But when in 1979 a group of writers tried openly to publish a small-circulation literary collection, *Metropol*, without going through the various censorship processes, it was suppressed; soon afterwards two of its contributors were expelled from the Writers' Union on grounds of 'insufficient merit'.

In painting, a noteworthy example of the complications of applying the new approach occurred in 1975, when a group of 'unofficial' artists (that is, of people who painted despite their non-membership of the Artists' Union) decided to stage their own, unapproved, exhibition. An open-air display of their work, which had little connection with Socialist Realism, was arranged. This display, and the artists, came under violent attack from 'an enraged public' (a euphemism, with roots in tsarist times, for officially-recruited or officially-inspired hooligans). To make quite sure of making their point, the authorities even recruited bulldozers to attack the paintings. All this occurred under the eyes of foreign visitors, some of whom had their cameras smashed, and the affair received worldwide publicity. But soon afterwards the local party secretary was transferred elsewhere, and approval was given to the artists to exhibit those pictures which could be patched up. It seemed that, as so frequently happens in Russian history, centrally-propagated policies were subject to all kinds of local aberrations. For example, in 1970 a Novosibirsk art gallery director who tried to organize an exhibition including works by Chagall and a dissident artist was promptly rewarded with an eight-year sentence: he had been accused, among other things, of offering help to a Chinese spy.

The population

The population of the USSR reached 263 million in 1979. There was still growth, but on average it was moderate. In urban areas of the Russian Republic (and to a lesser extent in other European republics) an increasing number of families seemed content to raise just one child, whereas the Asian nationalities still usually measured their worldly and spiritual success by the number of children they could bring into the world. By 1980 the Russian Republic contained only 52 per cent of the Soviet population; Great Russians still accounted for more than half of the USSR population, but only just. They would soon be in a minority. Meanwhile, the Moslem population was going through a classical 'population explosion'. This situation seemed likely to cause social strains.

In some ways the Soviet system seemed well adapted to cope with any racial disharmony. But time was needed: hence the anxiety about events in Iran and Afghanistan in 1979, for natural and religious outbursts were potentially contagious and could have had dire consequences if extended into Soviet Asia. Even party leaders in non-Russian republics were not always immune to the pulls of local and national emotions and interests. Party members with allegiance split between Moscow and Mecca could still be found in Central Asia. In that region the Moslem priesthood still retained great moral force among ordinary people and also, it seems, influenced party officials. In Transcaucasia, Georgia, as always, was exceptional. Georgians, although enjoying certain liberties unknown to other Soviet citizens, were quick to make protests. They staged street demonstrations against Khrushchev's dethronement of their compatriot Stalin, and they staged more street demonstrations in 1978, when the draft of the new Georgian constitution was published. This, like the draft constitutions for the other two Transcaucasian republics, no longer defined the local national language as a state language. This threatened boost for Russian at the expense of Georgian brought out the demonstrators, whose protest did succeed in restoring, in the final draft, the local languages to their previous position. Georgia was culturally and economically one of the richest republics of the USSR and, even after half a century of communism, preserved a spirit of free enterprise, not least among party officials who made good use of their power and influence to feather their own nests. Corruption and bribery among top officials is, of course, a weakness of one-party states, and such corruption was certainly not confined to Georgia. But the self-enrichment of Georgian party leaders became so blatant that Moscow set in train legal and party procedures. Resulting trials and condemnations ended in the dismissal of the Georgian party secretary and some of his associates. In the same year the Armenian party leader was removed after a state trial, and from Moscow came warnings about the threat of Ukrainian nationalism.

There was also a burgeoning of Great Russian nationalism, encouraged by several 'native' writers. These writers were not discouraged by the authorities, who appreciated the useful aspects of the movement. As for the possibility of interracial disharmony (which already existed among some social strata), this was not discussed. However, the occasional call for a proper 'population policy' did suggest that party and government were aware of the dangers.

An important feature of any population policy is birth control, but in the late 1970s the Soviet government still did not regard the production of modern contraceptives as very desirable. Small quantities of the contraceptive pill were imported from the peoples' democracies but they were, it seems, sent to Central Asia (where they were prescribed to local Russian women because Moslem doctors opposed their distribution to the Asian population). For most Russian women of the European regions abortion was the accepted practice. It was calculated that in the late 1960s, taking the population of the USSR as a whole (and thereby considerably under-estimating the average for Russian women), there were six legal abortions per woman-life. Despite this, it would seem that many babies were born to women ill-placed to look after them properly. Infant death-rates were deteriorating; they were highest in Central Asia where legal abortions, again for cultural and religious reasons, were fewer. In the mid-1970s towns in the Baltic republics (and the Baltic republics were regarded as the culturally most advanced parts of the Soviet Union) had infant death-rates of 17 to 22 per thousand, whereas in towns of Central Asia the rate was more than double this.

Rising death-rates in other age groups were another cause of concern. By the mid-1970s Soviet males had a life expectancy at birth of only sixty-three years, compared to sixty-nine for American males. The corresponding female expectancies were seventy-four and seventy-six. This deterioration at a time of rising living standards was puzzling. The average Russian diet, for example, had improved noticeably; between 1965 and 1978 the un-desirably high consumption of potatoes fell from 142 to 120 kilograms per person per year, while meat consumption grew from forty-one to forty-six kilograms. To some extent, though, better can mean worse: improved living standards since 1952 meant increased cigarette consumption, among other things. Moreover, alcoholic beverages in an age of more automobile traffic, more machinery in the factory and on the farm, and faster tempos of work, might be expected to raise the number of fatal accidents, especially of young males. Nor did improved living standards, of themselves, help to reduce deaths from prolonged exposure to alcohol, or the still quite high prevalence of suicide.

So far as infant deaths are concerned, the USSR had experienced a notable rise in the number of very young mothers, with their higher infant mortality. With most mothers going to full-time work (and with maternity leave terminating just two months after the birth), the number of infants in day-care centres was high, and such centres were breeding grounds for the influenza and pneumonia outbreaks which caused so many infant deaths. Indeed, the inability of so many mothers, for one reason or another, to give their full care and attention to the newborn, was probably the underlying factor in most types of infantile mortality. The lot of the Russian woman, especially if she had no mother or mother-in-law to help her, was more arduous than most. Because of labour shortages, the government did not make it easy for married women to give up the advantage of the second familial pay packet. To go to work, to attend to children, to look after the home (which included long hours spent queuing for food) was a heavy workload, especially as the Soviet male's characteristic good nature often did not extend to helping with 'women's business'. Possibly it was this continuing daily burden which kept the Soviet divorce rate at such a high level, but family life continued also to be threatened by poor housing conditions. In the 1960s great efforts had been made to relieve the abysmal housing situation left by the Stalinist years. Outside the cities huge expanses were covered with apartment blocks which, though sometimes ill-built and aesthetically unappealing, offered a new life to thousands of families. Under Khrushchev's successors residential building continued, and often made use of better or more pleasing designs. However, from 1969 the rate of construction fell behind the increase in the number of families. As before, accommodation that was in the better districts or was more spacious tended to be allocated to the privileged. The unprivileged had to be content (and they were) with cramped and remote apartments and, in the case of one design that was hurriedly altered to save materials, apartments where access from the kitchen to the living room was through the centrally placed bathroom. Housing, like other social services, was regarded as important, but had to take its place in the queue for resources. Defence, industry, and agriculture came first.

Some western specialists believed that the continuing problem of vandalism, petty crime, and hooliganism was partly a consequence of housing problems. The extent of 'hooliganism' was perhaps magnified by the tendency in the USSR to describe as a hooligan any young person whose tastes were not those generally accepted by society. Nevertheless, it certainly existed; for example, passengers on late evening commuter trains often complained that young people terrorized them while the train staff preferred to look the other way. In 1975, in the perhaps optimistic belief that children broke laws because they did not know what the laws were, a one-year course was introduced in schools on 'Principles of the Soviet State and Law'. Pilfering by workers of all ages was another problem. Armed guards had for decades been placed on freight trains carrying easily-stolen freight through populated areas, but thefts in transit continued. A trainload of automobiles, as they passed successive junctions, might be relieved first of their tool-kits, then of their window-wipers, then of their dials and gauges, and might arrive at their final destination stripped to their chassis frames.

One aspect of society in which Khrushchev had been the very reverse of a liberator was religion. Indeed, the devout could look back to the Stalin days with a certain nostalgia; after the war there had not been a relapse to the violent anti-religious campaigns of the thirties, and in many cases a blind eye had been turned on religious communities and priests who broke the strict letter of the anti-religious laws. Under Khrushchev, atheistic activity had returned to an abusive and physically violent course. In the Brezhnev years anti-religious legislation was not relaxed but, Khrushchev's policies having strengthened rather than weakened the hold of religion, official behaviour was more circumspect. In 1966 a revised law mentioned the criminality of 'deceitful actions calculated to arouse religious superstitions' and a new family law in 1968 stipulated that children should be brought up according to communist morals and that parents having a harmful influence over their children could lose their parental rights. Both these pieces of legislation were potentially of great utility in the campaign against religion, but they do not appear to have been widely used for that purpose.

The Orthodox Church remained the 'official' Church, with considerable advantages over other Christian denominations. Since 1946 the Uniate Church had been illegal. The Roman Catholics were a special case; in Lithuania the Catholic Church produced many dissidents and was closely linked with the Lithuanian nationalist movement, which was anti-Russian and remained strong despite frequent arrests. The *Chronicle of the Lithuanian Catholic Church* was one of the first well-known *Samizdat* publications in the USSR. Perhaps because the Lithuanian bishops had strong popular support, the Soviet authorities occasionally adopted a concessionary approach, allowing, for example, 10,000 copies of the New Testament to be published in Lithuania in 1972. Moslems were treated rather carefully, and there was a continuing policy of cultivating an officially-approved Moslem leadership, representatives of which were sent as spokesmen on visits to other Moslem countries. Buddhists, on the other hand, were treated badly.

Living standards rose sharply during the post-Stalin years. An effort to raise the lowest wages also resulted in a slight narrowing of the gap between the highest- and lowest-paid workers. However, the standards of many citizens were low, and there remained great inequalities in the size of incomes and, especially, in the distribution of privileges. While average pensions rose faster than average wages, most pensions were insufficient for a comfortable retirement. Moreover, higher wages could not always be translated into higher standards, because the desired goods were not to be found in the shops. In Moscow, Leningrad, and a few big cities (especially those open to foreign tourists) the inhabitants benefited from an unpublicized but very effective priority in supplies. Elsewhere in the Soviet Union, higher wages and unnaturally low prices meant that any allocations of the most wanted commodities were bought up in minutes. This situation was reflected in the growing propensity of Soviet citizens to increase personal savings. A particular victim of the unnatural price-and-supply relationship was meat. This was very cheap, thanks to a subsidy, but could only be obtained intermittently, and by queuing for long periods. This, obviously, aroused dissatisfaction, but the government felt that it was better that citizens should enjoy the thought of low meat prices, even if meat was very difficult to obtain, than that they should be antagonized by a raising of prices which would have resulted in more meat in the shops. Polish workers had several times shown what unfortunate things might happen to the vanguard of the working class if it decided to impose price increases on the working class's meat. Influential persons (that is, the privileged) could always buy their meat at the cheap official prices at the 'closed' shops which had been established for their exclusive benefit. There were only rare occasions when Soviet workers indulged in disorderly protests; the characteristic occasion for such public disturbances was a realization that treasured items of food were not forthcoming even after hours of queuing. In such cases the immediate government reaction was to release from state reserves a special allocation of supplies to that locality, in order to cool the situation. Investigations and perhaps selective arrests could then proceed unhurriedly.

Although ordinary citizens had many occasions for dissatisfaction, their irritation was usually directed, or channelled, towards lower officials. So long as living standards did not actually decline it could be assumed that the leadership was safe from popular discontent. After all, although the claim that there was no unemployment and no inflation in the USSR was exaggerated, these two scourges were unobtrusive minor irritants rather than the large-scale demoralizing phenomena of the western world of the 1970s.

But although the Soviet masses had little thought of changing the regime, just as in tsarist times there was a stratum of dissident opinion that was willing to take risks in its self-imposed task of fundamental criticism. There were signs of active dissidence in the sixties. Many intellectuals and others made known their distaste for such actions as the trial of Sinyavsky and Daniel, for the refusal to return their homeland to the Crimean Tartars even though their wartime deportation had been declared unjustified, and for the 1968 action in Czechoslovakia. Some of the protesters used the medium of the leaflet or of the petition, others actually tried to organize street demonstrations, while others embarrassed the government by voicing complaints to western pressmen which they could not publicize in the USSR. Dissidents whose opposition was blatant and attracting public attention were sometimes tried and sent to labour camps. Also, Nicholas I's practice of certifying intellectual critics as insane was repeated; this enabled suitable treatment to be administered in psychiatric institutions operated by the security services.

Also reminiscent of Nicholas's reign was the hand-to-hand circulation of writings which could not be printed because of censorship. With photocopying, these *Samizdat* editions could be circulated in hundreds of copies. A regular 'underground' periodical, *The Journal of Current Events*, provided information about what was really happening in the USSR and in the world. Another *Samizdat* 'publication' which attracted world-wide attention was *Thoughts on Progress, Peaceful Coexistence and Intellectual Freedom*. This studied the desirability, for the peace of the world, of a convergence of a freer USSR with a more socialized USA, a convergence which should be fostered by scientists. The author, Sakharov, was a respected and highly talented physicist.

Sakharov, being a top scientist, was not molested for this publication. Scientists, especially those attached to closed research establishments, had more intellectual freedom than ordinary citizens, and found all the more irksome those restrictions from which they continued to suffer. They were allowed to read western scientific and academic journals, but not always before censoring bureaucrats had removed those parts considered harmful or 'irrelevant'. They had contacts abroad, but their foreign correspondence was opened and examined. They had opportunities to travel abroad, but only after innumerable appearances and perhaps humiliations before party and state officials (they had to collect in triplicate, testimonials, then assemble their pedigrees and personal biographies, which were scrutinized by four party bureaux, the KGB, and the foreign ministry). It was from scientists and academics that the nucleus of a new 'public opinion' seemed to be emerging. As the purges receded further into the past, disturbed personal relationships between intellectuals were re-established and they developed a certain professional solidarity. They did not seek a revolution, but they wanted fair use of existing institutions. For example, they wanted the citizens' rights formally granted by the Constitution to be guaranteed in practice, they wanted the soviets to be genuine forums for discussion rather than gatherings of selected yes-men. They probably had little in common (apart from family connections) with the masses, whose preoccupations were still economic rather than political or moral. They probably did not even want to arouse the masses, whose rebellion might so easily be turned against themselves and their privileges; no doubt the Chinese Cultural Revolution reminded them how vulnerable they were. In a sense these discontented intellectuals resembled their predecessors of Nicholas II's time, talented men needed by the state, who strove to use their indispensability as a lever to extract political freedoms.

In the 1970s repression of the dissident movement seemed to intensify. The KGB scored a notable success in 1973, when after a long period of arrest and interrogation two prominent dissidents, P. Yakir and V. Krasin (both bearers of distinguished Bolshevik names), were persuaded to sign confessions that they were agents of foreign anti-Soviet organizations. Many dissidents were allowed to leave, or forced to leave, on one-way trips to the west. One prominent dissident, Bukovski, a specialist (through experience) of the 'psychiatric' treatment of dissidents, went west in a 'body-swap'; a prominent Chilean communist was released and sent to the USSR by the Chilean government in exchange. In 1978 a new law on citizenship made easier the formal deprivation of Soviet citizenship. Among those who were deprived of citizenship (that is, the right of residence in USSR) in the following year were the novelist V. Nekrasov, the philosopher A. Zinoviev (author of a long satirical and subversive novel, *Yawning Heights*), and the chess champion V. Korchnoi.

In the months preceding the 1980 Olympic Games the security services felt it prudent to shift many known dissidents away from Moscow, where they might have found audiences among the expected influx of foreign visitors. Sakharov was among those molested at this time, being sent to house arrest in the city of Gorki. Earlier, there had been several more trials of dissidents. Among these was that of Orlov, one of the leaders of a group

of concerned Soviet citizens which had established a committee to observe
how far the authorities were observing the agreements on human rights
enshrined in the Helsinki Agreement. Orlov was sentenced to seven years'
hard labour for 'anti-Soviet agitation' and his trial was so unsatisfactory
that several western communist leaders protested against it.

Other members of the intelligentsia, while refraining from activities that
would put them in the dissident camp, sometimes succeeded by discreet
pressure in achieving important aims. They had, for example, a large part
in the discouragement of moves to rehabilitate Stalin; the post-1956 line
was retained, that Stalin was 'positive' until 1934 and increasingly 'negative'
thereafter. Scientific opinion seems to have been a strong influence in the
leadership's acceptance of environmental pollution as a problem deserving
of attention. In the USSR, because of the scarcity of automobiles, air pollution was a lesser problem than water pollution, even though in some industrial cities air pollution was several times higher than the level acceptable
in Western Europe. In 1972 purification plants were planned, and a special
effort was made to start a gradual clean-up of the rivers flowing into the
Caspian. As elsewhere, ministries, enterprises, and local political interests
often suceeded in evading environmental regulations, but nevertheless a
start had been made. By 1980, it was stipulated, cities on the Volga and
Ural rivers would be forbidden to put unprocessed waste into the water (in
1990 these rivers were still polluted).

A rather novel, non-intellectual, protest attracted attention in 1977, when
six workers, including a coal miner, gave to western pressmen an account
of how they had variously lost their jobs after sending in complaints about
how their superiors were misbehaving in various ways. Managerial mis-
behaviour was quite common in the USSR, as the Soviet press indicated
from time to time. Neglect of safety precautions in order to help reach production targets, diversion of wages and bonuses from those who actually
earned them to administrative and managerial staff, the purloining for
private use or profit of state materials or products, were the usual fields of
such activity. Those who did protest to their trade union or party officials
usually received little sympathy. Sometimes they wrote to the newspapers,
and sometimes their letter gained a hearing and their complaint was publicized (although not necessarily with any result). If an enterprise was
meeting its production targets it was rare for criticisms of its management
to have any effect, but once an enterprise lost favour because of output difficulties its management was likely to be assailed by diverse accusations
accumulated during past years. Here, for example, is a little drama published by *Pravda* of 26 September 1979. Efimovski, a worker at a Tashkent
engineering factory, had many times complained about the neglect of

safety regulations. Finally, not having received any satisfaction, he decided to quit:

Efimovski was called to the director's office. There, already waiting for him, were the party secretary, the trade union chairman, and the head of the workshop. The conversation was begun with a threat:
'Well, you have decided to quit? Fine, we'll release you, but you won't be leaving voluntarily. We are going to dismiss you for absenteeism.'
'But I've not been absent', said the astonished Efimovski.
'If you haven't had any absences yet, you soon will have!' replied Yu. Pelishenko, head of the workshop.
They quickly put together a false document about Efimovski's absences, and similar faked minutes of a supposed meeting of the workshop trade union committee, which had 'demanded' the dismissal of the 'truant' . . .

So there was really nothing new about the complaint of the six dissident workers. But their chosen method of protest passed beyond what was acceptable in Soviet conditions. They tried to form a 'Free Trade Union of Soviet Workers'. This was more than individual protest (which was acceptable); it was the forming of an 'organization' (which was certainly unacceptable). In 1978 this 'Free Trade Union' appealed to the International Labour Organization at Geneva for support and recognition. Since the comfortably-installed executives of the ILO had much in common with those against whom the 'Free Trade Union' was protesting, it was hardly surprising that the ILO's response was disappointing.

Also outside the mainstream of the dissident movement were the protesters whose bomb in the Moscow Metro killed several passengers in 1977, and the lone assassin who shot at a motorcade conveying Soviet leaders in 1969. This assassin had wished to kill Brezhnev, but he fired at the wrong car, killing a driver.

One lone assassin does not make a revolutionary movement. Similarly, it would be a mistake to equate the dissidents of the 1970s with the revolutionaries of the preceding century. Whereas the nineteenth-century revolutionaries, from the Decembrists on, opposed not only the regime but also its philosophy, those who criticized the post-Stalin governments did usually accept socialist principles. Nevertheless, there was one common thread linking the oppositional movements of the twentieth and nineteenth centuries: the resentment aroused by the ever-present, ever-suspicious, and ever-interfering Russian bureaucratic mind. To examine such a mind would require a whole book. But, in brief, it had two major concepts: the elevation to a principle of the maxim that there is a proper time and place for everything, and the belief that the proper time and place may be specified only by a person adequately certified as someone-who-knows-best. In this mind, the ideal society is one where everyone acts according to a grand design, and yet within that design (prepared by experts) each individual is free to excel. In real life this ideal may be never quite attainable (although in the arts it is achieved by ballet; that ballet finds its most enthusiastic audience in administrative centres like St. Petersburg is perhaps unsurprising). When the bureaucrat's idea of perfection is backed by the power to impose it by coercion, well-known and perilous temptations arise.

The survival into Soviet times of an all-powerful and coercive bureaucracy repeatedly undermined the promise of 1917. Six decades after the Revolution the gap between 'official' and 'unofficial' Russia, which nineteenth-century visitors so much liked to point out, was still evident. The Russian communists had succeeded against all odds in proving that there was an attainable alternative to capitalism, but in doing so they had deliberately used the existing administrative apparatus, an apparatus which was coercive, repressive, and distrusted the people. They had changed the official ideology, but they had not changed the official arbitrariness and authoritarianism which had been the most disliked features of tsarism. Traditional bureaucratic attitudes weakened the state by arousing discontent and by repressing initiative (that is, by perpetuating traditional Russian inertia); therefore their continuation after 1917 could not entirely be justified by the need for a workable system of governing and guarding an enormous and incoherent state. Despite a realization of the dangers of bureaucracy, and sporadic efforts to curb its most alarming symptoms, both the party and the government came to rely more and more on the old methods. Inside the party, Democratic Centralism degenerated into bureaucratic centralization, so that by the thirties there was a wide gap between party officials and party members. In the administration, the old ministers, governors, and most heads of departments disappeared in 1917, but the majority of middle and lower officials seem to have remained in, or subsequently regained, their positions. Party members sent to watch over government departments seemed to share the bureaucratic outlook, or perhaps acquired such an outlook from those they were supposed to supervise. The pattern of the Red Army, most of whose commanders by the end of the Civil War were former tsarist officers, was duplicated in other departments of state; even the CHEKA made use of former *Okhrana* operatives. Patterns of bureaucratic thought and behaviour were thereby passed on from tsarist times, and later absorbed by new generations of state officials. Towards the end of his life Lenin seemed to realize what was happening. If he had been able to introduce an effective but less arbitrary and repressive mode of administration it would probably have been the most radical achievement of the Russian Revolution. But it is doubtful whether more than a minority of his supporters would have appreciated this. Too many Bolsheviks, both before and after Lenin's death, did not distinguish what was radical from what was merely excessive. Revolution, taking the form of removing church bells and arresting men wearing ties, was more attractive than radicalism. A result of this negligence was that from the 1930s ordinary Russians were enduring official repression more painful and more widespread than that of a century earlier. Subsequent 'destalinization' made life more bearable but was slow to touch the fundamentals. In the 1960s and 1970s the life of Soviet people visibly improved, and not only in material terms, but when the 1980s began there still seemed to be a discrepancy between what the Revolution had achieved on paper, and what the Revolution had achieved in practice.

This was the underlying situation that Brezhnev faced. He saw the symptoms but did not recognize the disease.

18. *Infirmity*

The end of Brezhnev

BREZHNEV'S last public appearance was in Red Square in early November 1982, at the 65th anniversary celebrations of the Revolution. A few days later he was dead. His last year in office had been unhappy and, although interpretations of the events of those months may vary, there can be little dispute that, for Brezhnev, they were months of humiliation and pathos.

The test of the real power of a Soviet leader was his ability to carry out far-reaching reforms that were unwelcome to powerful sections of the party and state bureaucracy. Since Brezhnev never attempted such reforms, the question of how much power he really had has never been convincingly answered. It could be argued that because he was not of a radical disposition the absence of vigorous policies was not a result of lack of power but of lack of interest in using it. On the other hand, trends under his successors suggested that the days of an all-powerful general secretary were over, and that the need to obtain a consensus in the Politburo was not at all an empty formality. On the question of authority, which is not quite the same as power, there can be little doubt that Brezhnev's position was deteriorating towards the end.

On the whole, his regime was benevolent, with a perceptible attitude of live-and-let-live. His rule was later characterized as 'the period of stagnation' but this stagnation did at least give the population something it had lacked for four decades: stability. One manifestation of this was his slogan 'Respect for Cadres', which reflected his wish to avoid upheavals in the party and state administration and to allow administrators to remain in office without fears of dismissal. By the end of his reign, this had ensured that he had broad support among elderly administrators, but also that a younger generation of middle-aged officials, denied promotion and opportunity for changing things, was dissatisfied. Added to this latent opposition were sizeable sections of the officer corps, which did not enjoy the same job security and opportunities for enrichment as the upper bureaucrats, and moreover was aware that these bureaucrats were not achieving much success in providing the forward-looking economic and social base on which military power ultimately depends.

In Soviet conditions such opposition had little opportunity to express itself openly and directly but, as impatience with Brezhnev and his clique of loyal cronies deepened, ways were found to embarrass him. The general tone, as indeed was reported by most western correspondents in Moscow at this time, was that Brezhnev had held on to office far too long. Not only was he a very sick man, but by character neither he nor those he had chosen as aides were fitted to take the radical measures needed to remedy what seemed to be economic stagnation and social decay.

For example, there was the occasion when, by a heroic physical and mental effort, Brezhnev was visiting Caucasian capitals and found himself reading a speech in one city intended for another. This scene, which was televised live, was evidently contrived to show that he hardly knew what he was doing, and the aide who is believed to have switched the speeches was promoted under Brezhnev's successor.

Even more wounding, the anti-corruption campaign, which the KGB had been pursuing energetically, probably more energetically than Brezhnev would have preferred, began to take in not only some of his supporters in the administration, but also his family. His daughter Galina, in conjunction with male friends of varying degrees of intimacy, and including the director of the celebrated State Circus and another character from the entertainment industry known as 'Boris the Gipsy', was allegedly involved in an illicit large-scale jewellery and valuables operation. This involved diamond-smuggling, collection of bribes, and currency specula-tion. The high positions of those involved (Galina was, additionally, mar-ried to a deputy minister of the interior) and the fact that the alleged crimes were grand enough to warrant the death penalty, made this an extra-ordinarily sensitive case. Eventually, some of the participants were arrested, but not Galina. Her husband, though, was demoted and posted to faraway and uncomfortable Murmansk, before justice and twelve years' hard labour caught up with him in 1988. A KGB general, Brezhnev's brother-in-law, who was believed to have protected her, died just as it was decided that the charges should be brought, and was assumed to have committed suicide. Brezhnev himself died before the case was finished.

The relations between Brezhnev and the Red Army appear to have deteriorated. The rewriting of military history so as to accord Brezhnev a decisive part in the war against Germany, when the senior officers, at least, knew that he had played a negligible role, must have been irritating, and this irritation would not have been eased by the succession of military decorations which he received. Since the highest orders were conferred by the Presidium of the Supreme Soviet, of which Brezhnev was chairman, he himself was in fact awarding the decorations, which included the rare and coveted Victory Medal, hitherto given only to a handful of outstanding generals in 1945. But these were superficial wounds. More serious, in the eyes of the higher military hierarchy, was that Brezhnev's regime was failing to provide the economic strength required by a great military power. A technological lag was painfully revealed in 1982, when Soviet missiles supplied to friendly Middle Eastern governments proved ineffective against the Israeli air force. This disquiet must have been felt, and probably expressed, by the armed forces' representative in the Politburo, the defence minister, Ustinov. Brezhnev, shortly before he died, arranged a conference between party and military leaders, in an attempt to restore confidence.

The Andropov phase

As Brezhnev's tenure of office was seen to be drawing to a close, most observers expected the succession to pass to Chernenko, another septuagenarian. Born in Siberia, Chernenko became a party official in 1933 and encountered Brezhnev when the latter led the party in Moldavia. Brought to Moscow in 1960, described by the irreverent as Brezhnev's closest drinking companion, Chernenko henceforth remained Brezhnev's most immediate aide and confidant, and there seems little doubt that the general secretary would have preferred him as his successor. However, Brezhnev had shown an unsurprising lack of enthusiasm for grooming possible heirs, and by the time his health made it clear that he would not remain at the helm much longer Chernenko was still not firmly in place as heir-apparent.

Indeed, Andropov, the head of the KGB, had been cementing his own claims to the top office. By this time, many Russians were beginning to hanker for strong leadership, for Brezhnev's brand of benign neglect had obvious drawbacks as well as obvious comforts. It seemed that only a strong leader could impose the change of direction that seemed more and more necessary in the face of disappointing economic performance. Moreover, Andropov's association, as head of the KGB, with the campaign against corruption must have enhanced his credit with those of his colleagues who felt the same way as he did about the blatant exploitation by party and state functionaries of the many opportunities they had for bribe-taking, nepotism, and empire-building. When Suslov, grand old man of the Politburo, relic of Stalin's regime, and party secretary in charge of ideological matters, died in 1982, it was Andropov who was transferred to succeed him in most of his offices. From May 1982, therefore, Andropov was in the party secretariat, and clearly many of his Politburo colleagues favoured him.

Born in the Stavropol region of the North Caucasus, son of a railway official, Andropov had worked on Volga riverboats before making a career in the Komsomol. As first secretary of the Komsomol at a sensitive time and place, Karelia in the 1940s, he had an opportunity to show his usefulness, and by the mid-1950s he was Soviet ambassador in Hungary, where he played a key role in the suppression of the 1956 rebellion. From 1967 to 1982 he was in charge of the KGB, where he pursued very successful offensives against political dissidents and against corruption.

He was clearly a man who could get things done, and it was with this reputation that his colleagues in the Politburo elected him general secretary of the party. Chernenko, the alternative, seemed all too likely to be merely a repetition of what went before. It was Chernenko, implicitly acknowledging that he had been outmanœuvred, who nominated Andropov but, contrary to expectations, he was not appointed head of state as a consolation prize. Instead the office of 'president' was left vacant, although Andropov assumed for himself the important office of chairman of the Defence Council.[1]

Unlike his predecessors, who needed years to assert their authority, Andropov appeared to be in charge right from the start, and his election as general secretary was announced only two days after Brezhnev's death. However, the ensuing weeks suggested that his colleagues in the Politburo did influence the pace and sometimes the direction of his initiatives.

Also noteworthy was that he did not find it necessary to denounce his immediate predecessor, as both Khrushchev and Brezhnev had done. Instead, it was indicated that the Brezhnev line would be followed, and only as time passed did it become clear, by implication, that the Brezhnev line, as continued by Andropov, had been shifted to a new and faster route. Although Andropov did not encourage a new personality cult for himself, and Brezhnev's personality cult ceased immediately, there was little attempt to reduce the late general secretary to a more modest place in history. That would come later and slowly; for the time being there was a spate of commemorative renamings. Whereas there had been little more grandiose than an irrigation canal to take the name of Suslov after the latter's death, Brezhnev's name was given to a new city, several districts in his old territory of Dnepropetrovsk where, as regional party secretary, he had met so many of those whom he later appointed to high positions, and

[1] The 1977 Constitution established that this was a state bureau, but it was closely tied with the party's Politburo.

in Moscow; also to collective farms, factories, institutes, a military academy, as well as to a nuclear icebreaker and an ocean liner.

Andropov's more relaxed approach was evident, among other things, from the magnanimous treatment of dismissed party leaders. When Podgorny, who had been retired in some degree of disgrace by Brezhnev, died in 1983, he was interred with full state honours, and the 'thick' party journal *Kommunist* made uncensorious mention of Khrushchev and Malenkov. The new trend outlasted Andropov, with the 94-year-old Molotov being readmitted to party membership in 1984.

As party secretary, Andropov's main attachment was to his kidney machine. Ill-health, which was not only renal but cardiac and diabetic as well, meant that he did not have enough time to carry out the changes that were expected of him. In the spring of 1983 both he and the emphysematic Chernenko disappeared temporarily into hospitals. He reappeared, but was last seen in public in August 1983, although from his sick-room he seems to have controlled events more or less up to his death in February 1984.

He continued the campaigns against corruption, dissidence, and idle workers, made a start in replacing some of the older or incompetent Brezhnev appointees in the bureaucracy, and took some hesitant steps towards decentralized economic decision-making. For the ordinary Russian, the most noticeable change was that the campaign against what was termed 'labour indiscipline' moved from exhortation under Brezhnev to energetic action under Andropov. Although foreign affairs were left largely in the experienced hands of Gromyko, Andropov needed to devote some of his all-too-few working hours to the deteriorating relationship with the USA, the unsettled state of Poland, the war in Afghanistan, and attempts to improve relations with China.

He was an interesting character, and one who demonstrated the inadequacy of the simple categorizations used by so many commentators on Soviet affairs. In particular, the division of Soviet leaders into so-called Stalinists and so-called liberals was shown, in Andropov's case, to be a misleading simplification. For he often contrived to appear a liberal while following policies and expressing views that were muted echoes from Stalin's time. As head of the KGB, he had been responsible for a sustained and harsh attack on the dissidents, yet they, the victims, somehow did not blame him for it. In his measures against the work-shy and corrupt, he favoured vigorous penalties more than an improvement of the situations which gave rise to their vices. On the other hand, his experience of Hungary, a country with which he maintained connections after leaving Budapest, made him tolerant of diversity within the socialist camp.

In an article under his name in *Kommunist* (March 1983), he acknow-ledged that Soviet society did not match Marx's idea of the socialist future, even though it was painfully treading in that direction. He doubted that the USSR could even be called a true socialist society, since although the people had won the right to become the owners of the common property, they had not become owners in terms of rights. He refused to accept that democracy and discipline were opposed; the USSR needed both and would get both. He pointed to the way local soviets were beginning to oppose ministries on questions involving town planning as an example of developing democracy. Democracy, he wrote, meant a widened participa-tion in arriving at decisions, but such decisions, once arrived at, needed discipline if they were to be carried out. This, evidently, was a variation on the theme of democratic centralism, but seemed to acknowledge that more democracy and less centralism might be an improvement. With such democratic processes, Andropov wrote, there was certainly a place for critics. Mixing 'Stalinism' and 'liberalism', he called for a freer atmosphere for those who would criticize while confining their remarks within certain guidelines, and for severe chastisement for those critics who refused to come inside the system; that is, for the dissidents.

Two other attitudes expressed in this article gave further clues to what Andropov's USSR might have been like had he lived. He made no attempt to claim that Soviet experience was a model for other countries; indeed, he leaned the other way and suggested that the peoples' democracies had a lot from which Moscow might learn. Finally, he concluded by affirming that nothing was more important for the party and state than preventing a nuclear war, which would be catastrophic for a humanity that was already facing perils enough.

Chernenko

After Andropov died the ancient city of Rybinsk was renamed in his hon-our, and then his memory faded. He had not been in power long enough either to delight or to disappoint; this was regretted by many citizens, who felt that this was a man who had the perception and the experience to put right so many of the things that were so visibly wrong.

On the eve of his retirement to hospital Andropov had prepared a speech to the central committee in which, among other things, he sug-gested that his protégé Mikhail Gorbachev should chair Politburo meet-ings in his absence. If this wish had been fulfilled Gorbachev would have had a stronger claim to the succession, but Andropov was too ill to deliver his speech; it was distributed in printed form, and somehow the paragraph about Gorbachev was deleted. So it was that the wheezy Chernenko who, having been rejected for the same office little more than a year previously, found enough support in the Politburo to ensure his selection as the next general secretary.

Just as it could be said that Andropov continued Brezhnev's policies with selective changes of speed and emphasis, so it might be argued that Chernenko continued Andropov's line, with some slackening of pace. Observers who, rather patronizingly, described Chernenko as a watered-down version of Brezhnev, were probably wrong. Despite his illness, it was possible to glimpse in him a man who had some ideas of his own, that were based on experience and an understanding of people. He emphasized, for example, the need to discover what ordinary people really wanted. His implied opinion that agriculture would benefit more from a comprehensive land improvement policy than from yet another reorganization was not without merit,[2] and when he discussed the new party programme (replacing that of 1961) he had the wisdom to remark that it was folly to lay down a specific timetable for the transition from socialism to communism, especially as it was clear that capitalism was a long way from being finished (or, as he put it, 'still has substantial reserves').

He died in March 1985. In accordance with Soviet practice, right up to the last moment his critical condition was not publicized. Indeed, in late February, when his proximity to death's door must have been intimate, he was shown on television receiving his credentials as a newly re-elected Supreme Soviet member. During the thirteen months of his appointment he was often absent, and business was largely left in the hands of Gromyko (foreign affairs), Gorbachev (economy), and Ustinov (defence). Gorbachev was allowed to act as Politburo chairman during these absences; this was one of several factors that facilitated his succession as general secretary after Chernenko's death.

Renovation of the KGB

Up to the 1960s, Beria excepted, the heads of the Soviet state security system did not remain long in office and often, Beria included, their careers ended nastily. The KGB itself was a post-Stalin creation originally designed to bring security under some kind of party control. But its early heads, themselves tainted with past misdeeds, did little to create a new image. Andropov was remarkable not only for his long tenure of the post,

---

[2] Land improvement had also been favoured by Brezhnev. Land exhaustion and erosion were Russian problems since medieval times, and the twentieth-century urge to maximize production at the expense of all else had made things worse. Just as Russian forests were damaged by the drive to obtain as much timber as possible at smallest cost, so the soil had been impoverished by over-exploitation and by the circumstance that nobody was held personally responsible for the state of the land.

but also for the revival of the service that took place under his supervision and initiative. Not only did he survive his office, but he also used it as a path to the top. Moreover, riding on his coat-tails, several professional security officers attained high political rank which they retained under Andropov's successors.

Andropov's management may be divided into three strands. First, he improved the techniques used by the service. Then he concentrated on dealing with two running sores: corruption in the state and party apparatus, and the activities of the dissidents. In his campaign against corruption he could count on the gratitude of the majority of Soviet citizens and perhaps most of the party, for inside the Politburo it could be assumed that honest, ascetic characters like Suslov and Ustinov would approve of it, as would some party officials in the middle and lower ranks. In the campaign against dissidents, who continued to be portrayed as anti-Soviet elements in the pay of western intelligence organizations, he could count on the blessing of all his party colleagues, which was far more important than the criticism he could expect from abroad.

In general, the KGB was tutored to act in a more sophisticated, yet more determined, way. Crude reliance on part-time informers seems to have diminished, being replaced by greater use of well-instructed and intelligent full-time undercover agents. Subtle means were evolved for going round, instead of crashing through, the legal rights which the accused might enjoy. For example, false information was fed to editors of underground journals who, having published this, could then be charged with spreading false reports; this was better than charging them with anti-Soviet propaganda, for it discredited them while making it impossible for them to plead that they had merely published facts. At the same time selectivity, indeed moderation, was applied in the matter of punishment. Internationally known dissidents were deprived of Soviet citizenship when abroad. Lesser-known dissidents were offered a choice of an exit visa or a trial which would put them in prison. It was at this time that psychiatric institutes were used to take certain dissidents out of circulation, a policy which finally, in 1984, led to the exclusion (until 1989) of Soviet representatives from the World Psychiatric Association. Those who merely dabbled in dissidence were warned off by such means as threats to promotion prospects or to their children's educational opportunities. Such measures began to wear down the dissident movement, and the KGB closed the mesh of its nets so that those who once felt themselves safe (notably, those who had carefully refrained from contacts with foreigners) also found themselves under threat. Although in the mid-1970s the dissident movement had seemed to stand fast, by the time Andropov left the KGB in

1982 it had diminished to a minor irritant, and Andropov's reputation had been enhanced.

In a society where a small class of administrators controlled the allocation to citizens of scarce resources like residence permits, visas, imported goods, housing, educational opportunities, and many other normal requirements of twentieth century life, the opportunities for bribe-taking and other forms of corruption were great. Under Stalin, corruption was not blatant, but under Brezhnev it was, and it excited disapproval and envy among those who witnessed it and venom among those who suffered from it. Brezhnev himself, by his easy-going reactions and his tolerance of the misdemeanours of his colleagues and supporters, and also by his taste for high living (shared by his family), did little to reverse this trend. It was left to Andropov, with occasional vocal but unspecific backing from Brezhnev, to tackle this problem, although the campaign against corruption continued into the Gorbachev years.

The campaign seems to have been conducted at all levels. It was not fully reported, but the newspapers did mention a selection of cases ranging from big scandals warranting executions to the minor sins of lesser mortals like headteachers and shop assistants, who were reprimanded, had their pay reduced, or were dismissed. A feature of the big cases was the long intervals between arrest, trial, and execution, and this is one of the circumstances that suggested that the accused, especially if they had party affiliations, had protectors in high places. More specifically, Brezhnev's death was followed by the execution of several offenders whose death sentences still awaited consummation. The events in Poland, where the ruling regime had collapsed amid revelations of gross corruption and self-enrichment, alerted party leaders to the dangers of widespread corruption in their own ranks, and in 1980 the Central Committee passed a resolution against official corruption which made a point of stressing that corrupt officials should be dealt with 'no matter who they might be'.

The 'great caviare scandal' was one of the bigger cases handled by the KGB in the late 1970s. It seemed to come to a head in 1979, but the execution of the convicted deputy minister for fisheries did not take place until 1982. This was a large-scale fraud in which caviare was despatched in tins labelled as herring. Much of it was exported, the foreign importing agents depositing pay-offs in western banks, to be used for currency speculation or high living when the conspiring soviet officials made their business trips abroad.

In 1981 a former mayor of Tbilisi was among those executed for bribe-taking. Georgia had long been a centre of corruption, and it was the KGB that was behind the purge of the Georgian party organization which resulted, among other things, in Shevardnadze being appointed first secretary of the Georgian party, charged with the continuation of the clean-up. In nearby Azerbaizhan the local party was similarly dealt with, and a KGB professional, Aliyev, became first secretary.

In 1982 the head of the state visa office, who was accused of demanding fees ten times higher than the official rate for exit visas, was dismissed. After Andropov became party secretary a number of deputy ministers resigned either because they were corrupt or had 'failed to prevent corruption' (probably a euphemism for 'not proven'). A public prosecutor in Kirgizia was among those executed for taking bribes. Meanwhile, Shevardnadze claimed that he had rooted out corruption and nepotism in Georgia, and turned his attention to drug abuse and alcoholism. Under Chernenko the campaign retained its impetus. Some officials were executed, several Ukrainian ministers were dismissed for incompetence or corruption, and the director of the State Circus finally came face to face with his sentence, which turned out to be only imprisonment. There were further dismissals in the Gorbachev years including, in 1985, that of a deputy minister of construction, said to have enriched himself by accepting bribes for new apartments. The rising status of the KGB was accompanied by a tide of books and articles that praised its work and its traditions. Meanwhile, the cunning of one of the KGB's foes, the foreign secret services, was kept in the public view, with calls for constant vigilance. At Tallinn it was reported that they were smuggling subversive T-shirts into the Soviet Union:

... They know that not every fashionable young man wants to put on a T-shirt with the Stars and Stripes. So they put on the T-shirts the slogan 'July is better than October'. This might seem quite inoffensive—many people prefer warm summer to chilly autumn . . . But our ideological enemies mean something else. In July the US constitution was adopted, and in October the USSR constitution.[3]

Above all, the KGB triumphed over the ministry of internal affairs (MVD), which had rival claims in security matters. Indeed, it seems quite likely that the protection of corrupt officials, which so often seemed to thwart or weaken KGB investigators, was inspired by MVD operatives. The minister of the interior, like so many Brezhnev appointees (including Tikhonov, the premier) had attended the same institute (Dnepropetrovsk Metallurgical Institute) as Brezhnev, and had been vice-chairman of the Moldavian republic government when Brezhnev had been first secretary of the Moldavian party organization. He had no police experience, was himself corrupt, and owed his career to Brezhnev. When Andropov became

---

[3] From the newspaper *Vodnyi transport*, 13 December 1984, p. 4, reporting on the responsible tasks of the port's officials.

general secretary he dismissed this man, replacing him with Fedorchuk, a KGB professional who had headed that organization in the months after Andropov's departure. The former interior minister was then put under investigation, one of the matters under study being the mysterious diversion of twenty Mercedes cars ostensibly imported for the police during his term of office. In late 1984 his sudden death was interpreted as suicide.

After Fedorchuk's promotion to interior minister, Chebrikov, a former Brezhnev protégé who saw no reason to put personal loyalty to the defunct party secretary before professional duty and advancement, became head of the KGB and it seemed likely that the latter, in charge of security policing, and the MVD, responsible for ordinary policing, would work more co-operatively together. The MVD, evidently, had its own problems, for there had been complaints in 1982 that ordinary street crime was becoming a menace in certain cities, with the police often turning a blind, or bribed, eye to it.

With its men in charge of the KGB and MVD, with five of its professionals in the Politburo of 1986 (Aliyev had been brought to Moscow by Andropov), the KGB was strongly represented in state and party. Further signs of its status were the restrictive laws and decrees that were passed in the early 1980s, almost certainly inspired by the requirements of the security service. In late 1982, new stricter frontier regulations were introduced to help the work of the KGB's military frontier guards. In 1983, further restrictions were placed on the movements and activities of foreign journalists. International direct dialling, introduced to the Soviet telephone system in time for the Moscow Olympics, was discontinued, as the system provided an unwelcome avenue for unofficial contacts between Soviet citizens and foreigners. It became unlawful to send printed material abroad without a permit. In 1984 a new law provided fines for citizens who without official permission gave excessive help to foreign visitors; apparently offering a lift could be an offence.

Meanwhile, the KGB, which in many ways was itself a military organization, worked closer with the armed services by providing intelligence and organizing some highly specialized auxiliary forces. Its operatives wore their uniforms more often, and in 1984 the rank of marshal was instituted for its head.

The economy

The slackening growth rates which caused anxiety in the 1970s continued into the 1980s. Labour shortages seemed likely to continue, and labour productivity was not by itself making up for this shortfall. By the time Gorbachev became party secretary the concept of 'intensive development' had been accepted, but ways of putting it into effect were still under discussion. The term implied a shift away from the concept of extensive development (the 'more and more' philosophy) as had been practised ever since the early five-year plans, towards development by the improvement of quality of output and quality of technique.

By the mid-1980s, even India was exporting grain to the USSR. Agricultural production remained disappointing. There were defects in the existing situation which for too long had been neglected; the party's emphasis on investment in production rather than services had meant that essential facilities had been starved of capital. The abysmal state of rural roads was one reason for agriculture's failure. Another was the lack of such essential services as storage and refrigeration, which meant that a high proportion of food output never reached the consumer. Brezhnev's 'Food Programme' sought to remedy some of these defects but in general it was one more attempt to solve a long-standing problem by massive investment that was not always wisely directed. Gorbachev was given responsibility for this plan but somehow avoided blame for its relative lack of success. In 1985 Gorbachev, by then general secretary, carried out a radical reorganization of the several ministries which shared responsibility for agriculture. This entailed the establishment of a kind of super-ministry, the State Agroindustrial Committee, which took over, among others, the functions of the former Ministry of Agriculture.

Agricultural failure was a main reason for the slow growth of national income. In 1984, for example, which was a relatively good year for industry with output growing by 4 per cent, a little higher than the plan, gross national income rose by only 2.6 per cent, rather less than planned.

A euphemism for economic reform, 'measures to improve the economic mechanism', became widely used. Various expedients were tried, and under Andropov there was a large-scale experiment in which hundreds of enterprises belonging to five ministries were transferred to a new system intended to give greater responsibility and greater independence to managers. The experiment included a reduction in the number of index figures used to specify and measure plan fulfilment; growth of output (in real rather than money terms), growth of labour productivity, and the extent to which delivery contracts were fulfilled were emphasized as criteria of performance. Achievement or over-achievement of delivery contracts resulted in substantial increases of rewards, in terms of wages and social services. In general, the results of this experiment were deemed satisfactory, even though the ministries were slow to lose their habit of interfering in management, and it was decided to extend the system to other industries. However, the best route to the new proposed 'intensive' economy was still not clear, and Gorbachev castigated the economics profession, which, he had belatedly discovered, was unable to provide clear answers to urgent questions.

Some sectors of industry, including engineering, did comparatively well, while others lagged. In the key energy sector, coal production by 1985 was substantially below the plan. West Siberian oil and gas, which earlier had been expected to be the jewel in the economic crown, were also disappointing, although this was largely because expectations had been too high, too remote from the very real difficulties of gaining access to the huge energy assets of that region. Oil and gas exports were needed to pay for the import of western technology and of American grain, so the shortfall here was especially serious; there were few other commodities which found a ready market abroad. When, in mid-decade, Soviet gas and oil production seemed poised to reach high outputs, it was at a time of falling world oil prices. Meanwhile, the nuclear generating programme was also behind schedule. The five-year plan specified that 12 per cent of electricity would be nuclear-generated by 1985, but this target had to be reduced to 9 per cent; then, in 1986, came the Chernobyl disaster which caused additional delays.

Another high-technology industry, computers, was still held back by lack of co-ordination between ministries and by its low order of priority. Although computers had been recognized as important in the 1960s, especially for processing the enormous quantity of paperwork originated by the planned economy, the promises of that decade were not kept. However, in the 1970s the utility of the microprocessor was noticed and clones of western chips were developed. Powerful computers were produced by connecting 'slices' of microprocessors in series, a technique that resulted in machines that were failure-prone compared to the complex integrated circuits favoured in the west. In the early 1980s it was realized that schools needed large numbers of microcomputers, but because they were scarce and needed elsewhere the educational system was largely deprived of this resource, threatening the future availability of computer-friendly users. To secure a reliable microcomputer a copy of the Apple machine was introduced, but this, too, could not be manufactured in large enough numbers. At this time three ministries were each producing IBM-compatible PC machines and they achieved the feat of producing three designs that were incompatible with each other and could not be used with western PCs either.[4] Later, in the Gorbachev years, legislation that eased the path of

---

[4] The international computer industry was on the inch standard but, perhaps to show how progressive it was, the Soviet industry used the metric system. This meant that an ostensibly IBM-compatible Soviet computer could not plug into western IBM-compatible equipment.

Soviet/non-Soviet partnerships encouraged several joint ventures in computer manufacturing, usually entailing the assembly in the USSR of computer parts supplied from the west. Some useful designs were introduced, but only enough to supply a fraction of the need.

With some sectors producing according to plan and with others lagging behind, it was evident that the industrial economy was badly co-ordinated. The planning system, and the State Planning Commission (*Gosplan*) in particular, was meant to eliminate the mismatching of supply and demand, so the existence of bottlenecks in the economy had an ideological and political significance which the party found disquieting. The performance of *Gosplan* began to be questioned, as did that of several ministries. One of Andropov's first acts was to dismiss the minister of transport, on the grounds that the railways were performing badly. In later years, other ministers were put aside in favour of supposedly more competent ones.

In late 1985, Gorbachev took a step that, in the opinion of many, was already too long-delayed: the chairman of *Gosplan* was removed. Since the notice of his retirement was published without the usual thanks for services rendered, the Soviet newspaper reader would have realized that this was a virtual dismissal. *Gosplan* had long been criticized, usually indirectly and by implication, for authoritarian interference in details of economic life and for the obstacles it raised to initiative and ideas originating from industry. With the individual enterprise subject to constant interference (or, equally damaging, delayed consents) from its ministry, and with ministries themselves subject to interference and obstruction from the all-powerful *Gosplan*, it had become progressively clearer that in the modern world, where industry needed to be agile and innovative, flexible and decisive, the Soviet economy was at a disadvantage. When to all these difficulties was added the circumstance that quite often the co-operation and co-ordination of several ministries were required to get a project moving, the inertia of much of Soviet industry seemed explicable. It was said that the reason why, in the 1970s, Japanese industrialists moved away from many of their expected co-operative ventures with Soviet industry in the Far East, was that they could never get a prompt, clear answer to their questions; the Soviet managers with whom they were dealing had to consult the Moscow ministries about quite minor details. In the end the Japanese showed a preference for doing business with the Chinese, who seemed less handicapped by bureaucratic constraints.

Estimates of the real growth of Soviet production vary, but it would be broadly accurate to describe 1960–5 as years in which, on average, the gross national product rose by 5 per cent annually, and in the next five years there was probably a small improvement, with an average of, perhaps 5.25.

Then came the decline to about 3.75 per cent in 1970–5, and a little more than 2.5 in 1976–80, with a further deterioration bringing growth close to 2 per cent for the first few years of the 1980s. Because the population was growing, output per head grew at a slower rate, declining from a little more than 4 per cent in 1966–70 to less than 2 per cent in 1976–80, with a further drop below 2 per cent in the next couple of years.

There were two broad interpretations of the drop in growth rates. The Soviet view was that this was a temporary fall below a long-term trend which would turn out to be higher, although probably not as high as in the 1950s and 1960s. Outside the USSR, many observers also held this view, while others suggested that what was happening was a long-term drop which had its origins in the nature of the Soviet system and would, therefore, be difficult to reverse.

Proponents of the first view could point to the failure of agriculture, which brought repercussions throughout the economy; better luck with the weather, and some organizational changes, would improve agricultural performance and this would soon be reflected in higher growth rates for the economy as a whole. Moreover, they said, there were certain other bottlenecks that had limited Soviet economic growth but which, when put right, would allow a new upward and onward surge. At the beginning of the 1980s three areas of the economy, apart from agriculture, were regarded as critical. These were ferrous metallurgy, whose average annual growth rate declined to little more than one per cent in 1976–80 and on whose output many other sectors depended: construction, suffering from a labour and steel shortage, and whose difficulties manifested themselves in very long building times for projects such as factories and housing; and transport, whose inadequacies affected practically all branches of the economy. Beginning with Andropov's leadership, some ministers and deputy ministers in sectors where performance was bad were replaced, but these were really symbolic acts, having the effect of making new and surviving ministers and managements try harder, rather than actually solving the physical problems which industries faced.

In the case of transport, for example, failures were hardly the fault of the minister and his deputies, but were the consequence of policies handed down from above and usually originating in *Gosplan*. The bulk of freight transport was handled by the railways; in fact their freight traffic already exceeded the freight traffic of all the rest of the world's railways added together. But *Gosplan*, right from the 1920s, had always held the view that rather than build new lines, the better policy would be to use existing lines more intensively. Possibly, in the 1920s and 1930s, this policy was justifiable, especially since other branches of the economy were in great need of all available investment. But Gosplan persisted with this policy far too long. New lines were almost always for the purpose of opening up new sources of raw materials; even the long Baikal–Amur Railway, which was in the final stages of construction in 1986 and which ostensibly provided a second route to the Pacific across eastern Siberia, had the effect of adding to the railways' traffic while doing little to reduce the intensity of use of existing lines. The result was that on some main lines, and especially the east–west trunk lines through the Urals, traffic density began to approach 100 per cent of what was theoretically possible, which meant, among other things, that a breakdown of one train could tie up traffic over hundreds of miles of track. Yet *Gosplan* still held to the view that certain technical innovations could obviate the need for more routes. Such innovations, which often had a 'quick-fix' character, included the introduction of eight-axle instead of four-axle freightcars (*Gosplan* economists seemed unaware that such vehicles would pose stability problems), longer loops and sidings (even though in the most serious bottlenecks there was no space for these), and wider freightcars (which, apparently unperceived by *Gosplan*, would risk the decapitation of any railwayman unwise enough to stand between two passing trains). Moreover, *Gosplan* did not limit its activity to broad planning, but interfered in detail. On the railways, for example, *Gosplan* insisted that a new diesel engine, designed for the Red Navy and then rejected by the latter, be used in a new locomotive type, even though Soviet Railways had designed a better one; the resulting locomotive, built in hundreds of units, was markedly inferior to the models it was designed to replace.

The question of how far bodies like *Gosplan*, and the Soviet planning system in general, were suited to modern economic conditions, was indeed discussed, but debate was hampered because an exhaustive discussion could easily enter onto the sensitive subject of the party's *raison d'être*. In the ultimate analysis, the all-encompassing, all-powerful party justified its position by its role as organizer and distributor of scarce resources for the general good. This was easy enough when industry was mainly heavy industry, and industrial units were large. It was not so easy when, as the experience of the west showed, it was small units which were beginning to make the most significant and useful advances. Possibly it was not just the economy, but the party itself, that was in need of 'new mechanisms'.

Brezhnev's successors did, however, exploit an additional string in their bow. They claimed, and backed their claim with energetic action, that industrial inertia was largely due to wrong attitudes and wrong behaviour. If managers who could not bother to manage, workers who could not bother to work, and citizens who could not bother to emerge from their alcoholic haze, were persuaded or forced to mend their ways, then the economy would assuredly pick up speed, it was said.

The lazy and the liquorish

Although the campaign against the work-shy seemed to come to a peak under Andropov, in reality it had its beginnings under Brezhnev. There was a decree, in 1980, aimed at workers who changed their jobs too frequently or who infringed labour discipline in other ways, and a strengthened 'Parasites' Law' of January 1983 had actually been prepared during the Brezhnev period. The campaign slackened halfway through Andropov's brief tenure of office, was barely kept in being under Chernenko, and was then revived by Gorbachev, although in his first year the latter directed his fire mainly at drunkenness.

Unemployment officially did not exist, and every worker's right to a job was enshrined in the constitution. Many workers, it seemed, did not feel any obligation to reciprocate by working hard at their jobs.[5] In any case, for other reasons apart from the sheer difficulty of doing so, managements were reluctant to shed workers. Even when factories were automated, the work-force was rarely reduced. In administrative jobs the situation was similar. When Gorbachev announced his new State Agro-industrial Committee, it was intimated that more than twenty thousand functionaries would be 'freed', but in fact they stayed on, albeit with different job titles. This meant that the labour shortage was worse than it need have been. In turn, the labour shortage strengthened the situation of individual workers; if a management took the step of enforcing stricter workplace discipline, by requiring workers to be at the workplace during working hours and to work properly while there, then a worker had no difficulty, apart from waiting out the statutory two weeks' notice, in quitting and finding a more compliant employer elsewhere.

Andropov's campaign was preceded and accompanied by meetings and letters to the press in which workers complained of the soft attitude taken towards drunkards, slackers, and 'rolling stones'. Favourable references were made to past Stalinist practices like the labour-book and the harsh punishments for lateness at work, which, it was claimed, might well be reinstituted; this was another example of the need felt by many for a 'strong' leader and which, probably mistakenly, was taken by western

---

[5] One of this author's fond memories is of the buffet car of the day train from Moscow to Leningrad in 1974. On this, the buffet closed at lunchtime because its attendant claimed he was entitled to a lunch-break. Hungry and resentful passengers were told that railway officials could not intervene because the attendant, being trade and not transport, was employed not by the railways but by the ministry of internal trade.

observers to be a resurgence of Stalinism. While comments from the working class tended to favour harsh punishments, those published in the more intellectual papers gave more emphasis to the living and working conditions which encouraged labour indiscipline.

In early 1983 it was clear that the new regime favoured the harsh approach. The police, aided by civilian volunteers, began to conduct raids in the cities during working hours. Fishing people out of queues, shops, hairdressers, swimming pools, public baths, buses, and underground trains, they demanded their identification papers and reasons why they were not at work. Those who had left their papers at home were taken to the police stations, as were those who could not explain why they were not at work. These latter were then reported to their managements and to their local party organizations, and could face reprimands and pay deductions.

This campaign may have done the state more harm than good, for it aroused a great deal of resentment, particularly among those who, though innocent, were greatly inconvenienced, if not insulted, by the police tactics. It was not long before the more extreme actions were abandoned, and more attention was paid to finding out precisely why so many workers were not at work. One very useful measure resulting from this was that shop opening hours were altered so that they were no longer closed at the times when workers were best placed to use them. It had been realized, belatedly, that the reason why workers went shopping in working hours was that, for many, this was the only time when queuing and shopping were possible.

Concurrently, a new campaign was mounted against workers having a second, 'black economy' job. This, apparently, was based on the shaky assumption that a worker deprived of his moonlighting opportunities would work harder at his regular job. The immediate result was that the Soviet citizen found it even harder than previously to obtain essential services like appliance repair, roof-mending, shoe repair, and countless others which the official service organizations were so bad at providing.

Gorbachev, once in power, continued the campaign, but placed more emphasis on drunkenness, which for some years had been regarded as a main cause of absenteeism, work accidents, and poor-quality output. In late 1982, for example, *Pravda* was naming drink as the reason why so many building sites were inactive on Mondays and on Friday afternoons. During Gorbachev's first year the massive propaganda campaign directed against alcoholism did at least change the atmosphere enough to embolden some managements to actually dismiss workers who were habitually drunk. But the problem was far from solved. Here again, the railways provided good examples of difficulties found throughout the economy. In the early 1980s railway accidents were increasing to an alarming frequency, and a majority of those attributed to human error involved drink. But existing labour legislation made it impossible, among other things, to prevent a driver taking out a train merely because his breath smelt of alcohol. Moreover, although it was possible to punish a driver for drunkenness by demoting him, labour legislation provided that at the end of a fixed term he had to be returned to his previous job.

In terms of pure alcohol consumption per head, the USSR was not the world's leader, but it was very close behind the world leaders (France and Italy). Unlike the two latter, though, a high proportion of its intake was in spirits, much more damaging than wine and beer. Although statistics for Soviet consumption are hard to construct, it seems likely that at least half the drink consumed was in the form of distilled spirits, mainly vodka, with average alcohol contents of more than 40 per cent. Also, Russians still tended to favour the drinking bout rather than the sipped glass; hence fatalities and hangovers were more common, and the death-rate was increased by the use of hangover remedies which were themselves liable to induce death. In the 1970s, increased Soviet consumption of wine brought little or no relief, probably because low-quality, and hence more toxic, alcohol was used to stiffen Soviet wines sold outside the traditional wine-consuming regions of the Crimea and Caucasus. *Samogon*, illicitly brewed spirits, which may have accounted for a quarter of total consumption, is usually reckoned to be more toxic than the factory-made brands.

Drunkenness in public was an increasing burden for the police, even though production-line methods were used in the form of sobering-up stations to which drunks could be taken, perhaps given a cold shower and a lecture, fined, and have their documents examined in order that their employers could be informed. Drunks who, by excessive intake or consequent accident, were too ill to follow this regime, were parked in special hospital wards. In Moscow, in the 1970s, there were about thirty sobering-up stations. A Soviet source estimated that in 1979 some 16–18 million drunks passed through sobering-up stations (that is, about 46,000 per day or 1 per cent of the urban population per month). Presumably these thirsty souls, all lit up and nowhere to go, were only the tip of an alcoholic iceberg, for many others would have enjoyed their hangovers in the privacy of their own homes or under the comradely protection of their workplace. In the mid-1970s a Soviet demographer estimated that the social costs attributable to alcohol actually exceeded the value of the profits and duties derived from its sale.

The man on the street had a difficult time in the mid-1980s:

My classmate, for example, was scared of going home by himself at the end of the month. He quite seriously stated that at that time the police would trap lone passers-by.

'But why?' we asked.

'The sobering-up stations have to fulfil their monthly plan', he explained . . .

There were many corroborating stories. 'We still have a plan,' N. Kirilenko, police captain, told me. 'Each year the Moscow City Executive's financial directorate demands 200,000. It's absurd, of course. How can you plan drunkenness?'

And in fact, looking back at the height of the anti-alcohol campaign, people were grabbed as they left restaurants, were 'taken' from weddings, banquets and funerals! And then the old dreary path of the report sent to the place of work, attendance before the trade union committee, loss of bonuses, going to the back of the queue for housing or for a car.[6]

In terms of ready availability in the stores, vodka rivalled Brezhnev's memoirs, with few interruptions of supply and little need for queuing. The growth in consumption had several likely causes: disposable incomes were rising faster than the supply of worthwhile things to buy; there was increased drinking by women; a campaign which was intended to reduce vodka consumption by encouraging wine-drinking ended up by increasing the sales of both; there was more drinking by teenagers; and there was loneliness and job frustration. Against these, the state deployed the price weapon in 1981, imposing considerable price increases. These did achieve a reduced per capita consumption of 'official' beverages, but larger sales of sugar (popularly used for making *Samogon*) as well as of alcohol substitutes, like anti-freeze and cleaning fluids, suggested that the health of the population did not necessarily benefit.

Gorbachev finally abandoned his anti-alcohol campaign in 1990. Just as with Nicholas II's prohibition of 1914, it had brought great unpopularity at a period when the regime could not afford to lose support. It had reduced the state's income, and it had limited citizens' opportunities of drowning sorrows in drink.

Soviet society

While campaigns against the drunk and the work-shy were the most conspicuous social measures in the early 1980s, other long-standing problems continued to cause anxiety. Among these was the existence and apparent growth of various kinds of nationalism within the USSR. What made the problem seem urgent was that the Great Russian population was not increasing, while other nationalities, especially those of Central Asia, continued to have a high natural increase. For economic planners, there was the added dimension that Central Asia was the one remaining labour reservoir which, through migration, might conceivably relieve labour shortages throughout the Soviet Union. Nationalism, which at times could

[6] *Gudok*, 21 May 1991, 3.

better be defined as chauvinism, was also on the upsurge among the Great Russians, who sometimes felt the other nationalities were being pampered at their expense and who were well aware of what seemed a threatening demographic trend. The January 1989 census would reinforce this fear with its figure of just 50.8 as the percentage of Russians in the USSR.

Open nationalist dissent was confined to the Caucasian and Baltic republics, although in the Ukraine it seemed to be barely contained below the surface. In Estonia, in 1980 and 1981, there were actual demonstrations, said to consist mainly of students, at which the banned Estonian national flag was exhibited and the official union-republican flag burned. It was also said that the authorities believed that part of the problem was the ease with which Estonians picked up Finnish television, from which they learned, among other things, harmful versions of what was happening in Poland. They had an attempted general strike in late 1981, but this was easily smothered by the authorities, and some participants were imprisoned. Meanwhile, in Georgia, there were demonstrations in favour of a professor who had been dismissed after stressing the importance of teaching Georgian history.

As elsewhere in the world, the question of nationalism was interwoven with the question of language, and the languages policy of the USSR inevitably raised hackles among the non-Russian nationalities. In principle, Russian was taught throughout the non-Russian republics' schools as a second language, and it could be claimed that this was necessary so as to provide a *lingua franca* for the whole of the USSR. But the non-Russian languages were hardly taught outside their own republics. This meant that whereas a Russian family moving to a non-Russian republic would find its own language, and hence culture, awaiting it in the new location, non-Russian emigrants would need to accept a degree of russianization if they were to be assimilated in the Russian Republic. Thus, apart from the historical circumstance that Muscovite expansion had naturally spread Russians throughout the territory of the developed USSR, Russian migration was further assisted by the language policies. In some republics (including Estonia at 28 per cent and Latvia at 33 per cent) the Russian proportion of the population was large enough to provoke social resentments on both sides. In 1983 the Politburo was discussing measures to actually intensify the teaching of Russian in the union republics; evidently the nationalist bull was to be taken by the horns.

Another critical social anxiety which the USSR shared with other countries concerned the way the younger generation was being brought up. Both Chernenko and Aliyev spoke of a generation which thought it could earn respect not by its knowledge and diligence but by the costly objects which its parents' money could buy for it. One element of this anxiety was expressed by criticism of the Komsomol organization. This was supposed to attract young adults to politically and socially useful leisure-time occupations, but apparently was having less and less success in pulling young people away from the unproductive pleasures and pastimes which modern times offered.

Meanwhile, a quite deep reappraisal of Soviet education resulted in 1984 guidelines for its reform. In part, this represented a new phase in the long-term struggle between academic and vocational education, and this time the swing was in favour of vocational. The educational system was turning out twice as many highly skilled graduates as were needed, at the same time as there was an increasing shortage of workers in the middle-skill categories. Entry to the two senior years of secondary school was, therefore, to be restricted, thereby diverting more pupils to vocational training. At the same time, the school starting age was reduced from seven to six, making the full school course eleven instead of ten years. The number of school hours to be devoted to 'labour training' remained con-troversial; in 1977 they had been doubled to four hours a week for the two senior years, mainly at the expense of foreign language teaching, and in the new reforms eight hours were proposed even though some critics foresaw a resultant erosion of academic standards. Teachers were to be trained for five instead of four years, a response to criticisms of their quality by, among others, Andropov. As for 'percentomania', the practice of taking into consideration the pupil's average marks over the year when entry to higher education was sought, and which created enormous pressure by parents on teachers and a consequent practice of bribery, blackmail, and threats in pursuit of inflated marks, this was expected to be contained by the requirement that this type of assessment be terminated.

Under Khrushchev, and even more so under his successors, the gap be-tween morality and legality remained obvious. But, as in other countries, those operating the legal system, unlike those drawn into it, believed in their propriety and effectiveness. For Soviet citizens the most obviously repellent feature of their system was the duality of justice. There was one privileged class, party and government officials, that was almost above the law. If one of these office-holders broke the law there might be a reprim-and from the party organization, but that would usually be the end of it; there would be no court action. Ordinary citizens who went to court found that the whole system was weighted in favour of the prosecution. At some periods acquittals were so rare that the legal profession regarded them as failures that had to be reinvestigated. This meant that the innocent were frequently punished and, moreover, that it was relatively easy for officials to get rid of troublemakers by concocting a criminal case against them. There was a phenomenon that became known as 'telephone law', in which high officials, by a telephone call to the procuracy or to a judge, could decide the outcome of a case. Judges, even that proportion that had a respect for truth, could not be independent; they came up for reappointment every five years and knew that if they displeased the local party organization they would be jettisoned.

Another social service in need of reform was the medical service. For the ordinary patient, the signs of a monstrously defective service included long waits for emergency ambulances, the occasional need to bribe doctors, nurses, and officials for such luxuries as anaesthetics or a place in a ward where there was some space between the beds, inability to actually find and obtain the drugs specified in doctors' prescriptions and, for alarmists, the dread possibility that the operating team might be too drunk to work safely but not drunk enough to be sent off duty. Doctors, who were largely female, were paid quite low salaries in comparison with other occupations, and this was said to be one of the reasons for demanding bribes. The existence of what in effect was a separate, superior medical service, with its own hospitals and facilities, for the privileged classes of the *nomenklatura* and certain top institutions, was probably one reason why the decline of the regular health service had been allowed to continue.

Ambulance services were poor and their staff mostly untrained in first aid. This helped to ensure that about 15 per cent of those who initially survived serious accidents died later, a rate which was about ten times higher than in the USA. This in turn was one reason why the USSR, with about one-tenth the vehicle ownership of the USA, had roughly the same annual total of road deaths. Other reasons were poor roads and abysmal vehicle maintenance and, according to some Russian citizens, the high car-ownership among Georgians, for whom spectacularly dangerous driving was irrefutable proof of manliness. Alcohol-related car accidents were comparatively rare, thanks largely to strict policing.

The world outside

In terms of maximum gains for least risk, foreign policy under Brezhnev seemed effective, although in some cases his successors had to deal with the negative side-effects of past successes. In general, what happened was that, taking advantage of what seemed a favourable 'correlation of forces' (to use a favourite Soviet term), the USSR succeeded in strengthening its influence among the uncommitted nations of the world and in bringing its strategic forces into a position of parity, or near-parity, with those of the USA. It was this equalizing of the strategic balance, together with perceived

American weakness after the Vietnam War, which seemed to give Soviet foreign and military policy its chance, but the price turned out to be high, for it helped to bring about the decay of the spirit of *détente*. Together with the emergence of an aggressive US administration in 1981, this meant that tension between the USA and the USSR tautened at a time when the Soviet Union, in order to tackle economic and other internal problems, needed relief from the arms race, good trading relations with the west, and an end to expensive competition for influence in the Third World. The use of Soviet power in Afghanistan, in particular, and also in other areas, including Ethiopia and Angola, was a powerful factor encouraging the USA, whose stance under President Carter had not been especially aggressive, to begin a new weapons programme. Meanwhile, the bolder Soviet policies had aroused anxieties that tended to push the USA, Western Europe, Japan, and China into a closer relationship. In Moscow, this coming together of outside powers aroused nightmare visions of a new encirclement, even though a real alliance between these four seemed highly unlikely. Finally, there was the Polish question.

Unrest in Poland grew during the Brezhnev years from simple meat riots, which proved little except that Poles were carnivorous, to the emergence of the Solidarity movement and the threat that this represented to all communist regimes of the Soviet type. The idea of a free trade union movement was disturbing in a Soviet Union which at that very time was experiencing weak, but unmistakable, signs of worker unrest. Indeed, a fleeting shift of trade union attention from output to welfare, which occurred at this time, may be attributed to a realization that unless the Soviet unions did something more to represent the true interests of the workers, then something like Solidarity might be reproduced within Soviet borders. In 1981, Brezhnev actually warned the Soviet unions that they should learn from Poland's painful experience and 'listen more sensitively to the voice of the masses.'

In late 1981 the decisive step was taken to master Solidarity and, with Soviet assistance, the Polish military leadership took over the government. Great care was taken to filter news from Poland, and the average Soviet citizen, however curious, would have been unable to obtain a clear picture of what was happening. For this and other reasons, domestic public opinion was decidedly hostile to the Polish workers, who were regarded as spoiled children, unable to show gratitude to their true friends, ready to betray socialist principles for the sake of a few material gains. However, the imposition of martial law in Poland and the subsequent suppression of Solidarity was not received favourably by many communist parties in countries outside the Soviet orbit, whose members had frequently pointed out that Solidarity had been merely demanding the kind of society which marxist revolutionaries had traditionally striven to create. The Italian communist party pushed opposition as far as a major break with the Soviet party, while the Central Committee of the Spanish party passed a resolution demanding the end of repression in Poland and a continuation of the Polish 'renewal'.

By the time Gorbachev came to power the Polish situation, though delicate, seemed well under control. Elsewhere in the communist bloc, Roumania continued to play its maverick role. When the Soviet Union, followed by the other countries of the Soviet bloc, decided to boycott the 1984 Olympic Games, held in the USA and with no guarantee that Soviet athletes would be securely isolated from politics, Roumania decided to participate nevertheless. In the fortieth anniversary celebrations of the liberation of Roumania from the fascists, the Russian and Roumanian accounts of 1944 varied, the Roumanian account minimizing the role of the Red Army. That this account was written by the brother of the Roumanian party leader added piquancy to the affair. Meanwhile, the USSR retaliated by criticizing Roumania's treatment of its Hungarian minority in Transylvania, a matter which for long had been in dispute between Bucharest and Budapest.

Successive Soviet leaders expressed a desire to improve relations with China. A possible alliance between the USA and China was frightening; even ordinary, unpolitical Russian citizens well understood this. When Andropov came to power he took advantage of the gathering of foreign leaders at Brezhnev's funeral to make conciliatory gestures and later referred to China as 'our great neighbour'. But China, although it too would have benefited from better relations, was deterred by the continued Soviet presence in Afghanistan, Soviet support for Vietnam's campaign against Campuchea (Cambodia), and the stationing of massive Soviet forces on the Russo-Chinese frontier.

In the early 1980s, expulsions of Soviet diplomats from foreign capitals became more frequent, almost resembling a mass movement. It was not only from capitals of the western world that alleged spies were returned to the Soviet Union, but from Third World states like Bangladesh and Thailand. Even Ethiopia, a Soviet protégé, took this action in 1984. Sweden, which had long maintained a careful neutral attitude in the confrontation between east and west, was offended by incursions of Soviet submarines into her territorial waters. Scandinavia, willy-nilly, was of great strategic interest, lying athwart a possible direct line of attack on European Russia from the west, and bordering on the Kola Peninsula with its large concentration of Soviet forces (the largest concentration of armed force anywhere in the world, according to some commentators). Soviet submarines were reported by the weak Swedish navy and coastguard more than fifty times in 1982, and when a Soviet nuclear submarine was temporarily stranded inside Swedish waters Stockholm made a very strong protest. It was believed that such incursions, which included the despatch of midget submarines into Swedish ports and fiords, were for the purpose of surveying possible landing points.

A number of countries imposed economic sanctions, notably curtailment of trade, as a reaction to the declaration of martial law in Poland. In general, however, the USA was unsuccessful in persuading her allies to take a strong line on trade. In 1981–2 Washington attempted to prevent certain West European companies supplying equipment for the pipeline being built to move West Siberian natural gas to eastern and western Europe. The thought of Soviet oil and gas being supplied to Western Europe in exchange for hard currency had long caused anxiety in Washington, and when western companies, subsidiaries of American companies or building American-designed equipment under licence, received Soviet orders, various bans were imposed on them. But the western European governments, in a rare outburst of protest at the way the USA was treating them, employed all kinds of legal and political means to frustrate the American intention. The European will was fortified by the knowledge that the USA was still profiting from its exports of grain to the USSR.

The homeward flow of Soviet diplomats was swollen by the expulsions which followed the 1983 shooting down, with heavy civilian casualties, of a South Korean civil airliner that had strayed over Sakhalin and Kamchatka on a flight between Alaska and Tokyo. How, or perhaps why, it had strayed was unclear, and its destruction by Soviet fighters was not at all prompt. But the fact remained that the Soviet forces had carried out what was seen as a barbaric act. Perhaps the most pointed lesson of this disaster was that the Soviet frontier was exceedingly sensitive, and the USSR would take no risks.

The deterioration of relations with the USA showed itself in many ways, including the end of the US–Soviet co-operation in space ventures, but notably in the question of arms policies. Several attempts to reach agreements on arms limitation failed, partly because of the western decision to place intermediate-range (Cruise and Pershing) missiles in Europe. Capable of reaching Soviet cities, the short flight-time of these missiles was a frightening new factor for the Soviet defences, and at one stage Andropov stated that they would compel the Soviet Union to adopt a 'launch on warning' policy; that is, Soviet missiles would be launched at the west as soon as the first (and hence unchecked) reports of oncoming Cruise and Pershing missiles were received. Thus this new stage of the arms race threatened to bring closer the possibility of nuclear war by accident. It was not the US government which had initiated the idea, but western governments, wanting a counter to the Soviet intermediate-range missiles that had been installed in eastern Europe.

Later, President Reagan's enthusiasm for his 'Strategic Defense Initiative', however unbalanced and starry-eyed it might have been, caused the USSR new anguish, and to a large extent poisoned, or re-poisoned, the waters; at a personal 'summit' meeting at Geneva in 1985 Gorbachev and Reagan appeared to have created a good relationship on the personal level, but this was a long way from being translated into political agreement. Earlier, the US President's public reference to the Soviet Union as an 'evil empire' could only reinforce Soviet suspicion that Washington had embarked on a really active anti-Soviet policy, the substance of which was that US pressure was to force the Soviet Union to devote increasing resources to armaments, thereby making it impossible to find the means required to cope with increasingly urgent economic and social problems.

The view inside

By the mid-1980s there were signs that environmental issues would be treated more seriously in the USSR or, more precisely, that their theoretical discussion would more often be translated into practical measures. The apparent abandonment of grandiose schemes for diverting northern rivers into the arid south seemed to suggest that the new leadership would be less reckless than its predecessors, a trend that could hardly fail to be reinforced by the Chernobyl accident.

Environmental problems had been discussed in scientific journals since at least the 1960s, and as the years passed this discussion moved also into popular publications, and the subject found itself mentioned in such diverse places as school curricula, the 1977 Constitution, and the party journal *Kommunist*; the latter, in September 1979, had an article acknowledging the environmental cost of the nuclear power programme.

The need of the Soviet regime to exploit natural resources as fast as possible meant that in its early decades wasteful and harmful decisions were made. The trough may have been reached in Khrushchev's time, with the near-conversion of the Virgin Lands into a new dust-bowl. It was at this time, too, that the party asserted in its 1961 Programme that communism '. . . raises mankind to an enormous level of superiority over nature, enabling a greater and more complete use of its inherent forces'. Such assertions had been made in the past, too, and Marx himself had written in the same key (although Engels with his greater perception remarked that the new socialist era should not flatter itself with its victories over nature because 'every such victory brings its own vengeance'). For long, misuse of the environment was treated in the Soviet Union as something that happens under capitalism but not under socialism.

What seems to have been the first of the large and public environmental disputes occurred in the 1960s, when the celebrated purity and scientific pricelessness of Lake Baikal appeared to be threatened by new wood-processing plants. In this instance, the combined weight of several scientific institutions won a partial, but significant, victory. Also in the mid-1960s, the Russian Republic issued a decree intended to protect the environment from wrong-headed or vandalistic industrial projects, but this seems to have been largely ignored; in Soviet conditions, a manager was not likely to pay a heavy penalty should he damage the environment in pursuit of his production target. This unsatisfactory situation continued until at least the mid-1980s, but by that time public opinion, as well as party opinion, was ready for more energetic defensive actions. Small and middle managers were increasingly taken to court, although their punishment hardly fitted the crime. Managers did not themselves pay fines, for that came out of their enterprises' budget; indeed, some enterprises maintained a fund from which such fines could be paid, a sure indication that it was cheaper to pay fines than take protective measures.

It was not until Gorbachev became general secretary that environmental issues received the attention they deserved. A State Committee for Environmental Protection was formed in 1988, and a Green Party was founded. Newly uncovered environmental horrors were well publicized. Among them was the shrinking of the Aral Sea due to so much water being diverted to irrigation, and the consequent unbalancing of the region surrounding it. Citizens became more conscious of bad air, and aware of, for example, the high rate of bronchial disease among children in certain industrial areas. Magnitogorsk, a socialist 'company town' dominated by the Lenin Steel Works, was said to exhale a million tons of solids from its smoke-stacks every year, and downwind there was a 100-mile stretch of grey snow in winter and brown grass in summer. In such towns car headlights were sometimes needed during the day, and children and the aged went to clinics for regular doses of oxygen.

Scientific institutes and local authorities, which sought to widen or enforce laws, found themselves handicapped not only by the priority given to industrial output but also by the familiar problem of bureaucratic structures. When a beach disappeared because building enterprises had removed sand and gravel at the same time as the electricity industry had dammed the rivers whose flow would normally have washed replenishing sand and gravel onto the depleted beaches, it was impossible to lay the blame against any one ministry. A horrifying source of atmospheric pollution in Georgia, the Zestafoni Ferro-alloy Works, was provided with a smoke-abating system only after managers, as well as district state and party officials, were dismissed or transferred, and this did not happen until nearly 300 meetings had been held to discuss the problem. Up in the Kola Peninsula, metallurgy poisoned vast areas of water and forest, with acid rain a particularly damaging agent. The opencast mining for iron ore around Kursk ruined extensive areas of agricultural land and there was little prospect of restoration.

For some new big projects various institutions were invited to make detailed environmental enquiries. The misfortune was that such research followed, rather than preceded, the beginning of construction. But in the case of the big river diversion schemes this sequence took a more intelligent course, with the result that in the mid-1980s it appeared that environmental considerations had prevailed. It would be wrong to describe this as a triumph of scientists over planners, because not all scientists gave priority to the environment over the economy, and not all planners scorned environmental arguments.

The party had not seized upon the environmental issue as one of those fields where its leadership could be shown as essential. The party, and especially its higher reaches, those select few who were listed as suitable for key *nomenklatura* appointments in the administration, enjoyed great privileges, ranging from priority acquisition of scarce goods to feudalistic rights like the use of private game reserves. These could be justified, ultimately, by the importance of the party's role in Soviet society. Every task that demanded a strong centralized response and the mobilization of large forces (that is, the kind of solution for which the party's experience had prepared it) was therefore, potentially, a task which might confirm the party's indispensability. So long as a belief in indispensability could be maintained, the question of 'what is the party for?' would contain no challenge. But the last quarter of the twentieth century was producing problems for which the traditional party approach was not self-evidently the best approach.

In the 1980s what the Soviet Union was trying to do was to modernize, but its modernization was uneasy. It had to come to terms with the modern world, with new technology, with the vastly more effective means of communication. Wary modernization, of course, had been exactly what the tsarist government was undertaking a century earlier. Then, it was the first modernization that was involved, moving from a peasant to an industrial economy, and it was the nature of Russian society and the nature of Russian government which made the process perilous. In the 1980s the first modernization having been achieved under Stalin, the second ('post-industrial') modernization had to be attempted, but again the nature of society and government presented certain problems.

In the nineteenth century, the tsarist regime had been increasingly questioned; its inconveniences could only be justified if it could show that it was doing a good job. The Communist Party in the 1980s also felt a need to show that it was fulfilling an essential role. Traditionally, it was as organizer, planner, and ultimately authority, at a time when scarce resources had to be rigorously allocated to the most necessary sectors of the economy, that the party could justify itself. With *Sputnik*, and more recently with other projects like the Baikal–Amur Railway, it demonstrated what it could do as organizer and inspirer. But the world was changing, and traditional party officialdom risked being seen as unnecessary, if not actually harmful, in a world where the spontaneity and diversity that come from absence of imposed control seemed to bring good rewards.

Under Witte and his immediate predecessors and successors, the Russian empire had been directed by the state into avenues which, it was hoped, would enable Russia to follow the German pattern of development rather than be left behind and dominated by other countries, as had happened to the Chinese Empire. In the end, under Stalin, the Russian economy followed neither the German nor the Chinese pattern but went its own tumultuous way. Because of the peculiarities of Russian society, it could hardly have followed western patterns.

One of those peculiarities, one of many, was the special status of truth in both tsarist and communist Russia. Truth, in its guise of information, was tightly controlled because it threatened, by chain reaction, to ravage a realm of myth which was the handiwork of generations of state servants, who believed that deception could be constructive and that deception in the interest of the state was ultimately deception in the interest of the people. This characteristic was not, and is not, confined to Russia, but in Russia its manifestation was extreme enough to make it unique and to contort, for better or for worse, Russian society.

In such circumstances new ideas could be inconvenient, perhaps dangerous, and therefore elicited a suspicious reception. All too often, innovation was regarded as subversion. Yet in the nineteenth and twentieth centuries it was innovation that was needed to keep up with the rest of the world and escape a relapse into the kind of humiliating decline classically demonstrated by the old Chinese Empire. Innovation, or rather lack of it, remained the essential obstacle to economic and social advance in the 1980s. Few bright new ideas in their right mind would settle in Russia, even though some older ideas lived there comfortably in retirement.

19. *From Red Flag to Double-headed Eagle*

Gorbachev

MIKHAIL Gorbachev was born in the Stavropol region of the North Caucasus in the period of mass collectivization. His father was a tractor driver and, as a teenager, Mikhail worked as a combine-harvester assistant driver in the summers. He went to Moscow University, where he graduated in law, and subsequently followed a correspondence course in agriculture. He began his political career in 1956 as the Komsomol first secretary in Stavropol town, made an impression on the first secretary of the party's Stavropol regional organization, and in 1970 himself succeeded to that post. He attracted the attention of Suslov (who had Stavropol connections) and of Andropov. His ascent was rapid; having become a member of the Central Committee in 1971, he was a full member of the Politburo in 1980. Charm and ability had made full use of his influential connections.

He took part in parliamentary delegations to Canada and Britain. His 1984 visit to England and Scotland came to a premature end at Holyrood House, when he learned that Ustinov had died. He flew home immediately but not before the British prime minister, Thatcher, had declaimed that Gorbachev was a man with whom 'we can do business together'.

Gorbachev was clearly a leading figure in the Politburo, favoured by those who realized that big changes were needed but distrusted by those who liked things as they were. The Politburo met to choose a new general secretary with almost unseemly haste after the demise of Chernenko. Gorbachev, as it happened, was in charge of the arrangements and the haste meant that one likely opponent, Shcherbitskii, who had been visiting the USA, did not arrive in time. The decision was arrived at without him, and Gorbachev became the new general secretary.

Unlike Brezhnev, who in his later years had a resuscitation team in constant attendance, and unlike Andropov and Chernenko, Gorbachev had good health and relative youth on his side. When he assumed power in March 1985 he was fifty-four, he knew what had to be done, and he could afford to hasten slowly. In his first year of office he took advantage of his leverage in the Politburo to exclude several long-standing members, including the party chiefs of Moscow and Leningrad, who represented the old ways.

It was yet one more paradox of Russian history that a man so inscrutable should so effectively have become a champion of openness. In public Gorbachev was outspoken, not seeking to cloak criticism with euphemism. He was willing to show himself among ordinary people and enter into impromptu discussions, frequently demonstrating that he had a good idea of what really went on in Soviet society. He referred to ministers who 'try to squeeze as much capital and materials as possible while proposing production targets as small as possible'. He acknowledged that service industries were so abysmal that when people needed something repaired they had to find a person in the 'black economy' to do it for them, and this moonlighter would depend on materials stolen from some state enterprise. Abroad, Gorbachev presented the Soviet case with more charm and intellectual distinction than had been seen since the days of Litvinov, and in his earlier meetings with American presidents seemed sometimes to stick out like a healthy thumb.

His political character had been shaped by his career as an *apparatchik*, and he was never able to throw off many of the assumptions and modes of behaviour of his class. At first he aimed to return to the aspirations and standards of Lenin's time, as he saw them. Very conscious of Khrushchev's fate, he proceeded cautiously; he could not afford to antagonize the bulk of the party apparatus, but what he intended to do would certainly be anathema to *apparatchiks*. He therefore moved slowly. His 1987 speech celebrating seventy years of Soviet power was possibly the point at which his intentions became plainer, but even that carefully crafted speech was fairly innocuous compared to what came later. In it, he made plain that Stalin had done bad things to be set against the good things, but even that admission was only grudgingly accepted by some of his Politburo colleagues.

By moving slowly, while steadily replacing the more conservative party administrators, Gorbachev hoped to transform the USSR through a transformed Communist Party. As things turned out, the party apparatus was very slow to reform itself, and he was faced with the same problem as other Russian reformers, how to make changes without unleashing a torrent of pent-up pressures. When the forces he had freed pushed much further than he intended, he tried to apply the brakes but did not reverse his course, although there were some pessimists who accused him of doing so.

The two catchwords of his policies were *glasnost'*, or frankness, and *perestroika*, or restructuring. Because the communist regime had maintained power largely through suppression of information, the new frankness threatened cataclysm for the party bureaucracy. As for restructuring, Gorbachev's realization that Soviet society needed a thorough rebuilding was sound, but in his six years of *perestroika* he succeeded mainly in the destructive phase of reconstruction.

But that destruction was an achievement wrought in the face of powerful opposition. When Gorbachev was awarded the Nobel Peace Prize in 1990, Soviet citizens made cynical observations about his greater popularity abroad than at home. But the honour was deserved, even though when he resigned in 1991 the USSR was in ruins and its people, though free, faced an uncertain future. He seemed destined to take his place in history alongside other great transformers; a Bismarck who managed without blood and iron and who, on balance, made the world not worse, but better.

In the beginning was the word

From 1985 to 1991 the USSR was weakened to the point where it actually disappeared, the Communist Party followed the same route, and the international situation relaxed. All this happened because freedom of speech and freedom of publication became real under Gorbachev's policy of *glasnost'*. Control of information, which really meant the suppression of truth and the construction of an all-embracing structure of falsehood, proved to be the vital support of communist bureaucracies in the USSR and in the peoples' democracies of central and eastern Europe. Vigilantly on guard against counter-revolution, they proved helpless against counter-revelation. Gorbachev had hoped to achieve a restructuring of Soviet society and especially of the Communist Party. But truth, once liberated, was too destructive to stop at mere restructuring.

Glavlit, the state censorship organization, was abolished only in 1990, but by 1988 the old barriers were clearly down. The process had not been instantaneous. At first just one or two publications printed material that previously would have been banned, and a few newspapers criticized what had previously been unimpeachable. When editors saw that such ventures attracted public interest and brought no undesirable consequences, the process spread and there developed a real variety of periodicals, ranging from the conservative to the radical. This change was uneven, with readers in many parts having access only to publications that stuck to the old standards, and this was one of the reasons why television was so important in changing the climate of opinion. With the central programmes receivable in most parts of the Union, and with many such programmes in the hands of reformist programme-makers, the viewing public (that is, the bulk of the population) was exposed to the release of new ideas and previously suppressed facts.

Discovering that their long-suppressed thoughts were shared by others, many ordinary people became ever bolder in their criticism and demands. Others, unable to accept the overturning of beliefs instilled since childhood, retired into their shells to cope as best they could with the new climate.

Television coverage of political debate was perhaps the most important means of informing the public, but a number of one-off programmes on sensitive issues, together with a few regular current-affairs programmes, were almost as important. For the first time, political problems could be presented from several points of view. One of the first of such occasions was when the British prime minister, Mrs Thatcher, was interviewed and, among other things, explained why she felt Britain should retain nuclear weapons; that the west might feel imperilled by the huge Red Army was a thought never previously explained to a mass Soviet audience.

An evening magazine programme, *Vzglyad* ('View'), soon attracted a growing audience with its well-informed outspokenness. Leningrad TV had a regular programme called '600 Seconds' with a reputation for unearthing scandals. Its presenter and leading spirit became something of a media hero until he criticized the conduct of the independence movements in the Baltic republics, after which rumours spread that he was really a KGB man. In the 1990–1 winter, when conservatives appeared to have won a controlling influence over Gorbachev, there was a move towards tighter control of radio and television. A more restrictive head of *Gostelradio* (the central state radio and television organization) was appointed, and one of his first moves was to eliminate *Vzglyad*. A parallel evening programme, the much blander *Vremiya* ('Time') was retained, but refrained from the politically controversial. In fact, when in July 1991 a Russian Republic decree banned party activity in enterprises, *Vremiya* waited two days before commenting, and when it did it gave coverage only to opponents of the decree. Meanwhile Gorbachev had decreed that Leningrad TV should be subordinated to *Gostelradio*.

Yeltsin, president of the Russian Republic, managed to get a Russian Republic TV programme into operation, broadcasting three times daily on an existing channel, and its magazine programme *Vesti* ('Tidings') soon became more popular than *Vremiya*. During the attempted coup of August 1991 several radio and television presenters showed reluctance to support the take-over, but the general television line was to conform (although on the first day this conformity simply meant little more than playing 'Swan Lake' over and over again, interspersed with the conspirators' press release). After the coup failed many of the conservative controllers, including the head of *Gostelradio*, were dismissed and replaced by more progressive figures. For the remainder of 1991 programmes, like much of the press, reverted to their previous outspokenness, only more so.

The 'thick' journals were also transformed by *glasnost'*, and were often the first to present fiction that had previously been unpublishable. *Novyi mir*, which had distinguished itself in Khrushchev's time, was again in the forefront of this liberalization, but was joined by several others, while even the journals that were unenthusiastic about reform showed a little more enterprise in defending the conservative position. Much of the Soviet fiction published in the 1920s but subsequently banned was reprinted, and some foreign literature was published for the first time; that Orwell's *Animal Farm* became available is testimony to the no-holds-barred character of *glasnost'*. The same author's *1984* was also published (as was the Soviet forerunner of this novel, Zamyatin's *We*).

Readers of these journals soon realized that many of the apparently turgid Stalinist novelists had written other novels which, far from winning a Stalin Prize, had hitherto been unpublishable. One of these surprises was Grossman's *Life and Fate*. Grossman had written several Stalinist best-sellers but in 1961, when he submitted this manuscript to the 'thick' journal *Znamya*, the KGB was informed and every copy of the manuscript confiscated. Grossman died in the belief that the novel was irretrievably lost, but a copy was found and published in 1988. The novel is truthful about World War 2 (some of its scenes take place in Soviet and German concentration camps, an ambience where the naked truth tends to survive) and there are hints Soviet Russia was not entirely unlike Nazi Germany, that there might be such a thing as Stalin's national bolshevism to parallel Hitler's national socialism.

Vladimir Dudintsev, who found that he could not get anything published in the aftermath of his *Not by Bread Alone*, reappeared with the novel *White Coats*. This was about the Lysenko affair, and reminded readers how ideology can, and did, make a mockery of science. Another notable writer, comparable to Solzhenitsyn in his portrayals of the horrifying realities of labour-camp life, was Varlam Shalamov, whose *Kolyma Tales* was published in *Novyi mir*. Many other unpublished manuscripts were taken from their hiding places and published.

Some new novels not only told the truth about the past, but also tried to explain it. In many cases this amounted to speculation about Stalin's real nature and motivation, as in Anatolii Rybakov's celebrated *Children of the Arbat*. The author, who had won a Stalin Prize in 1951, tried to get this book published by *Novyi mir* in the 1960s, but failed. It was finally published in 1987. Set in Moscow at the time of Kirov's murder, it has Stalin as a main character; his thoughts are portrayed to create a psychological study that is not necessarily valid but at least poses pertinent questions. Stray references, like Stalin's 'Hitler-like moustache' are not hard to interpret even though they may take artistic licence excessively far.

Whereas novelists seemed to have ready-to-use manuscripts secreted in their bottom drawers, the same could not be said of historians. Historians depended on archives that were not made freely available to them, and influential historians of the servile school, typically heads of departments or institutions, fought hard against *glasnost'*. Nevertheless, after a slow start, original history began to appear and much new light was shed on the recent past. In some cases surviving participants of the Stalinist period were interviewed, and in others long-suppressed documents were published. For the first time in decades Trotsky's work, and works, were publicly examined. Unsurprisingly, after the first burst of curiosity, the Soviet reading public relegated Trotsky to the trash-can of history. Bukharin, on the other hand, continued to arouse sympathetic interest, partly because he did seem to offer an alternative to Stalinism in the late 1920s and partly because he was perceived as the best of a bad bunch.

A good deal of archival material on the Stalinist purges and terror was unearthed and published, including bloodstained reports penned by torturers in the interrogation cells. Some statistics were located, but it seemed likely that Soviet researchers would have no more success than their western predecessors in accurately counting the number of victims. In 1989 Soviet responsibility was finally acknowledged for the Katyn (and other) mass killings. Not everything went smoothly for the new historians. As late as 1991 the director of the Military History Institute was denounced by the defence minister and had to resign after producing the first volume of a less tendentious history of the Red Army in World War 2. This recalled to mind the rapid exit, in Khrushchev's time, of the historian Nekrich, who had published an analysis of June 1941.

Not everything was cleared up. Past manifestations of anti-semitism were revealed but in a low-key and incomplete way. Whether Kirov had been murdered by Stalin remained unsettled, and it was reported that some of the documents seen by the members of Khrushchev's interrupted commission on this subject had since disappeared.

Plays and films made a great mark, just as in the past (probably more so, since many of them were repeated on television). Mikhail Shatrov, a long-established writer of historical plays, made an impression with his portrayals of dramatic events in the early years of the Soviet regime. He was one of the first to dig beyond the 1930s and raise questions about the real history of 1917 and 1918. In *Onward, Onward, Onward*, Shatrov covers the eve of the October Revolution. Prominent personalities are portrayed and they introduce themselves with autobiographies of their whole life. Thus Trotsky duly reports how he was murdered in Mexico (this was news for most, if not all, of the first audiences).

Perhaps because it was concentrated in a few units, the film industry made an exceptionally prompt jump from constraint to liberty. The Cinema Association, the body controlling the industry, normally found its executive committee by electing an officially nominated list of candidates. However, in 1986 its conference included enough rampant members to reject this list and to propose candidates from the floor of the meeting. The result was a completely transformed Cinema Association, one of whose first acts was to prepare for distribution the many films that in previous decades had been refused public showings. Sometimes underlining, sometimes merely implying, the evils of past decades, this collection of films helped to show why reform was necessary.

The film that made the biggest impression was a Georgian film, *Repentance*. Made in Stalin's homeland in the early 1980s before *glasnost'*, with the encouragement of the Georgian party secretary Shevardnadze, it could be regarded as an allegory of Stalinism. But its broad theme was that there were people with guilty consciences about, people who had behaved horrendously in the Stalin years, and that the best thing such people could do was to confess and hope for forgiveness. There was a secondary theme about Russians' insensitivity to non-Russian cultures, but this did not seem to diminish the film's popularity among Russians.[1]

Other notable film treatments of Stalinism included *Defence Lawyer Sedov*, which won prizes at western film festivals and was a low-key but highly effective exposé of the cruel legalities of the purge era. However, such subjects were over-exploited by film-makers. The result was often a kind of upturned socialist realism that did not enthuse audiences. In fact, the most popular films were not those of the new wave of Soviet cinema, but of the old Hollywood films that were imported in large numbers. Even a best-forgotten Hollywood 'B' movie could fill cinemas with audiences anxious to drain the cup of western culture down to the lower sediment. But despite the enormous popularity of films like *Crocodile Dundee*, cinema audiences were falling. The most popular Soviet films managed to reach audiences of rarely more than ten million, compared to 100 million in the Brezhnev period, although this was partly explicable by the larger

[1] Apart from its contribution to *glasnost'*, this film has another distinction, being the first in which, halfway through filming, the leading actor was removed to face trial and execution for participation in a failed aircraft hi-jack.

annual production of films (about 400, compared to 100–150 in the earlier period).

Newspapers, and the more popular periodicals, played a part in bringing day-to-day criticism to bear, and also, sometimes, devoted lengthy articles to long-standing evils or distorted history. Even *Pravda*, regarded as one of the conservative newspapers, played a big part in this; being the Central Committee's newspaper, a small shift by this paper was more important than a big shift in the views of another. However, as time passed and a spectrum of newspapers developed, *Pravda* and *Sovietskaya Rossiya* remained on the conservative wing. On the other hand *Komsoml'skaya pravda*, the newspaper of the Komsomol youth organization, transformed itself into one of the more crusading of the big newspapers. Some new titles appeared, *Nezavisimaya gazeta* ('Independent Newspaper') proving to be one of the most popular. Meanwhile an energetic editor transformed the popular illustrated magazine *Ogonyok* into an investigative, socially aware magazine with an ever-increasing circulation. Another journal, 'Arguments and Facts', thanks to its well-informed and highly factual articles, also reached a very high circulation.

Editors had to provide more of what the public wanted. *Pravda* made some kind of an effort to keep up with the times, but its views lost palatability just as did its owner, the Communist Party. By 1991 its circulation, which had once been about twelve million, had declined to about a million. In the August 1991 coup it was one of the nine papers that the plotters did not suspend; unsurprisingly, after the coup failed it was banned for a few days, during which its editorial board was changed. In its new form its title was bereft of the image of Lenin, it no longer called itself the communist party newspaper, but it was still the best-printed of the papers. Its future would henceforth depend on its commercial success; in late 1991 an issue even appeared with the top of its front page adorned by a page-wide advertisement offering stock-exchange opportunities.

Moves towards market pricing meant that newsprint, ever more scarce because of the problems of the timber industry, became more expensive. With the disappearance or diminution of subsidies, newspaper prices had to rise, and great efforts were made to increase circulations, but by the end of 1991 some of the more specialized newspapers were in difficulties. Newspaper managements in search of cheap newsprint reported bitterly that new popular and allegedly sleazy magazines, like those published by monarchists and religious interests and those taking advantage of new sexual freedoms, could afford to pay high prices for newsprint whereas more worthy papers, like their own, could not.Tsars, saints, and naked girls, they alleged, was where the money was. Obviously a fortune was awaiting the publisher of a Russian Orthodox *Playboy*, but by late 1992 such a money-spinner had yet to appear.

Gorbachev and the party

Like thousands of others, Gorbachev put his faith in the party that had made him. He realized that a reconstruction of the party was needed, a reconstruction to include demotions and promotions that would bring into leading positions men who, like himself, believed that the leading role of the party should be used to correct the distortions of society and economy that that same party had created. With charm, patience, and ruthlessness he succeeded in steadily replacing conservatives in the party bureaucracy. But this progress was not fast enough, although only at the thirteenth hour did he acknowledge that the party could not, after all, be the instrument of *perestroika*.

In his first two years Gorbachev achieved a faster rate of personnel changes among influential officials than had been seen since the days of Stalin's purges. In the Politburo, Central Committee, and elsewhere, these changes were facilitated by the large number of geriatric leftovers inherited from the Brezhnev years; time-worn officials, who usually tended to be against change, could be retired with dignity on account of age. Tikhonov was replaced as prime minister by Ryzhkov, and Gromyko as foreign minister by Eduard Shevardnadze. Gromyko had been one of Gorbachev's supporters and he was kicked upstairs (a new direction of departure for sacked ministers) to become head of state. His successor, Shevardnadze, was a very capable man who became interior minister and then party first secretary in Georgia, where he had distinguished himself as the scourge of both the corrupt and the nationalists. A history graduate, he was a man whose thoughts moved in mysterious ways. In Georgia he had anticipated *perestroika* in several ways, founding a centre for public opinion and adopting a more flexible attitude in agriculture.

Two early departures from the Politburo were the chiefs of the Moscow and Leningrad party organizations, elderly men who had regarded themselves as the rightful heirs to Chernenko. The new party chief for Moscow was Boris Yeltsin, a stalwart *apparatchik* in his previous post as head of the Sverdlovsk party organization, but soon showing himself as an implacable enemy of the deep-seated corruption he found in Moscow. As a somewhat tempestuous and impulsive enemy of corruption and sloth he made many enemies, but Gorbachev initially made him welcome in the Politburo.

In the other centre of power, the secretariat of the party's Central Committee (some of whose members also had Politburo seats), nine of the twelve members were appointed by Gorbachev in his first two years.

However, in the party apparatus as a whole the picture was patchy. Many party organizations, using familiar party methods, were able to keep reformers out. When the 27th party congress was called fifty weeks after Gorbachev's succession many party organizations contrived to send conservatively inclined representatives even when local members would have preferred reformers. This was a disappointment for Gorbachev and his advisers, who had hoped to make this congress a starting point for the transformation of the party and hence of the USSR. Nevertheless, the current was flowing in Gorbachev's favour, for at this congress only 59 per cent of the existing Central Committee members were re-elected (for comparison, at the previous 1981 congress about nine-tenths of the Central Committee had been re-elected). Although the new Central Committee members included some who could not be regarded as Gorbachev supporters, he was able to get some of his key advisers elected. Among them was Aleksandr Yakovlev, who was probably more enthusiastic than Gorbachev himself for *glasnost'* and was given responsibility in the secretariat for culture and propaganda.

The party congress was followed in April 1986 by the Chernobyl nuclear disaster which discredited the party, especially Shcherbitskii's Ukrainian party, and showed that *glasnost'* had still a long way to go. Meanwhile, conferences between Gorbachev and the US president, and a unilateral Soviet moratorium on nuclear tests (which brought no response from the west) showed that Gorbachev fully realized how damaging the east–west conflict had become, but it also aroused fears that he might 'sell out' to the west. Sakharov was released from internal exile in late 1986, one of several steps that emphasized that *glasnost'* was to be taken seriously. The jamming of the BBC (but not, at this point, of the more critical Radio Liberty or Radio Free Europe) soon ceased, and in February 1987 a large batch of political prisoners was released. Border talks with China were reopened after a gap of nine years. It became easier for Russians to obtain visas for foreign travel. From time to time Moscow intervened to overturn outrageous acts by local party organizations. Such interventions often resulted in the release of wrongly arrested individuals who had in one way or another displeased local officials, and news of such events, no longer suppressed, was cumulative, encouraging more and more citizens to decide that they were no longer going to be pushed around. This change of atmosphere was echoed in the new edition of the *Great Soviet Encyclopedia*, which replaced a curt, dismissive entry for Khrushchev with a longer, complimentary piece.

However, these first two years were hardly a honeymoon for Gorbachev. Apart from covert resistance to his initiatives there was the occasional overt opposition. This took a dramatic form in Kazakhstan, where the party leader was embroiled in a web of corruption of which leading officials and their families took blatant advantage. When he was forcibly retired it was hard to find a suitable, untainted, Kazakh to succeed him and a Russian was appointed. This led to violent riots in the capital, Alma Ata, and although order was restored the outbreak showed how carefully reformers needed to tread, and how easy it was for evil men to play the nationalist card.

A plenary meeting of the Central Committee was due in 1986, but was postponed until 1987 because of behind-the-scenes arguments about what should be done. At the plenum itself the final, decisive resolution was passed only because Gorbachev had suggested that if he could not do things his way then a new general secretary would have to be found. Many participants were firmly against Gorbachev's policies, but an even greater number, although worried, realized that Gorbachev might be their best hope for protection against something worse. Like Stalin, but more benignly, he was making himself indispensable by instigating crisis.

In his opening speech, in convoluted language that everyone understood, Gorbachev made clear his belief that the party had been twisted by Stalin and now must be untwisted. He referred to the fossilizing of so-called irrefutable truths which, among other things, had condemned the co-operative movement, prevented individual initiative, and robbed money of its role in measuring true value. He blamed past central committees for their role in this process and went on to make his main, devastating proposal, which was no less than the democratization of the party. The party was no longer to put itself above the state. It had to end secret nominations for posts and introduce the secret ballot in its decisions. It was to end its urge to dominate, to manage the smallest things, and to give orders to every individual. Truly independent courts were needed, and the soviets were to be properly elected and take a more genuine role in government at all levels, while non-party individuals should have the right to hold important offices.

He also proposed to hold in 1988 a party conference (the first since 1941) to review how these decisions, as passed by the plenum resolution, had been put into practice. Despite their unpalatability, most of Gorbachev's proposals were included in the final resolution and a day later, in a move unprecedented in the USSR, Gorbachev's final address to the plenum was televised. This secured him popular support that counterbalanced the opposition still evident in the Central Committee.

Gorbachev's next major policy speech was in celebration of the 70th anniversary of the Revolution, in November 1987. In the intervening period he worked on economic reforms directed at loosening old structures and permitting individuals greater freedom to become independent businessmen. In the summer, the independence movements in the Baltic republics, led by Lithuania, took advantage of the freedom to demonstrate by assembling crowds to listen to speeches and wave the hitherto banned national flags. An eccentric young German secured himself a niche in history by piloting his light plane across the frontier, over hundreds of miles of Soviet territory, to land triumphantly in Red Square. The failure of the armed forces to notice, let alone stop, this incursion, brought them into disrepute and Gorbachev took advantage of the situation to dismiss the defence minister and to appoint a more congenial general, Yazov, in his place.

In his November speech Gorbachev went out of his way to praise Khrushchev, and condemned Stalin's crimes. He also announced an enquiry into the victims of Stalin's purge (Bukharin, Zinoviev, Kamenev, and other old Bolsheviks were rehabilitated in the following months). Another, completely revised, history of the Communist Party was to be undertaken, he said. This speech brought no joy to the hearts of those who still hankered for the good old days of the 1970s, but their opposition was not the only problem facing the new reformist leadership.

Boris Yeltsin, whose rough-and-ready approach endeared him to a large public, began to press publicly for faster reform, and in June 1988 his indiscretions led to his expulsion from the Politburo and from the Moscow party leadership. Troubles were growing in the non-Russian republics, with unrest in the three Baltic republics, and inter-republican struggles in the Caucasus between Azerbaizhan and Armenia.

Among those most troubled by *glasnost'* and *perestroika* were the teachers, and it was appropriate that Nina Andreeva, whose lengthy, well-publicized letter appeared in the conservative newspaper *Sovietskaya Rossiya*, was a chemistry teacher. Published in March 1988, evidently with the connivance of high party officials including one or two in the Politburo, her piece portrayed Gorbachev's reforms and intentions as alarming and excessive. Reflecting the misgivings of many, and not without a nostalgic glance at Stalin's time and a hint that Jews were not Russians, the text became a rallying point for the controversy currently taking place, and served to assure other doubters that they were not alone in their fears and resentments.

Inside the Politburo Ligachev, who was regarded as number two in the leadership and had been appointed not by Gorbachev but by Andropov, was the inspiration of this opposition, the expression of which was itself a fruit of *glasnost'*. But Gorbachev, by flexibility and comments of the *après moi, le déluge* type, continued on his way. The Politburo continued to lose old and gain new, pro-Gorbachev, members; Aliyev had left in 1987 and Chebrikov and Shcherbitskii would go in 1989. Some of the members dropped from the Central Committee had previously held positions that Gorbachev had abolished; consistent with his intention of reducing the party's interventions, the departments of the Central Committee had been halved, with all the economic departments except agriculture being abolished. In September 1988 Ligachev himself was shunted to a less influential position, being entrusted with the agricultural department. He held his place in the Politburo until summer 1990, by which time that body had lost most of its importance. In October 1988 the Supreme Soviet voted unanimously (and, likewise in the old style, without an alternative candidate) to replace Gromyko as its chairman (and USSR president) with Gorbachev.

After the elections of spring 1989 Gorbachev was again elected president by the new parliament, known as the Congress of Peoples' Deputies. This was part of the transformed state structure resulting from the Supreme Soviet's substantial 1988 amendment of the 'Brezhnev Constitution'. The parliament had 2,250 seats, and from its membership was elected the new 542-member Supreme Soviet which, unlike its predecessor, became the scene of lively, well-reported debate. The parliament itself would meet only about twice a year for short periods, but as a fifth of the Supreme Soviet membership was to be renewed each year it was by no means a rubber stamp.

For this first, 1989, election the parliament had three classes of seat. One-third was contested in ordinary constituencies, one-third in large so-called national territorial constituencies, and one-third was reserved for 'public organizations'. This latter category guaranteed an advantage for certain interests, notably the Communist Party, which had 100 of these reserved seats. The Central Committee duly nominated 100 public figures (including Gorbachev but not Yeltsin) who were thus spared the necessity of descending into undignified vote-winning.[2] The trade unions and co-operatives also had 100 reserved seats each. In some public organizations, for example in the Academy of Sciences, fierce nomination struggles took place resulting, quite often, in 'old-guard' candidates falling victim to new reformist candidates. Among members elected by the Academy was Sakharov, most distinguished of the one-time dissidents.

Similar, truly democratic structures were created for republican and

---

[2] Nominees for the reserved seats did have to secure positive votes from 50 per cent of the voters. Some unpopular officials failed to clear this hurdle and new elections, with new nominees, had to be called. In December 1989 it was decided that reserved seats would be eliminated for the next election in 1994.

other local governments, although reserved seats were not provided in some of the republican elections that also took place in 1989–90. As for Yeltsin, he was elected to the USSR Congress of Peoples' Deputies for the national territorial seat of Moscow city with the record-breaking support of five million voters, despite all the efforts made to discredit him.

More than four-fifths of the electorate turned out to vote in the USSR election. Almost nine-tenths of the resulting Congress of Peoples' Deputies were party members, who both inside and outside the new parliament seemed so irrevocably divided between reformers and conservatives that a formal split would have been logical. However, Gorbachev did not encourage this; after all, he was the party's leader. There was therefore no dramatic split, but there were successive dramatic resignations by party reformers who declared that they could no longer remain in an organization so unwilling to correct its faults.

The parliamentary members tended to coalesce in blocs, which were alliances in support of particular philosophies. Soon after the Congress assembled, the *Soyuz* bloc formed, devoted to preserving the status quo, while about 400 deputies formed themselves into the so-called Interregional Bloc, of which Sakharov was a leading light until his death. This pressed for faster reform and was quick to publicize the arbitrary acts of repression that were still the stock-in-trade of old-type officials. Its supporters began to occupy key positions in the press and broadcasting; the media, too, tended to be divided into conservative and reformist camps, with television increasingly exploiting the new freedoms to expose the rottenness of the old ways and, increasingly, the failures of the new.

In 1989 more and more Soviet citizens lost faith in *perestroika*. Worsening shortages were obvious to all, *glasnost'* or no *glasnost'*, but it was media coverage that brought home the collapse of communist regimes in eastern Europe. This demonstration that communism was not, after all, permanent and irreplaceable, gave extra inspiration to the growing number of politically active reformers who were beginning to realize that reform without communists was quite feasible. In other words, the neutralization of the party had become a recognized option. The loss of party authority and repute was demonstrated by a shrinking membership and, even more emphatically, by the millions of members who kept their party cards but failed to pay their subscriptions.

In February 1990 a march on the Kremlin, said to involve 200,000 protesters, demanded an end of the party's monopoly, and a party plenum agreed that this would be a good idea. In March the Congress of Peoples' Deputies, after some argument, agreed with Gorbachev that a strong presidency was needed. The constitution was accordingly amended to provide for a US-style president, and a presidential council to advise him; the 'leading role' of the party was at the same time deleted. Gorbachev relinquished his lesser presidency (chairmanship of the USSR Supreme Soviet) when the Congress elected him as a new, executive president. It was agreed that the next presidential election would be a general election.

The president could be impeached by a two-thirds vote of the Congress, and his nominations for ministerial positions needed the approval of the Supreme Soviet. So although Gorbachev could issue decrees he was not all-powerful and, as time would show, not all his decrees would be obeyed in the republics. But these changes effectively sidetracked the Politburo and Central Committee, reflecting Gorbachev's intention of transferring power away from the party to the Soviets.

At the May Day parade in Moscow, a big day in the party's calendar, hostile placards and jeering resulted in the party's general secretary, Gorbachev, retreating in disgust. In July 1990 the party's 28th congress assembled. It put off the formulation of a new party programme, but Gorbachev made it plain that he envisaged a tolerant, humane, and socialist party that somehow would stay with 'democratic centralism' yet maintain total freedom of debate. The congress adopted new rules that allowed different 'platforms', if not 'factions', and provided for more information to be passed to lower party organizations and members.

While the new freedom for public organizations resulted in countless clubs and forums being established to pursue not only hobbies but also political and philosophical debate, and while new publications appeared, fell, or flourished, powerful political parties did not appear. Often it was hard to distinguish between a movement and a party, although in general it could be said that a movement was larger and might give its support to several parties that it found congenial. One important movement was *Pamyatnik* ('Memorial'), which began by urging the construction of appropriate memorials for the victims of Stalinism but naturally became a movement for defence against Stalinism. *Pamyat'* ('Memory') had a similar name but was very different. It was a strong Russian national movement whose members felt that there was such a thing as a Russian tradition and that it needed to be defended. But it had an extremist wing devoted to the pursuit of Jews and other real or imagined enemies of Russianism. By 1991 members of *Pamyat'* were distributing leaflets in which the real name of the Soviet prime minister, Pavlov, was said to be Goldberg, and that of the Leningrad mayor, Sobchak, to be Finkelstein. On the whole, *Pamyat'* would have found Nicholas I's philosophy of 'Orthodoxy, Autocracy, Nationality' quite congenial. Another movement, active in the Supreme Soviet and a definite conservative force opposed to most of Gorbachev's changes, was *Soyuz* ('Union'). There were hundreds of small parties, some consisting of just one individual. Among them were the Russian Nationalist Monarchist Party, one of whose aims was the canonization of Nicholas II, and the group calling itself the movement of 'Unity for Leninism and Communist Ideals', of which the leading light was Nina Andreeva. This wanted to put Gorbachev on trial, and to make Kaganovich its honorary president.

In the RSFSR (Russian Republic) parliament conservatives were fewer, and the Democratic Russia movement became a powerful group uniting radicals of various persuasions. Yeltsin, who by this time was offering what could be seen as an alternative to Gorbachev's *perestroika* (sovereignty for the republics, establishment of a free market, a directly elected presidency) soon became the inspiration of this movement, which scored a great electoral success in the municipal elections of March 1990. In these elections the official party organizations did particularly badly in Moscow, Leningrad, and Kiev. The Democratic Russia movement's Sobchak was elected mayor of Leningrad, Popov mayor of Moscow, and Yeltsin won a seat in the Russian parliament.

That summer Yeltsin, by now openly opposed by Gorbachev, succeeded in assembling a majority in the RSFSR parliament to elect him president of its presidium. Strengthened by this status, and by the provocative if ineffective declaration of independence by Lithuania, he succeeded in getting his parliament to declare Russian sovereignty. What precisely sovereignty meant was not clear, but other republics also made similar declarations and it was clear that the central, USSR government was losing authority. In the following months a 'war of laws' took place, as republics with some success insisted that republican laws took precedence over USSR laws.

The end of perestroika

An accelerated collapse of communist power was witnessed in 1989 in the peoples' democracies of eastern and central Europe. For the USSR itself the collapse was yet to come. The economy and its managers were failing to respond to treatment. The Union was threatened with break-up. Yeltsin, whose supporters were demanding more radical policies, with great publicity had resigned from the party during its 28th congress. Taken together, these circumstances represented a definite radical swing, which soon produced a reaction. From the autumn of 1990 Gorbachev seemed to ally himself with the more conservative elements, several of whom he had himself appointed to key posts.

Signs of this shift included Gorbachev's rejection of the Shatalin 500-day plan for a shift to the open market, which he had earlier favoured and which had been approved by Yeltsin's Russian Republic. It was not long before the fairly liberal Bakatin was replaced as interior minister by the harder Pugo, a Latvian with his roots in the KGB. Shevardnadze, alarmed at the trend, resigned his office and publicly stated that he was doing so because he feared the development of a dictatorship. In January 1991 the Soviet army and KGB took various actions against the independence movements in Latvia and Lithuania, with some deaths resulting, and with some newspapers condemning Gorbachev for this return to the old violent ways. In the same month the prime minister Ryzhkov, who had been ill, was replaced by Valentin Pavlov who, like his predecessor, was an economic administrator, but who, unlike Ryzhkov, was a pudgy man with a pudgy mind. A new, considerably less tolerant head of *Gostelradio* was appointed, although Gorbachev did not carry out his threat to repeal the laws on press freedom. The institution of joint army/police patrols in the cities aroused mixed feelings; they may have been necessary where crime was large-scale and violent, but they were thought to symbolize a reversion to coercive practices. The grant of automatic rights to the KGB and police to enter premises where economic crimes were suspected was another measure that had sinister overtones, but in early 1991 Gorbachev annulled this measure.

Among Pavlov's initiatives was a much-resented sales tax, and a sudden calling-in of all high-denomination (50- and 100-rouble) banknotes that caused immense inconvenience as well as loss to millions of citizens. The ostensible intention behind this return to arbitrary measures was to relieve speculators and other get-rich-quick citizens of their ill-gotten gains. In reality it was ordinary citizens and not the sharp operators who stored their wealth in banknotes. On later occasions, Pavlov spoke of western plots to ruin the economy by buying up roubles at low rates of exchange, to create inflation by injecting billions of roubles into the USSR, and to strangle development by means of a credit blockade. He never bothered to produce convincing evidence for these gigantic conspiracies, a sure sign of reversion to old-style bureaucratic practice.

Faced with what seemed a bit-by-bit return to authoritarianism, most reformers turned to Yeltsin for leadership. Meanwhile, Gorbachev, in an effort to stabilize the union, held a nationwide referendum in which voters were asked whether they supported the continuation of the USSR as a union of sovereign republics. The question was a classic misuse of the referendum technique. It actually implied several questions but only a single negative or positive response was possible: 'Do you think it necessary to preserve the Union of Soviet Socialist Republics as a renovated federation of equal sovereign republics in which human rights and freedom for every nationality will be guaranteed?' Three-quarters of that four-fifths of the electorate which voted agreed with the proposition, although in Leningrad and Moscow there were only bare majorities.

It was possible for republics, or districts, to append their own questions to the main referendum. Yeltsin ensured that there would be a supplementary question for voters in the Russian Republic. This asked whether the RSFSR should have an elected president. Voters agreed to this proposal, and to the distaste of Gorbachev (who had been elected to the presidency of the USSR only by an indirect vote of its parliament) a direct republic-wide presidential election was scheduled in Russia for June. Meanwhile, in Leningrad, 55 per cent of the voters surprised commentators by approving a reversion to the old name of St. Petersburg (they were not given the choice of Petrograd).

At this period the hostility between Yeltsin and Gorbachev became more open. An attempt by conservative communists to impeach Yeltsin in the Russian parliament failed. Yeltsin, finally granted a television interview, called for Gorbachev's resignation. In Moscow a rally in favour of Yeltsin attracted thousands of supporters.

Meanwhile, Yeltsin was backing one of the most threatening strikes called in this period. Not for the first time during *perestroika*, the miners downed tools. This time it was the Siberian miners, who in addition to their economic demands called for Gorbachev's resignation. For a country so dependent on coal this long strike was crippling. Finally Yeltsin stepped in to what was formally a USSR problem and negotiated a settlement that did not include Gorbachev's resignation but promised the transfer of the mines from the jurisdiction of the USSR to the respective republics.

The April '9 + 1' agreement was also largely engineered by Yeltsin. It was an understanding between the USSR (the '1') and nine of the republics. Gorbachev succeeded in including a passage on the need for work discipline and for limitation of strikes but on the other hand conceded, at least by implication, that the Baltic and Caucasian republics could secede. The transfer of much industrial and economic management to the other republics, and the fixing of 1992 for a new constitution and new free elections were other features. At about the same time Yeltsin secured the right for a Russian Republic television service and for a substantially independent Russian Republic KGB.

The freer atmosphere had encouraged many strikes throughout the USSR over the previous months, usually in support of wage claims or better conditions. In 1989 there had been a strike by the Donbas miners, once regarded as a Bolshevik stronghold. In April 1991 the workers of

Byelorussia, hitherto one of the most tranquil republics, came out on strike, and also in that month the new Independent Federation of Trade Unions called a one-hour strike involving millions (fifty million, it was said) of workers protesting against price rises. By this time, demands for an end to party organizations within workshops had also begun to figure in the workers' demands. One of the showpieces of Soviet industrialization, the Uralmash engineering works with its 32,000 workers, voted overwhelmingly for an end to party organizations within the plant.

In June came the municipal and presidential election in the RSFSR. For the Russian presidency, Yeltsin was the favourite, and his chosen running mate for vice-president, the fighter pilot and Afghanistan veteran Aleksandr Rutskoi, was also popular. The party organizations, anxious above all to defeat Yeltsin, mostly favoured Ryzhkov. There were four other candidates, and Yeltsin's margin might have been smaller if the election had been held less hurriedly; he had already built up his popularity but the other candidates had insufficient time to present their cases. Ryzhkov would have done better if there had been fewer candidates. As it was, he came second with 17 per cent of the votes cast. Yeltsin won 57 per cent and the next candidate received 8 per cent.

The latter was Zhirinovski, who styled himself as a liberal democrat but advocated views not far removed from those of the right-wing nationalists of the tsarist Fourth Duma. His support may well have grown in the later months of 1991 as he learned from experience the potential of populism; already in August he was suggesting it was time to return Finland to the Russian fold. He was adept at answering simplistic criticism with simplistic retorts:[3]

'Don't you think it's terrible to draw parallels between you and Hitler?'
'But I'm not making any parallels. Adolf was an uneducated corporal, whereas I'm a graduate of two higher institutes and know four languages.'

Yeltsin was sworn in as RSFSR president in the presence of Gorbachev and the Moscow patriarch Aleksii II. His seat was not to be in the Russian government building on the banks of the Moscow River, but in the Kremlin itself.

One of Yeltsin's first moves after the election was to issue a decree banning the activity of all political parties and organizations from factories and institutions. Potentially this could have affected trade unions but in fact was aimed, and seen to be aimed, directly at the Communist Party in the RSFSR. It was a devastating blow to the party organization in Russia, striking at the base of its pyramid.

[3] From an interview (*Gudok*, 4 September 1991, 1) in which he recommended sending half a million troops into East Germany to restore the status quo.

Gorbachev at this time was moving away from conservatism back to policies more palatable to the democrats. In March he had given a sign that he was ready to shift his ground, when he made a speech attacking 'dogmatic conservative forces supporting socialism without democracy', and by the summer he was clearly trying once again to put some life into *perestroika*. However, life had moved on and many of his old supporters were now determined to end the party's power, whereas Gorbachev still preserved his faith that the party would eventually become a vanguard of reform. Yakovlev, his old adviser, was summoned to defend himself before the party's higher officials after he had joined with Shevardnadze in July to publish the manifesto of the new Movement for Democratic Reform. Instead of waiting for expulsion, Yakovlev resigned from the party, a move that was more devastating than Yeltsin's earlier resignation because Yakovlev's membership had persuaded many that the party was not beyond redemption.

To varying degrees other republics were asserting their independence and a break-up of the USSR seemed closer. Quite apart from the political and psychological effects of this, there was a clear threat to the economy, which for a hundred years had been based on a specialized division of labour between the various parts of the empire. To avoid a catastrophic collapse and in the hope of stabilizing the situation, in July Gorbachev succeeded in drawing up a Union Treaty. With the Baltic and the southern republics intent on going their own way, the nine other republics appeared willing to sign this agreement, which gave them much greater power over their economic and financial affairs.

This greater autonomy for the republics was, for many, a sure sign that the USSR was on the verge of collapse. For many of Gorbachev's colleagues this was a last straw, added to the current disintegration of the economy, of the party, of the world as they had known it. Desperately trying to avert what they believed to be a catastrophe, some of them had tried by the political means available to them to change things in April, when there had been a move to oust Gorbachev at the party plenum, and in June, when an unsuccessful attempt was made to persuade the Supreme Soviet to transfer some of Gorbachev's powers to Pavlov. Gorbachev had skilfully defeated these moves, but the very fact that Pavlov stayed in office suggested that he was in a very weak situation.

In the days preceding the August crisis Gorbachev went to London to confer with western leaders about possible economic aid, then returned to a meeting of the Central Committee in which, although he had his back to the wall, he did not hesitate to suggest a new party programme that talked of a 'humane' socialism rather than Marxism–Leninism. Then he went with his family to his Crimean *dacha* to take a short holiday before returning to Moscow to sign the Union Treaty.

The handful of men who had decided to take unconstitutional action were very mixed, and the description of them as 'hardliners' was not helpful. Some had more misgivings than others, but persuaded themselves that in his heart of hearts Gorbachev felt the same as they did. He was invited either to sign a state of emergency or to transfer his powers to the USSR vice-president, and when he refused he was isolated in his *dacha*. The country was informed that he was ill and that an emergency committee (formed of the leading conspirators) was temporarily to take the helm.

In Moscow and Leningrad the plotters had made some half-hearted preparations, but elsewhere they relied on the army and KGB obeying their orders. In Moscow they failed to arrest key figures who might have been expected to oppose them. These included Shevardnadze, Sobchak, Yakovlev, and, most important, Yeltsin. Sobchak rushed back to Leningrad where by sheer force of word and intellect he frustrated officers and officials who were preparing to support the coup. The other leaders made their way to the Russian Republic's governmental headquarters, the so-called 'White House' in Moscow, where hundreds of other citizens joined them in a courageous show of defiance. Here, too, were the deputies of the Russian parliament, popularly elected just like Yeltsin and therefore with a better claim to legitimacy than the 'emergency committee'. The 'White House' remained in communication with the outside world; in fact both the US president and British prime minister telephoned Yeltsin to convey their best wishes at this critical time.

Inside the USSR, Zhirinovski and Alksnis (a prominent member of the *Soyuz* movement) supported the coup in radio and television interviews, while in the Russian Republic two-thirds of the Communist Party organizations willingly acquiesced and the remainder adopted a wait-and-see stance. As for ordinary people, they seemed to have no strong feelings. The emergency committee's instruction to live and work normally was unexceptional, but did not prevent pro-democracy demonstrations. What was significant, and seems to have surprised the plotters, was that not only the Red Army but also the KGB had doubts about the proceedings. When troops were ordered into Moscow to 'preserve order' they obeyed half-heartedly, and some men even took a handful of tanks to defend the White House, where they had a psychological effect out of all proportion to their numbers. There were enough disobedient members of a specialized KGB unit to prevent it accepting the instruction to fight its way into the White House. Having had several years of increasing freedom, having for the most part voted for Yeltsin as their president, having, in short, realized that people no longer had to be pushed around, the men in uniform showed that Gorbachev's *glasnost'* was not just a passing fashion.

However, Yeltsin's call for a general strike was only a partial success, with many workers ignoring it. The Ukrainian communist leader Kravchuk was among those urging their workers to stay on the job.

In the end the plot failed, its sponsors for the most part lacking the ruthlessness that might, just might, have overcome the reluctance of soldiers and police to obey orders. On the fourth day some of the conspirators, having decided to plead with Gorbachev, took off for the Crimea, hotly pursued by another jet airliner containing an armed party sent by Yeltsin's Russian government. In the end the main plotters were arrested. The interior minister Pugo and his wife gave much-needed dignity to the conspiracy by committing suicide, and the KGB head Kryuchkov, defence minister Yazov, prime minister Pavlov, the vice-president, and several others were arrested on charges of treason.

Yeltsin, who had led the continuous defiance outside the White House, and whose supporters managed to print and distribute news-sheets as well as run an anti-coup radio station, was rightly regarded as the hero of the hour. In his public statements he had been careful to centre his demands on the restoration of Gorbachev's presidential powers, but in reality those few days had elevated Yeltsin's stature and done nothing to enhance Gorbachev's. In popular perception, Gorbachev had been betrayed by men he had himself appointed and had been rescued by his political opponent.

In the next few days Yeltsin plainly exceeded his formal powers. Some of the instructions he had issued during the height of the crisis when, in a sense, he was acting on behalf of the USSR as well as of the Russian Republic, were confirmed; the dismissal of the head of *Gostelradio* had been an example of Yeltsin's encroachments and was not going to be undone. Although Yeltsin may not have approved the so-called witch-hunts in the party and government organizations, designed to sniff out and dismiss those who had actively or passively sympathized with the coup, much of his behaviour at this time was decidedly illiberal. But this could be explained by his belief that it would have been inexcusable to lose the opportunity of crushing that many-headed hydra, the party, once and for all.

He temporarily suspended the activities of the Communist Party in the Russian Republic, and some newspapers were banned until they had proved that they intended to mend their ways. Soon Yeltsin also banned party activity in military, KGB, and Tass news agency units stationed in his republic. The party headquarters buildings in Moscow and Leningrad were sealed. This latter move prevented party workers entering these buildings and put an end to the destruction of incriminating party documents that was already under way. A close study began of surviving documents, special interest being shown in those detailing financial transactions. Efforts of the party to secrete part of its immense wealth into foreign banks were studied, and several of the party's financial administrators died, apparently by suicide, in this period. Among other suicides was that of the former Red Army chief of staff Akhromeev, who apparently had taken no part in the unsuccessful coup but left a note which, in effect, was an explanation for both his own and others' suicides at this time: everything to which he had dedicated his life was being destroyed. At his funeral, relatives accused 'liberal fascists' of hounding him to death. He was buried in full uniform, and shortly afterwards nocturnal operators exhumed him in order to steal it.

Events in the last week of August meant the end of *perestroika*. Gorbachev himself finally acknowledged that it would not be the party that would carry out the changes. He resigned as general secretary, nationalized party property (an enormous but still-to-be-counted collection of assets), called for the dissolution of the Central Committee, and banned party activity in the Soviet forces, KGB, and police. Meanwhile the USSR Supreme Soviet suspended party activity in the USSR. It also signalled the end of the old USSR by proposing a new, looser union of sovereign states.

The remainder of 1991 was largely spent, or wasted, in coming to terms with the new situation. Transfer of power from Gorbachev's USSR to the republics was remorseless, with Yeltsin setting the pace and Gorbachev fighting a rearguard action to preserve the union. At the end of 1991, with the republics collecting and keeping the taxes and with the Ukraine voting for independence, it became clear that the USSR had run its unique course.

Nobody is in any doubt that the state known for decades as the Union of Soviet Socialist Republics has died and will be impossible to resuscitate, although the official funeral—putting an end to the validity of the present USSR Constitution—is yet to come. The problem which most worries us all now is, what kind of state are we going to live in?[4]

As for the Communist Party, it was returning to its roots almost literally, being driven to a near-underground existence. Its remnants had split, but each was trying to reorganize. In September 1991 the 'Democratic Party of the Communists of Russia' held its founding conference, and in November the 'Lenin Socialist Party of the Working Class' organized itself at a conference in Siberia. Just as some conservative groups seemed to be

---

[4] *Za rubezhom*, 22 November 1991, 1. This is an example of numerous editorials of the time, all saying very much the same thing.

resembling more and more the right-wing nationalists of the time of Nicholas II, so did the marxists seem to be reverting to the small, barely tolerated, and divided movement of late tsarist times. Some of them were beginning to interpret the Gorbachev revolution as the bourgeois revolution prescribed by Marx but obstructed by the Bolsheviks.

The economy

The decline of Gorbachev's reputation after 1988 was largely due to his inability to improve the economic situation, as seen by the woman in the street. The growing queues and scarcities were just one sign of an economic deterioration that could be traced back to the policies of previous decades, aggravated by new policies that crippled old managerial methods without providing an effective replacement.

The miserable inheritance from previous years was reflected, indeed symbolized, by a series of disasters that punctuated the Gorbachev years. The main reason for this catastrophic spate was the toleration of unsafe practices in the quest for ever-higher production figures; the toxic air breathed by a third of Soviet city-dwellers was itself visible testimony of decades of neglect.

The disaster at the Chernobyl nuclear power station, near Kiev, in spring 1986, was a test of Gorbachev's leadership, a warning of international significance, and above all an implied condemnation of the Soviet way of doing things. The plant was designed as a huge conglomerate of four reactors, one of which suffered a catastrophic explosion followed by a fire lasting, in its critical phase, two weeks, during which considerable radioactive material was released into the atmosphere. The initial hours were marked by a characteristic Russian blend of heroism, improvization, and muddle. Also characteristic was the reluctance to report bad news; local officials tried hard to conceal the scale of the accident but, out of tune with the times, seemed unaware that one kind of bad news is carried by the wind. Despite *glasnost'*, the Soviet public was not promptly informed, nor were proper precautions taken to protect the population from fall-out. Indeed, the party organization in Kiev decided to continue with the May Day celebrations so as to emphasize that there was nothing to worry about; this, however, did not prevent some party officials and others in the know dispatching their children to more salubrious regions. Parts of the Ukraine, Byelorussia, and the Baltic republics were contaminated to varying degrees, as well as Poland and, less severely, other parts of Europe. In a striking demonstration of professional solidarity transcending ideological frontiers, both Soviet and non-Soviet government scientists for years afterwards minimized the number of deaths that could be attributed to this accident. Five years later, large populations were still living in areas of dangerously high contamination.

The accident occurred in a non-Russian part of the Union and its fall-out affected other non-Russian parts. The Communist Party, since it claimed credit for all technical successes, could logically be blamed for the failures too. Thus Chernobyl was a blow to the concepts of the Union, of the leading role of the Communist Party, and of a high-technology future.

A different kind of *glasnost'* was lacking when a Soviet liner collided with a tanker in the Black Sea. The horrifying death toll would have been less if the passengers had been warned in good time that a collision was imminent. Russia's worst railway accident, however, was a consequence of negligent workmanship, negligent maintenance, and unheeded warnings. It occurred when gas from a leaking trunk pipeline accumulated around a railway line and was ignited by two passing passenger trains; hundreds of passengers were incinerated. Even natural disasters could show up the weaknesses of Soviet society. A high-scale earthquake in Armenia was made all the more lethal by the readiness with which poorly-constructed buildings collapsed.

These disasters were only the worst of scores of fatal occurrences in which negligence, incompetence, and often drunkenness were involved. Human and material shoddiness was commonplace. So much so, that when a New Zealand government investigation into the sinking of a Soviet cruise liner blamed New Zealand officials and praised the crew, its report was received with some incredulity in the USSR.

Empty shops and numerous accidents were symptoms of more fundamental ills. Although statistics showed continuing, though declining, economic growth up to the end of the 1980s, the real rate of growth (subtracting such items as environmental protection that should have been provided but was not, new equipment that was needed but not supplied, and so on) was probably zero before *perestroika* began. In 1990 industrial production was already falling, although this was partly accounted for by a drastic fall in defence output, which may have declined by a quarter. Interestingly, increasing shortages in the shops were accompanied by rising production of consumer goods.

Similarly, although harvests in 1989 and 1990 were good,[5] foodstuffs became scarce. Many local authorities introduced rationing schemes in 1990 and 1991. These were of varying types, many of them being designed not to allocate supplies evenly but to prevent certain people getting anything, the

---

[5] Grain production (million tonnes)

| 1985 | 178 | 1987 | 194 | 1989 | 197 |
| 1986 | 194 | 1988 | 180 | 1990 | 218 |

target being outsiders (often a euphemism for village-dwellers) who were alleged to visit localities (often a euphemism for cities) to buy available commodities. Because rationing was locally devised, there was no guarantee that coupons would be honoured. In late 1991 St. Petersburg, sausage coupons were being exchanged for butter, and sugar could be obtained with flour coupons, and there were innumerable other absurdities and paradoxes:

Staff at the corrective labour colony put forward their own equally strong claims and convincingly showed the commission that they eat worse than their prisoners. In particular, the monthly prisoner's ration in this specialized colony is 4.5 kg of meat, 1.2 kg of butter and 300 g of margarine. The colony staff get ration coupons for 1 kg of meat, 250 g of butter and 100 g of margarine.[6]

Shortage, as always, meant leverage. Those who controlled supply could control much else besides. But this power could sometimes be used positively. In Vorkuta, where work accidents were frequent, the town soviet in late 1991 was offering a kilo of meat to blood donors, and those lucky enough to belong to a rare blood group received 100 g of chocolate in addition.

For years people had been accumulating savings simply because there was so little to buy. This meant there was an enormous purchasing power at large in the economy that could keep the shops empty even if more goods were produced. This purchasing 'overhang' compromised any plan for economic reform; it may have provided one of the motives for Pavlov's 1991 calling-in of high-denomination banknotes (whose owners were promised reimbursement only if they could show that their wealth had been honestly obtained, and even then they could claim back only a small amount each month). Inflation, which in 1991 was bordering on hyperinflation, and which was a well-tried capitalist instrument of expropriation, could be expected to moderate, if not eliminate, this problem. Another possible solution was the privatization of industry and housing by means of private purchase.

A growing proportion of industrial and agricultural output never reached the market. It was used, instead, for barter, with a given factory undertaking to supply its products in exchange for products from another enterprise.

As we entered the Moven factory in the suburbs of Moscow the unmistakable smell of fresh-smoked fish filled our nostrils. The trouble was, this wasn't a fish factory. It produces industrial ventilators.

[6] *Gudok*, 5 November 1991, 1. This labour camp, near Chita, was for unhealthy prisoners. Other camps were not fed so well.

Alexander Mironov, president of the company, explained; he had taken delivery that morning of a couple of hundred cases of fish from the Baltic in part payment for ventilators supplied . . . The fish was sold at cost to the Moven's 490 workers who therefore won't have to join the Soviet Union's omnipresent queues which, according to estimates, waste 86 billion man hours a year.[7]

Individual republics, too, made barter agreements between themselves, and took measures to prevent other scarce products being exported across their borders. With the breakdown of the centralized administration, and with its replacement, the free market, slow to appear, this reversion to primitive modes of trade was unsurprising and indeed necessary at times. An unknown but growing proportion of output was stolen, although this eventually found its way through the black market into consumption. At the local level, environmental movements occasionally forced particularly obnoxious factories to close. In 1990, this resulted in an aspirin famine.

More strikes, ever-decreasing incentives to work hard, and supply problems meant that some vital products became rare. The spare-part problem had long plagued Soviet industry, and now became more acute. The old planning system in many cases had concentrated production of certain items on one factory, so interruption of production in one plant might have an enormous impact. The most obvious case of this phenomenon was when the factory making cigarette filters faltered, resulting in a prolonged cigarette shortage throughout the USSR.

A Communist Party plenum in 1985 had accepted the need for economic reform, and in the next six years a whole series of measures was passed, and even more discussed, but somehow things did not get better. The planned economy, with central institutions like *Gosplan* and the industrial ministries in Moscow making decisions and controlling activity, was plainly on the way out, but the free-market system which was to follow it was not clearly visualized. Few had experience of the free, or market, economy and indeed there were some doubts about whether Russians as a whole were psychologically prepared for it. Ideally the free economy should have been given decades to root itself, but this seemed impossible.

In the first years of *perestroika* the aim was a 'socialist market economy' in which central planning would be retained for the big matters like choice of investment but the 'market' (that is, prices) would regulate day-to-day production decisions. But by 1990 there was a growing belief that central planning and direction (that is, the planned economy) needed to be excluded from the big decisions as well. There were varying opinions about the degree of economic freedom and an increasing number of politically active people advocated the complete deregulation which, they imagined,

[7] *Guardian*, 10 May 1991, 21.

enhanced the economies of such countries as the USA and Britain. In the USSR there were very few people who understood how modern capitalism actually worked. The avidity with which the free-market ideology was grasped recalled Marx's cynical comment about the enthusiasm of Russian intellectuals for any new system of ideas, provided only that it originated in the west.

There was a burst of reform measures in 1987, not all of which were put into force. The most important was the law on State Enterprises. This gave enterprises independence in their decision-making and financial responsibility. But managers, who could now be elected by their workers, still knew that if their costs exceeded their revenues they could ask for a subsidy (and in 1988 24,000 of the 46,000 state enterprises made a loss). Moreover, as supplies were increasingly scarce managers preferred the old system of centrally allocated materials rather than the new system in which they were expected to seek out and bargain with suppliers. On the whole, this law weakened the old 'administrative command' system while not really encouraging the emergence of an effective market to replace it.

A price reform, aimed at securing the novel (for the USSR) advantage of prices actually informing buyers and sellers how valuable (in terms of production cost and scarcity) a product really was, had to be postponed when it was realized that freeing prices would inevitably result in a sudden and enormous price rise, something that Gorbachev was very unwilling to accept for political and social reasons. But enterprises did gain some freedom in price-setting and by calling their products new, or redesigned, or improved, they were able to ask considerably higher prices for what were virtually the same items; in this respect, at least, they showed they were quite ready for the western-style economic system.

In 1988, direct planning of output was in a formal sense abandoned. But central planners gave enterprises 'state orders' instead. These obliged them to deliver certain amounts of specified products (usually a high proportion of their total output), and materials for these were allocated from the centre as before. As time passed, however, enterprises showed decreasing enthusiasm for fulfilling state orders; sometimes they could get better prices by disposing of their products elsewhere, sometimes their own republican governments issued orders conflicting with those of the centre.

The 1988 Law on Co-operatives (tightened up later) should have been a decisive step forward in loosening the economy, given the popularity of co-operatives in pre-Stalin times. It enabled a new entrepreneurial class to set up as manufacturers or business people, actually employing others. Many badly needed products or services were thereby provided, often quite efficiently. But there were problems. Co-operatives usually depended on the goodwill of local authorities and where this was lacking they were soon in trouble. An official who did not like the new freedoms could usually find a way to ruin a local business; in one case a thriving new enterprise producing hothouse tomatoes was ruined when the power supply was cut off for a few hours in the winter. Some local authorities took 90 per cent of a co-operative's profits as tax. Successful co-operatives could offer higher pay and thus attract workers from state industries and this caused resentment, one of many examples of how general enthusiasm for a freeing of the economy could coexist with horror at its manifestations. The co-operatives also suffered from growing public distrust. The most successful entrepreneurs soon became rich, and this was hard to accept for an increasingly deprived public, culturally opposed to inequality in any case. What made things worse was that the new breed of entrepreneurs seemed to have easy access to capital and it was soon realized that many members of the Communist Party apparatus, seeing the writing on the wall, were making use of their existing power to entrench themselves as a new entrepreneurial class. In many cases it was suspected, rightly as it turned out, that these officials were obtaining capital by the fraudulent conversion of party assets. The term 'Mafia' was soon in general circulation to describe the invisible yet obvious underworld that sought to control newly emerging enterprise. Some of the shaky banks that appeared after the 1988 Law on Bank Specialization were believed to have dubious, if not illegal, foundations.

New freedoms were extended to agriculture, and thousands of 'family farms' were established. These only amounted to a small fraction of the cultivated area, and the new independent peasants depended very much on goodwill from their former collective farm administration. While lease of land by families was permitted, actual transfer of land ownership was a very emotional issue and Gorbachev was one of the many who could not face this departure from the morality on which they had been brought up. Land could be granted in perpetuity to a family, but the 'owner' was not allowed to sell it or to employ non-family workers on it. But Gorbachev did eventually relent to the extent of suggesting that referendums on the issue might be staged by the different republics. In industry, too, leasing was quite popular, and in due course workers who had leased their state enterprise were allowed to buy it, with a promise that there would be no expropriation later.

Financing by share issue became legal and so, therefore, did trading in shares. However, the 'stock exchanges' that appeared in various cities were mainly engaged in commodity trading. Despite some scandals, and the hostility aroused by so-called non-producers making good money, they provided a useful service and were a step towards the market economy.

From 1989 there was a succession of proposals for more radical changes, and in summer 1990 these debates resulted in two major plans for the transition to a market economy. The Ryzhkov and Shatalin plans had similar goals, but the latter envisaged a shorter (500-day) timescale, and more devolution of decision-making to republican governments (for example, unlike the Ryzhkov, or 'government' plan, it envisaged the replacement of Gosbank, the central bank, by a federal reserve system after the American model). Both plans aimed at privatization, and normal economic relations with the outside world (and hence a rouble freely convertible to other currencies). Both had difficulty in finding a non-explosive way to free prices. Even though indexation of wages and pensions was seen as a way to soften the impact, neither pretended that there could be full indexation.

Gorbachev for the USSR and Yeltsin for the Russian Republic announced that they favoured the Shatalin plan, but the Supreme Soviet would not make a choice and gave Gorbachev the right to decide, by decree. At first a combination of the two plans seemed likely, but by the end of 1990 it was clear that Gorbachev had lost his enthusiasm.

Essentially, nothing was then done for a year, during which the economy continued on its downward course. Inflation was accelerating fast. The budget deficit grew despite the introduction of a progressive income tax in 1990 with a rate of 50 per cent for the higher incomes. Thanks to relaxed controls, including the new right of industries to handle their own foreign-currency transactions, to increased imports, and to falling oil output and oil prices, hard currency reserves disappeared and the USSR was unable to pay its foreign debts. Finally, as the USSR was breaking up, Yeltsin announced a rapid jump to the market economy for the Russian Republic. Prices were to be freed, and privatization pushed forward with shops, among other assets, being offered for sale.

Money and credits, once so freely available for projects approved by the party, became scarce. The party had never overcome its fondness for lavish, premature expenditure on projects that took years to complete, and in 1991 funds for completing these disappeared; one grand project, the BAM railway, was at least open for traffic, but could not pay its debts. To soften what seemed likely to be a very difficult winter, western help in the form of grain and financial credits was sought and to some extent obtained. However, the steady transfer of powers from the centre to the republics meant that in 1991 western governments, like western companies, had difficulty in knowing which governments and institutions had the authority to make agreements. Equally important was the reluctance of western governments to find the necessary money, even though they were aware that failure to help the former Soviet people might open the way for extremist political movements. What was once the Soviet economy had come to depend on democratic western governments with their 'too little, too late' approach, a far cry from communist planning with its penchant for 'too much, too soon'.

In January 1992, immediately after the break-up of the USSR, consumer goods prices were freed in the Russian Republic, only a few basic items remaining under control (although simultaneously doubled or more). Yeltsin and his advisers, aware that this decision was very much a last throw, hoped that higher prices would bring more goods into the shops. The neighbouring governments of Ukraine and Byelorussia protested against this unilateral decision, fearing that their own scarce goods, still at the low prices, would drain into Russia. In the end, these two governments had to follow the Russian example, protesting that price deregulation before privatization was absurd and could only lead to exploitation by the producing monopolies.

Society

One of the new freedoms brought by *glasnost'* was the freedom to conduct and publish polls. At first they were amateurish, typically involving telephone calls that might be randomly chosen but inevitably recorded the opinions of that small sector that possessed telephones. But by the late 1980s techniques had improved.

Unsurprisingly, polls confirmed that the main care of people was not political freedom, or democracy, or economic reform, but how to obtain the necessities of life.[8] Shortages and poor services dominated lives and therefore thoughts. Of the non-material issues, lack of social justice caused by string-pulling and influence consistently ranked high. After 1987 most people believed that they had not benefited from *perestroika*, and by 1990 a majority thought it had worsened their standard of life, as reflected by the perceived gap between their incomes and rising price levels. Gorbachev's personal popularity fell in parallel; from October 1989 to June 1991 the number who fully trusted him fell from 52 to 10 per cent. Blame for the disappointments of *perestroika* was equally levelled at governmental indecisiveness and the machinations of the old *apparatchiki*.

Shortages and increasing crime meant that people were justified in saying, as they frequently did, that things were better in Brezhnev's time. The new political freedoms and the widened range of permissible activities were undervalued partly because most people did not have the leisure to enjoy them and partly because their advent was patchy. As always, local

[8] The verb 'to obtain', rather than 'to buy', had long been preferred by Soviet citizens, a semantic shift that perfectly fitted an economy structured on shortage.

officials and organizations could find ways of blocking change. But, in course of time, *glasnost'* ensured that many injustices were publicized and put right, and this encouraged others to defy overbearing bureaucrats. That defiance became an alternative to servility was an enormous step forward, but not everybody appreciated this, for imagining past outrage is rather like imagining past pain.

The disappearance of the old prohibitions against forming independent organizations gave birth not only to political parties but to interest groups of all kinds. Boy Scout troops began to compete for members with the Young Pioneers. Railway enthusiasts formed a society, and so did the surviving veterans of the atomic bomb tests of the 1950s, able to organize in pursuit of redress for the damage they had suffered when, as soldiers, they were marched into the detonation zone. Long-persecuted religious groups found relief both in the freedom to organize and in the new official tolerance. The Old Believers once more began to needle the official Church, and in 1991 even the Doukhobors resurfaced for a conference. Employers, especially private employers, were beginning to show a preference for recruiting sectarians like Baptists and Pentecostals, considered more resistant to temptation.

Under Gorbachev the Russian Orthodox Church recovered from the shattering experience of Khrushchev's anti-religious campaign and began to reassert its traditional functions. In 1988 Gorbachev implicitly promised a better status for the Church if it put its support behind *perestroika*, and a few weeks later the millenium of the Russian Orthodox Church was celebrated with public splendour. In print, the long-imposed 'god' reverted to the pre-revolutionary 'God'. Gorbachev, a man of morality, was probably sincere when he said that religion and communism had some common aims, and the Church was allowed to take up the charitable activities that had long been forbidden. This enabled it to fill a yawning gap in Soviet society, helping the poor, the sick, and the neglected, opening homes for orphans and old people who previously had only the excrementitious state institutions to look forward to.

Some confiscated churches were handed back, but the new atmosphere brought its complications. There was a split, more implied than blatant, between churchmen who had returned from the labour camps, and those who had progressed upwards by conformity and servility. There was also renewed friction between the Russian Orthodox Church and other, newly tolerated, religious organizations and sects. Among these were the Uniate Church in the Ukraine, that soon took back its confiscated churches from the Russian Orthodox Church. The Russian Orthodox Church seemed slow to condemn anti-semitism, but its head, Patriarch Aleksii II, handled the political upheaval of August 1991 quite deftly (he waited until the second day, and then declared that Gorbachev should have the right to state his case; this was just enough to escape accusations of supporting the coup).

From 1990 unemployment was officially recognized in the USSR, and it was no longer illegal to be unemployed. Labour exchanges and employment centres were set up and the way was open for a limited allowance of unemployment pay.

Freedom to organize, among other things, meant the end of the old trade unions. First one then another of the unions was taken over by real workers, usually by the democratic process of a conference and majority voting. The old subservient officials were ejected and the union renamed, with 'independent' usually incorporated in its new title. The new unions paid more attention to poor and unsafe working conditions and had the power to get things done; although several laws were passed to limit strikes, they had little effect. On the other hand, union power was limited in its ability to achieve better living standards. In key industries like mining a strike could eventually produce substantial wage increases but in conditions of scarcity such increases could not always be spent. Soon, union demands included allocations of scarce products. In some industries there was competition between unions, with the old union, perhaps under new management, struggling on without the benefit of its old monopoly. In 1991 Moscow there were, for example, three writers' unions: the USSR Writers' Union, the Russian Republic's Writers' Union and, newly formed in opposition to the latter, the Union of Russian Writers.

In 1991 a policewomen's union was formed, notable for being the first trade union to appear in the security forces and for its single-gender membership; the ordinary policeman, and especially the ordinary policewoman, had long been a very vulnerable worker and needed, especially, the legal support that could be offered by a union.

Women began to organize elsewhere, too. Dissatisfied with the official Soviet Women's Committee, which was party-dominated and disinclined to struggle against the prevailing patriarchism of Soviet society, various independent women's groups developed and in April 1991 held a nation-wide women's conference to discuss the real issues and to form a permanent all-Union organization. To help and advise women at the workplace, from 1990 the 'Eve' association organized regional centres which helped women to requalify and to set themselves up as businesswomen; it was also hoping to establish a women's bank.

The 'woman question' had been openly acknowledged in the 1920s and the party had even had a women's department with an interest in the possible restructuring of women's lives. But in 1930 the department was closed, the government claiming that the woman question had been solved. During the Khrushchev years the government, alarmed perhaps by declining fertility and unsatisfying female labour productivity, had been willing to allow studies of female problems, but little resulted from this. Under Gorbachev there was more official sympathy, but the underlying culture seemed likely to hold back the emergence of any real, pervasive, sex equality. The advent of democracy did not give women any more political power; women were less likely to win elective office, because of prevailing assumptions. In early 1991 women constituted 18 per cent of the USSR Supreme Soviet, whereas in the old days they had approached a third.

Women still composed half the labour force, and as a matter of course would take responsibility for running the home as well. Although they were not badly represented in middle management, very few reached the top. In 1991 the increasing unemployment seemed to hit women workers hardest.

Allegations that wife-beating was a mass phenomenon may have been exaggerated, but the prevalent attitude towards women, combined with poor housing, would certainly have created the conditions for it. Abortion was still considered the normal method of birth control; in 1991 it was said that there were 137 abortions for every 100 live births. As for rape, this was a subject from which the forces of law and order preferred to remain aloof. There were some technical reasons for this, not least the problem of proof, but the characteristic response of a policeman to a woman's desperate plea for help against a predatory male, 'How can I be sure he's not your husband?' implied something more.

In the health sector four-fifths of the workers were women; the high concentration of female workers in non-priority sectors like medicine and education was a legacy of the Stalinist years, as was the low pay in these services. The low quality of medical services was not always reflected in the statistics. For example, the increasing number of medical centres was publicized, but not the number of such centres where there was no running water and no telephone. Shortages of drugs and supplies, and not only of the rarely used varieties, were a daily fact of life and death.

The possibility that the epidemic of Aids, hitherto ignored or treated as a disease of capitalist society, might affect the USSR, was taken seriously only after the re-use of syringes (a necessary, and therefore normal, practice) infected a large number of children in one hospital. The disease then attracted some attention. Some posters were exhibited, the earliest of which suggested that avoiding promiscuous women was the best safeguard, but the criminality of homosexual acts hampered effective publicity. The interior minister, Pugo, shortly before his own demise, arranged for special police units to be formed with the aim of uncovering and prosecuting people concealing their Aids affliction. The limited study of this epidemic was hampered from 1990 by the disintegration of the Union, research data from the republics no longer being sent to the central statistical unit in Moscow. The official, and no doubt under-estimated, figure announced in 1991 was about 1,200 HIV-positives in the USSR, of whom a half were foreign residents.

Public health campaigns of a type seen in the west were virtually unknown, although under *glasnost'* they could be expected to develop. The level of smoking was reminiscent of 1940s Britain or America. Doctors were themselves among the heaviest smokers; this was part of the reason for their higher morbidity, but stressful work, poor living standards, exposure to radiation from low-standard equipment, and exposure to patients' infections also played a part. The Soviet public was unaware of the potential danger of asbestos; even if it had been told that Soviet Railways ballasted thousands of kilometres of track with asbestos waste it would not have cared.

Under Gorbachev, *glasnost'* meant that the defects of the health services could be criticized but the general lack of resources meant there could not be an instant remedy for six decades of neglect. There was the beginning of a drive to decentralize administration, and an experiment in which doctors played a role similar to the western general practitioner rather than performing impersonal functions within the polyclinic system, with its atmosphere of authoritarianism, bribe-taking, and abuse. Psychiatry was slow to improve; easy solutions, in the form of chemical treatments and diagnosing for life, meant a proliferation of cruelties.

With education, the situation was not so grave. There were abuses and defects, but the system was workable. No great changes were undertaken, but *glasnost'* did its job in exposing disgraceful and often remediable situations. Head teachers were able to make limited modifications to the syllabus. The chaos caused by the rewriting of history was manageable; pupils, after all, had a sense of humour.

However the teenager, more perhaps than other members of society, found it difficult to adjust in an atmosphere of overturned values. The 1986 law permitting the establishment of amateur clubs was followed by a surge of youth groupings that could generally be termed counter-cultural. Western models were often followed; mods and rockers, skinheads, punks and hippies all found their Soviet imitators. But there also appeared a counter-counter-culture; groups of teenage males whose object in life was to beat up those they considered to have deviated from proper Soviet (later, proper Russian) standards. Often addicts of bodybuilding and martial arts, these young toughs found late-night suburban trains and deserted town streets to be the best battleground for their kind of terrorism.

The grind of poverty, the overturning of morality, and above all the awareness that some undeserving people were doing very well indeed, combined with the weakening of the authoritarian state to produce a situation where crime flourished. The immense gains that could be made by the acquisition of scarce products led to inter-gang warfare that might end in murder. Various kinds of protection racket damaged honest traders. As so often happens when an authoritarian regime is liberalized, not only did trains run late but street and other crime increased. Mugging became an everyday occurrence and although the increase of crime was exaggerated in the popular imagination it was certainly true that it became inadvisable to be alone in certain places at certain times. Nor was home safe:

Endeavouring to safeguard themselves from the debauchery of robbed apartments, many inhabitants of Magnitogorsk have begun to acquire dogs of the bigger breeds like sheepdogs and Alsatians. A group of people describing themselves as members of the 'Alex' detective agency have turned up here and begun a lively trade in 'Hound of the Baskerville' puppies. Their outrageous prices do not discourage everybody, but when the puppies grow up they turn out to be not of pedigree blood, but ordinary Little-Russian mongrels. State officials are now investigating those private detectives.[9]

A special armed service of the Interior Ministry, the OMON or 'black berets', was formed to deal with armed gangs, but considerable imagination was required to find daily tasks for it:

Coastal and other tourist resorts of the Krasnodar region recently witnessed intense activity initiated by the newly formed MVD of the Russian Republic. Police helicopters, armed militia detachments of the regional OMON force, and the highway inspectorate's patrols all took part. Local residents thought a band of desperadoes was being hunted down, but the reality was that they were conducting a purge of undesirables, drunks and criminal elements in preparation for the summer season.[10]

The police and KGB were themselves weakened by the new political situation, although both tried hard to fit into the new norms of social behaviour. The KGB in 1988 was obliged to transfer its notorious psychiatric institutions to the health ministry, and began to engage in various public-relations endeavours, even showing journalists around its head office at the Lubyanka in Moscow. It proclaimed its readiness to answer all reasonable questions, but was the final judge of what was reasonable. It made successive concessions to public opinion, but when Kryuchkov was appointed as its head it seemed ready to relapse into its old ways. He was

---

[9] *Gudok*, 5 February 1991, 4.   [10] *Vodnyi transport*, 27 April 1991, 1 (edited).

arrested for his part in the August coup, and the continuing public distaste for the KGB was symbolized in the aftermath of that coup when the statue of Dzerzhinski, founder of the Soviet security service, received at the hands of aroused Muscovites injuries that proved fatal. The KGB was soon split into three separate functional organizations, and many of its officials were replaced. These personnel changes, however, were determined mainly on how a given official had behaved during the coup rather than on competence.

The concept of a 'civil society', long reviled by marxists as simply a class-based façade, but providing a set of institutions, standards, and laws that would act as a check and balance on the state, seemed to be taking birth. But it would not come easily. People who could group together over a single issue or on an ethnic basis found it difficult to unite around something that still seemed abstract and of which they had no experience. A reworking of legal norms and principles was accepted as desirable, but little was done in the years of *perestroika*. It is true that judges responded to the new climate by adjusting their verdicts to fit, and that had a great effect, but in an ideal civil society judges orientate themselves not by what politicians currently describe as right behaviour, but by their interpretation of the law.

All the same, in 1988 a 'socialist legal state' was promised. Ideologically this was a significant step; Lenin and his successors had considered the legal state as simply a bourgeois absurdity. In practice, the changes were limited to improvements rather than radical restructuring. For example, judges' terms were doubled to ten years and they were henceforth to be appointed by the higher soviets; these two changes made them more independent of local party officials. 'Telephone law' was officially abolished and in practice severely limited by the judges' greater independence. The notorious Article 70 of the criminal code concerning 'anti-soviet agitation and propaganda' was not really abolished; instead, it was replaced by a new, somewhat less threatening article about 'socially dangerous acts'. The death penalty was applied to a narrower range of offences, and sentences of internal exile abolished. In 1987 a new law gave citizens some legal rights of appeal against arbitrary decisions by officials.

Meanwhile, the new breed of liberal, democratic, radical activists seemed sometimes to forget the principles it preached; or, more ominously, persuaded itself, like previous ruling bureaucrats, that bad ways were acceptable so long as they were in good hands. An example of this was when the radical government of Moscow prevented the conservative secretary of the Russian party organization from taking up residence in Moscow, simply by refusing to grant him a residence permit.

Residence permits, the old bureaucratic, unjust, illogical and corruption-ridden method of selecting those permitted to settle in the cities, were condemned in late 1991 and scheduled for abolition in the Russian Republic. Earlier that year, in Moscow's first open auction for such permits (which took the form of a house and apartment action, the permits being attached to the properties), one changed hands for a million roubles. At the same period, a permit could also be obtained by marrying a Moscow resident, the going rate for such marriages of convenience being 30,000 roubles.

Housing seemed likely to prove a source of social tension in the 1990s. Although there seemed little ambition directed towards the western-style 'property-owning democracy', and little appreciation that property-ownership might be a contribution to personal freedom, the transfer of ownership from state authorities to the tenants was seen as a desirable form of privatization. Policies varied from place to place, and some local authorities were entirely opposed to the idea. From 1988 tenants were allowed to buy, if their local soviets allowed them to, and 1991 RSFSR legislation made the process slightly easier. But relatively few actually wanted to buy. In practice it was already possible for a tenant to bequeath his or her apartment, which in a sense implied 'ownership', and the tenant was not responsible for repairs (and, more important, for the backlog of disrepair). Faced with this reluctance (up to the end of 1990 only about 20,000 tenants had bought) some authorities experimented with the gratuitous transfer of apartments to their tenants. But even this was unwelcome. Such a policy was said to be grossly unfair; a tenant who by luck or string-pulling had highly desirable accommodation was much better off than someone who for years had struggled in a cramped and insalubrious hovel. Moreover, such schemes were unfair to members of co-operative associations, who had put their own resources into building their living quarters. Prohibitions against resale could reduce this friction, but only at the cost of preventing the emergence of a housing market which, in the long run, might prove the best way of regulating the housing problem. In the meantime, homelessness seemed to be on the increase, aggravated by the influx of refugees from areas where the break-up of the USSR was unleashing ethnic antagonisms.

The armed forces

For the armed forces, life under Gorbachev was one retreat after another. Since World War 2 they had enjoyed great prestige and privileges, and had first call on industry. But the campaign in Afghanistan had brought almost 14,000 deaths, little glory, and finally, under Gorbachev, a withdrawal. In Europe, the Red Army had left Czechoslovakia and Hungary by the end of 1991, and withdrawal from East Germany (partly financed by the German government) and from Poland was scheduled. Red Army life in these foreign garrisons was dull and austere, but even poorer housing and living standards awaited those returning to the USSR. Moreover, careers were threatened by successive reductions of manpower.

Reduction of military aid and advice to third-world countries not only involved a loss of military prestige, and a perceived loss of power and influence, but also cut down the opportunities for interesting missions abroad; exchange visits with NATO countries were becoming possible, but only a few officers took part in these. Relaxing tension, symbolized in such processes as the dissolution of the Warsaw Pact, aroused doubts about the purpose of being a soldier; the honourable duty of defending the socialist motherland seemed to be losing its point.

Top officers were not alone in feeling that Gorbachev was giving up long-held positions without receiving much in return, and some western observers were surprised that the Red Army did not rebel. But although within the forces there was a powerful group of officers who resented the spirit of the time, there was also a growing number in favour of reform.

To the disgust of conservative officers, the highly unofficial 'Shield' organization had appeared and survived. It was devoted to the welfare of its membership (which included a large number of middle and junior officers) and to the transfer into the forces of concepts of openness, restructuring, and even democracy. 'Shield', though its membership was small in relation to the size of the forces, was very much like an officers' trade union and therefore, in its own way, quite revolutionary.

Relaxation of the old repression meant that the general public began to make its voice heard. Mothers of men killed in Afghanistan spoke up. Mothers of other conscripts began to add their weight to existing misgivings about army life. 'Hazing' of recruits, bullying and beating, was shown to be widespread, with ethnic minorities, or young men who in one way or another were different, being especially vulnerable. Eventually the Supreme Soviet set up an enquiry which concluded that every year since 1945 thousands of conscripts had died, with suicides accounting for half the deaths.

From 1990 there was an increased reluctance of young men to answer the conscription summons. In the schools the emphasis on military training was weakening. The navy reduced its conscription term to two years, matching the other services. In 1991 it was announced that the call-up of students would cease. In that year, however, the break-up of the USSR implied the break-up of the forces. The new independent republics announced the establishment of 'national guards' while the Ukraine made plans for a strong army, to be formed of Ukrainians currently in the Red Army. Like other republics, the Ukraine also laid claim to military equipment and installations located on its territory. In late 1991 Azerbaizhan claimed the Caspian Sea fleet and Ukraine the Black Sea fleet; the latter's main base at Sevastopol was in the Crimea, which Khrushchev had transferred from Russia to the Ukraine in 1954.

Although in the Gulf crisis of 1990–1 the USSR did not support Iraq (whose armed forces were equipped and advised by the Soviet Union), high officers voiced their concern that the US-led forces were engaged in a massacre of civilians and raw conscripts. Many military commentators described the war in terms of American preparations for a new arms race, based on high-technology weaponry. Some pride was taken in the performance of the Soviet-built Syrian tanks (which in terms of defects per mile did better than US-built tanks), due notice was taken of the inability of the Americans to find and destroy the Soviet-built Scud missiles, and the poor Iraqi leadership was emphasized. Nevertheless, the conclusion had to be drawn that US weapons were far ahead of Soviet and that this would damage the prospects of Soviet arms exports. At the same time, high officers were not slow to point out the need of a new generation of weaponry for the Soviet forces. Electronic devices, and also a large military air transport service like the Americans had, were seen as first necessities. At the same time, those who had long been recommending a shift from conscription to a small but highly professional armed force could point to the example shown by the Americans in this war.

The qualitative inferiority of Soviet weapons was, paradoxically, why many high officers did not reject the Gorbachev regime. Life for them under Brezhnev had not been perfect, and defects of arms procurement dated from his time. Although not in the habit of making deep analyses and radical changes, Brezhnev had been obliged to look critically at conventional arms expenditure, and in effect made industry the dominant partner in the so-called military-industrial complex. The forces were no longer allowed to pursue several different designs to fulfil one role, and industry was to decide which designs to build as prototypes. This saved money, but meant that not only were the forces unable to ensure that they got the designs they wanted, but were sometimes compelled to buy designs they did not want. Small, but potentially important, design flaws would not be put right by the defence industry, and accidents in service were the result.

Under Gorbachev, the defence minister Yazov, among others, was clearly unhappy with the reduction of the Red Army. But the military interest accepted the conversion of some defence factories to civilian production, finding some compensation in the new possibility of airing their grievances in public, thanks to *glasnost'*. The loss of the experimental, titanium-hull, nuclear submarine *Komsomolets* in 1989 was promptly exploited as an example of what poor design and construction could lead to, and as a reason for greater military control over defence expenditure. Essentially, what the general staffs wanted was the right to decide which projects should receive financial support. Just as with the Third and Fourth Dumas eighty years previously, the existence of free parliamentary debate, and parliamentary defence committees, enabled the generals and admirals to put their arguments to the test of open discussion. The assumption that professional officers were inevitably opposed to the new freedoms was as wrong in the final Soviet years as it had been in the last tsarist years.

Empire's end

The USSR and its European 'satellite' communist republics were both largely the creation of Stalin, the first being the tsarist empire under a new type of management and the latter a gain of World War 2. This structure came to an end in 1989–91; unlike other great empires, it came to an end rapidly, relatively bloodlessly, and not as a result of defeat in war.

Until the very end Gorbachev resisted the break-up of the USSR, but it was his insistence on *glasnost'* and his reservations about the use of force that made this break-up possible. With the satellites his position was different; he did not regard them as essential. He saw that they could be a burden and he made it clear that the Red Army could no longer be used as the ultimate guarantor of the rule of their communist parties.

Rampant Poles had disturbed the tranquillity of Brezhnev's Politburo, and the resultant army-imposed government sympathetic to Soviet needs had a limited life. For years, the official Polish resistance to reform had been explained by 'geopolitical realities' (a euphemism for Soviet pressure), and as soon as Gorbachev made it plain that there would be no more Soviet pressure and no more 'Brezhnev Doctrine', the Polish ruling party and the powerful Solidarity dissident movement reached a compromise in which general elections were held but on terms that assured the communists a minimum of seats. For a time the communist military president coexisted with a non-communist government before he had the grace to withdraw. Henceforth Poland was left to its own devices and problems; only the evacuation timetable of the Red Army and the latter's communications through Poland to its units in East Germany remained as sources of anxiety.

In the other former satellites, events took different courses but arrived at the elimination of the former communist leaderships, with reform communists and open popular dissent providing the catalyst. Only in Roumania did this process produce substantial casualties. Events in the German Democratic Republic were the most dramatic; the East German government, after some personnel changes, acquiesced unresistingly to the new circumstances; some plain speaking from Gorbachev had its effect here. The Berlin Wall was dismantled, and eventually, offered some financial carrots by the West German chancellor, the East German population voted for a party that signified immediate reunion with the rest of Germany.

Comecon came to an end, and the former people's republics were faced with the prospect of paying both hard currency and world prices for their massive imports of Soviet fuel, while the USSR found itself unable to buy, except at world prices and for hard currency, the products supplied by its satellites (and, worse, spare parts of equipment already received). As both sides were usually lacking hard currency, much of this exchange petered out.

Multinational empires always present problems, and this was compounded in the case of the USSR by the absence of natural frontiers separating the constituent nations. The Bolshevik solution of a confederation of national territories with small, varying degrees of self-government, had proved to be workable so long as the central authoritarian regime kept national feelings under tight control. Under Gorbachev, *glasnost'*, the preference for political rather than authoritarian solutions, and the election of genuine republican parliaments gave pent-up national feeling an opportunity of expression. Nationalist unrest in the fifteen union republics, including Russia, was first to be noticed, but it soon became clear that smaller entities, the autonomous republics, the autonomous regions and in some cases nations with neither territory nor autonomy, also had ambitions.[11]

It was very hard to judge the real strength of national feeling. As always, there were those who knew how to inflame it, and how to make those

---

[11] Among the latter were the Crimean Tartars, who were finally allowed to return to the Crimea and were allocated some help to get settled. The Volga Germans, another nationality expelled by Stalin, were allocated territory near Saratov, thereby igniting local protests. Many of them were encouraged by the German government to settle in Germany where, however, they did not always find a warm welcome. Around Kazan leaders of the Tartar autonomous republic embarrassed Yeltsin by demanding independence from Russia, in the first place to be achieved by becoming a union republic to be called Tatarstan. In Georgia both the Abkhazian autonomous republic and the South Ossetian autonomous region demanded independence, and in the latter case began to fight for it.

immune to it feel guilty. On the other hand, the elections and referenda of this period certainly demonstrated a strong wish to throw off alien influences and alien powers. In the RSFSR, several of the many autonomous territories displayed their own national consciousness, and Russian nationalism was an old phenomenon, containing a touch of panslavism with a nostalgic regard for old Russian traditions and virtues. Its enemies preferred to call it Great Russian chauvinism. When the USSR began to break up in 1990 and 1991 it did sometimes seem that, for many, national feeling was little more than a desire for freedom from Moscow.

However, those who disdain national feeling often get a nasty surprise, and that is what happened to Gorbachev. He did not foresee the extent to which *perestroika* would be bedevilled by nationalism; he foresaw friction, but not the grinding, unrelenting movement towards independence from centralized Soviet power.

The first sharp shocks to the concept of the Soviet Union came from the periphery. The three union-republics of Lithuania, Latvia, and Estonia, as well as the Moldavian union-republic, dated from World War 2 and still had memories of old, pre-Soviet times.

The first, almost symbolic, move from the Baltic came in 1987, when the Estonian government claimed economic autonomy and in 1988 when it claimed Estonian sovereignty. Sovereignty was less drastic than independence, but nevertheless required that republic law should have precedence over all-union, Soviet, law; that resources listed in the Soviet Constitution as belonging to the state should be transferred to the republic; and that private ownership of the means of production would be legal in that republic. In 1989 Lithuania and Latvia claimed sovereignty, and Latvia and Estonia began to define citizenship to exclude some Russian immigrants. Gorbachev responded to these moves and other claims by repeating that all republics had the right to secede but only after fulfilling certain conditions, which implied a long waiting period.

Lithuania took the lead in early 1990 by declaring itself independent, but was induced to 'freeze' the declaration by pressure both from Moscow and from the French and German governments. Later in 1990 Estonia and Latvia issued their own, somewhat more moderate declarations of independence. In that year most of the other republics declared their sovereignty.

Pressure from the Baltic States was never relaxed; popular fronts had been formed between nationalists and those communists who supported independence, and fresh stimulus was provided by the acknowledgement by the Soviet parliament that the secret protocols of the Nazi–Soviet pact did in fact exist. Anniversaries of this 1939 pact, which had secured the

Soviet take-over of the three previously independent states, were occasions for impressive demonstrations. In the winter of 1990–1 the situation became more critical. In January 1991 OMON troops, and sometimes Red Army units, took part in a series of shows of strength and actual attacks on key installations. The Red Army's participation was excused on the grounds that too many local youths had refused to obey their conscription orders, but the use of tanks and security police against citizens surrounding public buildings in the Lithuanian capital and the central television transmitter in Latvia were really lethal shows of force. There were those in the local *apparat* of the communist parties who hoped that widespread riotous protests would follow, providing an excuse for full-scale intervention. But this did not happen. At the price of several deaths, enough barricades were held, and the Soviet authorities were unwilling to convert a bloody confrontation into a massacre. There were subsequent provocations, including the murder of frontier guards, but after the August coup even Gorbachev was prepared for the independence of these three states, which soon followed.

In Moldavia, after elections and political manœuvring, the Moldova Republic was declared, essentially for the benefit of the majority Roumanian population. But the areas inhabited mainly by Russian or Turks each set up their own dissident republic and used various means, including the blockage of strategic rail routes, to draw attention to their demands. In 1992 the Moldovan situation sharpened bloodily. Even the Roumanian part of the population was divided on whether or not to join Roumania.

In the Caucasus, Gorbachev's hard-pressed central government was faced with the duty of moderating quarrels between nations that hitherto had been held in check by authoritarian means. Nagorno-Karabakh seemed an insoluble problem. This autonomous region within the Azerbaizhan Republic had a majority of Armenians whose soviet demanded union with Armenia. The situation was inflamed into an Azeri versus Armenian argument that led to frequent armed conflicts. In pursuit of its goals Azerbaizhan cut oil pipelines and railways serving Armenia, and in the Azerbaizhan town of Sumgait there was a revival of the *pogrom* technique, with Azeris hunting down and killing Armenian residents with the alleged connivance of the police. In late 1991 there was a semblance of a ceasefire negotiated with the participation of Yeltsin, but this did not last .

The Red Army took part in a 'pacification' of Baku in these troubled times and was blamed, with some justification, for the high casualty rate. In Georgia, too, the Red Army fell into disgrace when its troops attacked an obviously peaceful, though banned, demonstration in Tbilisi. The demonstration, like the Nagorno-Karabakh problem a result of the

inter-ethnic complexities left behind by Stalin's Commissariat of Nationalities, was a rally of nationalists inflamed by the demand of the Abkhazian
autonomous republic for independence from Georgia. A high proportion
of the many dead were women and children, victims apparently of gas and
of shovel blades. Georgia shortly declared its independence under a nationalist coalition government. Soon it was in conflict with an autonomous
republic in its territory, Southern Ossetia, which it wanted to retain. By the
end of 1991 the Georgian president, popularly elected and with a brave
past as a dissident (persecuted by, among others, Shevardnadze), was under
shellfire from rebels alleging that he had become intolerant and authoritarian.

The smaller central Asian republics took different courses. Culturally
quite different from the rest of the USSR, they were still very dependent on
it. Their communist parties tended to survive, although after the August
1991 upheaval they began to metamorphose into new parties with the old
faces. With the break-up of the USSR there were signs of a return to the
old corrupt ways, and some leading officials who had been imprisoned for
large-scale fraud were released. The biggest of the Central Asian republics,
Kazakhstan, was among the most enthusiastic practitioners of *perestroika*,
involving itself early in privatization schemes, and until December 1991 its
president was one of Gorbachev's closest allies.

Gorbachev fought hard for the continuation of some form of central
government, but he remarked that without the Ukraine any such grouping
would be useless. In December 1991 an election and a referendum showed
that the Ukraine was as determined as Russia to go its own way. It was a
former communist leader who had embraced the nationalist cause, Kravchuk, who was elected as president; the nationalist party, *Rukh*, that had
kept the cause alive, was relatively unsuccessful in the electoral sense
though triumphant morally. The referendum had asked whether voters
wanted an independent Ukraine but did not ask what kind of independence they wanted. Unsurprisingly, they voted overwhelmingly for the
proposition, with majorities even in the mainly Russian eastern part.

The Ukraine and Byelorussia already had seats at the United Nations
and, in theory, their own foreign policies. Also, like Kazakhstan and
Russia, they provided the sites for nuclear missiles. This was one of the
reasons why western governments did not welcome the break-up of the
USSR. Another reason was that over the previous five years successive US
administrations had begun to appreciate Gorbachev as a reassuring, reliable performer.

The Soviet leadership had quietly abandoned the concept of equal
security, that the USSR needed enough armed strength to defeat all its

enemies simultaneously.[12] At the Reykjavik summit meeting of 1986 the US president, confronted with a Soviet readiness to overturn all the assumptions of the Cold War and scrap all nuclear weapons, almost reciprocated but was recalled to conventional behaviour by his advisers. But as Gorbachev continued on his course regardless, relaxing old tensions, speaking of a 'common European home', and disengaging from old allies, both the USA and other western powers realized the gains that could result from quietly supporting him.

The Red Army was withdrawn from Afghanistan (where, however, the Soviet-installed regime for a time resisted its enemies), Soviet help to Cuba was reduced, Moscow's ally Vietnam withdrew from Cambodia. In Africa, and elsewhere, regimes that had profited from Soviet support found that they were left to fend for themselves. The virtual end to the Cold War meant that all over the world conflicts that had continued because the USA and the USSR had taken opposite sides were seen to be irrelevant, or costly, or both. When in 1990 the former Soviet protégé Iraq invaded Kuwait the USSR, partly in accordance with Gorbachev's advocacy of a bigger peacekeeping role for the UN, approved the use of force while striving for a peaceful solution. In 1991 diplomatic relations with Israel were restored and Moscow participated in the Middle East conferences of that year. Finland was allowed to withdraw from the unique and restricting relationship with the USSR that at one time had been regarded as a possible, 'Finlandization', model for other countries in the Soviet orbit.

During these Gorbachev years progress was made, but only slowly, on reaching agreements for limiting both conventional and nuclear weapons. There were political figures on both sides discouraging such moves, and the US insistence on continuing with its 'Star Wars' programme held back Soviet initiatives. But in August 1991 a new START agreement, reducing nuclear weapons by about 30 per cent, was ready to be ratified by the US Congress and the Supreme Soviet. After August, Gorbachev decided to make further substantial reductions in nuclear forces irrespective of what the USA might do. The USA, for its part, seeing the prospect of Soviet nuclear weapons in the hands of newly formed states that might be involved in all kinds of conflicts, decided to respond in kind.

Despite internal pressures the western powers refrained from embarrassing Gorbachev by, for example, prematurely recognizing the independence of the Baltic republics. Right up to the August 1991 events,

[12] The crucial meeting took place in the foreign ministry in May 1986. Hitherto, a kind of two-power standard had been the aim, with a capability of fighting China and NATO simultaneously. This worst-case prescription, like Britain's earlier two-power standard, was unsustainable in the long run.

western governments treated Yeltsin with great caution; when he visited the European Community the offhand treatment he received verged on the insulting. Western powers were willing to promise, and to a lesser degree provide, economic and financial assistance. On the eve of the August disturbance Gorbachev was invited to attend a meeting of the 'Group of Seven' economically dominant governments to put the case for such help. After August, as the future of Gorbachev and his USSR became less hopeful, Yeltsin was regarded more favourably, but the inability of the Soviet republics to agree among themselves made it hard for the western powers to provide assistance, apart from postponing debt repayments and extending some credits for financing food shipments.

With Gorbachev's field of authority diminishing as the USSR's powers were assumed by the republics, and with his dependence on financial support from the Russian budget, it was clear in late 1991 that Yeltsin was dominant. This alarmed some observers; they could point to Yeltsin's despatch of security troops to suppress a nationalist coup in the Chechen-Ingush autonomous republic,[13] and of how after the August events Yeltsin had reanimated Ukrainian fears of 'Great Russian chauvinism' when he spoke of necessary rectifications of the Russian frontier in the event of a break-up of the USSR (although, as was often the case with Yeltsin, in both cases he proved ready to listen to advice and modify his stand without a blush). Both physically and mentally Yeltsin resembled the symbolic Russian bear; this brought him popularity among Russians and distrust among non-Russians.

In December the presidents of Russia, Ukraine, and Byelorussia held a quiet meeting at which the momentous decision was taken to form a new 'Commonwealth of Independent States' to replace the USSR. Although their main aim was to destroy the old Union, neatly depriving Gorbachev of his power, they were immediately accused of concocting a Pan-slav conspiracy. But at a meeting in Alma Ata the three original signatories were joined by Kazakhstan, Azerbaizhan, Uzbekistan, Armenia. Kirgizstan, Tadzhikstan, Turmenistan, and Moldova. This was sufficient for the new Commonwealth to take off.

With the Commonwealth replacing the USSR, there was clearly no place for Gorbachev. He resigned his presidency on 25 December 1991. In his last days he was subjected to petty humiliations by Yeltsin, who evidently had not forgotten the slights he had earlier endured. Nevertheless,

---

[13] On arrival the troops meekly allowed themselves to be ejected from the republic by chartered buses. Soon afterwards the Russian Republic's Supreme Soviet refused to approve Yeltsin's strong line, thereby emphasizing that the Russian president's powers were not unlimited.

apart from being the last leader of the USSR, Gorbachev was also the first to retire with dignity.

At the end of 1991, over official buildings, the red flag and the soviet republic flags were lowered for the last time, replaced by the various national flags. In the Russian Republic there was a design competition for a modern version of the old tsarist two-headed eagle symbol. Meanwhile, ordinary Russians were doing what they had always done, endeavouring in order to endure:

FLAGS INTO SKIRTS

Several score flags of the former USSR union republics have become the latest objects of trade, being offered for sale at the bargain shop in the centre of the Sanchur district in Kirov Region. But they are not being acquired as relics. Housewives have been quick see that they can make clothes and other things from that silk and crêpe de Chine.[14]

Although Gorbachev was no longer popular at home, his reputation abroad was intact, and he began to play the role of a world elder statesman, while largely withdrawing from Russian political life. As domestic difficulties mounted in 1992 that segment of the Russian population which held to the tradition that problems are best solved by denunciations began to call for his trial. He had for several years protected the communist party, whose officials had blatantly used their power to feather their own nests. Moreover, in playing the double game so necessary to protect his reforms, and himself, from powerful party interests he had undoubtedly left a record of deceptions that zealous, jealous, persecutors could utilize. The trial of the August 1991 plotters was expected to throw some unfavourable light on him, but trials of other former party luminaries for corruption and other offences were not being pursued energetically because, it was said, the web of past crimes was so dense, and so many of the perpetrators still occupied responsible positions. Nevertheless the investigation of the past financial activities of party organizations was proceeding, and the occasional revelation suggested that it was more than a formality.

The Commonwealth

That majority of the former union republics which had agreed to form the Commonwealth of Independent States had no agreed, collective, idea of what this meant. At first the British Commonwealth had been vaguely spoken of as a model, which was fair enough since nobody understood the

14   *Gudok*, 4 January 1992, 1.

British Commonwealth. As the months passed, the emphasis was increasingly on independence and less on commonwealth. Some changes cost nothing and meant much. For example, there was a move away from the Russian-style rendering of place-names. Belarus became the preferred rendering of White Russia, Kyrgyzstan was preferred to Kirgiziya. Meanwhile, in the English-speaking world *Ukraina* was no longer *the* Ukraine, but Ukraine. On the other hand, Ukraine's decision to replace the rouble by its own currency was a step of great economic and psychological significance.

Of the former union republics that refused to participate in a commonwealth whose strongest element was Russia, the Baltic republics seemed to have the best chance of economic survival. This was not because of their statesmanship, of which they demonstrated little, but because of their higher cultural level and their influential sympathizers in the west. Georgia with its natural endowments also seemed to have good economic prospects in the long term, but it was politically divided. Although the first, abrasive, president of independent Georgia was ousted his armed supporters remained strong enough to offer an internal resistance. The new state was moreover bedevilled by its own nationality problems and in 1992 Shevardnadze, who had returned to lead his native country, was berating Moscow for the latter's alleged support of the South Ossetian forces fighting for independence from Georgia.

In Central Asia the newly independent republics began to go their own separate ways. Former communist party stalwarts in some republics came to terms with the new situation while in others they were ejected from positions of influence. Culture and geography ensured that ties with Moscow were weakened. New economic ties began to develop with China and other more local states, while culturally there was a move towards Turkey, a state that had already gone through the stage of becoming secular and independent. Those who preferred an Islamic society sought ties with Iran, and the course of this contest for the souls of the central Asian republics was watched with anxiety in other capitals as well as Moscow.

Of the three big Slavic republics Belarus quietly went its own modest way, sometimes acting as intermediary in the quarrels between Russia and Ukraine. These quarrels were rooted in the Ukrainians' perceived need to assert themselves in order to survive alongside a naturally dominant power like Russia. Ukraine, which in its time had been occupied by both Russians and Poles, had substantial minorities of those nationalities, and its existing frontiers were contestable. But of the members of the new Commonwealth, it probably had the least need of economic help.

Ukraine's demand for the Black Sea fleet was primarily a means of making itself felt as a new power, but it had some simple logic behind it. Quite apart from the knowledge that Ukrainians had paid for a substantial part of the Red Navy, there was the circumstance that it was based in Ukraine, at Sevastopol. However, the Russian government was not prepared to concede on this issue, and took the precaution, much resented in Kiev, of evacuating a new aircraft carrier from the Black Sea to the Arctic. The Ukrainian response to this 'hi-jack' was to change its demand for the greater part of the Black Sea fleet to a statement that the whole fleet was Ukrainian property.

An equally emotional issue was the destiny of the Crimea. This, one of the more delectable territories of the USSR, had been transferred to Ukraine from Russia by Khrushchev. So long as the USSR existed this transfer was only a formality, but the highly russified Crimean population did not unanimously welcome its inclusion in the new independent Ukraine.

Inside Russia popular resentment on these issues tended to be channelled against the Ukrainian president, Kravchuk, who seemed to be a blatant and all-too-successful example of the party *apparatchik* who had jumped on the bandwagon of change and nationalism just in time to exploit the successes won by courageous and often-martyred rebels. The thought of losing the Crimea to such a man was painful, and the Russian parliament lost no time in declaring void the 1954 transfer of the Crimea to Ukraine. However, like most declarations of 1992, this made little difference and the quarrel, however resolved formally, seemed likely to poison Russo-Ukrainian relations for years. Both Russia and Ukraine quietly sought the support of the US government which, however, remained a well-intentioned neutral.

As 1992 progressed the impression strengthened that both Yeltsin and Kravchuk in their various quarrels were playing a mutually-acceptable game of brinkage, with both aware that the conflict should not go beyond angry words. In mid-1992 they decided to assume joint responsibility for the Black Sea fleet for three years, after which, it was hoped, the problem would have evaporated, if not oxidized. This mutual agreement was unpalatable to other members of the Commonwealth, for one of the most important provisions of that Commonwealth had been that the non-nuclear armed forces of the USSR would be jointly administered by the member-republics. That some republics, notably Ukraine, had partially by-passed this understanding by deciding to form their own national forces had not, in the opinion of several republican governments, rendered the agreement invalid.

Kravchuk stuck to the agreement that nuclear weapons stationed on

Ukrainian territory, like those in Kazakhstan and Belarus, should slowly be transferred to Russia, which would be responsible for storage or dismantlement. Any other course would have spoiled the essential good relationship with the USA, and it could also be argued that nuclear weapons had little practical value. Nevertheless, this continued acceptance that Ukraine would be a nuclear-free state bordering the potentially hostile nuclear power of Russia could plausibly be regarded as an act of statesmanship. Similarly, Kravchuk's reluctance to play the ultra-nationalist card by stirring up animosity against the non-Ukrainian part of the population (for example, he preferred to talk about the Ukrainian state rather than the Ukrainian nation) could be dismissed as mere commonsense; but commonsense at such a time was itself a rare and valuable quality. But whether Ukraine could feel secure without becoming a militarized state was still uncertain in 1992. There was talk in the Russian Republic of a reduced but 1,500,000-strong Russian armed force by the year 2000. If Ukraine was to match this it would not only create an enormous economic drain but also a certain kind of society, quite apart from alarming several of its weaker neighbours.

For the Russian Republic the reduction and then stabilization of the armed forces was just one of several painful problems faced by President Yeltsin and his government. Economic difficulties made solutions to all problems much harder. A reduction in the armed forces, for example, ideally required more housing and more job opportunities, two conditions that seemed unfulfillable in 1992.

The Russian economic situation, despite desperate measures, remained dire. Gorbachev's failure to tackle long-standing and progressively deepening crises had resulted in a situation that some observers believed was beyond cure. The freeing of prices did not bring the prompt flow of products into the shops that had been anticipated, except in a few special instances. Although some powerful interest groups were able to obtain relief from rising prices, most of the population was not only worse off but saw no hope of improvement. Another desperate measure, virtually the clutching of a last straw, was the import of western economists; however, these could at least affix the not-made-in-Russia seal of approval needed for the acceptance of radical proposals formulated by native economists.

The government survived the impoverished winter of 1991–2 but further moves along the road of market pricing, like increases in oil prices, were resisted fiercely and delayed by the parliamentary opposition. ('Market', rather than 'rational' pricing seems the more appropriate term for a period in which the market was producing all kinds of irrationalities; July 1992, for example, witnessed the phenomenon of fruit and vegetable prices actually rising in the summer). The continued existence of big industrial and commercial enterprises having a monopoly, or near-monopoly, for their products ensured that prices would be unrestrained by competitive forces. Enterprises were unwilling to reduce their prices in order to sell their products; they preferred the routine of high prices, low sales, and large work-forces, relying on bank credits to keep going. However, in August Yeltsin indicated that serious privatization would take place later in the year. His proposed method was to divide the total value of the state property to be privatized by the total population, with the resultant rouble figure taken as the value of a voucher to be distributed to each citizen. Such vouchers would be used to buy shares in the privatized enterprises, or could be themselves bought and sold. This was a plainly populist, but allegedly practical, way of transforming the Russian population into a nation of shareholders.

Foreign financial assistance was regarded as essential to provide backing for a stabilized rouble and to finance the imports that were plainly necessary at a time when both agricultural and industrial output was falling drastically. The International Monetary Fund imposed its usual good-housekeeping prerequisites for assistance, the main result of which was to limit the government's freedom of action. International capital was in short supply in the early 1990s, due largely to the financial weakness of the former big provider, the USA. America might have 'won' the arms race and the Cold War, but in doing so had badly damaged its own economic and financial health.

Yeltsin in Moscow, like Kravchuk in Kiev, preferred to rule by decree. But the Russian parliament (Congress of Peoples' Deputies), encouraged by its chairman ('speaker') Khasbulatov, resisted this. In April 1992 the Sixth Congress subjected both Yeltsin and Yeltsin's economic reforms to severe criticism. Khasbulatov, in particular, voiced the resentment of many Russians at growing Russian economic dependence on the west. To some, it seemed that the drastic and hurried economic changes were not simply the product of Yeltsin's young economic advisers but were imposed by potential western lenders. This congress resulted in neither a move towards a more parliamentary democracy nor to a reversal of the economic reforms, but nevertheless showed that the government needed to tread carefully.

Earlier, in February, there had been conflict between Yeltsin and the parliament over the former's determination to ensure his control of the ministry of state security (successor to the KGB). Up to late 1991 the old KGB had been shrinking, but in 1992 it was again expanding. Some of its operatives were being turned on to the other republics of the former

USSR, and there was evidence that the old KGB internal structure of information-gathering was still functioning, although part-time informers were becoming rare and the information was merely filed away for use in better times.

The ordinary police, at least in the Russian Republic, continued to fight what seemed to be a losing battle in 1992. Economic deprivation and the dissolution of old prohibitions had already, understandably, made crime a viable culture for a growing section of the population. The so-called 'mafia' was supplemented by a petty mafia subsisting off protection rackets, and some exceptionally nasty murders, for the most part unsolved, were ascribed to quarrels among 'mafia' groups and to exemplary retribution against private traders who had resisted protection demands. In the non-Russian parts of the former Union objects, and sometimes persons, that could be connected with the former regime began to suffer. These unpleasant events were given more than their fair share of coverage by a press that after decades of rose-tinted reportage was naturally inclined to swing to the opposite extreme. The actual situation was rarely as bad as the average citizen was led to believe; this newspaper extract gives some idea of the flavour:

The wives of locomotive drivers, seeing their husbands off to work, show as much anxiety as if they were setting off for the front. Will they come back safe and sound? When has it ever been like this before? Only in the Civil War and World War 2, and also in the first post-war years before order had been restored and the crime wave subdued . . . And what should we think of that incident in May, when a suburban train of the Moscow Railway was burned by a group of evil-intentioned people hurling bottles filled with inflammable liquid? It was with bottles like those that their fathers and grandfathers fought fascist tanks, and now their grandsons attack peaceful trains.[15]

Russians continued to display their ability to endure. They were suffering and they expected to continue to suffer, but even as their confidence in Yeltsin waned they showed no signs of revolt. The expected large-scale bankruptcies and unemployment, thanks to bank credits, were still to come. In mid-1992 Russians still seemed more like spectators than participants. So far as they could, they continued to work and to live as they had always done, and discussed political and economic events in the same way as they discussed a film or play. Optimists said that Russian inertia had at last come into its own, giving the government the long breathing space that it so badly needed. Pessimists said the Russians were waiting for someone to tell them what to do; someone with a new theory.

[15] *Gudok*, 14 July 1992, 1.

A NOTE ON STATISTICS

In this book statistics do not play a large role, for there seems little point in expressing the uncertain with an illusory precision. The following paragraph lists only a small selection of statistical snares.

Official statistics for tsarist Russia sometimes include Finland and Poland, and sometimes not, and do not always make clear this distinction. Soviet statisticians did distinguish between the 1913, inter-war, 1939–41, post-1945 territories and their own useful hypothetical 'the USSR as it would have been in 1913'; but writers quoting Soviet figures sometimes ignore these subtleties. Ill-defined categories can also mislead: comparative figures for coal production, for example, lose much of their significance if the changing ratio of lignite to hard coal is not recorded. Again, the official Soviet railway statistics refer only to the lines operated by the ministry of transport, but a third of Soviet railway mileage belonged to other ministries and was not operated as efficiently as the main lines. To mention, say, that 79 per cent of the US population was urban, compared with 64 per cent of the Russian population, is misleading because urban population is defined differently in the two countries. Educational statistics can be especially deceptive. To write that there were, say, 80,000 primary schools in 1900 is imprecise unless it is known how many local officials reported the existence of a primary school without revealing that it had no teacher or no pupils. Total student numbers, especially in higher education, lose much of their significance if they do not differentiate between full-timers and part-timers and between those who are actually attending and those who are merely registered. And so on.

Apart from these methodological problems, the gathering and collation of statistics is subject to human error and human nature. In wartime deserters may, in all sincerity, be classed as 'missing believed killed', and it is not uncommon for a soldier, statistically speaking, to be double- or treble-counted as missing, wounded, and killed. The 1897 census, the first full census in Russia, was bedevilled by omissions and double-counting. Lower authorities tend to inflate their performance statistics and when these are added together to make a national total the error may be considerable. In tsarist times import–export statistics were so unreliable because of double-counting that the government was seriously misinformed about the balance of trade.

Contrary to popular impression, Soviet statistics were not invented by propagandists. It is true that, especially in Stalin's time, figures were presented misleadingly, but even in the worst period there were western economists like Baykov and Jasny who could work out from them what they really meant. The most notorious instances of misleading presentation occurred in agricultural statistics after collectivization. The basis of grain production figures was quietly changed: output was no longer measured in terms of grain safely 'in the barn', but in terms of biological yield; that is, the estimated tonnage 'on the stalk' before harvesting, a classical instance of counting chicks before the hatching thereof. In 1950 the published grain production was 124 million tons but it later transpired that the real production, 'in the barn', was only 81 million tons. Again, some comparative figures for farm tractive power were based on an assumption that one tractor could do the work of so many average horses, the ratio chosen implying that the average Russian horse was a Shetland pony.

Thus any figure presented in this book should, strictly speaking, be accompanied by footnotes to explain how it was arrived at. In more specialized works this, in fact, is done, but in a short book covering one and a half centuries of Russian history this would not be the most productive use of space. So the reader is asked to take on trust the figures presented. He should bear in mind the American saying 'figures can't lie, but liars can figure', while accepting that an effort has been made to present reasonably reliable and unambiguous statistics.

BIBLIOGRAPHY

GENERAL

The titles mentioned below have been selected from a greater number, and several worthy books are not mentioned simply because they are alternatives to others which are more easily obtainable. For really complete listings the reader is advised to turn to specialized annual bibliographies like *The American Bibliography of Slavic and East European Studies*, and *European Bibliography of Soviet, East European and Slavonic Studies*. Scholarly journals, mentioned in the next paragraph, review and list new publications.

The *Slavic Review*, sometimes catalogued under its former title of *American Slavic and East European Review*, offers articles and book reviews covering history, politics, economics, and literature. Then there is the *Russian Review*, whose articles tend to be shorter but more varied. *Soviet Studies* is especially strong in economics and politics; it used to publish a separate *Information Supplement*, replete with relevant and often titillating items taken from the Soviet press, but this is now published commercially in the form of a quarterly under the title *ABSEES*. The *Slavonic and East European Review* devotes relatively little space to modern history, but what is there is good. A number of other journals have been established more recently, and a few have had short lives. Well worthy of mention are *Canadian Slavonic Papers*, *California Slavic Studies*, *Canadian-American Slavic Studies*, *Russian History*, *Soviet Union*, *Soviet Economy*, and *Russian Literature Triquarterly*. In French, the *Cahiers du Monde Russe et Soviétique* is useful, as are several other French- and German-language titles. Some journals have disappeared or changed their names. Among those that made no secret of their hostility to the USSR, but published serious commentaries, have been *Survey*, *Journal for the Study of the USSR*, and *Problems of Communism*. Recently established journals include *Journal of Communist Studies*; the twice-annual organ of the Study Group on the Russian Revolution, *Revolutionary Russia*; and *Journal of Soviet Military Studies*. The *Scottish Slavonic Review* sometimes has interesting historical pieces, while *Journal of Ukrainian Studies* devotes considerable space to history. Another journal, *Detente*, while pursuing its aim of studying ways in which the modern superpowers might arrive at a more mature relationship, threw perceptive illumination on the current scene.

Most of the books mentioned in this Bibliography contain their own bibliographies, although these often consist mainly of Russian-language material. Encyclopedias also provide suggestions for reading. Those which deal with modern Russia are S. V. Utechin, *Everyman's Concise Encyclopedia of Russia* (1961), M. T. Florinsky, *Encyclopedia of Russia and the Soviet Union* (1961), and, more recently, *The Cambridge Encyclopedia of Russia and the Soviet Union* (1982), edited by A. Brown and others. R. Maxwell, *Information USSR* (1962) consists of selective translations from the *Great Soviet Encyclopedia*, and may be regarded as a revealing presentation of the Soviet view of things in the late 1950s. For the quick reference, J. Paxton, *Companion to Russian History* (1984) can be useful. *The Soviet Union: A Biographical Dictionary* (1990), ed. A. Brown, is very informative.

Geography texts include L. Symons, J. Dewdney, *The Soviet Union* (1982), and J. P. Cole, *Geography of the USSR* (1967). Perhaps of more interest to history specialists are the two-volume collection, edited by J. Bater and R. French, *Studies in Russian Historical Geography* (1983), and W. H. Parker, *An Historical Geography of Russia* (1968). There are several historical atlases available, including A. Adams, *An Atlas of Russian and East European History* (1967), A. F. Chew, *An Atlas of Russian History* (1967), R. N. Taafe, *An Atlas of Soviet Affairs* (1965). An exquisite and enlightening work is R. Milner-Gulland, N. Dejevsky, *A Cultural Atlas of Russia and the Soviet Union* (1989). An informative textbook is edited by M. Bradshaw, *The Soviet Union: A New Regional Geography* (1991).

Textbooks may be torturesome both for their readers and their authors, but they are, nevertheless, convenient reference sources. Since each author has his own ideas of what should be included and what omitted, one textbook may usefully supplement another. H. Seton-Watson, *The Russian Empire 1801-1917* (1967) is of great help, as its 800-odd pages provide space for detailed interpretation as well as dense facts; it is particularly strong on foreign affairs and government. A. A. Kornilov, *Modern Russian History* (1916) is a translation of a noted liberal historian's view of the nineteenth century. Shorter coverage of the same period is provided by S. G. Pushkarev, *The Emergence of Modern Russia 1801-1917* (1963) and S. S. Harcave, *Years of the Golden Cockerel* (1970). The latter is more of a popularization than a textbook, perhaps, and so are two which deal with the period from the Decembrist to the 1917 rising, *The Shadow of the Winter Palace* (1976) by E. Crankshaw and *Russia's Failed Revolutions* (1981) by A. B. Ulam. A popularization of a longer period (1613-1917), with sound academic underpinning, is W. B. Lincoln, *The Romanovs* (1981). In the 1950s a succession of blockbuster textbooks were dropped into the US college market. Some of these failed to explode, but two by expatriate Russians deservedly became popular: M. T. Florinsky, *Russia, a History and an Interpretation* (2 vols., 1953), and N. V. Riasanovsky, *A History of Russia* (1969). There were others, too that may still be found on library shelves and for the most part they are reliable, if unexciting, but not always easy to read because so many American printers seem to prefer working with diluted ink. The British historian B. Pares, who lived through so much of what he wrote about, published his *History of Russia* (1949), but this is not good for the post-revolutionary years. Shorter texts include J. N. Westwood, *Endurance and Endeavour* (1973), criticized for its excruciating puns, and P. Dukes, *A History of Russia* (1974), which combines a brief narrative from medieval times with very interesting summaries of how different historians interpret the main events. Two textbooks which make a virtue of brevity are L. Kochan, *The Making of Modern Russia* (1963), which has chapters dealing with the pre-1812 period, and K. Charques, *Twilight of Imperial Russia* (1958). An older book by a distinguished Russian historian, M. Karpovich, *Imperial Russia 1801-1917* (1932), is very brief but of such quality as to make it well worth reading as an introduction. S. G. Pushkarev, *The Emergence of Modern Russia 1801-1917* (1963) is also instructive. More recent books include E. Acton's *Russia* (1986), which manages to compress ten centuries without sacrificing liveliness; J. Thompson's *Russia and the Soviet Union* (1985); and H. Rogger, *Russia in the Age of Modernisation and Revolution 1881-1917* (1983).

For the Soviet period there are B. Dymytryshin, *USSR: A Concise History* (1965), Ian Grey, *The First Fifty Years* (1967), G. von Rauch, *A History of Soviet Russia* (1957), D. W. Treadgold's exhaustive *Twentieth Century Russia* (1959), P. Sorlin's short *The Soviet People and their Society from 1917 to the Present* (1969), as well as some more recent works: M. K. Dziewanowski, *A History of Soviet Russia* (1985), W. McClennan, *Russia: A History of the Soviet Period* (1986), M. Kort, *The Soviet Colossus* (1990), the invariably informative M. McCauley's *The Soviet Union since 1917* (1981), and a very worthwhile paperback, G. Hosking, *A History of the Soviet Union* (1985). *Utopia in Power* (1986), by M. Heller and A. Nekrich, is halfway between a polemic and a history of the USSR; especially good on the attempt to annihilate public memory by creating a fictitious past, it can be read with caution and enjoyment. H. C. d'Encausse has undertaken a useful, and in places original, two-volume study, *History of the Soviet Union 1917–1953* (1981): volume 1 is called *Lenin* and volume 2 is *Stalin*. Both are translations from the French, and English-speakers might find the French-language editions more comprehensible. Also translated from French are C. Bettelheim. *Class Struggles in the USSR* (4 vols., 1976–), and D. Rousset, *A Critical History of the USSR* (vol. 1, 1982); both of these are marxist interpretations which seek to show that the Soviet Union was not really marxist at all, Bettelheim preferring to regard it as a final stage of capitalism and Rousset as a bureaucratic aberration. In a rather different class is E. H. Carr's multi-volume study of the first decade of Soviet history, whose individual titles are given in the chapter bibliographies. Although the author can occasionally be detected leaning ever so slightly backwards with one eye half-closed, this work is exemplary in its thoroughness. Shorter, more interpretative works on the USSR include a collection of essays edited by H. E. Salisbury, *The Soviet Union: the Fifty Years* (1967), which is especially good on society and culture. R. R. Abramovitch, *The Soviet Revolution, 1917–1939* (1962) is not quite outdated and offers a stimulating and controversial commentary. A little more specialized is P. Dukes, *October and the World* (1979) which relates the Revolution to movements in other countries. S. F. Cohen, *Rethinking the Soviet Experience* (1985), contains some interesting ideas by an expert on the 1920s and 1930s. O. A. Narkiewicz also has some perceptive ideas in her *Marxism and the Reality of Power 1919–1980* (1981), and so does M. Lewin in *The Making of the Soviet System* (1985).

Two books with rather short texts but enhanced by well-chosen and well-reproduced illustrations are O. Hoetzch, *The Evolution of Russia* (1966) and J. P. Nettl, *The Soviet Achievement* (1967).

Books which go deeper into Russian history, seeking and proposing plausible explanations of why things turned out the way they did, include T. G. Masaryk, *The Spirit of Russia* (1918) and J. H. Billington, *The Icon and the Axe* (1966), which stress permanent factors like religion, geography, and western contacts. W. Weidlé, *Russia Absent and Present* (1961), and N. Berdiaev, *The Russian Idea* (1947), explore Russian culture and attitudes, emerging with interesting though not incontrovertible conclusions. In the mid-1970s there appeared, almost simultaneously, T. Szamuely, *The Russian Tradition* (1974) and R. Pipes, *Russia under the Old Regime* (1974). These two were praised most highly by those reviewers least familiar with Russian history, but that is a common phenomenon and should not be held against them. More recently, R. V. Daniels has produced *Russia: the Roots of Confrontation* (1985), which describes how history, rather than Marxism, has made present-day Russia what it is. Then there are some interesting ideas, sometimes arguable, in M. Raeff, *Understanding Imperial Russia: State and Society in the Old Regime* (1984). The interacting attitudes of the Russians and their monarch are fascinatingly studied by M. Cherniavsky in his *Tsar and People* (1961). Intellectual history is extensively treated in *Continuity and Change in Russian and Soviet Thought* (1955), edited by E. J. Simmons, and R. Bartlett (ed.), *Russian Thought and Society 1800–1917* (1984), and is anthologized in M. H. Kohn, *The Mind of Modern Russia* (1962) and M. Raeff, *Russian Intellectual History* (1966), while R. Hare, *Pioneers of Russian Social Thought* (1951) provides biographies of some of the more notable thinkers. A. Walicki, *A History of Russian Thought from the Enlightenment to Marxism* (1979), gives, among other things, brief outlines of the ideas of all the important thinkers, including those, like Pobedonostsev, whose thought was remarkable for the power behind as much as for the power within. More specialized works in this field include E. C. Thaden, *Conservative Nationalism in Nineteenth Century Russia* (1964), H. Kohn, *Panslavism* (1953), and N. V. Riasanovsky, *Russia and the West in the Teaching of the Slavophils* (1952). One Slavophil gets full treatment in P. K. Christoff, *An Introduction to Nineteenth Century Russian Slavophilism. K. S. Aksakov: A Study in Ideas* (1982: vols. 1 and 2 were about Khomiakov and Kireevsky, and a forthcoming vol. 4 is to be devoted to Samarin). For the intelligentsia as a whole there is the collection, *The Russian Intelligentsia* (1961), edited by the indefatigable R. Pipes. S. R. Tompkins, *The Russian Intelligentsia: Makers of the Revolutionary State* (1957) is concerned largely with the radical intelligentsia of the nineteenth century.

A general introduction to Russian life in the nineteenth century is the well-illustrated *Russian Writers and Society 1825–1904* (1967) by R. Hingley, which deals more with society than with writers. The long and varied collection of essays edited by C. E. Black, *The Transformation of Russian Society: Aspects of Social Change since 1861* (1960) is still not quite outdated. D. S. Mirsky, *Russia, a Social History* (1952) is also worth reading. Perhaps the best understanding of Russian society, however, would be gained from Russian novels (not necessarily the best-known ones), and from the innumerable memoirs and autobiographies by former residents in Russia. A recent addition to the latter is E. Fraser, *The House on the Dvina* (1984), about pre-revolutionary Archangel. In a class of its own is D. Mackenzie-Wallace's unsurpassed *Russia* (1912), whose author spent several years as *The Times* correspondent in Russia, making a thorough study of Russian life and institutions of the late nineteenth century.

T. Talbot Rice, *Concise History of Russian Art* (1963), illustrates and describes painting, sculpture, and architecture of the tsarist period. There is also the rather bigger work by G. H. Hamilton, *The Art and Architecture of Russia* (1954), and *Art and Culture in Nineteenth Century Russia* (1983), edited by G. V. Stavrou. W. Brumfield's *Reshaping Russian Architecture* (1990) is an interesting account of how tsarist architecture was transformed into Soviet architecture. For literature there are scores of guides. Among the most useful of these are M. Baring, *Landmarks in Russian Literature* (1960), H. Gifford, *The Novel in Russia* (1964), R. Freeborn, *The Russian Revolutionary Novel: Turgenev to Pasternak* (1982), *Ideology in Russian Literature* (1990) edited by R. Freeborn and J. Grayson, *The Cambridge History of Russian Literature* (1989), edited by C. Moser, W. Kasack's *Dictionary of Russian Literature since 1917* (1988), *Handbook of Russian Literature* (1985) edited by V. Terras, and F. D. Reeve, *The Russian Novel* (1966). For a detailed who-wrote-what there are M. Slonim's three volumes, *The Epic of Russian*

Literature: To Tolstoy (1950), *From Chekhov to the Revolution* (1962), and *Modern Russian Literature* (1955). There is also *A History of Soviet Literature* (1963) by V. Alexandrovna. Beginning in 1977, successive volumes of *The Modern Encyclopedia of Russian and Soviet Literature* have appeared, edited by H. B. Weber and written by expert contributors. Other interpretative books are E. J. Brown, *Russian Literature Since the Revolution* (1963), R. W. Mathewson, *The Positive Hero in Soviet Literature* (1958), and the collection of specialized essays, edited by M. Haward and L. Labedz, *Literature and Revolution in Soviet Russia, 1917–1962* (1963). But it is better to read, rather than read about, the novels; the best are in English translation. In addition, the 'thick' journal, *Soviet Literature*, in which many Soviet novels were published for the first time, had an English-language edition. The journal *Russian Literature Triquarterly*, published in the USA, has also offered translations of Russian and Soviet fiction. Selected readings are provided by M. Crouch and R. Porter in *Understanding Soviet Politics through Literature* (1984). For the Russian theatre, M. L. Slonim, *Russian Theatre from the Empire to the Soviets* (1961) is useful. For music, R. A. Leonard, *A History of Russian Music* (1956) covers, rather thinly perhaps, both the tsarist and Soviet periods. For fuller coverage of the Soviet period there are *Soviet Composers and the Development of Soviet Music* (1970) by S. D. Krebs and *Music and Musical Life in Soviet Russia 1957–1981* (1983) by B. Schwarz. The latter, naturally enough, does not make a final judgement on the authenticity of Shostakovich's controversial memoirs, published as his *Testimony* in 1979. More specialized books are S. F. Starr, *Red and Hot* (1983), which details the alternating periods of repression and tolerance extended to jazz, culminating in permission to stage an original rock opera in Moscow during one of the happier periods of the Brezhnev regime, and R. C. Ridenour, *Nationalism, Modernism, and Personal Rivalry in Nineteenth Century Russian Music* (1981), a fascinating account of the formative 1860s.

For a study of nineteenth-century publishing, the rise of newspapers, and the increased demand for reading matter, C. A. Ruud, *Fighting Words* (1982) is very good, and it also makes considerable though patchy reference to the subject of its title, the censorship. For censorship in Soviet times see M. Dewhirst, R. Farrell, *The Soviet Censorship* (1973). *The Red Pencil* (1989), edited by M. Choldin and M. Friedburg, includes many examples of the absurdities created by the Soviet censorship.

The standard works on pre-1917 economic history are P. Lyashchenko, *History of the National Economy of Russia* (1949), a translation of the Soviet edition, which is inclined to portray Imperial Russia as some kind of colony; J. Mavor, *An Economic History of Russia* (1914); and the brief but good *The Industrialisation of Russia 1700–1914* (1972) by M. Falkus. O. Crisp, *Studies in the Russian Economy before 1914* (1976) is a collection of well-thought-out essays. A. Nove, *An Economic History of the USSR* (1969) is a readable introduction to post-1917 economic history. V. E. Bonnell, *The Russian Worker* (1983) consists of translations of five very interesting contemporary accounts of workers' lives under tsarism, while S. P. Turin, *From Peter the Great to Lenin* (1935) is a slightly outdated study of neither Peter nor Lenin nor the years between, but of the Russian labour movement. The collection edited by D. Lane, *Labour and Employment in the USSR* (1986), contains historical pieces, while A. Pravda and B. Ruble have edited *Trade Unions in Communist States* (1986) which, while not especially historical nor confined to the USSR, does provide a useful summary of the main features. That continuing problem of the Russian economy, the peasantry, receives attention in *The Peasant in Nineteenth Century Russia* (1968), edited by W. S. Vucinich and containing much fascinating detail about peasants' lives. G. Yaney in his *The Urge to Mobilize* (1982) deals with attempts at agrarian reform between 1861 and 1930 and shows how city people seemed to have no doubts about their ability to transform the rural situation, even though they never quite understood it. T. Shanin, *The Awkward Class* (1972) has some illuminating things to say about the peasantry in the years 1910–25. That continuing feature, the peasant commune, is featured in the collection *Land Commune and the Peasant Community in Russia* (1990), edited by R. Bartlett and covering the centuries up to 1930; the same subject, on a more concentrated time-scale, is dealt with by D. Atkinson's *The End of the Russian Land Commune 1905–1930* (1983). Two contributions by D. Christian, *Living Water: Vodka and Russian Society on the Eve of Emancipation* (1990), and *Bread and Salt* (1984), are good reading and throw considerable light on peasant society, among other things. Two very different angles on tsarist trade and commerce are provided by A. Fitzpatrick's many-faceted *The Great Russian Fair* (1990), which surveys the major trade fair of Nizhnii Novgorod from 1840 to 1890, and the somewhat legalistic but illuminating *The Corporation under Russian Law 1800–1917* (1991), by T. Owen. J. N. Westwood, *A History of Russian Railways* (1964) is useful, although its author seems to be more interested in railways than in history. Books about nineteenth-century capitalists, big and small, were until recently very rare, but much can now be learned from A. J. Rieber, *Merchants and Entrepreneurs in Imperial Russia* (1982), T. Owen, *Capitalism and Politics in Russia: A Social History of the Moscow Merchants 1855–1905* (1981), and J. A. Ruckman, *The Moscow Business Elite: A Social and Cultural Portait of Two Generations, 1840–1905* (1984). F. V. Carstensen, *American Enterprise in Foreign Markets* (1984) deals with the operations of the Singer and International Harvester companies, both of which proved that there was a latent consumer demand in Russia by offering their customers generous credit, something which native companies rarely did. This throws light on the still unsettled question of precisely why the tsarist economy was backward. Two pioneering attempts to answer this question, which are still not outdated even though their conclusions seem less firm as the years pass, are A. Gerschenkron, *Economic Backwardness in Historical Perspective* (1962) and T. H. von Laue, *Why Lenin? Why Stalin?* (1964). A more recent contribution to this debate is T. Shanin, *Russia as a 'Developing Society'* (1985), dealing with the late tsarist period.

P. Juvilier, *Revolutionary Law and Order* (1976) is a useful survey of the relationship between law and society, mainly but not exclusively in Soviet times. Of the many excellent books on Soviet government, the following are only a selection: D. J. R. Scott, *Russian Political Institutions*, M. Fainsod and J. Hough, *How the Soviet Union is Governed*, J. N. Hazard, *The Soviet System of Government*, L. G. Churchward, *Contemporary Soviet Government*, L. B. Shapiro, *Government and Politics in the Soviet Union*, and an excellent paperback, M. McAuley, *Politics and the Soviet Union*, which takes a historical approach (as these texts reprinted at frequent intervals, dates are not given). R. Sakwa's *Soviet Politics: An Introduction* first appeared in 1989 and included the changes of the early Gorbachev years. G. Smith's *Soviet Politics* (1992) is very useful. R. C. Tucker, *The Soviet Political Mind* (1972) examines the attitudes underlying the system. Histories of the Communist Party from before 1917 to the present day include L. B. Shapiro, *The Communist Party of the Soviet Union* (1960), B. Meissner, *The Communist Party of the Soviet Union* (1956), and J. S. Reshetar, *A Concise History of the Communist Party of the Soviet*

Union (1960). The Soviet textbook, *History of the Communist Party of the USSR, Short Course*, exists in many languages and editions; the pre-1956 and post-1956 editions are easily distinguished and both are tendentious. For a statistical analysis of the party's membership over the years, there is T. H. Rigby, *Communist Party Membership in the USSR 1917–1967* (1968). Differences inside the Communist Party from 1903 to 1939 are examined in R. V. Daniel, *The Conscience of the Revolution* (1960). For marxism as such there are many books, some of which are tedious. Perhaps I. Berlin, *Karl Marx* (1948), would make the most palatable beginning. C. Wright Mills, *The Marxists*, offers extracts of the works of leading marxists from Karl to Che, with some comment. A translation of the multi-volume post-Stalin version of Lenin's *Collected Works* is approaching completion. Stalin's *Collected Works* also exist in English, as do earlier versions of Lenin's.

Descriptions of how the tsarist government worked are still scarce, although that much-reviled institution, the bureaucracy, has recently received more detailed study, which tends to suggest that it has been a little misjudged, in so far as it did contain competent, hardworking men who had some sensible ideas for reform. W. M. Pintner and D. K. Rowney have edited a volume, *Russian Officialdom* (1980), which takes a look at the institution from the seventeenth century to the 1920s. W. B. Lincoln, *In the Vanguard of Reform* (1982), praises the officials who, in Nicholas I's time, quietly laid the foundations for the great reforms of his successor, D. Lieven's *Russia's Rulers under the Old Regime* (1989) consists largely of very informative biographies of those who rose to the top of the bureaucracy in the final tsarist decades, while D. T. Orlovsky in his *The Limits of Reform* (1981) looks at the structure and personnel of just one powerful ministry, the Ministry of the Interior, from Alexander I to Alexander II. S. Utechin, *Russian Political Thought* (1964) casts light on tsarist government and its spirit, as does, indirectly, M. Raeff's documentary survey of unsuccessful reform proposals, *Plans for Political Reform in Imperial Russia 1730–1905* (1966), J. Walkin, in *The Rise of Democracy in Pre-revolutionary Russia* (1962), looks at political institutions over the last sixty years of the Romanov regime and believes that participatory democracy had, possibly, a viable future. Memoirs by Russian statesmen and politicians are another source of information, while P. P. Gronsky and N. Astrov, in a posthumous kind of way, are quite informative in their *The War and the Russian Government* (1929).

A short but reliable guide to tsarist foreign policy is B. Jelavich, *A Century of Russian Foreign Policy 1814–1914* (1964). Her later *St Petersburg and Moscow* (1974) covers similar ground but carries on up to the Brezhnev years. For the Soviet period as a whole, A. B. Ulam, *Expansion and Coexistence 1917–1967* (1968) and M. Beloff's two-volume *The Foreign Policy of Soviet Russia 1929–1941* (1947) are still worth reading, although some of their assumptions might be questioned. *Russian Foreign Policy* (1962), edited by I. J. Lederer, has essays covering the nineteenth and twentieth centuries. Other useful books include R. Quested, *Sino-Russian Relations* (1984), which goes from Genghis Khan to Gromyko; L. Fischer, *The Soviets in World Affairs 1917–1929* (1951); E. H. Carr, *German–Soviet Relations Between the Two World Wars 1919–1939* (1952); G. F. Kennan, *Russia and the West under Lenin and Stalin* (1961); R. C. North, *Moscow and Chinese Communists* (1953); and W. A. Williams, *American–Russian Relations 1781–1947* (1952). M. M. Laserson, *The American Impact on Russia* (1950), is rather more than a study in foreign policies. The critical period of Soviet foreign policy leading to World War II has been examined by a dissident Czech, J. Hochman, in his *The Soviet Union and the Failure of Collective Security 1934–1938* (1984). The same subject is covered by *The Soviet Union and the Struggle for Collective Security in Europe 1933–1939* (1984) by J. Haslam, one of his four volumes covering inter-war foreign policy.

N. Hans, who worked in the tsarist educational system, dealt thoroughly with its history in his *History of Russian Educational Policy 1701–1917* (1931), while his *The Russian Tradition in Education* (1963) consists of biographies of leading tsarist educationists. W. H. E. Johnson, *Russia's Educational Heritage* (1950), is also useful, and so is P. L. Alston, *Education and the State in Tsarist Russia* (1969). The development of Soviet education can be followed in *The Changing Soviet School* (1960) by G. Z. F. Bereday, while N. Grant, *Soviet Education* (1964), describes how it was in Khrushchev's time. The story is carried further in M. Matthews, *Education in the Soviet Union* (1982), which runs from the 1950s to 1979. A more specialized study is S. Fitzpatrick, *Education and Social Mobility in the Soviet Union 1921–1934* (1979), which explains, implicitly at least, how the carrot of promotion brought forth a multitude of new Soviet men, educated but not imaginative. In a related field, J. Brooks, in *When Russia Learned to Read* (1985), describes the linked growth of literacy and popular literature in the final tsarist decades. The peak of the Soviet academic system, the Academy of Sciences, is treated by A. Vucinich in his *Empire of Knowledge* (1984), which concentrates on the relationship of science to ideology in the Soviet period. Another branch of learning, medicine, makes an interesting story, as is proved by N. M. Frieden, *Russian Physicians in an Era of Reform and Revolution 1856–1905* (1981).

As might be expected, the 1970s saw the beginning of a steady flow of books inspired by interest in the 'woman question'. The period from 1860 to 1930 is well covered in R. Stites, *The Women's Liberation Movement in Russia* (1978), while the Soviet period gets good coverage in a collection edited by D. Atkinson, A. Dallin, and G. W. Lapidus, *Women in Russia* (1977). B. A. Engel wrote *Mothers and Daughters* (1983), which is also quite informative about the nineteenth-century intelligentsia in general. L. H. Edmondson, in *Feminism in Russia 1900–1917* (1984) has written a readable book, but also a sad one, for it shows how participation in the liberation movement was followed by a loss, after October 1917, of most of the gains made. Also concerned with women, but throwing sidelights on industry, is R. L. Glickman, *Russian Factory Women: Workplace and Society 1880–1914* (1984). A new biography of a prominent liberated woman is B. Clements, *Bolshevik Feminist* (1979). This is about Alexandra Kollontai, a rather different kettle of fish from her contemporary Krupskaya, who has been given sensible treatment in R. McNeal's *Bride of the Revolution* (1973). The volume of essays edited by L. H. Edmondson, *Women and Society in Russia and the Soviet Union* (1991), covers a number of topics in the late tsarist and Soviet periods. Much more specialized but of relevance to several topics is S. Bridger's *Women in the Soviet Countryside* (1987), while G. Browning's *Women in Politics in the USSR* (1987) is a useful summary.

Religion is well covered in *The Modern Encyclopedia of Religions in Russia and the Soviet Union* (1988) by P. Steeves, and D. Pospielovsky's two-volume *The Russian Church under the Soviet Regime* (1984). See also G. Hosking's collection mentioned below. Other books on religion can be found in the bibliographies for Chapters 5 and 19, and on the Russian Jews in those for Chapters 5 and 15.

A. Parry's *Russian Cavalcade* (1944) is showing its age, but is one of the few books to cover the Russian army over the centuries. Most such books treat relatively short periods, although J. Keep's *Soldiers of the Tsar* (1985) does have a long span

(15th century to Alexander II's reform) and relates the army to society. A. Wildman's books (see the bibliography of Chapter 10) also have historical background. Memoirs and biographies fill some of the gaps. For the Soviet army, J. Erickson, *The Soviet High Command* (1962), is virtually a history of the armed forces from 1918 to 1941. Shorter, but continuing to a later date, is M. Mackintosh, *Juggernaut* (1967), while E. O'Ballance, *The Red Army* (1964), is a useful introduction. For the navy, D. Mitchell, *A History of Russian and Soviet Sea Power* (1974) ploughs wide but shallow waters. D. Woodward, *The Russians at Sea* (1965), starts around 1700 and is a reasonable, short account. Some libraries still have M. Mitchell's long *The Maritime History of Russia 848–1948* (1949), which covers exploration and commercial as well as naval matters. C. Benckendorff's attractive autobiography, *Half a Life* (1955), includes its author's experiences in the tsarist navy, as does D. Fedotov White, *Survival Through War and Revolution in Russia* (1939). For the air force there is R. Kilmarx, *A History of Soviet Air Power* (1962).

Coverage of nations and states that once formed part of the Russian Empire is patchy. A useful general history is B. Nahylo and V. Swoboda's *Soviet Disunion* (1990), whose point of view is succinctly expressed in the title. The following books in some cases are included because they are the best available, although not good, while in other cases they are the best, or more recent, of several books dealing with a given territory. For Poland, volume 2 of N. Davies, *God's Playground* (1983), is good, and so is the collection edited by R. Leslie, *The History of Poland since 1863* (1983). For the Ukraine there are B. Krawchenko's *Social Change and National Consciousness in Twentieth Century Ukraine* (1985), which is chronological but lingers on important questions, J. Armstrong's *Ukrainian Nationalism* (1963) which covers the Soviet period, O. Subtelny's *Ukraine; A History* (1984), and the collection edited by G. Hosking, *Church, Nation and State in Russia and Ukraine* (1991), which is partly devoted to the Church in the Ukraine. For Finland there are many sources, and two which are well represented in library collections are D. Kirby's *Finland in the Twentieth Century* (1979), and F. Singleton's *Short History of Finland* (1989). A. Bennigsen, S. Wimbush, *Muslims of the Soviet Empire* (1986), sets out to be a useful guide, and succeeds. *The Modern History of Soviet Central Asia* (1964) by G. Wheeler has worn well, although it can be usefully supplemented by the collection edited by E. Allworth, *Central Asia* (1967). A recent history of Georgia is R. Suny's *The Making of the Georgian Nation* (1988). For Armenia there is, among others, G. Walker's *Armenia* (1980). The Baltic republics between 1940 and 1980 are covered in R. Misiunas, R. Taagepera, *The Baltic States* (1983). Two slightly archaic but still useful books are J. H. Jackson, *Estonia* (1948), and A. Bilmanis, *History of Latvia* (1951). There is also T. Rawn's more up-to-date *Estonia and the Estonians* (1987). After the events of 1988–91, a flow of new books on these republics may be anticipated, of which a forerunner is A. Senn's *Lithuania Awakening* (1990), which deals mainly with 1987–90. Lithuania up to 1920 is covered by C. Jurgela's *A History of the Lithuanian Nation* (1947). A somewhat smaller ethnic minority (about two million in 1990) was the German, dealt with by I. Fleischauer and B. Pinkus in *The Soviet Germans: Past and Present* (1986).

CHAPTER 1

There are many books about Catherine the Great, most of which concentrate on her sex life, which was not really the centre of her own attention or of her importance. A good and recent study is J. Alexander's *Catherine the Great: Crises and Conquests* (1988), and S. de Madariaga's *Catherine the Great* (1990) can also be recommended. *Life in Russia under Catherine the Great* (1969) by M. Kochan gives a brief, readable, and well-illustrated description of the Russian society in which Alexander I grew up. The more ambitious student might like to tackle the 2,000-odd pages of W. Tooke, *View of the Russian Empire During the Reign of Catherine the Second, and to the Close of the Eighteenth Century* (1800),[1] the result of its author's long residence and research in St. Petersburg. A good account of Alexander's Russia, particularly in its institutional aspects, is conveyed by M. Raeff's biography, *Michael Speransky* (1961). Similarly, P. K. Grimsted, *The Foreign Ministers of Alexander I* (1969) reveals more than the title indicates, notably the Tsar's deviousness in dealing with his advisers. Alexander's friend Arakcheyev is described, readably but not profoundly, in M. Jenkin, *Arakcheev* (1969). Another useful biography, by M. and D. Josselson, is *The Commander: A Life of Barclay de Tolly* (1980). As for the Tsar himself, a good short study is A. McConnell, *Tsar Alexander I* (1970), and A. Palmer has written the longer, but popular in style, *Alexander I* (1974).

The war of 1812 is described by various eyewitnesses in A. Brett-James's collection, *1812: Napoleon's Defeat in Russia* (1966). L. Cooper, *Many Roads to Moscow* (1968) compares Napoleon's invasion with those of the Swedes and Nazis. An interesting post-mortem on the fire of Moscow is D. Olivier, *The Burning of Moscow* (1966). *The Memoirs of John Quincy Adams* (1874) contain in their second volume the US representative's impressions from on high, during his stay in St. Petersburg in 1809–14. An intelligent British observer's account of conditions in 1814 along the route of Napoleon's invasion is *Travels Through Part of the Russian Empire and the Country of Poland; Along the Southern Shores of the Baltic* (1816) by Robert Johnston. A specialized book, interestingly written, is *The Cossacks* (1969) by P. Longworth. J. S. Curtiss, *Church and State in Russia: the Last Years of the Empire, 1900–1917* (1940), has introductory sections dealing with the pre-1900 period. Part 1 of P. N. Miliukov, *Outlines of Russian Culture* (1943), is devoted to religion (Parts 2 and 3 are about literature, and art and architecture).

The classic account of the Decembrist Revolt is A. G. Mazour, *The First Russian Revolution, 1825* (1937). There is also M. Zetlin, *The Decembrists* (1958), while M. Raeff, in his *The Decembrist Movement* (1966), presents key documents, including the constitutional schemes composed by the plotters. An off-beat memoir by an off-beat character is N. Durova's *Cavalry Maiden* (1988), whose author was a gentlewoman who managed to serve as an officer in Alexander's hussars during the Napoleonic Wars.

CHAPTER 2

Probably the most useful view of Nicholas and his Russia is provided by N. V. Riasanovsky, *Nicholas I and Official Nationality in Russia 1825–1855* (1959): this deals not only with ideology but also with the Tsar and his entourage. For a straight biography, there are C. de Grunwald, *Tsar Nicholas I* (1954), and W. B. Lincoln, *Nicholas I* (1978); the latter, although patchy and repetitious, is well-informed. One

---

[1] Most of the nineteenth-century publications mentioned in this bibliography have been reprinted since the 1960s.

of the most enjoyable books about the reign is J. S. Curtiss, *The Russian Army under Nicholas I, 1825–1855* (1965), which conveys useful impressions of Nicholas and his generals, as well as information about the army and its campaigns. The life of the ordinary Russian soldier in the first half of the 19th century is studied in E. Wirtschafter's *From Serf to Russian Soldier* (1990). For the Crimean War, there are scores of British accounts, but J. S. Curtiss looks at things from the Russian side in *Russia's Crimean War* (1979). The Third Section is studied in two excellent and partly complementary monographs: *The Third Section* (1961) by S. Monas, and *The Third Department* (1968) by P. S. Squire. C. H. Whittaker, *The Origins of Modern Russian Education* (1984) is about Uvarov's contribution to education and his efforts to cope with the dilemma that he was intelligent enough to recognize, that of reconciling the spread of knowledge with continued respect for the regime.

Studies of individual writers are too numerous to mention in these bibliographies; the surveys of art and literature mentioned in the General Bibliography, which themselves are only a selection, contain suggestions for further reading. For the radical thinkers, a good start is E. Lampert, *Studies in Rebellion* (1957), which centres around the lives and times of Belinsky, Herzen, and Bakunin. For a full-length study of Bakunin there is G. Maximov, *Bakunin* (1953) and E. H. Carr, *Michael Bakunin* (1937), and for Herzen, M. Malia, *Alexander Herzen and the Birth of Russian Socialism* (1961). J. Seddon's *The Petrashevtsy* (1985) seems to be the only English-language book on this subject.

Two very detailed accounts by foreign observers, who in their time did much to illuminate Russia for the serious western reader, are Baron von Haxthausen, *The Russian Empire, its Peoples, Institutions and Resources* (1856), and J. G. Kohl, *Russia: St Petersburg, Moscow, Kharkoff, Riga, Odessa, the German Provinces on the Baltic, The Steppes, the Crimea, and the Interior of the Empire* (1844). With their Teutonic thoroughness these works stand favourable comparison with the rather poor travellers' tales of de Custine and A. Dumas.

CHAPTER 3

Two reliable, though not over-critical, biographies of Alexander II are S. Graham, *Tsar of Freedom* (1935), and E. Almedingen, *The Emperor Alexander II* (1962). For a very full history of the peasants up to 1861, J. Blum, *Lord and Peasant in Russia* (1961), should be consulted. For finding answers to questions that many historians skate around, G. T. Robinson, *Rural Russia Under the Old Regime* (1929), is admirable, although not easy reading. There are also the books already mentioned in the General Bibliography. D. Field, *The End of Serfdom* (1976) details the debates of 1855–61 which preceded and shaped the great liberation. T. Emmons, in his *The Russian Landed Gentry and the Peasant Emancipation of 1861* (1968), deals with an important aspect of the Emancipation, and the same author edited the short but useful collection of Russian and Western opinions, *The Emancipation of the Russian Serfs* (1970). Some of the books mentioned in the bibliography for Chapter 7 throw light on the results of the reform. A very detailed study of one Russian village is the basis of S. Hock's *Serfdom and Social Control in Russia* (1986). D. Moon, *Russian Peasants and Tsarism on the Eve of Reform*, was expected in 1992, while the peasants' lot after the Emancipation is studied in B. Eklof, S. Frank, *The World of the Russian Peasant* (1990).

An account of Kankrin and his economic policies is given in W. M. Pintner,

Russian Economic Policy under Nicholas I (1967). Early Russian industrialization and technology is detailed in W. L. Blackwell, *The Beginnings of Russian Industrialization, 1800–1860* (1968), while *The Beginnings of Railway Development in Russia* (1969) by R. M. Haywood deals not only with railway policy between 1835 and 1842 but also summarizes the development of pre-rail transport and incidentally throws some light on how decisions were reached in Nicholas's Russia. A. Parry, *Whistler's Father* (1939) is about the husband of Whistler's mother, and describes how he helped to build the St. Petersburg to Moscow Railway, dying in the process, while she attempted to convert Russians to her own brand of Christianity. For an extremely detailed examination of the lives and work of a few selected Russian peasants and workers in the last decade of serfdom, there is F. Le Play, *Les Ouvriers européens* (vols. 1, 2, 1877–9). *Labour and Society in Tsarist Russia: The Factory Workers of St. Petersburg 1855–1870* (1971) is the first of two volumes by R. E. Zelnik, dealing with the rise of industrial labour during Alexander's reign. M. Tugan-Baranovsky's nineteenth-century classic appeared in an edited translation in 1970, entitled *The Russian Factory in the Nineteenth Century*.

CHAPTER 4

Much of the work put into Alexander's reforms was actually carried out during the reign of his father, as is well brought out in R. Wortman, *The Development of a Russian Legal Consciousness* (1976), which describes how, in one department of state, competent bureaucrats developed useful ideas. In relation to their importance, the reforms of Alexander II have received meagre treatment by western scholars, but some of the books listed in later chapter bibliographies may also be consulted as they often deal with the consequences of what happened in the 1860s and 1870s. For the judicial reform, its antecedents and consequences, a former member of the Russian bar, S. Kucherov, wrote the very readable *Courts, Lawyers, and Trials under the Last Three Tsars* (1953). For the military reform, F. Miller, *Dmitri Miliutin and the Reform Era in Russia* (1968), is very useful and touches on other personalities and problems of the time, including education. For local government there is P. Vinogradoff, *Self-Government in Russia* (1915) and G. Fischer, *Russian Liberalism from Gentry to Intelligentsia* (1958). All these reforms are, of course, dealt with by the textbooks, and H. Seton-Watson, *The Russian Empire 1801–1917* (1967), is particularly useful. W. Mosse, *Alexander II and the Modernization of Russia* (1958), gives a clear but brief account. D. Mackenzie-Wallace, *Russia* (1877), provides eyewitness commentary on how the judicial and local government reforms worked out in practice, as does A. Leroy-Beaulieu, *Empire of the Tsars and the Russians* (3 vols., 1899–93). *The Politics of Autocracy; Letters of Alexander II to Prince A. I. Bariatinskii, 1857–1864* (1966) is also illuminating, especially the introduction by its editor, A. J. Rieber. Books on the individual writers and musicians of the period are too numerous to mention; the works mentioned in the General Bibliography contain useful book-lists. Perhaps N. Rimsky-Korsakov, *My Musical Life* (1924), deserves special mention, for it deals not only with music but also with life in the navy and St. Petersburg.

Volume 1 of A. S. Vucinich, *Science in Russian Culture* (1963), has something to say about technology but is largely, and interestingly, concerned with Russian scientists up to 1860, their thoughts and their opportunities. Relaxed censorship was one circumstance favouring thought and opportunity; the edited memoirs of

A. Nikitenko, *Diary of a Russian Censor* (1974) additionally illuminate a range of social topics rather wider than censorship, under Nicholas and Alexander. For education, A. Sinel's study of Dmitri Tolstoy's policies, *The Classroom and the Chancellery* (1973), provides a clear picture.

CHAPTER 5

An agreeable way of making acquaintance with this period is by reading R. Hare, *Portraits of Russian Personalities Between Reform and Revolution* (1959), which includes writers, revolutionaries, Stolypin, Witte, and Pobedonostsev among its subjects. The intellectual background of the revolutionary movement is covered by E. Lampert in *Sons Against Fathers* (1965), which centres around Chernyshevsky, Dobroliubov, and Pisarev. There is also P. Pomper, *Peter Lavrov and the Russian Revolutionary Movement* (1972). A readable general picture of revolutionary activity from 1825 to 1887 is provided by A. Yarmolinsky, *Road to Revolution* (1957). D. Offord's *The Russian Revolutionary Movement in the 1880s* (1986) describes, analyses, and interprets the several groups of that decade. A detailed and exemplary study of the Populists is F. Venturi, *Roots of Revolution* (1960). N. Naimark, *Terrorists and Social Democrats* (1983), is about the Narodniks up to 1895; its strength is its use of police archives and its weakness is its use of not much else, but it has some interesting things to tell, including an account of Narodnik activity within the imperial army. D. Hardy's *Land and Freedom* (1987) studies the break-up of Land and Liberty in 1879. A. Gleason's *Young Russia* (1980) examines the birth of radicalism from the 1860s and suggests how idealism was squeezed out by revolutionism, while V. Nahirny's *The Russian Intelligentsia* (1983) occasionally gives the impression that if psychiatry had been better developed many young people would have not needed to sublimate their hang-ups in revolutionary activity. D. Brower, *Training the Nihilists* (1975), studies the link between education and radicalism and supports the belief that students from the lower social classes were less likely than noble students to become revolutionaries. What happened to revolutionaries in emigration is studied by M. Miller in *The Russian Revolutionary Émigrés 1825–1870* (1986), and by W. McClennan in *Revolutionary Exiles* (1979). J. Slatter, in *From the Other Shore* (1984), deals with the Russian emigrants who came to Britain in 1880–1917. Vera Zasulich at last receives perceptive treatment in *Vera Zasulich* (1983) by J. Bergman, who concludes that she was too decent to be a truly effective revolutionary; her attack on Trepov was intended to be an act of self-sacrifice, not an incentive for a wave of bilateral terrorism. The assassination of the Emperor and its antecedents is covered in D. J. Footman's life of the leading conspirator, Zhelyabov, in *Red Prelude* (1944). R. Hingley, *Nihilists: Russian Radicals and Revolutionaries in the Reign of Alexander II* (1967) covers the same ground differently. In *The Unmentionable Nechayev* (1961), M. Prawdin handles his subject well, apart from what seems to be a laboured attempt to portray Lenin as some kind of Nechaevite Second Coming. Other biographies are J. H. Billington, *Mikhailovsky and Russian Populism* (1958), and S. H. Baron, *Plekhanov, the Father of Russian Marxism* (1963). Those who prefer the horse's mouth would enjoy *Underground Russia* (1883) by the celebrated assassin S. Stepnyak, *Memoirs of a Revolutionist* (1968) by Vera Figner (one of the last of the leading members of the People's Will to remain at large, being arrested in 1884 and sent to gaol for twenty years), and another *Memoirs of a Revolutionist* (2 vols., 1899, 1906) by Prince P. A. Kropotkin.

The latter, an anarchist so widely respected that Lenin allowed him a state funeral in 1921, was one of those who 'went to the people'. An edition of these memoirs, with commentary, was published in 1962 (ed. by J. A. Rogers). Turgenev's *Virgin Soil* (1877), while not the best of his novels, does convey how very varied in temperament and intentions were the young individuals who went to the peasants and workers. The 1887 attempt to bomb Alexander III is one of several episodes interestingly described in I. Deutscher, *Lenin's Childhood* (1970): the apparent leader of the conspiracy, Lenin's brother, is revealed as a young man having all of Lenin's qualities, plus a nobility of character which led to his downfall. How his execution shaped Lenin's own attitudes has to be left to the imagination, but certainly cannot be ignored.

Two other crosses borne by Alexander II are studied in R. F. Leslie, *Reform and Insurrection in Russian Poland* (1963), which is devoted mainly to the 1863 rebellion, and B. H. Sumner, *Russia and the Balkans* (1937).

There is very little material for the reign of Alexander III, although much may be gleaned from *The Memoirs of Count Witte* (1921) by S. I. Witte. This English version is abridged from the original and should be read with an awareness of the several axes which its author was grinding. R. Byrnes's study, *Pobedonostsev* (1968), also conveys much about the reign. K. P. Pobedonostsev, apart from numerous anonymous articles, also expressed his ideals in *Reflections of a Russian Statesman* (1898). How a bureaucracy, aligned towards liberalization in the previous reign, adjusted to the new atmosphere, can be studied with H. W. Whelan, *Alexander III and the State Council: Bureaucracy and Counter-Reform in Late Imperial Russia* (1982). The collection edited by W. Gurian, *Soviet Imperialism* (1953), contains much information on russification and tsarist policies towards the nationalities. Russification is also covered in E. C. Thaden (ed.), *Russification in the Baltic Provinces and Finland, 1855–1914* (1981), and S. A. Zenkovsky, *Pan-Turkism and Islam in Russia* (1960); the latter deals with 1905–21, and hence includes the Central Asian revolt of 1916. The enlightened governor of Bessarabia, S. D. Urussov, in his *Memoirs of a Russian Governor* (1908), has interesting comments on the pogroms, and much else besides.

Pogroms were a feature of Alexander III's reign, and much has been written about the condition of the Tsar's Jewish subjects. This paragraph includes works relating to the whole of the tsarist period. S. W. Baron, *The Russian Jew Under Tsars and Soviets* (1964) and S. Dubnow, *History of the Jews in Russia and Poland* are useful, as is the collection edited by J. Frumkin and others, *Russian Jewry, 1860–1917* (1966). More specialized books include Y. Peled's *Class and Ethnicity in the Pale* (1989); J. Klier, S. Lamboza (editors), *Pogroms* (1991); E. Mendelsohn, *Class Struggle in the Pale* (1970), describing the growth of the Jewish socialist movement up to 1905; J. Frankel's very carefully researched *Prophecy and Politics: Socialism, Nationalism, and the Russian Jews, 1862–1917* (1981); and H. Rogger, *Jewish Policies and Right-wing Politics in Imperial Russia* (1986). The latter touches on the Black Hundreds and provides material for discussing whether there was anything that might later be described as a fascist movement in tsarist Russia. One of the interesting points made by M. Stanislawski in his *Tsar Nicholas I and the Jews* (1983) is that because most writing about this subject was done in the reign of Nicholas II, it projects the contemporary feeling that Jewish policy was deliberately vicious back to Nicholas I's time, thereby distorting the view.

CHAPTER 6

G. Wheeler, *The Modern History of Soviet Central Asia* (1964) is perhaps the best introduction to that area, dealing with both nineteenth- and twentieth-century developments. M. Rywkin, *Russia in Central Asia* (1963) is mainly about the Soviet period but has a chapter on tsarist policies. *Russian Central Asia 1867–1917* (1960), by R. A. Pierce, concentrates on those forty important years. The alleged Russian threat to India called forth a host of books in the second half of the nineteenth century about Russian intentions in the area, but the less alarming *Tsarism and Imperialism in the Middle and Far East* (1940) by B. H. Sumner is preferable. D. Geyer's *Russian Imperialism* (1987) shows how foreign and domestic requirements clashed in the last half-century of tsarist Russia.

An agreeable introduction to the history of Siberia is G. Lensen, *Russia's Eastward Expansion* (1964), consisting of extracts, with commentary, from the writings of those who over the centuries had experience of that region. *The Great Siberian Migration* (1957) by D. W. Treadgold is an exhaustive study of the government's development policies. S. Marks, *Road to Power* (1991), is a very good account of how the Trans-Siberian Railway was pushed forward by Witte and others. Siberian development, from the 17th to the 20th century, is covered in various aspects by the collection edited by A. Wood and R. French, *The Development of Siberia* (1989). G. Kennan, *Siberia and the Exile System* (1891), is a classic exposé which greatly irritated the government. Asian Russia has always attracted western travellers with literary ambitions; three works which are useful and deserve prizes for endurance are: *Narrative of a Pedestrian Journey Through Russia and Siberian Tartary, from the Frontier of China to the Sea and Kamchatka* (1825) by Captain John Dundas Cochrane, R. N. (this was a pedestrian journey indeed, for the author set out from Dieppe on foot and covered about 30,000 miles); *Oriental and Western Siberia* (1858) by Mr Thomas W. Atkinson and *Recollections of Tartar Steppes and their Inhabitants* (1863) by Mrs Thomas W. Atkinson. The indefatigable Atkinsons covered nearly 40,000 miles, largely on horseback. Mr was an artist and included his landscapes in the book. Mrs was formerly a governess in a Russian family and a high point of her book is her conversations with wives of the Decembrists who were still in exile at mid-century. For a synthesis of travellers' tales, railway-building, and official policies, Harmon Tupper, *To the Great Ocean: Siberia and the Trans Siberian Railway* (1965) is comprehensive.

'*Matey' Imperialists* (1982) by R. K. I. Quested has a title which is not as out of place as it might seem at first sight, for it describes how the Russians behaved in Manchuria from 1895 to 1917. *The Russo-Chinese War* (1967), by the late and very lamented George Lensen, describes Russia's involvement in the Boxer Rebellion. There are many books about the Russo-Japanese War in English, but most of them say the same things, which are not always accurate. Somewhat superior is J. N. Westwood, *Russia Against Japan* (1986). The non-military side of the War is well-handled by J. A. White in his *Diplomacy of the Russo-Japanese War* (1964). For the military side, the fullest account is the multi-volume *Official History of the Russo-Japanese War* (1910), compiled by the British Committee of Imperial Defence. Of the scores of eyewitness accounts of the fighting, two are especially illuminating; Sir Ian Hamilton, *A Staff-Officer's Scrapbook* (1907) and A. N. Kuropatkin's explanation of his lack of success, *The Russian Army and the Japanese War* (1909). For the naval side, J. N. Westwood, *Witnesses of Tsushima* (1970), will gratify connoisseurs of gory sensations; the squeamish should content themselves with the Introduction, which deals with Russian naval policy in the Far East. The Russian navy's material, organization, and purpose, as seen from London, are treated in F. T. Jane, *The Imperial Russian Navy* (1904).

CHAPTER 7

M. Ferro's *Nicholas II* (1991) is a manageable account of the Emperor's life by an experienced practitioner. Of R. Massie, *Nicholas and Alexandra* (1968), it may at least be said that the book is better than the film. In addition, it treats very well the nature of haemophilia and, when all is said and done, to portray Nicholas as an essentially tragic figure is not really mawkish or sentimental. Another popular but not negligible biography is E. M. Almedingen, *The Empress Alexandra 1872–1918* (1961). Of the several books on Social Democracy, J. H. L. Keep, *The Rise of Social Democracy in Russia* (1963), takes the story up to 1905, as does the somewhat shorter *The Russian Marxists and the Origins of Bolshevism* (1955) by L. Haimson. R. Brym in *The Jewish Intelligentsia and Russian Marxism* (1978) makes the point that many Jews became revolutionaries out of the sheer frustration of being denied jobs appropriate to their abilities. D. W. Treadgold, *Lenin and his Rivals* (1955), treats the ideological struggles of 1898–1906 and includes useful accounts of the non-Bolshevik socialists and liberals. Other views of Lenin's ideological critics are contained in R. Williams, *The Other Bolsheviks* (1986), which apart from dealing with the misgivings of Gorki and Lunarcharsky in 1904–14 also deals with Bogdanov, possibly the most original of the Bolshevik thinkers and not loved by Lenin. The argument between these two is elaborated by Z. Sochor in *Revolution and Culture* (1988). R. Stites, in *Revolutionary Dreams* (1989), gives a quite touching account of how utopian ideas influenced Bolshevik behaviour. A. Besancon, in *The Intellectual Origins of Leninism* (1981), among other things gives the impression that Lenin's ideology squeezed out his humanity. D. Lane's *The Roots of Russian Communism* (1969) is very informative. For a general view of intellectual currents C. Read's *Religion, Revolution, and the Russian Intelligentsia* (1979) is quite interesting. Some of the writings of the most percipient 'Economist' are available in translation in J. Frankel, *Vladimir Akimov on the Dilemmas of Russian Marxism, 1895–1903* (1969); the introduction of this volume is an excellent summary of Russian marxist theory. R. Pipes, *Social Democracy and the St. Petersburg Labour Movement* (1963), attempts to correct exaggerated accounts of Lenin's significance in the early years of the social democratic movement. A. B. Ulam, *Lenin and the Bolsheviks* (U.S. title, *The Bolsheviks*: 1965), takes the story from the early days to Lenin's death. In *Octobrists to Bolsheviks* (1984), M. McCauley presents an interesting collection of documents from 1905–17. Among the best of the shorter biographies of Lenin are D. Shub, *Lenin* (1966) and H. Shukman, *Lenin and the Russian Revolution* (1966). These might be supplemented by the collection of essays by various specialists on aspects of Lenin's life edited by L. Shapiro and P. Reddaway, *Lenin: The Man, the Theorist, the Leader* (1967). The first of three volumes of R. Service, *Lenin: a Political Life* appeared in 1985 and takes him as far as 1910. Vol. 2 (1991) continues the story to 1918. Another multi-volume biography, absolutely devoid of convoluted language and with a definite viewpoint, is T. Cliff's *Lenin*, the three volumes of which appeared in 1975, 1976, and 1978. C. Rice's *Lenin* (1990) is succinct. Lenin's own works are available in a multiplicity of editions.

A. P. Mendel, *Dilemmas of Progress in Tsarist Russia* (1961), explains why movements such as Legal Populism and Legal Marxism split away from their parent movements, while R. Kindersley, *The First Russian Revisionists* (1962), concentrates on Legal Marxism. G. Swain, in his *Russian Social Democracy and the Legal Labour Movement 1906–14* (1983) reveals the gap, in those years, between Lenin's perceptions and reality.

P. Pomper gives the Bolsheviks a hard time in *The Russian Revolutionary Intelligentsia* (1970). The Socialist Revolutionaries are seen in action in C. Rice's *Russian Workers and the Socialist Revolutionary Party through the Revolution of 1905–7* (1988).

The Crisis of Russian Populism (1967) by R. Wortman examines the ideas and difficulties of three leading Populists. The politics of the rural situation are also covered by R. Hennesey in *The Agrarian Question in Russia 1905–1907* (1977), by L. Haimson's collection, *The Politics of Rural Russia 1905–1914* (1979), and by M. Perrie in *The Agrarian Policy of the Russian Socialist-Revolutionary Party* (1976). R. G. Robbin, *Famine in Russia 1891–1892* (1975) is about the previous reign, but helps to explain how peasants felt in the early twentieth century. Those of them who decided to move to Moscow and become workers are observed in *Peasants and Proletarians* (1979) by R. E. Johnson. *Radical Worker in Tsarist Russia* (1986), edited by R. Zelnik, is a fascinating autobiography of a Russian worker in the period up to 1905.

For Russian liberalism, whatever that might be, G. Fischer, *Russian Liberalism* (1958) goes up to about 1905, by which year T. Riha's biography of Milyukov, *A Russian European* (1969), is in full flow and takes the story up to the fiasco of 1917. Milyukov's explanation of his failure, among other more useful information, is conveyed by his autobiography, *Political Memoirs, 1905–1917* (1967 edn., ed. by A. P. Mendel). Another liberal is given generous two-volume treatment in R. E. Pipes, *Struve* (1970, 1980). A reliable guide to a more cheerful period for the liberals is S. Galai, *The Liberation Movement in Russia 1900–1905* (1973).

Many of the multitude of memoirs by revolutionaries begin their story around 1900. They should all be treated with caution (especially Trotsky's, whose deceptions and self-deceptions are superbly concealed by his fine style). Worth mentioning are V. Serge, *Memoirs of a Revolutionary, 1901–1941* (1963), B. Savinkov, *Memoirs of a Terrorist* (1931), the Menshevik Eva Broido, *Memoirs of a Revolutionary* (1967), and L. Trotsky, *My Life* (1930). The first volume of I. Deutscher's trilogy on Trotsky, *The Prophet Armed: Trotsky 1897–1921* (1954) is an advantageous substitute for Trotsky's autobiography. A useful biography covering the Mensheviks is I. Getzler's painstaking *Martov* (1967).

The immediate antecedents of 1905 are among the topics covered in E. H. Judge, *Plehve: Repression and Reform in Imperial Russia, 1902–1904* (1983), in which the subject appears as something of a pragmatist. This book might well be read concurrently with K. Frohlich, *The Emergence of Russian Constitutionalism 1900–1904* (1981). As for the 1905 rebellion, S. Harcave, *First Blood. The Russian Revolution of 1905* (1965; in some edns. the subtitle becomes the main title) is readable. Vol. 2 of T. Shanin's *The Roots of Otherness* (1986) deals, quite deeply, with 1905–7, while A. Ascher's *The Revolution of 1905* (1988) is a good straightforward treatment, beside which books like G. Gapon, *The Story of My Life* (1905), and G. Hough, *The Potemkin Mutiny* (1960), look very journalistic indeed. W. Sablinsky, in his *Road to Bloody Sunday* (1976), deals with Father Gapon and confirms that Bloody

Sunday occurred because nobody expected it to occur and because the authorities could think of no other way to deal with the situation that Gapon had created. Police Socialism gets good treatment in J. Schneiderman, *Sergei Zubatov and Revolutionary Marxism* (1976), and D. Pospielovsky; *Russian Police Trade Unionism* (1970). Some perceptive studies of this stormy period of Russian history are contained in J. Maynard, *Russia in Flux* (1948). Aspects of the rebellious workers are treated in L. Engelstein, *Moscow 1905* (1982) and V. E. Bonnell, *Roots of Rebellion* (1983); both of these concentrate on working-class organization. A sociological view of 1905 is presented in volume 2 of T. Shanin, *The Roots of Otherness* (1986). H. Reichman's *Railwaymen and Revolution* (1987), apart from having the rare virtue of depicting 1905 away from St. Petersburg and Moscow, also implies that the most rebellious railwaymen were those who had the closest ties with their villages. A. Verner's *The Crisis of Russian Autocracy* (1990) looks at the role, or non-role, of Nicholas II in 1905. A general picture of society is provided by G. Surh's *1905 in St. Petersburg* (1989), which is especially good on Gapon's 'Assembly of Russian Mill and Factory Workers'. Civil rights came into the foreground in 1905 and these are looked at from several different historical points of view in the collection edited by O. Crisp and L. Edmonson, *Civil Rights in Imperial Russia* (1989). Another collection, this time on varying historical topics between 1881 and 1917, is edited by R. McKean: *New Perspectives in Modern Russian History* (1991). A rare view of the 1905 events in the provinces and villages is an incidental benefit of S. Seregny's *Russian Teachers and Peasant Revolution* (1989), which is about educational politics in that year. The countryside is also involved in J. Bushnell's *Mutiny among Repression* (1985), which shows how in 1905–7 peasant soldiers would solve their internal conflict between loyalty and humanity by the desperate expedient of mutiny.

The post-1905 situation has been studied in several recent publications. A. Levin, who published *The Second Duma* in 1940, returned with *The Third Duma: Election and Profile* in 1973. The same period is covered differently in B. Pinchuk, *The Octobrists in the Third Duma, 1907–1912* (1974). T. Emmons adds to knowledge of the First Duma with *The Formation of Political Parties and the First National Elections in Russia* (1983), although it is mainly concerned with its immediate antecedents. How Stolypin tackled three main issues (agriculture, Finland, Zemstvo extension) is the substance of G. Tokmakoff, *P. A. Stolypin and the Third Duma* (1981). G. A. Hosking, *The Russian Constitutional Experiment* (1973), is devoted to the interaction between government and Duma up to 1914, thereby throwing much light on Stolypin's problems. The Stolypin Reform has been rather neglected by historians; the already-mentioned book by G. T. Robinson must suffice, together with L. Owen, *The Russian Peasant Movement, 1906–1917* (1937). D. Atkinson, *The End of the Russian Land Commune, 1905–1930* (1983), is an important contribution. The unsuccessful efforts to reform local government are related by N. B. Weissman in his *Reform in Tsarist Russia* (1981). In both agriculture and local government the role of the landowning gentry was sometimes decisive, and aspects of this situation are covered in R. T. Manning, *The Crisis of the Old Order in Russia* (1982), detailing relations between landowners and the government around 1905 and observing the importance of class antagonisms between the nobles and peasantry; G. M. Hamburg, *Politics of the Russian Nobility, 1881–1905* (1984); and D. Edelman, *Gentry Politics on the Eve of the Russian Revolution: The Nationalist Party, 1907–1917*. T. Pearson, in *Russian Officialdom in Crisis* (1989), deals with the problem of distributing authority in the countryside, and accordingly has much to say about *zemstva*, land captains, the traditional nobility, and the bureaucracy. L. Haimson's collection *The Politics of Rural Russia 1905–1914* (1979) contains some specialized essays that, for the most part, are still valid.

CHAPTER 8

Textbook coverage of Nicholas's reign is marked by the division between 'pessimistic' and 'optimistic' assessments of the regime's prospects on the eve of the war. Of the pessimists, the celebrated, but later disgraced, Soviet historian N. N. Pokrovsky is perhaps most uncompromising in his *Brief History of Russia* (1933). Florinsky's history also takes a pessimistic view, whereas Pushkarev believed that pre-1914 Russia had distinctly hopeful prospects. For reliable coverage of Nicholas's unhappy reign there are W. B. Lincoln, *In War's Dark Shadow* (1983), L. Kochan, *Russia in Revolution, 1890–1918* (1966), and R. Charques, *Twilight of Imperial Russia* (1958). A useful collection of essays is *Russia under the last Tsar* (1969), edited by T. G. Stavrou. A short collection of extracts from the writings of western and Soviet historians, *Russia in Transition, 1905–1914* (1970), edited by R. H. McNeal, presents opposing views on such themes as Russia's economic and political prospects, and on Stolypin.

Day-to-day life is agreeably presented by H. Troyat in *Daily Life in Russia under the Last Tsar* (1961). M. Kovalevsky's *Modern Customs and Ancient Laws of Russia* (1891) is fascinating for a reader already familiar with the period. W. H. Bruford, in his *Chekhov and his Russia* (1947), successfully makes a social survey of early twentieth-century Russia, using the writer's works as his raw material. F. H. E. Palmer, *Russian Life in Town and Country* (1901), is a reliable account, by the secretary of one of Nicholas's equerries, of what it was like to be a Russian under the last Romanov. Further sociological insight may be found in A. Kuprin's novel *Yama* (sometimes entitled *The Pit*) which is largely concerned with prostitution, and in his *The Duel*, which is about army life. A good account of the tsarist army's political influence is contained in W. C. Fuller, *Civil–Military Conflict in Imperial Russia 1881–1914* (1985), which shows that the War Ministry did not always get its own way. Another study is R. H. McNeal, *Tsar and Cossack 1855–1914* (1986), dealing with a unique military society. V. T. Bill's aptly-titled *The Forgotten Class* (1959) has some shortcomings but describes the Russian industrialists and merchants adequately enough, and has a useful section about the Old Believers. Both education and the 'woman question' are dealt with in A. H. Koblitz, *A Convergence of Lives* (1983), which is about Sofia Kovalevskaya, who, like so many other intelligent women, had to 'choose between knowledge and revolution'.

For the economy, there is T. H. von Laue, *Sergei Witte and the Industrialization of Russia* (1963), which is good but would have been better if its author had done some more homework in economics. M. Miller, *The Economic Development of Russia 1905–1914* (1926, 1968), is useful but patchy, and offers the rare courtesy of a conversion table for the old Russian weights and measures. The role of foreign capital and technology is described in J. P. McKay, *Pioneers for Profit; Foreign Entrepreneurship and Russian Industrialization 1885–1913* (1970). Two of that class of book which, ostensibly aimed at a very narrow subject, touches on a very broad spectrum of topics are A. Fenin, *Coal and Politics in Late Imperial Russia* (1990), which is the memoirs of an engineer, and J. Coppersmith, *The Electrification of*

Russia 1880–1926 (1991). The working class at this time receives attention in R. McKean, *St. Petersburg between the Revolutions* (1990), about the labour movement. Urbanization is dealt with by J. Bradley in *Muzhik and Muscovite* (1985), and other books covering the cities are the collection edited by M. Hamm, *The City in Late Imperial Russia* (1986), which details the situation in eight large cities, and R. Thurston's *Liberal City, Conservative State* (1987). The latter is about Moscow's critical situation in 1906–14 and suggests that half the problem was that a liberal city government had difficulty in co-operating with a conservative state. These difficulties are also illustrated in J. Hutchinson's *Politics and Public Health in Revolutionary Russia* (1990). Education is studied in J. McClelland, *Autocrats and Academics: Education, Culture and Society in Tsarist Russia* (1987), J. Johanson, *Women's Struggle for Higher Education in Russia 1855–1900* (1987), which is as much about inter-ministerial struggles as about women, and S. Kassow, *Students, Professors and the State in Tsarist Russia* (1989), which shows how universities formed a self- contained world in which radical ideas had more freedom to develop than elsewhere.

When Russia Learned to Read (1985), by J. Brooks, is about the spread of literacy in the last half-century of tsarist Russia. A related topic, the rise of a mass-circulation press after 1855, is covered by L. Reynolds in *The News under Russia's Old Regime* (1991), while C. Ruud in *Russian Entrepreneur* (1990) gives a biography of Ivan Sytin, the publisher responsible for the progressive popular newspaper *Russkoye slovo* (which eventually was metamorphosed into *Izvestiya*).

The Tsar's Viceroys (1987), by R. Robbins, deals with the provincial governors, and their quite hardworking lives are illustrated with many examples. At the opposite end of the scale were the social democrats, of whom some Ukrainian examples, cut off from their leadership and harried by the police, are studied by R. Elwood in *Russian Social Democracy in the Underground* (1974). N. Schleifman's *Undercover Agents in the Russian Revolutionary Movement* (1988) is involved with the travails of the Socialist Revolutionaries in 1902–14; Azeff is well covered, but still remains much of a mystery. There is very little in English on the Okhrana, but B. Nikolaevsky, *Azeff, the Russian Judas* (1934), is not as bad as its title suggests. A useful but inevitably incomplete account of the security organs is in R. Hingley, *The Russian Secret Police 1565–1970* (1970), a book which will be enjoyed especially by Russophobes. Of memoirs so far unmentioned, those by V. N. Kokovtsov, Stolypin's successor as prime minister, are quite valuable: *Out of my Past* (1935). Also worth reading are V. I. Gurko's recollections, *Features and Figures of the Past: Government and Opinion in the Reign of Nicholas II* (1939) and, especially, B. Pares, *My Russian Memoirs* (1931), which describe its author's experiences between 1898 and 1919.

CHAPTER 9

D. C. B. Lieven, *Russia and the Origins of the First World War* (1983), would be hard to surpass as a succinct account of how Russia was dragged into the war. Still very useful for a study of Russia at war are the several works published by the Carnegie endowment; most of them also provide the pre-war background for their topics. These books are: *Russian Public Finance during the War* (1928) by A. M. Michelson and others; *Russia in the Economic War* (1928) by B. E. Nolde; *State Control of Industry during the War* (1928) by S. O. Zagorsky; *The War and the*

Russian Government (1929) by P. P. Gronsky and N. J. Astrov; *Russian Schools and Universities in the World War* (1929) by N. Ignatiev and others; *The Cooperative Movement in Russia during the War* (1929) by E. M. Kayden and A. N. Antsiferov; *Russian Agriculture during the War* (1930) by A. N. Antsiferov and others; *Food Supply in Russia during the World War* (1930) by P. B. Struve and others; *Russian Local Government during the War and the Union of Zemstvos* (1930) by T. J. Polner and others; *The Russian Army in the World War* (1931) by N. N. Golovine; *The Cost of the War to Russia* (1932) by S. Kohn and A. F. Meyendorff; and *The End of the Russian Empire* (1931) by M. T. Florinsky. The last describes the disintegration of society and bureaucracy, and has been reprinted as a paperback. A more detailed account by one who was there is B. Pares, *Fall of the Russian Monarchy* (1939). The inside story is conveyed by A. N. Iakhontov's notes, taken at meetings of the Council of Ministers in 1915, edited by M. Cherniavsky and entitled *Prologue to Revolution* (1967). The same kind of inside story is conveyed by C. E. Vulliamy, *From the Red Archives* (1929), an edited translation of documents relating to the last pre-revolutionary years. The Rasputin episode is described, not always convincingly, by one of his murderers, F. F. Yusupov, in *Lost Splendour* (1953), and by A. de Jonge in *Life and Times of Grigorii Rasputin* (1982). F. A. Golder, *Documents of Russian History 1914–1917* (1969) is exactly what its title describes. C. J. Smith, *The Russian Struggle for Power 1914–1917* (1956), is actually an account of Russia's foreign relations, especially with the Allies. More recent titles include L. H. Siegelbaum's study of the War Industries Committees, *The Politics of Industrial Mobilization in Russia 1914–17* (1983), K. Neilson, *Strategy and Supply: The Anglo-Russian Alliance 1914–17* (1984), and R. Pearson's study of liberal travails, *The Russian Moderates and the Crisis of Tsarism 1914–17* (1977). A very good history of the regime's performance in the wartime years is N. Stone, *The Eastern Front* (1975).

What the generals saw is conveyed in A. I. Denikin, *The Russian Turmoil* (1922), A. A. Brusilov, *A Soldier's Notebook* (1930), and B. Gourko, *Memories and Impressions of War and Revolution in Russia 1914–1917* (1918), among many others. Three commendable accounts (and there are many others) from a less exalted viewpoint are G. P. Tschebotarioff, *Russia My Native Land* (1964), by a former Cossack artillery officer who participated in the Great and Civil wars; *The Grinding Mill* (1935) by another junior officer, A. Lobanov-Rostovsky; and *A Subaltern in Old Russia* (1944) by a Red Army general, A. A. Ignatiev. W. B. Steveni, *The Russian Army from Within* (1914) gives a westerner's observations. For the adventures of a Prussian pachyderm on the Eastern Front, see General Ludendorff, *My War Memories 1914–1918* (2 vols., n.d.).

CHAPTER 10

A very useful reference source, especially as it integrates much recent research, is *The Blackwell Encyclopedia of the Russian Revolution* (1988), edited by H. Shukman. A good and up-to-date account of the first revolution is T. Hasegawa, *The February Revolution: Petrograd 1917* (1981), which, among other things, suggests that the soviets were more symbolic than powerful, the Duma's provisional committee (which controlled the railways and had the confidence of both army and soviets) being the effective authority. M. Ferro has also written ground-breaking studies of the Revolution: *The Russian Revolution of February 1917* (1972) and

October 1917: A Social History of the Russian Revolution (1980). G. Katkov, *Russia 1917* (1967), is still useful, especially for the immediate antecedents. Another good account, with some emphasis on society, is S. Fitzpatrick, *The Russian Revolution* (1982). L. Shapiro, *1917: The Russian Revolutions* (1984), emphasizes the importance of power, its grasp and retention. A very brief account, but incorporating recent research, is R. Service, *The Russian Revolution* (1986). The same author's *Society and Politics in the Russian Revolution* was expected in 1992. There is also B. Williams, *The Russian Revolution 1917–1921* (1987), which is short but useful. J. Burbank's *Intelligentsia and Revolution* (1986) deals with the polemics exchanged between the Bolsheviks and their critics in 1917–21. How the Bolsheviks succeeded in taking over the leadership of the mass organizations after spring 1917, without those organizations' rank-and-file quite knowing what was going on, is described by J. Keep in his *The Russian Revolution: A Study in Mass Mobilisation* (1977). However, this book, like several others, needs to be read in conjunction with later books resulting from easier research conditions over recent years. Several of these concentrate on a particular area or group and collectively they demonstrate that there was no single pattern for the events that unrolled in 1917. Among them are: R. Suny, *The Baku Commune 1917–1918* (1972), G. Gill, *Peasants and Government in the Russian Revolution* (1979), O. Figes, *Peasant Russia, Civil War: The Volga Countryside in Revolution 1917–1921* (1989), D. Raleigh, *Revolution on the Volga* (1985), about Saratov in 1917, and R. Snow, *The Bolsheviks in Siberia 1917–1918* (1977). A very useful commentary on recent research is presented by E. Acton in his *Rethinking the Russian Revolution* (1990), while *Revolution in Russia: Reassessments of 1917*, edited by E. and J. Frankel, B. Knei-Paz, was expected in 1991. The period between February and October is well-detailed by several of the main participants, each grinding his own particular axe; Milyukov has already been mentioned. A. F. Kerensky published *The Catastrophe* (1927), *Crucifixion of Liberty* (1934), and *The Kerensky Memoirs* (1966): it is interesting to note which of his views are changed or unchanged, as not only time, but current events, influence his perspective. Kerensky also collaborated with R. P. Browder in *The Russian Provisional Government 1917: Documents* (1961), which is too selective, but useful. A sound biography of Kerensky was late in coming, but arrived with R. Abraham's *Alexander Kerensky* (1987). Among other biographies are a study of *Tseretelli* (1976) by W. Roobol, and R. Slusser's *Stalin in October* (1987), whose subtitle 'The Man who Missed the Revolution' seems a trifle unkind. For the Socialist Revolutionaries, V. M. Chernov, *The Great Russian Revolution* (1936), is sometimes revealing, and I. Sternberg, who was a Left S. R. and became a member of Lenin's original coalition government, lets a few cats out of various bags in his *In the Workshop of the Revolution* (1953). Another absorbing memoir is *Stormy Passage* (1961) by W. S. Woytinsky, who was a revolutionary student in 1905, broke with Lenin in 1917, and became an editor of *Izvestiya* and a member of the Petrograd Soviet. *On the Eve of 1917* (1982) is by A. Shlyapnikov, who later led the Workers' Opposition. What the Bolsheviks were doing, or not doing, before 1917 is described, not always sympathetically, by the prominent Menshevik T. Dan in his *The Origins of Bolshevism* (written 1940, published 1964). What Dan and his friends were doing, or not doing, in 1917, is covered in J. D. Basil, *The Mensheviks in the Revolution of 1917* (1983), but some of the author's interpretations are hard to swallow. Another bite at the same cherry is Z. Galili y Garcia's *The Menshevik Leaders in the Russian Revolution* (1989). The failure of the Kadets is chronicled in W. Rosenberg's

Liberals in the Russian Revolution (1974), which takes their story up to 1921. The collection edited by C. Timberlake, *Essays on Russian Liberalism* (1972), likewise covers an extended period. What the SRs were doing in 1917 is sympathetically examined by O. H. Radkey in *The Agrarian Foes of Bolshevism* (1958). The anarchists are covered, from 1905 to their suppression during the Civil War, by P. Avrich in *The Russian Anarchists* (1967). A sad story which examines one of the reasons for the failure of the Provisional Government is R. A. Wade, *The Russian Search for Peace February–October 1917* (1969). Equally melancholy is the more extensive *The Allies and the Russian Revolution, from the Fall of the Monarchy to the Peace of Brest-Litovsk* (1954) by R. D. Warth. L. Heenan's *Russian Democracy's Fatal Blunder* (1987) is about the summer offensive and seems to confirm that domestic considerations (like finding gainful employment at the front for the Petrograd garrison) were more important than military.

Much recent research has been devoted to the grassroots of the revolutions. O. Anweiler has studied the soviets from 1905 to 1921 in *The Soviets* (1974). D. Koenker, *Moscow Workers and the 1917 Revolution* (1981) is very informative, even though its strong statistical underpinning tends to reduce people to digits. D. Mandel has studied the Petrograd workers in *The Petrograd Workers and the Fall of the Old Regime* (1983) and *The Petrograd Workers and the Soviet Seizure of Power* (1984). D. Kaiser has edited *The Workers' Revolution in Russia 1917: The View from Below* (1987). A statistically based study of strikes between the two revolutions in D. Koenker, W. Rosenberg, *Strikes and Revolution in Russia 1917* (1989), suggests that violence was rare and that the workers were well capable of organizing themselves without the help of outsiders. R. A. Wade treats another important topic in his *Red Guards and Workers' Militias in the Russian Revolution* (1984). S. A. Smith, in his *Red Petrograd: Revolution in the Factories 1917–1918* (1983), suggests that workers took over their factories to protect their jobs rather than their revolution, and failed not because of managerial resistance or sabotage but simply because they had no idea what to do next.

A. Wildman, *The End of the Russian Army* (1980) is mainly concerned with the soldiers' revolts of spring 1917, but includes useful historical background for the tsarist army. The second volume (1987) continues the story. The role of the sailors in the Revolution is competently handled by E. Mawdsley in *The Russian Revolution and the Baltic Fleet* (1978) and by N. Saul in *Sailors in Revolt* (1978).

Outside the Soviet Union the best eyewitness account of the October Revolution and its time is deemed to be the first volume of W. H. Chamberlin, *The Russian Revolution* (1935); inside Russia this honour is accorded to John Reed's enthusiastic *Ten Days that Shook the World* (1919). There are many others, some of which are usefully anthologized in R. Pethybridge, *Witnesses to the Russian Revolution* (1964). Another revealing anthology, including the accounts of relatively humble participants, is D. von Mohrenschildt, *The Russian Revolution of 1917* (1971). Trotsky, like Chamberlin, combines personal experience with interpretation and narrative in his *History of the Russian Revolution* (1936), which is as reliable as one can expect from so committed a participant. For more serious history, the first volume of E. H. Carr's multi-volume history is thoroughly researched: *The Bolshevik Revolution 1917–1923* (1950). Two other books are *Red October* (1967) by R. V. Daniels, and *The Russian Revolution* (1970) by M. Liebman, which stresses the significance of the Revolution for socialism. A useful brief study is that edited by A. E. Adams, *The Bolshevik Revolution. Why and How.* (1960). A collection of documents was edited by I. Bunyan and H. H. Fisher in 1934: *The Bolshevik Revolution 1917–1918*. Other documents can be found in M. McCauley's collection, listed later.

CHAPTER 11

Two excellent books, incorporating recent research, are W. Lincoln's *Red Victory* (1989) and C. Mawdsley's *The Russian Civil War* (1987). Among older but still useful accounts of the Civil War are the second volume of W. H. Chamberlin, *The Russian Revolution* (1935), and D. Footman, *Civil War in Russia* (1961). The first volume of P. Kenez *Civil War in South Russia* (1971) deals with 1918 and the second volume with 1919–20. Both cover mainly the White Army and show that its failure was really because of non-military reasons. An edited transcript of Kolchak's eve-of-execution interrogation is the main item in E. Varneck's and H. H. Fisher's collection, *The Testimony of Admiral Kolchak and other Siberian Materials* (1953). *The Fate of Admiral Kolchak* (1963) by P. Fleming is readable but not searching. A soldier-participant in struggles against both Whites and Reds in Siberia, P. Dotsenko, has written the idiosyncratic *The Struggle for Democracy in Siberia* (1983). A. I. Denikin wrote five volumes of memoirs, which are summarized in English in his *The White Army* (1930). General P. N. Wrangel also had his say, in *Always with Honour* (1957). On foreign intervention there are: G. A. Brinkley, *The Volunteer Army and Allied Intervention in South Russia 1917–1921* (1966), J. A. White, *The Siberian Intervention* (1950), R. H. Ullman, *Britain and the Russian Civil War* (1968), J. F. C. Bradley, *Allied Intervention in Russia* (1968), and J. Silverlight, *The Victors' Dilemma* (1970). The latter is based mainly on British sources. Other sideshows are covered in M. Malet, *Nestor Makhno in the Russian Civil War* (1982), P. Arshinov's *History of the Makhnovist Movement* (1987), and O. H. Radkey's study of the Greens and the Tambov Revolt, *The Unknown Civil War in Soviet Russia* (1976). *The Day We Almost Bombed Moscow* (1986) by C. Dobson and J. Miller is a very readable account of the British participation, covert and overt, in the Russian Civil War. Its somewhat catchpenny title derives from an incident when British aircraft, transported by rail, were placed on airfields close enough to bomb Moscow, an idea that was soon squashed by the British war minister, Churchill. *Russia's Retreat from Poland 1920* (1990), by T. Fiddick, is a well-rounded view of the Bolsheviks' ill-judged and ill-fated march on Warsaw.

Political life in these troubled years is covered by *Party, State and Society in the Russian Civil War* (1989), edited by D. Koenker, W. Rosenberg, and R. Suny, which, like most such collections, is patchy but goes into enough detail to show the danger of simplifying the issues. How the Mensheviks, their leadership split, lost influence in 1918, is discussed by V. Brovkin in *The Mensheviks after October* (1987). O. Radkey wrote *The Election to the Russian Constituent Assembly of 1917* (1950), which tells of the true state of public opinion, and much else besides. L. Shapiro, in *The Origin of Communist Autocracy* (1955), claims that it was in the Civil War years that the rot set in inside the party, an idea that can be examined with the help of T. H. Rigby, *Lenin's Government* (1979), R. Service, *The Bolshevik Party in Revolution* (1979), and the collection of documents edited by M. McCauley, *The Russian Revolution and the Soviet State 1917–1921* (1975). How the Bolsheviks reacted with Moscow, and vice versa, in the Civil War years is recounted by R. Sakwa in *Soviet Communists in Power* (1988), while the opposition of the 'Left Communists' is covered by R. Kowalski in *The Bolshevik Party in Conflict* (1991). Lenin's responsibility for some of the unpleasant things that happened after his death is implied in M. Liebman, *Leninism under Lenin* (1975) and L. Gerson, *The Secret Police in Lenin's Russia* (1976). G. Leggett's well-researched *The Cheka* (1981) adds considerably to knowledge of this topic.

F. Benuventi's *The Bolsheviks and the Red Army 1918–1922* (1988), and M. von Hagen's *Soldiers in the Proletarian Dictatorship: The Red Army and the Soviet Socialist State 1917–1930* (1990), together present a well-rounded picture of the army's changing place in society. The fate of the émigrés is detailed in M. Raeff, *Russia Abroad: A Cultural History of the Russian Emigration 1919–1939* (1990), and in the first-hand accounts of several generations edited by M. Glenny and N. Stone, *The Other Russia* (1990). Two other, very different, first-hand accounts come in *The Memoirs of Anastas Mikoyan* (vol. 1, 1988) edited by S. Mikoyan, no more embellished than the memoirs of a typical western minister and dealing largely with revolution and civil war in the Caucasus, and *Alexis Babine in Saratov 1917–1922* (1988), edited by the indefatigable D. Raleigh. Babine's first claim to distinction was shooting a pine-cone off a friend's head, with fatal results, and his second was this diary. In between he was a grey, narrow-minded librarian interested in the small things of provincial life—which is why his diary is so valuable.

Economics and foreign relations are treated by E. H. Carr in the second and third volumes, respectively, of his *The Bolshevik Revolution* (1952–4), and the Bolsheviks' first major foreign affairs problem is dealt with by J. Wheeler-Bennett in *Brest-Litovsk: the Forgotten Peace* (1938). What went on inside the factories can be discerned from T. F. Remington, *Building Socialism in Soviet Russia: Ideology and Industrial Organization 1917–1921* (1984) and C. Sirianni, *Workers Control and Socialist Democracy: The Soviet Experience* (1982), although both books have broader ambitions: Remington seeks to show that the socialist state mobilized new elements of society to support it and thereby destroyed its own social base, while Sirianni argues that what happened to the Bolsheviks in these years was not simply a result of circumstances beyond their control, because they did make choices, and those choices were determined not by external circumstances but by their ideology. W. Husband's *Revolution in the Factory* (1990) is about the textile industry from 1917 to 1920.

Other books relating to this period are T. E. O'Connor, *The Politics of Soviet Culture* (1983), which is largely a study of Lunacharsky; *Bolshevik Culture* (1985), edited by A. Gleason, P. Kenez, and R. Stites, which deals with the first decade of Soviet culture; J. E. Mace, *Communism and the Dilemmas of National Liberation* (1983), about the problems caused by the ungrateful Ukrainians in 1918–33; A. Tuominen, *The Bells of the Kremlin* (1982), which is by a Finnish member of the Comintern in Lenin's time; and two books about British reactions, S. White, *Britain and the Bolshevik Revolution: A Study in the Politics of Diplomacy, 1920–1924* (1979), and M. H. Cowden, *Russian Bolshevism and British Labour 1917–1921* (1984). A useful biography of Trotsky, readable and unprejudiced, is I. Howe, *Leon Trotsky* (1978). Trotsky, of course, was the originator of lies about the Kronstadt Revolt that remained embedded in Soviet accounts. The western reader is lucky, for there are now available two good studies of this outbreak, J. Avrich, *Kronstadt 1921* (1970) having been followed by I. Getzler, *Kronstadt 1917–1921* (1983), which deals with the Revolution as well as the Revolt. Another Bolshevik's biography is W. Lerner's *Karl Radek: The Last Internationalist* (1970).

CHAPTER 12

E. H. Carr, *The Interregnum 1923–1924* (1954) bridges the gap between his three volumes on the Bolshevik Revolution and his three-volume *Socialism in One Country*. The first volume of the latter (1958) deals with the economy and with the main party personalities, the second (1959) with the party and government, and the third (1964) with foreign relations, from 1924 to 1926. A somewhat different perspective is offered by I. Deutscher in *The Prophet Armed, Trotsky 1921–1929* (1959). The same author's biography, *Stalin* (1961), may still be regarded as a standard work on the subject, even though subsequent revelations have accumulated much additional information. No doubt further biographies of Stalin will have appeared after this bibliography was compiled, but existing works should not be scorned, books like R. Hingley, *Joseph Stalin* (1974), and A. B. Ulam, *Stalin* (1974). A. Bullock's *Hitler and Stalin: Parallel Lives* (1991) is full and reliable; the two tyrants differed in one fundamental: Stalin, unlike Hitler, knew when to stop. R. Conquest's *Stalin: Breaker of Nations* (1991) is a good and not overlong synthesis but, like Bullock's book, almost ignores the five-year plans. R. McNeal's *Stalin: Man and Ruler* (1988) can be recommended. The subject of Stalin as a person is by no means exhausted, and new books will inevitably appear, either to go deeper into his psychology or to use materials that hitherto have been under lock and key. In the latter category is D. Volkogonov's *Stalin: Triumph and Tragedy* (1991), which is illuminating but not definitive. One of the earlier attempts to take a closer look at Stalin was E. Smith's *The Young Stalin* (1967), which is quite useful, although its attractive proposition that Stalin was once a police informer lacks proof. In a class by itself is R. Tucker's two-volume work. In his first volume, *Stalin as Revolutionary* (1973), he puts forward the proposition that Stalin's extraordinary nature was shaped by unconsciously modelling himself on a succession of heroes, beginning with a Caucasian warrior, then Lenin (whom he emulated by making his own revolution in 1928–41); like other biographers, Tucker accepts that the root cause of Stalin's neurosis (or whatever it was) was the childhood hammering he received from his drunken, violent father. In his second volume, *Stalin in Power* (1990), the author goes further and suggests that Stalin consciously and carefully followed in the footsteps of Peter the Great and Ivan the Terrible, a suggestion that is plausible but not really proven. Contemporary Russian researchers point out that Stalin's personal library provides evidence of greater interest in the Roman emperors, especially Augustus Caesar, than in Ivan and Peter.

Whether Stalin was anti-semitic is a question that biographers have not yet dealt with in a convincing way. L. Rappoport in his informative *Stalin's War against the Jews* (1991) considers that the Doctors' Plot was final proof of Stalin's anti-semitism, but this seems simplistic. When dealing with a probable case of paranoia (and Stalin's paranoia must have been inflamed by a feeling, quite justified, that he was surrounded by colleagues who did not like him) it is unhelpful to ascribe aggression to hatred of a particular group. As many Jews did well under Stalin as perished.

For Stalin's activities while Lenin was writing his 'Testament', M. Lewin, *Lenin's Last Struggle* (1968) is very well done. What he was doing after Lenin died forms part of N. Tumarkin's fascinating *Lenin Lives!* (1983), which is about how Lenin was canonized to become cult-fodder. The problem of what to do with the nationalities, one of the issues dividing Lenin and Stalin, is exhaustively treated in R. E. Pipes, *The Formation of the Soviet Union* (1954), dealing with the 1917–23 period. The problem of what to do with political enemies was solved violently, as can be illustrated by the 1922 show trial of SRs, described by M. Jansen in *A Show Trial under Lenin* (1982). The interaction between the grassroots and political developments in this period is studied by O. A. Narkiewicz in *The Making of the Soviet State Apparatus* (1970).

The industrialization debate is fully discussed in the two volumes of *Foundations of a Planned Economy 1926–1929* (1969), a further instalment from E. H. Carr, this time assisted by R. W. Davies. A prominent participant in these arguments was Bukharin, who receives superb biographical treatment in S. Cohen, *Bukharin and the Bolshevik Revolution* (1973). His thought on these matters is well set out in M. Haynes, *Nikolai Bukharin and the Transition from Capitalism to Socialism* (1985). R. B. Day, *Leon Trotsky and the Politics of Economic Isolation* (1973), gives the views of another participant. R. Pethybridge, *The Social Prelude to Stalinism* (1974), is a thoughtful attempt to explain how the emergence of alternatives to Stalin's way was stifled by social influences. The general political atmosphere of 1924–6 is well conveyed in the memoirs of an important economic official of the time, N. Valentinov, in his *The New Economic Policy and the Party Crisis after the Death of Lenin* (1971). More of the flavour of the NEP period can be enjoyed in A. Ball's *Russia's Last Capitalists; The Nepmen 1921–1929* (1987), the collection largely concerned with culture edited by S. Fitzpatrick, A. Rabinovitch, and R. Stites, *Russia in the Era of NEP* (1991), W. Chase's *Workers, Society, and the Soviet State: Labor and Life in Moscow 1918–1929* (1987), C. Ward's *Russia's Cotton Workers and the New Economic Policy* (1990), and P. Kenez's *The Birth of the Propaganda State* (1986), which deals with how the masses were influenced by the 'mass mobilizations' of 1917–29. C. Reiman's *The Birth of Stalinism* (1987) provides an excellent description of the USSR towards the end of NEP.

The Famine in Soviet Russia (1927) by H. H. Fisher is a detailed study of this tragedy from the viewpoint of the American relief organization. Lenin's internal contradictions on the subject of the peasantry (that is, his constant need, not always recognized, to reconcile his marxist analysis with the realities of Russian peasant life), are treated by E. Kingston-Mann in *Lenin and the Problem of Marxist Peasant Revolution* (1983). A useful background guide to collectivization is J. Maynard, *The Russian Peasant and Other Studies* (1942), which deals with the fundamental issues of peasant life from Nicholas I to Stalin. *Village Life under the Soviets* (1927 by K. Borders conveys the feel of rural Russia on the eve of collectivization. The events leading up to collectivization are analysed in J. Hughes, *Stalin, Siberia and the Crisis of the New Economic Policy* (1991), which makes the point that Stalin thought the dire state of grain supply in Siberia was typical of the whole country, and acted accordingly. How far collectivization was a manifestation of town-versus-country antagonism may be gauged, among many other things, from V. Lynne's *The Best Sons of the Fatherland: Workers in the Vanguard of Soviet Collectivization* (1987). For the still uncertain history of the collectivization itself, a good guide is M. Lewin, *Russian Peasants and Soviet Power* (1968). The Soviet Academy of Sciences prepared a massively researched study of collectivization which, had not Khrushchev been dethroned in 1964, might actually have been published then. As it was, V. Danilov's 1977 work appeared only in 1988, as *Rural Russia under the New Regime*. But an alternative exists in R. W. Davies's first two volumes under the general title of *The Industrialisation of Soviet Russia*: volume 1 is *The Socialist Offensive: The Collectivisation of Soviet Agriculture 1929–1930* (1980) and volume 2 is *The Soviet Collective Farm* (1980). *The History of a Soviet Collective Farm* (1955) is by a former collective farm chairman, F. Belov, who left Russia in the 1940s; its conclusions are expectedly negative, but it provides useful first-hand details of how things really were. A collection of research papers, *The Soviet Rural Community* (1970), edited by J. R. Millar, has some useful and original information on various aspects of Russian agriculture from Stalin to Brezhnev.

CHAPTER 13

'. . . every time you talk to one Russian you feel as if you were talking to them all. Not exactly that everyone obeys a word of command; but everything is so arranged that nobody can differ from anybody else.' These are a few lines from André Gide, *Back from the USSR* (1937). In the 1930s (and after 1953), a procession of foreigners visited the USSR for a few weeks and later published their revelations. Few of these are worth listing here, although few were totally bad. The impressions of brainy characters like Bernard Shaw and Gide could hardly fail to yield something, while the travel writers and journalists, beaming their professional insight onto the superficial to cook up semi-baked profundities, probably did little harm. The better first-person account is often by the unpretentious specialist who simply records what he sees without trying to make fancy interpretations. Perhaps a model of this kind of book is A. Monkhouse, *Moscow 1911–1933* (1934); the author was a British electrical engineer working in Russia most of his life, and had the additional distinction of being a defendant in the Metrovick Trial. Foreign technology was to play an important part in the five-year plans, but native technology was expected to learn fast. Technological aspects of Stalinist society are dealt with by K. E. Bailes in *Technology and Society under Lenin and Stalin* (1978). By the same author, *Science in Russian Culture* (1990), vol. 1, is also good. Various cultural topics are dealt with, sometimes heavily, in *The Culture of the Stalin Period* (1990), edited by H. Gunther. Somewhat more specialized topics are dealt with in books emanating from the Centre for Russian and East European Studies at Birmingham University: N. Lampert, *The Technical Intelligentsia and the Soviet State* (1979), dealing with the life and work of managers and technicians in 1928–35; R. Lewis, *Science and Industrialisation in the USSR* (1979), describing the organization of scientific research 1917–40; and J. N. Westwood, *Soviet Locomotive Technology during Industrialization 1928–1952* (1982), which has been known to petrify even the most fanatical of railway enthusiasts. As for economic progress in general, this is best reviewed in Nove's book, mentioned earlier, or with some of the titles listed on later pages. M. Lewin, *Political Undercurrents in Soviet Economic Debates* (1974), throws some light on the economic problems of the 1930s and later decades.

R. W. Davies presents the third volume of his *Industrialisation of Soviet Russia* (1989), which contains some mind-boggling examples of the chaos that attended the first five-year plan. Other books about the economy include D. Filtzer's *Soviet Workers and Stalinist Industrialization* (1986), which is challenging both in the profusion of ideas and the scarcity of commas. L. Siegelbaum's *Stakhanovism and the Politics of Productivity in the USSR* (1988) concentrates on that one aspect of the labour scene, incidentally suggesting that the need for an efficient industrial management was hard to reconcile with the party's hegemony. Workers in the first plan are the subject of H. Kuromiya's *Stalin's Industrial Revolution: Politics and Workers* (1988). Particular projects are covered by the eyewitness *Behind the Urals*

(1942) by J. Scott, which is about Magnitogorsk, and A. Rassweiler's *The Generation of Power* (1988). The latter is about the Dnieper hydroelectric scheme and especially the party's role; Stalin was not very keen on it, saying it reminded him of a peasant who bought a gramophone instead of mending his plough. How the party fitted into the upheaval of the 1930s is looked at from various angles by N. Shimotomai's *Moscow under Stalinist Rule 1931–34* (1992), C. Merridale's *Moscow Politics and the Rise of Stalin* (1990) which covers 1925–32, and D. Thorniley's *The Rise and Fall of the Soviet Rural Communist Party 1927–1939* (1988). The party's weapon against bureaucracy, the Workers' and Peasants' Inspectorate, lasted from 1924 to 1934, and its changing functions and influence are described by A. Rees in *State Control in Soviet Russia* (1987).

There are many books about the purges, not all of which can be recommended. A very complete study is R. Conquest, *The Great Terror* (1968). G. Katkov has written about *The Trial of Bukharin* (1969), while former Red Army General Gorbatov's memoirs, which include his arrest, torture, and incarceration before the war, have been translated as *Years off my Life* (1965). N. Mandelstam, widow of a talented and purged poet, revealed much about life during the purges and, unwittingly perhaps, about Russian spirituality, in her *Hope against Hope* (1970) and *Hope Abandoned* (1974). A scientist and a historian, F. Beck and W. Godin, after quitting the USSR, published their own analysis, based on their personal experiences, in *Russian Purge and the Extraction of Confession* (1951). Also still relevant is the collection edited by S. Wolin and R. M. Slusser, *The Soviet Secret Police* (1957), while R. Conquest, *The Soviet Police System* (1968), is a succinct account covering the fifty years after 1917. Of the several defectors from the NKVD, W. G. Krivitsky was sufficiently important to be murdered by his former colleagues, but not before he had written his *In Stalin's Secret Service* (1939). In *Origins of the Great Purges* (1985), J. A. Getty proposes that the earlier purges were for the sake of efficiency, and in particular aimed to ensure that distant party officials actually did what they were told by the centre. Much of the evidence comes from the Smolensk Archives. The latter provided the raw material for M. Fainsod, *Smolensk under Soviet Rule* (1958), which even in this abridged form reveals quite a lot about the NKVD's activities. A. Solzhenitsyn's multi-volume *The Gulag Archipelago 1918–1956* (1974–8) is a major literary and historical work. V. M. Petrov and E. Petrov published their *Empire of Fear* in 1956. M. Popovsky, once a Soviet science journalist, confirms in his *The Vavilov Affair* (1984) that Lysenko's hostility was the cause of the great biologist's downfall. S. Swianiewicz in *Forced Labour and Economic Development* (1965) examines the industrial significance of the labour camps. Two of the biggest NKVD complexes receive individual treatment in *Vorkuta* (1976) by a former Polish inmate, V. Buca, and *Kolyma* (1978) by R. Conquest.

For religion, there are J. S. Curtiss, *The Russian Church and the Soviet State 1917–1950* (1953), W. Kolarz, *Religion in the Soviet Union* (1961), which is especially good on the sects and the non-Christians, and J. Thrower, *Marxist–Leninist 'Scientific Atheism' and the Study of Religion and Atheism in the USSR* (1983), which is itself a marxist analysis. W. C. Fletcher, *The Russian Orthodox Church Underground 1917–1970* (1971) concentrates on unofficial and illegal activities.

The ever-debatable general nature of Stalinism is dealt with by G. Gill's *Stalinism* (1990), a short book which quite successfully comes to grips with the problem of defining that phenomenon, and his somewhat longer *The Origins of the Stalinist Political System* (1990), and there is also *Stalinism: Its Nature and Aftermath*

(1991), edited by N. Lampert. For general labour questions, in addition to the specialized titles mentioned earlier, there are S. Schwartz, *Labour in the Soviet Union* (1953), which is becoming dated although it was good in its time, and E. C. Brown, *Soviet Trade Unions and Labour Relations* (1960). Soviet law (and not just Stalinist law) is dealt with by S. Kucherov in *The Organs of Soviet Administration of Justice: Their History and Operation* (1970); by J. N. Hazard, *Law and Social Change in the USSR* (1953); and H. J. Berman, *Justice in the USSR* (revised edn., 1963). E. L. Johnson, *An Introduction to the Soviet Legal System* (1969), is short and clear. E. Huskey's *Russian Lawyers and the Soviet State* (1986) deals with the Soviet bar from 1917 to 1939. The sad story of the abandoned orphans of the 1920s is recounted in V. M. Zenzinov, *Deserted* (1931), while A. S. Makarenko's rehabilitation of some of these is described in his *Road to Life* (1953). Makarenko's ideas are competently examined in *Soviet Education: Anton Makarenko and the Years of Experiment* (1962) by J. Bowen. A. K. Geiger, *The Family in Soviet Russia* (1968) is mainly but not exclusively devoted to the Stalinist years, while R. Schlesinger, *The Family in Soviet Russia* (1949), presents documents for 1917–44. The shaping of Soviet minds is discussed in A. Inkeles, *Public Opinion in Soviet Russia* (1950). Another kind of mind-shaping, accomplished by banging of heads, figures in *Soviet Historians in Crisis 1928–1932* (1980) by J. Barber.

CHAPTER 14

To what extent Stalin and his generals were surprised by Hitler's invasion is a question that needs further research, which was impossible until it ceased to be a sensitive issue. In 1965 the Soviet historian Nekrich published a study on this matter, causing a dispute among historians which ended with Nekrich's expulsion from the party; the course of this dispute is described in V. Petrov, *June 22 1941* (1968). N. Tolstoy, in *Stalin's Secret War* (1981), goes into this question, too. The studies on foreign policy by Haslam and Hochman, listed earlier, also provide material for thought. To this period of Soviet foreign affairs also belongs E. H. Carr, *The Twilight of the Comintern* (1982). An eyewitness account of the Soviet take-over of Latvia is in P. Benton, *Baltic Countdown* (1984). Soviet foreign relations during the war itself are well chronicled in V. Mastny, *Russia's Road to the Cold War* (1979).

Probably the most informative and readable book about the war is A. Werth, *Russia at War* (1964), a product of its author's stay there during the period. For the campaigns, J. Erickson's highly detailed *The Road to Stalingrad* (1975) and *The Road to Berlin* (1983) are very complete, and as a consequence rather heavy going except for ardent war-gamers. *The Russo-German War* (1971) by A. Seaton is a workmanlike account. J. N. Westwood's short *Eastern Front* (1984) is redeemed by the illustrations. Readable but not especially perceptive are A. Clark, *Barbarossa* (1965), and P. Carell, *Hitler's War on Russia* (1964) and *Scorched Earth* (1970). G. Deborin, in *The Second World War* (1964), gives the Soviet view as it was in Khrushchev's time. A very exhaustive study of the Russian partisans is contained in the collection edited by J. A. Armstrong, *Soviet Partisans in World War II* (1964). For those unwilling to plough through H. Salisbury's long best-seller about Leningrad at war, there is L. Goure, *The Siege of Leningrad* (1962). German occupation policies are discussed in A. Dallin, *German Rule in Russia 1941–1945* (1957). The Vlasov movement is covered in G. Fischer, *Soviet Opposition to Stalin* (1952);

W. Strik-Strikfeldt, *Against Stalin and Hitler* (1970), covers the same ground differently. A more recent study is C. Andreyev, *Vlasov and the Russian Liberation Movement* (1987), while *Cossacks in the German Army 1941–1945* (1991), by S. Newland, looks at an important part of the Russian anti-soviet forces. How the Soviet planning system coped with the demands of war is described in M. Harrison, *Soviet Planning in Peace and War 1938–1945* (1985). There is also J. Barber, M. Harrison, *The Soviet Home Front 1941–1945* (1992). One important part of this topic is exhaustively examined in W. Moskoff, *The Bread of Affliction* (1990), which is about the rationing system. The wartime deportations are among the material to be found in R. Conquest, *The Nation Killers* (1970).

Many Red Army generals have written memoirs that have appeared in translated editions. An excellent and highly illuminating selection from the best of about fifty of such memoirs has been translated and included in S. Bialer, *Stalin and his Generals* (1969); most of these were published in Khrushchev's time and relate to the war, but some include comments on the army purge. Parts of Zhukov's memoirs have been published in H. Salisbury, *Marshal Zhukov's Greatest Battles* (1969). There is also a fuller English translation, *Memoirs of Marshal Zhukov* (Moscow, 1969). Neither the Russian nor the English editions contain all that Zhukov wrote, but an unexpurgated edition is expected. For Soviet strategy as a whole there is D. Glantz, *The Military Strategy of the Soviet Union* (1991), which covers several decades.

CHAPTER 15

Apart from the biographies already mentioned, Stalin is discussed from several angles in T. H. Rigby, *Stalin* (1966), which is a collection of comments and quotations. Stalin's daughter, Svetlana Allilueva, who from the 1960s lived several years in the USA, published *Twenty Letters to a Friend* (1967) and *Only One Year* (1969); these are both sensitive, subjective, yet honest accounts of her life, her father, and his associates. For a taste of the idolatry that was served up to the ordinary Soviet citizen, E. Yaroslavsky, *Landmarks in the Life of Stalin* (1942), is interesting, if only because it is something of a landmark in lying.

T. Dunmore surveys the political history of the period, in so far as it can be surveyed, in his *Soviet Politics 1945–1953* (1984). The same author in *The Stalinist Control Economy* (1980) suggests that after the war the bureaucracy had enhanced power, and that Stalin could not be sure that it would carry out his wishes. This thesis does not contradict the feeling that post-war politics were dominated by a struggle for influence over Stalin, with Zhdanov on the one side and an alliance of Malenkov and Beria on the other. W. G. Hahn, in his *Post-war Soviet Politics: the Fall of Zhdanov and the Defeat of Moderation 1946–53* (1982), argues that Zhdanov was a moderate whose views were rejected by Stalin, at Malenkov's prompting, and that the Leningrad Affair was intended to wipe out his supporters. W. O. McCagg, *Stalin Embattled, 1943–1948* (1978), suggests that Stalin had less control after the war than before, and that his policies were often manœuvres designed to deal with particular interest groups. In *International Policy Formation in the USSR* (1983), G. D. Ra'anan argues that there were two competing foreign policies at this time. Zhdanov's more aggressive policy, favourable perhaps to Tito, and the Beria–Malenkov line, which was very cautious. The origins and course of the Cold War over a long time-span are discussed in the collection edited by D. Armstrong and E. Goldstein, *The End of the Cold War* (1991).

Post-war Ukraine, and particularly the collectivization campaign in the western Ukraine, is the subject of *Stalinism in the 1940s* (1991) by D. Marples. Agriculture is also concerned in C. Kaplan's *The Party and Agricultural Crisis Management in the USSR* (1987) which has much to say about the lot of local party secretaries in the last Stalin years. The nature of Stalinism is condemned by R. A. Medvedev in *On Stalin and Stalinism* (1979), which is a kind of addendum to his celebrated *Let History Judge* (1972) and makes the same use of inside knowledge acquired by the author as a Soviet citizen and self-professed loyal Leninist. He also wrote *All Stalin's Men* (1983), consisting of biographies of Voroshilov, Mikoyan, Suslov, Molotov, Kaganovich, and Malenkov. His brother Z. A. Medvedev, a scientist, has written *The Rise and Fall of T. D. Lysenko* (1969) and *Soviet Science* (1979). The latter is especially good on what it was like to be a Soviet scientist in Khrushchev's time, and also shows how political pressures could lower the quality of scientific work. L. Badshah, in *Kapitsa, Rutherford, and the Kremlin* (1985), also has much to say about Stalinist science. He makes it clear that Kapitsa's stay in the USSR from the mid-1930s was involuntary.

The Soviet Citizen (1959), by I. Inkeles and R. Bauer, gives a full description and the feel of the daily life of citizens in the Stalin years. A more popularized study is R. Bauer, *Nine Soviet Portraits* (1955). Six former Red Army officers produced *Political Controls in the Soviet Army* (1954), edited by Z. Brzezinski. Aspects of Zhdanovism and propaganda are dealt with by F. C. Barghoorn, *The Soviet Image of the United States* (1950), H. Swayze *Political Control of Literature in the USSR 1946–1959* (1962), J. Keep's collection *Contemporary History in the Soviet Mirror* (1964), and C. E. Black, *Rewriting Russian History* (1956). M. Pundeff, *History in the USSR* (1967), is a collection of translated decrees, exhortations, and instructions, relating to the tasks of the Soviet historian. Those who prefer to get their information straight from the donkey's mouth should refer to A. A. Zhdanov, *Essays on Literature, Philosophy and Music* (1950). For a scholarly work on the tools of propaganda, see M. W. Hopkins, *Mass Media in the Soviet Union* (1970). A sensitive account of one woman's life under Stalin is E. S. Ginzburg, *Into the Whirlwind* (1967), which begins with the murder of Kirov and continues with the arrest and imprisonment of the author. The satirical sketches by M. M. Zoshchenko, *Scenes from the Bath-house* (1961), are amusing and often perceptive in their views of the ordinary Soviet citizen. Of good foreigners' accounts, which are rare because visas were scarce, and more often than not issued to visitors who could be relied on not to write too perceptively, the best may be M. Gordey, *Visa to Moscow* (1952), written by a Russian-speaking Frenchman. M. Granick, *The Red Executive* (1960), is a study of factory management as it had developed by the 1950s. The Soviet health services receive professional treatment from M. G. Field in *Doctor and Patient in Soviet Russia* (1957).

Nationalities are discussed extensively in W. Kolarz, *Russia and her Colonies* (1953), and succinctly in R. Conquest, *Soviet Nationality Policy in Practice* (1967). More specialized are O. Caroe, *Soviet Empire* (1953), which studies what used to be called Turkestan but which was divided into union republics by the Soviet constitution; G. Wheeler's brief *The Peoples of Soviet Central Asia* (1966); and *The Soviet Middle East* (1968), also about Central Asia, by A. Nove and J. A. Newth. The life of Soviet Jews is covered in S. M. Schwarz, *The Jews in the Soviet Union* (1951); the collection edited by L. Kochan, *The Jews in Soviet Russia since 1917* (1970); and *The Soviet Government and the Jews, 1948–1967* (1984) by B. Pinkus. The same author has produced *The Jews of the Soviet Union* (1988), covering seven decades. Y. Rapoport, one of the doctors involved, describes *The Doctors' Plot* (1990), with its anti-semitic overtones.

Apart from the general studies already mentioned, literature is discussed from various angles in E. J. Brown, *Russian Literature Since the Revolution* (1961), A. Kemp-Welsh, *Stalin and the Literary Intelligentsia 1928–1939* (1991), while the title of E. J. Simmons, *Through the Looking Glass of Soviet Literature: Views of Russian Society* (1961), is self-explanatory. A good reference for the Russian film, from the beginnings to 1958, is J. Leyda, *Kino* (1960).

The 'Khrushchev Memoirs' (N. S. Khrushchev, *Khrushchev Remembers*, 1971), which arrived in the west in 1970, say a lot about their subject's experiences with and under Stalin. Written by an accomplished polemicist, they need to be taken with a pinch of salt.

CHAPTER 16

Useful biographies of Khrushchev, although somewhat outdated, are E. Crankshaw, *Khrushchev* (1966) and M. Frankland, *Khrushchev* (1966). *Khrushchev: The Years in Power* (1977) by R. A. and Z. A. Medvedev is much fuller than these, and is supplemented by R. A. Medvedev, *Khrushchev* (1984), in which the author exhibits his characteristic mix of blind-spots and inside information. Most biographers are agreed on their subject's courage; they come to no definite conclusions about his role in the purges, but implicitly or explicitly accept that he had a guilty conscience. The collection edited by M. McCauley, *Khrushchev and Khrushchevism* (1988), sheds some useful light. Some filial comments come from S. Khrushchev's *Khrushchev on Khrushchev* (1990). Khrushchev's denunciation of Stalin is quoted and discussed in B. D. Wolfe, *Khrushchev and Stalin's Ghost* (1956) and T. H. Rigby, *The Stalin Dictatorship: Khrushchev's Secret Speech and other Documents* (1968). Khrushchev's manœuvrings inside the party are discussed in C. A. Linden, *Khrushchev and the Soviet Leadership 1957–1964* (1967), and also in R. Pethybridge's general survey, *A History of Post-War Russia* (1966). His uneasy relations with his generals is examined in R. Kolkowicz, *The Soviet Military and the Communist Party* (1967). His part in negotiating the Test-ban Treaty is covered by G. T. Seaborg, *Kennedy, Khrushchev, and the Test Ban* (1981), which also suggests that one of the obstacles to better understanding was that although the USA and USSR often developed similar views, they rarely held them at the same time. *Khrushchev and the Development of Soviet Agriculture: The Virgin Land Programme, 1953–1964* (1967) by M. McCauley deals with a favourite and grandiose project. Many of Khrushchev's colleagues are included in the forty-two biographical essays in *Soviet Leaders* (1967), edited by G. W. Simmonds. The easier atmosphere in the arts is treated in the collection of essays edited by M. Hayward, *Soviet Literature in the Sixties* (1965), and in G. Gibian, *Interval of Freedom* (1960), which discusses literature between 1954 and 1957. D. Brown, *Soviet Russian Literature since Stalin* (1978) covers a slightly longer period.

Soviet law is brought to fascinating life in G. Feiffer, *Justice in Moscow* (1964), and in B. A. Konstantinovsky, *Soviet Law in Action: The Recollected Cases of a Soviet Lawyer* (1953). Other books on law, not confined to the Khrushchev period, are G. van den Berg's *The Soviet System of Justice* (1985), and F. Feldbrugge (ed.), *The Distinctiveness of Soviet Law* (1987), which includes a study of the Stalinist legal system. Housing, which received a boost in the Khrushchev period, is discussed in G. Andrusz, *Housing and Urban Development in the USSR* (1984), which also deals with the post-Khrushchev years and throws much incidental light on Soviet society. Other books which cover more than the Khrushchev years are S. Fortescue, *The Communist Party and Soviet Science* (1986), P. Kneen, *Soviet Scientists and the State* (1984), and R. Humble, *The Soviet Space Programme* (1988). The uproarious memoir by an astronomer who lived through the Stalin, Khrushchev, and Brezhnev years also comes into this category: *Five Billion Vodka Bottles to the Moon* (1991), by I. Shklovsky. An original and sometimes irreverent comment on the theory of convergence is provided by Mervyn Jones, *Big Two* (US title, *The Antagonists*: 1962) which compares the USA and USSR and seems to have a high opinion of neither. Two books by western students who spent a year in Russia are W. Taubman, *The View from Lenin Hills* (1968) and H. Pitcher, *Understanding the Russians* (1964); both of these are good and informative. *Life in Russia Today* (1969) by J. Miller, *The Russian*, (1968) by L. Vladimirov, and *Russians Observed* (1969) by J. W. Lawrence can also be recommended for portrayals of Soviet life in the 1960s.

Soviet sociology was slow to recover from the Stalinist years, but some of its products have appeared in English as *Studies in Soviet Society*. No. 1 of this series was *Industry and Labour in the USSR*. No. 2, edited by G. V. Osipov, was *Town, Country and People* (1969). S. F. and E. Dunn made good use of Soviet sociological and ethnographical research in their *The Peasants of Soviet Russia* (1967), while another, off-beat but enjoyable, description of rural Russia as it really was in the 1960s is V. Soloukhin, *A Walk in Rural Russia* (1966). *The Soviet Family* (1963) by D. and V. Mace is another contribution. The experience of Russian Christianity in the 1950s and 1960s is included in M. Bourdeaux, *Opium of the People* (1965).

The USSR's relations with individual states have been dealt with by works too numerous to mention in these bibliographies. S. Galai's *The Soviet Union and National Liberation Movements in the Third World* (1988) deals with a subject that became important in the Khrushchev years.

CHAPTERS 17 AND 18

Books covering the Brezhnev, Andropov, and Chernenko years tend to overlap, so this bibliography covers two chapters. Books illuminating the mechanism, or messiness, of party leadership changes include: O. Narciewicz, *Soviet Leaders* (1986); D. Doder, *Shadows and Whispers* (1986); A. D'Agostino, *Soviet Succession Struggles* (1987); and R. Owen, *Crisis in the Kremlin* (1986). Biographies of the post-Khrushchev leaders tended to be written while they were in office and are therefore incomplete. J. Dornberg's *Brezhnev*, for example, was published in 1974. Z. A. Medvedev, *Andropov* (1983), says as much about Brezhnev's last years as it does about its ostensible subject. Inevitably it also deals with the KGB, a topic more fully explored in A. Myagkov, *Inside the KGB* (1976). Another book about Andropov, which in places goes quite deep, is *Andropov in Power* (1983) by J. Steele and E. Abraham. I. Zemtsov's *Chernenko: The Last Bolshevik* (1989) shares some of the characteristics of its subject. G. W. Breslauer, *Khrushchev and Brezhnev as Leaders* (1982), is especially good on authority-building. Several collections were published after Brezhnev's death, looking forward to the future. If their speculative parts are disregarded, they are good guides to the problems faced, or not faced, under

Brezhnev. Two of them are R. F. Byrnes (ed.), *After Brezhnev: Sources of Soviet Conduct in the 1980s* (1983), and H. Sonnenfeldt (ed.), *Soviet Politics in the 1980s* (1985). A good textbook on the party is R. J. Hill, P. Frank, *The Soviet Communist Party* (1983), while a political perspective for the period is provided by A. Nove, *Stalinism and After* (1981).

Aspects of Soviet society are dealt with in M. Dewhirst and W. Farrell (eds.), *The Soviet Censorship* (1973); D. Powell, *Antireligious Propaganda in the Soviet Union* (1975), which suggests that this propaganda was clumsy and ineffective, continuing only because nobody wanted to admit that it was useless; M. Matthews, *Class and Society in Soviet Russia* (1972) and the same author's *Privilege in the Soviet Union: A Study of Elite Life-styles under Communism* (1978); D. Lane, *The End of Social Inequality? Class, Status and Power under State Socialism* (1982); A. McAuley, *Women's Work and Wages in the Soviet Union* (1981); G. Littlejohn, *A Sociology of the Soviet Union* (1984); J. Brine, M. Perrie, A. Sutton (eds.), *Home, School and Leisure in the Soviet Union* (1980); Ellen Jones, *Red Army and Society* (1985); M. Kaser, *Health Care in the Soviet Union and Eastern Europe* (1976); J. Dunstan, *Paths to Excellence and the Soviet School* (1978); M. Matthews, *Education in the Soviet Union* (1983); J. Riordan, *Sport in Soviet Society* (1977); and A. McAuley, *Economic Welfare in the Soviet Union: Poverty, Living Standards, and Inequality* (1979). A. Roxburgh's *Pravda: Inside the Soviet News Machine* (1988) includes a history of the paper and is uniquely structured, short, and admirable. J. Riordan added to his studies of Soviet people a collection titled *Soviet Youth Culture* (1989). A study of Soviet emigrants from this and preceding periods led to J. R. Miller's *Politics, Work and Daily Life in the USSR* (1987). Fiction, in the form of J. Voznesenskaya's *The Women's Decameron* (1986), tells a lot about the tribulations of young women in the USSR at this period, while N. Lampert's *Whistleblowing in the Soviet Union* (1985) is about tribulation in general and the problem of making complaints. D. Kaminskaya, in *A Final Judgement* (1982), describes what it is like to walk the tightrope between ideology and justice as a Soviet defence lawyer. Some recommended first-hand impressions of life in the Soviet Union are: R. Kaiser, *Russia, the People and the Power* (1976), Hedrick Smith, *The Russians* (1976), M. Binyon, *Life in Russia* (1983), and A. Lee, *Russian Journal* (1981). In *Who are the Russians?* (1973), W. Miller gives his interpretation of the forces which made Russians what they are. The seamy side of Soviet life is revealed by K. M. Simis and V. G. Treml. The former, in *USSR: the Corrupt Society* (1982), discusses and condemns corruption, incidentally viewing the KGB as a sanitary and useful institution because it tries to improve matters. Treml has been taking his statistical breath-analyser to Soviet society for some years, and has produced *Alcohol in the USSR* (1982); his work underlies part of Chapter 18. In her *The KGB* (1988), A. Knight has written a book more sensible than most on that subject.

Problems faced by a multinational state include nationalisms, and these receive partial coverage in: Y. Ro'i (ed.), *The USSR and the Muslim World* (1984), M. Rywkin, *Moscow's Muslim Challenge* (1982), R. Karklins, *Ethnic Relations in the USSR* (1985), V. Zaslavsky, R. J. Bryan, *Soviet-Jewish Emigration and Soviet Nationality Policy* (1983), and J. Dunlop, *The Faces of Contemporary Russian Nationalism* (1983). Rywkin's book goes back to tsarist times; Dunlop is fairly optimistic, seeing no inevitable conflict.

Books by or about the dissident movement include N. Gorbanevskaya, *Red Square at Noon* (1972); A. Brumberg, *In Quest of Justice* (1970); P. Reddaway,

Uncensored Russia: The Human Rights Movement in the Soviet Union (1972);
A. Sakharov, *Sakharov Speaks* (1974); S. Bloch and P. Reddaway, *Russia's Political Hospitals* (1977); M. S. Shatz, *Soviet Dissent in Historical Perspective*
(1980); V. Bukovsky, *To Build a Castle* (1978); R. L. Tökes. *Dissent in the USSR*
(1975); and M. Hopkins, *Russia's Underground Press* (1983). The latter is about
Chronicle of Current Events, from its beginnings in 1968. Translations from dissident writings are to be found in R. A. Medvedev, *Samizdat Register* 11 (1981). Of the
several novels that were published in the west but not in the Soviet Union, G. Maximov, *Faithful Ruslan* (1975), is recommended for the skill with which the author has
fixed specific characteristics of the Stalinist personality in a series of individual dog
characters, V. Voinovich, *The Life and Extraordinary Adventures of Private Ivan
Chonkin* (1976), for its comedy, and A. Zinoviev, *The Yawning Heights* (1979), for
its amusing perception. N. Shneidman's *Soviet Literature in the 1980s* (1989) is
partly a social commentary.

General books on the Soviet economy include A. Nove, *The Soviet Economic
System* (1977), D. Dyker, *The Soviet Economy* (1976), M. Kaser, *Soviet Economics*
(1970). Science and technology is covered in: R. Hutchings, *Soviet Science, Technology, Design* (1976); R. Amann, J. Cooper, R. W. Davies, *The Technological Level
of Soviet Industry* (1977), which is a massive collection of case-studies; and
J. Thomas, U. Kruse-Vaucienne (eds.), *Soviet Science and Technology* (1977). How
new technology works in practice is one of the topics in V. Lysenko, *A Crime
Against the World* (1983) whose author, a defecting sea captain, describes how the
urge to meet high targets in the fishing fleet resulted in misuse of men and equipment, waste, and destruction of fish stocks all over the world. Environmental issues
are covered by P. Pryde in *Conservation in the Soviet Union* (1972), M. Goldman in
The Spoils of Progress (1972), and F. Singleton (ed.), *Environmental Misuse in the
Soviet Union* (1976). Later books include P. Pryde's *Environmental Management in
the Soviet Union* (1991), D. Weiner's *Models of Nature* (1988), and a collection
edited by J. Massey Stewart, *The Soviet Environment*, expected in 1992. Local
government is concerned in environmental issues, and some hints of its power and
powerlessness are given by C. Ross, *Local Government in the Soviet Union* (1987).

A comprehensive survey of relations with Eastern Europe is *Soviet Policy in
Eastern Europe* (1984), edited by S. M. Terry. There is also K. Gerner, *The Soviet
Union and Central Europe in the Post-War Era* (1985). R. F. Miller and F. Feher
have edited *Khrushchev and the Communist World* (1984). For the situation in
Brezhnev's time there is R. L. Hutching, *Soviet–East European Relations: Consolidation and Conflict 1968–1980* (1983), which naturally has a lot to say about
Czechoslovakia and Poland in particular. Czechoslovakia in 1968 gets full treatment in *The Kremlin and Prague Spring* (1985) by K. Dawisha, and by J. Valenta in
Soviet Intervention in Czechoslovakia 1968 (1979); both portray the Soviet leadership as divided and uncertain until the eleventh hour. Dawisha stresses the fear of
ideological infection, both in eastern Europe and in the USSR itself, as a main
motivation for the Soviet intervention. Also worth consulting are R. Remington,
The Warsaw Pact (1971), and T. Wolfe, *Soviet Power and Europe 1945–70* (1970).

Relations with other countries are covered in A. B. Ulam, *Dangerous Relations:
The Soviet Union in World Politics 1970–1982* (1983). Much of this excellent volume
is spent detailing the mismanagement by both the USA and the USSR of the
opportunities presented to them. There is also R. Edmonds, *Soviet Foreign Policy:
The Brezhnev Years* (1983). A. N. Shevchenko, *Breaking with Moscow* (1985), by a

defecting foreign affairs adviser, says much about the inside workings of Soviet diplomacy, while C. Keeble (ed.) in *The Soviet State. The Domestic Roots of Foreign Policy* (1985) sets forth some of the links between the internal situation and foreign policies. Policies towards the Third World and their results are described in R. Kanet (ed.), *The Soviet Union and the Developing Nations* (1974); C. Stevens, *The Soviet Union and Black Africa* (1976); A. Rubinstein, *Red Star over the Nile* (1977); B. D. Porter, *The USSR in Third World Conflicts: Soviet Arms and Diplomacy in Local Wars 1945–1980*, which is good at facts although some may question its opinions; and S. T. Hosmer and T. W. Wolfe, *Soviet Policy and Practice Towards Third World Conflicts* (1983). The application of naval power is dealt with by M. MccGwire and J. McDonnell (eds.), *Soviet Naval Influence* (1977); M. MccGwire (ed.), *Soviet Naval Policy* (1975); and B. Dismukes and J. McConnell (eds.), *Soviet Naval Diplomacy* (1979). An excellent, very full analysis of armament, disarmament, and foreign relations is D. Holloway, *The Soviet Union and the Arms Race* (1983), while S. Talbott, *Endgame* (1979) chronicles one complex set of arms negotiations, that involving SALT-1. A brief look at the nuclear weapons problem is contained in J. Haslam's *The Soviet Union and the Politics of Nuclear Weapons in Europe 1969–1987* (1989). The Soviet defence industry is studied in P. Almquist, *Red Forge* (1990) and J. Cooper, *The Soviet Defence Industry* (1991).

Lastly, A. Westoby's idiosyncratic but very rewarding *Communism since World War II* (1981) has historical chapters reviewing the successes and failures of communism in scores of countries, including communist states (which, regretfully, he defines as 'bureaucratic nationalized states').

CHAPTER 19

Books on the Gorbachev years have been appearing fast, and a number of titles, useful in their time but overtaken by events, have been omitted. Conversely, there will be many other books that have appeared since the compiling of this bibliography.

The horse's mouth has sometimes proved unrewarding; Gorbachev, Shevardnadze, Yeltsin, and Ligachev, together with Gorbachev's high-profile wife Raisa, have all published their memoirs, but they are not very revealing. A Sobchak's *For a New Russia* (1991) is better, and so is *Moscow and Beyond 1986–1989* (1991), by A. Sakharov. Another first-person account, covering previous decades of poetic and political activity also, is Ye. Yevtushenko's *Fatal Half-Measures: The Allure of Democracy in the Soviet Union* (1991).

G. Hosking's thoughtful *The Awakening of the Soviet Union* (1990) is largely concerned with the social forces behind the urge for a 'civil society'. *Glasnost'*, which brought quick results by 1989, is well covered by A. Nove in *Glasnost' in Action* (1989) and R. W. Davies in *Soviet History in the Gorbachev Revolution* (1989). The collection edited by J. Graffy and G. Hosking, *Culture and the Media in the USSR Today* (1989) also touches on this theme.

The political machinations attending Gorbachev's ascent are very well dissected with the aid of influential participants in A. Roxburgh's *The Second Russian Revolution* (1991). Some very necessary background information about the value of personal connections is conveyed in *Patronage and Politics in the USSR* (1992) by J. Willerton. Expected in 1992 is the collection edited by A. Rees about one of the pivotal moments in *perestroika*, the 28th party congress: *The Soviet Communist Party in Disarray*.

Some of the problems faced by the leadership are covered in P. Gregory's *Restructuring the Soviet Economic Bureaucracy* (1990) and S. Carter's *Russian Nationalism Yesterday, Today and Tomorrow* (1990). Nationalism is treated from several angles also in A. McCauley (ed.), *Soviet Federalism, Nationalism, and Decentralisation* (1991). How the nationalities problem was tackled, or not tackled, in the Gorbachev years is detailed in N. Diuk and N. Karatnycky, *The People Challenge* (1990).

The seamy side of life, as recalled by those who were there, is dealt with by the prominent reformist editor of *Ogonyok*, V. Korotich, in *The Waiting Room*, of which a translation is expected and should prove amusing. Another journalist, V. Vitaliev, tells all one needs to know about prostitution, racketeering, nazism, and privilege in *Special Correspondent* (1990).

Three quite specialized books are T. Ryback's *Rock Around the Bloc* (1990), about the fate of rock music in the USSR and eastern Europe in Gorbachev and pre-Gorbachev times, R. Rand's *Comrade Lawyer* (1991), based on first-hand experience of the work of defence lawyers in Gorbachev's time, and M. Bourdeaux's *Gorbachev, Glasnost and the Gospel* (1991), about the new situation with religion. The collection edited by E. Shirley and M. Rowe, *Candle in the Wind* (1989), also covers religion.

A. Aslund's *Gorbachev's Struggle for Economic Reform* (1991) is a well-informed and highly critical commentary on the biggest failure of Gorbachev. S. Woodby's *Gorbachev and the Decline of Ideology in Soviet Foreign Policy* (1989) throws some light on what appeared to be his biggest success. V. Tolz, in *The USSR's Emerging Multiparty System* (1991), steers the reader through a complex process. *Steeltown, USSR* (1991) is a very interesting impression of life in one of Russia's least salubrious cities by S. Kotkin, who endured several months there in the late 1980s.

Commentaries on the Gorbachev years as they unfolded include R. Sakwa's *Gorbachev and his Reforms* (1990) and S. White's *Gorbachev and After* (1991), both of which go quite deep. Then there are: *Gorbachev: Heretic in the Kremlin* (1991) by D. Doder and L. Branson, *Revolution and Evolution* (1989) by M. Crouch, *Why Gorbachev Happened: His Triumphs and his Failure* (1991) by R. Kaiser, *What Went Wrong with Perestroika* (1991) by M. Goldman, M. Sixmith's *Moscow Coup* (1991), and J. Parker's *Kremlin in Transition* (vol. 2, 1991). There are also two collections edited respectively by D. Spring and M. McCauley: *The Impact of Gorbachev* (1991), and *Gorbachev and Perestroika* (1990), and another is edited by C. Merridale and C. Ward: *Perestroika* (1991).

M. Urban, in *More Power to the Soviets* (1990), concentrates on the emergence of democratic processes. A flood of books about Yeltsin is to be expected, and among the first is J. Morisson's very competent *Boris Yeltsin* (1991).

MAPS AND TABLES

MAP 1. Communist Heartland, or Capitalist Encirclement?

Map 2. Union of Soviet Socialist Republics, 1950.

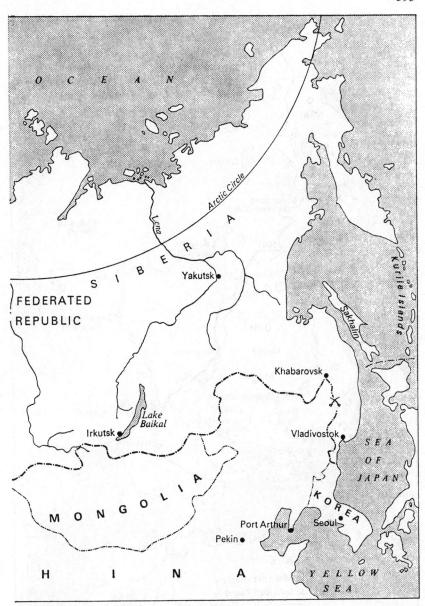

Based on J. N. Westwood: *Russia 1917–64* (Batsford 1966).

MAP 3. European Russia, 1950.
Based on J. N. Westwood: *Russia 1917–64* (Batsford 1966).

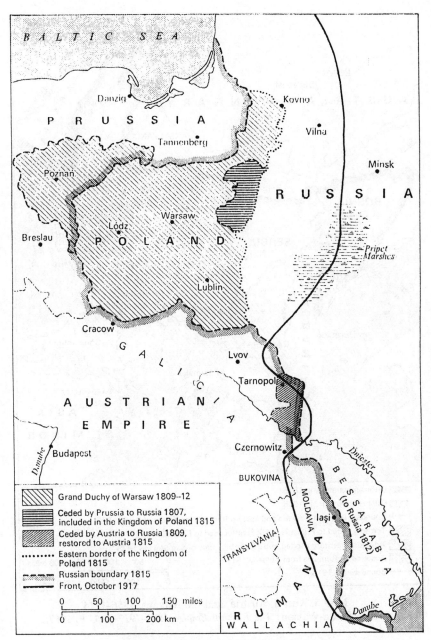

MAP 4. Russia's Western Border, 1809–1917.
Based on Seton-Watson: *The Russian Empire 1801–1917* (O.U.P. 1967).

RUSSIA

Pruth

Czernowitz
BUKOVINA

BESSARABIA

Danube

Budapest

AUSTRIA – HUNGARY

Sava

Drava

TRANSYLVANIA

Jassy
(Iasi)

Dniester

BLACK SEA

Braila

Belgrade

RUMANIA

BOSNIA
Sarajevo

Craiova

Bucharest

Silistra

HERCEGOVINA
Mostar

SERBIA
Nish

Plevna

Shumla

MONTE-
NEGRO

SANDJAK OF
NOVIBAZAR

Djakova

Sofia

BULGARIA

Varna

ADRIATIC SEA

ALBANIA

Skoplje

EASTERN ROUMELIA
Philippopolis

Burgas

Durazzo

Okhrid

MACEDONIA

Seres

THRACE

Constantinople

Salonika

Yanina

DARDANELLES

ASIA

Larissa

AEGEAN SEA

MINOR

GREECE

▰ Ottoman boundary in 1815
▨ Ottoman boundary in 1908
········ Boundary between Bulgaria and Eastern Roumelia by Treaty of Berlin 1878
▨ Territory ceded to Rumania in 1856, retroceded to Russia in 1878
▨ Additional territory allotted to Bulgaria by Treaty of San Stefano 1878
▦ Acquired by Rumania from Bulgaria 1913
--- Boundaries in 1913

0   50   100   150   200 miles
0   100   200   300 km

MAP 5. Russia, Austria, and the Balkans, 1856–1914.
Based on Seton-Watson: *The Russian Empire 1801–1917* (O.U.P. 1967).

MAP 6. The Conquest of Turkestan and Turkmenia.
Based on Seton-Watson: *The Russian Empire 1801–1917* (O.U.P. 1967).

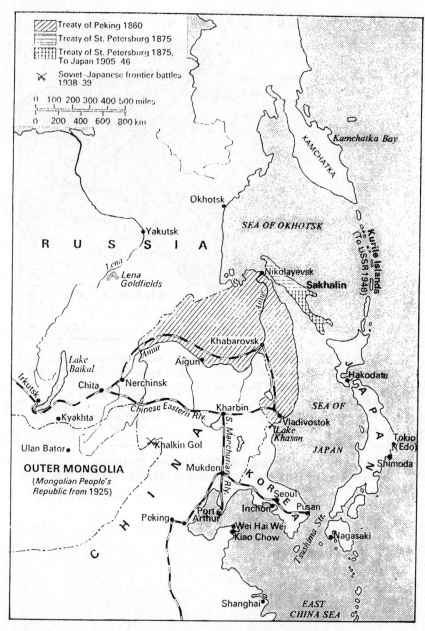

MAP 7. Russia as a Pacific Power.
Based on Seton-Watson: *The Russian Empire 1801–1917* (O.U.P. 1967).

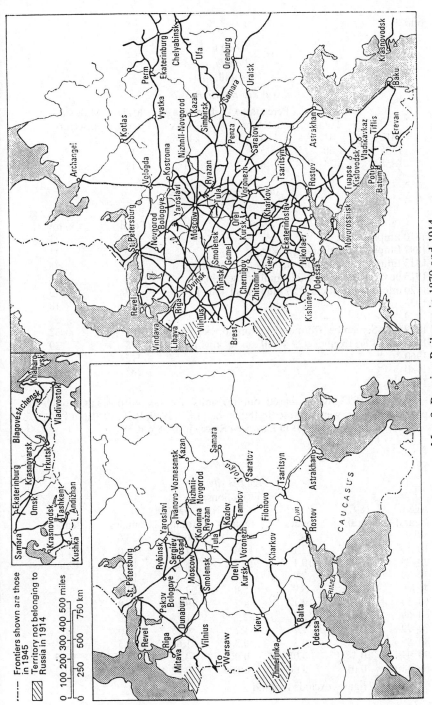

MAP 8. Russian Railways in 1870 and 1914.

Based on J. N. Westwood: *A History of Russian Railways* (Allen and Unwin 1964).

TABLE 1

Population
(in millions)

(*a*) *Pre-reform Russia*

	Total	Percentage in towns	Percentage of serfs	Male serfs	Male state peasants
1812	41	4	46	10	7
1835	60	5	36	11	10
1858	74	6	31*	11	13

(*b*) *Post-reform Russia*

	Total	Percentage in towns
1870 Empire	86	11
1897 Empire (22.4 millions sq. kms.)	125	15
1913 Empire (22.3 millions sq. kms.)	166	18
1913 post-1945 frontiers (22.4 millions sq. kms.)	159	18
1920 inter-war frontiers (21.7 millions sq. kms.)	137	15
1926 „ „ „ „	147	18
1939 „ „ „ „	171	33
1939 post-September frontiers (22.1 millions sq. kms.)	191	32
1950 post-1945 frontiers (22.4 millions sq. kms.)	178	39
1960 „ „ „ „	212	49
1980 „ „ „ „	265	63
1991 „ „ „ „	290	66

N.B. Pre-1897 figures based on 'revisions' for tax purposes, and only approximate. There were censuses in 1897, 1926, 1939, 1959, 1970, 1979 and 1989.

* The percentage of serfs in *European* Russia in 1858 was 38.

TABLE 2

Age Distribution
(millions)

Age (years)	1897 total	males	females	1959 total	males	female
0–9	38.6	19.2	19.3	46.3	23.6	22.7
10–19	26.4	13.1	13.4	31.8	16.0	15.7
20–29	20.4	10.1	10.2	38.5	18.9	19.6
30–39	15.8	7.9	7.9	30.6	13.1	17.4
40–49	11.7	5.9	5.8	22.6	8.7	13.9
50–59	8.3	4.1	4.2	19.1	6.9	12.1
60–69	5.4	2.7	2.7	11.7	4.0	7.6
70–79	2.4	1.1	1.2	6.2	2.0	4.1
80–89	0.6	0.3	0.3	1.6	0.5	1.1
90–99	0.1	0.05	0.06	0.2	0.05	0.15
over 100	0.01	0.006	0.009	0.02	0.005	0.02

N.B. 1897 figures exclude Finland.

TABLE 3

Average Expectation of Life (at birth)		*Child Mortality*

(Deaths in the age group 0–9 years as percentage of total deaths)

1897	(European Russia)	32 years	1910	64
1926	,, ,,	44 ,,	1926	61
1955	(USSR)	67 ,,	1960	11
1972	,,	70 ,,		
1990	,,	69 ,,		

TABLE 4

Birth and Death Rates

Births per thousand			Deaths per thousand		
1868–72	(European Russia)	50	1871–75	(European Russia)	37
1908–12	,, ,,	45	1906–10	,, ,,	29
1913	(all territory)	47	1913	,,	27
1916	,,	30	1913	(all territory)	29
1917	,,	24	1916	,,	29
1924	,,	43	1917	,,	28
1928	,,	42	1919	(European Russia	
1930	,,	39		excluding Caucasus)	47
1932	,,	31	1924	(all territory)	22
1935	,,	29	1929	,,	20
(Abortion restricted June 1936)			1940	,,	18
1937	(all territory)	39	1950	,,	10
1939	,,	36	1960	,,	7
1940	,,	31	1980	,,	10
1950	,,	27			
(Abortion de-restricted 1955)					
1960	(all territory)	25			
1980	,,	18			
1990	,,	17	1990	,,	10

N.B. Relatively low death-rates in First World War are partly a consequence of lower birth-rates.

TABLE 5

The Major Nationalities
(millions)

	1897	1959	1979
Great Russian	55.6	113.9	137.4
Ukrainian	22.4	32.7	42.3
White Russian	5.8	6.6	9.4
Polish	7.9	0.6	1.1
Jewish†	5.0	0.5	1.8
Kirgiz/Kaisats*	4.0	0.9	1.9
Tartar	3.4	4.6	6.3
Azerbaizhani	+	2.9	5.4
Uzbek*	0.7	5.9	12.5
Kazakh	+	3.6	6.5
German	1.8	1.2	1.9
Latvian	1.4	1.3	1.4
Bashkir	1.3	0.6	1.3
Lithuanian	1.2	2.3	2.8
Armenian	1.2	2.5	4.1
Roumanian/Moldavian	1.1	2.2	2.9
Estonian	1.0	0.9	1.0
Mordvinian	1.0	1.0	1.2
Georgian	0.8	2.6	3.5
Tadzhik	0.3	1.4	2.9
Turkmenian	0.3	1.4	2.0
Greek	0.2	0.1	0.3
Bulgarian	0.2	0.3	0.3

† Jews by faith were 5.2 million in 1897. By self-definition, as opposed to language, they were 2.3 million in 1959.

* Redefined in the Soviet period.

+ Not separately defined in 1897.

N.B. 1897 and 1959 populations are defined according to language, but 1979 census figures are based on self-definition. In the case of Great Russians, the Baltic nationalities, the Asian and Caucasian nations there is little difference between nationality by language and by self-definition, but in 1979 only 14 per cent of self-defined Jews spoke their national language, 29 per cent of Poles, 38 per cent of Greeks, 57 per cent of Germans, 67 per cent of Bashkirs, 68 per cent of Bulgarians, 72 per cent of Mordvinians, 74 per cent of White Russians, 83 per cent of Ukrainians, and 86 per cent of Tartars. In the 1979 census 153 million gave Russian as their mother-tongue. However, some doubts have been expressed about the precision of the language question asked by the census.

TABLE 6

Class Structure according to Official Categories
(per cent)

1897			1913	1928	1939	1978	1981
Hereditary nobles	1.0	Workers, white-collar included	17	18	50	85	86
Non-hereditary nobles, and non-noble bureaucrats	0.5	Workers, excluding white-collar	14	12	32	62	61
Christian priests	0.5	Collective farmers and workers in co-operative workshops	—	3	47	15	14
Hereditary and non-hereditary 'honoured citizens'	0.3	Independent peasants (excluding kulaks), independent artisans and handicraft workers	67	75	3	0.01	0.01
Merchants	0.2						
Petty commercial classes	10.6						
Peasants in rural areas	70.1						
Peasants in towns	7.0	Landowners, merchants, bourgeoisie, kulaks	16	5	—	—	—
Cossacks	2.3						
Settlers	6.6						
Foreigners	0.5						
Others (unclassifiable)	0.4						

TABLE 7

Urbanization

The twenty biggest cities 1897	Million inhabitants	The twenty biggest cities 1989	Million inhabitants
St. Petersburg	1.26	Moscow	8.77
Moscow	1.04	Leningrad (St. Petersburg)	5.02
Warsaw	0.68	Kiev	2.59
Odessa	0.40	Tashkent	2.07
Lodz	0.31	Baku	1.76
Riga	0.28	Kharkov	1.61
Kiev	0.25	Minsk	1.59
Kharkov	0.17	Gorki (Nizhnii Novgorod)	1.44
Tiflis (Tbilisi)	0.16	Novosibirsk	1.44
Tashkent	0.16	Sverdlovsk (Ekaterinburg)	1.37
Vilna (Vilno)	0.15	Tbilisi	1.26
Saratov	0.14	Kuibyshev (Samara)	1.26
Kazan	0.13	Erevan	1.12
Rostov on Don	0.12	Dnepropetrovsk	1.18
Tula	0.12	Omsk	1.15
Astrakhan	0.11	Chelyabinsk	1.14
Ekaterinoslav (Dnepropetrovsk)	0.11	Alma Ata	1.13
Baku	0.11	Odessa	1.12
Kishinev	0.10	Donetsk (Stalino, Yuzovka)	1.10
Helsinki	0.10 (approx.)	Kazan	1.09

TABLE 8

Growth of St. Petersburg/Petrograd/Leningrad
(million inhabitants)

1800	0.220	1900	1.44
1812	0.308	1914	2.2
1830	0.435	1920	0.6
1863	0.539	1939	3.38
1869	0.667	1959	3.32
1881	0.861	1970	3.95
1897	1.26	1989	5.02

N.B. Of the 1897 inhabitants, 58 per cent were classified as peasants.

TABLE 9

The Tsarist Economy: Annual Production
(million tons)

	Coal	Pig iron	Oil	Grain
1860	0.29	0.31	—	*
1870	0.68	0.33	0.03	*
1880	3.24	0.42	0.5	*
1890	5.9	0.89	3.9	*
1900	16.1	2.66	10.2	56
1910	26.8	2.99	9.4	74
1913	35.4	4.12	9.1	90
1916	33.8	3.72	9.7	64

* For European Russia only, grain production averaged 220 million *chetverts* 1857–63, and 179 million *chetverts* 1834–40 (a *chetvert* approximated 210 litres). Average annual production in European Russia 1886–90 was 36 million tons.

TABLE 10

The Soviet Economy: Annual Production

	1913 inter-war frontiers	1928	1940	1945	1960	1990	
Electricity	1.9	5.0	48.3	43.3	292	1726+	milliard KWH
Oil	9.1	11.6	31.1	19.4	148	571	million tons
Coal	29.1	35.5	166	150	510	703	million tons
Gas	0.017	0.3	3.4	3.4	47.2	815	milliard cu. metres
Steel	4.2	4.3	18.3	12.3	65.3	154	million tons
Mineral fertilizers	0.069	0.1	3.2	1.1	13.9	32	million tons (hypothetical units)
Tractors	—	1.3	31.6	7.7	238	495	thousand units
Plastics and synthetic materials	—	—	10.9	21.3	312	5536	thousand tons
Clocks and watches	0.7	0.9	2.8	0.3	26	77	million units
Cement	1.5	1.8	5.7	1.8	46	137	million tons
Leather footwear*	60	58	211	63	419	843	million pairs
Grain*	76	69	77	47	125	218	million tons
Meat*	4.1	4.2	4.0	2.6	8.7	20.0	million deadweight tons
Eggs*	10.2	9.2	9.6	4.9	27.4	81.7	milliard
Milk*	24.8	29.3	26.5	26.4	61.7	108.4	million tons

* Agricultural produce figures quoted for 1928 are annual averages for 1924–8, those for 1940 for annual averages for 1936–41. The 1913 figure for footwear may be understated. The larger figures have been rounded off to eliminate decimal points.

+ of the 1990 electricity output, 233 milliard KWH was hydro and 212 milliard was nuclear.

TABLE 11

Production per head of Population

			1913	1940	1960	1980	1990
Grain	tons per head		0.54	0.47*	0.58	0.71	0.75
Meat	,,	(dwt.)	0.031	0.024*	0.041	0.056	0.069
Coal	,,		0.22	0.89	2.4	2.7	2.4
Cement	,,		0.01	0.03	0.21	0.47	0.47
Clocks and watches units per head			0.005	0.015	0.12	0.25	0.26

* 1940 agricultural figures are based on an average of 1936–40.

TABLE 12

Development of Siberia and Central Asia
(percentage share of the regions east of the Urals in USSR totals)

	1940	1969
Population*	15	19
Electricity production	9	25
Natural gas production	0.5	28
Coal production	29	42
Steel production	11	9
Cement production	14	23
Meat production	23	21
Sawn timber production	25	28
Paper production	0.3	8
Tractor production	—	13

* The 1913 population of these regions was about 15 per cent of the Empire's population.

Sources

The tables in this section are mainly composite, being assembled, and sometimes calculated, from a number of sources. For the Tsarist period, figures have been taken from: F. Brokgaus and I. Efron, *Entsiklopedicheskii slovar* (dopolnitelnyi tom, 1907); P. Khromov, *Ekonomicheskoye razvitiye Rossii* (1967); P. Lyashchenko, *Istoriya narodnogo khozyaistva SSSR* (1956); and B. Urlanis, *Rozhdaemost i prodolzhitelnost zhizni v SSSR* (1963). The last-named was also used for the Soviet period. However the basic sources for post-1917 figures (and many 1913 figures) were the statistical annual *Narodnoye Khozyaistvo SSSR* and the 1959, 1979, and 1989 censuses.

INDEX

There are several conventions for transliterating the Cyrillic alphabet, but throughout this book such conventions have not always been followed. Common usage, convenience and even personal taste have had their influence. For example, Tchaikovsky is more correctly rendered as Chaikovskii, and there are grounds for preferring Gorbachov to Gorbachev.